COLLEGE ACCOUNTING
Principles and procedures

COLLEGE ACCOUNTING
Principles and procedures

JAMES DON EDWARDS, Ph.D., C.P.A.
J. M. Tull Professor of Accounting
University of Georgia

1977

RICHARD D. IRWIN, INC. Homewood, Illinois 60430
Irwin-Dorsey Limited Georgetown, Ontario L7G 4B3

First Printing, January 1977

ISBN 0-256-01879-0
Library of Congress Catalog Card No. 76–16234
Printed in the United States of America

LEARNING SYSTEMS COMPANY –
a division of Richard D. Irwin, Inc. – has developed a
PROGRAMMED LEARNING AID
to accompany texts in this subject area.
Copies can be purchased through your bookstore
or by writing PLAIDS,
1818 Ridge Road, Homewood, Illinois   60430.

Dedicated to
CLARA
and
JIM

Preface

Accounting has been defined as the process of collecting, recording, classifying, and reporting on the economic activities of business units to interested users of financial information. A concise definition of who these "interested users" are has yet to be found. Individuals in many fields are increasingly confronted with information presented in financial terms. *College Accounting: Principles and Procedures* was written for use by both students of accounting and business and for those who will need a working knowledge of accounting in their jobs.

This book is designed to provide an understanding of the total accounting process—from recording business transactions in the books of original entry to the preparation of periodic financial reports. The basic concepts of the accounting cycle are covered in the initial chapters. Later chapters deal more specifically with accounting problems encountered by the retailer, wholesaler, and manufacturer. Considerable space has been given to the discussion of accounting procedures applicable to the proprietorship, partnership, and corporate forms of business organization. In addition, specific procedures used in accounting for sales, purchases, prepaid expenses, inventories, payrolls, long-lived assets, payables, and owner's equity have been included.

College Accounting: Principles and Procedures is student oriented, and no previous study of accounting is assumed. Modern accounting terminology is used throughout the text. Each chapter contains visual illustrations, diagrams, and examples to illuminate the concepts presented. And, discussion of automated data processing has been integrated into the text material.

Each chapter is designed to reinforce the student's learning experience.

At the beginning of each chapter, a list of learning objectives is provided to give the student a perspective of the main points to be discussed in the chapter. Definitions of terms used in the text can be found in the glossary at the end of each chapter. Following the glossary, there is an ample number of questions, exercises, and problems for the instructor and student to use in reinforcing the learning experience.

Learning aids include a study guide and work book for the student to use in acquiring additional experience in answering questions and working problems. A set of working papers to accompany the text is also available.

Acknowledgments

Those following deserve mention for their assistance: Dan R. Johnson, Richland College; Shirley Glass, Macomb Community College; John Rich, Illinois State University; Lee C. Wilson, Mesa Community College; Jeff Hooper, Mesa Community College; Paul G. Markey, Massachusetts Bay Community College; and James Howe, Oakland Community College. Acknowledgment also goes to Joe Rhile, D. E. MacGuilvra, Donald Wilson, Deborah Wheless, John C. Richie, William Crosby, and Isabel L. Barnes.

December 1976   JAMES DON EDWARDS

Contents

1 Nature and purpose of financial accounting 1

The functions of accounting. Accounting versus bookkeeping. Basic elements of accounting: *Assets. Liabilities. Owner's equity.* Accounting equation. Transactions. Accounting equation illustration. Revenues and expenses. Financial statements: *Earnings statement. Statement of financial position. Statement of owner's equity.* Double-entry accounting. The account. Debits and credits illustrated. The balance column account form. The trial balance.

2 Recording accounting information 25

Recording transactions: *Business papers or source documents. Journalizing. The journal. Chart of accounts.* Journalizing illustrated: *Proving the journal.* Posting: *The general ledger. Posting and cross-referencing.* The trial balance: *Purpose of the trial balance. Preparing the trial balance.*

3 Worksheet, financial statements, and closing the books 51

Worksheet: *Form of the worksheet. Completing the worksheet.* Financial statements: *The earnings statement. Statement of financial position.* Closing the books: *Expense and Revenue Summary account. Closing revenue accounts. Closing expense accounts. Closing the Expense and Revenue Summary account. Closing the drawing account.* Post-closing trial balance.

4 Cash and cash records 69

Cash receipts. Cash disbursements. The cash journal. Cash receipts journal: *Posting the cash receipts journal.* Cash disbursements journal: *Posting the cash disbursements journal.* Petty cash: *The petty cash fund illustrated.* Bank credit card transactions.

5 Checking account procedures   93

Nature and purpose of checking accounts. Elements of a checking account: *Signature card. The deposit ticket. Endorsements. Dishonored checks. Mail and night deposits. Checks. Certified checks. The checkbook.* The bank statement: *The bank reconciliation. Journalizing the reconciliation.* Special checking accounts. Savings accounts. Bank statement for a company that accepts Master Charge cards.

6 Accounting for payroll   111

Earnings and payroll deductions: *Nature of payroll. Computing wages and salaries. Deductions from gross earnings. F.I.C.A. taxes. Income taxes withheld. Miscellaneous deductions.* Components of the payroll records: *Payroll register. Payroll checks. Individual earnings records.* Payroll preparation: *Recording gross wages and payroll deductions.* Employer payroll taxes: *Payroll tax expense. Recording employer payroll taxes.* Filing returns and paying payroll taxes.

7 Accounting for service enterprises – recording transactions   143

The cash basis of accounting for service enterprises. Accounting procedures: *Chart of accounts. The books of account. The cash journal. The general ledger. Extended illustration.* The trial balance.

8 Accounting for service enterprises – the accounting cycle   177

The worksheet. Financial statements. Adjusting and closing. The accounting cycle. Other adjusting entries. The matching concept. Bad debts: *Direct write-off. Allowance method. Bad debt recoveries.*

9 Accounting for a merchandising firm   203

Sales account. Sales tax accounting. Sales returns and allowances. Sales ticket or sales invoice. Bank credit cards. Sales journal. Accounts receivable: *Sales invoice method. Individual ledger accounts.* Purchase procedures: *Inventory methods. Purchases account. Purchase returns and allowances account. Purchase invoice. Purchases journal. Accounts payable.* Gross margin and cost of goods sold. Accounting procedures – a small merchandising business: *Recording. Posting. Schedule of accounts receivable. Schedule of accounts payable.*

10 Merchandising enterprise – end-of-period procedures   239

The trial balance. The worksheet: *Entry (a). Entry (b). Entries (c) and (d). Entry (e). Entry (f).* The financial statements: *The earnings statement. Statement of financial position.* Journalizing adjusting and closing entries.

11 Accounting for notes and interest   267

Computing interest: *Present value. The 60-day, 6 percent method.* Accounting for notes receivable: *Note received for cash loan. Note received in exchange for goods and services. Note received for extension of payment time on a previous obligation.* Note discounted before maturity. Reporting a contingent liability. Collection of note at maturity. Renewal of note at maturity. Notes receivable register. Notes Receivable account. Endorsement of notes. Accounting for notes payable. Notes issued for a cash loan: *Note issued in exchange for goods and services. Note issued for extension of payment time on a previous obligation. Payment of note at maturity. Renewal of note at maturity.* Notes payable register. Notes Payable account. Accrual of interest receivable. Accrual of interest payable.

12 Purchases 293

Purchase requisition. Purchase order. Invoice: *Back orders. Trade discounts. Cash discounts.* Common terms. Miscellaneous forms illustrated: *Bill of lading. COD. Freight and drayage. Debit and credit memoranda.* Invoice register: *Corrected purchase invoices. Proof of the invoice register. Posting procedure. Summary posting. Individual posting. Cash and COD purchases. Transportation costs. Purchase returns and allowances.* Automated accounting systems.

13 Accounting for sales 323

Sales for cash. Sales on credit. Sales on approval. COD sales. Sales on consignment. Installment sales. Handling of incoming purchase orders: *Examination. Credit approval. Review accuracy of purchase order. Transportation. Billing.* Purchases discount. Sales returns and allowances. Accounting procedure: *Recording sales. Posting procedure. Cash sales. COD sales. Sales returns and allowances. Shipping charges. Automated processing of sales transactions.*

14 Merchandise inventory and prepaid expenses 353

Merchandise inventory: *Purpose of taking inventory. Taking inventory. Valuation of inventory. Maintaining record of inventory.* Prepaid expenses: *Accounting for prepayments.*

15 Long-lived assets – tangible 377

Depreciation: *Determining depreciation expense.* Accounting for long-lived assets. Purchase of assets. Depreciation of assets. Disposal of assets: *Disposal through sale. Disposal through exchange. Disposal by retiring or discarding.* Statement presentation of assets. Asset records. Wasting assets.

16 Owner's equity: Proprietorship, partnerships 399

The proprietorship: *Proprietorship organization. Accounting procedure.* The partnership: *Partnership organization. Advantages and disadvantages of a partnership. Accounting for a partnership.*

17 Owners' equity: Corporation 423

Corporate advantages. Corporate disadvantages. Corporate organization. Corporate management. Corporate ownership. Corporate accounting procedure:

Incorporating a sole proprietorship. Incorporating a partnership. Owners' equity section.

18 Accrual accounting—wholesale business 445

Items affecting accounting records used: *1. Type of business. 2. Business volume. 3. Desired information. 4. Office machines.* Records and chart of accounts: *Sales register. Record of cash receipts. Invoice register. Record of checks drawn. General journal. General ledger. Accounts receivable ledger. Accounts payable ledger. Operating expense ledger. Supplementary records.* Accounting procedure illustrated.

19 Year-end accounting procedure—wholesale business 493

Summary and supporting worksheets: *Summary worksheet. Supporting worksheet—operating expenses. Completion of worksheets.* Adjusting entries—journalizing. Adjusting entries—posting. Closing entries—journalizing. Closing entries—posting. Post-closing trial balance. Reversing entries.

20 Voucher system 527

Purchase invoice. Voucher preparation. Voucher recording. Filing unpaid vouchers. Voucher register posting. Voucher payments. Filing paid vouchers. Recording voucher checks. Check register posting. Verifying vouchers payable. Fractional payments. Temporary voucher settlement. Purchase returns and allowances. Invoice corrections. Vouchers payable subsidiary ledger. Voucher system and the petty cash fund.

Index 551

Nature and purpose of financial accounting
Learning objectives

The contents of this chapter include a number of concepts which are basic to the accounting process. The learning objectives set forth are as follows:

1. Create awareness of the needs of present and potential users of financial information.
2. Become familiar with the "accounting equation" and its use in accounting for business transactions.
3. Illustrate the inclusion of revenues and expenses in the basic accounting equation.
4. Show how the basic accounting equation relates to the statement of financial position and to the earnings statement.
5. The use of double-entry accounting in recording financial transactions.
6. Underlying concepts—debits and credits, balance column account, "T-account," and trial balance.

1 Nature and purpose of financial accounting

Broadly speaking, the purpose of accounting is to provide useful information. This information typically relates to the financial activities or affairs of an individual, a business, or another organization (or a part of a business or an organization) and is expressed in terms of dollars. It is provided for a wide range of interested parties, some of whom have a legal right to know and to use the information in making many different types of decisions. Some of the more common users and uses of financial information concerning a business are:

1. *Owners* and *prospective owners* in deciding whether to increase, decrease, retain, or acquire an ownership interest in a business.
2. *Management* (who may also be owners) in deciding how the business is functioning, what its problem areas are, and whether additional financing is needed.
3. *Creditors* and *potential creditors* (creditors are those who supply goods and services in exchange for a promise by the business to pay later) in deciding whether to increase, decrease, or limit the amount of credit granted or whether to extend any credit at all.
4. *Government* in determining whether tax laws or other regulatory requirements have been met.
5. *Employees* and *prospective employees* (and the unions representing them) in deciding how large a salary increase to seek or to accept or whether to continue employment with a given business.

Other users of financial accounting information include customers or clients, stock exchanges, lawyers, trade associations, financial reporters for newspapers, and financial analysts. The information desired by all of the above users will vary according to the use to which it is to be put. But, generally, it will include information on the net earnings (profits) or lack of earnings (losses) of the most recent period and on the financial condition of the business at the present time. The accumulation and presentation of such information falls within what is known as *financial accounting* and is the primary subject matter of this book. Two other major, recognized areas of accounting are *management accounting* — the accumulation and presentation of information for internal management purposes — and *governmental accounting* — the accumulation and presentation of information on the financial affairs of governmental agencies.

While there are basically three recognized areas of accounting, there are considerably more than three areas of specialization in the profession of accounting. For example, an accountant may be employed by a private business enterprise, a public accounting firm, or a governmental agency as a specialist in taxation, cost accounting, budgeting, systems design and installation, or auditing. Auditing, which consists of the testing and checking of an organization's records to see whether it has followed proper policies and practices, is the primary activity of the **certified public accountant (CPA)**. In all states, an accountant may be granted the designation and be licensed to practice as a CPA upon passing a rigorous, uniform examination, reaching certain levels of education, and acquiring specified amounts of actual auditing experience. When employed by a public accounting firm, the services of the CPA are generally available to anyone at a fee. Public accounting firms typically are prepared to render services in tax planning, in the filing of tax returns, and in a wide range of services designed to assist clients in managing their affairs — an area often referred to as management or administrative services.

THE FUNCTIONS OF ACCOUNTING

Accounting is a measurement and communication process designed to provide useful information. This process includes identifying, recording, classifying, summarizing, and interpreting business transactions and events. The first step is the identification of those events which are financial in nature and which are to be recorded. In addition to writing by hand, recording includes the use of typewriters, bookkeeping machines, and machines for encoding information on magnetic tape, paper tape, or cards. Classifying is the grouping of similar items together in order to bring about a more efficient handling of the recording of many different events and transactions. Summarizing is the stating of various groups of data in concise form. Interpretation gives meaning to the information by way of explanations and through the development of significant relationships.

ACCOUNTING VERSUS BOOKKEEPING

Accounting includes designing forms and records to be used, designing accounting systems, data analysis, decision making, report and financial statement preparation, and the interpretation of these reports and statements. An accountant is a person involved with or responsible for these various functions. The recording phase of the accounting process is referred to as bookkeeping, and the person who actually records information in the books is a bookkeeper. Often, especially in small businesses, the accountant's role also includes the functions of a bookkeeper.

BASIC ELEMENTS OF ACCOUNTING

Financial information is commonly classified into the categories of assets, liabilities, owner's equity, revenues, expenses, and net earnings (or net loss), with the last three being essentially subdivisions of owner's equity. We will concentrate first on assets, liabilities, and owner's equity.

Assets

An **asset** is anything that is owned by a business and has value to a business (or other organization or entity). Common examples of assets include cash, accounts receivable, notes receivable, merchandise, machinery, building, land, furniture, and fixtures. The types and quantity of assets held vary with the enterprise. A manufacturer may have a large building with many machines as well as other assets. A doctor may require only a small office with relatively few items of equipment or furniture.

Liabilities

Basically, **liabilities** are obligations to disburse cash or other assets or to provide services in the future. A creditor's receipt of these assets or services cancels the obligations. Accounts payable and notes payable are the most common liabilities. Accounts payable arise from the receipt of items such as equipment, supplies, merchandise, and services in exchange for an unwritten promise to pay at a later date. Notes payable are written promises to pay others specified amounts at a future date. Taxes payable, which will be discussed later, are probably the most common of many other liabilities which may arise in a business.

Owner's equity

The term **owner's equity** refers to the owner's interest in or claim upon the business. It is the difference between the amount of assets and the amount of liabilities. Thus, assets are something owned, liabilities are something owed, and the difference is the owner's equity. Proprietorship, **capital,** and net worth are other terms for owner's equity.

It is important to separate a company's business activities from the owner's personal activities because entities, such as a corporation, are considered complete business units and exist separately from the individuals involved. This concept is referred to as the **entity** *concept.* For accounting purposes only the assets, liabilities, and economic activities of an economic unit are considered. Thus, if one person owns several businesses, caution must be taken to separate the accounting records of each business. It is important that the owner's personal economic activities not be included in the businesses' records.

ACCOUNTING EQUATION

All accounting information is recorded within the framework of the **accounting equation.** This equation is expressed as:

$$\text{Assets} = \text{Liabilities} + \text{Owner's Equity}$$

$$A \quad = \quad L \quad + \quad OE$$

An alternative form often used to express this equation is:

$$\text{Assets} - \text{Liabilities} = \text{Owner's Equity}$$

$$A \quad - \quad L \quad = \quad OE$$

As an example, at the end of one year H. C. Castor has assets of $10,620 and liabilities of $5,640. The accounting equation would appear as follows:

$$
\begin{array}{lr}
\text{Assets} & \$10,620 \\
- \text{Liabilities} & 5,640 \\
= \text{Castor's Equity} & \$\ 4,980 \\
\end{array}
$$

If, one year later, H. C. Castor had $12,490 of assets with no change in liabilities, the equation would appear as follows:

$$
\begin{array}{lr}
\text{Assets} & \$12,490 \\
- \text{Liabilities} & 5,640 \\
= \text{Castor's Equity} & \$\ 6,850 \\
\end{array}
$$

The change in owner's equity could have come about for a variety of reasons which will be illustrated shortly. The explanation of this change is one of the primary tasks of the accountant.

A balance sheet or **statement of financial position** is essentially a financial "picture" of a business at a particular date. A list of assets is compiled and added. Liabilities and owner's equity are also listed and totaled. Note that these totals are equal from the accounting equation (A = Λ + OE); hence the name "balance sheet." The balance sheet or statement of financial position lists the resources available to the firm (assets) and who provided them (liabilities and owner's equity) at a given point in time. A statement of financial position appears in Illustration 1–3.

TRANSACTIONS

Most accounting data arise from exchanges of value by a business with an outsider. Examples of exchanges include cash receipts from

Illustration 1–1

	Transaction	The business receives	The business gives up
a.	Original investment by owner in his or her business.	Cash	Ownership rights
b.	Purchased repair machine parts for cash.	Parts	Cash
c.	Purchased equipment on a credit basis.	Equipment	A promise to pay (accounts payable)
d.	Customers paid cash for services rendered.	Cash	Services
e.	Rendered services to customers on account.	Purchaser's promise to pay (accounts receivable)	Services
f.	Paid rent.	Building occupancy services	Cash
g.	Paid for advertising.	Advertising services	Cash

product sales, payment of wages for services rendered, and cash received from creditors. Such exchanges are called **transactions.** They are events which cause changes in the various asset, liability, and owner's equity accounts. Since the accounting equation must always balance, each transaction involves giving up something in order to receive something else. Accountants rely upon exchanges in which a business engages as evidence that economic activity has occurred and that something should be recorded. Some common transactions are shown in Illustration 1–1 (as looked at from the viewpoint of the business).

ACCOUNTING EQUATION ILLUSTRATION

The functioning of the accounting equation will be illustrated by assigning dollar values to the above transactions. The effect of transactions (*a*), (*b*), and (*c*) are shown in the chart or "transaction worksheet" of Illustration 1–2. The transactions affect the financial position of the Speedy Radio Repair Shop.

The first transaction is a contribution of capital. Assets and owner's equity both increase by $5,000. The second transaction is the exchange of one asset for another. The composition of the assets changed, but

Illustration 1–2

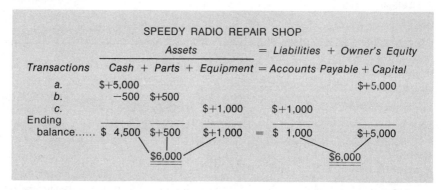

		SPEEDY RADIO REPAIR SHOP			
		Assets		= *Liabilities* + *Owner's Equity*	
Transactions	*Cash* +	*Parts* +	*Equipment* =	*Accounts Payable* +	*Capital*
a.	$+5,000				$+5,000
b.	−500	$+500			
c.			$+1,000	$+1,000	
Ending balance......	$ 4,500	$+500	$+1,000 =	$ 1,000	$+5,000
		$6,000			$6,000

their total amount did not change; owner's equity was unaffected. The third transaction increased assets by $1,000. Owner's equity did not change, but liabilities did change. Thus, the accounting equation remained in balance. At the conclusion of these three transactions, all of which we will assume took place on September 30, the statement of financial position would be as shown in Illustration 1–3.

Illustration 1–3

```
           SPEEDY RADIO REPAIR SHOP
           Statement of Financial Position
                September 30, 1978

                      Assets
Cash ................................................... $4,500
Parts ...................................................    500
Equipment ...........................................  1,000
       Total Assets ................................ $6,000


                    Liabilities
Accounts payable ................................... $1,000

                  Owner's Equity
Owner's equity .......................................  5,000
       Total Liabilities and Owner's Equity.............. $6,000
```

REVENUES AND EXPENSES

Thus far, the only change in owner's equity has come from the capital contribution of the owner. Of course, owner's equity could be reduced in an exactly reverse manner if the owner withdrew assets from the business. These capital transactions of the owner are only one way of changing the owner's equity section of the accounting equation. The other way is through the operation of the business.

When a business sells its product or service, the resulting cash receipts or other assets are called **revenue.** The cash disbursements made or the liabilities incurred in order to produce revenue are called **expenses.** Examples of expenses are wages, rent, and advertising. Most revenues are in the form of cash receipts. Since liabilities are not changed, there must be a corresponding increase in owner's equity so that the accounting equation remains in balance. Likewise, when a decrease in assets results from paying expenses, owner's equity is reduced.

To illustrate this concept, let's return to the Speedy Radio Repair Shop and examine transactions (d) through (f) and their effect on the accounting equation. (See Illustration 1–4.)

Illustration 1–4

SPEEDY RADIO REPAIR SHOP

	Assets				= Liabilities + Owner's equity	
Transactions	Cash +	Accounts Receivable +	Parts +	Equipment	= Accounts Payable +	Capital
Beginning balance ...	$ 4,500	$ 0	$500	$1,000	$1,000	$5,000
d.	+1,000					1,000
e.		+800				+800
f.	−400					−400
g.	−300					−300
Ending balance ...	$ 4,800 +	$800 +	$500 +	$1,000	= $1,000 +	$6,100
	$7,100				$7,100	

We could record revenues and expenses directly in the owner's equity account. But as the number of transactions increases, it becomes more difficult to decide which changes came about from operations and which pertained to capital transactions. This distinction is of great importance. One of the major financial statements is the **earnings statement** which is a summary of the changes in owner's equity due to operations. Capital transactions are excluded from the earnings statement because they are not events related to commercial operations.

Illustration 1–5

SPEEDY RADIO REPAIR SHOP

Transactions	Assets				= Liabilities +	Owner's equity		
	Cash +	Accounts Receivable +	Parts +	Equipment =	Accounts Payable =	Owner's Equity (Capital) +	Revenues –	Expenses
Beginning balance........	$ 4,500	$ 0	$500	$1,000	$1,000	$5,000	$ 0	$ 0
d.	+1,000						+1,000	
e.		+800					+800	
f.	–400							+400
g.	–300							+300
Ending balance........	$ 4,800 +	$ 800 +	$500 +	$1,000 =	$1,000 +	$5,000 +	$ 1,800 –	$ 700
	$7,100					$7,100		

Note: An increase in expense is a *decrease* in owner's equity.

The accumulation of data for the earnings statement is made much easier by first classifying changes in owner's equity. Revenue from operations is used to describe increases in owner's equity from operations. Expenses are used to describe decreases in owner's equity from operations.

The new accounting equation is Assets = Liabilities + Owner's Equity + Revenues − Expenses. The manner in which business transactions affect this equation is illustrated through the use of the last four example transactions of the Speedy Radio Repair Shop (Illustration 1–5).

Transaction (d) consists of the receipt of $1,000 in cash from customers for services performed by the repair shop. The receipt of the cash increases assets, and the related increase must be in owner's equity on the right side of the accounting equation. The objective in rendering services is to bring about an increase in owner's equity. Rather than record the increase directly in owner's equity, it is classified first as a new element in the equation—revenue.

In a similar manner, the $800 of services rendered on account is recorded as an increase in assets (accounts receivable) and as an increase in revenue. The fact that cash has not been received does not prevent us from recording revenue when it is earned. (Note: An **account receivable** is a customer's promise to pay at a later date.)

The $400 rent payment and the $300 advertising payment are recorded as a reduction in assets (cash in this case) and as a corresponding reduction in owner's equity. Again, the reduction is made by increasing the expense account rather than by decreasing the owner's equity account directly.

In essence, the revenue and expense accounts serve temporarily as part of the owner's equity account to make it easier to accumulate data for statements. The credit side of the revenue accounts represents increases in owner's equity, and the debit side of the expense accounts represents decreases in owner's equity. (Debits and credits will be explained in full detail in a later section.) At the end of the accounting period, the revenues and expenses are matched to determine the net increase or decrease in owner's equity.

FINANCIAL STATEMENTS

One function of accounting records is to serve as the basis for financial statements. The two most common financial statements are the earnings statement and the statement of financial position.

Earnings statement

The earnings statement shows the net earnings for a stated period and how it was derived. This statement is sometimes called a profit and loss

Illustration 1-6

```
                    SPEEDY RADIO REPAIR SHOP
                        Earnings Statement
                  For the Month Ended October 31, 1978

Revenue:
  Radio repair fees.................................................................        $1,800
Expenses:
  Rent..............................................................................  $400
  Advertising .....................................................................   300
    Total Expenses .............................................................              700
Net Earnings........................................................................        $1,100
```

statement, an operating statement, or an income statement. The earnings statement shows the changes in owner's equity during some time period, exclusive of owner's contributions or deductions. As an example, the earnings statement of the Speedy Radio Repair Shop would appear as shown in Illustration 1-6, assuming that transactions (*d*) through (*g*) were the only transactions that took place in October.

Statement of financial position

The statement of financial position (balance sheet) shows the assets, liabilities, and owner's equity of a business at a specific point in time. For

Illustration 1-7

```
                    SPEEDY RADIO REPAIR SHOP
                    Statement of Financial Position
                          October 31, 1978


                              Assets
Cash................................................................................        $4,800
Accounts receivable.................................................................          800
Parts .............................................................................          500
Equipment .........................................................................        1,000
    Total Assets ..................................................................        $7,100

                            Liabilities
Liabilities ........................................................................       $1,000

                          Owner's Equity
Capital, October 1, 1978............................................................  $5,000
Add net earnings for October.......................................................   1,100
Capital, October 31, 1978..........................................................          6,100
    Total Liabilities and Owner's Equity............................................        $7,100
```

example, the statement of financial position for the Speedy Radio Repair Shop prepared at the end of October would appear as shown in Illustration 1–7.

Statement of owner's equity

The statement of owner's equity starts with the owner's equity (or capital) at the beginning of the period. To the amount of owner's equity at the beginning of the period, additional investments of capital made by the owner are added. Similarly, withdrawals of capital by the owner are subtracted. Then the amount of **net earnings** for the period is added or the amount of **net loss** is subtracted. The resulting figure is the amount of owner's equity (or capital) at the end of the period. This procedure involves five steps.

1. Amount of capital or owner's equity at the beginning of the period.
2. Add additional capital investments by the owner.
3. Subtract capital withdrawals by the owner.
4. Add the net earnings for the period or subtract the net loss.
5. Amount of capital or owner's equity at the end of the period.

The statement of owner's equity for the Speedy Radio Repair Shop is shown in Illustration 1–8.

Illustration 1–8

SPEED RADIO REPAIR SHOP
Statement of Owner's Equity
October 31, 1978

Capital, October 1, 1978	$5,000
Add net earnings for October	1,100
Capital, October 31, 1978	$6,100

DOUBLE-ENTRY ACCOUNTING

The previous examples have shown that each transaction has a double effect on the accounting equation. This system provides a means of verifying the arithmetic accuracy of the recorded business transactions. The system of double-entry accounting evolved from the accounting equation Assets = Liabilities + Owner's Equity. If we did not have this automatic check on arithmetic accuracy, the only alternative check would be complete duplication of the record-keeping process. This would be very costly and time-consuming.

THE ACCOUNT

The financial records of a business must contain more detailed information than just total assets, total liabilities, and owner's equity. Each of these major classifications is composed of many items. In the example of the radio repair shop, the total assets were composed of cash, accounts receivable, parts, and equipment. Even a very small business would usually have more types of assets than these. An **account** is the form of record kept for each type of item. It is used to classify similar types of information.

The number of accounts depends mainly upon the desired detail of financial records. For example, the asset classification "cash" could be composed of cash on hand, a checking account balance, a savings account balance, and a petty cash fund for small expense disbursements. Parts could consist of bolts, washers, screws, and nails. If desired, separate accounts or financial records could be maintained for each specific type of item. Obviously, it is more expensive to keep elaborate and detailed records. This additional cost must be weighed against the benefits of the additional information available from more detailed financial records.

An account is often represented in a form called a "T-account." The T-account receives its name from its shape:

Account Title

Debits	Credits

The left side of the T-account is the **debit** side, and the right side is the **credit** side. Thus, to debit an account is to record a dollar amount on the left side of the account, and to credit an account is to record a dollar amount on the right side. Credit is often abbreviated Cr.; debit is abbreviated Dr.

The recording process still consists of recording increases and decreases, but the increases and decreases are now recorded by debiting and crediting the accounts in question. The general classification T-accounts below are set up in the form of the accounting equation, $A = L + OE + R - E$, and they show the rules for increasing and decreasing each kind of account.

Assets		=	**Liabilities**		+	**Owner's Equity**	
Debit	Credit		Debit	Credit		Debit	Credit
Increase	Decrease		Decrease	Increase		Decrease	Increase
+	−		−	+		−	+

Expense		**Revenues**	
Debit	Credit	Debit	Credit
Increase	Decrease	Decrease	Increase
+	−	−	+

Using the above rules, the accounting equation will always balance, and the dollar value of the debits and credits will always be equal. The asset and expense accounts will normally have debit balances. The liability, owner's equity, and revenue accounts will normally have credit balances.

DEBITS AND CREDITS ILLUSTRATED

Increases in assets are called debits and are recorded on the left side of the account. An asset may be increased in any of the following ways:

1. Additional cash or other property may be invested by the owner.
2. Liabilities of the business may increase.
3. Revenues may be derived from the sale of goods and services or from other sources.
4. Another asset may be decreased.

Decreases in assets are called credits and are recorded on the right side of the account. An asset may be decreased in any of the following ways:

1. Cash or other property may be withdrawn from the business by the owner.
2. Liabilities of the business may decrease.
3. Expenses may be incurred in operations.
4. Another asset may be increased.

As might be expected, assets comprise the left (debit) portion of the accounting equation:

$$\text{Assets} = \text{Liabilities} + \text{Owner's Equity}$$
$$\text{Debits} = \qquad\qquad \text{Credits}$$

Increases in liabilities and owner's equity, however, are called credits and are recorded on the right side of the accounts. Liabilities may be increased in any of the following ways:

1. Assets may increase.
2. Expenses may be incurred.
3. Other liabilities may be decreased.

Owner's equity on the other hand can be increased only in the following ways:

1. The owner may invest additional cash or other property (assets) in the business.
2. Revenue may be derived from the sale of goods and services or from other sources.

Decreases in liabilities and owner's equity are called debits and are recorded on the left side of the accounts. Liabilities may be decreased in either of the following ways:

1. Assets may decrease; or
2. Other liabilities may increase.

Owner's equity can also be decreased in only the two following ways:

1. Cash or other property (assets) may be withdrawn from the business by the owner; or
2. Expenses may be incurred in operations.

As might be expected, liabilities and owner's equity form the right (credit) portion of the accounting equation:

Assets = Liabilities + Owner's Equity
Debits =   Credits

The process of increasing and decreasing accounts with debits and credits will be illustrated by reworking the Speedy Radio Repair Shop transactions using T-accounts. The transactions will be keyed by using the transaction letter used to refer to the individual transactions earlier.

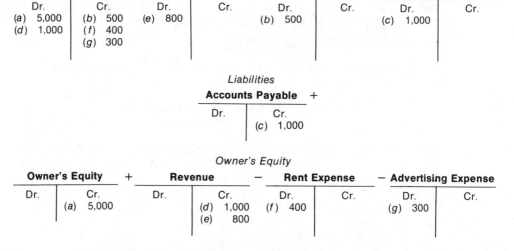

Transaction (a): Original investment by owner in his or her business. This illustrates an increase in an asset offset by an increase in owner's equity. The amount of money invested ($5,000) represents the owner's equity in the business; and at this point, the amount of the asset cash is equal to the owner's equity. As shown by the T-accounts, separate accounts are maintained for the owner and for the asset "cash." In recording the transaction, Cash was debited for $5,000 and Owner's Equity was credited for $5,000, thus keeping the accounting equation in balance.

Transaction (b): Purchased parts for cash. This transaction illustrates an increase in an asset offset by a decrease in another asset. As a result of this transaction, a new asset, parts (an inventory item), was acquired. This acquisition, however, was offset by a decrease in the asset cash. In recording the transaction, Parts was debited for $500 and Cash was credited for $500, thus keeping the accounting equation in balance.

Transaction (c): Purchased equipment on a credit basis. This transaction illustrates an increase in an asset which is offset by an increase in a liability. As a result of this transaction, a new asset, equipment, was acquired and, at the same time, a liability, accounts payable, was incurred. Again, separate accounts are maintained. In recording the transaction, Equipment was debited for $1,000 and Accounts Payable was credited for $1,000. Hence, the accounting equation is kept in balance.

Transaction (d): Customers paid cash for services rendered. This transaction illustrates an increase in an asset offset by an increase in owner's equity resulting from revenue. Cash was increased as a result of customers' payments for services rendered; and at the same time, owner's equity increased as a result of revenue generated. In recording the transaction, Cash was debited for $1,000 and Revenue was credited for $1,000, thus keeping the accounting equation in balance.

Transaction (e): Rendered services to customers on account. This transaction illustrates an increase in an asset offset by an increase in owner's equity. As a result of this transaction, accounts receivable was increased, and at the same time owner's equity was increased as a result of the revenue generated. In recording the transaction, Accounts Receivable was debited for $800 and Revenue was credited for $800. Hence, the accounting equation remains in balance.

Transaction (f): Paid rent. This transaction illustrates the decrease in an asset offset by a decrease in owner's equity. As a result of this transaction, cash was decreased and owner's equity was decreased (as a result of the expense incurred). In recording the transaction, Rent Expense was debited for $400 and Cash was credited for $400. The accounting equation remains in balance.

Transaction (g): Paid for advertising. This transaction is essentially the same as transaction (f) except that advertising expense rather than rent expense is the reason for the decrease in owner's equity. Also, the transaction illustrates that separate accounts are maintained for different types of expenses. In recording the transaction, Advertising Expense was debited for $300 and Cash was credited for $300. Again, the accounting equation remains in balance.

At any point in time, the total dollar value of the debits must equal the total dollar value of the credits. If this is not the case, an error has been made. But, if there has been a large number of transactions, then the account balances are not readily apparent. The balances are arrived at by

footing (adding) the columns in each account and subtracting the lesser amount from the greater amount to obtain the account balance. As an example, the balance in the Cash account is:

Cash

Dr.	Cr.
(a) 5,000	(b) 500
(d) 1,000	(f) 400
	(g) 300
6,000	1,200
−1,200	
4,800	

The revenue and expense accounts would be used to prepare the earnings statement. The balances in the asset, liability, and owner's equity accounts would be combined with the net earnings figure to prepare the statement of financial position. In summary the debit and credit rules are:

	Assets	Liabilities	Owner's Equity	Revenues	Expenses
Increase	Debit	Credit	Credit	Credit	Debit
Decrease	Credit	Debit	Debit	Debit	Credit

THE BALANCE COLUMN ACCOUNT FORM

In actual practice the T-account is often abandoned in favor of a more convenient form called the balance column account. This form has a column for the balance as well as the debit and credit columns. This allows a running balance for the account in question. The Cash account for Speedy Radio Repair Shop would appear as follows:

Cash   Account No._____

Date	Explanation	P.R.	Debit	Credit	Balance
	Owner's investment		5,000		5,000
	Purchased parts			500	4,500
	Revenue from services		1,000		5,500
	Paid rent			400	5,100
	Paid for advertising			300	4,800

The use of the account number and the P.R. (posting reference) column will be discussed later. The Date column contains the date of the transaction. A brief explanation of the transaction appears in the Explanation column. The appropriate debit or credit column contains the amount of the transaction. The Balance column shows the balance in the account at the conclusion of each transaction.

THE TRIAL BALANCE

As a result of the fundamental accounting equation and the rules of debits and credits, double-entry accounting always results in an equal dollar amount of total debits and total credits. A way of verifying that

Illustration 1-9

SPEEDY RADIO REPAIR SHOP
Trial Balance
October 31, 1978

Account Title	Debit	Credit
Cash	$4,800	
Accounts receivable	800	
Parts	500	
Equipment	1,000	
Accounts payable		$1,000
Owner's equity		5,000
Revenue		1,800
Rent expense	400	
Advertising expense	300	
	$7,800	$7,800

the accounts are in balance is to prepare a trial balance. A **trial balance** is simply a listing of all the asset, liability, owner's equity, revenue, and expense account balances at a point in time. The trial balance for the Speedy Radio Repair Shop would appear as shown in Illustration 1-9. Note the order in which the accounts are listed and that the accounts "balance"; that is, total debits ($7,800) equal total credits ($7,800). A trial balance is also often used as a worksheet for financial statement preparation. Refer to the earnings statement in Illustration 1-6 and the statement of financial position in Illustration 1-3. It should be apparent that the trial balance helps in the preparation of these financial statements.

GLOSSARY

Account   a device used for measuring and storing financial information regarding the activity of a business unit or other organization.

Accounting   the process of collecting, measuring, and reporting financial information of a business unit or other organization. The three basic types of accounting are: financial accounting, which reports financial information to interested parties outside the organization; management accounting, which reports information to the organization's management for internal decision-making purposes; and governmental accounting, which reports on the financial affairs of government agencies.

Accounting equation   basically, Assets = Liabilities + Owner's Equity.

Accounts receivable an asset account that is used by a company to keep a record of amounts due from its customers.

Assets roughly, anything that is owned by and has value to a business (or other organization or entity).

Capital investment in a business by its owner(s).

Certified public accountant (CPA) an accountant who has passed a rigorous examination and met other requirements and has been granted a license to be a CPA. He or she is often called upon by organizations to attest to the fairness of financial information which they release.

Credit the right-hand side of an account; placing an entry on the right-hand side of an account.

Debit the left-hand side of an account; placing an entry on the left-hand side of an account.

Earnings statement a financial statement which summarizes the expenses and revenues of an organization for a specified period of time.

Entity a business unit or other organization which is viewed as being completely separate from its owners and creditors.

Expenses the costs incurred in the production of revenues.

Footing adding the left-hand and right-hand sides of an account and subtracting the smaller amount from the larger amount to obtain the account balance.

Liabilities basically, the debts or obligations owed by a business concern to its creditors.

Net earnings the amount by which the revenues of a business unit exceed its expenses over a specified period of time.

Net loss the amount by which the expenses of a business unit exceed its revenues over a specified period of time.

Owner's equity roughly, the owner's interest in the assets of an organization.

Revenue the cash receipts or cash claims that result from selling a product or service to customers.

Statement of financial position also called the balance sheet; it is a financial statement which presents the assets, liabilities, and owner's equity of a business unit as of a specific date.

Transactions events or exchanges which affect the assets, liabilities, or owner's equity of an organization.

Trial balance a listing of all the asset, liability, owner's equity, revenue, and expense account balances at a point in time.

QUESTIONS AND EXERCISES

1. What is the purpose of accounting?

2. Name some common users and uses of financial information.

3. Distinguish between bookkeeping and accounting.

4. Define the following terms and give some examples of each:

    a. Asset.
    b. Liability.
    c. Owner's equity.

5. What is the entity concept? Why is it important?

6. What are transactions? What are some typical examples of transactions?

7. What are revenues and expenses?

8. Define the following:

    a. Earnings statement.
    b. Statement of financial position.

9. What are debits and credits? Which accounts normally have debit balances, and which accounts normally have credit balances?

10. What is a trial balance?

PROBLEMS

1-1. During the month of February, the following transactions were completed by J. C. Thomas. Insert the dollar amounts under the proper headings below to indicate the effect of each transaction on the accounting equation. A dollar amount should be preceded by a plus sign if it is an increase and by a minus sign if it is a decrease.

    a. Sold a typewriter, used by the office secretary, for $125 cash.
    b. Purchased a desk for the office, on account, $175.
    c. Purchased office supplies for cash, $100.
    d. Paid $275 for February office rent.

		Assets		=	*Liabilities*	+	*Owner's Equity*
	Cash +	*Office Supplies* +	*Office Equipment* =		*Accounts Payable* +		*J. C. Thomas, Capital*
Bal.	$1,500	$25	$3,000		$1,200		$3,325
a.	___	___	___		___		___
Bal.							
b.	___	___	___		___		___
Bal.			=				
c.	___	___	___		___		___
Bal.							
d.	___	___	___		___		___
Bal.	═══	═══	═══		═══		═══

1-2. R. L. Roberts is a television service person. As of April 30, Roberts owned the following business-related property:

Cash...................... $1,425   Repair equipment...... $1,500
Office equipment...... 2,500   Repair parts............. 2,800

As of the same date, Roberts owed business creditors as follows:

TV Supplies, Inc. $1,700
Johnson Office Supplies and Equipment Co.......... 750

a. On the basis of the above information, fill in the following spaces in the accounting equation:

Assets $_____ = Liabilities $_____ + Owner's Equity $_____

b. Assuming that during the month of May there is an increase in business assets of $275 and an increase in business liabilities of $625, give the resulting accounting equation:

Assets $_____ = Liabilities $_____ + Owner's Equity $_____

c. Assuming that during June there is a decrease in business assets of $225 and a decrease in business liabilities of $850, give the resulting accounting equation:

Assets $_____ = Liabilities $_____ + Owner's Equity $_____

1-3. J. T. Adams, M.D., has just retired from the U.S. Navy and established a local practice. Adams's business transactions during the first month were:

a. Personally invested $3,000 in the business.
b. Paid office rent for one month, $500.
c. Purchased professional equipment from Super Office Supplies, $27,500, on account.
d. Received $8,350 for services rendered to patients during the month.
e. Paid $700 salary to office secretary.
f. Paid telephone bill, $150.

Required:

1. Set up eight T-accounts with the following titles: Cash; Professional Equipment; Accounts Payable; J. T. Adams, Capital; Professional Fees; Salaries Expense; Rent Expense; and Telephone Expense.
2. Record transactions (*a*) through (*f*) directly in these accounts.
3. Foot the accounts and enter balances as necessary.
4. Prepare a trial balance of the accounts.

1-4. J. E. Drake owns and operates Economy Cleaners. At the beginning of the month, the books show the following account balances:

Cash... $ 1,750
Accounts receivable 850
Accounts payable... 1,000

Dry cleaning equipment	7,500
Office equipment	1,500
Delivery truck	3,000
Revenue	1,500
Expense	500
J. E. Drake, capital	12,600

Set up an accounting equation form using the given balances, and then record the effects of the following transactions on the equation (using plus, minus, and equal signs). Compute new balances after each transaction.

a. Rendered services for cash, $300.
b. Paid salaries, $750.
c. Performed services worth $1,800 on account.
d. Purchased adding machine for office on account, $300.
e. Received $2,100 from customers in payment of their accounts.
f. Paid creditors, $350.
g. Paid rent, $400.
h. Purchased a new steam press on account, $1,500.

1-5. W. C. Smith is a barber, and on February 1, 1978, Smith's business, Smith's Barbershop, had the following statement of financial position!

SMITH'S BARBERSHOP
Statement of Financial Position
February 1, 1978

Assets

Cash	$ 750
Equipment	350
Building	5,000
Total Assets	$6,100

Liabilities

Accounts payable	$ 250

Owner's Equity

W. C. Smith, capital	5,850
Total Liabilities and Owner's Equity	$6,100

The following transactions were made during the month. Indicate their effect on the accounting equation:

a. Purchased equipment on account, $150.
b. Withdrew $100 for personal expenses.
c. Paid $250 on accounts payable.
d. Receipts for the month totaled $500 (all in cash).
e. Cash expenses for the month totaled $200.

		Assets		=	Liabilities	+	Owner's Equity
	Cash +	Equipment +	Building =		Accounts Payable +		W. C. Smith, Capital
Bal.	$750	$350	$5,000		$250		$5,850
a.	————	————	————		————		————
Bal.							
b.	————	————	————		————		————
Bal.							
c.	————	————	————		————		————
Bal.							
d.	————	————	————		————		————
Bal.							
e.	————	————	————		————		————
Bal.							

1-6. J. W. Childs started a real estate business on June 1, and during the month Childs made the following transactions:

a. Personally put $5,000 into the business.
b. Paid $200 rent for the office building for the month of June.
c. Sold a house and received a commission of $400.
d. Purchased some office furniture for the business giving a note for $1,500. (Childs agreed to pay $250 at the end of each month.)
e. Purchased some office equipment and agreed to pay for the office equipment within 30 days. Total bill, $450.
f. Sold a building and received a commission of $750.
g. Paid telephone bill of $100.
h. Paid for advertising in the local newspaper, $75.
i. Sold a house, receiving a commission of $200.
j. Paid electric bill of $15.
k. Paid the water bill of $5.
l. Put car worth $1,000 into the business.
m. Paid for gasoline and oil for the car, $35.
n. Paid secretary for the month, $350.
o. Sold a house and received a commission of $750.
p. Paid the monthly installment of $250 on the office furniture.
q. Paid for the office equipment.

Required:

PART A
1. Analyze each transaction and post it to the T-accounts.
2. Prepare a trial balance.

PART B   From the trial balance, what is the amount of—
1. Assets.
2. Liabilities.
3. Owner's Equity + Revenue − Expenses.

1-7. Dr. F. E. Thomas opened a dentist's office on March 1, 1978. During the month of March, Dr. Thomas completed the following transactions:

a.   Personally invested $5,800 in the business.
b.   Paid office rent for one month, $300.
c.   Purchased office furniture costing $900.
d.   Purchased professional equipment costing $2,500.
e.   Paid the telephone bill, $80.
f.   Paid secretary for the month, $600.
g.   Paid the utilities bill, $60.
h.   Received $10,200 for services rendered to patients during the month.

Required:

1.   Set up nine T-accounts with the following titles: Cash; Office Furniture; Professional Equipment; F. E. Thomas, Capital; Professional Fees; Rent Expense; Telephone Expense; Utilities Expense; and Salaries Expense.
2.   Record transactions (*a*) through (*h*) directly in these accounts.
3.   Foot the accounts and enter balances as necessary.
4.   Prepare a trial balance of the accounts.

Recording accounting information
Learning objectives

This chapter introduces several procedures and practices used in recording accounting information. They are:

1. The use of business transaction papers and records as a source of the information contained in the journal entry.

2. Establishing a chart of accounts as a method of identifying and locating accounts.

3. The procedures used in journalizing a transaction in a journal.

4. Necessity of proving the general journal prior to posting as a means of reducing possible journalizing errors.

5. The posting process and the procedures used to cross-reference the posted amounts.

6. The purpose of the trial balance in the preparation of financial statements.

2

Recording accounting information

In Chapter 1, the basic accounting elements of assets, liabilities, owner's equity, revenues, and expenses and the basic accounting equation were introduced. Different types of transactions were analyzed for their effects on this equation. In each instance, it was shown that every transaction has a dual effect and that the recording of these two effects was a distinguishing feature of the double-entry system of accounting. In Chapter 1, little attention was paid to recording procedures since our concern was with obtaining an understanding of the basic elements of accounting and their relationship in double-entry accounting. Now it is time to introduce some of the recording procedures used to handle the many transactions entered into by even a small business.

RECORDING TRANSACTIONS

Broadly speaking, the flow of information concerning the transactions of every business is from (1) business papers, source documents, or other recording devices to (2) journal entries to (3) the accounts to (4) the financial statements.

Business papers or source documents

In almost every business, a written record of some sort is prepared for every transaction that takes place. These **business papers** may be handwritten or prepared mechanically. They consist of payroll timecards, purchase or sales invoices, cash register tapes, deposit slips, check stubs or carbon copies of checks, duplicate sales tickets, and similar items.

Journalizing

To record the evidence of transactions contained in business papers in the accounting system, the accountant engages in a process known as **journalizing.** The accountant analyzes the transaction to determine its debit and credit effects upon the accounts and then prepares a **journal entry** which is recorded in a **journal.** Every journal entry contains (1) the date of the transaction, (2) the titles of the accounts to be debited and credited, (3) the dollar amounts of the debits and credits, and (4) a brief explanation of the transaction.

The journal

Journal entries are recorded in a record or book called the journal. Although a transaction may originally be recorded on a business paper or in a business machine, the first recording of that transaction in terms of double-entry accounting is found in the journal. For this reason, the journal is called a *book of original entry.* The actual form of the journal may vary among firms of different size and with different types of activities. The simplest form of journal – often called the general journal – contains only two money columns. A typical general journal page is shown below. Because of its simplicity, a journal entry for *any* business transaction can readily be entered in the general journal.

	GENERAL JOURNAL			Page 1	
Date	Accounts and Explanation	P.R.	Debit	Credit
1978 Dec. 10	Cash		10,000	
	D. Edwards, Capital			10,000
	Investment by owner.			

The first item entered in the Date column on each journal page is the year. It is not repeated on the page unless an entry is to be made for a transaction occurring in a *new* year. The next items entered in the Date column are the month and day of the transaction. The month is not repeated on the page for following transactions unless a transaction of a *new* month is entered. Instead, only the day of the transaction is entered in the Date column.

The Accounts and Explanation column is used to record the titles of the ledger accounts (at least two) affected by each transaction. It is also used to provide a brief explanation of the transaction. Each account title and only the account title is recorded on a separate line. The titles of the accounts *debited* are entered first and are started at the left-hand margin of the Accounts and Explanation column. The titles of the accounts *credited* are started approximately one-half inch to the right of the margin. The explanation of the transaction is written on the next line and is usually indented slightly, but not as much as the titles of the accounts credited.

The P.R. (posting reference) column is not used during the journalizing process. It is used for cross-referencing (as explained below).

The debit column is used to record the dollar amount of the debit to each account that is to be debited. Similarly, the credit column is used to record the dollar amount of the credit to each account that is to be credited. The dollar amount of the debit should be written on the same line as the title of the account to be debited. Likewise, the dollar amount of the credit should be written on the same line as the title of the account to be credited.

Journalizing procedure. To summarize, the complete journalizing procedure consists of a number of distinct steps. The transaction must be analyzed (1) to determine the type of accounts affected — asset, liability, owner's equity, revenue, or expense; (2) to identify the specific accounts affected; (3) to determine and express the dollar amount of the increase or decrease in terms of debits and credits; and (4) to formulate the required explanation. The journal entry is then written in the journal. The entry is made either at the time the transaction takes place or very shortly thereafter. In either case, the transactions are entered in the journal in chronological order — that is, according to the dates on which they occurred.

In entering journal entries in the journal, the debit portion of the entry is traditionally recorded first. When a transaction requires entries in three or more accounts, the resulting entry is referred to as a *compound journal entry*. In compound entries, all debits are recorded first followed by all of the credits; but debits must still equal credits.

Chart of accounts

Because even a small business may have many different accounts in its accounting system, a plan should be established to permit accounts to be easily identified and quickly located. Such a plan consists of identifying all accounts by means of a number as well as by name. A list of all of the accounts and their numbers is known as a **chart of accounts.**

The names chosen for the accounts and the total number of accounts employed depend upon the detail of information required, the size of the firm, and the nature of its activities. Generally, a separate account is kept for each type of asset, liability, owner's equity, revenue, and expense. In a chart of accounts, the individual accounts are usually grouped into these five major classifications. They are assigned numbers in such a way that every account is easily identified as being either an asset, a liability, an owner's equity, a revenue, or an expense account. For example, all accounts may be assigned a three-digit number with all asset accounts beinning with "1," all liabilities with "2," all owner's equities with "3," all revenues with "4," and all expenses with "5." The other two digits in the account number identify a specific account within the general classification.

Presented in Illustration 2–1 is the chart of accounts as established for The Staple Employment Agency, a business owned and operated by J. D. Staple.

Illustration 2–1

Account No.	Name of Account
THE STAPLE EMPLOYMENT AGENCY	
Chart of Accounts	
100–199	*Assets:*
110	Cash
147	Office Furniture
200–299	*Liabilities:*
212	Accounts Payable
300–399	*Owner's Equity:*
320	J. D. Staple, Capital
330	J. D. Staple, Drawing
400–499	*Revenue:*
420	Fees earned
500–599	*Expenses:*
505	Office Rent Expense
514	Advertising Expense
521	Office Supplies Expense
523	Dial-A-Phone Expense
570	Wages Expense
590	Miscellaneous Expense

Note that the accounts are not numbered within classifications in exact numerical sequence. The gaps in the numbering permit the easy insertion of additional accounts when they are needed. Also note that with a chart of accounts available, the accountant does not have to "thumb through" records to locate the accounts involved every time he or she wishes to make a journal entry.

JOURNALIZING ILLUSTRATED

The following illustration shows the journal entries made to record the transactions of The Staple Employment Agency from May 30 through

June 30, 1978. Sufficient information is provided to permit analysis of each transaction. A detailed explanation of each transaction is given, followed by the required journal entry. The firm's general journal with all of its recorded entries is reproduced in Illustration 2–2.

J. D. Staple founded The Staple Employment Agency by investing $2,500 in the business. Thus, the firm acquired an asset, cash, in the amount of $2,500 and gave up an equal amount of ownership rights. This increase in the Cash account is recorded by a debit of $2,500. The owner's equity account, J. D. Staple, Capital, is also increased by $2,500. To record an increase in an owner's equity account, it must be credited. Thus, the required entry in the general journal is:

GENERAL JOURNAL					Page 1
Date		Accounts and Explanation	P.R.	Debit	Credit
1978 May	30	Cash		2,500	
		J. D. Staple, Capital			2,500
		Investment by owner.			

The journalizing process consisted of the following steps:

1. The year, 1978, was written at the top of the Date column.
2. The month and the day were entered in the Date column.
3. On the same line as the month and day, the title of the account to be debited, Cash, was written to the extreme left of the Accounts and Explanation column. The amount of asset increase, $2,500, was entered in the debit column on the same line.
4. Indented about one-half inch on the next line is the title of the account to be credited, J. D. Staple, Capital. The amount of the increase in the owner's equity, $2,500, was entered on the same line in the credit column. (Note: Only the title of the account is entered in the Accounts and Explanation column on the line where a debit or credit is entered.)
5. Indented about one quarter of an inch on the next line is a brief explanation of the transaction.

May 31, 1978

Office rent for the remainder of May and for all of June was paid in cash, $310.

31	Office Rent Expense	310	
	Cash		310
	Paid rent through June, 1978.		

The effect of the transaction is to decrease the asset cash and to decrease owner's equity. The decrease in owner's equity is made by increasing the expense account Office Rent Expense. (Theoretically, an asset—prepaid rent—was acquired in this transaction because rent paid in advance is a thing of value—an asset. But, because the asset will expire before financial statements are next presented, the accountant seeks to save himself or herself the work of making a further entry transferring an amount from an asset account to an expense account. Thus, the accountant anticipates the expiration of the asset and records the item as an expense originally. Transactions of this type will be dealt with in depth in later chapters.)

May 31, 1978

Office furniture is ordered from the Brand Furniture Store. Because the furniture must be ordered from the factory, no delivery date can be promised by the store. No journal entry is necessary until delivery of the furniture and receipt of the bill.

June 1, 1978

Dial-A-Phone, Inc., installed a telephone in the office. Both the $10 installation fee and the $25 June service charge are paid on this date.

```
June   1   Dial-A-Phone Expense .............................................. 35
               Cash ............................................................      35
           Payment of phone bill.
```

The transaction results in a decrease in the asset, cash, and an increase in an expense. The journal entry consists of a debit to Dial-A-Phone Expense for $35 and a credit to Cash for $35.

June 2, 1978

Office supplies costing $72 were purchased on account from Big Fudd's Supply.

```
       2   Office Supplies Expense.............................................72
               Accounts Payable .................................................      72
           Purchased office supplies from Big Fudd's Supply
           Store.
```

This transaction results in an **account payable** which is an obligation to pay cash at some future time and in the incurrence of an expense. It is most likely that the supplies will be used during the current accounting period. If some supplies are left unused at the end of the period and are therefore an asset, an adjustment will be made. This will be discussed later.

June 4, 1978

Services were rendered to J. P. Cowell. Cash of $125 was received as payment in full.

```
4   Cash................................................................. 125
         Fees Earned .............................................         125
    Revenue received for services.
```

The transaction resulted in an increase in the asset, cash, and an increase in owner's equity. This increase in owner's equity was recorded by increasing a revenue account. The journal entry consists of a debit to Cash and a credit to Fees Earned for $125.

June 6, 1978

Brand Furniture Store delivered the office furniture ordered from them on May 31, 1978. An invoice (bill) payable in 90 days for $1,140 accompanied the delivery.

```
6   Office Furniture ...............................................1,140
         Accounts Payable .......................................       1,140
    Purchased office furniture from Brand Furniture
    Store; payment due in 90 days.
```

This transaction increases the asset account, Office Furniture, and increases the liability account, Accounts Payable.

June 8, 1978

Membership dues of $20 were paid to the Nationwide Personnel Placement Association.

```
8   Miscellaneous Expense............................................ 20
         Cash ................................................................         20
    Paid membership dues.
```

Assets and owner's equity are both decreased. The reduction in owner's equity results from the incurrence of an expense. The journal entry reads debit Miscellaneous Expense and credit Cash for $20.

June 15, 1978

Cash of $940 was received for professional placement services rendered for various individuals.

```
5   Cash................................................................. 940
         Fees Earned .................................................         940
    Revenue received for services.
```

This transaction results in an increase in the asset, cash, and an increase in owner's equity which is recorded by way of a temporary owner's equity revenue account, Fees Earned.

June 18, 1978

Cash of $73 was paid to a local newspaper for advertising.

```
18   Advertising Expense .................................................. 73
         Cash ...............................................................        73
     Advertising payment.
```

This transaction results in a decrease in owner's equity (expense increase) and a reduction in the asset, cash. Thus, journalizing requires a debit to Advertising Expense and a credit to Cash for $73.

June 19, 1978

A part-time secretary is hired at an agreed-upon rate of pay of $2 per hour. No journal entry is necessary at this time because an exchange, a transaction, has not taken place. Only after the employee has performed services will the business be liable to pay for such services.

June 29, 1978

Cash of $640 for professional placement services was received during the period of June 16 to June 29.

```
29   Cash................................................................. 640
         Fees Earned ..................................................        640
     Revenue received for services.
```

This transaction increases assets and increases owner's equity through the revenue account.

June 30, 1978

The secretary is paid wages of $60 for June work.

```
30   Wages Expense...................................................... 60
         Cash ...............................................................        60
     Secretary's salary.
```

This transaction results in a decrease in the asset account, Cash, and an increase in the expense account, Wages Expense.

June 30, 1978

Staple withdraws $400 from the firm.

```
30   J. D. Staple, Drawing ............................................. 400
         Cash................................................................        400
     Withdrawal by owner.
```

The owner's equity is decreased as is the asset cash. Withdrawals of equity are recorded in a **drawing account** to separate additions and withdrawals of the owner's equity during an accounting period and to simplify the preparation of the statement of financial position.

For illustration, all of the above transactions are shown in Illustration 2–2 as they would appear when entered in the general journal of the Staple Employment Agency. Disregard the numbers in the P.R. column. They will be explained later.

Illustration 2–2

		GENERAL JOURNAL			Page 1
Date		Accounts and Explanation	P.R.	Debit	Credit
1978 May	30	Cash	110	2,500	
		J. D. Staple, Capital	320		2,500
		Investment by owner.			
	31	Office Rent Expense	505	310	
		Cash	110		310
		Paid rent through June, 1978.			
June	1	Dial-A-Phone Expense	523	35	
		Cash	110		35
		Payment of phone bill.			
	2	Office Supplies Expense	521	72	
		Accounts Payable	212		72
		Purchased office supplies from Big Fudd's Supply Store.			
	4	Cash	110	125	
		Fees Earned	420		125
		Revenue received for services.			
	6	Office Furniture	147	1,140	
		Accounts Payable	212		1,140
		Purchased office furniture from Brand Furniture Store; payment due in 90 days.			
	8	Miscellaneous Expense	590	20	
		Cash	110		20
		Paid membership dues.			
	15	Cash	110	940	
		Fees Earned	420		940
		Revenue received for services.			
	18	Advertising Expense	514	73	
		Cash	110		73
		Advertising payment.			
	29	Cash	110	640	
		Fees Earned	420		640
		Revenue received for services.			
	30	Wages Expense	570	60	
		Cash	110		60
		Secretary's salary.			
	30	J. D. Staple, Drawing	330	400	
		Cash	110		400
		Withdrawal by owner.			
				6,315	6,315

Proving the journal

As each page in the journal is filled with entries, the accuracy of the journalizing process should be checked. This is done simply by adding all of the debits in the debit column on the page and adding all of the credits in the credit column on the page. If the total of the debit column equals the total of the credit column, the journal has been proven. That is, the debits are equal to the credits in the entires on that page. The totals are expected to be equal because the debits must equal the credits in *each individual entry*. It would require an extremely rare combination of errors for the totals to agree and for the debits not to be equal to the credits in each of the individual entries.

The totals, or footings as they are often called, are entered on the last line of each filled page of the journal. Footings are also entered on the horizontal line below the last entry on partially filled pages.

POSTING

We have seen how the accountant prepares a chronological record of the transactions of a business by making journal entries in a journal. But, in a sense the information contained in a journal is still in "raw" or unusable form. To be of any value to the users of the data, it must be summarized. It would make little sense to offer as a financial statement a listing of several thousand individual cash receipts. When properly categorized and summarized, the details of the various transactions can yield useful information. This summarization/categorization process is carried out through the use of ledger accounts.

The general ledger

Ledger accounts are actually printed forms on sheets of paper or on computer cards. If on a sheet of paper, the accounts may be kept in a loose-leaf notebook or may be bound in a book. If the accounts are in card form, the cards are usually kept in a tray. The entire collection of account records of a business is referred to as its *general ledger,* or simply as its **ledger.** Usually the accounts are grouped in the ledger according to whether they are asset, liability, owner's equity, revenue, or expense accounts. The groupings are arranged so as to aid in the preparation of the financial statements; and the individual accounts are kept in numerical order, as shown by the chart of accounts.

Posting and cross-referencing

In a sense, a journal entry is a set of written instructions stating specifically what dollar amounts are to be entered in which accounts and whether the accounts are to be debited or credited. The process of entering in the accounts the amounts stated in journal entries is known as **posting.** In this way, information about the transactions of a business which is contained in the journal is transferred to the ledger accounts. Journal entries may be posted (1) immediately after the journal entry is recorded in the journal; (2) at the end of a specific period of time such as a day, a week, or a month; or (3) after each journal page is filled.

In posting, the actual information transferred from the journal to each account posted consists of (1) the date of the transaction, (2) the dollar amount of the debit or credit, and (3) the number of the page in the journal which contains the item posted. This number is recorded in the P.R. column in the account. It provides a **cross-reference** between the journal and the ledger. After a dollar amount has been posted in an account from the journal, the number of the account is entered in the P.R. column in the journal on the same line as the amount just posted. This shows that the journal has been posted, and in this way serves as a check upon the completeness of the posting process. A transaction can be quickly traced from the journal to the ledger or in the reverse direction by using the cross-reference numbers. Errors that may occur in the posting process can be readily corrected.

To illustrate, the first transaction of the general journal of the Staple Employment Agency is properly posted and cross-referenced in Illustration 2–3.

Illustration 2–3

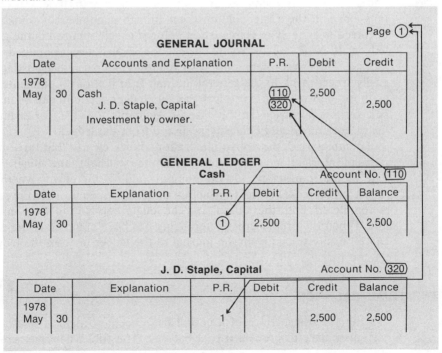

The first line of the first entry on page 1 of the general journal indicates that a transaction occurred on May 30 which caused cash to increase by $2,500. This means that an entry must be made for $2,500 as a debit in the Cash ledger account. This ledger entry was properly made as is shown by the date and the dollar amount entered in the Cash account. The P.R. column in the Cash account contains the number "1" to show that it was posted from page 1 of the general journal. In like manner, the second line of the entry in the journal was properly posted to the J. D. Staple, Capital account, and the proper cross-reference was inserted in the P.R. column.

When the debit was posted to Cash, the number of the Cash account, 110, was entered in the P.R. column in the journal on the same line as the $2,500 debit. Also, after the credit was posted to J. D. Staple, Capital, the number of the account to which it was posted, 320, was entered in the P.R. column in the journal on the same line as the $2,500 credit. The appearance of these two numbers, 110 and 320, in the P.R. column of the journal indicates that the entry has been completely posted. The absence of such numbers in the P.R. column immediately signals the fact that a journal entry has not been posted to the general ledger.

The complete ledger of the J. D. Staple Employment Agency is shown in Illustration 2–4 with all items properly posted from its journal (as shown in Illustration 2–2). The year 1978 has been entered at the top of the Date column in every account. Note, also, that in the Cash account and in the Fees Earned account the name of the month, June, was entered only once in the Date column even though a number of transactions occurred in June. The Explanation column is seldom used in the general ledger. It is not necessary to repeat the explanation contained in the journal. The cross-referencing system allows any particular posting to be easily traced back to the general journal. Informational comments, such as those shown in the Accounts Payable ledger account, can be made to suit various purposes. In the case of Accounts Payable, for example, a list of creditors could be easily prepared from the ledger.

To summarize, the above illustration shows clearly that three bits or items of information are transferred from the journal to the ledger: (1) the date of the transaction, (2) the amount, and (3) the effect (whether increase or decrease) of the transaction upon the account. After the posting is completed, both the journal and the ledger contain the same information. When the proper cross-referencing has been completed, the entries can be easily traced from the journal to the ledger or from the ledger to the journal.

THE TRIAL BALANCE

After the transactions of a period have been journalized and posted, it is customary to prepare a trial balance. The trial balance is simply a

Illustration 2–4

GENERAL LEDGER

Cash   Account No. 110

Date		Explanation	P.R.	Debit	Credit	Balance
1978						
May	30		1	2,500		2,500
	31		1		310	2,190
June	1		1		35	2,155
	4		1	125		2,280
	8		1		20	2,260
	15		1	940		3,200
	18		1		73	3,127
	29		1	640		3,767
	30		1		60	3,707
	30		1		400	3,307

Office Furniture   Account No. 147

Date		Explanation	P.R.	Debit	Credit	Balance
1978						
June	6		1	1,140		1,140

Accounts Payable   Account No. 212

Date		Explanation	P.R.	Debit	Credit	Balance
1978						
June	2	Big Fudd's Supply Store	1		72	72
	6	Brand Furniture Store	1		1,140	1,212

J. D. Staple, Capital   Account No. 320

Date		Explanation	P.R.	Debit	Credit	Balance
1978						
May	30		1		2,500	2,500

J. D. Staple, Drawing   Account No. 330

Date		Explanation	P.R.	Debit	Credit	Balance
1978						
June	30		1	400		400

Fees Earned   Account No. 420

Date		Explanation	P.R.	Debit	Credit	Balance
1978						
June	4		1		125	125
	15		1		940	1,065
	29		1		640	1,705

Illustration 2–4 (*continued*)

Office Rent Expense   Account No. 505

Date		Explanation	P.R.	Debit	Credit	Balance
1978 May	31		1	310		310

Advertising Expense   Account No. 514

Date		Explanation	P.R.	Debit	Credit	Balance
1978 June	18		1	73		73

Office Supplies Expense   Account No. 521

Date		Explanation	P.R.	Debit	Credit	Balance
1978 June	2		1	72		72

Dial-A-Phone Expense   Account No. 523

Date		Explanation	P.R.	Debit	Credit	Balance
1978 June	1		1	35		35

Wages Expense   Account No. 570

Date		Explanation	P.R.	Debit	Credit	Balance
1978 June	30		1	60		60

Miscellaneous Expense   Account No. 590

Date		Explanation	P.R.	Debit	Credit	Balance
1978 June	8		1	20		20

listing of all the accounts in the general ledger and the debit or credit amounts of their balances.

Purpose of the trial balance

There are three reasons for preparing a trial balance: (1) to decide whether the ledger is in balance by determining whether the total of the accounts with debit balances equals the total of the accounts with credit balances, (2) to aid in locating errors, and (3) to assist in the preparation of financial statements.

Before preparing financial statements, the accountant seeks to test the arithmetic accuracy of his or her record of the financial activities of the business. Since every journal entry must contain an equal amount of debits and credits, it follows that the accounts must have an equal amount of debit and credit balances. Or, as it is often said, the books must *balance*. This means simply that a trial balance must balance. If the trial balance does not balance, an error has been made. This error has been made in the period following the date of the last correct trial balance. A trial balance may be prepared daily, weekly, monthly, or at the end of a longer period of time. Usually it is prepared monthly, and one is always prepared at the end of the accounting period prior to the preparation of financial statements.

The fact that a trial balance balances does not mean that no errors have been made. A trial balance would balance even though any of the following errors had been made: (1) no entry was made for a certain transaction, (2) an entry was posted twice, or (3) a debit or a credit was posted or journalized to the wrong account. Since a common reason for an out-of-balance trial balance is an arithmetical error in determining the balance of an account, care should be exercised in computing the running balance of an account. Also, if the accounts are hand-posted, the writing should be clear and legible so that it will not be misread and lead to a mistake in determining the balance of the account or in transcribing the balance of the account in the trial balance.

Preparing the trial balance

To draw up a proper trial balance, the following procedures should be carefully observed:

1. The heading of the trial balance should state the name of the business, the title of the statement, and the date of the statement. Usually a trial balance is prepared a few days after the last day of the period for which transactions are included in the trial balance.
2. The number and title of each account should be listed after the heading in the order in which they are found in the ledger.
3. The account balances should be listed in parallel columns — debit balances on the left and credit balances on the right.
4. Each column should be totaled, and these totals entered at the bottom of the column; a single line should be drawn above each total, and a double line below each total.

The trial balance of The Staple Employment Agency, prepared in accordance with these procedures, is shown in Illustration 2–5.

Illustration 2–5

THE STAPLE EMPLOYMENT AGENCY			
Trial Balance			
June 30, 1978			
Account No.	Account Title	Debit	Credit
110	Cash	$3,307	
147	Office furniture	1,140	
212	Accounts payable		$1,212
320	J. D. Staple, capital		2,500
330	J. D. Staple, drawing	400	
420	Fees earned		1,705
505	Office rent expense	310	
514	Advertising expense	73	
521	Office supplies expense	72	
523	Dial-A-Phone expense	35	
570	Wages expense	60	
590	Miscellaneous expense	20	
		$5,417	$5,417

The trial balance will serve a useful purpose in the preparation of financial statements as will be shown in Chapter 3.

GLOSSARY

Accounts payable   a liability account that is used by a company to keep a record of amounts due to creditors within one year.

Business papers   written records, either handwritten or mechanically prepared, for every transaction that takes place in a business. They consist of payroll timecards, purchases or sales invoices, cash register tapes, deposit slips, check stubs or carbon copies of checks, duplicate sales tickets, and similar items.

Chart of accounts   a complete listing of all the accounts in the ledger and their identifying numbers.

Cross-referencing   the acts of entering in the P.R. column of the book of original entry the ledger account number to which an entry was posted and entering the page number of the book of original entry in the P.R. column of the ledger.

Drawing account   an account used to record withdrawals of equity by the owner.

Journal   a book of original entry which contains a chronological record of business transactions showing the changes to be recorded in terms of debit and credit as a result of each transaction.

Journal entry   an entry recorded in a journal which analyzes the effects of a business transaction in terms of debit and credit. A compound journal entry is a journal entry which affects three or more accounts.

Journalizing   the act of entering a transaction in a journal.

Ledger   the entire collection of the account records of a business; often referred to as the general ledger.

Posting   the act of transferring journal entries to a ledger.

QUESTIONS AND EXERCISES

1. Describe the flow of information concerning transactions of a business.

2. Why is a journal called a book of original entry?

3. Describe the journalizing procedure.

4. Define the following terms:

    a. Chart of accounts.
    b. Posting.
    c. Cross-referencing.

5. When may journal entries be posted?

6. What are three reasons for preparing a trial balance?

7. Elaine Combe has just prepared a trial balance for her proprietorship. The total of the debits column equals the total of the credits column. Does this mean that no errors have been made? Explain.

8. What journal entries should be made to record the following transactions?

    a. Office supplies costing $55 were purchased on account from Selby's Supply Company.
    b. Cash of $22 was received for services rendered to customers.
    c. The secretary was paid wages of $105.

9. What is a drawing account? What journal entry should be made when M. C. Owner withdraws $600 from the firm?

10. What are four procedures that should be carefully observed when preparing a trial balance?

PROBLEMS

2-1. J. T. Smith, a local CPA, completed the following transactions during March.

Required:

Journalize each transaction.

Mar. 1 Paid the rent for March, $175.
      1 Paid February's telephone bill, $37.
      2 Received $25 for services from A. B. Smith.
      2 Paid February's electric bill, $17.
      3 Received $40 for services from Bill Tooley.

Mar. 3 Paid the secretary's weekly salary, $75.
      4 Paid'dues to the AICPA, $25.
      4 Paid business license fee, $100.
      5 Received $50 for services from Jim Jones.
      8 Received $45 for services from Jane Payne.
      8 Withdrew $100 from the business.
      9 Gave $25 to the Community Chest.
     10 Paid secretary's weekly salary, $75.
     11 Received $60 for services from Big Jim Walker.
     11 Purchased a new calculator for the business giving a note for $750.
     11 Purchased office supplies on account for $50.
     12 Billed Tom Williams for services, $480.
     12 Sold an old typewriter for $25. It was listed on the books for the sale value.
     12 Borrowed $500 from the bank giving a 90-day note.
     12 Paid gasoline bill for car used in the business, $40.
     12 Billed J. A. Pennyworth Company for services, $450.
     12 Paid for repair services on the typewriter, $15.
     15 Paid $35 for maintenance on the new calculator.
     15 Received $45 for services from P. T. O'Riley.
     15 Withdrew $100 for living expenses.
     15 Paid for office supplies purchased on March 11.
     16 Paid monthly rent on the duplicating machine, $30.
     16 Received Tom Williams's check for the services previously billed.
     17 Billed Bruce Company for services, $850.
     17 Invested $1,500 in the business.
     17 Paid the secretary's weekly salary, $75.
     17 Paid the note on the calculator.
     18 Received $65 for services from L. P. Zenn.
     18 Purchased a dictaphone on account, $150.
     19 Purchased a new office desk and chair for $225.
     19 Received from J. A. Pennyworth Company a check for services previously billed.
     19 Hired a student to post ledgers at $2.50 per hour. She worked ten hours and was paid.
     22 Paid for the dictaphone.
     22 Received a check from the Bruce Company in payment of their bill.
     23 Paid water bill, $8.
     24 Paid secretary's weekly salary, $75.
     25 Withdrew $100 for personal expenses.
     26 Paid home electric bill on a company check, $6.

2-2. W. A. Smith Company had the following trial balance as of June 1, 1978. None of the journal entries for the month of June have been posted or included in the trial balance.

Required:

1. Open general ledger balance column accounts for the accounts listed in the trial balance. Post the June 1, 1978, balances to accounts.

2. Post the journal entries to the ledger.
3. Prepare a trial balance as of June 30, 1978.

W. A. SMITH COMPANY
Trial Balance
June 1, 1978

Account No.	*Account Title*	*Debit*	*Credit*
111	Cash	$ 750	
130	Office equipment	1,830	
150	Automobile		
211	Accounts payable		$ 300
232	Notes payable		1,000
310	W. A. Smith, capital		1,720
350	W. A. Smith, drawing	400	
410	Fees earned		1,250
501	Gas and oil expense	25	
511	License expense	50	
532	Wages expense	250	
540	Utilities expense	35	
565	Office supplies expense	55	
588	Rent expense	750	
590	Telephone expense	125	
		$4,270	$4,270

GENERAL JOURNAL

Page 1

Date		Accounts and Explanation	P.R.	Debit	Credit
1978					
June	1	Office Supplies Expense		25	
		Accounts Payable			25
		Purchased office supplies on account.			
	2	Wages Expense		100	
		Cash			100
		Paid payroll.			
	5	Rent Expense		150	
		Cash			150
		Paid rent for June.			
	6	Cash		225	
		Fees Earned			225
		Received fees for professional services.			
	7	W. A. Smith, Drawing		75	
		Cash			75
		Withdrew money for personal expense.			
	7	Telephone Expense		15	
		Cash			15
		Paid telephone bill.			
	8	Cash		85	
		Fees Earned			85
		Received fees for professional services.			
	9	Automobile		2,000	
		Cash			500
		Notes Payable			1,500
		Purchased a car.			
	9	Accounts Payable		25	
		Cash			25
		Paid for office supplies.			
	10	Utilities Expense		10	
		Cash			10
		Paid for water.			

GENERAL JOURNAL

Page 2

Date		Accounts and Explanation	P.R.	Debit	Credit
1978 June	14	Office Equipment Accounts Payable Purchased a file cabinet on account.		45	45
	15	Gas and Oil Expense Cash Paid gas bill for company car.		35	35
	16	Cash W. A. Smith, Capital Invested cash in business.		450	450
	20	Accounts Payable Cash Paid for the file cabinet.		45	45
	21	Cash Fees Earned Received fees for professional services.		100	100
	21	License Expense Cash Paid for business license.		25	25
	22	Wages Expense Cash Paid payroll.		175	175
	26	Utilities Expense Cash Paid electric bill.		20	20
	27	Cash Fees Earned Received fees for professional services.		85	85
	30	Notes Payable Cash Paid on car.		250	250

2-3. W. R. Roberts, a local business executive, owns a small business. During the month of July several transactions were made that are listed below. The trial balance for July 1, 1978, is also listed below.

Required:

1. Journalize the transactions.
2. Post from the journal to the ledger.
3. Prepare a trial balance as of July 31, 1978.

W. R. ROBERTS
Trial Balance
July 1, 1978

Account No.	Account Title	Debit	Credit
101	Cash..	$ 2,350	
110	Accounts receivable	1,750	
140	Office equipment...........................	2,750	
152	Automobile...................................	-0-	
201	Accounts payable...........................		$ 850
301	W. R. Roberts, capital		6,210
310	W. R. Roberts, drawing...................	1,100	
405	Fees earned		4,300
508	Rent expense	2,100	
515	Utilities expense	125	
517	Telephone expense.........................	285	
541	Wages expense	900	
		$11,360	$11,360

July 1 Paid the monthly rent, $350.
   2 Received from Robert Rawlings a check for $750 for services previously billed.
   3 Paid electric bill of $25.
   5 Billed Dorothy Hazeltine $850 for services rendered.
   5 Paid telephone bill, $65.
   8 Paid the secretary's salary, $150.
   9 W. R. Roberts put personal car worth $2,000 into the business.
  15 Billed Walter Haller $1,500 for services rendered.
  18 Received a check for $850 from Dorothy Hazeltine.
  19 Paid water bill, $15.
  25 Withdrew $200 for personal expense.
  28 Purchased a typewriter on credit for $450.

2-4. J. C. Jones, a local attorney, completed the following transactions during July.

Required:

Journalize each transaction.

July	1	Paid June's electric bill, $28.
	1	Paid June's telephone bill, $80.
	2	Paid the rent for July, $300.
	3	Received $200 for services from Jay Haynes.
	4	Paid $60 for office supplies.
	4	Received $90 for services from Connie Clark.
	5	Billed Joe Lynch for services, $150.
	6	Purchased a new typewriter on account, $400.
	6	Received $115 for services from Katherine Rogers.
	7	Withdrew $150 for living expenses.
	7	Received $250 for services from Smithbro Company.
	8	Paid gasoline bill for car used in the business, $85.
	8	Sold the old typewriter for $100. It was listed on the books at $100.
	9	Purchased office furniture costing $1,050. Paid $350 in cash and gave a $700 note.
	10	Billed Tom Adams for services, $70.
	11	Received $150 from Joe Lynch for services previously billed.
	12	Paid for typewriter purchased on the 6th.
	13	Paid insurance premiums on policies taken out in the name of the business, $90.
	14	Paid the secretary's salary, $275.
	14	Paid home electric bill on a company check, $15.
	15	Invested $600 in the business.
	16	Received a check from Tom Adams for services previously billed, $70.
	17	Paid the note on the office furniture.
	18	Paid the water bill, $20.
	19	Received $70 from Barbara Clay for services rendered.
	19	Purchased office supplies on account, $50.
	20	Hired a person to clean the office once a week and paid $25 for the service.
	21	Billed Glenn Taylor for services, $300.
	22	Paid home telephone bill on a company check, $25.
	23	Paid business license fee, $65.
	24	Withdrew $150 for living expenses.
	25	Received $85 from Wesley Company for services.
	25	Paid for office supplies purchased on the 19th.
	26	Received check from Glenn Taylor for services previously billed.
	27	Paid the cleaning person, $25.
	28	Paid the secretary's salary, $275.
	29	Received $110 for services from Gail Cox.
	29	Received $80 for services from Gary West.
	30	Gave $50 to the Community Chest.
	31	Withdrew $100 for living expenses.

2-5. R. A. Johnson, a management consultant, had the following trial balance on November 1, 1978:

R. A. JOHNSON
Trial Balance
November 1, 1978

Account No.	Account Title	Debit	Credit
101	Cash...	$ 1,600	
121	Accounts receivable	2,500	
151	Office equipment.............................	1,900	
221	Accounts payable............................		$ 700
301	R. A. Johnson, capital......................		4,500
321	R. A. Johnson, drawing....................	3,800	
421	Consulting fees earned.....................		12,500
501	Rent expense..................................	1,000	
511	Telephone expense..........................	150	
521	Salaries expense	6,000	
531	Utilities expense	500	
541	Office supplies expense....................	250	
		$17,700	$17,700

During November, Johnson completed the following transactions:

Nov. 1 Paid November rent, $100.
1 Paid October phone bill, $20.
3 Billed Allen Reeves for services rendered, $475.
4 Paid $80 for office supplies.
6 Received $300 for services from Olsen Company.
7 Purchased an adding machine on account, $400.
10 Withdrew $200 for living expenses.
11 Paid electric bill, $35.
12 Paid water bill, $20.
15 Paid secretary's salary, $300.
17 Invested $800 in the business.
20 Received check from Allen Reeves for services previously billed.
22 Received $600 for services from Carmen Company.
26 Received $50 for services from Jean Wilson.
28 Paid for adding machine purchased on the 7th.
29 Paid home electric bill with a company check, $15.
30 Paid secretary's salary, $300.
30 Withdrew $300 for living expenses.

Required:

1. Open general ledger balance column accounts for the accounts listed in the trial balance. Post the November 1, 1978, balances to accounts.
2. Journalize the above transactions.

3. Post the journal entries to the accounts.
4. Prepare a trial balance for November 30, 1978.

2-6. On July 31, 1978, Lynn Barrow prepared the following trial balance for her service business:

LYNN BARROW
Trial Balance
July 31, 1978

Account Title	Debit	Credit
Cash		$ 5,000
Accounts receivable	$12,000	
Office equipment		20,000
Accounts payable	10,000	
Lynn Barrow, capital	6,000	
Lynn Barrow, drawing		4,100
Fees earned	31,000	
Wages expense		4,400
Rent expense		1,400
Telephone expense	100	
	$59,100	$34,900

Required:

It is apparent that the trial balance does not balance. Given the following information, prepare a corrected trial balance.

1. All of the accounts have normal balances.
2. The debits to the Cash account total $14,000, and the credits to the Cash account total $8,900.
3. A $200 cash receipt from a customer was not posted to the Accounts Receivable account.
4. The balance in the Fees Earned account is $13,000 instead of $31,000.
5. The debits to the Office Equipment account total $30,900, and the credits to the Office Equipment account total $18,800.
6. The balance in Lynn Barrow's capital account is $16,000.

Worksheet, financial statements, and closing the books
Learning objectives

The contents of this chapter will provide a working knowledge of the procedures used when preparing financial statements from the accounting records. This chapter introduces the following material:

1. The form, contents, and completion of a worksheet.
2. The significance of the earnings statement and the statement of financial position.
3. The form of earnings statement and the statement of financial position.
4. Theoretical justifications for closing the books.
5. The procedures used in closing the expense, revenue, and drawing accounts.
6. The purpose of and procedures employed in preparing a post-closing trial balance.

3

Worksheet, financial statements, and closing the books

WORKSHEET

One of the major objectives of an accounting system is the preparation of the earnings statement and the statement of financial position. The preparation of these statements is greatly facilitated by the use of the **worksheet.** It provides an opportunity for the early detection of errors and arranges the trial balance data in an efficient form for financial statement preparation. If the number of accounts in a trial balance is small, the worksheet's usefulness may not be apparent. However, as the number of accounts increases, the worksheet becomes a very valuable tool.

Form of the worksheet

The worksheet shown in Illustration 3–1 is called a six-column worksheet. The six columns referred to are actually three pairs of columns. Each pair contains a column for debits and a column for credits.

The worksheet should have a proper heading. This includes the name of the firm, the designation that this is a worksheet, and the date of the trial balance which appears on the worksheet.

The first two columns are used as identification for the accounts that appear on the worksheet. The account title is the name of the account as it appears in the general ledger. The account number is the identification number that has been assigned to that particular account. This is the same identification scheme that was used in the preparation of the trial balance in the last chapter.

The first pair of debit and credit columns is used to record the appro-

51

Illustration 3–1

		FIRM NAME Worksheet For the Period Ended "Date"						
Acct. No.	Account Title	Trial Balance		Earnings Statement		Statement of Financial Position		
		Debit	Credit	Debit	Credit	Debit	Credit	

priate account balances in each of the individual accounts. Thus, the first four columns are in effect the same as the trial balance that has already been discussed in Chapter 2.

The last two pairs of columns are used to classify data for the earnings statement and the statement of financial position. These columns will contain only those account balances that affect each particular financial statement.

The worksheet in Illustration 3–2 is for the Staple Employment

Illustration 3–2

		THE STAPLE EMPLOYMENT AGENCY Worksheet For the Year Ended June 30, 1978						
Acct. No.	Account Title	Trial Balance		Earnings Statement		Statement of Financial Position		
		Debit	Credit	Debit	Credit	Debit	Credit	
110	Cash	3,307						
147	Office furniture	1,140						
212	Accounts payable		1,212					
320	J. D. Staple, capital		2,500					
330	J. D. Staple, drawing	400						
420	Fees earned		1,705					
505	Office rent expense	310						
514	Advertising expense	73						
521	Office supplies expense	72						
523	Dial-A-Phone expense	35						
570	Wages expense	60						
590	Miscellaneous expense	20						
		5,417	5,417					

Agency as of June 30, 1978. Only the Trial Balance columns have been completed at this point. The completed worksheet is shown in Illustration 3–3.

Completing the worksheet

After the trial balance has been properly recorded on the worksheet, the accounts are sorted according to the statement in which they appear. All the dollar amounts of the revenue and expense accounts are placed in the Earnings Statement columns. The dollar amounts of the assets, liabilities, and owner's equity accounts are transferred to the Statement of Financial Position columns.

Unlike the Trial Balance columns, the Earnings Statement columns usually will not be equal. If the debit column equaled the credit column that would mean that expenses equaled revenues. Thus, the firm would have just "broken even." If the debits are greater than the credits, the expenses are greater than the revenues, and the firm has incurred a net loss. When the credits are greater than the debits, the firm has made a profit called net earnings. The Staple Employment Agency worksheet is shown in Illustration 3–3 after the trial balance amounts have been transferred to the appropriate financial statement columns.

Illustration 3–3

THE STAPLE EMPLOYMENT AGENCY
Worksheet
For the Year Ended June 30, 1978

Acct. No.	Account Title	Trial Balance		Earnings Statement		Statement of Financial Position	
		Debit	Credit	Debit	Credit	Debit	Credit
110	Cash	3,307				3,307	
147	Office furniture	1,140				1,140	
212	Accounts payable		1,212				1,212
320	J. D. Staple, capital		2,500				2,500
330	J. D. Staple, drawing	400				400	
420	Fees earned		1,705		1,705		
505	Office rent expense	310		310			
514	Advertising expense	73		73			
521	Office supplies expense	72		72			
523	Dial-A-Phone expense	35		35			
570	Wages expense	60		60			
590	Miscellaneous expense	20		20			
		5,417	5,417	570	1,705		
	Net Earnings			1,135			1,135
				1,705	1,705	4,847	4,847

In the case of the Staple Employment Agency, the credits exceed the debits by $1,135 in the Earnings Statement columns. This amount represents the net earnings for the period. In order to get the Earnings Statement columns to balance, $1,135 must be added to the debit column. When this is done, the two columns balance at $1,705. Since the trial balance was in balance when it was entered on the worksheet, an offsetting credit must be made to keep the accounts in balance. Thus, $1,135 is added to the credit column of the statement of financial position. When this is done, the two columns balance at $4,847.

The Statement of Financial Position columns include the account balances for all asset, liability, and owner's equity accounts along with the net earnings or loss for the period. If there are net earnings for the period, the amount is recorded in the credit column (increase in owner's equity). If a net loss occurs, the amount appears in the debit column (decrease in owner's equity).

In the Staple Employment Agency example, the $1,135 of net earnings appears in the credit column. The $1,135 that was entered as a debit in the Earnings Statement column is offset with a credit in the Financial Position column.

When each pair of columns balances, a double line is drawn under the total of the two columns. When the worksheet is completed, each pair of columns should balance. If the Statement of Financial Position columns do not balance after the above procedures have been followed, an error has been made. The error must be located before the formal financial statements can be prepared. While errors are never desirable, it is wise to locate them early in the accounting process.

Once the worksheet has been completed, the formal financial statements may be prepared. The statements can be prepared directly from the data on the worksheet.

FINANCIAL STATEMENTS

The general journal, general ledger, and trial balance all provide information about the firm. But they are insufficient because the firm's progress cannot be readily determined from them. To correct this deficiency, two statements are prepared. One is called the earnings statement, and the other is known as the statement of financial position.

The earnings statement

One measure of a firm's progress is the change in owner's (proprietor, J. D. Staple) equity that has occurred from operations within a specified time period. The effects of transactions resulting from operations and affecting owner's equity are recorded in the revenue and expense accounts. These accounts are called temporary accounts since they are closed out to owner's equity normally once a year. Changes caused by additional investment or withdrawal of equity are not included. The summarization of the revenue and expense account balances is called the earnings statement.

The earnings statement is often said to be the most important financial statement. It shows how well the business has done in its primary activity — selling a product or rendering a service and thereby earning a profit. It is also suggested that the firm's ability to generate net earnings is the best measure of its ability to meet future obligations such as mortgage payments and dividend payments.

Net income or net earnings is a flow concept. Net earnings must be considered in reference to some time period. The statement that a person earned $2,000 means little without a time reference. If the $2,000 refers to a year, the person is well below the national average. If it is $2,000 a month, the person is doing much better than the national average.

In a similar manner, a firm may prepare an earnings statement for a month, a quarter (three months), a semiannual period, or a year. Virtually all firms prepare an earnings statement *at least* once a year. All earnings statements must state the period of time that they cover.

Every earnings statement should have a heading consisting of the firm's name, statement title, and the time period covered by the statement. A proper statement arrangement shows the total of the individual expenses deducted from the total of the revenue sources. If the expense total exceeds the revenue total, the business suffers a net loss and a decrease in owner's equity. If the revenue total is greater than the expense total, then the business has net earnings and an increase in owner's equity.

As an illustration, the earnings statement for the Staple Employment Agency for the period May 30 to June 30, 1978, has been reproduced in Illustration 3–4.

Illustration 3–4

THE STAPLE EMPLOYMENT AGENCY
Earnings Statement
For the Month Ended June 30, 1978

Revenue:		
Fees earned		$1,705
Expenses:		
Office rent expense	$310	
Advertising expense	73	
Office supplies expense	72	
Dial-A-Phone expense	35	
Wages expense	60	
Miscellaneous expense	20	570
Net earnings		$1,135

Since the revenue total ($1,705) exceeded the expense total ($570), the firm had net earnings or an increase in owner's equity amounting to $1,135 during this time interval. The worksheet served as the preparation source; all revenue and expense account balances were taken directly from it.

Statement of financial position

The statement of financial position (often called the "balance" sheet) is merely a statement of the accounting equation, Assets = Liabilities + Owner's Equity. It is a formal arrangement of the firm's asset, liability and owner's equity accounts as of a given date. Progress of the firm may be evaluated by comparing such statements over a period of time.

The statement of financial position is prepared at a point in time. At any other point in time, any or all of the accounts in the statement may have a different balance. A trained investment analyst can often obtain a great deal of information about a firm by noting the changes in the various account balances from one statement to another.

Every statement of financial position should have a heading consisting of the name of the firm, the name of the statement, and the date of the statement. The statement's format usually consists of a listing of all the asset accounts and their balances on the left side and all the liability and owner's equity accounts and their balances on the right side. Totals are computed and recorded for each side to test for the equality of debits and credits. As an illustration, the statement of financial position as of June 30, 1978, for the Staple Employment Agency has been reproduced in Illustration 3–5. The worksheet was also the source of the information contained in the statement of financial position in Illustration 3–5. All account balances were derived from information contained in it. The total

Illustration 3–5

THE STAPLE EMPLOYMENT AGENCY
Statement of Financial Position
June 30, 1978

Assets		*Liabilities and Owner's Equity*			
Cash......................	$3,307	Liabilities:			
Office furniture	1,140	Accounts payable..........................			$1,212
		Owner's Equity:			
		J. D. Staple, capital,			
		May 30, 1978.............................		$2,500	
		Net earnings.................................	$1,135		
		Less withdrawals...........................	400	735	
		J. D. Staple, capital, June 30, 1978 ...			3,235
		Total Liabilities and			
Total Assets...	$4,447	Owner's Equity..................			$4,447

of Staple's equity, $3,235, may be checked by solving the accounting equation for owner's equity. Total assets minus total liabilities equals total owner's equity ($4,447 − $1,212 = $3,235).

The owner's equity section in the statement of financial position explains how any change in total owner's equity, either through operations or proprietary action, has occurred. Operations for a period that result in net earnings will increase total equity while the incurrence of a net loss decreases total equity. Proprietary action in the form of additional investment increases total equity. On the other hand, asset withdrawal will decrease total equity.

The format of the owner's equity section presents the above relationships in detail. For example, Staple's owner's equity was presented in the following manner:

Owner's Equity:		
J. D. Staple, capital, May 30, 1978..........................		$2,500
Net earnings..	$1,135	
Less withdrawals..	400	735
J. D. Staple, Capital, June 30, 1978......................		$3,235

The first figure, $2,500, was taken from the firm's trial balance account, J. D. Staple, Capital. The net earnings figure of $1,135 was taken from the firm's earnings statement. It represents the link between the statement of financial position and the earnings statement. The figure $400 came from the trial balance account called J. D. Staple, Drawing.

CLOSING THE BOOKS

As mentioned in Chapter 1, revenue and expense accounts are **temporary owner's equity accounts.** They are used to record the increases and decreases in owner's equity due to operations for a period of time. At the end of each accounting period, the data contained in the revenue and expense accounts are transferred to the permanent owner's equity account. This transfer process is referred to as **closing** the books. It is accomplished by making journal entries which are called **closing entries** or clearing entries.

Closing the books accomplishes two fundamental goals. First, it zeros out the balances in all the revenue and expense accounts. Since the earnings statement covers a period of time, it is absolutely essential that it contain only revenue and expenses of that period. Therefore, the revenue and expense accounts must have a zero balance at the start of each accounting period.

Second, closing the books brings the permanent owner's equity account up to date at the end of each period. The ending balance of one period becomes the beginning balance of the next period since only an instant in time has elapsed.

Expense and Revenue Summary account

The revenue and expense accounts are usually not closed *directly* to the Owner's Equity account. Instead, they are closed to another temporary account called the **Expense and Revenue Summary account.** When all the revenue and expense accounts are closed, the Expense and Revenue Summary account should have a balance equal to the net earnings or loss for the period. This provides an additional check for errors. If no errors are found, the Expense and Revenue Summary account is closed to the Owner's Equity account.

Closing revenue accounts

Revenue accounts are closed by transferring their credit balances to the Expense and Revenue Summary account. This is done by debiting each revenue account for its balance to decrease it to zero and crediting the Expense and Revenue Summary account for the same amount.

In the case of the Staple Employment Agency, the journal entry to close the Fees Earned account would be as follows:

Date		Accounts and Explanation	P.R.	Debit	Credit
GENERAL JOURNAL					Page
1978 June	30	Fees Earned Expense and Revenue Summary To close the revenue account.		1,705	1,705

When this entry is posted, the revenue account will have a zero balance. The Expense and Revenue Summary will have a $1,705 credit balance. In this case, the Staple Employment Agency had only one revenue account. If there had been several revenue accounts, they would have been handled in the same manner.

Closing expense accounts

Expense accounts are closed by transferring their debit balances to the Expense and Revenue Summary account. This is accomplished by crediting each of the expense accounts for its debit balance to decrease it to –0– and debiting the Expense and Revenue Summary for the same amount.

The journal entry to close the expense accounts of the Staple Employment Agency is as follows:

GENERAL JOURNAL					Page
Date		Accounts and Explanation	P.R.	Debit	Credit
1978 June	30	Expense and Revenue Summary		570	
		Office Rent Expense			310
		Advertising Expense			73
		Office Supplies Expense			72
		Dial-A-Phone Expense			35
		Wages Expense			60
		Miscellaneous Expense			20
		To close the expense accounts.			

The above journal entry is a compound entry. Each account could have been closed with a separate journal entry. But since each entry would have included a debit to the Expense and Revenue Summary account, the compound entry saves time and space when making closing entries. After posting this entry, the expense accounts all have zero balances, and the Expense and Revenue Summary account has a $1,135 credit balance. You will recall that this was the net earnings figure for the period.

Closing the Expense and Revenue Summary account

The Expense and Revenue Summary account is closed by transferring its balance to the permanent owner's equity account. If the Expense and Revenue Summary account has a credit balance, it will be debited and owner's equity (J. D. Staple, Capital) credited for the amount of the balance in the Expense and Revenue Summary. If a loss has occurred, the Expense and Revenue Summary must be credited and owner's equity (J. D. Staple, Capital) debited.

The Staple Employment Agency example is continued as follows:

GENERAL JOURNAL					Page
Date		Accounts and Explanation	P.R.	Debit	Credit
1978 June	30	Expense and Revenue Summary		1,135	
		J. D. Staple, Capital			1,135
		To close the Expense and Revenue Summary account.			

Closing the drawing account

If the owner has made withdrawals during the period, the drawing account should be closed at the end of the period. This is done by crediting the drawing account and debiting the capital account for the amount of the withdrawals. This will leave the drawing account with a zero balance at the end of the period.

The J. D. Staple, Drawing account is closed out below:

GENERAL JOURNAL					Page ____
Date		Accounts and Explanation	P.R.	Debit	Credit
1978 June	30	J. D. Staple, Capital		400	
		J. D. Staple, Drawing			400
		To close out J. D. Staple's Drawing account.			

Using simple T-account forms, the closing procedure is diagrammed in Illustration 3–6. This may help in understanding the transfer or flow process in closing entries.

Illustration 3–6

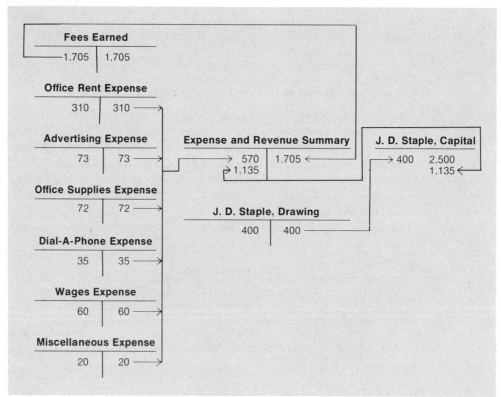

POST-CLOSING TRIAL BALANCE

The **post-closing trial balance** is prepared after all the closing entries have been journalized and posted. Errors can easily be made in the closing process. Many of these may be revealed by an out-of-balance post-closing trial balance. Thus, the post-closing trial balance is one way of checking for errors. It also insures that the books will be in balance at the start of the new accounting period. If subsequent trial balances are not in balance, it must be due to errors in the new accounting period.

The post-closing trial balance should only include those ledger accounts appearing on the statement of financial position. Earnings statement accounts, which are all revenue and expense accounts, and the owner's drawing account have already been closed and hence have zero balances. (Note the illustration of closing procedures presented above.) The post-closing trial balance of the Staple Employment Agency is presented in Illustration 3–7.

Illustration 3–7

THE STAPLE EMPLOYMENT AGENCY
Post-Closing Trial Balance
June 30, 1978

Account No.	Account Title	Debits	Credits
110	Cash	$3,307	
147	Office furniture	1,140	
212	Accounts payable		$1,212
320	J. D. Staple, capital		3,235
		$4,447	$4,447

GLOSSARY

Closing   the act of transferring the balances in the expense and revenue accounts to the Expense and Revenue Summary account and then to the Owner's Equity account.

Closing entries   those entries made which transfer the balances in the expense and revenue accounts to the Expense and Revenue Summary account.

Expense and Revenue Summary   a temporary clearing account to which all revenue and expense account balances are closed at the end of an accounting period.

Post-closing trial balance   a trial balance taken after the expense and revenue accounts have been closed.

Temporary owner's equity accounts   the revenue and expense accounts which are closed to the Expense and Revenue Summary account when financial statements are prepared.

Worksheet   an informal accounting statement which summarizes the trial balance and other information which is needed to prepare the financial statements and the closing entries.

QUESTIONS AND EXERCISES

1. What is the purpose for preparing a worksheet?

2. Explain why the Earnings Statement columns on a worksheet are not usually equal.

3. Which of the following accounts would appear in the Earnings Statement columns of the worksheet, and which of the following accounts would appear in the Financial Position columns of the worksheet?

    E a.   Wages Expense.
    E b.   Accounts Payable.
    F c.   Office Equipment.
    E d.   Advertising Expense.
    F e.   Accounts Receivable.
    F f.   Cash.
    F g.   John Ames, Capital.
    F h.   John Ames, Drawing.
    E i.   Fees Earned.
    E j.   Office Supplies Expense.

4. The Earnings Statement columns of the worksheet have been totaled. The total of the debit column is $6,045, and the total of the credit column is $8,600. What does the difference represent?

5. The Corner Rental Agency earned revenue of $2,500 during April. It also incurred the following expenses during April: advertising, $200; office supplies, $300; wages, $600; telephone, $50; and utilities, $30. Compute the Corner Rental Agency's net earnings or loss for the month of April.

6. What effect does each of the following items have on owner's equity?

    + a.   Net earnings.
    − b.   Net loss.
    + c.   Additional investment by the owner.
    − d.   Withdrawal of assets by the owner.
    S e.   The purchase of office equipment on account.
    S f.   The purchase of office furniture for cash.

7. What two fundamental goals are accomplished by closing the books?

8. Given the account balances shown below, make the entries to (*a*) close the revenue account, (*b*) close the expense accounts, (*c*) close the expense and revenue summary account, and (*d*) close the drawing account.

    Cash .... $ 6,000
    Fees earned............................   12,000

Telephone expense	60
Wages expense..........................	4,840
Rent expense............................	2,400
Insurance expense	200
Accounts payable	1,000
R. M. Nifer, drawing..................	5,000
R. M. Nifer, capital	5,500

All of the accounts have normal balances.

9. At what point in the accounting cycle is a post-closing trial balance prepared?

10. What accounts appear in the post-closing trial balance?

PROBLEMS

3–1. The W. L. Nelson Company had the following trial balance at the end of the year:

W. L. NELSON COMPANY
Trial Balance
December 31, 1978

Account Title	*Debit*	*Credit*
Accounts payable....		$ 950
Accounts receivable	$ 4,000	
Cash...................	1,250	
Revenue from services.....		12,550
Rent expense........	2,400	
Wages expense	8,000	
Miscellaneous expenses.......	600	
Notes payable		2,500
Office equipment....	2,000	
Office furniture	1,850	
Taxes payable		750
W. L. Nelson, capital....		4,550
W. L. Nelson, drawing....	1,200	
	$21,300	$21,300

Required:

Prepare a statement of financial position.

3–2. The C. R. Olson Company had the following accounts in their trial balance at December 31:

Gas and oil expense...	135
Miscellaneous expenses..	85

Rent expense.. 2,000
Revenue from services 8,000
Taxes expense 1,000
Telephone expense 150
Utilities expense 150
Wages expense 2,500

Required:

1. Prepare an earnings statement for the year ended December 31.
2. Prepare closing entries.

3-3. The R. J. Williams Company had the following worksheet on December 31, 1978:

R. J. WILLIAMS COMPANY
Worksheet
For the Year Ended December 31, 1978

Account Title	Trial Balance		Earnings Statement		Statement of Financial Position	
	Debit	Credit	Debit	Credit	Debit	Credit
Accounts payable		700				
Accounts receivable	2,250					
Cash	850					
Rent expense	350					
Revenue from services		2,500				
R. J. Williams, capital		1,500				
R. J. Williams, drawing	380					
Salary expense	750					
Telephone expense	85					
Utilities expense	35					
	4,700	4,700				

Required:

1. Complete the worksheet.
2. Prepare in good form an—

   a. Earnings statement.
   b. Statement of financial position.

3. Prepare the closing entries.

3-4. The J. C. Roberts Company had the following worksheet at the end of the year.

J. C. ROBERTS COMPANY
Worksheet
For the Year Ended December 31, 1978

Account Title	Trial Balance		Earnings Statement		Statement of Financial Position	
	Debit	Credit	Debit	Credit	Debit	Credit
Accounts payable		675				
Accounts receivable	1,500					
Cash	650					
Depreciation expense	150					
Gas and oil expense	150					
J. C. Roberts, capital		6,100				
J. C. Roberts, drawing	1,500					
Merchandise inventory	1,850					
Miscellaneous expense	75					
Mortgage payable		2,500				
Notes payable		4,000				
Notes receivable	3,500					
Office equipment	4,000					
Office furniture	1,500					
Repair parts expense	2,000					
Revenue from services		4,000				
Taxes payable		550				
Telephone expense	125					
Utilities expense	50					
Wages expense	775					
	17,825	17,825				

Required:
1. Complete the worksheet.
2. Prepare in good form an—

    a. Earnings statement.
    b. Statement of financial position.

3. Prepare the closing entries.

3–5. J. F. Bell, owner of Bell Company, has just given you the following list of accounts and wants you to prepare a statement of financial position for December 31, 1978. Each account has a normal balance.

Accounts payable	$ 500
Accounts receivable	1,400
Cash	1,250
J. F. Bell, capital	1,700
J. F. Bell, drawing	800

Revenue from services... 13,250
Rent expense 1,800
Wages expense 9,600
Miscellaneous expenses 600

3–6. J. C. Athens, owner of Athens Company, has just given you the following list of accounts and wants you to prepare an earnings statement for the year ended December 31, 1978. Each account has a normal balance.

Gas and oil expense... $ 200
Rent expense... 450
Repair parts expense... 1,500
Revenue from services 2,500
Salaries expense... 500
Telephone expense 150

Cash and cash records
Learning objectives

The contents of this chapter are intended to provide
a working knowledge of accounting for cash. The
following material is introduced.

1. A description of cash items or items considered
   to be cash.
2. The procedures used in recording in and posting
   from the cash journal.
3. The procedures used in recording cash receipts
   in the cash receipts journal.
4. Posting from the cash receipts journal to the
   appropriate accounts.
5. Recording cash disbursements and posting from
   the cash disbursements journal to the
   appropriate accounts.
6. The use of a petty cash fund and the related
   accounting procedures.
7. The procedures used for bank credit card
   transactions.

4

Cash and cash records

To most individuals **cash** consists of coins and currency. But in a business, cash usually has a much broader meaning. It includes coins, currency, and any instrument a bank will accept for immediate deposit. These include personal checks, traveler's checks, cashier's checks, money orders, and bank drafts.

Some items are often handled like cash but are not cash. Stamps, IOUs, and postdated checks are examples. (A check received on June 5 but dated June 7 is an example of a postdated check. It cannot be deposited on June 5.) Stamps and IOUs cannot be deposited. Consequently, they should be recorded in other ledger accounts, such as Accounts Receivable and Office Supplies.

It is customary to list assets in the statement of financial position in the order of their **liquidity** (the relative ease of converting assets to cash without loss of value). Thus, cash is listed first because it is the most liquid and the most readily spendable form of asset if there are no legal restrictions on its use. Most businesses have a large number of cash transactions. Cash is commonly received from cash sales, collections on accounts receivable, and the sale of other assets. Such receipts are debited to the Cash account, thus increasing the asset. Common types of cash disbursements which are credited to the Cash account and decrease the asset include payment of wages, payment of accounts payable, the purchase of assets, and the payment of various expenses.

Because currency cannot be identified if it is stolen and because cash transactions are quite numerous, special procedures are established to handle and account for cash. Usually, this involves the separation of the duties of handling cash from the recording of entries to account for cash.

69

CASH RECEIPTS

One means of verifying cash receipts is to have the employee collecting cash, such as a salesclerk or receptionist, make two lists of all cash receipts in a given period of time. One copy of the list remains with the receipts until a deposit is made. The **deposit slip** is verified by a comparison with the list of the actual receipts. The list should include the name of the party from whom the cash was received, the date, the form (currency or check) of cash received, and the amount received. Formal receipts can be prepared in duplicate with the original given to the customer and the copy to the bookkeeper. In businesses where cash receipts are quite numerous, they may be recorded in cash registers with the cash register tape providing the list of receipts. Regardless of the method used, the bookkeeper should not handle the cash. The temptation to steal the cash and attempt to conceal the theft by altering the accounting records may be too great.

CASH DISBURSEMENTS

A disbursement, or payment, may be made by either currency or check. It is usually better to use checks since the check will serve as a receipt for the payment. If currency is used, a receipt is an absolute necessity. Furthermore, if currency is used, the amount of currency kept on hand at all times may have to be very large. This creates an additional problem of preventing the theft of the currency.

THE CASH JOURNAL

As you will recall, the journal is the book of original entry. Up to this point, we have used only one—the general journal. A business often uses several journals. Normally, any given transaction is recorded in *only one journal.* If certain types of transactions occur frequently, a special journal may be designed to permit easy recording of these transactions. For example, **cash journals** are designed to make the recording of receipts and disbursements of cash easier than if such transactions were recorded in a two-column general journal. Since cash transactions always include either a debit or a credit to the Cash account, a four-column journal may be appropriate. An example of such a journal is shown below. The transactions include a cash sale of $100 on June 14. The $100 of cash received is recorded in the Cash debit column. The date is entered, the name of the account credited—Sales—is placed in the Description column, and the $100 is entered in the General credit column.

CASH JOURNAL								**Page 1**
Cash		Date		Description	P.R.	General		
Debit	Credit					Debit	Credit	
100		1978 June	14	Sales			100	
	50		14	Telephone expense		50		

The second entry records the payment of the telephone bill by entering a debit to the Telephone Expense account and a credit to Cash of $50. Note that the use of the four-column journal eliminates the writing of the account title Cash every time a cash transaction is recorded. This can save a considerable amount of time if many cash transactions occur. There can also be time savings in the posting process as will be seen later. Also, note that cash transactions are recorded on a single line.

When a journal page is filled with entries, the page should be proved. This is also done for partial pages when the accounting period ends and the journal must be posted to the general ledger. Each column is totaled separately. If the total debits and credits are not equal, the entries are not in balance, and a search must be started to find the error. No further steps should be taken until the error is located. The total of each column is placed in small pencil figures just below the last line containing an entry.

CASH JOURNAL								**Page 1**
Cash		Date		Description	P.R.	General		
Debit	Credit					Debit	Credit	
100		1978 June	14	Sales			100	
	50		14	Telephone expense		50		
100	50					50	100	

In addition, the journal is usually footed and ruled at the end of each month. It is common practice to enter the footing totals on the line below the last entry and to draw two lines across all amount columns beneath the footing totals.

CASH JOURNAL					Page 1	
Cash		Date	Description	P.R.	General	
Debit	Credit				Debit	Credit
		1978				
100		June 14	Sales			100
	50	14	Telephone expense		50	
100	50				50	100
100	50	14			50	100

At the end of each month, the cash balance is often placed in small figures in the Description column. This amount is obtained from last month's balance plus the cash debits minus the cash credits.

CASH JOURNAL					Page 1	
Cash		Date	Description	P.R.	General	
Debit	Credit				Debit	Credit
		1978	500			
100		June 14	Sales			100
	50	14	Telephone expense		50	
100	50		550		50	100
100	50	14			50	100

For the next month, a new page is started with the cash balance placed in small figures at the very top of the Description column in the same manner as the $500 in the illustration.

Posting the cash journal includes the posting of the *totals* from the Cash debit and credit columns to the Cash account and the *individual items* to the general ledger accounts. The cash is posted only after it has been proved, which is usually weekly or even daily. The other debit and credit items are usually posted at the same time. The ledger account number is placed below the cash totals in parentheses to indicate that the figures have been posted. When the general debits and credits are posted, a check in parentheses (✔) is penciled below the double rulings under the General columns. As the individual general items are posted to the ledger accounts, the appropriate account numbers are placed in the P.R. (posting reference) columns (see Illustration 4–1).

After the cash journal is proved, the bank account balance and the currency on hand should equal the cash balance in the journal. The current cash journal balance should also be equal to the opening cash balance plus the receipts minus the disbursements. This may be com-

Illustration 4–1

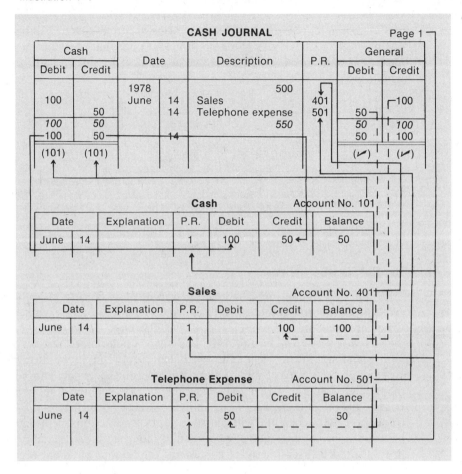

pared to the balance in the check register (assuming the check register also shows deposits) plus the cash on hand which should be verified by actual count. Check registers will be described in a later chapter.

When cash is handled, there are usually some mistakes. For example, too much or too little change may have been given to a customer. As a result, actual cash collections may differ from the amount of cash we should have on hand. This difference is recorded in a separate ledger account called **Cash Short and Over.** In the long-run, shortages and overages often tend to balance each other out. When financial statements are prepared at the end of an accounting period, the account is closed out to the Expense and Revenues Summary account. If there is a debit balance in the Cash Short and Over account at the end of the accounting period, it is treated like an expense. A credit balance is handled like a revenue account.

For example, assume that the accounting record showed cash receipts (all from cash sales for a given day) of $100 but that only $98 in coins, currency, and checks were actually on hand. The entry in the journal would look like this:

	CASH JOURNAL				Page 1	
Cash		Date	Description	P.R.	General	
Debit	Credit				Debit	Credit
98		1978 July 1	Sales			100
			Cash short and over		2	

CASH RECEIPTS JOURNAL

When the volume of cash receipt transactions is very large, a **cash receipts journal** may be used. This journal is used to record transactions which involve only the *receipt* of cash. The exact form of this special journal will vary from firm to firm. The form is determined largely by the nature and size of the firm. The journal presented in Illustration 4–2 is an example of a typical multicolumn cash receipts journal. The number of special columns (such as sales and accounts receivable) depends largely on the preference of the individual firm. If an account is used frequently in connection with cash receipts transactions, it is likely to have its own column in the cash receipts journal. As an example, if a firm granted a discount to its customers for prompt payment on credit

Illustration 4–2

					CASH RECEIPTS JOURNAL		Page		
Date	Account	Cash, Dr.	Sales, Cr.	Accounts Receivable, Cr.	P.R.	General	P.R.	Dr.	Cr.

Illustration 4–3

CASH RECEIPTS JOURNAL

Page

Date		Account	Cash, Dr.	Sales, Cr.	Accounts Receivable, Cr.	P.R.	General	P.R.	Dr.	Cr.
1978										
Aug.	1	Cash sales	1,250	1,250						
	2	A Co.	500		500	121				
	2	B Co.	700		700	122				
	3	Sold office equipment	900				Office equip.	151		900
	6	Cash sales	1,000	1,000						
	9	Borrowed from bank	7,000				Notes payable	220		7,000
	10	Cash sales	1,300	1,300						
	10		12,650	3,550	1,200					7,900
			(101)	(401)	(120)					(✓)

sales (discussed in Chapter 9), the cash receipts journal would usually contain a column for the account, "Sales Discounts."

The following example will illustrate the use of the cash receipts journal (see Illustration 4–3) and its advantages. The list of transactions which follows contains only cash receipt transactions. All other transactions are recorded in the general journal or other special journals that the firm may use. These other journals will be discussed later in this chapter and in Chapter 9.

Date		Transaction
1978		
Aug.	1	Cash sales of $1,250.
	2	A Company paid $500 on its account.
	2	B Company paid $700 on its account.
	3	Sold office equipment for $900 cash that was purchased earlier this year for $900.
	6	Cash sales of $1,000.
	9	Borrowed $7,000 from the bank on a note payable.
	10	Cash sales of $1,300.

As shown in Illustration 4–3, in each transaction the receipt of cash is recorded by placing the amount in the Cash debit column. When the cash was received for sales, the amount was recorded in the special Sales credit column. When the cash received represented a collection on an account receivable, the amount was entered in the special Accounts Receivable Credit column. No special columns are included in the journal for recording the credit part of the entries for the sale of the equipment or the borrowing of money from the bank. Thus, the titles of the accounts credited must be written in the column headed "General." This column is used whenever an entry must be made in an account for which a special column does not exist.

Note that cash does not have to be written out and that common transactions such as cash received from sales and collections on accounts receivable require no account title to be written. This can save a substantial amount of time.

Posting the cash receipts journal

At any time during the month, the individual items in the General accounts column may be posted to the appropriate accounts in the ledger. At that time, the account number is written in the P.R. (posting reference) column of the cash receipts journal. At the same time, the page number and the journal name are placed in the P.R. column of the account to show the source of the ledger entry.

At regular intervals, often daily or weekly, the individual amounts recorded in the special columns are posted to the individual ledger accounts. Once again, the system of cross-referencing is used to allow easy tracing of the entries. The individual amounts in the Accounts Receivable credit column are posted to the individual accounts at frequent intervals. The appropriate account number is placed in the P.R. column. For example, $500 was posted to A Company's individual account receivable, Account No. 121. The Account No. 121 was then placed in the P.R. column (next to the Accounts Receivable credit column) of the cash receipts journal.

All columns are usually footed and ruled at the end of the month. The totals of the special columns are posted to the appropriate ledger accounts. For example, the total of the Accounts Receivable credit column is posted to the ledger account, Accounts Receivable. When a column total is posted, the appropriate account number is placed below the total in that column to show that it has been posted. The journal page number and journal name are placed in the posting reference column of the ledger account. The totals of the General accounts columns are not posted since they do not represent a single account. The items in these columns have already been posted individually.

CASH DISBURSEMENTS JOURNAL

The volume of cash disbursement transactions might dictate the need for a special journal to handle cash disbursements. Just as we saw in the case of cash receipts, this may allow for a logical division of accounting labor and may save time in the recording and in the posting of cash disbursement transactions.

The exact form of the **cash disbursements journal** may vary substantially. The form used is determined by the size and nature of the business as well as by the requirements for accounting information. Illustration 4–4

Illustration 4–4

	CASH DISBURSEMENTS JOURNAL								Page	
Date	Check No.	Account	Cash, Cr.	Accounts Payable, Dr.	P.R.	General	P.R.	Dr.	Cr.

Illustration 4–5

	**CASH DISBURSEMENTS JOURNAL**　　　　　Page 1
Date	Check No.	Account	Cash, Cr.	Accounts Payable, Dr.	P.R.	General	P.R.	Dr.	Cr.
1978									
Aug. 2	302		120			Advertising exp.	511	120	
3	303	X Co.	600	600	210				
4	304	Y Co.	700	700	211				
6	305		1,200			Salaries exp.	520	1,200	
9	306	Z Co.	1,500	1,500	212				
10	307		2,000			Delivery equip.	161	10,000	
						Notes payable	220		8,000
16	308		8,025			Notes payable	220	8,000	
						Interest exp.	531	25	
16			14,145	2,800				19,345	8,000
			(101)	(201)				(✔)	(✔)

is an example of a cash disbursements journal page. It contains the special columns commonly found in cash disbursements journals.

The number of special columns for individual accounts can vary from firm to firm. Often there will be many more special columns than the number shown in the example. If an account is used quite frequently in connection with cash disbursements, it usually has its own column in the cash disbursements journal.

The transactions listed below represent some typical cash disbursements for the month of August. These transactions will illustrate the special cash disbursements journal (see Illustration 4–5). Transactions not involving cash disbursements have been omitted since they would be recorded in other journals.

Date	Check No.	Transaction
1978		
Aug. 2	302	Paid $120 for newspaper advertising.
3	303	Paid $600 to X Company for supplies purchased earlier on credit.
4	304	Paid $700 on account to Y Company.
6	305	Paid $1,200 for weekly salaries.
9	306	Paid $1,500 on account to Z Company.

Date	Check	
1978	No.	Transaction
Aug. 10	307	Paid $2,000 down for a $10,000 delivery truck and borrowed the remainder.
16	308	Paid loan on delivery truck plus $25 interest—$8,025.

In each transaction, the credit to Cash was recorded by placing the appropriate amount in the special Cash credit column (Illustration 4–5). The payments on accounts payable taking place on August 3, 4, and 9, were completed by placing the appropriate amount in the special Accounts Payable debit column. The other transactions require the writing of the individual account titles in the General accounts column. The transactions on the August 10 and August 16 required that two accounts be written in the General column. As you may remember, these are called compound journal entries. Any of the accounts that were written in the General column could have its own special column if it was used frequently enough to need a special column.

Posting the cash disbursements journal

Posting the cash disbursements journal is similar to posting the cash receipts journal. At intervals during the month, the items in the General accounts column are posted to the ledger accounts. The account number of each account posted is placed in the P.R. column of the cash disbursements journal after the account is posted. A coding for the appropriate journal name and page is placed in the P.R. column of the ledger account at the same time. For example, the transaction of August 10 is shown in Illustration 4–6 as it would be posted. Note that only the *totals* of the special columns are posted, in this case, Cash. In this example the abbreviation "CDJ" is used for the cash disbursements journal when it is referenced in the ledger account.

The individual amounts in the Accounts Payable debit column are posted to the individual accounts at frequent intervals, daily if possible. Frequent posting is necessary if a company desires current information about its transactions with creditors. Again, the same cross-referencing system is used.

All columns are footed and ruled at the end of the month. The totals of the individual special account columns are posted to their respective accounts in the ledger. As each total is posted, the account number is written below the column total. Likewise, the appropriate journal name and page number are recorded in the ledger account P.R. column. The *total* of the Accounts Payable debit column is posted to a control or master account for accounts payable in the general ledger. At any point in time when posting is completed, the total of the *individual* accounts

Illustration 4–6

CASH DISBURSEMENTS JOURNAL Page 1

Date		Check No.	Account	Cash, Cr.	Accounts Payable, Dr.	P.R.	General	P.R.	Dr.	Cr.
1978										
Aug.	2	302		120			Advertising exp.	511	120	
	3	303	X Co.	600	600	210				
	4	304	Y Co.	700	700	211				
	6	305		1,200			Salaries exp.	520	1,200	
	9	306	Z Co.	1,500	1,500	212				
	10	307		2,000			Delivery equip.	161	10,000	
							Notes payable	220		8,000
	16	308		8,025			Notes payable	220	8,000	
							Interest exp.	531	25	
	16			14,145	2,800				19,345	8,000
				(101)	(201)				(✓)	(✓)

Cash   Account No. 101

Date		Explanation	P.R.	Debit	Credit	Balance
1978 Aug.	16		CDJ-1		14,145	

Delivery Equipment   Account No. 161

Date		Explanation	P.R.	Debit	Credit	Balance
1978 Aug.	10		CDJ-1	10,000		

Notes Payable   Account No. 220

Date		Explanation	P.R.	Debit	Credit	Balance
1978 Aug.	10		CDJ-1		8,000	

payable should equal the balance in the general ledger account for accounts payable. The *totals* for the General accounts columns are not posted; rather, the individual items are posted to the accounts named.

PETTY CASH

For control purposes, most cash disbursements are made by check. But, for some small expenditures, the convenience of having coins and currency immediately available outweighs the safeguard of using checks. The amounts expended are not usually large. Hence, a small supply of

Illustration 4-7

PETTY CASH VOUCHER

Number ___22___ Date August 15, 1978

Amount Six Dollars _____ $ 6.00

Paid to Marlane Gruver

For Coffee Supplies

Approved BKN Received by M. Gruver

Expense account Miscellaneous

cash (a fund) can be maintained. Whenever the fund becomes low or at the end of an accounting period, the cash supply is replenished. The **petty cash fund,** like all assets, should have adequate controls placed on it to insure its proper use. Usually one person, called the petty cash custodian, is given the responsibility of operating the petty cash fund. This person makes the disbursements and keeps a record of the fund's activity.

Each time a disbursement is made from the petty cash fund, a **petty cash voucher** is filled out. The exact form of the voucher may vary from firm to firm. However, several characteristics are quite common. Vouchers are often prenumbered for control purposes. The date of the disbursement and the name of the recipient are also necessary. Illustration 4-7 is a typical petty cash voucher.

At any point in time, the coins and currency plus the total of the completed petty cash vouchers on hand should equal the amount originally placed in the fund. This voucher system is known as the *imprest fund* method of handling petty cash. This is the most common method used by firms.

The petty cash fund illustrated

To begin the use of a petty cash fund, a check is cashed for the amount of the fund. For example, suppose a fund will be created for $100. The necessary journal entry to create the fund is shown below in a four-column cash journal:

CASH JOURNAL						General		Page 1
Cash		Date	Description	P.R.				
Debit	Credit				Debit	Credit
	100	1978 June 15	Petty cash To create a petty cash fund		100	

When the fund runs short of currency, the vouchers will be totaled for each type of expense. The total amount of the vouchers should be the amount of cash needed to bring the petty cash fund to its *original balance*. In this example, cash totaling $27 and petty cash vouchers of $73 make up the fund at the time of replenishment. The necessary journal entry to restore the fund's cash balance to $100 is as follows:

CASH JOURNAL						General		Page 2
Cash		Date	Description	P.R.				
Debit	Credit				Debit	Credit
	73	1978 June 30	Postage expense Office repair expense Telephone expense Miscellaneous expense		9 18 31 15	

The expense debit information is taken from the vouchers turned in by the fund custodian, who must turn in completed vouchers to receive additional cash.

Note that no additional debit has been made to the petty cash fund. The fund is debited only when it is *created* or *increased* in size. The petty cash fund is credited only when it is *decreased* in size. Changes in the fund size would be made if it became apparent that the fund was either too small or too large to meet the firm's needs.

As was mentioned earlier, errors may sometimes occur when handling cash. When such errors occur in connection with the operation of a petty cash fund, the cash and vouchers no longer total to the original amount. The difference between the original amount and the total of the coins, currency, and petty cash vouchers is recorded in the account "Cash Short and Over." For example, if the fund has excess cash and vouchers on hand, a credit is recorded. At the end of the accounting period, the Cash Short and Over account is considered an expense if it has a debit balance and a revenue if it has a credit balance.

Continuing the example, at the end of July the fund had coins and currency of $21 and petty cash vouchers totaling $71. The following entry would be recorded (the expense details are computed from the returned vouchers):

CASH JOURNAL						Page 3	
Cash		Date	Description	P.R.	General		
Debit	Credit				Debit	Credit
	79	1978 July 31	Postage expense		17	
			Office maintenance expense		22	
			Telephone expense		15	
			Miscellaneous expense		17	
			Cash short and over		8	

At the end of August, the office manager decided that the fund should be increased to $150 to meet all petty cash demands for the month. At this time, a count of the petty cash fund shows coins and currency of $8 and vouchers of $92. The journal entry is:

CASH JOURNAL						Page 4	
Cash		Date	Description	P.R.	General		
Debit	Credit				Debit	Credit
	142	1978 Aug. 31	Petty cash		50	
			Postage expense		13	
			Telephone expense		16	
			Telegraph expense		10	
			Office supplies expense		23	
			Miscellaneous expense		30	

Large petty cash funds may have a book similar to the one found below to summarize transactions.

PETTY CASH BOOK

Date	Voucher or Check No.	Receipts	Payments	Postage	Freight	Office Supplies	General	
							Amount	Description

A statement of petty cash disbursements can be made by listing the totals of each type of disbursement and totaling all of them for the total disbursements.

It should be noted that the petty cash book is *not* a journal. The transactions must still be recorded in the cash journal.

BANK CREDIT CARD TRANSACTIONS

There has been a recent trend toward the frequent use of bank credit cards. Two of the more common bank credit cards are Master Charge and Bank Americard.

Bank credit card transactions are handled in a manner similar to cash transactions.

When a customer uses a bank credit card to pay a bill, three or four copies of a special sales slip are filled out by the cashier. A Master Charge sales slip is shown in Illustration 4–8. The number in the upper right-hand corner of the sales slip is the authorization number. It is designated by the bank for a specific business such as Landers Dry Cleaners. When services are charged on the Master Charge card, the spaces on the sales slip are filled in for the date of the transaction, the department number, and the cashier's or clerk's name or initials. The other spaces provide information about the nature of the transaction; they are labeled Quantity, Class, Description, Unit Cost, Amount, Tax, and Total.

After the special sales slip has been completed by the cashier, it is placed in a credit card recorder. The customer's Master Charge card is placed on the upper left-hand section of the sales slip. When a lever is pulled across the sales slip, all the raised lettering on the Master Charge card is printed on the sales slip. The raised lettering includes such information as the customer's name, credit card number, and the expiration date on the credit card. The sales slip and Master Charge card are re-

Illustration 4-8
Master Charge sales slip

Illustration 4-9

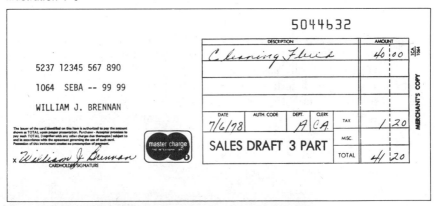

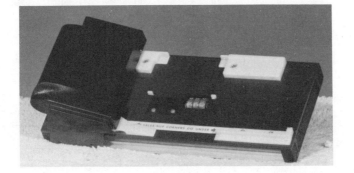

Illustration 4–9 (*continued*)

moved from the credit card recorder. The customer is then asked to sign the sales slip in the space marked Cardholder's Signature. The customer receives one copy of the sales slip. A completed Master Charge sales slip is shown in Illustration 4–9 along with a Master Charge credit card and a credit card recorder.

Just as cash should be deposited in the bank daily, Master Charge credit card sales slips should also be deposited daily.

The total number of Master Charge sales slips and the total dollar amount represented on the sales slips should be determined. Then a Merchant Draft should be prepared (see Illustration 4–10). The business's name, address, bank account number, and member number all appear on the Merchant Draft. The date, the number of sales slips, the gross dollars and cents amount, the amount of refunds made to credit

Illustration 4–10
Merchant draft

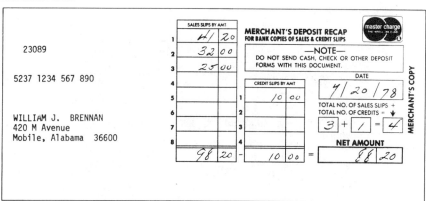

card customers, and the net sales total must be filled in by the bookkeeper. There are three copies of the Merchant Draft: one copy is retained by the business, and the other copies are forwarded to the bank with the Master Charge sales slips.

GLOSSARY

Cash   coins, currency, and anything else a bank will accept for immediate deposit. This includes personal checks, traveler's checks, cashier's checks, money orders, bank drafts, and credit card receipts from sales.

Cash disbursements journal   a special journal used when the volume of cash transactions is quite large to record only transactions involving cash disbursements.

Cash journal   a special journal used to record only transactions involving cash receipts and cash disbursements.

Cash receipts journal   a special journal used when the volume of cash transactions is quite large to record only transactions involving cash receipts.

Cash short and over   a separate account used to record the difference between actual cash collections and the amount that should be on hand.

Deposit slip   a written record which shows and acknowledges the receipt of a deposit by a bank.

Liquidity   the relative ease of converting certain assets into cash without loss of value.

Petty cash fund   usually, a small sum of money established as a separate fund from which minor cash disbursements for authorized purposes are to be made. When the imprest fund method is used, the cash in the fund plus the vouchers covering disbursements from the fund must equal the balance which is shown in the ledger for the fund.

Petty cash voucher   a form provided with spaces for recording data concerning disbursements from the petty cash fund. The information recorded often includes the amount of the disbursement, to whom it was made, for what purpose, and an authorizing signature for the disbursement.

QUESTIONS AND EXERCISES

1. What are the components of cash from the viewpoint of a business? checks money orders

2. Why is cash listed first in the statement of financial position? most liquid

3. Why are special procedures established to handle the Cash account. What are some of these special procedures? safety.

4. When is it necessary to debit an account called Cash Short and Over? When should the account be credited?

5. What is a petty cash fund? What is the imprest fund method? *Small fund for minor transactions (cash)* *recording of paym*

6. When is the Petty Cash account debited, and when is it credited?

7. The Martin Company established a petty cash fund of $100. At the end of May, the total of the completed petty cash vouchers was $80. Coins and currency amounted to $19. The expenses were as follows:

Telephone expense $25
Office supplies expense 20
Postage expense.. 15
Freight expense 20

What entry should be made in the cash journal to replenish the petty cash fund?

8. Describe a cash receipts journal and a cash disbursements journal. What advantages result from using these special journals?

9. What cash journal entry should be made to create a $200 petty cash fund?

10. Record the following transactions in a four-column journal:

May 3   Purchased office supplies for cash, $75.
     18   Paid telephone bill, $26.
     22   Had cash sales totaling $300.
     29   Received $80 in payment of an account receivable.
     31   Paid secretary's salary, $600.

11. Name two widely used bank credit cards.

12. What information can be found on a merchant draft?

13. Describe the procedures that are followed by a cashier when a customer presents a bank credit card in exchange for goods or services.

PROBLEMS

4-1. E. F. Jones Company completed the following cash transactions during the month of May 1978.

1978
May 1   Paid the rent for May, $150.
      3   Paid the secretary's salary, $450.
      4   Received for services $855 cash.
      6   Received a check from D. A. Bain in payment of an account, $1,350.
    15   Paid the utility bill, $45.
    18   Received a check from William Brown in payment of an account, $1,000.
    23   Received for services $750 cash.
    24   Purchased a calculator paying cash $845.

25 Received for services $325 cash.
26 Paid the telephone bill, $38.

Required:

Journalize the transactions in the cash journal and total and rule at the end of the month.

4–2. J. A. Wilson Company had the following cash receipts during the month of June 1978:

1978
June 1 Received a check for $850 from B. B. Carson in payment of an account.
    4 Counted cash at the end of the day finding $93 in the cash register while sales totaled $95.
    5 Received a check in payment of an account from A. L. Knight for $1,500.
    8 Counted cash at the end of the day finding $106 in the cash register; sales totaled $105.
    15 Received a check for $250 from K. K. Corbett in payment of an account.
    20 J. A. Wilson put $350 into the business.
    23 Received a check for $350 from the Atlanta Company in payment of an account.
    24 Cash sales were $75; cash of $74 was in the cash register.

Required:

Journalize the transactions in the cash receipts journal and total and rule at the end of the month.

4–3. Wilton John's Company completed the following cash disbursements during July 1978.

Date	Check No.	Transactions	
1978			
July 1	301	Purchased a typewriter.............................	$ 450
3	302	Paid rent for the month	100
5	303	Purchased an office desk...........................	300
5	304	Paid a note payable.................................	1,200
8	305	Purchased an adding machine....................	125
15	306	Paid an account payable to X Co.	255
18	307	Owner withdrew cash	250
22	308	Paid for telephone	85
25	309	Paid wages...	475
29	310	Purchased a calculator	850
29	311	Paid an account payable to W Co.	1,250

Required:

Journalize the transactions in the cash disbursements journal and total and rule at the end of the month.

4-4. W. W. Thrower, contractor, began operations on June 1, 1978. On this date Thrower invested $5,000 cash in the operations. In addition to this initial investment, Thrower completed the following transactions during the month of June:

1978

June 1 Paid rent for June, $150.

3 Received a check from Spots, Inc., for services rendered, $385.

5 Paid telephone bill, $27.85.

7 Paid utility bill, $23.50.

10 Received a check from Wonder World for services rendered, $875.

11 Withdrew $350 for personal use.

12 Received a check from J. D. Swift for services rendered, $1,875.

15 Paid secretary for the first half of the month, $225.

20 Received a check from C. O. Dunn for services rendered, $1,250.

21 Withdrew $200 for personal use.

25 Paid Janitorial Service $25 for cleaning the office.

27 Received a check from A. B. Thompson for services rendered, $650.

29 Paid secretary's salary for the second half of the month, $225.

29 Withdrew $500 for personal use.

Thrower established a chart of accounts as follows:

Account No.	*Name of Account*
101	Cash
310	W. W. Thrower, Capital
311	W. W. Thrower, Drawing
410	Professional fees
510	Utilities Expense
515	Telephone Expense
520	Rent Expense
525	Salary Expense
530	Miscellaneous Expense

Required:

1. Using a four-column cash journal, journalize the above transactions.
2. Total and rule each journal.
3. Open ledger accounts and post the journal entries.
4. Prepare a trial balance.

4-5. Give the general journal entry for the replenishment of a $150 petty cash fund when the cashier reports the following authorized disbursements. The cash on hand at the time of replenishment was $23.75.

Postage $56.75

Office supplies 23.40

Taxicabs 12.75
Telephone 3.50
Repairs 26.85

4–6. The A. B. Cohen Company wants to have a petty cash fund and you have been asked to set it up and handle the transactions for it. The transactions are as follows:

1978
June 1 Set up petty cash fund with $75.
     30 Replenish petty cash with the following expenses:

Postage.. $25
Office supplies 28
Miscellaneous... 15

July 15 Replenish petty cash with the following expenses:

Postage.. $ 3
Travel expense 55
Office supplies 2
Miscellaneous... 3

     30 Replenish petty cash and increase the fund to $100.

Travel expense $45
Postage.. 15
Office supplies 5

Required:

Journalize the transactions in the cash journal.

Checking account procedures
Learning objectives

The material in this chapter is intended to provide a basic understanding of the use and maintenance of a checking account. The following items are discussed.

1. The nature and purpose of a checking account.
2. A description of the various items and procedures associated with a checking account.
3. The mechanics of maintaining a checkbook.
4. The purpose and method of performing a bank reconciliation.
5. Journalizing the entries resulting from the bank reconciliation.

5

Checking account procedures

NATURE AND PURPOSE OF CHECKING ACCOUNTS

A very large part of the cash that flows through the business community is transferred by check. Currency is very difficult to control since it is hard to identify specifically. The use of checks greatly reduces the risk of a firm's cash being misused. With proper control procedures which include the use of checks, a firm can be relatively certain that its cash disbursements are being properly handled. The fundamental features, documents, and procedures relating to the maintenance of a checking account are discussed in this chapter.

ELEMENTS OF A CHECKING ACCOUNT

A checking account (sometimes referred to as a bank or commercial account) is opened by obtaining the permission of the bank and making deposits of items acceptable to the bank. Items commonly accepted for deposit include money, checks, bank drafts, and money orders. Terms are set up with the bank with the restrictions that pertain to each account. Such restrictions might include a requirement for the signatures of two different company officials on each check over a specified amount. The bank specifies which checks and deposit tickets are to be used.

Signature card

The **signature card** contains the signature of each of the individuals authorized to sign checks drawn against the account. The bank is au-

thorized to honor checks drawn on the account which have been signed
by any individual whose signature appears on the signature card for that
account. A check drawn on the account and signed by anyone else should
not be honored by the bank. The bank will check the signature card if
there is doubt about the authenticity of a check signature. The signature
card thus serves to protect both the bank and the depositor.

The deposit ticket

The **deposit ticket** contains the name of the bank, the company's
name, the account number, and the date. The first three items are usually

Illustration 5–1
Deposit ticket

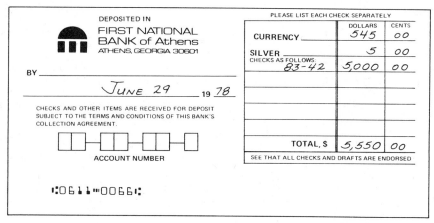

preprinted on the deposit ticket. The date is inserted when filling out the
ticket. Currency and coin are totaled separately, and the amounts are
entered on the ticket. The amount of each check is listed along with the
check's bank number which is found in the upper right-hand corner. The
numerals above the line designate the bank on which the check was
drawn. This is the bank's transit number assigned by the American
Bankers Association. The numbers below the line indicate the Federal
Reserve District in which the bank is located and other routing information. The deposit ticket shown in Illustration 5–1 lists a check for $5,000.
The bank number for this check is 83–42.

Endorsements

Typically, a check will be endorsed before a bank will accept it for
deposit. To endorse a check, the depositor places his or her signature on
the reverse side of the check at the end opposite the check writer's signa-

ture. A check is usually endorsed whenever it is transferred from one person to another. An **endorsement** has the legal effect of transferring ownership of the check.

The simplest endorsement is a blank endorsement. The current owner of the check merely signs his or her name. This makes the check payable to whoever presents the check for payment. A check that has a blank endorsement can be cashed by anyone regardless of the original payee.

If a check is to be transferred to another party and the check will be sent by mail, a blank endorsement is not very safe. Instead a *full* endorsement should be used. The phrase "Pay to the order of" would precede the name of the person to whom the check was being transferred. The owner would then sign his or her name as before.

When a person endorses a check, his or her rights are transferred to the check guaranteeing its payment. For this reason, persons depositing blank endorsement checks in their own accounts are often required to endorse these checks to protect the bank.

Another type of endorsement is the restrictive endorsement. Such an endorsement terminates further negotiation of the check and specifies the use of the check proceeds. Restrictive endorsements are usually used on checks being deposited in the payee's account. Examples of endorsements are shown below:

Blank	*Full*	*Restrictive*
J. Q. Jones	Pay to the order of Merchants National Bank J. Q. Jones	Pay to the order of Merchants National Bank For deposit only J. Q. Jones

Endorsements such as these are commonly placed on a check by means of a rubber stamp. The phrase "For deposit only" limits the use of the check to that purpose.

Dishonored checks

The receipt of a check is not actual payment. If the writer of the check does not have sufficient funds in his or her checking account to cover the check, the bank will refuse to pay it, and the check will be **dishonored.** If the check had been included in a bank deposit, it will be charged against the depositor's account. Thus, the total amount of any deposit depends upon the deposited checks clearing the bank upon which they were drawn since a depositor guarantees all checks he or she deposits. A depositor must adjust his or her records for dishonored or NSF (not sufficient funds) checks charged against his or her account.

Mail and night deposits

Some firms are not able to get their daily cash receipts to the bank before the bank closes. Since it is usually not wise to leave the receipts on the firm's premises until morning, many banks provide a night depository service. The deposit slip and cash receipts are assembled and dropped through a night deposit slot at the bank. The duplicate deposit slip is returned to the depositor the following day. Often a special depository is available to commercial customers for overnight safekeeping. Valuables, including cash, can be picked up the next morning or deposited as desired.

A similar service is provided by "bank by mail services." If the entire deposit is made up of checks, the depositor may choose to mail the deposit. The duplicate deposit slip would then be returned by mail. For obvious reasons, it is unwise to use this approach if the deposit includes coins and currency.

Checks

A check is a written document, signed by an authorized person, directing the company's bank to pay a specified amount of money to a particular party (known as the payee). Checks are widely used in business because of their great convenience and safety. Checks can be written for exact amounts. Since the payee is specified, checks are safe to mail. They are returned to the company after clearing the bank, and, hence, serve as a receipt. Cleared checks are traceable documents in evaluating past transactions.

Illustration 5–2 is an example of a typical check.

Illustration 5–2
Typical check

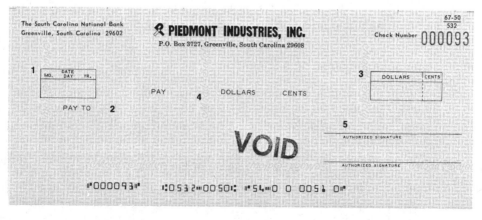

A check is made out in the following manner:

1. Date.
2. Payee.
3. Amount in figures.
4. Amount in words.
5. Authorized signature.

Checks may take on a variety of forms. They come in various sizes and a multitude of colors. But the basic characteristics that were pointed out in the example check are standard. The number 523 appearing in the upper right-hand corner of the example is the check number. For control purposes, each check is prenumbered in consecutive order. Thus, no two checks written on a given account would have the same number. All numbers should be accounted for with none missing. The number in the lower left-hand corner of the example is printed in magnetic ink and is used for automatic check-sorting by the bank. The company name and the bank name also appear on the check. The fraction-like number below the check number is the bank transit number and the routing information.

Observing a few simple rules will greatly reduce the possibility of a check being altered by dishonest persons. When the amount of the check is written in numbers in item No. 3, care should be taken to write the numbers close enough together so that no extra numbers can be inserted. When the check amount is written out in words in item No. 4, the words should start at the far left of the line. If any blank space remains on the line after the amount is written, a straight line should be drawn up to the word "Dollars" on the check. Many companies use a machine called a **checkwriter** to print the check amount in numbers and in words on the check. This machine is designed to prevent check alterations.

The company or individual entitled to the check proceeds is known as the payee. The payee's name is written in item No. 2. When a company desires to draw currency out of its own account, the payee is often "cash." Preparing the check in this manner allows any holder of the check to cash it and is a convenient way of replenishing petty cash funds, but it is not recommended. When a company issues a check to an outside party, the payee's name should always be filled in to provide a proper receipt after the check clears the bank.

The customer's account on the bank's books is a liability of the bank. The bank may directly charge or credit a customer's account. If a customer's deposit contained an endorsed check with was subsequently returned as dishonored, the bank would charge the account and issue a debit memo. This memo would be mailed to the company along with the dishonored check to notify them of the reduction in their account balance. A charge is called a debit memo since it reduces the bank's liability

Illustration 5–3
Debit memo

Illustration 5–4
Credit memo

to the customer. An example of a debit memo is shown in Illustration 5–3.

Many banks will collect notes receivable for their customers. A small handling fee is charged for this service and is deducted from the note proceeds. A credit memo is mailed to the customer which notifies that his or her account balance has been increased. A credit entry in a customer's account increases the bank's liability to that customer. An example of a credit memo is shown in Illustration 5–4.

Certified checks

Sometimes an ordinary check is not an acceptable form of payment. Perhaps the person receiving the check is concerned about the check being dishonored. In such a case, the recipient may require a **certified check.** A certified check is similar to a regular check except the bank on which the check is drawn has guaranteed its payment by stamping "certified" and the bank's name on the check. When the bank certifies a check, it examines the writer's account to see that sufficient funds are available to cover the check. Then it immediately deducts the amount of the check from the writer's account.

The checkbook

Usually checks are received from the bank in a prenumbered sequence and are printed with information identifying the individual or firm using the account. This information may be in the form of magnetic printing used for automatic sorting as well as conventional printing. The exact form of the checkbook may vary somewhat just as checks may vary somewhat.

Typically, there are two basic forms of checkbooks. One form has all of the checks attached in sequential order with the record-keeping forms in the back of the checkbook. After each check is written, the writer turns to the back of the checkbook and records the pertinent data such as: (1) the date of the check, (2) the check number, (3) the payee, (4) the nature of the payment, (5) the amount of the check, and (6) the new balance in the account. This type of checkbook is most often used by individuals who do not need detailed financial records.

The second form of checkbook has the record-keeping system attached to the check itself. After each check is written, it is detached along a perforated line and the check stub upon which the pertinent information is *first* recorded remains in the checkbook for record-keeping purposes. This type of checkbook may have one check on top of another or several checks and check stubs on each checkbook page. In either case the record-keeping system is the same. This type of checkbook is preferred by most businesses since more information can be entered on a check stub than is possible with the first checkbook form. An example of a check with attached stub is shown in Illustration 5–5.

Regardless of the form of the checkbook, it should provide a sequential numbered record of all checks written. Sequential numbered checks are easier to account for. If a check is spoiled or destroyed, it should be so described in the records. In any event, all checks should be accounted for.

Illustration 5–5
Check with attached stub

701	May 17, 1978		The Joker Company					701
To:	Robert Burns					May 17, 1978		93-59 / 921
For:	Inventory		Pay to the Order of	Robert Burns				$ 105.00
PREV. BAL.	470	00	One Hundred Five and 00/100 – Dollars					
DEPOSIT	400	00						
TOTAL	870	00	Gallatin Bank					
THIS CHECK	105	00						
BALANCE	765	00	1:0921-0059 : 22 076 0' '					

THE BANK STATEMENT

The bank must keep a record of all transactions which affect any given account. Periodically the bank sends out a **bank statement** to its customers to report upon the status and past transactions of each account for a certain period of time. The periodic reports may be monthly, weekly,

Illustration 5–6
Bank statement

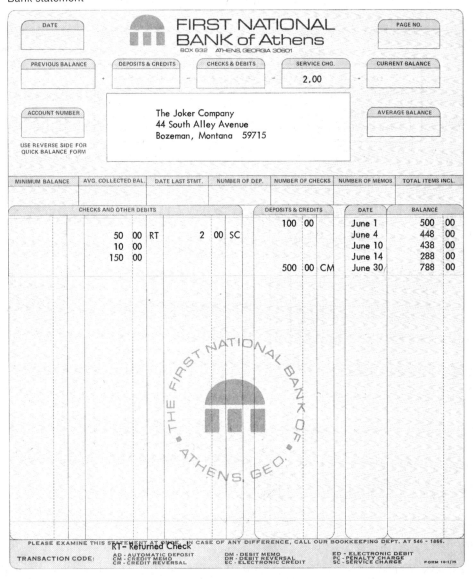

DATE		**FIRST NATIONAL BANK of Athens** BOX 632 ATHENS, GEORGIA 30601	PAGE NO.

PREVIOUS BALANCE	DEPOSITS & CREDITS	CHECKS & DEBITS	SERVICE CHG. 2.00	CURRENT BALANCE
	+	−	−	−

ACCOUNT NUMBER

The Joker Company
44 South Alley Avenue
Bozeman, Montana 59715

AVERAGE BALANCE

USE REVERSE SIDE FOR
QUICK BALANCE FORM

MINIMUM BALANCE	AVG. COLLECTED BAL.	DATE LAST STMT.	NUMBER OF DEP.	NUMBER OF CHECKS	NUMBER OF MEMOS	TOTAL ITEMS INCL.

CHECKS AND OTHER DEBITS			DEPOSITS & CREDITS	DATE	BALANCE
			100 00	June 1	500 00
50 00 RT	2 00 SC			June 4	448 00
10 00				June 10	438 00
150 00				June 14	288 00
			500 00 CM	June 30	788 00

PLEASE EXAMINE THIS STATEMENT AT ONCE. IN CASE OF ANY DIFFERENCE, CALL OUR BOOKKEEPING DEPT. AT 546 – 1866.

RT – Returned Check

TRANSACTION CODE:	AD - AUTOMATIC DEPOSIT CM - CREDIT MEMO CR - CREDIT REVERSAL	DM - DEBIT MEMO DR - DEBIT REVERSAL EC - ELECTRONIC CREDIT	ED - ELECTRONIC DEBIT PC - PENALTY CHARGE SC - SERVICE CHARGE

FORM 10-1/75

or even daily, depending upon the agreement between the customer and the bank. However, monthly statements are the most common.

The form of the statements may vary but basically the statement contains:

1. The balance at the beginning of the period.
2. Deposits and other additions to the account.
3. Checks and other deductions from the account.
4. The balance at the end of the period.

Also included in the bank statement will be the canceled checks written on the account which have been *paid* by the bank during the period. Illustration 5–6 is an example of what a bank statement may look like.

The bank reconciliation

The bank statement is prepared by the bank as of a point in time. It shows all the transactions that affected the account since the last bank statement according to their records. The balance in the Cash account on the company's books probably is not the same as the balance per the bank statement (on the bank statement).

There are several reasons for this discrepancy. Some items that have been recorded as cash disbursements on the company books have not had time to clear the bank. A common example is outstanding checks. These are checks that have been written but which have not come through the banking system to the point of being paid by the company's bank.

Other items are not known by the company until the bank statement arrives. The bank service charge is a good example of this.

Sometimes, errors are made by the bank or the company. The bank may charge one company's account with a check written by another company. This can sometimes happen when two firms have very similar names. The company may make an error in recording a check. It is easy to transpose two figures (e.g., recording 18 as 81) when recording a check.

Any or all of these items may combine so that the bank statement and the book balance are not equal at a given point in time. A **bank reconciliation** is prepared whenever a bank statement is received to explain the difference between the bank and company figures. This reconciliation provides a check on the accuracy of the records kept by the bank and by the company. When errors do arise, they are quickly recognized and can be corrected.

To prepare the reconciliation, first compare the deposits shown by the bank during the month to those shown on the books. If some have not been recorded by the bank yet, they should be added to the *bank balance*.

These deposits are called "deposits in transit" or late deposits (made too late to appear on this statement).

Take all the checks returned with the bank statement and compare them to check stubs or check register entries. Place a check mark ($\checkmark$) on the check stub or in the check register to indicate each check that has been paid by the bank. Those that have not passed through the bank will have to be deducted from the *bank balance*. These are outstanding checks since they have not been presented for payment.

The service charge shown on the bank statement must be subtracted from the *book balance*. From the reconciliation prepared for the *previous* period, determine that all deposits in transit at that time have been properly credited by the bank. Also, place a mark in the check register beside the outstanding checks that have been paid. Any checks from the previous reconciliation that are still outstanding must be included in the new reconciliation.

Items that have been properly recorded by the bank but not by the business should be added to or subtracted from the *book balance*. Similarly, any items properly recorded on the books but not on the bank statement should be added to or subtracted from the *bank balance*. Deposits in transit, outstanding checks, dishonored checks, service charges, and notes collected by the bank for the account of the company are examples of the items which may be encountered in reconciling bank statements.

Illustration 5–7

THE JOKER COMPANY
Bank Reconciliation
June 30, 1978

Balance per books, June 30, 1978		$100
Add:		
Noninterest-bearing note collected by bank (net of $10		
collection charge)	$500	500
		$600
Subtract:		
Service charge	$ 2	
Error on check recording – 198	20	22
Adjusted book balance, June 30, 1978		$578
Balance per bank statement, June 30, 1978		$788
Add:		
Deposit in transit		70
		$858
Subtract:		
Outstanding checks:		
No. 189	$ 60	
No. 200	80	
No. 201	140	280
Adjusted Bank Statement Balance, June 30, 1978		$578

The bank reconciliation of the Joker Company is presented as an example in Illustration 5–7. Note that reconciliations are always made at a specific date. The bank balance was taken from the bank statement presented in Illustration 5–6. The book balance came from the ledger account at the end of June 30, 1978. The information needed to complete the reconciliation is accumulated from the company records and the bank statement.

The above example (Illustration 5–7) is relatively simple. Many bank reconciliations will have a large number of checks outstanding and a substantial number of other items in the statement. In any event when the reconciliation is completed, the adjusted book and bank balances should be equal. If they are not, an error has been made, and an additional search must be made to locate the cause of the difference.

Journalizing the reconciliation

The items that appeared in the book's side of the reconciliation must be journalized to correct the company's Cash account. In general journal form, the journal entry for the additions to the Cash account would be:

```
Cash ................................................................................ 500
Collection Charge .........................................................  10
    Notes Receivable.......................................................        510
  To correct cash.
```

The entry for the deductions would be:

```
Bank Service Charge..................................................... 2
Accounts Payable........................................................ 20
    Cash ......................................................................        22
  To correct cash.
```

The items on the bank's side of the reconciliation affect the *bank's books*. Thus, the firm makes no journal entry for these items. However, if the bank has made an *error*, the company should notify the bank of the error so that it can be corrected on the bank's books.

SPECIAL CHECKING ACCOUNTS

Many firms have more than one checking account. Several accounts may aid in an appropriate division of responsibility and may insure proper control. Commonly, accounts are separated by the function that they serve. A payroll cash account and a dividend cash account are often employed in addition to the regular cash account. These accounts are typically used to pay the payroll and dividends when they come due. A separate ledger account is usually established for each different bank account.

For example, the payroll account will usually have a nominal balance in it, say $100, to insure against any minor errors causing the account to be overdrawn. When the total of the payroll checks is determined, a check for the total is written on the general checking account and deposited in the payroll account. When the payroll checks are prepared, they are written on the payroll account. If any serious errors have been made in preparing the payroll checks, it will be easier to trace the errors than if the checks were written directly on the general account which may have a large number of checks drawn on it for a variety of purposes. The dividend checking account operates in essentially the same way.

The number of special checking accounts a firm has is subject to the needs of management. A firm may choose to have several payroll accounts — one for each plant as an example. The added control over cash and the increased cost of multiple accounts should be the major factors considered.

SAVINGS ACCOUNTS

Banks also offer savings accounts. Such accounts usually bear a stated rate of interest whereas the checking account does not. There are a large variety of plans that may loosely be defined as savings accounts. These various plans have different interest rates from plan to plan, from town to town, and from time period to time period.

Savings accounts are usually not considered to be as liquid as checking accounts because savings accounts are not always payable *on demand*. Sometimes a certain amount of advance notice is required before the bank will pay out the savings account funds. Withdrawals from savings accounts must usually be made in person.

Other financial institutions such as savings and loan organizations can provide savings account services. Only commercial banks can provide checking account services, however.

BANK STATEMENT FOR A COMPANY THAT
ACCEPTS MASTER CHARGE CARDS

Landers Dry Cleaners accepts Master Charge credit cards from its customers. The bank statement for Landers Dry Cleaners for the month of May is shown in Illustration 5–8. The $40 Master Charge Debit Item is the fee charged by the Second Central Bank for handling Master Charge sales slips. The Landers Dry Cleaners' account has been debited for $40 on the bank's books. According to the bank statement, the company's Cash account should have a $975 balance. On the company's book, the cash balance is $1,020. The difference is explained by the Master Charge fee and the bank service charge. The following journal

Illustration 5–8

```
BANK STATEMENT:

    Landers Dry Cleaners                          Second Central Bank
    603 Lumpkin Drive                             480 Peach Avenue
    Zebra, Georgia                                Zebra, Georgia
```

CHECKS	DEPOSITS	DATE	BALANCE
Amount Brought Forward			750.00
200.00		May 2	550.00
50.00	400.00	May 9	900.00
80.00		May 16	820.00
40.00 MC	200.00	May 24	980.00
5.00 SC		May 28	975.00

```
CODE: MC –   Master Charge Debit Item
      SC –   Service Charge
```

entry is required to adjust the Landers Dry Cleaners' Cash account balance to the correct amount.

Master Charge Fee	40	
Bank Service Charge	5	
Cash		45

To correct the Cash account.

GLOSSARY

Bank reconciliation   a statement which points out and reconciles the differences between the company's bank balance on the company's books and the company's bank balance on the bank's books.

Bank statement   a periodic statement sent by a bank to its customers which presents the current balance of each account and provides a detailed list of past transactions of each account for a certain period of time. Monthly statements are the most common.

Certified check   a check whose payment has been guaranteed by the bank on which it is drawn.

Check   a written document, signed by an authorized person, directing the company's bank to pay a specified amount of money to a particular party.

Checkwriter   a machine used to print the check amount in numbers and words on the check instead of doing it manually.

Deposit ticket   a document showing the name and number of the account into which a deposit is made, the date, and the items which make up the deposit.

Dishonored check   a check which the bank has refused to pay because the writer of the check does not have sufficient funds (NSF) in his or her checking account to cover the check.

Endorsement   the act of placing one's signature on the back of a check which is to be cashed or deposited. This is usually required by a bank before it will accept the check for cash or deposit.

Signature card   a card which contains the signature of each individual authorized to sign checks drawn against a firm's checking account.

QUESTIONS AND EXERCISES

1. What is the purpose of a checking account?

2. What is a signature card?

3. Distinguish among a blank endorsement, a full endorsement, and a restrictive endorsement.

4. Give some precautions that should be taken in order to reduce the possibility of a check being altered by dishonest persons.

5. When might a customer receive a debit memo from a bank? A credit memo?

6. Define the following types of checks:

 a. Dishonored.
 b. Certified.

7. What are the basic parts of a bank statement?

8. Usually there is a difference between the balance in the Cash account on the company's books and the balance per the bank statement. Why might this difference exist?

9. How does a savings account differ from a checking account?

10. The Acton Company's Cash account has a balance of $1,100. The balance per the bank statement is $1,070. The difference is because of a $10 service charge and a $20 NSF check. What journal entry is necessary to correct the company's cash account?

11. The Barnett Company's Cash account has a balance of $1,655. The balance per the bank statement is $1,085. The difference is because of the following items:

$ 50   Master Charge debit item
 10   Service charge
 40   Outstanding check
 185   NSF check
 365   Deposit in transit

What journal entry is required to correct the Cash account on the company's books?

PROBLEMS

5–1. R. Cook, an electrician, completed the following transactions with the Park Avenue Bank during the month of February:

Feb.	1	Balance in bank per checkbook......................	$3,500.00
	2	Check No. 251..	83.75
	3	Check No. 252..	175.00
	4	Check No. 253..	346.00
	5	Check No. 254..	855.00
	6	Deposit...	1,832.00
	7	Check No. 255..	453.00
	7	Check No. 256..	261.00
	7	Check No. 257..	138.95
	12	Deposit...	3,408.00
	14	Check No. 258..	1,253.47
	14	Check No. 259..	893.06
	14	Check No. 260..	613.78
	14	Check No. 261..	796.49
	14	Check No. 262..	853.60
	17	Deposit...	1,575.00
	21	Check No. 263..	656.09
	21	Check No. 264..	713.21
	21	Check No. 265 *outstanding*..........................	195.37
	21	Check No. 266..	141.14
	21	Check No. 267..	202.63
	21	Deposit...	1,893.00
	28	Check No. 268..	428.04
	28	Check No. 269..	515.65
	28	Check No. 270 *outstanding*..........................	313.93
	28	Check No. 271 "	406.16
	28	Deposit.......*In transit*...............................	2,843.56

The February bank statement showed a balance of $2,825 on February 28. Check Nos. 265, 270, and 271 were outstanding. A service charge of $3.14 was made by the bank during February.

The deposit on February 28 was still in transit at that date.

Required:

Prepare a bank reconciliation for the month ended February 28.

5–2. Prepare a bank reconciliation from the following information:

Balance per bank statement of Blaine & Jones Co., Inc.,		
April 30, 1978		$3,487.16
Balance per checkbook, April 30, 1978		4,189.01
Checks outstanding:		
No. 351........................	57.63	
No. 362........................	89.95	
No. 374........................	102.45	

No. 376........................ 63.37
No. 380........................ 450.50
Deposit of April 30, 1978, not recorded on bank
  statement 1,163.00
Returned check NSF 335.00
Check No. 365 for $315 returned with the statement had
  been recorded in the books as $351.
Bank service charge... 3.75

5–3. D. L. Cambridge, an interior decorator, has just received the October bank statement. It shows a balance of $1,672. Cambridge's books show a balance of $1,776. Given the information below, prepare a bank reconciliation for the month ended October 31, 1978.

a. The bank had not received the October 31 deposit of $600.
b. A bank service charge of $25 was not recorded on the books.
c. The following checks were outstanding on October 31, 1978:

Check
No.

176......................... $156
179......................... 78
183......................... 94
184......................... 202

d. A customer's check for $9 had been stamped "NSF" and had been returned with the bank statement.

5–4. Dr. H. M. Hamster, a veterinarian, completed the following transactions with the Barber Street Bank during the month of July:

July	1	Balance in bank per Cash account	$8,000.00
	2	Deposit..	500.00
	3	Check No. 448...	25.76
	5	Check No. 449...	102.50
	6	Check No. 450...	400.00
	6	Check No. 451...	75.24
	9	Deposit..	600.00
	11	Check No. 452...	55.75
	12	Check No. 453...	84.25
	14	Check No. 454...	26.00
	15	Check No. 455...	94.68
	16	Check No. 456...	82.32
	18	Deposit..	300.00
	21	Check No. 457...	500.00
	24	Check No. 458...	101.67
	26	Deposit..	600.00
	27	Check No. 459...	93.33
	28	Check No. 460...	45.00
	29	Check No. 461...	78.00
	30	Check No. 462...	12.00
	31	Deposit..	406.00

urnolized check book balance additions and subtractions

The bank statement for July showed a balance of $8,726.33. Check Nos. 459, 460, 461, and 462 were outstanding. The deposit on July 31 was still in transit at that date. The bank had collected a $300 note receivable and had deducted a $10 collection charge from the proceeds. The collection had not been recorded on Dr. Hamster's books. The bank service charge for July was $15.50.

Required:

1. Prepare a bank reconciliation for the month ended July 31, 1978.
2. Prepare the general journal entries that are necessary to adjust Dr. Hamster's cash balance to the reconciled figure.

5–5. Prepare a bank reconciliation from the following information:

Balance per bank statement of Lysae Company,
    January 31, 1978 .... $6,777.77
Balance per checkbook, January 31, 1978 .... 7,333.10
Check outstanding: No. 179 .... 31.00
Deposit of $400 on January 31, 1978, has not been
    recorded by the bank.
Returned check NSF 55.23
Bank service charge 14.10

The bookkeeper for Lysae Company had recorded several checks incorrectly:

Check no.	Amount recorded on books	Correct amount
Wages 159	$112	$211
Supplie 173	58	85
Misc 180	76	67

5–6. The Denton Company's Cash in Bank account has a balance of $6,745 on February 28, 1978. The balance shown on the bank statement is $4,600. Using the following information, (1) prepare a bank reconciliation for the Denton Company on February 28, 1978, and (2) prepare the general journal entries that are required to correct the company's Cash in Bank account.

Checks outstanding:
    No. 762 .... $100
    No. 770 25
    No. 772 50
    No. 779 35
Deposit of February 28, 1978, not recorded on the bank
    statement $1,000
Returned check NSF 300
Bank service charge 15
Check No. 766, returned with the bank statement, had been
    written for $851 but had been recorded in the books at
    $581. It was written in payment of an account.
The bank had charged the Denton Company with two checks
    written by the Benton Company. The checks were for
    $360 and $410.

Accounting for payroll
Learning objectives

The law requires an employer to maintain detailed records for employee earnings and related deductions. Careful study of the following material will provide a basic understanding of the procedures used when accounting for payroll:

1. The definition and computation of gross wages and gross salaries.
2. The determination of the appropriate payroll deductions for each employee.
3. Example of tables used in calculating payroll tax deductions.
4. Procedures used in preparing and recording payroll checks.
5. Calculation of employer payroll liabilities and the recording of such payables.
6. Procedures used in paying payroll deductions and employer payroll liabilities.

6

Accounting for payroll

Many business enterprises find that disbursements for wages and salaries and related payroll taxes make up a good portion of the firm's total expenses. Therefore, it is especially necessary that these charges be recorded correctly if the enterprise is to determine accurately its net earnings for each accounting period.

This further implies that the employer is able to pay each employee according to the employment agreement or contract. The employer will supply the employee and all appropriate governmental organizations with the required information on each employee's earnings. This information is necessary so the employees can file their income tax returns and so the employer can pay the appropriate payroll taxes.

EARNINGS AND PAYROLL DEDUCTIONS

There are four principal phases in **payroll accounting.** Each of these aspects is covered in the next sections of this chapter. The first concern in payroll accounting is the computation of total gross earnings for each employee during a payroll period.

A payroll period may vary from firm to firm and from one class of employee to another class within a given firm. Common payroll periods are weekly, biweekly, semimonthly, and monthly.

Second, once the gross pay has been calculated, the deductions must be determined. The deductions will be based on governmental regulations and employee instructions.

When the first two steps are completed, they must be recorded in the permanent payroll records. This third step is essential to the firm in meeting governmental requirements. Finally, the total payroll activity must be summarized to facilitate recording in the company's general records.

Nature of payroll

During any period, a firm is likely to require the services of a great many individuals. Not all, however, are considered employees of the firm. Some individuals offer their services as **independent contractors.** A lawyer or a public accountant may offer his or her services to a firm but is not considered an employee. An employee has a more permanent relationship with the firm. He or she is under the direct supervision of the firm's management. Payroll accounting refers to accounting for the cost of *employees.*

Computing wages and salaries

Compensation for skilled and unskilled employees is typically classified as **wages** which are usually expressed in terms of an individual hourly rate. When an employee's hourly rate is multiplied by the total hours worked during the payroll period, the resulting figure is the employee's gross earnings. In contrast, compensation for administrative and managerial personnel is usually termed a **salary.** Salaries are customarily expressed as monthly or annual amounts.

The basic salary or hourly wage is sometimes supplemented by sales commissions or bonuses, production piece rate payments, cost-of-living adjustments, and profit sharing plans. These payments vary from firm to firm since each of these has a unique computational formula.

Each employee's basic compensation is based on the total time worked during a particular payroll period. If the number of people is small, this time figure might be a mental record kept by the manager or a brief entry in his or her memorandum book. As the number of employees increases, however, the business will probably use a **time clock.** Use of a time clock provides a printed record of when each employee arrived for work and when he or she departed for the day. A specimen clock card is shown in Illustration 6–1. Time clocks are only infrequently used with *salaried* personnel. Instead, they or their immediate supervisor will submit a written summary of hours worked.

Wages and salaries for employees who have not worked any overtime are easy to compute using the recorded hours. The gross earnings of an hourly employee is simply the base rate per hour times the total hours the employee has worked during the period. For salaried employees, it is simply their prescribed salary for the payroll period. Usually, however, employees are entitled to extra compensation for working overtime. The

Illustration 6–1
Specimen clock card

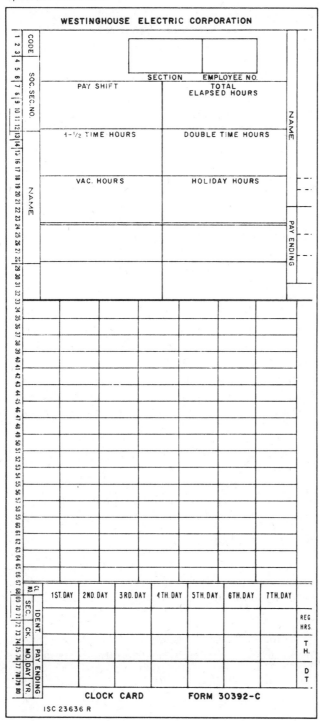

Federal Fair Labor Standards Act, which applies to all employers engaged in interstate commerce, specifies that covered employees shall be paid a premium rate—$1\frac{1}{2}$ times their regular hourly rate—for all hours worked in excess of 40 per week. Provision is made in the act so that certain managerial and supervisory employees may elect to be exempt from its regulations. There is nothing in the act which limits specific labor-management agreements to these exact terms. In fact, many labor agreements have significantly more generous provisions. Oftentimes, premium pay is paid for excess hours worked in any one day or for work on a holiday. Some contracts specify that a standard workweek be shorter than 40 hours.

To illustrate the computation of gross earnings, suppose an hourly employee, Henry Abbott, has worked 55 hours during the weekly payroll period ended October 24. Abbott's regular hourly rate is $4, and the company pays time and a half for all hours worked hours over 40 per week. His gross earnings are computed as follows:

40 hours @ $4	$160
15 hours @ $6	90
Gross Earnings for the Week	$250

When the employee is salaried, the computations are similar once his or her *hourly rate* is established. To do this, the employee's salary is first converted to an annual amount which is then converted to an hourly figure. This can best be shown with an example. Suppose a second employee, Jean Larch, has a salary of $520 per month. Her overtime rate would be:

$$\$520 \times 12 \text{ months} = \$6,240 \text{ annual rate}$$
$$\$6,240 \div 52 \text{ weeks} = \$120 \text{ per week}$$
$$\$120 \div 40 \text{ hours} = \$3 \text{ per hour}$$
$$\$3 \times 1\frac{1}{2} = \$4.50 \text{ per overtime hour}$$

Deductions from gross earnings

Employers are required by law to withhold amounts from every employee's gross earnings to cover the payroll taxes levied by federal, state, or local governmental units. These would include the following:

1. F.I.C.A. taxes (social security)—employee's share.
2. Federal income taxes—employee.
3. State and local income taxes, where applicable—employee.

In addition to the above, many employers deduct amounts for such things as:

1. U.S. savings bonds or other savings plans.
2. Premiums on employee's life, health, or accident insurance.
3. Union dues.
4. Contributions to charitable organizations.
5. Payments to pension or profit sharing funds.
6. Repayment of loans – employer or credit union.

F.I.C.A. taxes

These **F.I.C.A. taxes** (or social security taxes) are collected under the provisions of the Federal Insurance Contributions Act in equal amounts from both the employee and employer. These proceeds are paid into a fund which provides disability and old age payments to employees covered by the act. The original Social Security Act of 1935 has been modified considerably by congressional amendments. Not only has the payment size increased but also the coverage has been extended to many more employee classifications.

As presently amended, the act requires that 5.85 percent of the first $16,500 annually paid an employee be withheld. All employers with covered employees must contribute a matching amount. Thus, the total amount remitted to the F.I.C.A. fund is 11.7 percent of gross wages. For the moment, any discussion of the employer's share will be postponed until a later section. While Congress has established rates for all years after 1972, only those through 1980 are listed below:

Year	Rate
1973 through 1977	5.85%
1978 through 1980	6.05

Income taxes withheld

Federal law requires that an employer withhold an appropriate amount from each employee's paycheck for income tax. The amount withheld in each case is based on (1) the employee's total earnings, (2) the number of exemptions, and (3) the employee's marital status.

Every employee is allowed to claim an exemption for himself or herself plus additional exemptions for qualifying **dependents.** The regulations state which family relationships qualify as *dependents.* They also explain the financial support test that a dependent must meet.

All employees must fill out an Employee's Withholding Allowance Certificate (Form W-4). A sample W-4 is shown in Illustration 6–2. Not only does it provide for the number of exemptions claimed but it also allows the employee to specify additional withholdings or credits.

The credits, known as withholding allowances, are based on the employee's estimated tax deductions for the coming year. To the extent that the estimated itemized deductions exceed an amount based on normal deductions as determined by the Internal Revenue Service, the employee is entitled to **withholding allowances** (line j on the W-4). One additional allowance is permitted for every $750 excess, for example, two for

Illustration 6-2

Employee's Withholding Allowance Certificate

The explanatory material below will help you determine your correct number of withholding allowances, and will indicate whether you should complete the new Form W—4 at the bottom of 'his page.

How Many Withholding Allowances May You Claim?

Please use the schedule below to determine the number of allowances you may claim for tax withholding purposes. In determining the number, keep in mind these points: If you are single and hold more than one job, you may not claim the same allowances with more than one employer at the same time; If you are married and both you and your wife or husband are employed, you may not claim the same allowances with your employers at the same time. A nonresident alien other than a resident of Canada, Mexico or Puerto Rico may claim only one personal allowance.

Figure Your Total Withholding Allowances Below

(a) Allowance for yourself—enter 1	*1*
(b) Allowance for your wife (husband)—enter 1	*1*
(c) Allowance for your age—if 65 or over—enter 1	
(d) Allowance for your wife's (husband's) age—if 65 or over—enter 1	
(e) Allowance for blindness (yourself)—enter 1	
(f) Allowance for blindness (wife or husband)—enter 1	
(g) Allowance(s) for dependent(s)—you are entitled to claim an allowance for each dependent you will be able to claim on your Federal income tax return. Do not include yourself or your wife (husband)*	*3*
(h) Special withholding allowance—if you have only one job, and do not have a wife or husband who works— enter 1	
(i) Total—add lines (a) through (h) above	*5*
If you do not plan to itemize deductions on your income tax return, enter the number shown on line (i) on line 1, Form W—4 below. Skip lines (j) and (k).	
(j) Allowance(s) for itemized deductions—If you do plan to itemize deductions on your income tax return, enter the number from line 5 of worksheet on back	*1*
(k) Total—add lines (i) and (j) above. Enter here and on line 1, Form W—4 below	*6*

*If you are in doubt as to whom you may claim as a dependent, see the instructions which came with your last Federal income tax return or call your local Internal Revenue Service office.

See Table and Worksheet on Back if You Plan to Itemize Your Deductions

Completing New Form W—4

If you find that you are entitled to one or more allowances in addition to those which you are now claiming, please increase your number of allowances by completing the form below and filing with your employer. If the number of allowances you previously claimed decreases, you must file a new Form W—4 within 10 days. (Should you expect to owe more tax than will be withheld, you may use the same form to increase your withholding by claiming fewer or "0" allowances on line 1 or by asking for additional withholding on line 2 or both.)

▼ Give the bottom part of this form to your employer; keep the upper part for your records and information ▼

Form **W-4** (Rev. Aug. 1972) Department of the Treasury Internal Revenue Service	**Employee's Withholding Allowance Certificate** (This certificate is for income tax withholding purposes only; it will remain in effect until you change it.)	
Type or print your full name *William Henry Powell, III*	Your social security number *250 -80 -9799*	
Home address (Number and street or ural route) *113 Ocean Drive*	Marital status ☐ Single ☒ Married	
City or town, State and ZIP code *Daytona Beach, Fla. 50123*	(If married but legally separated, or wife (husband) is a nonresident alien, check the single block.)	

1 Total number of allowances you are claiming	*6*
2 Additional amount, if any, you want deducted from each pay (if your employer agrees)	$ *0*

I certify that to the best of my knowledge and belief, the number of withholding allowances claimed on this certificate does not exceed the number to which I am entitled.

Signature ▶ *William Henry Powell, III*   Date ▶ *January 2* 19 *78*

Illustration 6–2 (continued)

What If You Itemize Deductions?

If you expect to itemize deductions on your income tax return, you may be entitled to claim one or more additional withholding allowances on line (j) on page 1. You may claim one additional withholding allowance for each $750, or fraction of $750, by which you expect your itemized deductions for the year to exceed the amounts shown in columns (A), (B), or (C) below.

Estimated salaries and wages	Single employees (with one job) (A)	Married employees with one job (wife or husband is not working) (B)	Married employees (both husband and wife working) and employees working in more than one job (C)
Under $8,000	$1,700	$1,700	$1,700
$8,000—10,000	1,800	1,800	2,000
10,000—12,000	2,200	2,200	2,700
12,000—15,000	2,400	2,400	2,700
15,000—20,000	2,400	2,400	3,300
20,000—25,000	2,400	2,400	4,000
25,000—30,000	2,900	2,400	4,900
30,000—35,000	3,800	2,400	5,900
35,000—40,000	4,900	2,700	6,900
40,000—45,000	6,400	3,500	7,900
45,000—50,000[1]	7,900	4,500	9,100

[1] If your annual salary or wages exceeds $50,000, you may claim one additional withholding allowance for each $750, or fraction of $750, by which your expected itemized deductions will exceed the following: A single employee with one job—19 percent of annual salary or wages; A married employee with one job whose wife or husband is not working—13 percent of annual salary or wages; A married employee whose wife or husband is also working, or an employee who holds more than one job—22 percent of the combined or total annual salary or wages.

Determining Withholding Allowances For Itemized Deductions

The worksheet below will be helpful to you in determining whether your expected itemized deductions entitle you to claim one or more additional withholding allowances.

Worksheet

1 Total estimated annual salary or wages (from all sources)	1	$ **20,000**
2 Total expected itemized deductions for the year	2	$ **3,150**
3 Appropriate amount from column (A), (B), (C) or footnote 1, above	3	**2,400**
4 Balance. Subtract line 3 from line 2. (If "0" or less, you are not entitled to additional allowance(s) for itemized deductions)	4	$ **750**

5 If the amount on line 4 is:

Between	Enter on line 5	Between	Enter on line 5	Between	Enter on line 5	
$0— $750	1	$2,251—$3,000	4	$4,501—$5,250	7	
751—1,500	2	3,001— 3,750	5	5,251— 6,000	8	
1,501—2,250	3	3,751— 4,500	6	6,001— 6,750	9	

Note: If the amount on line 4 is over $6,750 you get 9 allowances, plus 1 allowance for each $750 or fraction thereof by which the amount on line 4 exceeds $6,750. If the balance on line 4 is less than "0," you may be having too little tax withheld. You can generally avoid this by claiming one less allowance (than the total number to which you are entitled) for each $750 by which the estimated deductions on line 2 are less than the amount on line 3.

5 ▶ **1** Enter this number on line (j), page 1.

☆ U.S. GOVERNMENT PRINTING OFFICE: 1973-0-458-177 E.I. NO. 31-0271450

$1,500, three for $2,250, and so on. On the other hand, should the employee expect that his or her withheld taxes are going to be significantly less than the estimated year-end tax liability, the employee can request additional withholdings (line 2 on the W-4) to avoid owing a large amount when the tax return is filed.

There are several methods for computing the required standard withholding. The first, and probably the most prevalent among smaller businesses, is the **wage bracket method.** It relies on a set of withholding tables provided by the Internal Revenue Service. Each table covers a payroll period of specified length: daily, weekly, biweekly, semimonthly, and monthly. Within each table there is a detailed breakdown both by wage brackets and by number of exemptions. Since marital status is one of the determining factors, there are separate tables for single and married taxpayers.

We have included a portion of the weekly table for married taxpayers as Illustration 6–3. To illustrate its usage, assume that James Harrison's weekly income is $175.40 and that he claims four exemptions. Entering

Illustration 6–3

WEEKLY PAYROLL PERIOD — MARRIED PERSONS

WAGES: $0–$319.99

At least	Less than	0	1	2	3	4	5	6	7	8	9	10 or more
		\$.10										
$0	$48											
48	49	$.10										
49	50	.20										
50	51	.40										
51	52	.60										
52	53	.80										
53	54	.90										
54	55	1.10										
55	56	1.30										
56	57	1.40										
57	58	1.60										
58	59	1.80										
59	60	1.90										
60	62	2.20										
62	64	2.50	$.10									
64	66	2.90	.40									
66	68	3.20	.80									
68	70	3.60	1.10									
70	72	3.90	1.40									
72	74	4.20	1.80									
74	76	4.60	2.10									
76	78	4.90	2.50									
78	80	5.30	2.80	$.40								
80	82	5.60	3.10	.70								
82	84	5.90	3.50	1.00								
84	86	6.30	3.80	1.40								
86	88	6.60	4.20	1.70								
88	90	7.00	4.50	2.10								
90	92	7.30	4.80	2.40								
92	94	7.60	5.20	2.70	$.30							
At least	Less than	0	1	2	3	4	5	6	7	8	9	10 or more
94	96	8.00	5.50	3.10	.60							
96	98	8.30	5.90	3.40	1.00							
98	100	8.70	6.20	3.80	1.30							
100	105	9.40	6.80	4.30	1.90							
105	110	10.40	7.70	5.20	2.70	$.30						
110	115	11.40	8.60	6.00	3.60	1.10						
115	120	12.40	9.60	6.90	4.40	2.00						
120	125	13.40	10.60	7.70	5.30	2.80	$.40					
125	130	14.40	11.60	8.70	6.10	3.70	1.20					
130	135	15.40	12.60	9.70	7.00	4.50	2.10					
135	140	16.40	13.60	10.70	7.80	5.40	2.90	$.50				
140	145	17.40	14.60	11.70	8.80	6.20	3.80	1.30				
145	150	18.40	15.60	12.70	9.80	7.10	4.60	2.20				
150	160	19.90	17.10	14.20	11.30	8.40	5.90	3.50	$1.00			
160	170	21.90	19.10	16.20	13.30	10.40	7.60	5.20	2.70	$.30		
170	180	23.90	21.10	18.20	15.30	12.40	9.50	6.90	4.40	2.00		
180	190	25.60	23.10	20.20	17.30	14.40	11.50	8.60	5.10	3.70	$1.20	
190	200	27.30	24.80	22.20	19.30	16.40	13.50	10.60	7.80	5.40	2.90	$.50
200	210	29.00	26.50	24.10	21.30	18.40	15.50	12.60	9.80	7.10	4.60	2.20
210	220	30.70	28.20	25.80	23.30	20.40	17.50	14.60	11.80	8.90	6.30	3.90
220	230	32.40	29.90	27.50	25.00	22.40	19.50	16.60	13.80	10.90	8.00	5.60
230	240	34.10	31.60	29.20	26.70	24.30	21.50	18.60	15.80	12.90	10.00	7.30
240	250	35.80	33.30	30.90	28.40	26.00	23.50	20.60	17.80	14.90	12.00	9.10
250	260	37.50	35.00	32.60	30.10	27.70	25.20	22.60	19.80	16.90	14.00	11.10
260	270	39.20	36.70	34.30	31.80	29.40	26.90	24.50	21.80	18.90	16.00	13.10
270	280	41.70	38.40	36.00	33.50	31.10	28.60	26.20	23.70	20.90	18.00	15.10
280	290	44.20	40.60	37.70	35.20	32.80	30.30	27.90	25.40	22.90	20.00	17.10
290	300	46.70	43.10	39.50	36.90	34.50	32.00	29.60	27.10	24.70	22.00	19.10
300	310	49.20	45.60	42.00	38.60	36.20	33.70	31.30	28.80	26.40	23.90	21.10
310	320	51.70	48.10	44.50	40.90	37.90	35.40	33.00	30.50	28.10	25.60	23.10

the table at the appropriate line—"At least $170 but less than $180"—and proceeding to the column for four exemptions, we find the correct withholding to be $12.40.

A second method, the one often used when payrolls are prepared on electronic data processing equipment, utilizes an estimated withholding rate. First, the employee's gross earnings for a payroll period are adjusted according to the number of exemptions claimed. To calculate the amount to be withheld, this adjusted gross figure is multiplied by the appropriate percentage rate. Like the previous computational method, the employee's marital status is considered when selecting the rate.

Many states and an increasing number of cities have also enacted some form of income tax. While the extent of coverage and the taxation rates vary widely, most require systematic withholdings from the employee's paychecks in a manner similar to that of the federal plan. Due to their diversity, it is difficult to make any generalizations about their computational features. Yet most of them allow **exemptions** for the employee and his or her dependents, if any. Like the federal income tax, the actual withholding can be calculated using either the **wage-bracket method** or the **percentage rate method.** The nature of the tax rate varies from a fixed percentage of gross earnings to a progressive scale based on the individual's overall earnings level. Often, municipal income taxes contain different tax rates for employees who both live and work in the municipality and for those who just work there.

Miscellaneous deductions

The employee may request that additional amounts be deducted from his or her paycheck. The additional withholdings may be for a variety of items. Some common examples are union dues, insurance premiums, savings bonds, and charitable contributions.

All these items require that the employee give specific authorization indicating he or she wants these amounts to be withheld. The employer usually acts only as an intermediary between the employee and the final recipient. These payroll deduction plans are offered as a convenience to a company's employees.

COMPONENTS OF THE PAYROLL RECORDS

From the preceding sections it has become clear that certain records must be maintained for each employee. These payroll records are not only to satisfy the information needs of management but also the requirements of various federal and state agencies. In addition, the employee must be provided with sufficient information to complete income tax forms. From such records we should be able to determine:

1. The employee's name, address, and social security number.
2. The gross earnings, period covered, and date paid for each payroll.
3. The employee's cumulative gross earnings since the beginning of the year.

4. The details of all taxes and other deductions withheld from the employee's paycheck.

For most businesses, regardless of size or number of employees, these requirements are met through the use of three records. They are: (1) the **payroll register** or journal; (2) the **payroll check,** generally with an attached earnings statement; and (3) the **earnings records** of each employee on a cumulative basis. These records can be maintained manually or prepared electronically.

Payroll register

An example of a manually prepared payroll register is shown in Illustration 6–4. While this example lists the employees in alphabetical order, this form is by no means universal. In fact, many businesses keep track of their employees by means of individual identification numbers: employee number, clock card number, department number, and so on. The number of columns allotted to "deductions" in a particular payroll register also varies widely. Some registers have provisions for many types of deductions while others rely on a "Miscellaneous column" for small or infrequent deductions.

Although F.I.C.A. (assuming the employee is below the $16,500 cutoff) and income taxes are withheld every pay period, the same may not be true for all deductions. It is not unusual to deduct the entire monthly insurance premium from the first payroll of the month. Nor is it unusual to find union dues or charitable contributions also being deducted in a lump sum during the month.

Looking at the first two employees, Henry Abbott and James Harrison, we find that their gross earnings for the weekly payroll period ended December 13, 1978, were $187.50 and $150.00, respectively. These earnings are based upon the total hours worked during the period as recorded either on their clock cards or by some other system. Amounts withheld for federal income tax are based on their respective exemption certificates (W-4). For this example, all employees are subject to a city income tax equal to 1 percent of gross earnings. There are no deductions for health insurance premiums since they were withheld in total on the previous payroll for December. The remaining deductions are computed using the authorizations filed by each employee.

Once all the employees' names have been entered and all necessary deductions have been made, each column in the register should be footed (added). These column totals can then be checked by crossfooting them. If all deductions have been properly subtracted and every column correctly footed, then:

$$\frac{\text{Net Pay}}{\text{Column}} + \frac{\text{All Deductions}}{\text{Columns}} = \frac{\text{Gross Earnings}}{\text{Column}}$$

Illustration 6–4
Manually prepared payroll register

Employee No.	Name	No. of Exemp.	Marital Status	Earnings				Taxable Earnings		Deductions								Date	Net Pay	Ck. No.
				Regular	Over-time	Total	Cumula-tive Total	Unem-ploy. Comp.	FICA	FICA Tax	Fed. Inc. Tax	City Inc. Tax	Life Ins.	Priv. Hosp. Ins.	Credit Union	Other	Total			
1.	Henry Abbott	3	M	160.00	27.50	187.50	9,200.00		187.50	10 97	20 40	1 88			2 00		35.25	12/31/78	152.25	501
2.	James Harrison	3	M	150.00		150.00	8,400.00		150.00	8 78	15 60	1 50			2 00	SAVINGS BOND 10 00	37.88	12/31/78	112.12	502
	Total			310.00	27.50	337.50	17,600.00		337.50	19 75	36 00	3 38			4 00	10.00	73.13		264.37	

For this example, details have been included for only the first two employees. The reader should, however, satisfy himself or herself that the column totals — net pay and deductions — crossfoot to the gross earnings figure. Note also how the column totals have been ruled with single and double lines.

The required entry for the general journal can be made by using these column totals directly as supporting detail. For the specimen payroll register, the following entry would be made:

Dec. 13	Wages Expense	337.50	
	F.I.C.A. Taxes Payable		19.75
	Income Taxes Payable — Federal Employee...........		36.00
	Income Taxes Payable — City Employee................		3.38
	Credit Union Payable — Employee........................		4.00
	Cash..		264.37
	Savings Bond Payable — Employee......................		10.00

The exact nature of these accounts is covered in a later section.

Companies with sizable numbers of employees will probably utilize an automated payroll system to increase efficiency. These systems often reduce costs and human errors. Their data output can be structured to provide more information on the breakdown and allocation of payroll expenses. The types of systems currently being used range from small-capacity bookkeeping machines to ultra-high-speed electronic digital computers.

With an automated payroll system, the three basic payroll records — register, check, and earnings record — are generally prepared simultaneously. Since a complete discussion of the merits and shortcomings of such systems is beyond the scope of this chapter, the following discussion is limited to several broad observations. Given a medium- to large-sized payroll, these systems have greater accuracy, frequently have lower operating costs, and provide more information than manual systems. Yet, regardless of the complexity of the system, the basic objectives remain the same as those listed in the early sections of this chapter. A specimen payroll register from an electronic data processing system is shown as Illustration 6–5. As can be seen from the example, the column headings and other information closely parallel the previous manual example in Illustration 6–4.

Payroll checks

Most payroll checks, whether prepared manually or by machine, have several unique features that distinguish them from general disbursement checks. This is because of the special requirements of the payroll procedures. For example, in addition to the check the company provides a detachable stub which contains much the same information as the pay-

Illustration 6–5
Specimen payroll register from an electronic data processing system

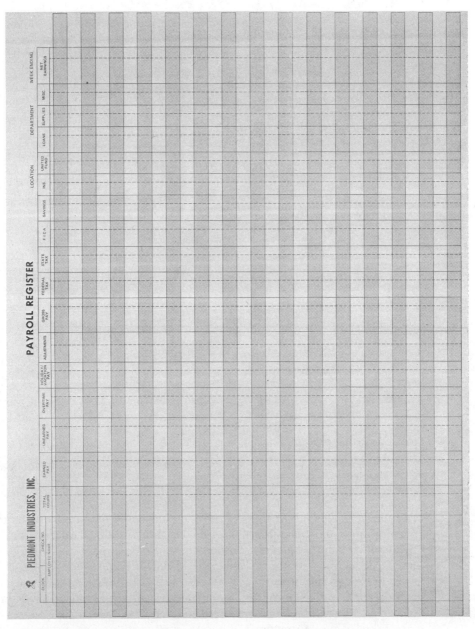

Illustration 6–6
Manually prepared payroll check and stub

	PAYROLL	No.
	DIVERSIFIED DISTRIBUTORS, INC.	1205
	1321 Industrial Drive	
	West Palm Beach, Fla. 37604	

DATE:

December 31, 1978

	Dollars	Cents
	$ *189*	*79*

PAY TO THE
ORDER OF   *Sam Rogers, Jr.*

One hundred eighty nine and ⁷⁹/₁₀₀ ————— DOLLARS

DIVERSIFIED DISTRIBUTORS, INC.

FIRST STATE BANK
West Palm Beach, Fla. 37604

By *James H. Harland*

1:☐72☐···☐☐6:

DIVERSIFIED DISTRIBUTORS, INC.

this is a statement of your payroll payments and deductions

PLEASE DETACH FOR YOUR RECORDS   No. 1205

Home Dept. Acct.	Dist Code	Soc. Sec. No.	Employee Name	Regular Pay	Comp.	Gross Pay
1011GH1960001	459	255-74-3326	ROGERS, S.	220 00		220 00

Fed. W/H	State W/H	FICA	Hosp. Ins.	Life Ins.	Other	Net Pay
13 02	5 19		6 00	6 00		189 79

Payment Date *Dec. 31, 1978*   Pay Period Ending *Dec. 24, 1978*

NOT NEGOTIABLE

---

roll register. This stub can be seen on the manually prepared version in Illustration 6–6. The stub provides the employee with an **earnings statement** which includes a permanent record of gross earnings and a detailed list of deductions. Before cashing the check, the employee should detach and retain this stub.

For comparative purposes, a machine prepared payroll check is included as Illustration 6–7. It can be seen that both checks have approximately the same information on their respective stubs. These two checks are assumed to have been drawn on a special payroll bank account. There are several advantages to handling payroll transactions in a specialized account. First, to provide better control over cash, the company can limit the amount of any check, perhaps less than $500. Second, the company may feel that a single signature check gives adequate control over payroll disbursements considering the scope of activity in this account. This would allow the company to retain a dual signature requirement on its general checking account. Third, the reconciliation procedure can generally be simplified and streamlined since the payroll account's activity is rather standardized and check volume is high.

One alternative to a payroll bank account is the use of payroll drafts. Briefly, this system requires that the company repurchase all payroll drafts from the recipient banks where they were presented for payment.

Illustration 6–7

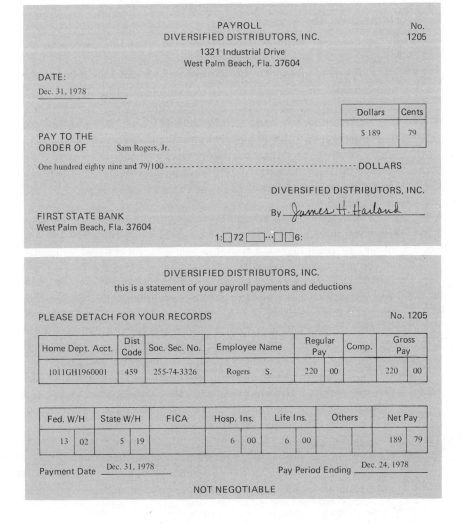

Unlike a checking account, the company does not maintain a cash balance with the bank but instead gives its promise to repurchase immediately all such drafts. Usually, such a system entails a service charge per item to cover bank handling charges. Unless the company has an established working relationship with the area banks, it is apt to find that the banks are hesitant to establish a payroll draft procedure.

Although the discussion has been limited to only payment by check, it should be noted that a few businesses still pay with currency. The number of these firms, however, is small and has been declining. Under such a system, the employee's earnings are placed in an envelope which is delivered to the employee on payday. The employee is asked to sign a receipt showing that the pay envelope has been received.

Individual earnings records

A detailed earnings record must be kept for every employee. This record shows gross earnings, deductions, and net pay. During the year, this record is updated each payroll period and new cumulative year-to-date totals are computed. As previously noted in the discussion of F.I.C.A. taxes, these gross earnings cumulative totals provide a signal for the employer to stop withholding F.I.C.A. taxes. These same gross earnings amounts are utilized when the employer files and pays his or her share of the F.I.C.A. taxes. They also constitute the basis for calculating the employer's liability for the federal and the various state unemployment taxes. A discussion of these employer tax reports will be discussed in a later section.

A manually prepared employee's earnings record for Henry Abbott is Illustration 6–8. Similar records would be maintained for each of the company's employees. From this example, we see that it duplicates much of the information in the payroll register. The principal difference is that the payroll register is a summary of the earnings of all employees for a specific pay period while the earnings records summarize the annual earnings of each employee.

These gross earnings become the basis for the withholding statement (Form W-2) which the employer is required to furnish employees following the end of the calendar year. Depending upon local requirements, the W-2 form should have at least four copies—two for the employee, one for the Internal Revenue Service, and one for the employer's files. If there are state or local income taxes on the employee's earnings, the number of copies increases accordingly.

Machine prepared earnings records have the same information as their manually prepared counterparts. Only their method and order of presentation differ. With many electronic data processing systems, they are prepared simultaneously with the payroll register and check. More-

Illustration 6–8
Manually prepared earnings record

Sex	Department	Occupation	SS No.	Marital Status	Exemptions		Pay Rate	Date of Birth	Date Employed	Name Last — First — Middle			Emp. No.
M F ✓	Shipping	Loader	255-74-3627	M	3		$160 wk.	10-29-51	2-25-74	Abbott,	Henry	William	1

Period Ending	Earnings				Taxable Earnings		Deductions			Deductions							Net Pay	
	Regular	Overtime	Total	Cumulative Total	Unemp. Comp.	FICA	FICA Tax	Fed. Inc. Tax		City Inc. Tax	Life Ins.	Private Hosp. Ins.	Credit Union	Other		Total	Ck. No.	Amount
7/7	160.00		160.00	4520 00		160.00	9.36	17.20		1.60	10.00	4.00	2.00			44.16	112	115 84
7/14	160.00		160.00	4680 00		160.00	9.36	17.20		1.60			2.00	SAVINGS BOND 10 00		40.16	125	119 84
7/21	160.00	40.00	200.00	4880 00		200.00	11.70	23.60		2.00			2.00			39.30	156	160 70
7/28	160.00		160.00	5040 00		160.00	9.36	17.20		1.60			2.00			30.16	170	129 84
8/4	160.00		160.00	5200 00		160.00	9.36	17.20		1.60	10.00	4.00	2.00			44.16	180	115 84
8/11	160.00		160.00	5360 00		160.00	9.36	17.20		1.60			2.00	SAVINGS BOND 10 00		40.16	199	119 84
8/18	160.00		160.00	5520 00		160.00	9.36	17.20		1.60			2.00			30.16	206	129 84
8/25	160.00		160.00	5680 00		160.00	9.36	17.20		1.60			2.00			30.16	231	129 84
9/1	160.00	20.00	180.00	5860 00		180.00	10.53	20.40		1.80	10.00	4.00	2.00			48.73	240	131 27
9/8	160.00		160.00	6020 00		160.00	9.36	17.20		1.60			2.00	SAVINGS BOND 10 00		40.16	262	119 84
9/15	160.00		160.00	6180 00		160.00	9.36	17.20		1.60			2.00			30.16	280	129 84
9/22	160.00		160.00	6340 00		160.00	9.36	17.20		1.60			2.00			30.16	295	129 84
9/29	160.00		160.00	6500 00		160.00	9.36	17.20		1.60			2.00			30.16	303	129 84
3d QTR.	2080.00	60.00	2140.00			2140.00	125.19	233.20		21.40	30.00	12.00	26.00		30 00	477.79		1662 21
10/6	160.00		160.00	6660 00		160.00	9.36	17.20		1.60	10.00	4.00	2.00			44.16	345	115 84
10/13	160.00	20.00	180.00	6840 00		180.00	10.53	20.40		1.80			2.00	SAVINGS BOND 10 00		44.73	370	135 27
10/20	160.00		160.00	7000 00		160.00	9.36	17.20		1.60			2.00			30.16	401	129 84
10/27	160.00		160.00	7160 00		160.00	9.36	17.20		1.60			2.00			30.16	420	129 84
11/3																		
11/10																		
11/17																		

over, most electronic systems are programmed so that withholding of
F.I.C.A. taxes will cease when the employee's earnings exceed the statutory limit of $16,500.

PAYROLL PREPARATION

Up to this point, the discussion has centered around an employer-operated payroll system. There are some alternatives, however. As noted in previous sections there are certain advantages to utilizing an electronic payroll system. But sometimes the size of the company is small enough that it cannot justify the purchase or rental of such a system. Increasingly, data processing services have been offered both by **service bureaus** and by some *commercial banks*.

Typically, the service organization maintains a complete record of vital statistics on every employee: wage rate, exemptions, deductions, and so on. Each payroll period, the employer furnishes the service organization with the total hours every employee has worked plus any corrections or data needed to update the withholding or deduction information. One unique feature, which is sometimes offered with bank operated systems, is to include a payroll bank account reconciliation as part of the normal service work.

Recording gross wages and payroll deductions

The accounts used in accounting for payrolls range from those expense accounts charged with the gross earnings to the various liability accounts used to record the different deductions. It is advisable to establish separate accounts for each type of deduction. The use of these accounts is illustrated in this section.

Wages expense. This expense account is charged with the total gross earnings of all employees for the period. For larger payroll systems, the total expense may be broken down into several expense accounts which more fully describe the type of services (for example, Factory Wages Expense and Sales Salaries Expense). In addition, some systems provide separate accounts for overtime and other special premiums. Thus, charges to the account would be made in the debit column (1) with the cumulative total being shown in the Balance column (2).

Wages Expense

Date	Explanation	P.R.	Debit	Credit	Balance
			(1)		(2)

F.I.C.A. Taxes Payable. This liability account can be used to record both the amounts withheld from employees and the employer's matching amount. Both types of items would be credits (1) to the account. When these taxes are paid, a debit (2) is made to the account. Any outstanding balance (3) in the account represents unremitted taxes as of a particular point in time.

F.I.C.A Taxes Payable

Date	Explanation	P.R.	Debit	Credit	Balance
			(2)	(1)	(3)

Income taxes payable – employee. Depending upon the particular circumstances, there may be several income taxes payable accounts: federal, state, or municipal (where applicable). These liability accounts should be credited (1) with the total amount withheld from the employees' earnings. The account is debited (2) whenever the taxes are remitted. Again, the balance (3) in the account at any time represents the unremitted portion of these taxes. Accounts for state and municipal income taxes withheld are handled identically.

Income Taxes Payable — Federal — Employee					
Date	Explanation	P.R.	Debit	Credit	Balance
			(2)	(1)	(3)

Insurance Premiums Payable — Health.   This liability account is credited (1) with amounts deducted from the employees' earnings. Since the company is only an intermediary, it would pay these premiums to the proper insurance company and debit (2) the account at that time. Like the other payroll liability accounts, the balance (3) represents collected premiums which have yet to be forwarded. Accounts for recording the multitude of other deductions would be handled in a similar manner.

Insurance Premiums Payable — Health					
Date	Explanation	P.R.	Debit	Credit	Balance
			(2)	(1)	(3)

EMPLOYER PAYROLL TAXES

The earlier sections of this chapter have concentrated on payroll taxes which are withheld from the employee's earnings. We shall now turn our attention to payroll taxes imposed directly on the employer. Unlike the previous taxes, these taxes are considered an additional expense to the employer for the services performed by the employees. While the costs of various employee fringe benefits are also paid by the employer and likewise represent additional employment expense, only payroll taxes will be considered. These include: (1) the matching portion of the F.I.C.A. taxes, (2) the Federal Unemployment Tax Act (F.U.T.A.), and (3) depending upon local statutes, a state unemployment tax.

Payroll tax expense

All payroll taxes imposed on the employer are considered expenses of the business and should be debited to the Payroll Tax Expense account count. If a more detailed expense breakdown is desired, separate accounts should be established for each tax. Thus, we might have (1) F.I.C.A. Tax Expense, (2) F.U.T.A. Tax Expense, and (3) State Unemployment Tax Expense. The computation and payment of these taxes is enumerated below.

F.I.C.A. tax—employer. Under the Federal Insurance Contributions Act, the tax rate applies equally to both employee and employer. Since the rates and limits are the same as those discussed in the "Employee" section of the chapter on page 115, readers should refer back to it for the exact amounts. Because the employer is liable for both the withheld amount and the matching liability, they can be combined into a single liability account as discussed in the preceding section. Otherwise, the company can maintain separate accounts for the employee and the employer. Their operation is the same as previously described.

F.U.T.A. tax—employer. The federal government participates with the states to provide a jointly administered unemployment insurance program. The **F.U.T.A. tax** is levied only on employers and only on those employers who employ one or more individuals for some portion of a day in each of 20 weeks in the calendar year or who paid $1,500 or more in wages during any quarter of the current or preceding calendar year. Certain types of employment are exempt: agricultural labor, employees of federal and state governments, and employees of charitable and religious organizations.

The current federal unemployment tax rate is 3.4 percent of the first $6,000 paid to a covered employee during the calendar year. There is, however, a substantial credit against the federal tax for amounts paid into state unemployment funds. Currently, the allowable credit for qualifying state plans is 2.7 percent of the wages taxable under the federal plan. Thus, the effective rate becomes 0.7 percent (3.4 − 2.7). As is true of F.I.C.A. rates, this tax is also subject to change by Congress.

Typically, the F.U.T.A. tax liability is kept in a separate account entitled F.U.T.A. Taxes Payable. Credits (1) to this account represent the computed tax amount. The corresponding debit should be to the aforementioned Payroll Tax Expense account. Payments on the tax liability should be debited (2) to this account. The balance (3) in the account represents the outstanding tax liability at a point in time.

F.U.T.A. Taxes Payable					
Date	Explanation	P.R.	Debit	Credit	Balance
			(2)	(1)	(3)

State unemployment taxes. Virtually every state has enacted unemployment compensation laws that provide benefits to qualified unemployed workers. Although there is considerable uniformity in the provisions of each state law, there are substantial differences in coverage, tax rates, and size of benefits.

The types of exempt employment vary among the state laws as does the minimum number of employees. Further complications arise because some states allow employers who are subject to the federal tax to be optionally covered by the state law. In general then, the employer must become familiar with the unemployment laws in those states in which the employer has one or more employees.

Like the federal plan, most state plans are financed entirely by taxes imposed on the employer. Although the rate structure varies among states, most have a maximum rate of less than 2.7 percent (the maximum allowable credit on the federal tax). Most states provide for a **merit-rating system,** whereby the employer's tax rate is based on past unemployment experience. Thus, volatile industries with large fluctuations in their employment rolls are likely to have correspondingly high rates.

If the employer is subject to the unemployment tax laws of several states, it is customary to maintain a separate liability account for the amounts owed to each state. These liability accounts should be credited (1) with the computed tax liability of the employer. Conversely, the account should be debited (2) when payments are made on the tax. The balance (3) in the account represents the outstanding tax liability at a point in time.

State Unemployment Taxes Payable						
Date	Explanation	P.R.	Debit	Credit	Balance
			(2)	(1)	(3)

Recording employer payroll taxes

Technically speaking, employers are liable for payroll taxes on payrolls *paid*. But, because a payroll may be paid in a period following the one in which it is earned, it is customary to record payroll taxes in the period to which the payroll relates.

To illustrate, suppose the earnings subject to F.I.C.A. taxation for a particular pay period totaled $730. Given the current rate of 5.85 percent, the computation would be:

F.I.C.A. Taxes — 5.85 percent of $730 = $42.71

Assume also that the earnings subject to federal and state unemployment taxes equaled $550. If the state tax rate is 2.7 percent; the effective federal rate is 0.5 percent. The computation would be as follows:

State Unemployment Taxes — 2.7 percent of $550 = $14.85
F.U.T.A. Taxes — 0.7 percent of $550 = $3.85

The following general journal entry would be made to record these employer payroll taxes:

Payroll Tax Expense	61.41	
F.I.C.A. Taxes Payable		42.71
F.U.T.A. Taxes Payable		3.85
State Unemployment Taxes Payable		14.85

FILING RETURNS AND PAYING PAYROLL TAXES

All federal income taxes withheld and F.I.C.A. taxes imposed on employees and employer must be deposited with an authorized commercial bank depository or a Federal Reserve Bank. However, the exact remittance schedule for these deposits varies depending upon the amount of such taxes. If the employer has less than $100 of F.I.C.A. and withheld federal income taxes, payment is due at the end of the month following the end of the quarter. It should be pointed out that F.I.C.A. taxes refers to the combined employee and employer amounts. Should the combined taxes total at least $100 but less than $2,500 per month, monthly deposits are required. For amounts in excess of $2,500 per month, the employer must make semimonthly deposits. Each deposit should be accompanied by a Federal Tax Deposit Form 501 which will then be authenticated by the receiving bank.

Following the end of every quarter (March 31, June 30, September 30, December 31), the employer must file a quarterly return on Form 941. This form summarizes the taxable wages paid every employee during the quarter and computes the combined F.I.C.A. tax liability. From this total, the employer would deduct any monthly or semimonthly deposits (Form 501) made during the quarter. An example of a partially completed Form 941 is shown in Illustration 6–9.

The actual steps involved in completing this form can best be described by using an example. First, every employee's taxable wages must be detailed with supporting information in columns 4, 5, 6, and 7. Their total line — 8 — is then entered at line 14 where the combined tax calculation is made. For this example the total taxable wages and quarterly tax liability are $10,550 and $1,234.35, respectively. This is not the required payment, however, since the employer made monthly deposits totaling $3,500 (line 20). While not shown for our specimen, these deposits are summarized in Schedule B which is provided on the reverse side of Form 941. The actual balance due would be $184.35 — line 21. Notice that this includes both F.I.C.A. and withheld federal income taxes.

A check would be drawn to the Internal Revenue Service for $184.35 and sent to the nearest District Director's office. If the $184.35 is at-

Illustration 6–9

Form 941
(Rev. July 1973)
Department of the Treasury
Internal Revenue Service

Employer's Quarterly
Federal Tax Return

SCHEDULE A—Quarterly Report of Wages Taxable under the Federal Insurance Contributions Act—FOR SOCIAL SECURITY
IF WAGES WERE NOT TAXABLE UNDER THE FICA MAKE NO ENTRIES IN ITEMS 1 THROUGH 9 AND 14 THROUGH 18

| 1. (First quarter only) Number of employees (except household) employed in the pay period including March 12th ▶ | 2. Total pages of this return including this page and any pages of Form 941a ▶ 2 | 3. Total number of employees listed ▶ 5 |

List for each nonagricultural employee the WAGES taxable under the FICA which were paid during the quarter. If you pay an employee more than $10,800 in a calendar year report only the first $10,800 of such wages. In the case of "Tip Income" see instructions on page 4.

Please report each employee's name and number exactly as shown on his Social Security card.

4. EMPLOYEE'S SOCIAL SECURITY NUMBER	5. NAME OF EMPLOYEE (Please type or print)	6. TAXABLE FICA WAGES Paid to Employee in Quarter (Before deductions) Dollars / Cents	7. TAXABLE TIPS REPORTED (See page 4) If amount in this column are not tips check here ☐ Dollars / Cents
000 00 0000			
268-44-5061	Tom R. Baker	2100.00	
301-74-1112	Bud E. Brown	2280.00	
250-80-3334	Thomas E. Davis	1870.00	
242-74-0689	Tom T. Hall	2200.00	
351-54-1072	John J. Jones	2100.00	

If you need more space for listing employees, use Schedule A continuation sheets, Form 941a.
Totals for this page—Wage total in column 6 and tip total in column 7 ▶   10550.00

8. TOTAL WAGES TAXABLE UNDER FICA PAID DURING QUARTER.
(Total of column 6 on this page and continuation sheets.) Enter here and in Item 14 below . . $ 10550.00

9. TOTAL TAXABLE TIPS REPORTED UNDER FICA DURING QUARTER.   (If no tips reported, write "None.")
(Total of column 7 on this page and continuation sheets.) Enter here and in Item 15 below ▶ $ None

```
                 Name (as distinguished from trade name)          Date quarter ended
                 Sheet Metal Products, Inc.                        June 30, 1978
Employer's       Trade name, if any                               Employer Identification No.
name,         ▶  Sheet Metal                                      44-7896545709
address,         Address and ZIP code
employer         2200 Beech Island Drive, Miami, Florida.  35786
identification   ....Entries must be made both above and below this line; if address different from previous return check here ☐
number, and
calendar         Name (as distinguished from trade name)          Date quarter ended
quarter.         Sheet Metal Products, Inc.                        June 30, 1978
(If not          Trade name, if any                                Employer Identification No.
correct,      ▶  Sheet Metal                                       44-7896545709
please           Address and ZIP code
change)          2200 Beech Island Drive, Miami, Florida 35786
```

10. TOTAL WAGES AND TIPS SUBJECT TO WITHHOLDING PLUS OTHER COMPENSATION ▶	10550	00
11. AMOUNT OF INCOME TAX WITHHELD FROM WAGES, TIPS, ANNUITIES, etc. (See instructions)	2450	00
12. ADJUSTMENT FOR PRECEDING QUARTERS OF CALENDAR YEAR		
13. ADJUSTED TOTAL OF INCOME TAX WITHHELD ▶	2450	00
14. TAXABLE FICA WAGES PAID (Item 8) . . . . $ 10550.00 . . . multiplied by 11.7%=TAX	1234	35
15. TAXABLE TIPS REPORTED (Item 9) . . . . $ . . . multiplied by 5.85%=TAX		
16. TOTAL FICA TAXES (Item 14 plus Item 15) ▶	1234	35
17. ADJUSTMENT (See instructions)		
18. ADJUSTED TOTAL OF FICA TAXES ▶	1234	35
19. TOTAL TAXES (Item 13 plus Item 18)	3684	35
20. TOTAL DEPOSITS FOR QUARTER (INCLUDING FINAL DEPOSIT MADE FOR QUARTER) AND OVERPAYMENT FROM PREVIOUS QUARTER LIST IN SCHEDULE B (See instructions on page 4)	3500	00

Note: If undeposited taxes at the end of the quarter are $200 or more, the full amount must be deposited with an authorized commercial bank or a Federal Reserve bank. This deposit must be entered in Schedule B and included in Item 20.

| 21. UNDEPOSITED TAXES DUE (ITEM 19 LESS ITEM 20)—THIS SHOULD BE LESS THAN $200. PAY TO INTERNAL REVENUE SERVICE AND ENTER HERE ▶ | 184 | 35 |
| 22. IF ITEM 20 IS MORE THAN ITEM 19, ENTER EXCESS HERE ▶ $ AND CHECK IF YOU WANT IT ☐ APPLIED TO NEXT RETURN, OR ☐ REFUNDED. | | |

23. If not liable for returns in succeeding quarters write "FINAL" here ▶   and enter date of final payment of taxable wages here ▶

Under penalties of perjury, I declare that I have examined this return, including accompanying schedules and statements, and to the best of my knowledge and belief it is true, correct and complete.

Date 6/30/78   Signature Paul W. Williams   Title (Owner, etc.) Treasurer tributed to F.I.C.A. Taxes Payable, this transaction would be recorded with the following journal entry:

F.I.C.A. Taxes Payable	184.35	
Cash		184.35

Every employer subject to F.U.T.A. taxes (see page 130) must file an annual federal unemployment tax return, Form 940, on or before January 31. Like the taxes in the previous section, the payment schedule depends upon the size of the employer's tax liability. Deposits are required if the tax liability exceeds $100 for any one quarter or if the total cumulative liability exceeds $100.

Likewise, any state unemployment taxes imposed on the employer must be paid to the proper state offices. Each state will provide the employer with the necessary official forms to be used in filing and paying the tax liability. Although there is no universal rule, most states require that payments be made at least quarterly.

GLOSSARY

Dependents   under the tax law, people for whom the taxpayer is allowed a deduction of a specified amount. These people must meet four conditions relating to support, income, relationship, and no joint return.

Earnings record   a detailed record which summarizes the annual earnings of each employee. It shows the employee's gross earnings, deductions, and net pay for each payroll period along with a cumulative total of gross earnings.

Earnings statement   a stub attached to an employee's payroll check that provides the employee with a permanent record of gross earnings and a detailed list of deductions.

Exemptions   deductions of a specified amount which a taxpayer can claim for himself or herself, his or her spouse, and his or her qualifying dependents.

Federal Fair Labor Standards Act   an act which applies to all employers engaged in interstate commerce; it specifies that covered employees shall be paid a premium rate — $1\frac{1}{2}$ times their regular hourly rate — for all hours worked in excess of 40 per week.

F.I.C.A. taxes   social security taxes collected under the provisions of the Federal Insurance Contributions Act in equal amounts from both the employee and employer. Proceeds are paid into a fund which provides disability and old age payments to employees covered by the act.

F.U.T.A. taxes   taxes levied only on certain employers under the provisions of the Federal Unemployment Tax Act.

Independent contractor   an individual who sells services to a firm for a fee. The independent contractor is not an employee of the firm.

Merit rating   a system whereby a firm's unemployment tax rate is based on its past unemployment experience. Its unemployment taxes may be reduced if it has a stable history of employment.

Payroll accounting   accounting for disbursements for wages and salaries and related payroll taxes. It involves four phases: (1) computation of total gross earnings for each employee, (2) determination of deductions for each employee, (3) recording of gross earnings and deductions in the permanent payroll records, and (4) summarization of the total payroll activity to facilitate recording in the company's general records.

Payroll check   one of the components of a firm's payroll records. It can be distinguished from general disbursement checks by a detachable stub which contains much the same information as the payroll register.

Payroll register (journal)   a summary of the earnings and deductions of all employees for a specific pay period.

Percentage rate method   a method used to compute the required standard withholding. The employee's gross earnings are adjusted for the number of exemptions claimed, and this adjusted gross figure is multiplied by an estimated withholding rate to obtain the required standard withholding.

Salary   a term often used to refer to the compensation for administrative and managerial personnel. It is customarily expressed as a monthly or annual amount.

Service bureau   a business which offers data processing services to small- and medium-size businesses on a contract basis.

Time clock   a card used to provide a printed record of when each employee arrived for work and when he or she departed for the day.

Wage-bracket method   a method often used by small businesses to compute the required standard withholding. It relies on a set of withholding tables provided by the Internal Revenue Service.

Wages   a term often used to refer to compensation for skilled and unskilled employees which is expressed in terms of an individual hourly rate.

Withholding allowances   credits which an employee can claim if his or her estimated itemized deductions exceed an amount based on normal deductions as determined by the Internal Revenue Service.

QUESTIONS AND EXERCISES

1. What is the difference between an independent contractor and an employee? Give some examples of independent contractors.

2. Distinguish between salaries and wages. Name five other types of compensation besides salaries and wages.

3. Connie Cast works for an employer who is engaged in interstate commerce. Her regular rate of pay is $6 per hour. According to the regulations set forth in the Federal Fair Labor Standards Act, what is the minimum amount of total earnings that Connie should receive if she works 50 hours per week?

4. Nearly all employers are required to withhold part of each employee's earnings for federal income tax and for social security (F.I.C.A.) taxes. Besides these required deductions, what are six other types of deductions that might be withheld from an employee's earnings?

5. What four factors must be considered in determining the amount of income tax to be withheld from an employee's earnings?

6. What are three types of payroll records that are usually prepared by an employer? What information can be obtained from these payroll records?

7. What is a service bureau?

8. What payroll taxes are expenses of the employer?

9. What is a wage and tax statement, Form W-2?

10. Steve Melton receives a monthly salary of $1,080. He is entitled to overtime pay at one and one-half times his regular hourly rate for all hours worked in excess of 40 per week. How much should he be paid for each hour of overtime?

PROBLEMS

6–1. PART A   The Hardwin Company pays its employees time and a half for all hours worked in excess of 40 per week. For the first week of May, compute the gross earnings for each of the company's six employees.

No.	Employee name	Hours worked in first week of May	Regular hourly rate
1	Allen, Rick	45	$2.50
2	Busbee, Kay	50	4.00
3	Foster, Mark	40	3.00
4	Keller, Julie	46	3.50
5	Mackey, Tom	50	2.75
6	Murphy, Diane	42	3.25

PART B   The Hardwin Company also has three salaried employees who are entitled to time and a half for all hours worked in excess of 40 per week. Compute their gross earnings for the first week of May.

No.	Employee name	Hours worked in first week of May	Monthly salary
7	Cost, Kathy	45	$1,040
8	Hutto, Sally	49	1,300
9	Mehra, Debbie	53	1,560

6–2. The employees of the Kelly Jelly Company are paid time and a half for all hours worked in excess of 8 per day òr 40 per week. The following chart summarizes relevant payroll information about the company's employees for the week ended May 8, 1978:

No.	Employee name	Exemptions claimed	Regular hourly rate	Hours worked M T W T F S	Cumulative earnings Jan. 1–May 1
1	Alred, Jack	2	$2.60	10 8 8 9 0 5	$1,800
2	Bomar, Jane	1	2.50	8 8 8 8 8 3	1,700
3	Sapp, Jerry	3	3.00	8 8 9 8 8 4	2,000
4	Staley, Jean	2	2.90	8 8 8 8 8 0	2,100
5	Taylor, Joseph	4	2.80	8 9 8 8 7 5	1,900
6	Welch, John	3	3.20	9 8 8 8 8 4	2,300
7	Wyatt, Julia	2	3.10	8 8 8 8 8 5	2,200

The employees have requested the following deductions for the week ended May 8, 1978:

Alred....................	$5 group life insurance
Bomar...................	10 savings bond
Sapp'....................	4 private hospital insurance
Staley	5 United Fund
Taylor..................	10 savings bond
Welch	5 group life insurance
Wyatt	4 private hospital insurance

Required:

1. Prepare a payroll register similar to the one in Illustration 6–4 for the week ended May 8, 1978. Of each employee's taxable wages, 5.85 percent is to be withheld for F.I.C.A. tax. All of the employees are married. Use the weekly income tax table (Illustration 6–3) to determine the amount of federal income tax to be withheld from each employee's earnings.

   Check Nos. 607 through 613 were issued to the employees. Complete the payroll register by totaling and ruling the amount columns. Also, check the column totals by crossfooting them.

2. Make the journal entry to record the payment of the payroll.

6–3. The Murray Davis Company pays its employees on the 15th and last day of the month. Each payday, the journal entry to record the payroll includes liabilities for amounts withheld from employees' earnings. The employer's payroll tax expenses and liabilities are also recorded each payday.

Required:

Journalize the following transactions which relate to payrolls and payroll taxes.

1978
Jan. 15   Payroll:

Total earnings		$4,500.00
Less withholdings:		
F.I.C.A. tax...............................	$263.25	
Employees' federal income tax........	300.00	563.25
Net Earnings Paid...........................		$3,936.75

    15 Employer's social security taxes:
        F.I.C.A. tax, 5.85 percent.
        State unemployment tax, 2.7 percent.
        F.U.T.A. tax, .7 percent.
    30 Paid December's payroll taxes:
        F.I.C.A. tax, $175.
        Employees' federal income tax, $550.
    30 Paid state unemployment tax for quarter ended December 31, 1977,
        $70.20.
    31 Paid F.U.T.A. tax for quarter ended December 31, 1977, $13.

Jan. 31 Payroll:

Total earnings		$5,200.00
Less withholdings:		
F.I.C.A. tax	$304.20	
Employees' federal income tax	375.00	679.20
Net Earnings Paid		$4,520.80

    31 Employer's social security taxes:
        Same rates as on 15th,
        All earnings are still taxable.
Feb. 13 Paid January's payroll taxes which included employees' federal in-
        come tax withheld and both employees' and employer's shares of
        F.I.C.A. taxes.

 6-4. Pamela Dawn Wells is employed as a bookkeeper in the accounting department of the Henry Cole Company. Her social security number is 255-92-7689,
and her employee number is 105. She is married, and she claims four exemptions on her income tax return. Ms. Wells' regular rate of pay is $200 per
week. However, she receives time and a half for all hours worked in excess
of 40 per week. Federal income taxes (See Illustration 6–3), city taxes at a
1 percent rate, and F.I.C.A. taxes at a 5.85 percent rate are deducted from
her paycheck every week. Also, weekly deductions of $2.50 are made for the
company credit union. The first paycheck for each month contains a $12
deduction for life insurance and a $5 deduction for private hospital insurance.
The third paycheck for each month contains a $10 deduction for savings
bonds. During the first month of 1978, Pamela Wells worked the following
number of hours:

                    Week ended 1/9 .... 50 hours
                    Week ended 1/16 40
                    Week ended 1/23 48
                    Week ended 1/30 52

She was issued Check Nos. 681, 706, 750, and 808.

Required:

    Prepare an employee's earnings record like the one in Illustration 6–8
for Pamela Dawn Wells for the first four weeks of 1978. (Date of birth is
2/27/54, and date employed is 1/15/74.)

6-5. The Harrison Company has 45 employees who earned a total of $560,000 during 1978. Twenty employees earned $13,500 each. The remainder of the payroll was divided equally among the other employees.

Required:

1. What amount did each of the remaining 25 employees earn during 1978?
2. Compute both the employees' and the employer's shares of F.I.C.A. tax for 1978.
3. Compute the amounts of F.U.T.A. tax and state unemployment tax imposed on the employer during the year. The effective F.U.T.A. tax rate is 0.7 percent, and the state rate is 2.7 percent.
4. What was the employer's total payroll expenses for 1978?

 6-6. The Honeycake Food Store, operated by J. C. Honeycake, has six employees, all of whom are paid on the last day of each month. The following tax rates are effective for 1978:

F.I.C.A. tax — employee.................. 5.85%
F.I.C.A. tax — employer.................. 5.85
F.U.T.A. tax 0.70
State unemployment tax 2.70

Accounts related to the payroll and the payroll taxes are listed below along with their account numbers and their balances on April 1, 1978.

Account No.	Account Title	Balance, 4/1/78
101	Cash..	$32,000.00
212	F.I.C.A. taxes payable.................................	547.56
213	Income taxes withheld payable–Federal–employee...	590.00
214	Insurance premiums payable – life – employee..	60.00
215	Insurance premiums payable – hospital – employee...	30.00
216	F.U.T.A. taxes payable	70.20
217	State unemployment taxes payable.................	126.36
502	Wages expense...	14,040.00
509	Payroll tax expense	1,270.62

Required:

1. Using the balance column account form, open the nine accounts listed above and enter the April 1 balances.
2. Journalize the following transactions, and post the journal entries to the ledger accounts.
3. Prepare a list of the accounts and their balances on July 1, 1978.

1978

Apr. 15 Paid insurance premiums deducted from employees' wages during March:

Life.............................. $60
Hospital....................... 30

25   Paid payroll taxes for March:

F.I.C.A. tax $547.56
Employees' federal income tax.................. 590.00

26   Paid state unemployment tax for March, $126.36.
27   Paid F.U.T.A. tax for first quarter of 1978, $70.20.
30   Payroll for April:

Total earnings................................. $4,680.00
Less withholdings:
F.I.C.A. taxes............................. $273.78
Employees' federal income taxes..... 590.00
Insurance premiums – life.............. 60.00
Insurance premiums – hospital 30.00   953.78
                                                    $3,726.22

30   Recorded employer's social security taxes for April – all earnings
     were taxable.
May 15   Paid insurance premiums deducted from employees' wages during
         April.
25   Paid F.I.C.A. tax and employees' federal income tax for April.
26   Paid state unemployment tax for April.
31   Payroll for May – same as April's.
31   Recorded employer's social security taxes for May.
     All wages are taxable for F.I.C.A. $4,080 are taxable for F.U.T.A.
     and state unemployment.
June 15   Paid insurance premiums deducted from employees' wages during
          May.
25   Paid F.I.C.A. tax and employees' federal income tax for May.
26   Paid state unemployment tax for May
30   Payroll for June – same as that for April and May.
30   Recorded employer's social security taxes for June. All wages are
     taxable for F.I.C.A. $1,680 are taxable for F.U.T.A. and state
     unemployment.

Accounting for service enterprises – recording transactions
Learning objectives

The increasing portion of service enterprises, when compared with all types of business organizations, indicates that attention should be directed to the accounting problems of such a business. The high failure rate of service enterprises is further cause for concern. A study of the following material will provide a basic understanding of accounting for the service enterprise:

1. The procedures used when accounting for a service enterprise on the cash basis.
2. The organization of the chart of accounts for the service enterprise.
3. An understanding of the cash journal as a book of original entry when accounting on a cash basis.
4. A detailed illustration of the procedures used in recording the transactions of a service enterprise.
5. The trial balance as the final step in the recording process.

7 Accounting for service enterprises — recording transactions

A firm is classified as a **service enterprise** if its major source of revenue is derived from services performed for customers. A large number of firms can be characterized as service enterprises. Common examples are professional practices such as doctors, lawyers, accountants, and management consulting firms or service businesses such as barber shops, shoe repair shops, and realtors. Some of these firms may sell a certain amount of merchandise. For example, it is common for a shoe repair shop to sell shoe laces and polish in addition to providing shoe repair service. But, the *main* source of revenue is from providing a service.

THE CASH BASIS OF ACCOUNTING FOR SERVICE ENTERPRISES

The **cash basis of accounting** is frequently used for recording the revenue of a service enterprise. This means that the revenue is not recorded by the firm until the cash has been received from the customer. This may mean that the services are performed in one period but the cash is received in a later period. Under the cash basis of accounting, the revenue would be recorded in the later period when the cash was received. The mere promise of a customer to pay is not considered valid evidence of earned revenue. One reason for this point of view is that there is less likelihood of collecting a past-due account receivable in the service enterprise. In a merchandising firm, a washing machine or automobile can be repossessed, but it is not possible to take back a service once it has been performed for a client.

Typically, when the cash basis of accounting is used for revenue, expenses are also accounted for on a cash basis. This means that the expense is recorded only when paid even though it may have been incurred in a prior period. For example, if an employee is paid on the 15th of each month, the payment of January 15 will be for the last half of December and the first half of January, but (on the cash basis) it will all be recorded as a January expense. This fact is of minor importance, however, because the same thing happened at the beginning of the year. Thus, the effect on net earnings is negligible. The total amount actually paid in cash and recorded as expense for the year will be close to the amount actually "earned" by the employees. The cash basis of accounting is acceptable because most expenses are of a recurring nature and are similar in amount from period to period.

However, some items which are not recurring in nature or which vary substantially in amount may cause distortion in the financial statements if treated on a cash basis. As an example, if supplies are purchased in large amounts for cash during a period and a large portion of them remain unused at the end of the period, it would be undesirable to treat the entire amount as a period expense. In such a case, it would be desirable to estimate the dollar amount of the supplies used and charge only that amount to the period in question.

Another common example is the acquisition of long-term assets such as buildings and machinery. A building typically has a useful life far in excess of one year. Buildings often have useful lives of 25 years or more. If such a building was purchased for cash, it would not be sound accounting practice to charge the entire cost of the building to the year of purchase. The first year of service would have a very large expense for the building, and the remaining years of service would show no expense. Clearly, this would not be a very informative way of handling the expense of the building.

It is much more desirable to charge a portion of the total cost of the building to each of the years of service of the building. In this way the cost of the building is spread over the years of benefit. This allocation procedure is called **depreciation,** and the portion which is charged, or "written off," each year by means of an adjustment is called **depreciation expense.** Depreciation expense is the total cost of the asset less the estimated salvage (or scrap) value at the end of the asset's useful life spread in some systematic way over that life. A common method is to divide the cost less scrap value by the estimated useful life in years and thus charge an equal amount of depreciation expense to each year. The depreciation expense is an *estimated* figure, since no one can say exactly how "much" the ownership of the building helped the firm earn revenue in each of the years. In addition, the useful life of an asset and the scrap value figures are estimates.[1] (Adjustments such as depreciation will be discussed in Chapter 8.)

Almost all accountants and business executives would agree that this estimated depreciation charge to each year is more desirable than the distortion which would result from use of the strict cash basis. It is important to understand that the estimates involved in depreciation procedures are but one of the reasons why a firm's net earnings as computed for a time period are really an *estimate* of the earnings for that period. Knowledgeable accountants and business executives realize that the computed dollar amount of the net earnings is not as precise as it often appears. They know that the general size and trend of the earnings, as well as the ratio of the earnings to the investment of the owner, are more important than the exact dollar amount.

ACCOUNTING PROCEDURES

An extended illustration will be presented to aid in the understanding of the procedures involved in the recording of transactions for a service enterprise on the cash basis. The example will illustrate the records of J. T. Adams, M.D. After presenting some typical transactions for a month, financial statements will be presented in Chapter 8. Even though unique problems arise in the operation of any enterprise, the basic principles of recording transactions and preparing financial statements remain fundamentally the same. The system illustrated for Dr. Adams could easily be adapted to meet the needs of almost any small service firm or professional person.

Chart of accounts

Dr. Adams's chart of accounts is reproduced in Illustration 7–1. Each account has been assigned a three-digit code number where the first digit indicates the type of account: Those beginning with 1 are assets; 2, liabilities; 3, owner's equity; 4, revenue; and finally 5, expenses. The second and third digits identify specific accounts, and the accounts are numbered in such a way that accounts can be added later without disturbing the coding of the original accounts.

---

[1] It should also be understood that depreciation is an *allocation* process, and it is not related directly to the current physical condition or current resale value of the asset. This will be covered in more depth in later chapters.

Illustration 7-1

J. T. ADAMS, M.D.
Chart of Accounts

Assets:

110   Second National Bank
120   Petty Cash Fund
130   Drugs and Medical Supplies on Hand
140   Office Equipment
150   Accumulated Depreciation—Office Equipment

Liabilities:

210   F.I.C.A. Taxes Payable
220   Income Taxes Payable–Federal–Employee

Owner's Equity:

310   J. T. Adams, Capital
320   J. T. Adams, Drawing
330   Expense and Revenue Summary

Revenue:

410   Professional Fees—Office
420   Professional Fees—Hospital

Expenses:

505   Rent Expense
510   Drugs and Medical Supplies Expense
515   Salary Expense
520   Payroll Tax Expense
525   Telephone Expense
530   Nonmedical Supplies Expense
535   Automobile Expense
540   Depreciation Expense
545   Insurance Expense
550   Cleaning Expense
555   Charitable Contributions Expense
560   Miscellaneous Expense

The books of account

The following books are used in Dr. Adams's accounting system:

1.   Cash journal.
2.   General ledger.
3.   Petty cash disbursements book.

Many other records are kept, of course, such as detailed payroll records, drug purchase and use records (also required by state law), copies of bills sent to patients, and papers related to the tax returns. These records are not illustrated in this chapter. The petty cash disbursements book is also not shown since it has already been covered in Chapter 4.

The cash journal

Dr. Adams uses only one book of *original entry* — a cash journal. This journal provides for the recording of all transactions, end-of-period adjustments such as depreciation, and closing entries. The vast majority of transactions will, of course, be for cash. The journal, Illustration 7–2, has the typical date and description columns and ten amount columns. The first two provide for debits (deposits) and credits (checks issued) to the Cash account in the Second National Bank. Note the column for the check number next to the credit side. Six special columns provide for the two types of professional fees, salaries, and the related tax withholding, and drugs and medical supplies purchases. These special columns are for the most frequent transactions of Dr. Adams and thus save time in the posting process since only the totals need to be posted. Finally, at the far right, the General columns provide for all other transactions — that is, for those which involve accounts not listed in one of the special columns. Almost every transaction, of course, will have either a debit or credit in the Second National Bank pair of columns. The **P.R. column** is used to show the posting reference for the entries in the General pair of columns. The transactions of Dr. Adams for December are described on pages 147–60 and entered in the cash journal, Illustration 7–2.

The general ledger

The standard form of general ledger, as presented in Chapter 2, is used by Dr. Adams. This ledger, with the transactions of December posted, is given in Illustration 7–4. Note that the balance of December 1 has been entered in each account before the posting.

Extended illustration

The following transactions of Dr. Adams's practice are recorded in the cash journal, Illustration 7–3, and are posted to the general ledger, Illustration 7–4. The transactions are recorded daily with various activities being necessary at the end of each week as described on pages 148–49.

First week

December 1

Received checks from patients and insurance companies totaling $495. Of this, $318 represents charges for hospital services and $177 for office calls.

December 2

Received checks totaling $235 for professional services, of which $35 was for hospital services and $200 for office calls.

Issued Check No. 480 to Quality Drug Company for drugs and medical supplies to be dispensed to office patients; total cost of $48.53.

Issued Check No. 481 to Medical Building, Inc., for $400 for the December rent.

December 3

Issued Check No. 482 to Standard Oil Company for gasoline and other automobile expenses charged during the prior month. All of the charges were related to the leased car which is used by Dr. Adams for business only. The total was $33.18.

December 4

Received checks from patients and insurance companies for a total of $426.50, of which $125 was for hospital and $301.50 for office calls.

Issued checks for the weekly payroll to the two office nurses and the office girl. The detail of the payroll:

Name	Check No.	Gross Pay	Federal Income Tax Withheld	F.I.C.A. Tax Withheld	Net Pay
Betty Brown........	483	$150	$20.26	$ 7.20	$122.54
Carol Conner	484	138	23.23	6.62	108.15
Doris Davis	485	105	14.28	5.04	85.68
Totals........		$393	$57.77	$18.86	$316.37

Issued Check No. 486 for insurance premiums of $158. The check was to the Safeguard Insurance Agency and covers several policies, all business related. The same premium is due on the fourth day of each month.

December 5

Issued Check No. 487 to Quality Drug Company for drugs and medical supplies for office use. The total cost was $45.16.

Dr. Adams issued Check No. 488 for personal use in the amount of $250. (This is a debit to the J. T. Adams, Drawing account.)

Issued Check No. 489 for supplies, payable to the Central Company in the amount of $14.95. These supplies included paper, envelopes, and other office supplies, all of a nonmedical nature.

End of the week

At the end of each week it is desirable, but not absolutely necessary, to prove the equality of debits and credits in the cash journal and to post the entries in the General columns. This will help to isolate quickly any errors which may have been made and will also save posting time at the end of the period.

The proof of equality of debits and credits is shown by taking the total of each column, entering it in small figures in the column, and then checking to see if debits equal credits. At the end of the first week the proof is:

Account Column	Debit	Credit
Second National Bank	$1,156.50	$1,266.19
Fees — office		678.50
Fees — hospital		478.00
Salary expense	393.00	
F.I.C.A. taxes payable		18.86
Income taxes payable		57.77
Drugs and medical supplies expense	93.69	
General	856.13	
Totals	$2,499.32	$2,499.32

The posting of the individual items in the General pair of columns to the General Ledger can be done at any time during the period, but it should not all be postponed until the end. In Dr. Adams's case, postings are made at the end of each week. Note that the account number has been entered in the P.R. column of the Cash Journal, and the page number of the Cash Journal has been entered in the P.R. column of the ledger. This shows which items have been posted and also provides a **cross-reference system.** An "X" entered in the P.R. column of the journal indicates that there is no entry in the General column on that line. Also note that the December 1 balance of each account has been entered in the ledger before the posting started. The transactions for the first week have been recorded in the cash journal as shown in Illustration 7–2.

The transactions for the remainder of December are described and are recorded in the cash journal in Illustration 7–3.

Second week

December 7

Checks totaling $340 were received for professional fees. Of this amount, $160 was from hospital and $180 from office patients.

Check No. 490 was issued to Ajax Cleaning Service Company for $52. This is an amount paid weekly for the cleaning of the offices after hours every evening except Sunday.

December 8

Check No. 491 was issued to Physicians Supply Company for $18 for medical supplies for office use.

Illustration 7-2

Page 42

Cash Journal
For Month of December 1978

Date	Description	P.R.	Second National Bank Debit 110	Second National Bank Credit 110	Check Number
1978 Dec. 1	Professional fees	X	495 00		
2	Professional fees	X	235 00		
2	Quality Drug Company-drugs & med.	X		48 53	480
2	Medical Building, Inc.-rent	505		400 00	481
3	Standard Oil Company-automobile	535		33 18	482
4	Professional fees	X	426 50		
4	Betty Brown-salary	X		122 54	483
4	Carol Conner-salary	X		108 15	484
4	Doris Davis-salary	X		85 68	485
4	Safeguard Ins. Agency-insurance	545		158 00	486
5	Quality Drug Company-drugs & med.	X		45 16	487
5	Dr. Adams-drawings	320		250 00	488
5	Central Company-nonmedical supplies	530		14 95	489
			1156 50	1266 19	

Issued and cashed Check No. 492 for $20.47 to replenish the petty cash fund. The following expenses were compiled from the petty cash records:

Telephone expense	$ 1.80
Nonmedical supplies expense	4.67
Automobile expense	3.50
Miscellaneous expense	5.50
J. T. Adams, drawing	5.00
Total	$20.47

December 9

Received checks for professional fees of $510, $460 of which was from hospital patients and $50 from office calls.

Issued Check No. 493 for $381.96 for the amount of F.I.C.A. and federal income taxes withheld from employees, plus Dr. Adams's share of F.I.C.A.

The December 1 balances of F.I.C.A. Taxes Payable and Income Taxes Payable–Federal–employee represent the amounts withheld in November.

(There were four paydays in November, and the salaries were at

Fees — Office Credit 410	Fees — Hospital Credit 420	Salary Expense Debit 515	Payroll Deductions FICA Credit 210	Income Tax Credit 220	Drugs & Med. Supp. Exp. Debit 510	General Debit	Credit
177 00	318 00						
200 00	35 00						
					48 53		
						400 00	
						33 18	
301 50	125 00						
		150 00	7 20	20 26			
		138 00	6 62	23 23			
		105 00	5 04	14 28			
						158 00	
					45 16		
						250 00	
						1 495	
678 50	478 00	393 00	18 86	57 77	93 69	856 13	

the same rate as in December, so the F.I.C.A. represents $4 \times \$18.86$ or $\$75.44$, and the income tax is $4 \times \$57.77 = \$231.08$.) Dr. Adams's share of F.I.C.A. as an employer will also be $\$75.44$, which is recorded as a debit to Payroll Tax Expense and is credited to F.I.C.A. Taxes Payable in the first entry, and then the total liability is paid in the second entry related to this transaction. The total paid is $\$75.44 + \$75.44 + \$231.08 = \$381.96$.

December 10

Received checks for total fees of $790, of which $416 was hospital and $374 office calls.

Issued Check No. 494 for $61.80 to Quality Drug Company for drugs for office use.

December 11

Paid the regular weekly payroll in the same amounts as last week (see transaction of December 4). The payroll was paid with Check Nos. 495, 496, and 497.

Issued Check No. 498 to Medical Building Drug Store for $4 for drugs for office use.

December 12

Issued Check No. 499 to Dr. Adams for $180 for personal use.

End of the week

The equality of debits and credits in the cash journal is proved again by writing small totals in the journal and then adding to get total debits and total credits:

Account Column	Debit	Credit
Second National Bank	$2,796.50	$2,300.79
Fees—office		1,282.50
Fees—hospital		1,514.00
Salary expense	786.00	
F.I.C.A. taxes payable		113.16
Income taxes payable		115.54
Drugs and medical supplies expense	177.49	
General	1,566.00	
Totals	$5,325.99	$5,325.99

Notice that the totals are cumulative totals for all of the transactions on that page of the journal. The posting of the General columns has also been brought up to date, as shown in the general ledger.

Third week

December 14

Received checks for professional fees, $80 from hospital and $236 from office patients for a total of $316.

Issued Check No. 500 for the regular weekly cleaning. (See transaction of December 7.)

December 15

Received checks from patients and insurance companies for a total of $139, of which $39 was office and $100 hospital.

Issued Check No. 501 to Quality Drugs for $36.80 for medical supplies for office use.

Mailed Check No. 502 to Bell Telephone Company to pay the phone bill for the past month. The total bill was $63.

At this point, page 42 of the cash journal has been filled and a new page must be started. Each column of page 42 is totaled, and the totals entered and ruled. These totals are then entered on the first line of the new page as "Balance forward." It is also convenient to check the equality of debits and credits at this point:

Account Column	Debit	Credit
Second National Bank	$3,251.50	$2,452.59
Fees — office		1,557.50
Fees — hospital		1,694.00
Salary expense	786.00	
F.I.C.A. taxes payable		113.16
Income taxes payable		115.54
Drugs and medical supplies expense	214.29	
General	1,681.00	
Totals	$5,932.79	$5,932.79

Issued Check No. 503 to Dr. Adams for $50 for personal use.

December 16
Received checks for $225 for professional fees, all office patients.

December 17
Received a check for $125 from a hospital patient.

Issued and cashed a check, No. 504, for $22.69 to replenish the petty cash fund. The expenses were:

Telephone expense	$ 3.60
Nonmedical supplies expense	15.34
Automobile expense	1.30
Miscellaneous expense	2.45
Total	$22.69

December 18
Paid regular weekly payroll with Check Nos. 505, 506, and 507.

Issued Check No. 508 for $400 to Dr. Adams for personal use.

December 19
Issued Check No. 509 to Medical Building Drug Store for $32 for drugs for office use.

End of the week

The proof of equality of debits and credits:

Account Column	Debit	Credit
Second National Bank	$3,601.50	$3,273.65
Fees — office		1,782.50
Fees — hospital		1,819.00
Salary expense	1,179.00	
F.I.C.A. taxes payable		132.02
Income taxes payable		173.31
Drugs and medical supplies expense	246.29	
General	2,153.69	
Totals	$7,180.48	$7,180.48

Fourth week

December 21

Received checks totaling $405 for fees, $200 of which was hospital and $205 office.

Issued Check No. 510 for office supplies in the amount of $17.50. The check was made payable to Business Forms Supply House, Inc.

Check No. 511 for $100 was issued to the United Fund (the debit is to Charitable Contributions Expense).

Issued Check No. 512 for $52 for the regular weekly cleaning bill.

December 22

Check No. 513 was issued to Quality Drug Company for $10.60 for drugs and medical supplies for office use.

December 23

Checks for $264 were received, all from office patients.

December 24

Check Nos. 514, 515, and 516 were issued for the regular weekly payroll. Since December 25 and 26 are "paid holidays," the checks were for the usual amounts.

Check No. 517 was written to Medical Building Drug Store for $14 for drugs for office use.

End of the week

The usual "end-of-the-week" procedures were omitted since December 21–24 was a short workweek.

Fifth week

December 28

Checks totaling $526 were received, of which $420 was for hospital services and $106 for office calls.

The cleaning bill for last week was $34.75 instead of the usual amount because the office was only cleaned four times. It was paid with Check No. 518.

December 29

Check No. 519 was written to Dr. Adams for personal use. It was for $125.

December 30

Checks received for professional services totaled $455. Of this, $250 was for hospital and $205 for office calls.

Issued Check No. 520 to Quality Drug Company for $34 for medical supplies for office use.

Issued Check No. 521 to United Car Leasing Company for the monthly lease of Dr. Adams's car. The total was $89.

December 31

Issued and cashed Check No. 522 for the petty cash fund. The total was $22.73, and the expenses were:

Nonmedical supplies expense	$ 4.68
Miscellaneous expense	13.05
J. T. Adams, drawing	5.00
Total	$22.73

End of the month

The end-of-the-month procedures include the proof of the equality of debits and credits in the cash journal and the complete posting of the data contained therein to the ledger. There are no separate "end-of-the-week" steps, since these steps were merely to catch errors and save posting time at the end of the month. First, each column of the cash journal is totaled and the totals entered and ruled. The final totals for December, as shown in Illustration 7–3, are:

Amount Column	Debit	Credit
Second National Bank	$5,251.50	$4,089.60
Fees — office		2,562.50
Fees — hospital		2,689.00
Salary expense	1,572.00	
F.I.C.A. taxes payable		150.88
Income taxes payable		231.08
Drugs and medical supplies expense	304.89	
General	2,594.67	
Totals	$9,723.06	$9,723.06

The posting procedure is to first complete the posting of the individual items in the General pair of columns. Remember that an "X" in the P.R. column indicates that there is no General entry on that line. The second step is to post the total of each special column. For example, the total of $5,251.50 in the debit column of the Second National Bank pair of columns must be posted to the debit column of the Second National Bank account in the general ledger. This total is posted because none of the individual items of which it is composed have been posted (nor should they be posted as individual items). The account number, 110, is entered below the total in the journal to show that the total has been posted. A "✔" below the General totals shows that these totals are not to be posted (they have already been posted as individual items.) As amounts are posted to

Illustration 7-3

Page 42   Cash Journal
For Month of December 1978

Date	Description	P.R.	Second National Bank Debit 110	Credit 110	Check Number
1978 Dec. 1	Professional fees	X	495 00		
2	Professional fees	X	235 00		
2	Quality Drug Company-drugs & med.	X		48 53	480
2	Medical Building, Inc.-rent	505		400 00	481
3	Standard Oil Company-automobile	535		33 18	482
4	Professional fees	X	426 50		
4	Betty Brown-salary	X		122 54	483
4	Carol Conner-salary	X		108 15	484
4	Doris Davis-salary	X		85 68	485
4	Safeguard Ins. Agency-insurance	545		158 00	486
5	Quality Drug Company-drugs & med.	X		45 16	487
5	Dr. Adams-drawings	320		250 00	488
5	Central Company-nonmedical supplies	530		14 95	489
			1156 50	1266 19	
7	Professional fees	X	340 00		
7	Ajax Cleaning Service Co.-cleaning	550		52 00	490
8	Physicians Supply Co.-drugs & med.	X		18 00	491
8	Petty cash - telephone	525		20 47	492
	-nonmedical supplies	530			
	-automobile	535			
	-miscellaneous	560			
	-drawings	320			
9	Professional fees	X	510 00		
9	FICA - employer's share (payroll tax)	520			
9	Federal Gov't. - withholding debit	220		381 96	493
	-FICA debit	210			
10	Professional fees	X	790 00		
10	Quality Drug Company-drugs & med.	X		61 80	494
11	Betty Brown - salary	X		122 54	495
11	Carol Conner - salary	X		108 15	496
11	Doris Davis - salary	X		85 68	497
11	Medical Building Drug Store-drugs & med.	X		4 00	498
12	Dr. Adams-drawings	320		180 00	499
			2796 50	2300 79	
14	Professional fees	X	316 00		
14	Ajax Cleaning Service Co.-cleaning	550		52 00	500
15	Professional fees	X	139 00		
15	Quality Drug Company-drugs & med.	X		36 80	501
15	Bell Telephone Company-telephone	525		63 00	502
	Totals - forward		3251 50	2452 59	

Fees – Office Credit 410	Fees – Hospital Credit 420	Salary Expense Debit 515	Payroll Deductions FICA Credit 210	Payroll Deductions Income Tax Credit 220	Drugs & Med Supp. Exp. Debit 510	General Debit	General Credit
177 00	318 00						
200 00	35 00						
					48 53		
						400 00	
						33 18	
301 50	125 00						
		150 00	7 20	20 26			
		138 00	6 62	23 23			
		105 00	5 04	14 28			
						158 00	
					45 16		
						250 00	
						14 95	
678 50	478 00	393 00	18 86	57 77	93 69	856 13	
180 00	160 00						
						52 00	
					18 00		
						1 80	
						4 67	
						3 50	
						5 50	
						5 00	
50 00	460 00						
			75 44			75 44	
						231 08	
						150 88	
374 00	416 00						
					61 80		
		150 00	7 20	20 26			
		138 00	6 62	23 23			
		105 00	5 04	14 28			
					4 00		
						180 00	
1282 50	1514 00	786 00	113 16	115 54	177 49	1566 00	
236 00	80 00						
						52 00	
39 00	100 00						
					36 80		
						63 00	
1557 50	1694 00	786 00	113 16	115 54	214 29	1681 00	

Illustration 7–3 (continued)

Cash Journal
For Month of December 1978

Page 43

	Date	Description		P. R.	Second National Bank Debit 110	Second National Bank Credit 110	Check Number
		Balances forward		X	3251 50	2452 59	
1978 Dec	15	Dr. Adams – drawings		320		50 00	503
	16	Professional fees		X	225 00		
	17	Professional fees		X	125 00		
	17	Petty cash – telephone		525		22 69	504
		– nonmedical supplies		530			
		– automobile		535			
		– miscellaneous		560			
	18	Betty Brown – salary		X		122 54	505
	18	Carol Conner – salary		X		108 15	506
	18	Doris Davis – salary		X		85 68	507
	18	Dr. Adams – drawings		320		400 00	508
	19	Medical Building Drug Store – drugs & med.		X		32 00	509
					3601 50	3273 65	
	21	Professional fees			405 00		
	21	Business Forms Supply House – nonmedical		530		17 50	510
	21	United Fund – charitable contrib. exp.		555		100 00	511
	21	Ajax Cleaning Service Co. – cleaning		550		52 00	512
	22	Quality Drug Company – drugs & med.		X		10 60	513
	23	Professional fees		X	264 00		
	24	Betty Brown – salary		X		122 54	514
	24	Carol Conner – salary		X		108 15	515
	24	Doris Davis – salary		X		85 68	516
	24	Medical Building Drug Store – drugs & med.		X		14 00	517
	28	Professional fees		X	526 00		
	28	Ajax Cleaning Service Co. – cleaning		550		34 75	518
	29	Dr. Adams – drawings		320		125 00	519
	30	Professional fees		X	455 00		
	30	Quality Drug Company – drugs & med.		X		34 00	520
	30	United Car Leasing Co. – automobile		535		89 00	521
	31	Petty cash – nonmedical supplies		530		22 73	522
		– miscellaneous		560			
		– drawings		320			
		Totals – December			5251 50	4089 60	
					(110)	(110)	

Fees–Office Credit 410	Fees–Hospital Credit 420	Salary Expense Debit 515	Payroll Deductions FICA Credit 210	Income Tax Credit 220	Drugs & Med. Supp. Exp. Debit 510	General Debit	General Credit
1557 50	1694 00	786 00	113 16	115 54	214 29	1681 00	
						50 00	
225 00							
	125 00						
						3 60	
						15 34	
						1 30	
						2 45	
		150 00	7 20	20 26			
		138 00	6 62	23 23			
		105 00	5 04	14 28			
						400 00	
					32 00		
1782 50	1819 00	1179 00	132 02	173 31	246 29	2153 69	
205 00	200 00						
						17 50	
						100 00	
						52 00	
					10 60		
264 00							
		150 00	7 20	20 26			
		138 00	6 62	23 23			
		105 00	5 04	14 28			
					14 00		
106 00	420 00						
						34 75	
						125 00	
205 00	250 00						
					34 00		
						89 00	
						4 68	
						13 05	
						5 00	
2562 50	2689 00	1572 00	150 88	231 08	304 89	2594 67	
(410)	(420)	(515)	(210)	(220)	(510)	(✓)	(✓)

the general ledger, the P.R. column in the ledger is cross-referenced to the cash journal.

This completes the recording of the transactions of December for Dr. Adams. The cash journal and general ledger as of the end of December, before adjustments and closing entries, appear in Illustrations 7–3 and 7–4.

Illustration 7–4

GENERAL LEDGER
Second National Bank — Account No. 110

Date		Explanation	P.R.	Debit	Credit	Balance
1978 Dec.	1	Balance	✓			12,117.80
	31		CJ43	5,251.50		17,369.30
	31		CJ43		4,089.60	13,279.70

Petty Cash Fund — Account No. 120

Date		Explanation	P.R.	Debit	Credit	Balance
1978 Dec.	1	Balance	✓			25.00

Drugs and Medical Supplies on Hand — Account No. 130

Date	Explanation	P.R.	Debit	Credit	Balance

Office Equipment — Account No. 140

Date		Explanation	P.R.	Debit	Credit	Balance
1978 Dec.	1	Balance	✓			18,350.00

Accumulated Depreciation — Office Equipment — Account No. 150

Date		Explanation	P.R.	Debit	Credit	Balance
1978 Dec.	1	Balance	✓			3,670.00

F.I.C.A. Taxes Payable — Account No. 210

Date		Explanation	P.R.	Debit	Credit	Balance
1978 Dec.	1	Balance	✓			75.44
	9		CJ42	150.88		(75.44)
	31		CJ43		150.88	75.44

Illustration 7–4 (continued)

Income Taxes Payable–Federal–Employee   Account No. 220

Date		Explanation	P.R.	Debit	Credit	Balance
1978 Dec.	1	Balance	✓			231.08
	9		CJ42	231.08		–
	31		CJ43		231.08	231.08

J. T. Adams, Capital   Account No. 310

Date		Explanation	P.R.	Debit	Credit	Balance
1978 Dec.	1	Balance	✓			14,352.72

J. T. Adams, Drawing   Account No. 320

Date		Explanation	P.R.	Debit	Credit	Balance
1978 Dec.	1	Balance	✓			10,940.00
	5		CJ42	250.00		11,190.00
	8		CJ42	5.00		11,195.00
	12		CJ42	180.00		11,375.00
	15		CJ43	50.00		11,425.00
	18		CJ43	400.00		11,825.00
	29		CJ43	125.00		11,950.00
	31		CJ43	5.00		11,955.00

Professional Fees–Office   Account No. 410

Date		Explanation	P.R.	Debit	Credit	Balance
1978 Dec.	1	Balance	✓			28,588.00
	31		CJ43		2,562.50	31,150.50

Professional Fees–Hospital   Account No. 420

Date		Explanation	P.R.	Debit	Credit	Balance
1978 Dec.	1	Balance	✓			29,234.00
	31		CJ43		2,689.00	31,923.00

Rent Expense   Account No. 505

Date		Explanation	P.R.	Debit	Credit	Balance
1978 Dec.	1	Balance	✓			4,400.00
	2		CJ42	400.00		4,800.00

Illustration 7–4 (continued)

Drugs and Medical Supplies Expense   Account No. 510

Date		Explanation	P.R.	Debit	Credit	Balance
1978						
Dec.	1	Balance	✓			3,289.79
	31		CJ43	304.89		3,594.68

Salary Expense   Account No. 515

Date		Explanation	P.R.	Debit	Credit	Balance
1978						
Dec.	1	Balance	✓			18,864.00
	31		CJ43	1,572.00		20,436.00

Payroll Tax Expense   Account No. 520

Date		Explanation	P.R.	Debit	Credit	Balance
1978						
Dec.	1	Balance	✓			829.84
	9		CJ42	75.44		905.28

Telephone Expense   Account No. 525

Date		Explanation	P.R.	Debit	Credit	Balance
1978						
Dec.	1	Balance	✓			816.40
	8		CJ42	1.80		818.20
	15		CJ42	63.00		881.20
	17		CJ43	3.60		884.80

Nonmedical Supplies Expense   Account No. 530

Date		Explanation	P.R.	Debit	Credit	Balance
1978						
Dec.	1	Balance	✓			653.04
	5		CJ42	14.95		667.99
	8		CJ42	4.67		672.66
	17		CJ43	15.34		688.00
	21		CJ43	17.50		705.50
	31		CJ43	4.68		710.18

Automobile Expense   Account No. 535

Date		Explanation	P.R.	Debit	Credit	Balance
1978						
Dec.	1	Balance	✓			1,515.78
	3		CJ42	33.18		1,548.96
	8		CJ42	3.50		1,552.46
	17		CJ43	1.30		1,553.76
	30		CJ43	89.00		1,642.76

Illustration 7–4 (concluded)

Depreciation Expense   Account No. 540

Date	Explanation	P.R.	Debit	Credit	Balance

Insurance Expense   Account No. 545

Date		Explanation	P.R.	Debit	Credit	Balance
1978 Dec.	1	Balance	✓			1,738.00
	4		CJ42	158.00		1,896.00

Cleaning Expense   Account No. 550

Date		Explanation	P.R.	Debit	Credit	Balance
1978 Dec.	1	Balance	✓			2,101.25
	7		CJ42	52.00		2,153.25
	14		CJ42	52.00		2,205.25
	21		CJ43	52.00		2,257.25
	28		CJ43	34.75		2,292.00

Charitable Contributions Expense   Account No. 555

Date		Explanation	P.R.	Debit	Credit	Balance
1978 Dec.	1	Balance	✓			300.00
	21		CJ43	100.00		400.00

Miscellaneous Expense   Account No. 560

Date		Explanation	P.R.	Debit	Credit	Balance
1978 Dec.	1	Balance	✓			210.34
	8		CJ42	5.50		215.84
	17		CJ43	2.45		218.29
	31		CJ43	13.05		231.34

THE TRIAL BALANCE

The trial balance is the third step in the sequence. It is a list of all the balances in the general ledger at the end of an accounting period. It is the "raw material" for the preparation of financial statements and the closing process, which are covered in the next chapter. The December 31 trial balance for Dr. Adams is Illustration 7–5.

Illustration 7–5

J. T. ADAMS, M.D.
Trial Balance
December 31, 1978

Account No.	Account Title	Debit	Credit
110	Second National Bank	$13,279.70	
120	Petty cash fund	25.00	
140	Office equipment	18,350.00	
150	Accumulated depreciation—office equipment		$ 3,670.00
210	F.I.C.A. taxes payable		75.44
220	Income taxes payable—federal—employee		231.08
310	J. T. Adams, capital		14,352.72
320	J. T. Adams, drawing	11,955.00	
410	Professional fees—office		31,150.50
420	Professional fees—hospital		31,923.00
505	Rent expense	4,800.00	
510	Drugs and medical supplies expense	3,594.68	
515	Salary expense	20,436.00	
520	Payroll tax expense	905.28	
525	Telephone expense	884.80	
530	Nonmedical supplies expense	710.18	
535	Automobile expense	1,642.76	
545	Insurance expense	1,896.00	
550	Cleaning expense	2,292.00	
555	Charitable contributions expense	400.00	
560	Miscellaneous expense	231.34	
		$81,402.74	$81,402.74

GLOSSARY

Cash basis of accounting   recording revenue only when cash is received and recording expenses only when cash is paid.

Cross-reference system   a system which allows transactions to be traced from the book of original entry to the ledger accounts or from the ledger accounts to the book of original entry. The ledger account number is entered in the P.R. column of the book of original entry, and the page number of the book of original entry is entered in the P.R. column of the ledger account.

Depreciation   the systematic procedure used to allocate the cost of a long-lived asset to each of the years of service of the long-lived asset.

Depreciation expense   the portion of a long-lived asset's cost that is charged to expense or "written off" each year. It is the total cost of the asset less the estimated salvage value at the end of the asset's useful life spread in some way over that life.

P.R. column   a Posting Reference column that indicates which items have been posted and that provides a cross-reference system for tracing transactions from the book of original entry to the ledger accounts, or vice versa.

Service enterprise   a firm whose major source of revenue is derived from providing services to customers. Examples would be professional practices, barber shops, and realtors.

QUESTIONS AND EXERCISES

1. What is a distinguishing characteristic of service enterprises? Give some examples of service enterprises.

2. How are revenues and expenses accounted for when the cash basis of accounting is used?

3. A service enterprise does not usually follow a strict cash basis of accounting. What are some exceptions to the cash basis? Why are they exceptions?

4. Why is there only a small chance of collecting a past-due account receivable in a service enterprise?

5. What should be considered more important than the exact dollar amount of net earnings? Why?

6. What procedure is followed when each page in a cash journal is filled?

7. What are "end-of-the-week" procedures? What is their purpose?

8. What are "end-of-the-month" procedures?

PROBLEMS

7-1. Boot's Shoe Repair Shop is owned and operated by B. C. Boot. Boot records all transactions in a cash journal. During the month of August, Boot completed the following transactions:

1978
Aug. 1 Issued Check No. 618 to Conyers Company for shoe repair supplies. The amount was $75.
      2 Received $40 for shoe repair services.
      3 Received $50 for shoe repair services.
      4 Issued Check No. 619 to Martin Landers to pay the rent for August. The amount was $150.

Aug. 5 Received $60 for shoe repair services.
      5 Paid telephone bill for July, $15. Check No. 620.
      6 Received $80 for shoe repair services.
      7 Paid utilities bill for July, $20. Check No. 621.
     10 Issued Check No. 622 for personal use. The amount was $100.
     11 Received $55 for shoe repair services.
     12 Purchased shop equipment costing $150 on account. It was bought from the Calvin Equipment Company.
     13 Issued Check No. 623 to KCEB radio station for advertising. The amount was $25.
     14 Received $90 for shoe repair services.
     17 Issued Check No. 624 to Conyers Company for shoe repair supplies. The amount was $100.
     18 Received $65 for shoe repair services.
     19 Issued Check No. 625 to Calvin Equipment Company in partial payment of an account. The amount was $75.
     20 Received $75 for shoe repair services.
     21 Issued Check No. 626 for $25 to the Community Chest.
     22 Received $100 for shoe repair services.
     28 Issued Check No. 627 for $75 to Calvin Equipment Company in payment of an account.
     29 Received $25 for shoe repair services.
     30 Issued Check No. 628 for personal use. The amount was $150.
     31 Received $95 for shoe repair services.

Required:

Journalize the above transactions in the cash journal. The cash journal has columns headed Date, Description, P.R., Cash (debits and credits), Check No., Shoe Repair Revenue, Shoe Repair Supplies Expense, and General (debits and credits). Total and rule the cash journal.

7-2. Jan Baskin opened a beauty parlor in March 1978. The transactions for the first month have already been recorded in the cash journal shown on the next page. The chart of accounts is show below:

Chart of Accounts

Account No.	Name of Account
109	Cash
113	Shop Equipment
309	Jan Baskin, Capital
313	Jan Baskin, Drawing
409	Beauty Parlor Revenue
509	Beauty Parlor Supplies Expense

513	Rent Expense
517	Advertising Expense
521	Miscellaneous Expense

Page 3

Cash Journal
For Month of March 1978

Date	Description	P. R.	Cash Debit	Cash Credit	Check Number	Beauty Parlor Revenue	Beauty Parlor Supplies	General Debit	General Credit
1978 Mar. 1	Jan Baskin, capital		4000 00						4000 00
1	Shop equipment			1000 00	101			1000 00	
2	Beauty parlor supplies			300 00	102		300 00		
5	Beauty parlor revenue		60 00			60 00			
8	Beauty parlor revenue		80 00			80 00			
9	Rent expense			125 00	103			125 00	
11	Beauty parlor revenue		120 00			120 00			
12	Advertising expense			20 00	104			20 00	
15	Beauty parlor revenue		100 00			100 00			
16	Jan Baskin, drawing			100 00	105			100 00	
18	Beauty parlor revenue		30 00			30 00			
19	Beauty parlor supplies			95 00	106		95 00		
22	Beauty parlor revenue		120 00			120 00			
23	Shop equipment			500 00	107			500 00	
25	Miscellaneous expense			20 00	108			20 00	
26	Beauty parlor revenue		140 00			140 00			
29	Beauty parlor revenue		90 00			90 00			
30	Jan Baskin, drawing			50 00	109			50 00	

Required:
1. Open the above ledger accounts, and post the journal entries for March.
2. Prepare a trial balance for March 30, 1978.

7-3.
DR. H. P. CLAXTON
Trial Balance
November 30, 1978

Account No.	Account Title	Debit	Credit
101	Cash..	$15,200	
111	Petty cash...	40	
121	Office equipment...................................	10,000	
131	Accumulated depreciation — office equipment		$ 2,000
201	F.I.C.A. taxes payable............................		199
211	Income taxes payable — federal — employee...		169
301	H. P. Claxton, capital		50,000
311	H. P. Claxton, drawing	15,250	
401	Professional fees — office........................		9,600
411	Professional fees — hospital		7,500
501	Rent expense	2,200	
511	Drugs and medical supplies expense...........	4,500	
521	Salary expense	18,700	
531	Payroll tax expense	2,662	
541	Telephone expense.................................	150	
551	Nonmedical supplies expense....................	60	
561	Automobile expense...............................	126	
571	Insurance expense..................................	330	
581	Miscellaneous expense............................	250	
		$69,468	$69,468

Required:
1. Open the above ledger accounts and record the November 30 balances.
2. Journalize the December transactions in the cash journal (column headings should be the same as those used in the example of J. T. Adams.)
3. Post the journal entries to the ledger accounts.
4. Prepare a trial balance for December 31, 1978.

Dec. 1 Issued Check No. 852 to Randall Drug Company for drugs and medical supplies for office use. The total was $50.
    2 Checks totaling $310 were received for professional fees — $160 from hospital patients and $150 from office patients.
    3 Issued Check No. 853 for nonmedical supplies to Carry Supply Company. The amount was $20.
    4 Checks totaling $400 were received for professional fees — $150 from hospital patients and $250 from office patients.
    6 Issued and cashed Check No. 854 for $21 to replenish the petty cash fund. The following expenses were compiled from the petty cash records:

Telephone expense...................................... $ 5
Automobile expense   10
Nonmedical supplies expense........................   6

　　　Total.. $21

Dec.　7　Issued Check No. 855 for $368 for the amount of F.I.C.A. and federal income taxes withheld from employee plus Dr. Claxton's share of F.I.C.A. taxes.

　　8　Received checks totaling $250 from hospital patients.

　　8　Issued Check No. 856 to Dr. Claxton for personal use, $175.

　　9　Mailed Check No. 857 to Independent Telephone Company for November's phone bill of $86.

　10　Issued Check No. 858 to Randall Drug Company for drugs for office use. The cost was $90.

　11　Received checks totaling $494 from office patients.

　13　Issued Check No. 859 to Helpful Insurance Company to pay premium for December. The amount was $30.

　14　Issued and cashed Check No. 860 to replenish petty cash fund. The expenses were:

Nonmedical supplies expense........................ $10
Miscellaneous expense................................   15
H. P. Claxton, drawing   10

　　　Total.. $35

　15　Received checks totaling $690 — $500 from hospital patients and $190 from office patients.

　16　Issued Check No. 861 for $200 to Lance Skinner in payment of December's rent.

　17　Issued Check No. 862 to Medic Company for medical supplies for office use. The total cost was $50.

　18　Received checks totaling $475 for professional fees — $270 from office patients and $205 from hospital patients.

　20　Issued Check No. 863 to Randall Drug Company for drugs for office use. The cost was $120.

　21　Issued Check No. 864 to Medic Company for medical supplies for office use. The cost was $75.

　22　Received checks totaling $500 from office patients.

　23　Issued and cashed Check No. 865 to replenish petty cash fund. The expenses were:

Automobile expense $10
Telephone expense......................................   5
Miscellaneous expense................................   5
H. P. Claxton, drawing   10

　　　Total.. $30

　27　Received checks totaling $500 from hospital patients

　27　Issued Check No. 866 to Harris Equipment Company for a new typewriter. The total cost was $300.

Dec. 28   Issued Check No. 867 to Carry Supply Company for nonmedical supplies. The amount was $20.

29   Issued Check No. 868 to the Community Chest for $15.

30   Received checks totaling $325 — $150 from office patients and $175 from hospital patients.

31   Paid the December payroll:

Total earnings		$1,700.00
Less: F.I.C.A. taxes............	$ 99.50	
Federal income taxes....	169.00	268.50
Net Amount Paid		$1,431.50

Check Nos. 869, 870, and 871 were issued to employees.

31   Recorded the payroll tax expense for December: F.I.C.A. taxes, $99.50.

31   Issued and cashed Check No. 872 to replenish the petty cash fund. The expenses were:

Miscellaneous expenses	$15
H. P. Claxton, drawing	10
Total...	$25

7-4.   Jimmy Carson, owner and operator of Carson's Radio Repair Shop, completed the following transactions during September, 1978:

1978

Sept.   1   Issued Check No. 382 for September's rent, $125.

2   Issued Check No. 383 for $25 to pay the utility bill for August.

3   Received $100 from Clyde O'Hara for radio repair revenue.

4   Paid telephone bill of $15 for August with Check No. 384.

6   Received $20 from Ronnie Keats for radio repair revenue.

7   Issued Check No. 385 to Bonner Supply Company for shop supplies. The total cost was $60.

8   Received $30 for radio repair revenue from Karen Kirby.

9   Issued Check No. 386 to the Tinsley Company for a piece of shop equipment. The total cost was $100.

9   Received $15 from Connie James and $25 from Debbie Butler for radio repair revenue.

13   Received $40 from Steve Melton for radio repair revenue.

14   Invested an additional $500 in the business.

15   Issued Check No. 387 to Mann's Supply Company for $25 worth of shop supplies.

16   Purchased a company truck costing $4,000. Issued Check No. 388 for $1,000 as a down payment.

17   Received $35 from Jim Kline and $45 from Byron Wells as radio repair revenue.

18   Issued Check No. 389 to the Atlanta Journal for newspaper advertising that cost $30.

20   Issued Check No. 390 to Jimmy Carson for personal use. The amount was $25.

Sept. 23 Issued Check No. 391 to Bonner Supply Company for $50 worth of shop supplies.

    24 Issued Check No. 392 for $500 as a payment on the truck purchased on September 16.

    27 Received $30 from Satish Mehra, $25 from Bobby Moore, and $60 from David Bishop for radio repair revenue.

    28 Issued Check No. 393 for $20 to the United Fund.

    29 Issued Check No. 394 for $150 to Jimmy Carson for personal use.

    30 Received $25 from Ting Chan and $75 from Harvey Hightower for radio repair revenue.

Required:

Record the above transactions in a cash journal with the following column headings: Date, Description, P.R., Cash (debit and credit), Check No., Radio Repair Revenue, Shop Supplies, and General (debit and credit).

7–5. Lane Jordan is a management consultant. Jordan's transactions for the month of May have already been recorded in the cash journal which is shown on the next page. The trial balance for April 30, 1978, is shown below.

Required:

1. Open ledger accounts and post the journal entries.
2. Prepare a trial balance for May 31, 1978.

LANE JORDAN
Trial Balance
April 30, 1978

Account No.	Account Title	Debit	Credit
104	Cash	$ 1,200.00	
114	Office equipment	700.00	
124	Accumulated depreciation — off. equip.		$ 150.00
204	F.I.C.A. taxes payable		21.06
214	Income taxes payable–federal— employee		20.40
224	F.U.T.A. taxes payable		14.40
234	State unemployment taxes payable		77.76
304	Lane Jordan, capital		4,111.90
314	Lane Jordan, drawing	4,000.00	
404	Consulting fees earned		6,500.00
504	Salary expense	2,880.00	
514	Payroll tax expense	755.52	
524	Telephone expense	160.00 ·	
534	Utilities expense	60.00	
544	Rent expense	800.00	
554	Postage expense	50.00	
564	Office supplies expense	200.00	
574	Miscellaneous expense	90.00	
		$10,895.52	$10,895.52

Page 7   Cash Journal
For Month of May 1978

Date	Description	P.R.	Cash Debit	Cash Credit	Check Number	Consulting Fees Earned (Cr.)
May 3	Karen Lupo		50 00			50 00
4	Hardy Company		150 00			150 00
5	Telephone expense			50 00	298	
6	Utilities expense			15 00	299	
6	Postage expense			10 00	300	
7	Maverick Company		200 00			200 00
7	Secretary's salary			149 07	301	
7	Payroll tax expense					
10	Rent expense			200 00	302	
11	Barker Company		75 00			75 00
12	Torbert Company		150 00			150 00
13	Office equipment			300 00	303	
13	Leitch and Sons		250 00			250 00
14	Secretary's salary			149 07	304	
14	Payroll tax expense					
14	Lane Jordan, capital		900 00			
17	Office supplies expense			30 00	305	
18	Johny Sousa		125 00			125 00
19	Miscellaneous expense			10 00	306	
20	Lennon Beadle		250 00			250 00
21	Secretary's salary			149 07	307	
21	Payroll tax expense					
24	Postage expense			20 00	308	
25	Miscellaneous expense			15 00	309	
26	Orange Company		100 00			100 00
27	Office supplies expense			25 00	310	
28	Secretary's salary			149 07	311	
28	Payroll tax expense					
31	Lane Jordan, drawing			250 00	312	
31	Membro and Sons		150 00			150 00

7–6. June Bennett recently graduated from law school. She decided to open her own practice in January 1978. During January, Ms. Bennett completed the following transactions:

1978
Jan. 2   Invested $2,000 cash in the law firm, June Bennett, attorney.
     4   Rented an office, and issued Check No. 101 for $150 for January's rent.

| Salary Expense (Dr.) | FICA Taxes (Cr.) | Payroll Deductions | | | General | |
		Income Taxes (Cr.)	FUTA Taxes (Cr.)	St. Un. Taxes (Cr.)	Debit	Credit
					50 00	
					15 00	
					10 00	
180 00	10 53	20 40				
	10 53		0 90	4 86	16 29	
					200 00	
					300 00	
180 00	10 53	20 40				
	10 53		0 90	4 86	16 29	
						900 00
					30 00	
					10 00	
180 00	10 53	20 40				
	10 53		0 90	4 86	16 29	
					20 00	
					15 00	
					25 00	
180 00	10 53	20 40				
	10 53		0 90	4 86	16 29	
					250 00	

Jan. 4 Issued Check No. 102 for $175 to purchase a typewriter.

    5 Issued Check No. 103 for $80 to purchase office supplies.

    6 Established a petty cash fund of $30 by issuing and cashing Check No. 104.

    6 Issued Check No. 105 to purchase office furniture costing $500.

    8 Paid her two employees their weekly salaries.

Total payroll..................................... $285
Less: F.I.C.A. taxes.......................... $17
          Federal Income taxes...............   33   50
Net Amount Paid............................. $235

The employees received Check Nos. 106 and 107.

Jan. 8 Recorded the following payroll tax expense:

F.I.C.A. taxes $17
F.U.T.A. taxes   1
State unemployment taxes   8

11 Received $250 from Allen Burke for legal fees.
12 Paid insurance premiums totaling $50 with Check No. 108.
13 Received $150 from Mead & Sons for legal fees.
14 Issued and cashed Check No. 109 to replenish the petty cash fund. Expenses were as follows:

Postage expense .... $ 5
Office supplies expense   3
Travel expense   8
Miscellaneous expense................................   10
      Total.. $26

15 Paid the weekly payroll with Check Nos. 110 and 111. The payroll was identical to last week's.
15 Recorded the payroll tax expense which was the same as last week's.
18 Received $200 for legal fees from Don Turkey.
19 Received $85 for legal fees from Kay Carter.
20 Issued Check No. 112 for $90 for office supplies.
22 Paid the weekly payroll with Check Nos. 113 and 114. It was the same as the previous weeks' payrolls.
22 Recorded the payroll tax expenses which were the same as last week's.
25 Received $300 for legal fees from Kurt Lewis.
26 Issued and cashed Check No. 115 to replenish the petty cash fund. Expenses were as follows:

Travel expense $10
Miscellaneous expenses   12
Jane Bennett, drawing.................................   5
      Total.. $27

27 Issued Check No. 116 to June Bennett for personal use. The amount was $250.
28 Received $400 for legal fees—$200 from Clay Chang and $200 from Sunit Past.

Jan. 29 Paid the weekly payroll (same as before) with Check Nos. 117 and 118.

 29 Recorded the payroll tax expenses which were the same as last week's.

Required:

1. Open a cash journal with the following column headings:
   Date
   Description
   P.R.
   Cash — debits and credits
   Check No.
   Legal Fees Earned — credit
   Salaries Expense — debit
   Payroll Deductions
      F.I.C.A. Taxes — credit
      Income Taxes — credit
   F.U.T.A. Taxes — credit
   State Unemployment Taxes — credit
   General — debits and credits
2. Record the January transactions in the cash journal.
3. Open the following ledger accounts (account numbers are in parentheses): Cash (105); Petty Cash (110); Office Equipment (115); Office Furniture (120); F.I.C.A. Taxes Payable (205); Income Taxes Payable-federal-employee (210); F.U.T.A. Taxes Payable (215); State Unemployment Taxes Payable (220); June Bennett, Capital (305); June Bennett, Drawing (310); Legal Fees Earned (405); Salaries Expense (505); Payroll Tax Expense (510); Rent Expense (515); Office Supplies Expense (520); Postage Expense (525); Insurance Expense (530); Travel Expense (535); and Miscellaneous Expenses (540).
4. Post the journal entries to the ledger accounts.
5. Prepare a trial balance for January 29, 1978.

Accounting for service enterprises
— the accounting cycle
Learning objectives

The material in Chapter 7 concerned the accounting for transactions for a service enterprise. This chapter discusses the completion of the accounting cycle for a service enterprise. Careful study of the following areas will provide an understanding of the completed accounting cycle for a service business.

1. The matching concept and how it affects the adjusting entries of a service enterprise.
2. Preparation and completion of a worksheet in constructing financial statements.
3. Journalizing and posting the adjusting and closing entries.
4. Application of the matching concept when accounting for bad debts.

8

Accounting for service enterprises — the accounting cycle

The preceding chapter illustrated in detail the recording of the transactions of a service enterprise. The operations of the medical practice of J. T. Adams, M.D., were recorded in a cash journal, posted to a general ledger, and the December 31 balances of the ledger were summarized in a trial balance. The figures in the trial balance represent the net results of all the transactions of the year. From this point, the process of preparing financial statements is quite similar to that described in Chapter 3. The only difference is that two of the accounts need *adjusting* so that they will reflect the correct balances in the financial statements.

The two accounts are the Drugs and Medical Supplies on Hand account and Depreciation Expense on the office equipment. Some transactions have an effect on more than one accounting period. The effect of these transactions must be apportioned over the accounting periods affected. Adjustments are necessary so that financial statements can provide as much information as possible. **Adjusting journal entries** are necessary because there is no source document which would normally "trigger" an entry in the journal.

THE WORKSHEET

In Chapter 3, a six-column worksheet was used. It provided a pair of debit and credit columns for the trial balance, the earnings statement, and the statement of financial position. However, in Chapter 3 no adjustment was made to any of the account balances. In this chapter, two additional pairs of columns will be added. They are a pair of debit and credit columns for adjustments and a pair of debit and credit columns for the adjusted trial balance.

The **adjusted trial balance** is merely the original trial balance taken from the general ledger plus the adjustments that were made. Many of the account balances will be the same since no adjustment is necessary. Other accounts will be increased or decreased to reflect the correct balance. There may be several new accounts that were not present in the unadjusted trial balance. These accounts were not necessary in the recording of transactions, but they became necessary when adjustments were made.

The worksheet presented in this chapter is a ten-column worksheet. As explained in Chapter 3, worksheets aid in the detection of errors and in the preparation of financial statements. An example of a ten-column

Illustration 8–1
Ten-column worksheet

J. T. ADAMS, M.D.
Worksheet
For the Year Ended December 31, 1978

Acct. No.	Account Title	Trial Balance	
		Debit	Credit
110	Second National Bank	13,279.70	
120	Petty cash fund	25.00	
130	Drugs and medical supplies on hand		
140	Office equipment	18,350.00	
150	Accumulated depreciation—office equipment		3,670.00
210	F.I.C.A. taxes payable		75.44
220	Income taxes payable—federal—employee		231.08
310	J. T. Adams, capital		14,352.72
320	J. T. Adams, drawings	11,955.00	
410	Professional fees—office		31,150.50
420	Professional fees—hospital		31,923.00
505	Rent expense	4,800.00	
510	Drugs and medical supplies expense	3,594.68	
515	Salary expense	20,436.00	
520	Payroll tax expense	905.28	
525	Telephone expense	884.80	
530	Nonmedical supplies expense	710.18	
535	Automobile expense	1,642.76	
540	Depreciation expense		
545	Insurance expense	1,896.00	
550	Cleaning expense	2,292.00	
555	Charitable contributions expense	400.00	
560	Miscellaneous expense	231.34	
	Net Earnings	81,402.74	81,402.74

worksheet is found in Illustration 8–1. This worksheet contains all the ledger accounts of Dr. J. T. Adams, M.D., as shown in the previous chapter.

The first step in preparing a worksheet is to enter the unadjusted trial balance. Second, any necessary adjustments are entered in the Adjustment columns. In this example there are only two adjustments, but often there are many more. Here, there are adjustments for drugs and medical supplies on hand and for depreciation expense on the office equipment.

On December 31 of the current year, the drugs and medical supplies are counted, and Dr. Adams finds that supplies with a cost of $350 are on hand. In the worksheet in Illustration 8–1 the $350 has been entered in the Adjustments debit column on the line for "Drugs and medical Supplies on Hand" and in the Adjustments credit column on the line for "Drugs and medical supplies expense." This will have the effect of re-

Illustration 8–1 (continued)

Adjustments		Adjusted Trial Balance		Earnings Statement		Statement of Financial Position	
Debit	Credit	Debit	Credit	Debit	Credit	Debit	Credit
		13,279.70				13,279.70	
		25.00				25.00	
(a) 350.00		350.00				350.00	
		18,350.00				18,350.00	
	(b) 1,835.00		5,505.00				5,505.00
			75.44				75.44
			231.08				231.08
			14,352.72				14,352.72
		11,955.00				11,955.00	
			31,150.50		31,150.50		
			31,923.00		31,923.00		
		4,800.00		4,800.00			
	(a) 350.00	3,244.68		3,244.68			
		20,436.00		20,436.00			
		905.28		905.28			
		884.80		884.80			
		710.18		710.18			
		1,642.76		1,642.76			
(b) 1,835.00		1,835.00		1,835.00			
		1,896.00		1,896.00			
		2,292.00		2,292.00			
		400.00		400.00			
		231.34		231.34			
2,185.00	2,185.00	83,237.74	83,237.74	39,278.04	63,073.50		
				23,795.46			23,795.46
				63,073.50	63,073.50	43,959.70	43,959.70

cording the asset with a debit balance. The credit to the expense account is necessary since all supplies purchased, including the beginning amount on hand, have been recorded as an expense on the cash basis. The credit will reduce the expense account balance to the amount actually used during the year which is the proper amount. Labeled adjustment (*a*).

For depreciation of the office equipment, an expense account for the amount of the depreciation for the current year needs to be established. Depreciation is the process of spreading the cost of an asset, less its salvage value, over the estimated useful life of the asset. Depreciation is recorded by debiting an expense account, Depreciation Expense, and crediting a contra asset account, **Accumulated Depreciation.** A **contra asset account** (sometimes called a negative asset account) is one shown as a deduction from its related asset account in the statement of financial position. The contra asset account Accumulated Depreciation shows the total amount of depreciation on the asset as of the date of the statement of financial position. The Accumulated Depreciation account is used to reduce the Office Equipment asset account to its estimated value. The depreciation rate used by Dr. Adams is based upon an estimated life of ten years with no scrap value remaining at that time. The depreciation expense for any year is therefore 10 percent of $18,350 (the original cost of the equipment) which is $1,835. Another method of calculating the amount of depreciation expense in this example is to divide the original cost less the salvage value by the number of years in the life of the asset. In this example, original cost less salvage value is $18,350, and the life of the asset is ten years. Thus, $18,350 ÷ 10 = $1,835 depreciation expense.

The adjustment, then, is to enter $1,835 in the debit column of the Adjustments pair of columns on the worksheet on the line for "Depreciation expense." The corresponding credit entered in the Adjustments credit column is to "Accumulated depreciation – office equipment." (The balance already in accumulated depreciation is the result of two full years of depreciation before the current year: $1,835 + $1,835 = $3,670.) Labeled adjustment (*b*).

After the adjustments have been entered in the Adjustment columns of the worksheet, the two columns are footed (added) to be certain of the equality of the debits and credits. If any errors have been made in making adjustments, it is important to identify them as soon as possible. One check is the footing of the Adjustment columns.

The next step is to extend the unadjusted trial balance, plus or minus the effect of the adjustments, to the adjusted Trial Balance columns. As mentioned earlier, some accounts will not be affected, some will have new balances, and there may be some new accounts which were not included in the original trial balance.

Once again the adjusted Trial Balance columns are footed to be certain that the debits and credits are equal. When their equality is proven,

Illustration 8–2

J. T. ADAMS, M.D.
Earnings Statement
For the Year Ended December 31, 1978

Revenue from professional fees:

Office	$31,150.50	
Hospital	31,923.00	$63,073.50

Expenses:

Rent	$ 4,800.00	
Drugs and medical supplies	3,244.68	
Salaries	20,436.00	
Payroll tax	905.28	
Telephone	884.80	
Nonmedical supplies	710.18	
Automobile	1,642.76	
Depreciation	1,835.00	
Insurance	1,896.00	
Cleaning	2,292.00	
Charitable contributions	400.00	
Miscellaneous	231.34	39,278.04
Net Earnings		$23,795.46

J. T. ADAMS, M.D.
Statement of Owner's Equity
For the Year Ended December 31, 1978

J. T. Adams, capital — January 1, 1978	$14,352.72
Add net earnings	23,795.46
	$38,148.18
Less withdrawals	11,955.00
J. T. Adams, Capital — December 31, 1978	$26,193.18

J. T. ADAMS, M.D.
Statement of Financial Position
December 31, 1978

Assets

Cash — Second National Bank		$13,279.70
Petty cash		25.00
Drugs and medical supplies on hand		350.00
Office equipment	$18,350.00	
Less: Accumulated depreciation	5,505.00	12,845.00
Total Assets		$26,499.70

Liabilities

F.I.C.A. taxes payable	$ 75.44	
Income taxes payable — federal — Employee	231.08	$ 306.52

Owner's Equity

J. T. Adams, capital	26,193.18
Total Liabilities and Owner's Equity	$26,499.70

the worksheet is completed by extending the amounts in the various accounts to the appropriate financial statement columns. These procedures will not be discussed here as they were covered in detail in Chapter 3.

FINANCIAL STATEMENTS

Once the worksheet is completed, the formal financial statements may be easily prepared. As you will recall from Chapter 3, the necessary information for preparing financial statements can be taken directly from the completed worksheet. The financial statements for J. T. Adams, M.D., are presented in Illustration 8-2.

Illustration 8-3

CASH JOURNAL

For Month of December 1978   Page 44

Date		Description	P.R.	General Debit	General Credit
		Adjusting Entries			
Dec.	31	Drugs and Medical Supplies on Hand	130	350.00	
		Drugs and Medical Supplies Expense	510		350.00
	31	Depreciation Expense	540	1,835.00	
		Accumulated Depreciation—Off. Equip.	150		1,835.00
		Closing Entries			
	31	Professional Fees—Office	410	31,150.50	
		Professional Fees—Hospital	420	31,923.00	
		Expense and Revenue Summary	330		63,073.50
	31	Expense and Revenue Summary	330	39,278.04	
		Rent Expense	505		4,800.00
		Drugs and Medical Supplies Expense	510		3,244.68
		Salary Expense	515		20,436.00
		Payroll Tax Expense	520		905.28
		Telephone Expense	525		884.80
		Nonmedical Supplies Expense	530		710.18
		Automobile Expense	535		1,642.76
		Depreciation Expense	540		1,835.00
		Insurance Expense	545		1,896.00
		Cleaning Expense	550		2,292.00
		Charitable Contributions Expense	555		400.00
		Miscellaneous Expense	560		231.34
	31	Expense and Revenue Summary	330	23,795.46	
		J. T. Adams, Capital	310		23,795.46
	31	J. T. Adams, Capital	310	11,955.00	
		J. T. Adams, Drawings	320		11,955.00

ADJUSTING AND CLOSING

After the financial statements are prepared, the final step at the end of the fiscal period is to prepare the ledger for the transactions of the next period. The first step in this process is to journalize and post the adjusting entries so that the ledger balances will agree with the figures which appeared on the financial statements. Up until this point, the adjustments only appear in the Adjustments columns of the worksheet. Thus, they do not appear in the formal records of the company until they are journalized. In our example, there were two adjusting entries. These appear in the cash journal (Illustration 8–3). These journal entries will then be posted to the ledger accounts (see Illustration 8–4).

After the adjusting entries have been journalized and posted, it is time to close the books. This process brings the equity accounts up to date, and it eliminates any existing balances in the expense and revenue accounts. Thus, all the accounts are up to date and ready for the recording of transactions in the new accounting period.

Illustration 8–4
Ledger accounts

Second National Bank — Account No. 110

Date		Explanation	P.R.	Debit	Credit	Balance
1978 Dec.	1	Balance	✔			12,117.80
	31		CJ43	5,251.50		17,369.30
	31		CJ43		4,089.60	13,279.70
1979 Jan.	1	Balance	✔			13,279.70

Petty Cash Fund — Account No. 120

Date		Explanation	P.R.	Debit	Credit	Balance
1978 Dec.	1	Balance	✔			25.00
1979 Jan.	1	Balance	✔			25.00

Drugs and Medical Supplies on Hand — Account No. 130

Date		Explanation	P.R.	Debit	Credit	Balance
1978 Dec.	31	Adjusting entry	CJ44	350.00		350.00
1979 Jan.	1	Balance	✔			350.00

Illustration 8-4 (*continued*)

Office Equipment   Account No. 140

Date		Explanation	P.R.	Debit	Credit	Balance
1978 Dec.	1	Balance	✓			18,350.00
1979 Jan.	1	Balance	✓			18,350.00

Accumulated Depreciation—Office Equipment   Account No. 150

Date		Explanation	P.R.	Debit	Credit	Balance
1978 Dec.	1	Balance	✓			3,670.00
	31	Adjusting entry	CJ44		1,835.00	5,505.00
1979 Jan.	1	Balance	✓			5,505.00

F.I.C.A. Taxes Payable   Account No. 210

Date		Explanation	P.R.	Debit	Credit	Balance
1978 Dec.	1	Balance	✓			75.44
	9		CJ42	150.88		(75.44)
	31		CJ43		150.88	75.44
1979 Jan.	1	Balance	✓			75.44

Income Taxes Payable—Employee   Account No. 220

Date		Explanation	P.R.	Debit	Credit	Balance
1978 Dec.	1	Balance	✓			231.08
	9		CJ42	231.08		—
	31		CJ43		231.08	231.08
1979 Jan.	1	Balance	✓			231.08

J. T. Adams, Capital   Account No. 310

Date		Explanation	P.R.	Debit	Credit	Balance
1978 Dec.	1	Balance	✓			14,352.72
	31	Closing entry	CJ44		23,795.46	38,148.18
	31	Closing entry	CJ44	11,955.00		26,193.18
1979 Jan.	1	Balance	✓			26,193.18

Illustration 8–4 (continued)

J. T. Adams, Drawing   Account No. 320

Date		Explanation	P.R.	Debit	Credit	Balance
1978						
Dec.	1	Balance	✔			10,940.00
	5		CJ42	250.00		11,190.00
	8		CJ42	5.00		11,195.00
	12		CJ42	180.00		11,375.00
	15		CJ43	50.00		11,425.00
	18		CJ43	400.00		11,825.00
	29		CJ43	125.00		11,950.00
	31		CJ43	5.00		11,955.00
	31	Closing entry	CJ44		11,955.00	—

Expense and Revenue Summary   Account No. 330

Date		Explanation	P.R.	Debit	Credit	Balance
1978						
Dec.	31	Closing entry	CJ44	39,278.04		(39,278.04)
	31	Closing entry	CJ44		63,073.50	23,795.46
	31	Closing entry	CJ44	23,795.46		—

Professional Fees — Office   Account No. 410

Date		Explanation	P.R.	Debit	Credit	Balance
1978						
Dec.	1	Balance	✔			28,588.00
	31		CJ43		2,562.50	31,150.50
	31	Closing entry	CJ44	31,150.50		—

Professional Fees — Hospital   Account No. 420

Date		Explanation	P.R.	Debit	Credit	Balance
1978						
Dec.	1	Balance	✔			29,234.00
	31		CJ43		2,689.00	31,923.00
	31	Closing entry	CJ44	31,923.00		—

Rent Expense   Account No. 505

Date		Explanation	P.R.	Debit	Credit	Balance
1978						
Dec.	1	Balance	✔			4,400.00
	2		CJ42	400.00		4,800.00
	31	Closing entry	CJ44		4,800.00	—

Illustration 8–4 (*continued*)

Drugs and Medical Supplies Expense   Account No. 510

Date		Explanation	P.R.	Debit	Credit	Balance
1978						
Dec.	1	Balance	✔			3,289.79
	31		CJ43	304.89		3,594.68
	31	Adjusting entry	CJ44		350.00	3,244.68
	31	Closing entry	CJ44		3,244.68	—

Salary Expense   Account No. 515

Date		Explanation	P.R.	Debit	Credit	Balance
1978						
Dec.	1	Balance	✔			18,864.00
	31		CJ43	1,572.00		20,436.00
	31	Closing entry	CJ44		20,436.00	—

Payroll Tax Expense   Account No. 520

Date		Explanation	P.R.	Debit	Credit	Balance
1978						
Dec.	1	Balance	✔			829.84
	9		CJ42	75.44		905.28
	31	Closing entry	CJ44		905.28	—

Telephone Expense   Account No. 525

Date		Explanation	P.R.	Debit	Credit	Balance
1978						
Dec.	1	Balance	✔			816.40
	8		CJ42	1.80		818.20
	15		CJ42	63.00		881.20
	17		CJ43	3.60		884.80
	31	Closing entry	CJ44		884.80	—

Nonmedical Supplies Expense   Account No. 530

Date		Explanation	P.R.	Debit	Credit	Balance
1978						
Dec.	1	Balance	✔			653.04
	5		CJ42	14.95		667.99
	8		CJ42	4.67		672.66
	17		CJ43	15.34		688.00
	21		CJ43	17.50		705.50
	31		CJ43	4.68		710.18
	31	Closing entry	CJ44		710.18	—

Illustration 8–4 (*continued*)

Automobile Expense   Account No. 535

Date		Explanation	P.R.	Debit	Credit	Balance
1978 Dec.	1	Balance	✔			1,515.78
	3		CJ42	33.18		1,548.96
	8		CJ42	3.50		1,552.46
	17		CJ43	1.30		1,553.76
	30		CJ43	89.00		1,642.76
	31	Closing entry	CJ44		1,642.76	—

Depreciation Expense   Account No. 540

Date		Explanation	P.R.	Debit	Credit	Balance
1978 Dec.	31	Adjusting entry	CJ44	1,835.00		1,835.00
	31	Closing entry	CJ44		1,835.00	—

Insurance Expense   Account No. 545

Date		Explanation	P.R.	Debit	Credit	Balance
1978 Dec.	1	Balance	✔			1,738.00
	4		CJ42	158.00		1,896.00
	31	Closing entry	CJ44		1,896.00	—

Cleaning Expense   Account No. 550

Date		Explanation	P.R.	Debit	Credit	Balance
1978 Dec.	1	Balance	✔			2,101.25
	7		CJ42	52.00		2,153.25
	14		CJ42	52.00		2,205.25
	21		CJ43	52.00		2,257.25
	28		CJ43	34.75		2,292.00
	31	Closing entry	CJ44		2,292.00	—

Charitable Contributions Expense   Account No. 555

Date		Explanation	P.R.	Debit	Credit	Balance
1978 Dec.	1	Balance	✔			300.00
	21		CJ43	100.00		400.00
	31	Closing entry	CJ44		· 400.00	—

Illustration 8–4 (concluded)

		Miscellaneous Expense			Account No. 560	
Date		Explanation	P.R.	Debit	Credit	Balance
1978 Dec.	1	Balance	✔			210.34
	8		CJ42	5.50		215.84
	17		CJ43	2.45		218.29
	31		CJ43	13.05		231.34
	31	Closing entry	CJ44		231.34	—

The procedure for closing the books is explained in detail in Chapter 3. This same procedure is applied here in the example of J. T. Adams, M.D. The **closing entries** are found in the cash journal (Illustration 8–3).

Once the closing entries are journalized, they may be posted to the ledger accounts (see Illustration 8–4). The revenue and expense accounts should all have zero balances after the closing entries are posted. All the accounts should be ruled by drawing two horizontal lines beneath the December 31 balance. The January 1 balances of the asset, liability, and owner's equity accounts are entered on the following line in each ledger account. To test this fact and to again prove the equality of debits and credits, a **post-closing trial balance** is prepared. This appears in Illustration 8–5.

Illustration 8–5

J. T. ADAMS, M.D.
Post-Closing Trial Balance
December 31, 1978

Account No.	Account Titles	Debit	Credit
110	Second National Bank	$13,279.70	
120	Petty cash fund	25.00	
130	Drugs and medical supplies on hand	350.00	
140	Office equipment	18,350.00	
150	Accumulated depreciation – office equip.		$ 5,505.00
210	F.I.C.A. taxes payable		75.44
220	Income taxes payable – employee		231.08
310	J. T. Adams, capital		26,193.18
		$32,004.70	$32,004.70

THE ACCOUNTING CYCLE

All of the steps involved in the recording of transactions during the entire accounting period and the end-of-fiscal period procedures are referred to collectively as the **accounting cycle.** A complete accounting cycle for J. T. Adams, M.D. has been illustrated in Chapters 7 and 8. In this case, the accounting cycle is one year in length. The following is a summary of the steps:

1. Journalize the transactions.
2. Post to the ledger.
3. Prepare a trial balance.
4. Determine the necessary adjustments.
5. Complete the worksheet.
6. Prepare the financial statements.
7. Journalize and post the adjusting and closing entries.
8. Rule the closed accounts and bring down the balance in the open accounts.
9. Prepare a post-closing trial balance.

The transactions should be journalized as soon as possible during the year after the actual event occurs, and the posting should be done during the period as time permits. Steps (3) through (9) are dated as of the last day of the period even though they are actually performed during the first few days or weeks of the next period. For example, it might be January 15 before the statements for Dr. Adams are actually prepared, yet they are dated December 31 which was the last day of the accounting period. It may be January 22 before the ledger is closed and the post-closing trial balance prepared. During this period of time, the transactions of January would be recorded as usual in the journal, but could not, of course, be posted until the ledger is prepared for new entries.

OTHER ADJUSTING ENTRIES

A large number of other adjustments is often necessary in a firm. This is particularly true if the firm is not using the cash basis of accounting illustrated in this chapter. While the actual number of adjustments may be quite large, the nature of the adjustments may be classified into two broad categories. These broad categories are:

1. Adjusting entries for data already recorded.
   a. Asset expiration or asset becoming an expense.
   b. Expiration of a liability or liability becoming revenue.
2. Adjusting entries for which no data has yet been recorded.
   a. Asset growth or equal growth of asset and revenue.
   b. Growth of a liability or equal growth of an expense and a liability.

Examples of these adjusting entries are shown below.

1.   *a. Asset expiration.* Many assets are purchased during an accounting period and are only partially used up during that period. In such a
case the portion of the asset used up should be charged to an expense
account. The remaining portion should remain in the asset account because of its future economic value to the firm.

A common example of this adjustment is rent paid in advance. If the
accounting period ends before all the rent has expired, an asset remains.

As an example, suppose that $1,800 was paid on October 1 for one
year's rent. It was recorded with a debit to the asset account Prepaid
Rent and a credit to Cash. On December 31, the end of the accounting
period, $450 of rent has been used up and should be transferred to an
expense account. The adjusting entry would be:

```
Rent Expense .........................................................................   450
    Prepaid Rent.....................................................................            450
```

This entry records a $450 reduction of the asset, prepaid rent, and recog-
nizes $450 of rent expense.

1.   *b. Expiration of a liability.* Sometimes a firm will receive payment in advance for some service which is yet to be rendered. In such a
case, the asset account Cash would be debited and a liability account
would be credited. A liability account is used instead of a revenue account because the service has not yet been *performed;* thus, the revenue
is not yet *earned.* Either the services must be performed or the payment
must be returned.

Suppose that a dance studio sells contracts for dancing lessons. These
contracts require advance payment at the time the contract is signed. The
journal entry is to debit Cash and to credit the liability account, Unearned
Dance Contracts. At the end of the year, this account probably contains
some contracts which have been partially performed. Suppose that
$1,200 is the amount that has already been earned. The adjusting entry is:

```
Unearned Dance Contracts...................................................   1,200
    Dance Contracts Revenue .............................................            1,200
```

2.   *a. Asset growth.* Sometimes an asset will grow over time even
though no specific transaction has taken place to require a journal entry.
A common example is the growth of interest on a note receivable. The
interest may not be payable until some future accounting period, but the
interest is actually earned day by day.

Assume that a 6 percent, $3,000, 12-month note is received on Sep-
tember 1 of this year. The principal and interest are payable when the note
is due. If the accounting period ends on December 31, four months of
interest have already been earned by the passage of time. The journal
entry to record the adjustment is:

Interest Receivable (an asset)... 60

    Interest Revenue 60

The calculation of the interest is as follows: Principal × Rate × Time or $3,000 × 0.06 × 4/12. The 0.06 is 6 percent expressed in decimal form. The $3,000 is the principal of the note, and 4/12 represents the fraction of a year that interest has been accumulating. Interest is typically stated at an annual rate unless otherwise indicated.

2. *b. Growth of a liability.* At the end of any accounting period, there are usually some liabilities which have increased but have not been recorded. This happens because no transaction has occurred which would necessitate a journal entry. A very common example is wages.

At the end of an accounting period, there is usually a certain amount of wages which has been earned by employees during the current accounting period but which will not be paid until the next accounting period. Since these wages are for services performed in the current accounting period, they should be recorded as an expense in this accounting period.

For example, if $2,000 of wages have been earned at the end of the accounting period but they are not to be paid until the next accounting period, the adjusting entry would be:

Wages Expense.. 2,000

    Wages Payable (a liability).. 2,000

THE MATCHING CONCEPT

The preceding examples of adjustments and almost all other end-of-period adjustments are based on the accounting **matching concept.** This concept states that net earnings for a given accounting period should include only the revenue *earned* during the period and the various expenses that were necessary to generate the earned revenue. Therefore, earned revenues are "matched" with the necessary expenses. The resulting net earnings for the period should then be the best indication of the firm's performance during that period of time. The matching concept is the fundamental basis for accrual accounting which will be discussed in further detail in the next chapter.

BAD DEBTS

In the process of operating almost any business, it is common to grant credit to customers. In a few cases, the majority of the business is for cash with only a few preferred customers receiving credit. Other businesses do almost all their business with credit customers. Although the service business illustrated in this chapter uses a cash basis of accounting, it should not be assumed that all service businesses are on a cash basis.

When granting credit, there is always the risk that the customer will not pay his or her account. If this happens, the firm incurs an additional cost or expense of operating on a credit basis which is usually called a **bad debts expense.**

If it could be determined in advance which customers would not pay their accounts, credit would not be granted to those customers. This, however, is not possible. It is only after the account is opened that it becomes apparent the amount will not be collected. The indication may be a formal notice such as a court statement declaring the customer bankrupt. Whatever the form of the notice, once the account is known to be uncollectible, it should not be considered an asset since no future payment is expected. There are two methods of accounting for bad debts.

Direct write-off

When the **direct write-off method of accounting for bad debts** is used, the entry is to debit the expense account and to credit the account receivable. As an example:

Bad Debts Expense	150	
Accounts Receivable		150
To record account written off.		

This method is convenient because no entry is required until the account is known to be uncollectible. No prior estimations are necessary, and no elaborate record keeping is necessary.

This approach is not entirely consistent with proper accounting. Revenue is usually recorded in the period when the sale is made on a credit basis. The account becomes uncollectible at a later date which may be in the next accounting period. This violates the matching concept which was just discussed. But, if the amount of bad debts is quite small, this approach is acceptable. For example, since most small businesses use the cash basis of accounting and seldom sell services or merchandise on credit, the direct write-off method is commonly used by small businesses.

Allowance method

If a large portion of a firm's sales are on credit, it is common to use the **allowance method of accounting for bad debts.** This method is considered preferable because the expense of the bad debt is matched with the revenue generated by the sale. Also the accounts receivable are shown on the statement of financial position at the amount that is expected to be collected in cash called the net realizable value.

When the allowance method is used, an *estimate* is made of the total dollar value of receivables that are expected to be *uncollectible* from the current period's sales. This amount is then debited to the Bad Debts Expense account and the credit is to the **Allowance for Doubtful Accounts** account which is a contra asset account used to reduce accounts receivable. When individual accounts become uncollectible, the allowance account is debited, and the Accounts Receivable account is credited.

The estimate of bad debts is based on expectations of the collectability of this period's sales. It is typically derived from previous experience. If a firm's credit policy has not changed a great deal, past experience is usually a good basis upon which to make this period's estimate.

Example:

Sales, $1,200,000. Past experience has shown that $1\frac{1}{2}$ percent of sales become uncollectible. Accounts receivable are $160,000 at the end of the period.

Recording the allowance:

Allowance should be $1,200,000 \times 0.015 = $18,000.

```
Bad Debts Expense..........................................................  18,000
    Allowance for Doubtful Accounts..................................           18,000
    To record estimated bad debts.
```

On the statement of financial position, the accounts receivable would appear as follows:

```
Accounts receivable ..................................................  $160,000
    Less allowance for doubtful accounts .......................    18,000   $142,000
```

On the earnings statement, bad debts expense would be deducted from sales thus matching revenue and expenses in the appropriate time period.

Assume that during the next accounting period three individual accounts receivable are determined to be uncollectible and should be written off. The journal entry required is:

```
Allowance for Doubtful Accounts..................................  2,100
    Accounts Receivable – Black Co. ............................           900
    Accounts Receivable – Blue Co. ..............................           800
    Accounts Receivable – White Co. ............................           400
    To record accounts written off.
```

Bad debt recoveries

Sometimes an account that has been written off will be paid. In such a case, the account receivable should be reinstated, and the payment should then be recorded in the usual manner. The reinstatement of the account is a reversal of the entry made to write off the account. The entry to record the payment then is the same as if the account had not been written off. The entries would be:

Direct write-off method:

Accounts Receivable—J. J. Co.	200	
Bad Debts Expense		200
To record the reinstatement of account written off.		

Cash	200	
Accounts Receivable—J. J. Co.		200
To record receipt on account.		

Allowance method:

Accounts Receivable—J. J. Co.	200	
Allowance for Doubtful Accounts		200
To record the reinstatement of account written off.		

Cash	200	
Accounts Receivable—J. J. Co.		200
To record receipt on account.		

GLOSSARY

Accounting cycle   a collective term used to refer to all of the steps involved in the recording of transactions during the entire accounting period and the end-of-fiscal period procedures. The steps can be summarized as follows:

1. Journalize the transactions.
2. Post to the ledger.
3. Prepare a trial balance.
4. Determine the necessary adjustments.
5. Complete the worksheet.
6. Prepare the financial statements.
7. Journalize and post the adjusting and closing entries.
8. Rule the closed accounts and bring down the balance in the open accounts.
9. Prepare a post-closing trial balance.

Accumulated Depreciation account   an account used to reduce its related long-lived asset account to its proper value or book value. The account balance is the sum of all amounts taken as depreciation on the asset thus far.

Adjusted trial balance   a trial balance taken after the adjusting entries have been made. It is the sum of the original trial balance plus the effects of the adjustments.

Adjusting journal entries   journal entries made at the end of an accounting period so that the accounts will reflect the correct balances in the financial statements. These entries are necessary because some transactions have an effect on more than one accounting period, and their effects must be apportioned over the accounting periods affected.

Allowance for Doubtful Accounts account   a contra asset account used to reduce accounts receivable to its estimated collectible amount.

Allowance method of accounting for bad debts   a method which matches the expense of the bad debt with the revenue generated by the sale. An estimate is made of the total dollar value of receivables that are expected to be uncollectible from the current period's sales. This amount is debited to Bad Debts Expense and credited to the Allowance for Doubtful Accounts. When individual accounts become uncollectible, the allowance account is debited and the Accounts Receivable account is credited.

Bad debts expense   an expense incurred by a business when it grants credit to customers. It occurs because some customers fail to pay their accounts.

Closing entires   journal entries made at the end of an accounting period to bring the equity accounts up to date and to eliminate the balances in the expense and revenue accounts.

Contra account   an account which is directly related to another account but has an opposite balance. For example, Accumulated Depreciation — Machinery is the contra account to Machinery. Accumulated Depreciation — Machinery has a credit balance which is the opposite of the Machinery account's debit balance.

Direct write-off method of accounting for bad debts   a method commonly used by small businesses to account for bad debts. When an individual account receivable becomes uncollectible, it is written off by debiting Bad Debts Expense and crediting Accounts Receivable.

Matching concept   an accounting concept which states that net earnings for a given accounting period should include only the revenue earned during the period and the various expenses that were necessary to generate the earned revenue.

Post-closing trial balance   a trial balance taken after the closing journal entries have been made.

QUESTIONS AND EXERCISES

1. What is the difference between a six-column worksheet as discussed in Chapter 3 and a ten-column worksheet as discussed in Chapter 8?

2. What is an *adjusted trial balance?*

3. What is the *accounting cycle?* Summarize the steps in the accounting cycle.

4. When are the steps in the accounting cycle performed?

5. Name four general classifications or categories of adjustments. Give a specific example of each classification.

6. What is the *matching concept?*

7. Describe the two methods of accounting for bad debts. When is each method commonly used?

8. The Blue Tube Company wrote off a $500 account receivable which was owed by the Greenway Company. Six months later, the account was paid. What entries should be made to record the payment of the account using (*a*) the direct write-off method and (*b*) the allowance method?

9. An office equipment account has a balance of $16,480. The straight-line depreciation rate is based upon an estimated life of eight years with no scrap value remaining at that time. What entry should be made to record one year's depreciation expense?

10. Dr. Thomas Turkey, a local optometrist, had a capital balance of $15,650 on January 1, 1978. His earnings statement showed net earnings of $16,500 for 1978. Before closing entries were made, his drawing account had a balance of $12,750. What is Dr. Turkey's capital account balance on December 31, 1978?

PROBLEMS

8–1. R. C. Helms is a plumber. Helms's trial balance for December 31, 1978 is shown below:

R. C. HELMS
Trial Balance
December 31, 1978

Account No.	Account Title	Debit	Credit
10	Cash...	$ 1,500	
11	Office equipment...	400	
12	Accumulated depreciation – office equipment.......		$ 75
13	Truck	3,500	
14	Accumulated depreciation – truck		500
20	Accounts payable		1,000
30	R. C. Helms, capital..		6,000
31	R. C. Helms, drawing......................................	11,250	
40	Plumbing revenue		12,700
50	Truck expense...	750	
51	Advertising expense..	100	
52	Plumbing supplies expense	2,700	
53	Miscellaneous expense....................................	75	
		$20,275	$20,275

Required:

1. Prepare a ten-column worksheet. Use the following information for adjustments:

   a. The depreciation rate for office equipment is $12\frac{1}{2}$ percent.

    b. The depreciation rate for the truck is 10 percent.

    c. On hand at the end of the year are $1,200 worth of plumbing supplies.

2. Prepare an earnings statement for the year ended December 31, 1978.
3. Prepare a statement of owner's equity for the year ended December 31, 1978.
4. Prepare a statement of financial position for December 31, 1978.

Note: The Depreciation Expense account No. is 54 and Plumbing Supplies on Hand is No. 15.

8-2.

COASTAL REALTY COMPANY
Trial Balance
December 31, 1978

Account Title	*Debit*	*Credit*
Cash	$10,100	
Unexpired insurance	720	
Prepaid rent	1,200	
Office equipment	800	
Accumulated depreciation — office equipment		$ 200
Automobiles	6,000	
Accumulated depreciation — automobiles		1,000
F.I.C.A. taxes payable		25
Employees' income taxes payable		45
Unearned management fees		510
Greg Coastal, capital		10,540
Greg Coastal, drawing	10,500	
Revenue from commissions		20,000
Revenue from management fees		9,200
Salary expense	8,500	
Payroll tax expense	1,100	
Advertising expense	200	
Automobile expense	750	
Office supplies expense	100	
Rent expense	1,200	
Insurance expense	300	
Miscellaneous expense	50	
	$41,520	$41,520

Required:

1. Record the following adjustments in general journal form:

    a. On July 1, 1978, six months' rent was paid, and the debit was to Prepaid Rent.

    b. On May 1, 1978, $720 was paid for one year's insurance coverage. The debit was made to Unexpired Insurance.

    c. On November 1, 1978, the company received an advance payment of $510 to manage an apartment building for six months. The credit was made to Unearned Management Fees.

    d. The depreciation rates are 15 percent for office equipment and 25 percent for automobiles.

2. Prepare an adjusted trial balance for December 31, 1978.

8-3. Robert West owns and operates West's TV and Radio Repair Shop. His trial balance for December 31, 1978, is shown below:

WEST'S TV AND RADIO REPAIR SHOP
Trial Balance
December 31, 1978

Account No.	Account Title	Debit	Credit
100	Cash...	$ 600	
110	Shop supplies on hand............................		
120	Shop equipment.....................................	1,000	
130	Accumulated depreciation – shop equipment........		$ 500
140	Truck..	3,000	
150	Accumulated depreciation – truck....................		1,200
200	Accounts payable....................................		400
210	Employees' income tax payable.....................		120
220	F.I.C.A. tax payable................................		80
300	Robert West, capital................................		10,000
310	Robert West, drawing...............................	10,675	
400	TV repair revenue...................................		10,000
410	Radio repair revenue................................		4,000
500	Salary expense.......................................	5,000	
510	Payroll tax expense..................................	800	
520	Rent expense...	2,100	
530	Depreciation expense................................		
540	Shop supplies expense...............................	3,000	
550	Miscellaneous expense...............................	125	
		$26,300	$26,300

Required:

1. Prepare a ten-column worksheet with the following adjustments:

    a. Shop equipment, 10 percent depreciation rate.

    b. Truck, 20 percent depreciation rate.

    c. Shop supplies on hand, $1,700.

2. Prepare an earnings statement for the year ended December 31, 1978.
3. Prepare a statement of owner's equity for the year ended December 31, 1978.

4. Prepare a statement of financial position for December 31, 1978.

5. Prepare the adjusting and closing entries.

8–4. The trial balance for Rivers Realty for the fiscal year ended November 30, 1978, is shown below:

RIVERS REALTY
Trial Balance
November 30, 1978

Account No.	Account Title	Debit	Credit
106	Cash..	$ 9,000	
112	Prepaid rent..	1,800	
118	Unexpired insurance	480	
124	Office equipment..	1,500	
130	Accumulated depreciation—office equipment.........		$ 360
136	Automobile...	4,000	
142	Accumulated depreciation—automobile		1,000
206	F.I.C.A. taxes payable......................................		100
212	Employees' income taxes payable......................		80
218	Unearned management fees...............................		780
306	Lee Rivers, capital..		21,290
312	Lee Rivers, drawing...	11,750	
406	Revenue from commissions		15,000
412	Revenue from management fees		1,200
506	Salary expense	9,600	
512	Payroll tax expense..	780	
518	Advertising expense...	150	
524	Automobile expense...	500	
530	Office supplies expense.....................................	150	
536	Rent expense		
542	Insurance expense		
548	Depreciation expense		
554	Miscellaneous expense......................................	100	
		$39,810	$39,810

Required:

1. Prepare a ten-column worksheet with the following adjustments:

   a. Expired insurance, $240.

   b. Expired rent, $1,200.

   c. The unearned management fees were recorded on October 1, 1978. The advance payment covered six months' management of an apartment building.

   d. Depreciation rates:
   Office equipment, 12 percent.
   Automobile, 20 percent.

2. Prepare an earnings statement for the year ended November 30, 1978.
3. Prepare a statement of owner's equity for the year ended November 30, 1978.
4. Prepare a statement of financial position for November 30, 1978.
5. Record the adjusting and closing entries.

8-5. The December 31, 1978, trial balance for Sandra Gibbs' Dance Studio is shown below:

SANDRA GIBBS' DANCE STUDIO
Trial Balance
December 31, 1978

Account No.	Account Title	Debit	Credit
107	Cash	$ 3,000	
112	Office equipment	600	
117	Accumulated depreciation — office equipment		$ 240
122	Automobile	5,000	
127	Accumulated depreciation — automobile		1,500
207	F.I.C.A. taxes payable		20
212	Employees' income taxes payable		40
307	Sandra Gibbs, capital		7,000
312	Sandra Gibbs, drawing	10,500	
407	Dance contracts revenue		19,500
507	Salary expense	5,600	
512	Payroll tax expense	600	
517	Advertising expense	200	
522	Automobile expense	250	
527	Rent expense	2,400	
532	Depreciation expense		
537	Miscellaneous expense	150	
		$28,300	$28,300

Required:
1. Prepare a ten-column worksheet for the year ended December 31, 1978. Depreciation rates are 10 percent for the office equipment and 20 percent for the automobile.
2. Prepare an earnings statement for the year ended December 31, 1978.
3. Prepare a statement of owner's equity for the year ended December 31, 1978.
4. Prepare a statement of financial position for December 31, 1978.
5. Prepare adjusting and closing entries.

8-6. The Spiral Department Store sold $2,000,000 worth of merchandise during 1978. At the end of 1978, the Allowance for Doubtful Accounts contained a balance of $5,500. Past experience has shown that $1\frac{1}{2}$ percent of sales become uncollectible.

Required:

1. Make the journal entry to record the allowance for doubtful accounts for 1978.
2. Record the following events which occurred in 1979:

    a. Wrote off the following accounts with a compound entry: James Kaminsky, $1,000; Jerry Nutting, $225; and Alice Stone, $75.
    b. Reinstated and recorded the collection of Marshall Babcock's account, $250.
    c. Wrote off the account of Charles Welch, $1,500.
    d. The allowance was increased by $1\frac{1}{2}$ percent of sales for 1979. Sales for 1979 were $1,750,000.

3. Record entries given in 2—(*a*), (*b*), and (*c*)—using the direct write-off method.

Accounting for a merchandising firm
Learning objectives

Because of the large volume of transactions, the merchandising firm must have a different accounting system that will satisfy the needs of the business. Careful study of the following material will provide a basic understanding of the accounting procedures used by a merchandiser:

1. The use of the matching concept in the form of accrual basis accounting when determining expenses and revenues of period.

2. Accounting for sales: the sales account, sales taxes, and sales returns and allowances.

3. The procedures used in recording sales transactions in the sales journal and the manner in which the transactions are posted and cross-referenced to the subsidiary accounts.

4. Accounting for purchases: periodic or perpetual inventory system, Purchases account, purchases invoices, purchases journal, and purchases returns and allowances.

5. Illustrative schedules of accounts receivable and accounts payable.

6. Determination of gross margin and cost of goods sold for the merchandising firm.

9

Accounting for a merchandising firm

A **merchandising firm** is one that derives most of its revenue from selling merchandise to customers. Accounting for a merchandising firm is still based on the fundamental concepts that have been presented in previous chapters. But certain characteristics of a merchandising firm require several new techniques for accumulating and presenting accounting data for such a firm.

Chapter 7 (Accounting for service enterprises—recording transactions) presented an example of a service enterprise using the cash basis of accounting which was acceptable in that case for matching purposes. When accounting for a merchandising firm, the problem of properly matching revenues and expenses becomes more difficult. Merchandising firms usually stock a large inventory of items for future sale to customers. Seasonal fluctuations and inventory purchasing policies would often cause an unacceptable distortion of the matching concept if the cash basis of accounting were used.

To correctly implement the matching concept, the **accrual basis of accounting** is generally used for merchandising enterprises. Using this basis, revenue is recognized in the period in which it is earned, and expenses are recognized in the period in which they cause revenues to be earned. Many items entering into the computation of the business's net earnings are recorded before or after they involve the receipt or payment of cash. The adjusting entries discussed in Chapter 8 are examples of the application of the accrual accounting concept to adjust cash basis records. Moreover, records kept on the accrual basis will also need adjustment.

Merchandise sales are the principal means of earning revenue in a merchandising firm. Sometimes the Sales account is divided into several classifications of merchandise. You will recall that Revenue from Services or Fees was typically the title of the revenue account in a service enterprise.

Revenue is recorded at the *time of sale* in a merchandising enterprise even though a good portion of the sales may be on account. This is different from the cash basis of accounting illustrated in Chapter 7 for the service enterprise. The point of sale is considered to be the appropriate time to recognize revenue in a merchandising firm because it is assumed to be the *critical event* in the generation of the revenue. All of the other activities that are necessary to the operation of a merchandising firm are important, but the sale is considered to be the critical event for recognizing earned revenue.

Sales may be for cash or on credit (also called "on account," or "charge sales"). The portion of credit sales depends largely on the nature of the merchandise and the type of customer. If the company is in the retail trade where sales are to the ultimate customer and the sales price of most merchandise is not large, then most sales will be for cash. If, however, the merchandise consists of large durable goods (major appliances), then most sales will be on credit. If the company's business consists of selling to other businesses (a wholesaler), then almost all of the sales will be on credit.

There are no general business standards for granting credit. The credit terms depend upon the industry in which the firm operates. Certain types of merchandising firms may use a relatively common practice. For example, most large department stores have similar credit policies and payment terms.

To determine net earnings for a merchandising firm using accrual accounting, it is necessary to record transactions in the following accounts:

1. Sales.
2. Sales Returns and Allowances.
3. Purchases.
4. Purchases Returns and Allowances.
5. Merchandise Inventory.

SALES ACCOUNT

Merchandise sales for the period are recorded in the **Sales account.** Since these sales are applicable to a specific accounting period, the account is a revenue account or a temporary owner's equity account. That is, it will be closed out at the end of every accounting period. We will have more to say on closing procedures in subsequent chapters. For the present time, it is sufficient to note that the balance in the account as of a point in time represents the cumulative sales from the *beginning* of the accounting period.

To show how the Sales account is used, we have included two typical ledger postings below:

Date		Explanation	P.R.	Debit	Credit	Balance
Sales					Account No. 110	
1978 Oct.	9		GJ1		127.50	127.50
	9		CR1		48.27	175.77

Assume that during the week ending October 9 the company sold $127.50 of merchandise on account. When this transaction was recorded in the general journal, it required a credit to Sales with a matching debit to Accounts Receivable. Suppose that during the same week the company sold $48.27 of merchandise for cash. This was journalized in the cash receipts journal by crediting Sales and debiting Cash for the sales amount.

For the above transaction, it was assumed that the company was not subject to a retail sales tax. Had this not been the case, the company would have had two options. First, assuming the sales tax to be 4 percent of the $127.50, it could credit Sales for $127.50, credit Sales Tax Payable for $5.10, and debit Accounts Receivable for $132.60. Or, the entire amount $132.60 ($127.50 sale + $5.10 tax) could be credited to Sales with a matching debit to Accounts Receivable. At the end of the period, the cumulative sales figure would be multiplied by 4/104 to compute the sales tax liability. For example, suppose the total credits to Sales for the month were $9,984, then the tax would be $9,984 × 4/104 = $384. This amount would be transferred from Sales to Sales Tax Payable by the following journal entry:

```
Oct. 31   Sales ........................................................... 384
                Sales Tax Payable ..................................            384
```

SALES TAX ACCOUNTING

Many business enterprises are required by state or municipal statute to collect sales tax from their customers. While the tax is generally levied on the gross sales price of retail merchandise — **a retail sales tax** — it is sometimes extended to persons furnishing services at retail, in which case gross receipts become the taxable basis. With merchandise, the tax may apply only to specific items such as automobiles, televisions, radios, and selected appliances. Alternatively, the tax may be imposed on all merchandise except essentials such as drugs or food products.

To minimize the computations on smaller amounts, it is customary for the taxing authority to provide a sales tax schedule. One such schedule for the 3 percent retail sales tax imposed by one of the states is shown below:

Amount of sale	Tax amount
1¢–10¢	None
11¢–34¢	1¢
35¢–64¢	2¢
65¢–$1.10	3¢
$1.11–$1.34	4¢

Continued in a similar manner.

One further complication is the provision in many tax statutes for exempt sales. Under such provisions, numerous nonprofit organizations are exempt from paying sales tax on their purchases. Consequently, the merchandiser must devise some procedure whereby these exempt sales can be excluded from the sales tax liability computation.

The sales tax liability is accumulated in the **Sales Tax Payable account.** An example of such an account is shown below:

	Sales Tax Payable					Account No. 53
Date	Explanation		P.R.	Debit	Credit	Balance
				(2)	(1)	(3)

The computation of the tax liability can be the actual amount from each and every invoice, or once a month the company can compute its total liability based on its taxable sales for the period. The method selected will depend on the governing statutes or the business's preference. Either way, the tax liability is credited (1) to the account. When the taxes are remitted to the proper authorities, the account is debited (2). The balance in the account (3) at any point in time represents the total of the unremitted items.

SALES RETURNS AND ALLOWANCES

Occasionally a customer will receive a larger quantity of a particular merchandise item than originally ordered, or a customer may receive the incorrect items, style, or color. Similarly, the merchandise may be damaged or spoiled. When this happens, the company can request that the merchandise be returned, usually at its expense, and a credit will be recorded in the customer's account. If the sale was for cash or if the customer has already paid the account, a cash refund will be made. Sometimes, however, the buyer is willing to keep the merchandise provided a reduction in the price is received. Like a merchandise return, this entitles the customer to a cash refund or a credit which reduces the customer's account balance.

Since both types of transactions reduce the total sales for the period, they could be debited directly to the Sales account. Yet, there are several reasons for recording these items in a separate contra account called **Sales Returns and Allowances.** For instance, a large balance may indicate inadequate ordering, packing, or shipping procedures. In addition, any unusual fluctuations will be highlighted. When computing the net sales for the period, the balance of the Sales Returns and Allowances account must be deducted from the Sales account. Similarly, before calculating the company's sales tax liability, the Sales account should be adjusted for any returns and allowances.

The postings made to such an account are demonstrated as follows:

Sales Returns and Allowances					Account No. 111	
Date		Explanation	P.R.	Debit	Credit	Balance
1978 Oct.	12		GJ1	67.00		67.00
	23		GJ1	36.00		103.00

On October 12, a customer informed the company that $67 worth of merchandise was being returned from the customer's most recent order because of incorrect style. The required entry is a debit to Sales Returns and Allowances for $67 with a matching credit to Accounts Receivable. During the month, another customer informed the company that slightly damaged merchandise had been received. An agreement was reached with the company, however, to keep the items and receive an allowance of 20 percent on the $180 purchase price. The entry recording this transaction of October 23 consists of a debit to Sales Returns and Allowances for $36 (20 percent × $180) and a credit to Accounts Receivable for the same amount. Had the original transaction been for cash and a cash refund made, the entries would be the same except the credit would be to Cash, not to Accounts Receivable.

SALES TICKET OR SALES INVOICE

Whether sales are for cash or on credit, a **sales ticket** or **sales invoice** should be filled out by the salesperson. These tickets are usually prepared in duplicate or triplicate with the original copy going to the bookkeeping department and a duplicate going to the customers. Sales tickets are pre-numbered, and the salesperson is held accountable for each of his or her

Illustration 9–1
Sales ticket

Western Supply Company				
112 Main St., Tampa, Florida				

Sold To *Paul S. Stone*

Address *Lake Bluff Drive*

City *Tampa*   State *Florida*

Salesperson Initials	Date	Cash	Charge	
JRD	*3-26-78*		✓	
Quantity	Stock No. & Description	Price		
2	*F 1926 Headlights*	*7*	*56*	
1	*A 2607 Wrench set*	*3*	*59*	
	Total	*11*	*15*	

No.	Sales tax		*34*
46	Total	*11*	*49*

tickets. By sorting the tickets by number, management can determine the quantity, type, and amount of sales made by each salesperson. For credit sales, the name and address of the customer are always entered. The type of information required on a sales ticket or invoice is shown in Illustration 9–1.

BANK CREDIT CARDS

The use of bank credit cards has become very common in retail merchandising. Two well-known cards are "Bank Americard" and "Master Charge." Many retail businesses use this form of credit exclusively; therefore, they do not bear the risk of uncollectible accounts receivable. Credit card transactions can be accounted for in nearly the same manner as cash sales.

After the sale of goods where the customer uses a bank credit card, the merchant's copy of the sales ticket is taken to the bank where it can be discounted or the amount can be credited to the merchant's account and paid at the end of the month. The total amount of the sale is credited to Sales; the amount of cash received from the bank is debited to Cash. If the tickets are discounted at the bank, the discount is debited to Interest Expense.

SALES JOURNAL

All credit sales of merchandise could be initially recorded in the general journal. With many businesses, however, the volume of credit sales transactions is sufficiently large to use a special **sales journal.** This journal can have either one or three columns depending on whether the company is subject to a sales tax. If the company is not subject to a sales tax, there will be a single column representing the credit to Sales and the debit to Accounts Receivable. Otherwise, there will be three columns: Accounts Receivable—a debit, Sales—a credit, and Sales Tax Payable—a credit. Cash sales are not entered in the sales journal but rather in the cash receipts journal.

A sample one-column sales journal is given in Illustration 9–2.

Illustration 9–2

	Sales Journal			Page 4
Date	Sold To	Invoice No.	Accounts Receivable, Dr. Sales, Cr. Amount	P.R.
1978 Oct. 2	Dr. Jones	7837	127.13	✔
6	Kamins Mfg. Co.	7838	637.20	✔
8	L. Dunn	7839	42.73	✔
13	S. Mair	7840	61.20	✔
16	Beer's Drug Store	7841	142.50	✔
19	H. Smith	7842	23.15	✔
24	T. Howard	7843	13.70	✔
26	Midwest Specialty	7844	147.88	✔
31	Acc. Rec., Dr.—Sales, Cr.		1,195.49	
			(15/110)	

When using a sales journal like the one in Illustration 9–2, a single line is sufficient to record a transaction. If more detail is desired on any transaction, all required information is readily available from the sales invoice.

If the company maintains only a single Accounts Receivable account, then every invoice is filed by customer name immediately after recording the transaction in the sales journal. When the company maintains a separate account for each customer, then the sales invoice should be posted to the appropriate customer's account before being filed. The posting could be made from the sales journal. However, it is preferable for the posting to be made from the invoice because it provides efficiency and accuracy. After the invoice is posted, a check (✔) should be made in the far right-hand column of the sales journal. Note that this posting is to customer accounts found in a subsidiary accounts receivable ledger, to be explained later, not to the Accounts Receivable account.

At the end of the month, this single column is footed and ruled as illustrated. The total can now be posted to the general ledger. For our example, the required entries are:

a.   Debit Accounts Receivable for $1,195.49.
b.   Credit Sales for $1,195.49.

To provide a cross-reference in the general ledger, the source for the entry should be indicated in the P.R. column of the affected accounts. This can best be done by using an "S" to indicate sales journal, followed by the page number. For our illustration, the notation would be "S4."

For a company that is subject to retail sales tax, the three-column sales journal in Illustration 9–3 would be maintained. Assume the same facts as the last example except that the company must pay a 3 percent sales tax. This 3 percent tax would increase proportionately the amount that the customer must pay.

Assume that Midwest Specialty returned merchandise of $103 (Invoice No. 7844). The entry would be made in the general journal (page 8).

Illustration 9–3

			SALES JOURNAL				Page 4
Date		Sold To	Invoice No.	Accounts Receivable, Dr.	Sales, Cr.	Sales Tax Payable, Cr.	P.R.
1978							
Oct.	2	Dr. Jones	7837	130.95	127.13	3.82	✔
	6	Kamins Mfg. Co.	7838	656.32	637.20	19.12	✔
	8	L. Dunn	7839	44.02	42.73	1.29	✔
	13	S. Mair	7840	63.04	61.20	1.84	✔
	16	Beer's Drug Store	7841	146.78	142.50	4.28	✔
	19	H. Smith	7842	23.85	23.15	.70	✔
	24	T. Howard	7843	14.12	13.70	.42	✔
	26	Midwest Specialty	7844	152.32	147.88	4.44	✔
				1,231.40	1,195.49	35.91	
				(15)	(110)	(40)	

Accounts Receivable should be credited for $103; Sales Tax Payable should be debited for $3; and Sales Returns and Allowances should be debited for $100.

At the end of the month, the columns are footed and the totals posted to the proper accounts in the general ledger as follows:

Accounts Receivable   Account No. 15

Date		Explanation	P.R.	Debit	Credit	Balance
1978 Oct.	31		S4	1,231.40		1,231.40
			GJ8		103.00	1,128.40

Sales   Account No. 110

Date		Explanation	P.R.	Debit	Credit	Balance
1978 Oct.	31		S4		1,195.49	1,195.49

Sales Tax Payable   Account No. 40

Date		Explanation	P.R.	Debit	Credit	Balance
1978 Oct.	31		S4		35.91	35.91
			GJ8	3.00		32.91

Sales Returns and Allowances   Account No. 111

Date		Explanation	P.R.	Debit	Credit	Balance
1978 Oct.	31		GJ8	100.00		100.00

The posting reference, "S4," refers to the sales journal (S), page 4. This cross-referencing of the general ledger entries to the sales journal is necessary in order that the accounting records may be examined to see that they agree with one another.

ACCOUNTS RECEIVABLE

During the accounting period the company must keep a record of amounts due from its customers. Furthermore, this account — **Accounts Receivable** — must not only reflect activity for the period but it must also indicate the unpaid balances as of any point in time. Since these balances are due in less than a year, the account is classified as a *current asset*. (Current assets will be discussed further in Chapter 10.)

To be useful, the company must know not only the total but also a detailed breakdown of what amount each customer owes. One alternative would be to have separate accounts in the general ledger for each customer. However, if the number of customers is large, this is cumbersome and awkward. For this reason, a single general ledger account — Accounts Receivable — is often used for *all* customers. This account is considered the **control account.** Supporting this account are subsidiary records, usually called **subsidiary ledgers,** which disclose the balance owed by each customer. Of course, the total of the subsidiary ledgers should equal the control account balance.

Sales invoice method

Under this method, all sales invoices are kept in a file organized by customer name until paid. Any allowance or partial payments are noted on the face of the invoice, but it is still retained in the open file until the total amount is paid. By adding up a customer's invoices, the receivable balance can be readily determined. The total of all of the customers' receivable balances should equal the control account — Accounts Receivable — balance, assuming no errors or omissions have been made.

Individual ledger accounts

Under this system, the company maintains a separate account for each customer in a special subsidiary ledger. Like the above invoice system, the sales invoice is still the main document. Whenever a sale is made, the amount is debited to the appropriate customer's ledger account. Likewise, any payments or allowances are credited to the account. Thus, an account balance will represent only unpaid items. If all individual balances are footed, they should equal the control account — Accounts Receivable — balance in the general ledger. The final section of the chapter contains an example of this method.

PURCHASE PROCEDURES

A merchandising firm purchases inventory for resale to customers. While a service enterprise also purchases items such as supplies, they are not held for resale to customers. The purchase procedures about to be discussed relate to the accounting for **merchandise inventory.**

Inventory methods

A merchandising firm may use either a **periodic inventory system** or a *perpetual inventory system.* With a periodic system, the physical amount or inventory need be counted only at the close of an accounting period. The general ledger contains only the beginning balance in inventory, while inventory purchases for the period are recorded in a separate ledger account. The perpetual inventory system is covered in detail in a subsequent chapter. This chapter is based on a periodic inventory system. The purchase procedure discussed below is appropriate for a periodic system.

Purchases account

Purchases of merchandise during the current period are entered in an account entitled **Purchases.** Since this account is closed out at the end of the accounting period, it is considered a temporary owner's equity account. Below is a sample Purchases account with several transactions illustrated.

Purchases					Account No. 210
Date	Explanation	P.R.	Debit	Credit	Balance
1978 Oct. 14		GJ1	254.00		254.00
17		CD1	38.00		292.00

All merchandise purchases, whether for cash or on credit, are debited to this account. Suppose that on October 14 the company purchases $254 of mechandise on account. There would be a debit to Purchases — as shown — with an offsetting credit to Accounts Payable. Likewise, if the company purchased $38 of merchandise on October 17 for cash, then Purchases is debited for $38 while Cash is credited for the same amount. The vast majority of transactions, however, would be on account, especially those of larger enterprises. Sometimes there are additional expenses, such as transportation charges and insurance costs on the goods, and these could also be debited to the Purchases account. If such expenses are common and their amounts significant, separate ledger accounts should be established for them.

Purchase returns and allowances account

It is not unusual for the business to occasionally receive merchandise which was either not ordered or was in excess of the requested amount. Likewise, the merchandise may be damaged or impaired in some way so that its resale value is reduced. The purchaser has two options: The goods can be returned or the merchandise can be kept and a deduction from the regular price accepted. Either way, the buyer is entitled to a credit on his or her account, if the purchase was on account, or a refund if it was a cash purchase.

The refund or allowance can be credited either to the Purchases account or to a separate account, **Purchase Returns and Allowances** which is also a temporary owner's equity account. By using a separate account, the total returns and allowances for the period is made readily available to the user of this type of data. Should this total be large or show a significant increase within the period, it may indicate problems in the purchasing procedures. Since the costs of handling and accounting for returned merchandise are likely to be significant, proper corrective action is important.

To demonstrate the operations of the Purchase Returns and Allowances account, an example is presented below:

Purchase Returns and Allowances			Account No. 211		
Date	Explanation	P.R.	Debit	Credit	Balance
1978 Oct. 16		GJ1		54.00	54.00
30		GJ1		50.00	104.00

Assume that the company received goods totaling $54 in the October 14 shipment which it never ordered. These items were returned to the seller which results in a credit to the Purchase Returns and Allowances account and a matching debit to Accounts Payable. On October 28, the company received some slightly damaged merchandise. The seller and the company agreed that the price of each of the 100 damaged units should be reduced by $0.50. Consequently, the Purchase Returns and Allowances account is credited for $50 with an offsetting debit to Accounts Payable. Purchases Returns and Allowances is a reduction in the recorded cost of Purchases.

Purchase invoice

A **purchase invoice** is a document the buyer receives from the seller that is used to record a purchase transaction. This document provides information such as the seller of the merchandise or goods, the date of purchase, the invoice number, the means of shipment, the terms of the purchase transaction, and the type and quantity of goods ordered and shipped. Frequently, the buyer will imprint a form on the face of the invoice. This imprinted form is used to indicate (1) that goods have been received in a satisfactory condition, (2) the date received, (3) who received the goods, (4) whether they were correctly priced, and (5) the number of the account where the transaction is recorded. Illustration 9–4 is an example of a purchase invoice.

Illustration 9–4
Purchase invoice

Southgate Wholesale, Inc.
Jacksonville, Florida
33001

Sold To: _W. D. Bates, Inc._

1113 N. Main, Jacksonville, Fla. 33002

Date _May 5, 1978_   Invoice No. _5002_

Terms _30 days_   Customer Order No. _612_

Date Shipped _May 5, 1978_   Via _Brown Transport_

Quantity		Stock No. & Description	Unit Price		Amount	
Ordered	Shipped					
12	12	F2122 Rims	3	50	42	00
1	1	F2741 Bicycle	56	79	56	79
12	12	P4104 Paint	3	18	38	16
					136	95

Date received
Quantity
Items
Price
Received by
Acct. No.
Ent. & Foot.

5/5/78
PPS
PPS
PPS
BPD
000
KKg

Purchases journal

We have assumed that all of our transactions were recorded in the general journal. For a larger business, however, such purchase transactions will occur frequently, and recording them individually in the general journal would be not only time-consuming but would also lead to very cumbersome ledger accounts. For this reason, a special journal is used called the **purchases journal.** Using it, we make only one summary posting to the ledger account every month. Additionally, its columns are headed in such a way that a single entry suffices for both the debit to Purchases and the offsetting credit to Accounts Payable. Should the purchase be for cash, it would not be entered here, but instead would be recorded with the other cash disbursements. An example of a purchases journal is shown in Illustration 9–5. The columns in the purchases journal are self-explanatory except for the "Terms" column. In this column the payment terms from each invoice are entered. Thus, the first invoice listed in the journal should normally be paid within ten days after the date of the invoice. Since every creditor sets his or her own terms of sale, they will vary considerably. Often, the creditor will offer a *cash discount* to encourage rapid payment of an invoice. We shall, however, postpone further discussion of discounts until Chapter 12.

At the end of the month, the Amount column is totaled and ruled as indicated. This total then becomes the basis for the summary posting to the general ledger. The entries would be:

a. Debit Purchases for $3,364.40.
b. Credit Accounts Payable for $3,364.40.

When posting these amounts, a "P5" should be placed in the P.R. column of each ledger account to indicate that the posting source is the purchases journal, page 5.

As in the case of sales invoices if the company maintains a *separate subsidiary ledger account* for each creditor, purchase invoices should be posted to these accounts before filing. If the enterprise uses the **invoice method,** the invoices would be placed in the unpaid file according to payment date as determined from the terms of the purchase. It is easy to

Illustration 9–5

					PURCHASES JOURNAL		Page 5
Date		Terms	Invoice		Creditor	Purchases, Dr. Accounts Payable, Cr.	P.R.
			No.			Amount	
1978 Oct.	5	Net 10	973		Lash Distributors	237.44	✔
	9	Net 30	1243		Midwest Carpet Co.	1,567.40	✔
	15	Net 20	47		White Installation Service	113.00	✔
	20	Net 10	3743		Armstrong Brothers	985.21	✔
	29	Net 30	6771		Central Specialty	461.35	✔
	31					3,364.40	
						(210/50)	

determine what payments are due on any date by simply looking in the unpaid file under any particular date. If partial payment on purchases is made, this amount is noted on the face of the invoice and also in the cash disbursements journal.

When purchase invoices are fully paid, they are removed from the unpaid file and placed in a paid file in alphabetical order according to the sellers' names. This system is similar to the sales invoice method mentioned earlier in this chapter.

Postings to the Accounts Payable and Purchases accounts from the purchases journal are illustrated below. This posting is done at the end of each month and is called a **summary posting.**

	Accounts Payable				Account No. 50	
Date	Explanation	P.R.	Debit	Credit	Balance
1978 Oct. 31		P5		3,364.40	3,364.40

	Purchases				Account No. 210	
Date	Explanation	P.R.	Debit	Credit	Balance
1978 Oct. 31		P5	3,364.40		3,364.40

If a separate subsidiary ledger account is maintained for each supplier, it is necessary to record each purchase and payment individually in the proper ledger account. Returns and allowances would also be recorded in these ledger accounts. The remaining balance is shown in the ledger account.

Accounts payable

In several of our previous entries, we have used the **Accounts Payable** ledger account. This account is classified as a current liability account because the balance in the account represents amounts due to creditors within one year. The credit balance in the account represents the total amount owed by the company for merchandise purchases.

The fact that the account shows only the total liability to all vendors dramatizes the need for some form of subsidiary record for each creditor. These supporting records should reflect the outstanding balance owed to a particular creditor. The sum of these supporting records should equal the Accounts Payable controlling account balance. Basically, there are two accounting methods used to maintain supporting records.

Invoice method. As indicated previously, under this method all unpaid invoices are kept in an open file according to their due dates. This insures their being paid when they become due. After payment, which is typically for the full face amount of the invoice, the purchase invoices are removed from the open file and placed in a paid file according to vendor name. If, however, only a partial payment is made, then an appropriate notation should be made on the invoice explaining the amounts paid, and the invoice should be retained in the open file. When we speak of this open file, it may be as simple as a single manila folder or as complex as a magnetic computer tape. At any point in time, barring errors, the total of open invoices should agree with the Accounts Payable control account balance.

Ledger account system. With this system it is customary to maintain a separate ledger account for each creditor. The handling of the invoice, however, is exactly the same as in the invoice system. These subsidiary accounts are not maintained in the general ledger, but instead they are kept in a ledger for subsidiary payable records. When a purchase on account is made, the supporting invoice becomes the basis for the credit to the particular creditor's ledger account. When a payment is made, it is debited to the appropriate creditor's account. Like the open invoice method, most payments cover the entire amount of a particular invoice. When this is not the case, a notation should be made on the invoice explaining the amount, and it should remain in the unpaid file until payment is completed. Therefore, a credit balance in any subsidiary account represents unpaid invoices to that particular creditor. By totaling all the account balances in the subsidiary ledger, we should arrive at the control total. The technique of using a control account (Accounts Payable in this case) in the general ledger with underlying subsidiary records was also employed when accounts receivable were discussed in an earlier section.

The working of the control account, Accounts Payable, will now be demonstrated.

		Accounts Payable			Account No. 50	
Date		Explanation	P.R.	Debit	Credit	Balance
1978 Oct.	14		GJ1		254.00	254.00
	16		GJ1	54.00		200.00
	24		GJ1	150.00		50.00
	30		GJ1	50.00		—
	31		P5		3,364.40	3,364.40

The set of hypothetical transactions are those from the previous two sections:

a. Merchandise purchase: October 14, $254.
b. Merchandise returns: October 16, $54.
c. Payment on account: October 24, $150.
d. Merchandise damage allowance: October 30, $50.
e. Merchandise purchases, month of October, $3,364.40.

The balance in the account on October 31, $3,364.40, represents the total amount owed to all creditors.

GROSS MARGIN AND COST OF GOODS SOLD

A merchandising firm, unlike a service firm, has a product cost or **cost of goods sold.** This is what the product purchased for resale costs the seller. The selling price of the merchandise must be high enough to cover the product cost *and* the operating expenses if a merchandising firm is to earn a profit.

The total cost of products sold during a period is called the cost of goods sold. The difference between the net sales of the period and cost of goods sold is called the **gross margin** or **gross profit.**

Net sales for the period are calculated as follows:

Net Sales = Total Sales − Sales Returns and Allowances

These amounts should be readily available in the general ledger accounts.

Cost of goods sold is determined according to the following equation:

Cost of Goods Sold = Merchandise Inventory (Beginning of Period)
            + Net Purchases − Merchandise Inventory (End of Period)

where the **net purchases** are computed as:

Net Purchases = Total Purchases − Purchase Returns and Allowances

The amounts needed to calculate net purchases come directly from the Purchases and Purchase Returns and Allowances accounts in the general ledger. Determining the merchandise inventory balance requires that the company physically count the merchandise on hand at the end of the accounting period. This quantity of inventory is then multiplied by its unit cost to arrive at a dollar value for ending inventory. The ending inventory of one period is the beginning inventory of the next period so that inventory need be counted only once—at the end of the accounting period.

Revenue:		
Sales..		$110,000
Less: Sales returns and allowances............................		4,000
Net sales		$106,000
Cost of goods sold:		
Merchandise inventory, beginning of period.................		$10,700
Purchases	$85,500	
Less: Purchase returns and allowances	2,100	
Add: Net purchases..		83,400
Cost of goods available for sale......................................		$94,100
Merchandise inventory, end of period...........................		12,300
Cost of goods sold		81,800
Gross margin on sales...		$ 24,200

From this point, the company would deduct operating expenses and other items to arrive at its net earnings for the accounting period.

ACCOUNTING PROCEDURES – A SMALL MERCHANDISING BUSINESS

The transactions of a merchandising business are recorded in much the same manner as those of any other enterprise. If the number of transactions is small, the only book of original entry will be a standard two-column general journal or a modified cash journal. As the volume of activity increases, however, the company is likely to use a combination of special journals such as the purchases journal, sales journal, cash receipts journal, and cash disbursements journal to supplement its general journal. At the end of every month, these special journals will be summarized, and postings will be made to the appropriate general ledger accounts.

A trial balance of all accounts in the general ledger should be made at the end of every month. Its purpose is to prove the equality of the debit and credit account balances. At the same time the Accounts Receivable control balance from the general ledger should be reconciled to the total of the amounts in the underlying subsidiary records. A detailed listing of customer balances is often prepared for this purpose. Likewise, the balance in the Accounts Payable control account should be reconciled to a list of amounts owed each supplier which is recorded in the subsidiary Accounts Payable accounts.

To illustrate these accounting procedures, we will (1) record selected transactions from a representative month in the applicable journals, (2) post all required entries to the general ledger accounts, (3) prepare a schedule of accounts receivable balances, and (4) prepare a similar schedule of accounts payable balances. Since the accounts we are concerned with are only one segment of the total general ledger, no trial balance will be prepared.

The particular merchandising business, "Jones Floor Coverings," uses a purchases journal, a sales journal, separate journals for cash receipts and disbursements, and a general journal. The company maintains an unpaid invoice file as supporting detail for its accounts payable. For accounts receivable, however, an individual subsidiary ledger account is maintained for each customer. The company is not subject to a retail sales tax.

The following chart of accounts has intentionally been limited to only those accounts affected by our selected transactions:

Chart of Accounts (Partial)

Assets:	Revenues:
10 Cash	110 Sales
15 Accounts Receivable	111 Sales Returns and Allowances
Liabilities:	Cost of Goods Sold:
50 Accounts Payable	210 Purchases
	211 Purchase Returns and Allowances

Explanation of transactions

Nov. 2 Received Invoice No. 6734 from Midwest Wholesale for merchandise purchased, $374.51. Terms are ten days net.

3 Sold merchandise on account to P. Corby, $38.50. Sales Invoice No. 7881.

4 Purchased merchandise on account from Kamins Manufacturing Corporation, $132.18. Terms are 20 days net. Invoice No. 13838.

5 Sold merchandise on account to M. Walters for $17.45. Sales Invoice No. 7882.

6 Issued Check No. 282 to McKenzie Wholesalers for payment on account, $482.91. (This would be recorded in the cash disbursements journal.)

Purchased merchandise for cash from Wilson Brothers Company with Check No. 283, $78.

7 Cash sales from the totals on the cash register tape, $347.81. These totals represent all cash sales made during the week up through closing time on Saturday. They should be recorded in the cash receipts journal by debiting Cash and crediting Sales. They would not be recorded in the sales journal because it is used only for sales on account.

9 Received $73 from S. Wills for payment on account.

10 Sold merchandise on account to Modern Pharmacy, $318. Sales Invoice No. 7883.

12 Paid account with Midwest Wholesale, $374.51. Check No. 284.

13 Received $38.50 from P. Corby as payment on account.

14 Issued Check No. 285 for cash purchase of merchandise from Campbell Distributors, $47.50.

Cash sales for the week were $451.37.

15 Sold merchandise on account to G. White for $417.50. Sales Invoice No. 7884.

16 Issued a credit to Modern Pharmacy for merchandise returned, $13.50.

Nov. 17 Received an invoice, No. 913, from Midwestern Hardware Company for merchandise purchases, $148.91. Terms, net ten days.

18 Sold merchandise on account to H. Sherman, $118.50. Sales Invoice No. 7885.

19 Received a purchase allowance from Midwestern Hardware Company for damaged merchandise in the November 17 shipment, $21.

20 Received $37.45 from M. Walters in full payment on Walter's account.

21 Cash sales for the period, $513.40.

22 Received an invoice from Fox Carpet Company for merchandise purchases, $671.40. Terms, net ten days. Invoice No. 41243.

24 Issued Check No. 286 to Kamins Manufacturing Corporation for payment on account, $132.18.

26 Received an invoice from Northwest Supply Company for merchandise purchased, $210. Terms, net 20 days. Invoice No. 67742.

27 Issued Check No. 287 to Midwestern Hardware Company for $127.91. This represents the original purchase $148.91, less the allowance, $21.00, received on November 19.

28 Cash sales for the week were $462.43.

30 Received $304.50 from Modern Pharmacy for payment on account. This covered the sale of November 10, $318, less the merchandise returned on November 16, $13.50. Cash sales for November 29 and 30, $56.70.

Recording

The above transactions were recorded in the applicable journals in Illustration 9–6, 9–7, and 9–8. The purchases and sales journals (Illustra-

Illustration 9–6

CASH RECEIPTS JOURNAL　　　　　　　　　　　　　　　　Page 1

Cash, Dr.	Date		Description	Sales, Cr.	Accounts Receivable, Cr.			Sundry Accounts, Cr.		
					Amount		✔	Acct. No.	Amount	✔
347.81	1978 Nov.	7	Cash sales	347.81						
73.00		9	S. Wills		73	00	✔			
38.50		13	P. Corby		38	50	✔			
451.37		14	Cash sales	451.37						
37.45		20	M. Walters		37	45	✔			
513.40		21	Cash sales	513.40						
462.43		28	Cash sales	462.43						
304.50		30	Modern Pharmacy		304	50	✔			
56.70		30	Cash sales	56.70						
2,285.16		30		1,831.71	453	45				
(10)				(110)	(15)					

Illustration 9–7

CASH DISBURSEMENTS JOURNAL

Page 1

Accounts Payable, Dr.		Sundry Accounts, Dr.			Date	Description	Check No.	Cash, Cr.
Amount	✓	Acct. No.	Amount	✓				
482.91	✓				1978 Nov. 6	McKenzie Wholesalers	282	482.91
		210	78.00	✓	6	Wilson Brothers Co.	283	78.00
374.51	✓				12	Midwest Wholesale	284	374.51
		210	47.50	✓	14	Campbell Distributors	285	47.50
132.18	✓				24	Kamins Manufacturing Corp.	286	132.18
127.91	✓				27	Midwestern Hardware Co.	287	127.91
1,117.51			125.50		30			1,243.01
(50)			(✓)					(10)

Illustration 9–8
Purchases, sales, and general journals

PURCHASES JOURNAL   Page 1

Date		Terms	Invoice No.	Creditor	Purchases, Dr. Accounts Payable, Cr.	P.R.
					Amount	
1978 Nov.	2	Net 10	6734	Midwest Wholesale	374.51	✔
	4	Net 20	13838	Kamins Manufacturing Corp.	132.18	✔
	17	Net 10	913	Midwestern Hardware Co.	148.91	✔
	22	Net 10	41243	Fox Carpet Company	671.40	✔
	26	Net 20	67742	Northwest Supply Co.	210.00	✔
	30			Purchases, Dr.—Acct. Pay., Cr.	1,537.00	
					(210/50)	

SALES JOURNAL   Page 1

Date		Sold To	Invoice No.	Accounts Receivable, Dr. Sales, Cr.	P.R.
				Amount	
1978 Nov.	3	P. Corby	7881	38.50	✔
	5	M. Walters	7882	17.45	✔
	10	Modern Pharmacy	7883	318.00	✔
	15	G. White	7884	417.50	✔
	18	H. Sherman	7885	118.50	✔
	30			909.95	
				(15/110)	

GENERAL JOURNAL   Page 1

Date		Accounts and Explanation	P.R.	Debit	Credit
1978 Nov.	16	Sales Returns and Allowances	111	13.50	
		Accounts Receivable—Modern Pharmacy	15/✔		13.50
		To record credit issued for returned merchandise—Modern Pharmacy.			
	19	Accounts Payable—Midwestern Hardware Co.	50	21.00	
		Purchase Returns and Allowances	211		21.00
		To record purchase allowance from Midwestern Hardware Co.			

Illustration 9–9

ACCOUNTS RECEIVABLE—SUBSIDIARY LEDGER
Accounts Receivable—S. Wills · Account No. 15–1

Date		Explanation	P.R.	Debit	Credit	Balance
1978 Nov.	1	Balance	✔			73.00
	9		CR1		73.00	—

Accounts Receivable—M. Walters · Account No. 15–2

Date		Explanation	P.R.	Debit	Credit	Balance
1978 Nov.	1	Balance	✔			20.00
	5		S1	17.45		37.45
	20		CR1		37.45	—

Accounts Receivable—P. Corby · Account No. 15–3

Date		Explanation	P.R.	Debit	Credit	Balance
1978 Nov.	3		S1	38.50		38.50
	13		CR1		38.50	—

Accounts Receivable— Modern Pharmacy · Account No. 15–4

Date		Explanation	P.R.	Debit	Credit	Balance
1978 Nov.	10		S1	318.00		318.00
	16		GJ1		13.50	304.50
	30		CR1		304.50	—

Accounts Receivable—H. Sherman · Account No. 15–5

Date		Explanation	P.R.	Debit	Credit	Balance
1978 Nov.	18		S1	118.50		118.50

Accounts Receivable—G. White · Account No. 15–6

Date		Explanation	P.R.	Debit	Credit	Balance
1978 Nov.	15		S1	417.50		417.50

tion 9–8) include all transactions for the month, and the amount columns foot to the illustrated totals. Since the company maintains individual accounts for each customer, these were posted simultaneously with the sales journal and cash receipts journal (Illustration 9–9). Note that parentheses around the balances shown in the accounts indicate a debit balance in an account that normally has a credit balance, such as Accounts Payable (Illustration 9–10). Likewise, a credit balance in an account that normally has a debit balance, such as Cash, would be in parentheses. See Accounts No. 15 and No. 50 in Illustration 9–10 for examples of **"negative" account balances.**

Illustration 9–10

GENERAL LEDGER (Partial)
Cash   Account No. 10

Date		Explanation	P.R.	Debit	Credit	Balance
1978						
Nov.	1	Balance	✓			1,741.50
	30		CR1	2,285.16		4,026.66
	30		CD1		1,243.01	2,783.65

Accounts Receivable   Account No. 15

Date		Explanation	P.R.	Debit	Credit	Balance
1978						
Nov.	1	Balance	✓			93.00
	30		CR1		453.45	(360.45)
	30		S1	909.95		549.50
	30		GJ1		13.50	536.00

Accounts Payable   Account No. 50

Date		Explanation	P.R.	Debit	Credit	Balance
1978						
Nov.	1	Balance	✓			482.91
	30		CD1	1,117.51		(634.60)
	30		P1		1,537.00	902.40
	30		GJ1	21.00		881.40

Sales   Account No. 110

Date		Explanation	P.R.	Debit	Credit	Balance
1978						
Nov.	1	Balance	✓			28,147.23
	30		CR1		1,831.71	29,978.94
	30		S1		909.95	30,888.89

Illustration 9–10 (continued)

Sales Returns and Allowances — Account No. 111

Date		Explanation	P.R.	Debit	Credit	Balance
1978						
Nov.	1	Balance	✓			313.10
	30		GJ1	13.50		326.60

Purchases — Account No. 210

Date		Explanation	P.R.	Debit	Credit	Balance
1978						
Nov.	1	Balance	✓			16,433.66
	6		CD1	78.00		16,511.66
	14		CD1	47.50		16,559.16
	30		P1	1,537.00		18,096.16

Purchase Returns and Allowances — Account No. 211

Date		Explanation	P.R.	Debit	Credit	Balance
1978						
Nov.	1	Balance	✓			413.09
	30				21.00	434.09

Posting

Only those general ledger accounts affected by the selected transactions are shown. Since the enterprise has been in operation some time, all accounts have a balance carried forward from the previous month. With regard to accounts receivable, any customer account with an unpaid balance as of November 1 is shown in the subsidiary ledger.

The order of posting to the general ledger accounts was (1) cash receipts journal, (2) cash disbursements journal, (3) purchases journal, (4) sales journal, and (5) general journal. For each of these, the columns were footed and ruled as indicated. While the "Sundry Accounts" columns in the cash journals are totaled, this is for crossfooting purposes only. Each item in that column must be posted individually since different ledger accounts are contained within this column. Posting is indicated by the check mark (✓). For the other columns, their totals are posted directly to the respective ledger accounts. Note that the ledger account number is shown below or next to its respective total to indicate posting.

When the company utilizes a number of special journals, it is recommended that the source of each entry in the general ledger be indicated. For our example this was done using the following code:

CR = cash receipts journal
CD = cash disbursements journal
S   = sales journal
P   = purchases journal
GJ = general journal

These initials are followed by the page number of the journal.

Schedule of accounts receivable

At the end of the month, the company should prepare a list of the amounts due from each customer. This **schedule of accounts receivable** can be readily prepared utilizing the balances from the individual ledger accounts. If this total does not agree with the balance in the Accounts Receivable control account from the general ledger, then the reason for this difference must be determined. The schedule of accounts receivable for Jones Floor Coverings, as of November 31, 1978, is shown below:

JONES FLOOR COVERINGS
Schedule of Accounts Receivable
November 30, 1978

H. Sherman $118.50
G. White... 417.50
                                                                                                                $536.00

Schedule of accounts payable

Like the accounts receivable, a detailed list of amounts owed each creditor should be prepared at the end of the month. For our example, this **schedule of accounts payable** would be compiled from the file of unpaid invoices. Again, the schedule total should agree with the balance in the Accounts Payable control account from the general ledger. Should these differ, postings to the Accounts Payable control account and invoices in the unpaid file must be rechecked until the error is found. The schedule of accounts payable for Jones Floor Coverings, as of November 30, 1978, is shown below:

JONES FLOOR COVERINGS
Schedule of Accounts Payable
November 30, 1978

Fox Carpet Company... $671.40
Northwest Supply Company 210.00
                                                                                                            $881.40

GLOSSARY

Accounts Payable account   a current liability account that is used by a company to keep a record of amounts due to creditors within one year.

Accounts Receivable account   a current asset account that is used by a company to keep a record of amounts due from its customers.

Accrual basis of accounting   recognizing revenue in the period in which it is earned and recognizing expenses in the period in which they cause revenues to be earned. Thus, many items will be recorded before or after they involve the receipt or payment of cash.

Control account   a general ledger account that is supported by detailed information in a subsidiary ledger.

Cost of goods sold   the cost of the products sold by a company. It is computed as follows: Merchandise Inventory (beginning of period) + Net Purchases − Merchandise Inventory (end of period).

Gross margin (or gross profit)   the difference between the net sales of the period and the cost of goods sold.

Invoice method   one of two basic accounting methods used to maintain supporting records for control accounts. Under the *sales* invoice method, all sales invoices are kept in a file organized by customer name until paid. Under the *purchases* invoice method, all unpaid invoices are kept in an open file according to their due dates. Under both methods, allowances or partial payments are noted on the face of the invoice, but the invoice is retained in the open file until the total amount is paid.

Merchandise inventory   amount of goods on hand and available for sale at a particular point in time. When a periodic inventory system is used, the balance in the Merchandise Inventory account is known only at the beginning and end of the year.

Merchandising firm   a firm that derives most of its revenue from selling goods (merchandise) to customers.

"Negative" account balances   credit balances in accounts that normally have debit balances or debit balances in accounts that normally have credit balances.

Net purchases   total purchases minus purchase returns and allowances. (Later, the definition will be extended to add transportation-in and subtract purchases discounts.)

Net sales   total sales minus sales returns and allowances. (Later, the definition will be extended to subtract sales discounts.)

Periodic inventory system   a system of accounting for merchandise in which the physical amount of inventory is counted only at the close of an accounting period. The general ledger account Merchandise Inventory contains only the beginning balance in inventory, while inventory purchases for the period are recorded in a separate ledger account.

Purchase invoice   a document the buyer receives from the seller and uses to record a purchase transaction. It provides such information as the seller of the merchandise, the date of purchase, the invoice number, the means of shipment, the terms of the purchase transaction, and the type and quantity of goods ordered and shipped.

Purchase Returns and Allowances account   an account on the buyer's books which is credited when the buyer returns unsatisfactory merchandise to the seller or when the buyer receives a discount (allowance) from the regular price because the merchandise was damaged or impaired.

Purchases account   a temporary owner's equity account that is debited for purchases of merchandise during the current period. Sometimes, the transportation charges and insurance costs are also debited to the Purchases account.

Purchases journal   a special journal in which all purchases of merchandise on account are recorded.

Retail sales tax   a tax that is levied on the gross sales price of retail merchandise. Sometimes, the tax is levied on persons furnishing services at retail, in which case gross receipts becomes the taxable basis.

Sales account   a temporary owner's equity account that is credited for merchandise sales during the current period. The balance in the account at a point in time represents the cumulative sales from the beginning of the accounting period.

Sales invoice (ticket)   a document the seller prepares and sends to the buyer. (See purchase invoice above.)

Sales journal   a special journal in which all credit sales are recorded.

Sales Returns and Allowances account   an account that is debited on the seller's books for the sales price of unsatisfactory merchandise returned by the customer or for a reduction in price granted when merchandise is damaged or spoiled.

Sales Tax Payable account   a current liability account that is credited for the amount of sales taxes collected from customers because of state or municipal statutes.

Schedule of accounts payable   a detailed list of the amounts owed to each creditor.

Schedule of accounts receivable   a detailed list of the amounts due from each customer.

Subsidiary ledger   a group of supporting records which shows the details of the balance of a General Ledger control account.

Summary posting   recording the column total from a journal in a ledger account rather than recording the individual amounts in the column.

QUESTIONS AND EXERCISES

1. What is the accrual basis of accounting? Why is it generally used for merchandising enterprises?

2. What is the principal source of revenue in a merchandising enterprise?

3. What five accounts which are not found in a service enterprise are needed in order to determine net earnings for a merchandising firm using accrual accounting?

4. Why is it better to record sales returns and allowances in a separate account rather than to debit them to the Sales account?

5. How does a periodic inventory system operate?

6. What is a purchase invoice? What type of form is imprinted on the face of the invoice?

7. What two accounting methods are used to maintain supporting records? Describe both methods.

8. Use equations to define the following terms:

   a. Net sales.
   b. Net purchases.
   c. Cost of goods sold.
   d. Gross margin.

9. Describe a sales journal.

10. Describe a purchases journal.

PROBLEMS

9-1. Candy Snow has decided to open a children's clothing store called Snow's Clothes for Kids. She maintains the following books of original entry: a purchases journal, a sales journal, and a cash journal. However, this problem relates only to the purchases journal and the cash journal. Ms. Snow completed the following selected transactions during March 1978:

1978
Mar. 1 Invested $5,000 in Snow's Clothes for Kids.
     2 Purchased office equipment for cash, $550.
     3 Purchased merchandise for cash, $150.
     4 Received Invoice No. 402 dated March 1, 1978, from Houston Brothers for merchandise purchased, $250. Terms, net 30.
     5 Received Invoice No. 907 dated March 1 from Flanders, Inc., for merchandise purchased, $200. Terms, net 10.
     8 Purchased shop furniture on account, $300.
     9 Received Invoice No. 850 dated March 8 from Henley Company for merchandise purchased, $175. Terms, net 10.
    10 Returned defective merchandise to Houston Brothers, $100.
    11 Paid Flanders, Inc., in full for Invoice No. 907 dated March 1.
    15 Paid $150 on account for shop furniture purchased on March 8.
    16 Received Invoice No. 190 dated March 9 from Crosby Company for merchandise purchased, $75. Terms, net 20.
    17 Purchased merchandise for cash, $100.
    18 Paid Henley Company the full amount of Invoice No. 850 dated March 8.

Mar. 22   Paid $150 on account for shop furniture purchased on March 8.
24   Received Invoice No. 1002 dated March 20 from Flanders, Inc., for merchandise purchased, $150. Terms, net 10.
26   Returned defective merchandise to Crosby Company, $20.
29   Paid the Crosby Company the full amount owed to them.
30   Paid Houston Brothers the full amount owed to them.
31   Received Invoice No. 515 dated March 29 from Linsey, Inc., for merchandise purchased, $200. Terms, net 30.

Required:

1. Record the foregoing transactions in the appropriate journals. Use the following accounts:

120   Cash
130   Office Equipment
140   Shop Furniture
220   Accounts Payable
320   Candy Snow, Capital
520   Purchases
521   Purchase Returns and Allowances

2. Open the above accounts and post the journal entries for March.
3. Prepare a trial balance for March 31, 1978.

9–2.   P. L. Walker has decided to open a shoe store. During the month of June 1978 the following selected transactions were completed:

June   1   Invested $8,000 in Walker's Shoes.
7   Sold merchandise to John Hollingsworth on account, $80, Invoice No. 101.
8   Sold merchandise to Susan Marsh on account, $50. Invoice No. 102.
11   Sold merchandise to Carol Flint on account, $35. Invoice No. 103.
14   Received $50 from John Hollingsworth in partial payment of his account.
15   Sold merchandise to Carey Kellum on account, $65. Invoice No. 104.
18   Susan Marsh returned merchandise for credit, $25.
21   Carol Flint returned merchandise for credit, $15.
22   Received $30 from John Hollingsworth in payment of his account.
23   Received $25 from Susan Marsh in payment of her account.
24   A customer returned merchandise that had been purchased for cash. He received a cash refund of $20.
28   Sold merchandise to Brenda Sanders on account, $75. Invoice No. 105.
29   Received $20 from Carol Flint in payment of her account.
30   Cash sales for June, $1,500.

Required:

1. Record the above transactions in the appropriate journals. (Assume that Walker maintains a sales journal and a cash journal.) Use the following accounts:

　　　101　Cash
　　　106　Accounts Receivable
　　　301　P. L. Walker, Capital
　　　401　Sales
　　　406　Sales Returns and Allowances

2. Open the above accounts and post the journal entries for June.
3. Prepare a trial balance for June 30, 1978.

9–3. S. G. Coleman has decided to open a furniture store. Coleman's books of original entry include a purchases journal, a sales journal, and a cash journal. During the month of February 1978, Coleman completed the following transactions:

Feb. 2　Invested $12,000 in Coleman's Furniture Store.
　　3　Received Invoice No. 818 dated January 27 from Haven Brothers for merchandise purchased, $2,000. Terms, net 30.
　　4　Paid rent expense for February, $250.
　　5　Purchased office equipment for cash, $550.
　　6　Received Invoice No. 601 dated January 30 from Maddox and Sons, $750. Terms, net 20.
　　9　Sold merchandise to Michael Cook on account, $250. Sales Invoice No. 10.
　　10　Returned defective merchandise to Haven Brothers, $500.
　　11　Received Invoice No. 690 dated February 7 from Joplin Company, $1,000. Terms, net 10.
　　12　Sold merchandise to Mary Myers on account, $150. Sales Invoice No. 11.
　　13　Sold merchandise to Bruce Cooper on account, $50. Sales Invoice No. 12.
　　16　Paid $50 to the local newspaper for advertising.
　　17　Michael Cook paid $150 on his account.
　　18　Mary Myers returned a defective chair for credit, $75.
　　19　Sold merchandise to Bill Groover on account, $200. Sales Invoice No. 13.
　　20　Paid Joplin Company in full for Invoice No. 690 dated February 7.
　　23　Michael Cook paid $100 on his account.
　　24　Mary Myers paid her account in full, $75.
　　25　Received Invoice No. 109 dated February 20 from Gresham's Store for merchandise purchased, $750. Terms, net 20.
　　26　Paid Maddox & Sons in full for Invoice No. 601 dated January 30.
　　27　Cash sales for February, $700.

Required:

1. Record the above transactions in the appropriate journals.
2. Open the following accounts and post the journal entries for February:

　　　110　Cash
　　　120　Accounts Receivable
　　　130　Office Equipment

210   Accounts Payable
310   S. G. Coleman, Capital
410   Sales
415   Sales Returns and Allowances
510   Purchases
515   Purchase Returns and Allowances
520   Rent Expense
530   Advertising Expense

3.   Prepare a trial balance for February 28, 1978.

9–4.   Martha Stone operates a clothing store called Stone's. Three books of original entry are kept — a sales journal, a purchases journal, and a cash journal. This problem involves only the sales journal. All sales are subject to a 3 percent retail sales tax which is computed on each and every invoice. During the first half of December 1978 Ms. Stone completed the following selected transactions:

Dec.   1   Sold merchandise to Joan Wilson on account, $55, plus sales tax $1.65. Invoice No. 803.

2   Sold merchandise to Albert Boggs on account, $15, plus sales tax $0.45. Invoice No. 804.

3   Sold merchandise to Lewis Tummins on account, $80, plus sales tax $2.40. Invoice No. 805.

4   Sold merchandise to Beverly Scoggins on account, $33, plus sales tax $0.99. Invoice No. 806.

6   Sold merchandise to Charlotte Buchanan on account, $27, plus sales tax $0.81. Invoice No. 807.

7   Sold merchandise to Linda Merley on account, $14, plus sales tax $0.42. Invoice No. 808.

8   Sold merchandise to Russ Hilley on account, $39, plus sales tax $1.17. Invoice No. 809.

9   Sold merchandise to Dan Kelly on account, $48, plus sales tax $1.44. Invoice No. 810.

10   Sold merchandise to Linda Merley on account, $28, plus sales tax $0.84. Invoice No. 811.

11   Sold merchandise to Albert Boggs on account, $26, plus sales tax $0.78. Invoice No. 812.

13   Sold merchandise to Beverly Scoggins on account, $16, plus sales tax $0.48. Invoice No. 813.

14   Sold merchandise to Joan Wilson on account, $18, plus sales tax $0.54. Invoice No. 814.

15   Sold merchandise to Charlotte Buchanan on account, $26 plus sales tax $0.78. Invoice No. 815.

Required:

1.   Open the following general ledger accounts and record the December 1, 1978, balances:

Account No.	Account Title	Balance 12/1/78
116	Accounts receivable	$ 600
216	Sales tax payable	56
403	Sales...	9,800

2. Open a subsidiary ledger for individual accounts receivable. The accounts had the following balances on December 1, 1978:

Albert Boggs...........................	$ 25
Charlotte Buchanan.................	80
Russ Hilley.............................	105
Dan Kelly..............................	65
Linda Merley..........................	96
Beverly Scoggins.....................	82
Lewis Tummins.......................	76
Joan Wilson............................	71

3. Record the transactions in the sales journal and post to the individual customer's accounts.
4. Foot the sales journal and post the totals to the general ledger accounts.
5. Prepare a schedule of accounts receivable as of December 15, 1978.

9–5.

THE INDIA STORE
Trial Balance
December 31, 1978

Account No.	Account Title	Debit	Credit
101	Cash..	$ 5,000	
111	Accounts receivable	1,500	
121	Merchandise inventory, 1/1/78	5,000	
131	Office supplies.............................	500	
141	Office equipment..........................	3,000	
151	Accum. depreciation, office equip. ...		$ 600
201	Accounts payable..........................		800
301	Thota Hamsa, capital....................		20,000
311	Thota Hamsa, drawing...................	12,000	
401	Sales..		52,600
411	Sales returns and allowances...........	200	
501	Purchases	35,000	
511	Purchase returns and allowances		300
521	Salaries expense	9,000	
531	Rent expense	1,800	
541	Insurance expense.........................	600	
551	Advertising expense	200	
561	Utilities expense	500	
		$74,300	$74,300

Merchandise inventory, 12/31/78, is $4,000.

Required:

Compute (1) cost of goods sold and (2) gross margin on sales.

6. Tony Partridge has decided to open a retail store called The Partridge Shop. He keeps a sales journal, a purchases journal, a cash receipts journal, a cash disbursements journal, and a general journal as books of original entry. During the month of August, the following transactions were completed:

1978

Aug. 2   Invested $10,000 in The Partridge Shop.

3   Received Invoice No. 182 dated July 30 from Sportsco for merchandise purchased, $300. Terms are ten days net.

4   Paid rent for August with Check No. 101, $250.

5   Received Invoice No. 102 dated August 2 from Corbin Brothers for merchandise purchased, $450. Terms, net 10.

6   Purchased office equipment from Drake Equipment Company on account, $500.

7   Paid Sportsco the full amount of Invoice No. 182, $300. Check No. 102.

9   Sold merchandise to Kathy Mason on account, $75. Sales Invoice No. 10.

10   Sold merchandise to Della Swan on account, $55. Sales Invoice No. 11.

11   Received Invoice No. 95 dated August 7 from Ramsey Company for merchandise purchased, $400. Terms, net 10.

12   Paid Corbin Brothers the full amount of Invoice No. 102, $450. Check No. 103.

13   Sold merchandise to Ronnie Akins on account, $125. Sales Invoice No. 12.

14   Received Invoice No. 316 dated August 11 from Sportsco for merchandise purchased, $200. Terms, net 20.

14   Withdrew $150 for personal use. Check No. 104.

16   Allowed a credit of $35 to Ronnie Akins for merchandise returned.

16   Sold merchandise to Ravi Jain on account, $80. Sales Invoice No. 13.

17   Kathy Mason paid her account in full, $75.

17   Paid Ramsey Company the full amount of Invoice No. 95, $400. Check No. 105.

18   Returned unacceptable merchandise to Sportsco, $75.

19   Sold merchandise to Glenn Hawkins on account, $65. Sales Invoice No. 14.

19   Paid $30 for newspaper advertising. Check No. 106.

20   Received Invoice No. 168 dated August 17 from Corbin Brothers for merchandise purchased, $175. Terms, net 20.

21   Paid Drake Equipment Company for part of the office equipment purchased on the 6th, $250. Check No. 107.

23   Della Swan paid her account in full, $55.

Aug. 23 Sold merchandise to Kathy Mason on account, $95. Sales Invoice No. 15.

24 Ronnie Akins paid his account in full, $90.

24 Paid Sportsco the full amount owed on Invoice No. 316, $125. Check No. 108.

25 Purchased office supplies on account from Ace Supply Company, $50.

26 Kathy Mason returned defective merchandise that cost $55.

27 Paid Drake Equipment Company $250 for office equipment purchased on the sixth. Check No. 109.

28 Sold merchandise to Ronnie Akins on account, $50. Sales Invoice No. 16.

28 Received Invoice No. 155 dated August 26 from Ramsey Company, $200. Terms, net 10.

30 Withdrew $150 for personal use. Check No. 110.

31 Returned defective merchandise to Ramsey Company, $80.

31 Cash sales for August, $500.

Required:

1. Using the following accounts and account numbers, record each of the above transactions in the appropriate journal:

Cash.. 101
Accounts receivable 111
Office equipment.. 121
Accounts payable 201
Tony Partridge, capital 301
Tony Partridge, drawing.. 311
Sales.. 401
Sales returns and allowances.. 411
Purchases... 501
Purchase returns and allowances 511
Rent expense 521
Advertising expense 531
Office supplies expense.. 541

2. Open a general ledger that contains the foregoing accounts and open subsidiary ledgers for individual accounts receivable and accounts payable.

3. Post the transactions that occurred during August.

4. Prepare a trial balance for August 31, 1978.

5. Prepare a schedule of accounts receivable and a schedule of accounts payable as of August 31, 1978.

Merchandising enterprise— end-of-period procedures
Learning objectives

The material in Chapter 9 concerned the daily accounting procedures of a merchandising firm. The contents in this chapter are designed to provide an understanding of the end-of-period procedures used by a merchandiser. The items below are introduced in the following pages:

1. Importance of taking a periodic trial balance as well as taking a trial balance before the adjusting entries and financial statement worksheets are prepared.

2. Illustration and description of typical adjusting entries and the recording of such entries in a worksheet.

3. Presentation of the earnings statement and the statement of financial position for the merchandising firm.

4. Journalizing and posting the adjusting and closing entries.

5. The advantages of preparing a post-closing trial balance.

10 Merchandising enterprise— end-of-period procedures

The preceding chapter introduced a number of new concepts that were necessary to properly account for the activities of a merchandising enterprise. The last part of the chapter contained an example which illustrated the accumulation of accounting data for the month of November for Jones Floor Covering.

The example included selected transactions for the month of November. These selected transactions dealt with the purchase and sale of merchandise, the return of merchandise, cash collections from customers, and cash payments to vendors (or suppliers). Other transactions such as the payment of salaries and the purchase of office supplies were not shown. These transactions would be recorded in the same manner as they were for the service enterprise.

At the end of the accounting period, a merchandising firm will follow procedures which are very similar to those followed in a service enterprise. The example from Chapter 9 recorded transactions for the month of November. Assume that November 30 is the end of the accounting period for Jones Floor Covering. Thus, its accounting year would run from December 1 to November 30. The practice of ending an accounting period at some date other than December 31 is quite common. The accounting year is called the **fiscal year** if it does not coincide with the calendar year.

The data accumulated in the Jones Floor Covering example will be used in this chapter as the basis for illustrating end-of-period procedures for a merchandising enterprise. A number of procedures will be very similar to those of a service firm. Illustrations of some of the adjustments explained in Chapter 8 will be presented. We will also deal with new accounts such as Merchandise Inventory, Sales, Sales Returns and Allowances, Purchases, and Purchase Returns and Allowances. The financial statements will be more carefully analyzed, and we will look at a number of key relationships within the financial statements.

THE TRIAL BALANCE

A trial balance is usually taken at the end of each month. This is because it is desirable to isolate as quickly as possible any errors that may have occurred.

At the end of each accounting period, the regular end of the month trial balance is entered on the worksheet from which financial statements will evolve.

The financial data presented in Chapter 9 from Jones Floor Covering are compiled only from selected transactions.

A trial balance could not be prepared from this data alone.

In order to complete our example, the omitted transactions have been summarized; and the trial balance presented in Illustration 10-1 consists

Illustration 10-1

JONES FLOOR COVERING
Trial Balance
November 30, 1978

Account Title	Debit	Credit
Cash	$ 1,340.00	
Accounts receivable	536.00	
Allowance for doubtful accounts		$ 50.00
Merchandise inventory	7,220.00	
Unexpired insurance	240.00	
Prepaid rent	1,800.00	
Office equipment	6,000.00	
Accumulated depreciation—office equipment		1,500.00
Accounts payable		881.40
Notes payable		1,000.00
Joe Jones—capital		15,951.88
Joe Jones—drawing	5,217.50	
Sales		30,888.89
Sales returns and allowances	326.60	
Purchases	18,096.16	
Purchase returns and allowances		434.09
Advertising expense	600.00	
Delivery expense	900.00	
Rent expense	1,400.00	
Repairs and maintenance expense	255.00	
Salaries expense	6,500.00	
Utilities expense	275.00	
	$50,706.26	$50,706.26

of the data in Chapter 9 and the necessary additional accounting information.

THE WORKSHEET

The worksheet in a merchandising enterprise performs the same function that it does in a service enterprise. It facilitates the preparation of financial statements and provides a check against errors before the formal financial statements are prepared.

Worksheets have already been discussed in Chapter 3 and Chapter 8. Therefore, it will be assumed that the student has an understanding of the operation of a worksheet. This section will emphasize the aspects of the worksheet which are unique to a merchandising firm and will illustrate some common adjustments explained in Chapter 8.

The first step in completing a worksheet is to enter in the first pair of debit and credit columns the trial balance for the end of the period. The trial balance for Jones Floor Covering was taken directly from the ledger account balances at the end of the period and is referred to as the unadjusted trial balance. Thus, the trial balance shown in Illustration 10–1 is transferred to the worksheet in Illustration 10–2.

The second step is to make the necessary adjustments in the pair of columns designated for adjustments. The information necessary for making the adjustments is found in various company records. For example, the information necessary to adjust the asset, unexpired insurance, is found in the insurance policy itself. The adjustment for depreciation on office equipment is based upon previously determined information: the cost of equipment, the expected useful life, and the salvage value. Each adjustment is based on information which the firm would already have.

Below is a list of six adjustments that are common in a merchandising firm. All the necessary information has been given to make each of the adjustments. If you were an accountant employed by a merchandising firm, you would have to secure this information before you could make the adjustments.

a. A physical count of the merchandise inventory at the end of the period indicates that the ending balance is $9,640.

b. Past experience has shown that 0.5 percent of net sales will be uncollectible.

c. On November 1, 1978, the firm purchased a 12-month fire insurance policy for $240 covering a period of one year from that date.

d. On October 1, 1978, the firm paid $1,800 for the next 12 months' rent. It was recorded in the Prepaid Rent account.

e. The Office Equipment was purchased three years ago for a cost of

Illustration 10-2

Jones Floor Covering
Worksheet
For the Year Ended November 30, 1978

Account Title	Trial Balance		Adjustments	
	Debit	Credit	Debit	Credit
Cash	1340 00			
Accounts receivable	536 00			
Allowance for doubtful accounts		50 00		(b) 152 81
Merchandise inventory	7220 00		(a)(2) 9640 00	(a)(1) 7220 00
Unexpired insurance	240 00			(c) 20 00
Prepaid rent	1800 00			(d) 300 00
Office equipment	6000 00			
Accumulated depreciation— Office equipment		1500 00		(e) 500 00
Accounts payable		881 40		
Notes payable		1000 00		
Joe Jones—capital		15951 88		
Joe Jones—drawing	5217 50			
Sales		30888 89		
Sales returns & allowances	326 60			
Purchases	18096 16			(a)(3) 18096 16
Purchase returns & allowances		434 09	(a)(3) 434 09	
Advertising expense	600 00			
Delivery expense	900 00			
Rent expense	1400 00		(d) 300 00	
Repairs & maintenance expense	255 00			
Salaries expense	6500 00		(f) 800 00	
Utilities expense	275 00			
	50706 26	50706 26		
Cost of goods sold			(a)(1) 7220 00 (a)(3) 17662 07	(a)(2) 9640 00
Doubtful accounts expense			(b) 152 81	
Insurance expense			(c) 20 00	
Depreciation expense— office equipment			(e) 500 00	
Salaries payable				(f) 800 00
			36728 97	36728 97
Net Earnings				

Adjusted Trial Balance		Earnings Statement		Financial Position	
Debit	Credit	Debit	Credit	Debit	Credit
1340 00				1340 00	
536 00				536 00	
	202 81				202 81
9640 00				9640 00	
220 00				220 00	
1500 00				1500 00	
6000 00				6000 00	
	2000 00				2000 00
	881 40				881 40
	1000 00				1000 00
	15951 88				15951 88
5217 50				5217 50	
	30888 89		30888 89		
326 60		326 60			
600 00		600 00			
900 00		900 00			
1700 00		1700 00			
255 00		255 00			
7300 00		7300 00			
275 00		275 00			
15242 07		15242 07			
152 81		152 81			
20 00		20 00			
500 00		500 00			
	800 00				800 00
51724 98	51724 98	27271 48	30888 89		
		3617 41			3617 41
		30888 89	30888 89	24453 50	24453 50

$6,000. The equipment has an estimated useful life of 12 years with no salvage value anticipated.

f. At the end of the period, salaries of $800 have been earned but will not be paid until December 15, 1978.

The above adjustments appear on the worksheet shown in Illustration 10–2. The adjustments are "keyed" with a small letter to identify which debit and credit made up each adjustment. This system can be very helpful if there are a large number of adjustments and an error is made. A quick check of each set of entries will usually locate the error.

Each adjustment will be briefly explained. Most of the adjustments have been explained in previous chapters.

Entry (a)

The first adjustment is unique to merchandising firms. It deals with the product cost portion of the earnings statement. This adjustment is necessary to calculate the cost of goods sold for a merchandising firm that uses a periodic inventory. A quick reference to Chapter 9 will refresh your memory on cost of goods sold. One starts with the beginning inventory, adds the purchases, subtracts the purchase returns and allowances, and subtracts the ending inventory. The resulting figure is the cost of goods sold. This is accomplished in the Adjustments columns of the worksheet as follows:

1. Debit Cost of Goods Sold and credit Merchandise Inventory for the dollar amount of the beginning inventory.
2. Debit Merchandise Inventory and credit Cost of Goods Sold for the dollar amount of the *ending* inventory.
3. Debit Purchase Returns and Allowances for the balance in the Purchase Returns and Allowances account, credit Purchases for the balance in the Purchases account, and debit Cost of Goods Sold for the difference between the balance in the Purchases account and the balance in the Purchase Returns and Allowances account.

The first entry reduces the Merchandise Inventory account balance to zero and adds the original balance to the Cost of Goods Sold account. This is appropriate because the balance in the Merchandise Inventory account is correct only at the beginning of the period. No running record is kept of the account's balance during the period if a periodic inventory system is used. Also, we recall that the starting point in calculating Cost of Goods Sold is the beginning inventory of the period. Thus, the beginning inventory balance is added to the Cost of Goods Sold account with a debit.

The second entry creates the correct ending balance in the inventory account by a debit to the account for the ending balance which has just been calculated. Since the first entry left the Merchandise Inventory account with a zero balance, the second entry places the appropriate balance in the account for the end of the period.

The second half of the entry subtracts the ending inventory from Cost of Goods Sold. This is appropriate because the cost of inventory on hand cannot be part of the cost of the merchandise sold. The credit to Cost of Goods Sold has the effect of reducing the account balance.

The third entry closes out Purchases and Purchase Returns and Allowances to the Cost of Goods Sold account. When all the adjustments are completed, the balance in the Cost of Goods Sold account is $15,242.07. The same amount will be calculated in the formal earnings statement using the form shown in the previous chapter. By making these adjusting entries on the worksheet, the cost of goods sold can be determined before the formal financial statements are prepared.

Entry (*b*)

The second adjustment is the adjustment for bad debts or credit losses. Past experience has shown that 0.5 percent of net sales is the dollar amount of bad debts that probably will be incurred on sales revenue earned during the accounting period. The calculation of the appropriate bad debts expense is:

$$(\text{Sales} - \text{Sales Returns and Allowances}) \times 0.005$$

$$(\$30,888.89 - \$326.60) \times 0.005 = \$152.81$$

The entry is a debit to Bad Debts Expense and a credit to Allowance for Doubtful Accounts, which is an accounts receivable contra account. If the purpose of this adjustment or the following four adjustments is not clear, you should refer to the section on adjustments in Chapter 8.

Entries (*c*) and (*d*)

The third and fourth adjustments deal with the expiration of an asset. An asset must have future economic value to the firm. When any part of that value expires, the expired portion should be charged off as a current expense, leaving only the unexpired portion remaining as an asset. In the third adjustment a portion of the fire insurance policy which was purchased on November 1 has expired. The cost of the one month of protection that is gone is charged off with a debit to Insurance Expense and a credit to Unexpired Insurance. The amount to be charged off is $1/12 \times$ $240, which is $20. This reduces the Unexpired Insurance account to its appropriate remaining value, and it matches the expense of the fire insurance protection for the period with the revenue generated in the period.

The next adjustment is very similar in nature. The portion of the rent which has been used up is charged to the Rent Expense account, and the unexpired portion remains an asset recorded in the Prepaid Rent account. The journal entry is a debit to Rent Expense and a credit to Prepaid Rent for $300 (2/12 × $1,800 = $300).

Entry (e)

The fifth adjustment is necessary to spread the cost of the office equipment over its useful life. This apportioned cost is called depreciation expense. The office equipment has a cost of $6,000, a 12-year useful life, and no salvage value. Therefore, calculation of the annual depreciation charge is as follows:

$$\frac{\text{Cost} - \text{Salvage Value}}{\text{Useful Life}} = \frac{\$6,000 - 0}{12} = \$500$$

The entry is a debit to Depreciation Expense − Office Equipment and a credit to Accumulated Depreciation − Office Equipment, a contra asset account. The method of calculating depreciation in this case is the *straight-line method* since each annual charge is the same. Other methods will be discussed in a future chapter.

Entry (f)

The last adjustment is for the accrual of salaries earned but unpaid at the end of the period. A firm may have more than one accrued expense at the end of the period. In this case, however, salaries is the only accrued expense. The entry is a debit for $800 to Salaries Expense and a credit of the same amount to Salaries Payable, a liability account. Since the salaries have been accrued, it is common to call this account Accrued Salaries Payable rather than Salaries Payable.

The above adjustments are presented here as an example of some very common adjustments. A firm may well have many more adjustments. Regardless of the number, they should be handled in the same general manner as presented in the above examples.

After the adjustments have been entered on the worksheet, the two Adjustment columns should be footed to prove the equality of the debits and credits. If an error has been made, it is much better to identify it now than to have to search for it later. Our Adjustment columns balance at $36,728.97 in debits and credits.

Next, the trial balance plus the effects of the adjustments are entered in the Adjusted Trial Balance columns. Once again our primary objective with the adjusted trial balance is to locate any errors that might have been made in adjusting the unadjusted trial balance. In the example, the Adjusted Trial Balance columns balance at $51,724.00.

The asset, liability, permanent owner's equity, and owner's drawing account balances are then transferred to the Financial Position columns. All the revenue and expense accounts are placed in the Earnings Statement columns. These columns will not balance unless no net earnings or net loss resulted during the period. If the credit column is greater than the debit column, net earnings have occurred. A net debit balance would indicate a net loss. In our example, the firm had net earnings of $3,617.41.

This amount is then transferred to the credit column of the statement of financial position, as explained in Chapter 3. The two Financial Position columns balance at $24,453.50. If the two had not balanced, a search would be made to locate the apparent error. After net earnings are added to the debit column of the earnings statement, the two Earnings Statement columns will also balance. In our example, they balance at $30,888.89.

THE FINANCIAL STATEMENTS

Once the worksheet has been completed, the financial statements can easily be prepared. These financial statements are sometimes referred to as **classified financial statements.** The term classified is used because financial statements are often prepared so that the accounts are grouped into classifications in order to present more meaningful information. While the exact classifications in financial statements may vary somewhat, the major classifications are rather standard.

The earnings statement

The earnings statement of a merchandising firm has three basic classifications: (1) the revenue section showing net sales, (2) the product cost section showing the cost of goods sold, and (3) the operating expense section. The revenue section consists of the Sales account, which is usually reduced by a Sales Returns and Allowances account. Sometimes a firm will grant a cash discount if payment is received within a specified period of time. This discount is usually recorded in the Sales Discount account. The Sales Returns and Allowances and Sales Discounts accounts are subtracted from the Sales account to calculate net sales.

The cost of goods sold section is used to show the product cost of goods sold during the period. This is what the firm had to pay for the merchandise that is sold during the period. The cost of goods sold section

Illustration 10–3

JONES FLOOR COVERING
Earnings Statement
For the Year Ended November 30, 1978

Revenue:

Sales		$30,888.89	
Less: Sales returns and allowances		326.60	
Net sales			$30,562.29

Cost of goods sold:

Merchandise inventory, December 1, 1977		$ 7,220.00	
Purchases	$18,096.16		
Less: Purchase returns and allowances	434.09		
Net purchases		17,662.07	
Goods available for sale		$24,882.07	
Merchandise inventory, November 30, 1978		9,640.00	
Cost of goods sold			15,242.07
Gross margin from sales			$15,320.22

Operating expenses:

Advertising expense	$ 600.00	
Bad debts expense	152.81	
Delivery expense	900.00	
Depreciation expense—office equipment	500.00	
Insurance expense	20.00	
Rent expense	1,700.00	
Repairs and maintenance expense	255.00	
Salaries expense	7,300.00	
Utilities expense	275.00	
Total Operating Expense		$11,702.81
Net Earnings		$ 3,617.41

which appears in the example earnings statement in Illustration 10–3 is for a firm that uses the periodic inventory technique. The cost of goods sold is subtracted from the net sales to compute gross margin on sales, sometimes called gross profit.

The operating expenses must be subtracted from gross margin before the net earnings or net loss can be determined. Thus, a merchandising firm must sell its merchandise for a price which will cover both the product cost and the operating costs if it is to make a profit. Operating expenses, also known as selling and administrative expenses, may be broken into a number of different categories.

Statement of financial position

We already know that the statement of financial position consists of assets, liabilities, and owner's equity. Nonetheless, it is often beneficial to divide these broad classifications more specifically.

The first classification in the asset section is **current assets.** Common examples of current assets are cash, accounts receivable, merchandise inventory, and **prepaid expenses.** An asset is considered to be a current asset if it is expected to expire or to be converted into cash within one year or one operating cycle of a business, whichever is longer. An operating cycle is the length of time required before cash spent on merchandise purchases is returned to the company by its customers. Current assets are considered to be very important to creditors and others because they are the most liquid of the firm's assets. That is, they can be converted to cash easier than other types of assets. Cash, of course, is the most liquid asset.

The next classification of assets is usually called **long-term investments.** This category consists of securities which have been purchased with the intention of holding them for a relatively long period of time. If securities are intended to be held for only a short period of time, they should be classified as current assets. Note that Jones Floor Covering, Illustration 10–4, has no long-term investments. The nature and size of the firm often

Illustration 10–4

JONES FLOOR COVERING
Statement of Financial Position
November 30, 1978

Assets

Current Assets:			
Cash		$1,340.00	
Accounts receivable	$536.00		
Less: Allowance for doubtful accounts	202.81	333.19	
Merchandise inventory		9,640.00	
Unexpired insurance		220.00	
Prepaid rent		1,500.00	
Total Current Assets			$13,033.19
Property, plant, and equipment:			
Office equipment		$6,000.00	
Less: Accumulated depreciation—office equipment		2,000.00	
Total Property, Plant, and Equipment			4,000.00
Total Assets			$17,033.19

Liabilities

Current Liabilities:		
Accounts payable	$ 881.40	
Salaries payable	800.00	
Notes payable	1,000.00	
Total Current Liabilities		$ 2,681.40

Owner's Equity

Joe Jones, Capital—November 30, 1978	14,351.79
Total Liabilities and Owner's Equity	$17,033.19

dictate the detail of account classification used for the financial statements.

The **plant asset** section of the statement of financial position includes such items as equipment, building, and land. These items are characterized by a relatively long useful life, and they are used in the normal operation of the firm instead of being held for their resale value. All the items except land are subject to depreciation. Jones Floor Covering has only one type of plant asset—office equipment. Note that the **net book value** of the asset is the difference between the cost of the asset and the accumulated depreciation at that point in time. The net book amount of an asset is also known as the **carrying value.**

Intangible assets are usually presented below the plant asset classification. These assets have no physical form associated with them. Patents,

Illustration 10–5

JONES FLOOR COVERING Statement of Owner's Equity For the Year Ended November 30, 1978		
Joe Jones, capital—December 1, 1977		$15,951.88
Net earnings	$3,617.41	
Less: Withdrawals	5,217.50	(1,600.09)
Joe Jones, Capital—November 30, 1978................................		$14,351.79

copyrights, and trademarks are common examples of intangible assets. Again, Jones Floor Covering has no assets which would be classified as intangible assets.

The first classification in the liabilities section is **current liabilities.** These are liabilities which must be paid within one operating cycle or one year, whichever is longer. Accounts payable, accrued taxes payable, **accrued wages payable,** and short-term notes payable are current liabilities.

A liability which is not due within one operating cycle is a **long-term liability.** For example, mortgages payable and long-term notes payable are long-term liabilities.

Jones Floor Covering is a single proprietorship. Thus, the owner's equity section of the statement of financial position reflects only the proprietor's capital account. As such, the section starts with the beginning balance, adds the net earnings, subtracts the owner's withdrawals, and arrives at the ending account balance. A formal statement of owner's equity is presented in Illustration 10–5. Additional discussion of the owner's equity section will be postponed until later chapters.

JOURNALIZING ADJUSTING AND CLOSING ENTRIES

Once the formal financial statements are prepared, the adjusting entries should be journalized and posted. Up until this time, the adjustments have only appeared on the worksheet. They have not been journalized. The journal entries will be the same as the worksheet entries made in the Adjustments column of the worksheet. After the adjusting entries are journalized, the journal will be posted to the ledger accounts. The journal entries are shown in Illustration 10–6.

The closing entries are made after the adjusting entries have been posted. The necessary information is available by referring to the worksheet. All of the revenue and expense accounts in the Earnings Statement

Illustration 10–6

		GENERAL JOURNAL			Page 1
Date		Accounts and Explanation	P.R.	Debit	Credit
1978		Adjusting Entries			
Nov.	30	Cost of Goods Sold	215	7,220.00	
		Merchandise Inventory	20		7,220.00
		Merchandise Inventory	20	9,640.00	
		Cost of Goods Sold	215		9,640.00
		Purchase Returns and Allowances	211	434.09	
		Cost of Goods Sold	215	17,662.07	
		Purchases	210		18,096.16
		To record adjusting entry (a).			
	30	Bad Debts Expense	220	152.81	
		Allowance for Doubtful Accounts	16		152.81
		To record adjusting entry (b).			
	30	Insurance Expense	225	20.00	
		Unexpired Insurance	25		20.00
		To record adjusting entry (c).			
	30	Rent Expense	245	300.00	
		Prepaid Rent	30		300.00
		To record adjusting entry (d).			
	30	Depreciation Expense—Office Equipment	230	500.00	
		Accumulated Depreciation—Office Equipment	41		500.00
		To record adjusting entry (e).			
	30	Salaries Expense	225	800.00	
		Salaries Payable	55		800.00
		To record adjusting entry (f).			

columns will be closed. Also, the drawing account which appears in the debit column of the Financial Position column will be closed. After the closing entries are journalized and posted, the post-closing trial balance will be prepared to insure that the records are ready for recording trans-

Illustration 10-7

GENERAL JOURNAL					Page 2
Date,		Accounts and Explanation	P.R.	Debit	Credit
1978		Closing Entries			
Nov.	30	Sales	110	30,888.89	
		Sales Returns and Allowances	111		326.60
		Expense and Revenue Summary	290		30,562.29
		To close revenue accounts to Expense and Revenue Summary.			
	30	Expense and Revenue Summary	290	26,944.88	
		Bad Debts Expense	220		152.81
		Insurance Expense	225		20.00
		Depreciation Expense	230		500.00
		Advertising Expense	235		600.00
		Delivery Expense	240		900.00
		Rent Expense	245		1,700.00
		Repairs and Maintenance Expense	250		255.00
		Salaries Expense	255		7,300.00
		Utilities Expense	260		275.00
		Cost of Goods Sold	215		15,242.07
		To close expense accounts to Expense and Revenue Summary.			
	30	Expense and Revenue Summary	290	3,617.41	
		Joe Jones Capital	80		3,617.41
		To close Expense and Revenue Summary to Joe Jones Capital.			
	30	Joe Jones Capital	80	5,217.50	
		Joe Jones Drawing	90		5,217.50
		To close drawing to Joe Jones Capital.			

actions in the next accounting period. (The word *post* means *after*. Thus, we prepare an "after-closing entries" trial balance.) The closing journal entries are shown in Illustration 10-7. Following these entries, the ledger accounts are reproduced (Illustration 10-8) to further illustrate the adjusting and closing process. The post-closing trial balance is not shown. The student should, however, assure himself or herself of the equality of debits and credits of the account balances.

Illustration 10–8

Cash — Account No. 10

Date		Explanation	P.R.	Debit	Credit	Balance
1978 Nov.	30	Balance	✓			1,340.00

Accounts Receivable — Account No. 15

Date		Explanation	P.R.	Debit	Credit	Balance
1978 Nov.	30	Balance	✓			536.00

Allowance for Doubtful Accounts — Account No. 16

Date		Explanation	P.R.	Debit	Credit	Balance
1978 Nov.	30	Balance	✓			50.00
	30	Adjusting entry	GJ1		152.81	202.81

Merchandise Inventory — Account No. 20

Date		Explanation	P.R.	Debit	Credit	Balance
1978 Nov.	30	Balance	✓			7,220.00
	30	Adjusting entry	GJ1		7,220.00	-0-
	30	Adjusting entry	GJ1	9,640.00		9,640.00

Unexpired Insurance — Account No. 25

Date		Explanation	P.R.	Debit	Credit	Balance
1978 Nov.	30	Balance	✓			240.00
	30	Adjusting entry	GJ1		20.00	220.00

Prepaid Rent — Account No. 30

Date		Explanation	P.R.	Debit	Credit	Balance
1978 Nov.	30	Balance	✓			1,800.00
	30	Adjusting entry	GJ1		300.00	1,500.00

Illustration 10–8 (*continued*)

Office Equipment   Account No. 40

Date		Explanation	P.R.	Debit	Credit	Balance
1978 Nov.	30	Balance	✔			6,000.00

Accumulated Depreciation— Office Equipment   Account No. 41

Date		Explanation	P.R.	Debit	Credit	Balance
1978 Nov.	30	Balance	✔			1,500.00
	30	Adjusting entry	GJ1		500.00	2,000.00

Accounts Payable   Account No. 50

Date		Explanation	P.R.	Debit	Credit	Balance
1978 Nov.	30	Balance	✔			881.40

Salaries Payable   Account No. 55

Date		Explanation	P.R.	Debit	Credit	Balance
1978 Nov.	30	Adjusting entry	GJ1		800.00	800.00

Notes Payable   Account No. 60

Date		Explanation	P.R.	Debit	Credit	Balance
1978 Nov.	30	Balance	✔			1,000.00

Joe Jones—Capital   Account No. 80

Date		Explanation	P.R.	Debit	Credit	Balance
1978 Nov.	30	Balance	✔			15,951.88
	30	Closing entry	GJ2		3,617.41	19,569.29
	30	Closing entry	GJ2	5,217.50		14,351.79

Joe Jones—Drawing   Account No. 90

Date		Explanation	P.R.	Debit	Credit	Balance
1978 Nov.	30	Balance	✔			5,217.50
	30	Closing entry	GJ2		5,217.50	-0-

Illustration 10–8 (*continued*)

Sales
Account No. 110

Date		Explanation	P.R.	Debit	Credit	Balance
1978 Nov.	30	Balance	✓			30,888.89
	30	Closing entry	GJ2	30,888.89		-0-

Sales Returns and Allowances
Account No. 11

Date		Explanation	P.R.	Debit	Credit	Balance
1978 Nov.	30	Balance	✓			326.60
	30	Closing entry	GJ2		326.60	-0-

Purchases
Account No. 210

Date		Explanation	P.R.	Debit	Credit	Balance
1978 Nov.	30	Balance	✓			18,096.16
	30	Adjusting entry	GJ1		18,096.16	-0-

Purchase Returns and Allowances
Account No. 211

Date		Explanation	P.R.	Debit	Credit	Balance
1978 Nov.	30	Balance	✓			434.09
		Adjusting entry	GJ1	434.09		

Cost of Goods Sold
Account No. 215

Date		Explanation	P.R.	Debit	Credit	Balance
1978 Nov.	30	Adjusting entry	GJ1	7,220.00		7,220.00
	30	Adjusting entry	GJ1		9,640.00	(2,420.00)
	30	Adjusting entry	GJ1	17,662.07		15,242.07
	30	Closing entry	GJ2		15,242.07	-0-

Bad Debts Expense
Account No. 220

Date		Explanation	P.R.	Debit	Credit	Balance
1978 Nov.	30	Adjusting entry	GJ1	152.81		152.81
	30	Closing entry	GJ2		152.81	-0-

Illustration 10–8 (*continued*)

Insurance Expense   Account No. 225

Date		Explanation	P.R.	Debit	Credit	Balance
1978 Nov.	30	Adjusting entry	GJ1	20.00		20.00
	30	Closing entry	GJ2		20.00	-0-

Depreciation Expense   Account No. 230

Date		Explanation	P.R.	Debit	Credit	Balance
1978 Nov.	30	Adjusting entry	GJ1	500.00		500.00
	30	Closing entry	GJ2		500.00	-0-

Advertising Expense   Account No. 235

Date		Explanation	P.R.	Debit	Credit	Balance
1978 Nov.	30	Balance				600.00
	30	Closing entry	GJ2		600.00	-0-

Delivery Expense   Account No. 240

Date		Explanation	P.R.	Debit	Credit	Balance
1978 Nov.	30	Balance	✔			900.00
	30	Closing entry	GJ2		900.00	-0-

Rent Expense   Account No. 245

Date		Explanation	P.R.	Debit	Credit	Balance
1978 Nov.	30	Balance	✔			1,400.00
	30	Adjusting entry	GJ1	300.00		1,700.00
	30	Closing entry	GJ2		1,700.00	-0-

Repair and Maintenance Expense   Account No. 250

Date		Explanation	P.R.	Debit	Credit	Balance
1978 Nov.	30	Balance	✔			255.00
	30	Closing entry	GJ2		255.00	-0-

Illustration 10–8 (*concluded*)

Salaries Expense   Account No. 255

Date		Explanation	P.R.	Debit	Credit	Balance
1978						
Nov.	30	Balance	✓			6,500.00
	30	Adjusting entry	GJ1	800.00		7,300.00
	30	Closing entry	GJ2		7,300.00	-0-

Utilities Expense   Account No. 260

Date		Explanation	P.R.	Debit	Credit	Balance
1978						
Nov.	30	Balance	✓			275.00
	30	Closing entry	GJ2		275.00	-0-

Expense and Revenue Summary   Account No. 290

Date		Explanation	P.R.	Debit	Credit	Balance
1978						
Nov.	30	Closing entry	GJ2		30,562.29	30,562.29
	30	Closing entry	GJ2	26,944.88		3,617.41
	30	Closing entry	GJ2	3,617.41		-0-

GLOSSARY

Accrued liability   an obligation which exists at the end of an accounting period but is not recorded until adjusting entries are made. An example is accrued salaries payable.

Carrying value   cost less accumulated depreciation of a depreciable asset.

Classified financial statements   financial statements which group the accounts into classifications in order to present more meaningful information. The basic classifications on a merchandising firm's earnings statement are revenue, cost of goods sold, and operating expenses. A statement of financial position might contain the following classifications: current assets, long-term investments, plant assets, intangible assets, current liabilities, long-term liabilities, and owners' equity.

Current assets   assets which will expire or be converted into cash within one year or one operating cycle, whichever is longer. Examples are cash, accounts receivable, prepaid expenses, and inventory.

Current liabilities   liabilities which must be paid within one operating cycle or one year, whichever is longer. Accounts payable, accrued taxes payable, accrued wages payable, and short-term notes payable are current liabilities.

Fiscal year   a 12-month accounting period which ends on a date other than December 31.

Intangible assets   assets which have no physical form associated with them. Patents, copyrights, and trademarks are intangible assets.

Long-term investments   securities which have been purchased with the intention of holding them for a relatively long period of time.

Long-term liability   a liability which is *not* due within one operating cycle. Examples are mortgages payable and long-term notes payable.

Net book value   carrying value, that is, cost less accumulated depreciation.

Plant assets   assets which are characterized by a relatively long useful life and which are used in the normal operation of the firm instead of being held for their resale value.

Prepaid expenses   current assets which represent expenses that have already been paid but which were not consumed during the current period. Prepaid rent and unexpired insurance are examples of prepaid expenses.

QUESTIONS AND EXERCISES

1. What is the function of a worksheet in a merchandising enterprise?

2. What three basic classifications are found on an earnings statement for a merchandising enterprise?

3. Name four classifications found in the asset section of the statement of financial position. Specifically, what assets would be found under each classification?

4. Distinguish between current liabilities and long-term liabilities. Give examples of each type.

5. What adjusting entries should be made on the worksheet in order to calculate the cost of goods sold?

6. What steps must be followed to complete a worksheet?

7. Given the following information concerning operations for 1978, compute Holly Pyle's capital balance on December 31, 1978:

     Net earnings $4,606
     Withdrawals..................................... 1,700
     Holly Pyle, capital, 1/1/78.................. 6,505

8. On August 1, 1978, the Harley Company paid $2,400 for the next 12 months rent. It was recorded in the Prepaid Rent account. What adjustment is necessary on December 31, 1978.

9. Office equipment costing $9,000 was purchased four years ago. The equipment has an estimated useful life of ten years with no salvage value antici-

pated. What adjusting journal entry is needed to record the annual depreciation charge? (Use the straight-line method of depreciation.)

10. Sales and sales returns and allowances had the following balances on December 31, 1978:

Sales..	$99,000
Sales returns and allowances..................	8,000

Past experience has shown that 0.5 percent of net sales will be uncollectible. What adjusting entry should be made to record bad debts expense for 1978?

PROBLEMS

10-1. The Redford Drug Store has just completed its fiscal year ending October 31, 1978. Given the following information, prepare the adjusting entries that are required at the end of the year.

   a. The Merchandise Inventory account had a balance of $9,600 on November 1, 1977.
   A physical count of the merchandise inventory on October 31, 1978, indicates that the ending balance is $10,400.
   At the end of the fiscal year, salaries of $500 have been earned but will not be paid until November 20, 1978.
   b. Office equipment costing $7,000 was purchased three years ago. The equipment has an estimated useful life of seven years with no salvage value anticipated.
   c. The Purchases account has a balance of $95,000.
   The Purchase Returns and Allowances account has a balance of $3,500.
   d. On October 1, 1978, the firm purchased a 12-month fire insurance policy for $300. The payment was recorded in the Unexpired Insurance account. The policy's coverage began on October 1, 1978.

10-2. The Collier Department Store has just completed its fiscal year ending June 30, 1978. Given the following information, prepare the adjusting entries that are required at the end of the fiscal year.

   a. The Merchandise Inventory account had a balance of $20,700 on July 1, 1977.
   A physical count of the merchandise inventory on June 30, 1978, indicates that the ending inventory is $16,400.
   The Purchases account has a balance of $106,000.
   The Purchase Returns and Allowances account has a balance of $5,500.
   b. At the end of the fiscal year, salaries of $650 have been earned but will not be paid until July 1, 1978.
   c. On April 1, 1978, the firm purchased a 12-month fire insurance policy for $480. The payment was recorded in the Unexpired Insurance account. The policy's coverage began on April 1, 1978.

d. Office equipment costing $8,000 was purchased five years ago. The equipment has an estimated useful life of ten years with no salvage value anticipated.

e. Store equipment costing $5,000 was also purchased five years ago. It has an estimated useful life of 20 years with no salvage value anticipated.

f. On March 1, 1978, the firm paid $2,940 for the next 12 months' rent. The payment was recorded in the Prepaid Rent account.

g. All purchases of office supplies are debited to the Office Supplies (on Hand) account. At the end of the fiscal year, the account had a balance of $650. A physical count revealed that $150 worth of office supplies were on hand on June 30, 1978.

h. Twenty dollars of interest has accrued on notes payable but has not been recorded yet. The interest will be paid on the note's maturity date.

10–3.

NIXON'S MUSIC STORE
Trial Balance
July 31, 1978

Account Title	*Debit*	*Credit*
Cash	$ 12,390	
Accounts receivable	2,500	
Allowance for doubtful accounts		$ 200
Merchandise inventory	15,700	
Unexpired Insurance	360	
Prepaid rent	2,400	
Office equipment	6,000	
Accumulated depreciation – office equipment		2,250
Accounts payable		4,000
Clyde Nixon, capital		6,000
Clyde Nixon, drawing	10,000	
Sales		150,000
Sales returns and allowances	500	
Purchases	99,600	
Purchase returns and allowances		700
Advertising expense	500	
Rent expense	900	
Salaries expense	11,600	
Utilities expense	700	
	$163,150	$163,150

C. R. Nixon has prepared the foregoing trial balance for Nixon's music store. The following information was gathered which will be used to prepare adjusting entries:

a. A physical count of the merchandise inventory at the end of the period indicates that the ending balance is $13,200.

b. Past experience has shown that 0.4 percent of net sales will be uncollectible.

    c. On April 1, 1978, a 12-month fire insurance policy was purchased for $360. Coverage began on April 1, 1978.

    d. On February 1, 1978, Nixon paid $2,400 for the next 12 months' rent. The payment was recorded in the Prepaid Rent account.

    e. The office equipment was purchased four years ago for a cost of $6,000. The equipment has an estimated useful life of eight years with no salvage value anticipated. The straight-line method is used to record depreciation expense.

Required:

1. Prepare a worksheet for Nixon's Music Store for the fiscal year ended July 31, 1978.
2. Prepare an earnings statement for the fiscal year ended July 31, 1978.
3. Prepare a statement of financial position for July 31, 1978.

10–4. The trial balance of the Marvel Book Store for December 31, 1978, is shown below:

MARVEL BOOK STORE
Trial Balance
December 31, 1978

Account Title	*Debit*	*Credit*
Cash	$ 20,000	
Accounts receivable	6,304	
Allowance for doubtful accounts		$ 300
Merchandise inventory	20,243	
Store supplies	845	
Office supplies	636	
Unexpired insurance	432	
Prepaid rent	1,620	
Office equipment	4,000	
Accumulated depreciation—office equipment		800
Store equipment	9,100	
Accumulated depreciation—Store equipment		4,200
Accounts payable		6,280
Beth Wooten, capital		45,000
Beth Wooten, drawing	20,000	
Sales		109,000
Sales returns and allowances	2,200	
Purchases	65,500	
Purchase returns and allowances		2,500
Advertising expense	600	
Rent expense	800	
Salaries expense	15,000	
Utilities expense	800	
	$168,080	$168,080

Required:

1. Prepare a worksheet for the year ended December 31, 1978. The following information will be needed for adjustments:

   a. Merchandise inventory, December 31, 1978, $19,780.
   b. Store supplies on hand at December 31, 1978, $150.
   c. Office supplies on hand at December 31, 1978, $200.
   d. Unexpired insurance, December 31, 1978, $288.
   e. Prepaid rent, December 31, 1978, $1,080.
   f. Bad debts expense for 1978, $534.
   g. Depreciation expense for 1978:

   Office equipment.................. $800
   Store equipment $700

2. Prepare an earnings statement for the year ended December 31, 1978.
3. Prepare a statement of financial position for December 31, 1978.

10–5. The trial balance for the Burger Carpet Shop for December 31, 1978, is shown below:

BURGER CARPET SHOP
Trial Balance
December 31, 1978

Account Title	*Debit*	*Credit*
Cash	$ 15,000	
Accounts receivable	6,500	
Allowance for doubtful accounts		$ 200
Merchandise inventory	30,600	
Office equipment	1,500	
Accumulated depreciation—office equipment		750
Delivery equipment	6,000	
Accumulated depreciation—delivery equipment		3,000
Accounts payable		20,700
Elmo Burger, capital		39,000
Elmo Burger, drawing	12,000	
Sales		95,000
Sales returns and allowances	1,500	
Purchases	78,700	
Purchase returns and allowances		2,450
Advertising expense	600	
Insurance expense	480	
Miscellaneous expense	120	
Rent expense	1,740	
Salaries expense	5,720	
Utilities expense	640	
	$161,100	$161,100

Required:

1. Prepare a worksheet for the year ended December 31, 1978. Use the following information to make adjustments:

a.   Merchandise inventory at the end of the year, $36,850.
b.   Prepaid rent, December 31, 1978, $348.
c.   Unexpired insurance, December 31, 1978, $96.
d.   Bad debts expense has been estimated to be 0.4 percent of net sales.
e.   Depreciation expense for 1978:

Office equipment .... $ 250
Delivery equipment.................   1,000

2.   Prepare an earnings statement for the year ended December 31, 1978.
3.   Prepare a statement of financial position for December 31, 1978.
4.   Prepare adjusting and closing journal entries.

10–6.   The trial balance for the Random Store for December 31, 1978, is shown below:

RANDOM STORE
Trial Balance
December 31, 1978

Account Title	Debit	Credit
Cash..	$ 3,815	
Notes receivable...	500	
Accounts receivable	4,200	
Allowance for doubtful accounts		$ 110
Merchandise inventory	16,580	
Office supplies..	350	
Store supplies..	500	
Unexpired insurance	540	
Prepaid rent..	4,320	
Office equipment...	2,500	
Accumulated depreciation—office equipment...........		500
Store equipment	5,000	
Accumulated depreciation—store equipment		625
Delivery equipment...	8,400	
Accumulated depreciation—delivery equipment		2,100
Notes payable		2,500
Accounts payable		6,000
Rudolph Wheless, capital		52,100
Rudolph Wheless, drawing	10,500	
Sales...		130,545
Sales returns and allowances..............................	2,985	
Purchases..	90,320	
Purchase returns and allowances		3,450
Advertising expense	480	
Miscellaneous expense.......................................	240	
Payroll taxes expense	4,200	
Salaries expense	41,600	
Utilities expense..	900	
	$197,930	$197,930

Required:

1. Prepare a worksheet for the year ended December 31, 1978. Use the following information to make adjustments:

   a. Merchandise inventory, Dec. 31, 1978, $12,250.
   b. Office supplies on hand, December 31, 1978, $75.
   c. Store supplies on hand, December 31, 1978, $125.
   d. Expired insurance, $360.
   e. Expired rent, $2,160.
   f. Bad debts expense for 1978, $450.
   g. Depreciation expense for 1978.
      Office equipment, $500. Store equipment, $625.
      Delivery equipment, $2,100.

2. Prepare an earnings statement for the year ended December 31, 1978.
3. Prepare a statement of financial position for December 31, 1978.
4. Prepare the adjusting and closing journal entries.
5. Prepare a post-closing trial balance.

Accounting for notes and interest
Learning objectives

The extensive use of credit in commercial buying and selling has made it necessary to account for credit transactions in a detailed manner. A study of the following material will provide a working knowledge of the accounting procedures used when accounting for notes receivable and notes payable:

1. Discussion concerning the legal and physical attributes of a promissory note.
2. The difference between an interest-bearing note and a noninterest-bearing note and the manner in which interest is computed for each type of note.
3. A description of a contingent liability and its presentation in the statement of financial position.
4. Accounting for notes receivable and notes payable: payment, collection, renewal, maturity, and endorsement.
5. Accounting procedures for accruing interest receivable and interest payable.

11

Accounting for notes and interest

The extensive use of credit has become a characteristic of modern business. Credit is used by individuals as well as by all types and sizes of business organizations. Millions of credit transactions occur daily that involve the exchange of goods and services for promises to pay at later dates. "On credit," "on account," and "charge" are commonly used to describe credit sales. Although some credit transactions involve a written promise to pay, the majority of credit sales simply involve a signature on a sales receipt by the buyer as acknowledgment of the receipt of the goods or services. This type of credit arrangement is called an "open account." Other kinds of credit devices commonly used are the credit card and the **promissory note.**

Promissory notes are used in several different transactions. A promise to repay borrowed cash usually takes the form of a note. Promises for later payment other than for borrowed cash sometimes take the form of a note, especially when credit is extended for periods of more than 60 days or when large sums of money are involved.

The characteristics associated with a promissory note cause it to be a negotiable instrument. Such notes must evidence the following legal attributes:

1. Unconditional promise to pay a specified sum of money.
2. Payable either at a fixed future time or on demand.
3. Payable to a specific person, firm, or to bearer.
4. Must be signed by the person or firm making the promise.

The promissory note in Illustration 11–1 has all the required legal characteristics. Tom Jones, the person to whom the amount of money will be paid, is called the **payee.** The promissory note is a *note receivable* to the payee. Ed Wheeler, the person who promises to pay money, is known as the **maker** of the note. The promissory note is a *note payable* to the maker.

The note in Illustration 11–1 is interest bearing. In other words, **interest** paid at 8 percent is in addition to the repayment of the face amount at maturity date. A noninterest-bearing note would not show an interest rate on its face. The interest would be included in the face amount

Illustration 11–1
Promissory note

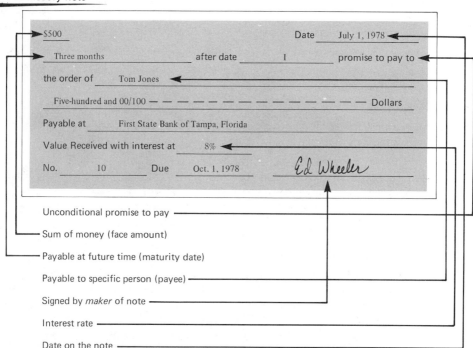

$500   Date   July 1, 1978

Three months _____ after date _____ I _____ promise to pay to

the order of   Tom Jones

Five-hundred and 00/100 — — — — — — — — — — — — — — — — — — Dollars

Payable at   First State Bank of Tampa, Florida

Value Received with interest at   8%

No.   10   Due   Oct. 1, 1978   *Ed Wheeler*

Unconditional promise to pay
Sum of money (face amount)
Payable at future time (maturity date)
Payable to specific person (payee)
Signed by *maker* of note
Interest rate
Date on the note

of the note. Noninterest-bearing notes are issued at a **discount.** The maker of the note receives an amount less than the face amount that he or she promises to repay. The difference between the amount received by the maker and the face amount equals the amount of the discount. The discount amount is the amount of total interest expense at maturity. For example, a borrower gives a $500 note payable in 90 days to a bank in return for cash of $492.50. The $7.50 difference between the face amount of the note and the amount received by the borrower is equal to the interest expense at the maturity date.

COMPUTING INTEREST

There are three factors that must be considered when computing interest: (1) principal, (2) interest rate, and (3) time period.

The **principal** is the amount of money borrowed. The amount of interest is based on this figure.

The interest rate is usually given on the face of the note. If the note is interest bearing and the interest rate is not given on the face of the note, the legal rate must be used. The legal rate varies among the different states. The interest rate shown on the face of the note is always an annual percentage rate unless stated otherwise. For example, 12 percent is assumed to be an annual percentage rate unless otherwise stated. Twelve percent is equivalent to 1 percent per month.

The time period of the note is determined by the number of days or months from the date of the note until the date of maturity. Interest computations are based on this time period. When the maturity date is specified in months, the fraction of the year the months represent is used to calculate interest. For example, if a note specifies maturity in four months, interest is calculated for $\frac{4}{12}$ or $\frac{1}{3}$ of a year. If maturity is specified in days, interest is calculated based on the fraction of the year those days represent. Three hundred sixty days is customarily used to compute interest for one year. For example, if a note matures in 60 days, interest is based on $\frac{60}{360}$ or $\frac{1}{6}$ of a year. Some institutions such as banks or government agencies may use 365 days as the base in computing daily interest.

If the due date is specified on a note, the exact number of days from the date of the note through the due date or maturity date must be determined. For example, if a note is issued on January 1 and is due on March 17, the time period is computed as follows:

Days in January	31
Date of note, January	1
Days remaining in January	30
Days in February	28
Days in March	17
Time period in days	75

Notice in the above computation that the date of maturity is included but the date of the note is excluded.

After determining the proper factors, interest is calculated using the following formula:

Principal × Rate × Time Period = Amount of Interest

Remember, the time period is usually a fraction of a 360-day year.

To illustrate the application of the formula, the note in Illustration

11–1 is used. The principal amount is $500; the interest rate is 8 percent; the time period is three months. The interest payable is $10, computed as follows:

$$\$500 \times 8 \text{ Percent} \times {}^{3}\!/_{12} = \$10 \text{ Interest}$$

Assume the same facts as in the above example except that the note matures 90 days after issuance instead of three months. The interest is $10, computed as follows:

$$\$500 \times 8 \text{ Percent} \times \frac{90}{360} = \$10 \text{ Interest}$$

Present value

The **present value of a note** increases as the number of days to maturity decreases. The value increases because interest is accruing on the note. The present value of an interest-bearing note is equal to the face amount of the note plus accrued interest. If the note is noninterest bearing (does not show an interest rate on its face), the present value is computed by subtracting from the face amount an amount determined at the discount rate.

The present value of a note must be determined if the note is exchanged for credit or for cash. For example, the original payee may endorse the note and buy goods and services, or the payee may exchange the note at the bank for cash. Consider these situations involving the note in Illustration 11–1.

1. On August 1 (one month after date of note), Tom Jones exchanges the note for merchandise at McKinney Wholesale. McKinney agrees to allow Jones merchandise worth the present value of the note. The present value, $503.34, is calculated as follows:

    Present Value = Principal + Accrued Interest

    a. Principal = $500,000.
    b. Accrued Interest = $500 × .08 × $^{1}\!/_{12}$ = $3.33.
    c. Present Value = $500 + $3.33 = $503.33.

2. Tom Jones decides to exchange the note at the bank for cash. The bank will buy the note if it is discounted at 10 percent. The following steps are necessary to compute the discount:

    a. Determine the maturity value of the note. The maturity value is the sum of principal and interest.

    Interest = Principal × Rate × Time
    Interest = $500 × 8 Percent × $^{3}\!/_{12}$ = $10
    Maturity Value = Principal + Interest
    Maturity Value = $500 + $10 = $510

    b. Determine the discount time or discount period.

$$3 \text{ Months} - 1 \text{ Month} = 2 \text{ Months}$$

Two months is the remaining life of the note on August 1, the date on which the note is discounted.

    c. Calculate the amount of discount charged by the bank.

> Discount = Maturity Value × Discount Rate × Discount Period
> Discount = $510 × 10 Percent × $^{2}/_{12}$
> Discount = $8.50

Now, the present value of the note can be computed as follows:

> Present Value = Maturity Value − Discount
> Present Value = $510 − $8.50
> Present Value = $501.50

It is customary for banks to calculate the discount on the value of the note at the maturity date. The present value of the note is equal to the **maturity value** of the note less the discount.

The party discounting a note or exchanging a note is usually liable for its maturity value in the event the maker defaults (does not pay) at the maturity date. This possible future liability is known as a **contingent liability.**

Notice in the past illustrations that accrued interest is computed with the principal of the note used as a base, while the discount is computed with the maturity value of the note used as a base.

In summary:

$$\text{Principal} \times \text{Rate} \times \text{Time Period} = \text{Interest}$$

$$\text{Maturity Value} = \text{Principal} + \text{Interest}$$

$$\text{Maturity Value} \times \text{Discount Rate} \times \text{Discount Period} = \text{Discount}$$

$$\text{Maturity Value} - \text{Discount} = \text{Present Value}$$

The 60-day, 6 percent method

When a 360-day year is used to calculate interest, the 60-day, 6 percent method can be used as a shortcut. The interest amount for the period is determined by taking 1 percent of the principal. The 1 percent is determined in the following manner:

Factors:

1. Interest rate—6 percent or $^{6}/_{100}$.
2. Time period—60 days.

Calculation:

$$\frac{6}{100} \times \frac{60}{360} = \frac{6}{100} \times \frac{1}{6} = \frac{1}{100} \quad \text{or} \quad 1 \text{ Percent}$$

Thus, the interest on $445 for 60 days at 6 percent interest is $4.45.

The 60-day, 6 percent method can now be used to calculate interest when the time period is *greater or less than 60 days.* For example:

1. The interest on a $500 note for 30 days at 6 percent is $2.50, calculated as follows:
   a. 1 percent × 500 = $5 Interest for 60 Days.
   b. 30 days = ½ of 60 days.
   c. ½ × $5 = $2.50, interest for 30 days.
2. The interest on a $4,000 note for 120 days at 6 percent is $80, calculated as follows:
   a. 1 percent × $4,000 = $40, interest for 60 days.
   b. 120 days = 2 × 60 days.
   c. 2 × $40 = $80, interest for 120 days.

When the *interest rate is not 6 percent,* the 60-day, 6-percent method is used as illustrated below:

1. $8 is the interest on a $1,200 note for 60 days at 4 percent, computed as follows:
   a. $1,200 × 1 Percent = $12, interest at 6 percent.
   b. 4 Percent = ⅔ of 6 Percent.
   c. ⅔ × 12 = $8, interest at 4 percent.
2. $39 is the interest on a $2,600 note for 60 days at 9 percent, computed as follows:
   a. $2,600 × 1 percent = $26, interest at 6 percent.
   b. 9 Percent = 1½ × 6 Percent.
   c. 1½ × $26 = $39, interest at 9 percent.

When interest is not 6 percent and the number of days is not 60, the amount of interest is calculated in the following manner.

1. The interest on a $3,000 note for 30 days at 9 percent is $22.50.
   a. $3,000 × 1 Percent = $30, interest at 6 percent for 60 days.
   b. ½ × $30 = $15, interest at 6 percent for 30 days.
   c. $15 × 1½ = $22.50, interest at 9 percent for 30 days.
2. The interest on a $4,600 note for 120 days at 10 percent is $153.34.
   a. $4,600 × 1 percent = $46, interest at 6 percent for 60 days.
   b. 2 × $46 = $92, interest at 6 percent for 120 days.
   c. 1⅔ × $92 = $153.34, interest at 10 percent for 120 days.

ACCOUNTING FOR NOTES RECEIVABLE

Notes are received in several types of transactions. The most common transactions are notes exchanged for (1) cash loan, (2) goods and services, and (3) extension of payment time on a previous obligation.

Note received for cash loan

First National Bank received a note from John Martin in exchange for a loan of $800. The bank records the note receivable as indicated by the following general journal entry:

Notes Receivable	800	
Cash		800
Loaned John Martin $800.		

Note received in exchange for goods and services

SGA Wholesale Company received a note from Ken Baker in exchange for merchandise valued at $375. The general journal entry for SGA Wholesale Company is the following:

Notes Receivable	375	
Sales		375
Sale of merchandise to Ken Baker.		

Note received for extension of payment time on a previous obligation

Earl Roger requested a time extension on $200 due William's Department Store. William's agreed to the time extension in exchange for a note from Roger. The general journal entry for William's Department Store is the following:

Notes Receivable	200	
Accounts Receivable–Earl Rogers		200
Note from Earl Roger.		

Accounts Receivable is credited, therefore, balancing the account receivable account of Earl Roger to zero.

Assume the same facts except Roger makes a partial payment of $50 on the account receivable balance due and issues a note for the $150 remaining balance. The general journal entry on the books of William's Department Store is:

Cash	50	
Notes Receivable	150	
Accounts Receivable–Earl Rogers		200
Note from Earl Roger.		

Again the Account Receivable is credited for $200 to remove the previous $200 debit balance from the books.

NOTE DISCOUNTED BEFORE MATURITY

As previously illustrated, notes are often discounted before their maturity dates. Instead of issuing a promissory note of his or her own, a person could **discount notes receivable** to obtain cash. For example, on April 2, Tom Odom issues a $600 face amount, 8 percent note due in 90 days to Thompson Company in exchange for merchandise. Thompson Company discounts the note at Citizens Bank at 9 percent on April 4. The proceeds from the note equal the discounted present value. The present value of the note discounted at 9 percent is calculated as follows:

1. $600 × 8 percent × $^{90}/_{360}$ = $12, accrued interest at maturity date.
2. $600 + $12 = $612, value of note at maturity date.
3. $612 × 9 percent × $^{88}/_{360}$ = $13.46, discount on maturity value of the note.
4. $612 − $13.46 = $598.54, present value of the note discounted at 9 percent.

The following is the general journal entry to record the note discounted before maturity date on the books of the Thompson Company:

```
Apr.  4   Cash.................................................................... 598.54
          Interest Expense ..................................................   1.46
              Notes Receivable .............................................          600
          Discounted Tom Odom's note at bank.
```

Notice that the $1.46 difference between the face value of the note and the cash proceeds from discounting the note is interest expense. However, if the cash proceeds from discounting the note are greater than the face amount, then the difference is accounted for as interest revenue. For example, assume the same facts as the previous problem except Thompson Company does not discount the note at Citizens Bank until May 2. The present value of the note discounted at 9 percent is:

1. $600 × 8 Percent × 90/360 = $12, accrued interest at maturity date.
2. $600 + $12 = $612, value of note at maturity date.
3. $612 × 9 Percent × 60/360 = $9.18, discount on maturity value of the note.
4. $612 − $9.18 = $602.82, present value of the note discounted at 9 percent.

The following is the general journal entry on Thompson's books:

```
May 2   Cash .................................................................... 602.82
            Notes Receivable............................................          600.00
            Interest Revenue ............................................            2.82
        Discounted Tom Odom's note at bank.
```

REPORTING A CONTINGENT LIABILITY

As previously explained, the person discounting a note is guaranteeing that the note will be paid. If the maker fails to pay the note when due, the holder of the note can collect from the person who discounted the note. For example, if Cox Corporation discounts a $3,000 note received from Tom Wilkes at First National Bank, Cox Corporation must report a contingent liability for the discounted note until the note is paid.

The contingent liability generally is disclosed in a footnote to the statement of financial position. If Cox Corporation has other notes receivable of $10,000 that are not discounted, the statement of financial position would have the following disclosure:

Current Assets:
Notes receivable (see Note No. 1) $10,000
       Note No. 1: Contingent liability on notes receivable discounted, $4,000.

COLLECTION OF NOTE AT MATURITY

When a note matures, it is usually collected by the holder. Occasionally, the holder may want to turn the note over to a bank for collec-

Illustration 11–2

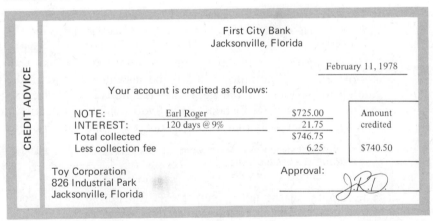

First City Bank
Jacksonville, Florida

February 11, 1978

CREDIT ADVICE

Your account is credited as follows:

NOTE:	Earl Roger	$725.00	Amount
INTEREST:	120 days @ 9%	21.75	credited
Total collected		$746.75	
Less collection fee		6.25	$740.50

Toy Corporation
826 Industrial Park
Jacksonville, Florida

Approval:

tion because it is inconvenient to personally collect the note. If the note is collected, the bank charges a fee for this service and notifies the holder that the note was collected and credited to his or her account. The bank uses a credit advice similar to the one in Illustration 11–2 to notify the holder of collection.

The entry on Toy Corporation's books after the bank's collection of Earl Roger's note (Illustration 11–2) is the following:

```
Cash................................................................... 740.50
Collection Expense ........................................      6.25
   Notes Receivable ........................................            725.00
   Interest Revenue.........................................             21.75
```
Bank collection of Earl Roger's note plus interest.

If the maturity value of a note is paid directly to the payee at the due date of the note, the transaction is recorded on the payee's books in the following manner. Assume Tat Thompson pays a $400 note plus $6 interest directly to Cooper's Wholesale on the maturity date:

```
Cash................................................................... 406.00
   Notes Receivable ........................................            400.00
   Interest Revenue.........................................              6.00
```
Tat Thompson paid $400 note plus $6 interest.

RENEWAL OF NOTE AT MATURITY

The maker of a note may be permitted to renew the note or part of the note at the maturity date if he or she is unable to pay and the payee agrees to a renewal.

For example, assume Tat Thompson is granted a renewal of his note for $400 and pays interest at the maturity date. Cooper's Wholesale would make the following general journal entry:

```
Cash...................................................................   6.00
Notes Receivable (new note).......................... 400.00
   Interest Revenue.........................................              6.00
   Notes Receivable (old note) .........................            400.00
```
Tat Thompson renewed note for $400 and paid accrued interest.

If Thompson fails to pay the note when it becomes due and the note is not renewed, the note is said to be **dishonored.** The maker has defaulted in payment of the note, and the note is no longer negotiable. Assuming Thompson dishonored a $560 noninterest-bearing note, the following general journal entry would be made on Cooper's books:

```
Accounts Receivable–Tat Thompson.................. 560.00
   Notes Receivable ........................................            560.00
```
Tat Thompson's note dishonored.

The amount of the note receivable is transferred to the Accounts Receivable account until some future time when it is determined that the obligation will not be paid. If the account is not paid, Cooper would debit Allowance for Doubtful Accounts and credit Accounts Receivable.

NOTES RECEIVABLE REGISTER

It is advisable to keep a separate record of each note receivable. This record is commonly called a **notes receivable register.** Illustration 11–3 indicates one form of the notes receivable register used by the B. E. Camp Company.

Illustration 11–3

NOTES RECEIVABLE REGISTER

Date	No.	Name	Where Payable	Date Made	Time Period	Maturity Date	Amt.	Interest Rate	Amt.	Discounted Bank	Discounted Date	Date Paid	Remarks
2/1/78	1	Becker Co.	First National/Tampa	2/1/78	90 days	5/2/78	$600	9%	$13.50			5/2/78	
2/3/78	2	J. D. Nelton	First National/Pensacola	2/3/78	60 days	4/4/78	$400	10%	$ 6.67			4/4/78	
2/6/78	3	Harry Smith	First National/Tampa	2/6/78	90 days	5/7/78	$750	10%	18.75	First National	3/6/77		
2/9/78	4	David Jones	Second National/Miami	2/9/78	60 days	4/10/78	$545	9%	$ 8.18			4/10/78	
2/14/78	5	Donna Clay	Second National/Miami	2/14/78	90 days	5/15/78	$615	8%	$12.30				
2/16/78	6	Rogers Co.	First National/Tampa	2/16/78	90 days	5/17/78	$430	10%	$10.75	First National	2/23/77		
2/21/78	7	Grimm Co.	First National/Pensacola	2/21/78	30 days	3/23/78	$300	10%	$ 2.50			3/23/78	

Although most of the information recorded in the register comes directly from the face of the note, other information is also reported. The total amount of interest is calculated; if the note is discounted, the bank that bought the note is recorded; the date the note is paid is recorded.

NOTES RECEIVABLE ACCOUNT

The Notes Receivable account shown in Illustration 11–4 should agree with the notes recorded in the register. Notice that the amounts in the account are cross-referenced to the register by using the numbers of the notes. The Notes Receivable account shows both uncollected notes receivable and the notes receivable that have been collected. The balance in the account can be determined easily as shown in Illustration 11–4.

Illustration 11–4

	Notes Receivable	Account No.	
No. 1	600	No. 1	600
No. 2	400	No. 2	400
No. 3	750	No. 4	545
No. 4	545	No. 7	300
No. 5	615		
No. 6	430		
No. 7	300		
Balance	1,795		

The notes receivable register and the Notes Receivable account are periodically compared to prove the accuracy of the account. This comparison usually is made monthly.

The purpose of maintaining a Notes Receivable account separately from a notes receivable register is to insure proper internal control. The account and register are maintained by separate people. This will help reduce errors in the accounting records and will possibly discourage fraud.

ENDORSEMENT OF NOTES

Before a note can be transferred to another party, the holder must endorse the note unless it is a bearer note, and even then it should be endorsed. The two most important types of endorsements are the **blank endorsement** and the **special endorsement.** The payee makes a blank endorsement when only his or her name is signed on the back of the note.

Illustration 11–5
Note endorsements

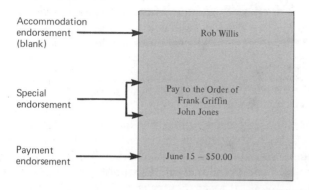

Accommodation
endorsement
(blank)

Rob Willis

Special
endorsement

Pay to the Order of
Frank Griffin
John Jones

Payment
endorsement

June 15 – $50.00

If the payee signs "pay to the order of" followed by someone's name, a special endorsement is made. The endorser becomes contingently liable for the note in the event the maker is unable to pay at maturity. The blank endorsement makes the note payable to the bearer of the note, while the special endorsement specifies to whom payment is to be made.

Occasionally the payee may require either a **cosigner** of a note or an endorser of a note before the promissory note is accepted. The cosigner puts his or her signature below the maker's name on the face of the note. In the latter event, commonly called an **accommodation endorsement,** a person endorses in blank on the back of the note. In either instance, the payee is assumed to have additional security because there is more than one person from whom the payee can collect the note at maturity. **Endorsing the payment** occurs when a partial payment is made on a note.

To illustrate endorsements, assume a note from Jack Greiner was given to John Jones (Illustration 11–5). Rob Willis signs an accommodation endorsement on the note. Jones signs a special endorsement to Frank Griffin. Jack Greiner later makes a partial payment of $50 on June 15.

ACCOUNTING FOR NOTES PAYABLE

When promissory notes are issued (notes payable), the same types of transactions occur that are common to the receipt of notes (notes receivable). The common transactions involve (1) cash loan, (2) exchange for goods and services, (3) extension of payment time on a previous obligation, (4) payment at maturity, and (5) renewal at maturity.

NOTES ISSUED FOR A CASH LOAN

It is common for many businesses to experience periods when they need more cash than is available from internal sources of the business. For example, during periods of inventory build-up, cash from within the business may be inadequate to purchase additional goods or materials. The business may then issue a promissory note to a bank in exchange for a cash loan. For example, assume Martin Company issues an interest-bearing note to Peoples Bank in exchange for a loan of $1,000 for 90 days at 9 percent. Martin's general journal entry would be:

```
Cash........................................................................  1,000
     Notes Payable......................................................            1,000
     Borrowed $1,000 from Peoples Bank 90-day, 9 percent
     note issued.
```

If the note is noninterest bearing, the difference between the cash received and the maturity value of the note is accounted for as interest expense. Assume Martin Company issued a noninterest-bearing note for $1,000 for 90 days and Peoples Bank discounted the note at 9 percent. Martin Company's general journal entry is as follows:

```
Cash........................................................................  977.50
Interest Expense......................................................   22.50
     Notes Payable......................................................          1,000.00
     Issued noninterest-bearing note to Peoples Bank for 90
     days, discounted at 9 percent.
```

Note issued in exchange for goods and services

Ken Baker issued a $400 note for 60 days at 10 percent to Wayne Company in exchange for merchandise. Baker makes the following general journal entry:

```
Purchases................................................................  400
     Notes Payable......................................................            400
     Issued 60-day, 10 percent note to Wayne Company.
```

Note issued for extension of payment time on a previous obligation

K. C. Roberts Company owes a $200 account payable to Glenn Company. Glenn agrees to accept a 9 percent note in exchange for an extension of 60 days. Roberts's general journal entry is:

```
Accounts Payable–Glenn Company...............................  200
     Notes Payable......................................................            200
     Issued 60-day, 9 percent note to Glenn Company.
```

If Roberts made a partial payment of $50 and issued a note for the balance, the following general journal entry would be made:

```
Accounts Payable–Glenn Company...............................  200
     Cash................................................................             50
     Notes Payable......................................................            150
     Issued 60-day, 9 percent note to Glenn Company.
```

In both cases, the remaining balance for Roberts's account payable to Glenn Company is zero.

Payment of note at maturity

Payment of a note may be made directly to the payee or directly to a bank the payee designates to collect the payment. A bank will always send the maker of a note a notice similar to the one in Illustration 11–6 notifying him or her that the note is due.

Illustration 11–6

First State Bank				
Maker	Number	Date Due		
Bill Brown	40-125	8/31/78	Principal Interest Total	$500.00 34.15 $534.15
	To:	Bill Brown 1235 Main Street Jacksonville, Florida 40572		

In either case, Bill Brown's general journal entry is:

```
Notes Payable...............................................................    500.00
Interest Expense .......................................................     34.15
   Cash.......................................................................               534.15
   Payment of note plus interest.
```

Renewal of note at maturity

If the payee agrees, the maker may renew the note at maturity for all or part of the amount. For example, Joan Miller agrees to renew an $800 note of Lynn Drake, but Drake must pay accrued interest of $40. Drake's general journal entry is:

```
Notes Payable (old note)...............................    800.00
Interest Expense .......................................     40.00
   Cash.......................................................                40.00
   Notes Payable (new note) .........................               800.00
   Note to Joan Miller renewed; accrued interest is paid.
```

NOTES PAYABLE REGISTER

It is often advisable to record notes payable in a separate register from the general journal record. All information shown on the face of the

Illustration 11-7

NOTES PAYABLE REGISTER

Date	No.	Payable to Whom	Where Payable	Date Made	Time Period	When Due	Amt.	Int. Rate	Date Paid	Remarks
1/2/78	1	Ross Bros.	First State Bank	1/2/78	90 days	4/2/78	1,000	9% $22.50		
1/4/78	2	Robb Co.	Peoples Bank	1/4/78	15 days	1/19/78	3,000	9% $11.25	1/19/78	
1/5/78	3	Martin Co.	First State Bank	1/5/78	15 days	1/20/78	200	10% $ 0.84	1/20/78	
1/18/78	4	Harris Bros.	Second National Bank	1/18/78	30 days	2/17/78	400	9% $ 3.00		
1/22/78	5	Harvey Co.	First State Bank	1/22/78	60 days	3/23/78	500	9% $ 7.50		

note is recorded here, and, in addition to this information, the amount of interest payable at maturity is recorded. The **notes payable register** is shown in Illustration 11-7.

NOTES PAYABLE ACCOUNT

The amounts recorded in the Notes Payable account (illustrated below) agree with amounts shown in the notes payable register. Amounts recorded are cross-referenced to the notes payable register by indicating the number of the note. Both notes payable and notes payable already paid are shown in the account for a period. The balance in the account is found by taking the difference between debits and credits as shown in the illustration.

		Notes Payable		Account No.
No. 2.	3,000	No. 1.		1,000
3.	200	No. 2.		3,000
		No. 3.		200
		No. 4.		400
		No. 5.		500
		Balance		1,900

The notes payable register and the Notes Payable account are kept separately by different people within the firm. This provides better internal control, and thus greater reliability can be placed on the accounting records. The register and account are periodically compared to indicate the accuracy of the records. This comparison is usually made monthly or annually, depending on the needs of a particular firm. A schedule of outstanding notes payable is usually prepared, similar to the one below:

Notes payable at January 31, 1978

No. 1	$1,000
No. 4	400
No. 5	500
Total	$1,900

ACCRUAL OF INTEREST RECEIVABLE

If there are any interest-bearing notes receivable outstanding at the end of an accounting period, it is necessary to account for the interest

Illustration 11–8

Accrued interest on outstanding notes receivable on March 31, 1978					
Note No.	Principal	Issue Date	Interest Rate	Days Outstanding	Accrued Interest
3	$ 500	Dec. 31, 1977	8%	90	$10.00
4	400	Jan. 10, 1978	9	80	8.00
7	1,000	Mar. 1, 1978	9	30	7.50
	Total accrued interest				$25.50

that accrues until the last day of the period. Because interest accrues on a day-to-day basis, net earnings would be understated and current assets would be understated if the accrued interest adjustment were not made. It is necessary to debit Accrued Interest Receivable and credit Interest Revenue to adjust for the interest at the end of the period.

To illustrate the problem, assume that Baker Company has three interest-bearing notes receivable outstanding at its March 31 fiscal year-end. The schedule in Illustration 11–8 would be prepared from information obtained from the face of the notes or from the notes receivable register.

The following journal entry is made on Baker's books:

Mar. 31	Accrued Interest Receivable	25.50	
	Interest Revenue		25.50
	Accrued interest earned on notes receivable.		

Accrued Interest Receivable is disclosed as a current asset in the statement of financial position. Interest Revenue is disclosed in the earnings statement, thus increasing net earnings.

ACCRUAL OF INTEREST PAYABLE

If interest-bearing notes payable are outstanding at the close of a fiscal period, an adjusting entry must be made by debiting Interest Expense and crediting Accrued Interest Payable. If the entry is not made, net earnings will be overstated, and current liabilities in the statement of financial position will be understated. The calculation for accrued interest payable is just like that for accrued interest receivable. Assume that Baker Company in the last example has accrued interest payable of $25.50. The following general journal entry is made at the close of the fiscal year:

```
Mar.  31   Interest Expense......................................................... 25.50
           Accrued Interest Payable....................................         25.50
```

Accrued Interest Payable is disclosed as a current liability in the statement of financial position. Interest Expense is disclosed in the earnings statement, thus decreasing net earnings.

GLOSSARY

Accommodation endorsement   a blank endorsement made by a person other than the payee on the back of a note. It gives additional security to the note because the payee can look to more than one person for payment of the note.

Blank endorsement   the payee's signature on the back of a note making the note payable to the bearer of the note.

Contingent liability   a possible future liability or obligation that can materialize if certain events occur. A person who discounts a note has an obligation to pay the note if the maker does not pay.

Cosigner (of a note)   one who puts his or her signature below the maker's name on the face of a note, thus providing an additional guarantee that the note will be paid.

Discount (on a noninterest-bearing note)   the difference between the face amount of a note and the amount of cash received by the maker.

Discounting notes receivable   exchanging a note at the bank for cash and being held liable for its maturity value if the maker defaults. The amount of cash received from the bank will be equal to the maturity value of the note less a discount computed with the maturity value used as a base.

Dishonored note   a note which the maker failed to pay at the due date. It is no longer negotiable.

Endorsing a payment   recording on the back of a note the amount of a partial payment and the date on which it was made.

Interest   money paid for the use of money; it is equal to the principal × interest rate × time period. The time period is usually a fraction of a 360-day year.

Maker   the person who promises to pay money by signing his name on the face of a note.

Maturity value   the principal plus interest accrued until the due date; the amount which the holder of a note should receive on the due date.

Notes payable register   a record separate from the general journal which contains detailed information about each note payable—the date made, date due, payable to whom, payable where, time period covered, face amount of note, interest, and date paid.

Notes receivable register   a separate record in which detailed information is recorded about each note receivable—date made, date due, payable by whom, when payable, time period covered, face amount of note, interest, bank at which discounted, date of discount, and date paid.

Payee   the person to whom the amount of money specified on a note will be paid.

Present value (of a note)   face amount or principal of the note plus accrued interest for an interest-bearing note: principal amount less a discount for a noninterest-bearing note; maturity value less a discount for a note discounted at the bank.

Principal   the amount of money borrowed or the face amount of a note which must be paid on the maturity date.

Promissory note   a negotiable instrument which has the following legal attributes: (1) unconditional promise to pay a specified sum of money; (2) payable either at a fixed future time or on demand; (3) payable to a specific person, firm or to bearer; and (4) signed by the person or firm making the promise.

Special endorsement   an endorsement which specifies to whom payment is to be made. The payee signs "pay to the order of" followed by someone else's name and the payee's signature.

QUESTIONS AND EXERCISES

Assume a 360-day year in these questions and exercises.

1. What amount of interest is due at maturity on a $650 note at 9 percent for 90 days?

2. Tim Brown issued a 9 percent, $220 promissory note to Davis Construction Company for materials on April 15. The maturity date of the note is November 1.

   a. How much interest will Tim have to pay at maturity?
   b. What general journal entries would Davis have to make on April 15 and November 1?

3. On June 1, John Greiner issues a 60-day, 8 percent, $450 promissory note to James D. Brown Company for landscaping a piece of property. On June 11, Brown discounts the note at Miami Federal Bank at 10 percent.

   a. What is Brown's general journal entry on June 11?
   b. What is John Greiner's general journal at date of maturity?

4. On April 30, Roberts Company issues an $800 note at 11 percent interest for three months to the Bank of Key Largo for a cash loan. After paying the accrued interest, Roberts renews the note on July 31. What is Roberts's general journal entry on July 31 for this transaction?

5. Thompson Company has an interest-bearing note receivable from Barclay for $300 at 9 percent for four months. First Financial Bank collected the note and interest at maturity for Thompson and charged a $5 service charge. After receiving notification of collection, Thompson would make what general journal entry to record the transaction?

6. Thomas Manufacturing Company has a noninterest-bearing note receivable for $500 from Shirley Distributors, Inc. Shirley Distributors, Inc., failed to pay the note at maturity. What is Thomas's journal entry to record this transaction?

7. What is the purpose of maintaining a separate register and ledger account for both notes receivable and notes payable?

8. How is a contingent liability from a discounted note reported in the financial statements?

9. On June 1, Weather's Wood, Inc., issued a six-month, 9 percent, $2,500 note to Cloud Equipment Company for several chain saws.

   a. What general journal entries would Weather's Wood, Inc., make on June 1 and also at maturity?
   b. What general journal entries would Cloud make on June 1 and also at maturity?

10. On March 1, Sherry Wynne issued a 90-day, 10 percent note for $1,000. What is the present value of the note on March 31?

PROBLEMS

11-1. Assume that a 360-day year is used to calculate interest. Use the 60-day, 6 percent method to calculate the interest amount on each of the following notes (show steps of computation):

   a. $2,345 note for 60 days at 6 percent.
   b. $720 note for 60 days at 6 percent.
   c. $400 note for 40 days at 6 percent.
   d. $2,000 note for 90 days at 6 percent.
   e. $500 note for 60 days at 9 percent.
   f. $250 note for 60 days at 3 percent.

    g. $1,500 note for 30 days at 8 percent.

    h. $4,600 note for 120 days at 12 percent.

11-2. PART A On May 3, 1978, Lee Foster requested a time extension on $300 owed to Trellis Supply Company. The time extension was granted to Foster in exchange for a 90-day, 9 percent, $300 note. On June 2, 1978, Trellis Supply Company exchanged the note at the bank for cash. The note was discounted at 10 percent.

Required:

    On the books of the Trellis Supply Company, make the journal entries to record (1) the receipt of the note and (2) the discounting of the note.

PART B On September 10, 1978, Sherrie Cheves issued a note to Beauty Best, Inc., for merchandise valued at $450. The $450 note was for 60 days at 8 percent interest. Beauty Best, Inc., sent the note to a bank for collection. On November 12, 1978, Beauty Best, Inc., was notified that the note had been collected on November 9, 1978. Beauty Best's bank account was credited for the amount of the note plus interest less a $4.75 collection fee.

Required:

    On the books of Beauty Best, Inc., record (1) the receipt of the note and (2) the collection of the note.

11-3. Trice Wholesale Company often accepts notes in exchange for merchandise and for extension of payment time on previous obligations.

Required:

    Record the following transactions, related to notes receivable, that occurred in 1978.

1978

Jan. 16   Accepted a 60-day, 9 percent note for $200 from Hugh Nail. The note was dated January 16 and is payable at First National Bank, Forsyth. Mr. Nail issued the note for $200 worth of merchandise.

Feb. 20   Accepted a 90-day, 8 percent note for $500 from Pat Bailey. The note was dated February 18 and is payable at Farmer's Bank, Thomaston. Ms. Bailey received extension of payment time on a previous obligation.

Mar. 17   Renewed Hugh Nail's 60-day, 9 percent note for $200. Received interest that was due on the original note.

Apr. 19   Discounted Pat Bailey's note at 10 percent at the First National Bank, Forsyth.

May 16   Received a check from Hugh Nail in payment of his note plus interest.

July 8   Accepted a 90-day, 9 percent note for $400 from Ray Malone in exchange for merchandise. The note was dated July 6 and is payable at County Bank, Woodland. This note was turned over to a bank for collection.

Sept. 24   Accepted a 120-day, 10 percent note for $800 from Tina Evans. The note was dated September 22 and is payable at Farmer's

Bank, Thomaston. Ms. Evans received extension of payment time on a previous obligation.

Oct. 6   Received a memo stating that the company's bank account had been credited for the amount of Ray Malone's note plus interest less a collection fee of $6.

Dec. 31   Recorded the interest that had accrued on Tina Evans's note.

11–4. D. M. Blum, owner and operator of Blum's Department Store, often finds it necessary to issue notes in exchange for cash loans, for goods and services, or for an extension of payment time on a previous obligation. During 1978, Blum was engaged in the following notes payable transactions:

1978

Jan. 15   Issued a $500, 30-day, 9 percent note to Cotton Wholesale Company in exchange for merchandise.

Feb. 14   Issued a check to Cotton Wholesale Company in payment of the note plus interest.

Mar. 1   Issued a note to Merchant's Bank in exchange for a loan of $800 for 90 days at 9 percent.

Apr. 19   Issued a $450, 60-day, 10 percent note to Hair Brothers in exchange for merchandise.

May 30   Issued a check to Merchant's Bank in payment of the note plus interest.

June 18   Renewed note issued to Hair Brothers and paid accrued interest.

July 16   Issued a $300, 90-day, 8 percent note to Tejero Company for an extension of payment time on a previous obligation.

Aug. 17   Issued a check to Hair Brothers in payment of the note plus interest.

Oct. 14   Issued a check to Tejero Company in payment of the note plus interest.

Nov. 11   Issued a $700, 90-day, 9 percent note to Gable & Sons, Inc., in exchange for merchandise.

Dec. 31   Recorded the interest that had accrued on the note issued to Gable & Sons, Inc.

Required:

Record the above transactions in general journal form.

11–5. J. D. Shea operates a furniture and appliance store. Sometimes Shea accepts notes from customers and extends their payment time on accounts that are due. During the current year, Shea was involved with the following notes receivable transactions:

Jan. 15   Received a 90-day, 8 percent note for $300 from Abe Lewis. The note was dated January 12 and is payable at Corpus State Bank, Atoka.

Feb. 5   Received a 60-day, 6 percent note for $500 from Bill Nelson. The note was dated February 4 and is payable at First City Bank, Hachita.

Mar. 18   Received a 120-day, 9 percent note for $800 from Candy Olsen. The note was dated March 16 and is payable at First National Bank, Berino.

Apr.   5   Received a check from Bill Nelson in payment of his note plus interest.

     12   Received a check from Abe Lewis in payment of his note plus interest.

May 15   Discounted Candy Olsen's note at 10 percent at First National Bank, Berino.

July 12   Received a 60-day, 9 percent note for $400 from Dawn Pelt. The note was dated July 12 and is payable at Corpus State Bank, Atoka.

Sept. 10   Dawn Pelt was granted a renewal of her note for $400. She also paid the interest due on the old note.

Nov.   9   Received a check from Dawn Pelt in payment of her note plus interest.

Dec.   5   Received a 90-day, 10 percent note for $700 from Elaine Quartz. The note was dated December 1 and is payable at First National Bank, Berino.

Dec. 31   Made an adjusting entry to record accrued interest on notes receivable.

Required:

1. Record the transactions in the general journal.
2. Prepare a notes receivable register to serve as a detailed record of notes received by Shea.

11–6.   Christina Rosado owns and operates Rosado's Furniture Store. Occasionally she issues notes in exchange for cash loans, for goods and services, or for an extension of payment time on a previous obligation. During 1978, Ms. Rosado was involved in the following notes payable transactions:

1978

Jan. 29   Issued a $1,000, 90-day, 10 percent note to First National Bank in exchange for a $1,000 loan.

Mar. 12   Issued a $550, 60-day, 9 percent note to Akruk Wholesale Company in exchange for merchandise.

Apr. 29   Issued a check to First National Bank in payment of the note plus interest.

May 11   Renewed note issued to Akruk Wholesale Company and paid accrued interest.

June 14   Issued a $740, 90-day, 9 percent note to Chang Equipment Company for office equipment costing $740.

July 10   Issued a check to Akruk Wholesale Company in payment of the note plus interest.

Sept. 12   Issued a check to Chang Equipment Company in payment of the note plus interest.

Oct.   5   Issued a $300, 30-day, 8 percent note to the Sigalos Company for an extension of payment time on a previous obligation.

Nov. 4   Issued a check to the Sigalos Company in payment of the note plus interest.
Nov. 16   Issued a $360, 30-day, 10 percent note to First National Bank in exchange for a $360 loan.
Dec. 11   Issued a $405, 60-day, 10 percent note to Korker Manufacturing Company for merchandise.
Dec. 16   Renewed note issued to First National Bank and paid accrued interest.
Dec. 31   Recorded the interest that had accrued on the notes issued to 1st National Bank and Korker Manufacturing Company.

Required:

1.   Record the above transactions in the general journal.
2.   Prepare a notes payable register to serve as a detailed record of notes issued by Ms. Rosado. (All notes are payable at the First National Bank.)

Purchases
Learning objectives

Business managers are becoming aware of the large amounts of working capital (the difference between current assets and current liabilities) that can be released through the use of proper purchasing and payment practices. A study of the following material will provide an understanding of purchasing terminology and accounting procedures:

1. The role of the purchase requisition and purchase order in the purchasing cycle.

2. The manner in which the purchase invoice and carbon copies are used in the purchasing process.

3. Treatment of trade discounts and cash discounts in determining amounts payable.

4. Discussion of the various methods of accounting for transportation charges.

5. A detailed illustration of how purchase invoices are recorded in the invoice register.

6. Procedures used in handling: debit and credit memoranda, corrected invoices, COD purchases, prepaid freight, insurance, and purchase returns and allowances.

12

Purchases

The term "purchase" not only refers to the purchase of merchandise for resale but also includes the buying of various types of property for use within a business. The procedures followed in purchasing activities depend upon the type and size of the business enterprise. The owner of a small retail store may do all the purchasing, or one employee may devote part of his or her time to purchasing. In larger firms, a purchasing department consisting of a manager and staff who devote full time to the purchasing operation may be required.

PURCHASE REQUISITION

Any department within an enterprise may request the purchasing department to purchase merchandise or other items by submitting a form called a **purchase requisition.** Purchase requisitions are generally prenumbered consecutively to prevent their misuse or loss. The requisitions are prepared in duplicate with the original going to the purchasing department and the duplicate being retained by the department preparing the requisition.

Illustration 12–1 is an example of a purchase requisition. The requisition shows merchandise requested by Department A and originates with the head of the department. Upon approval, an order was placed with General Supply Corporation by the purchasing agent, as indicated by the purchasing agent's memorandum. The approved purchase requisition is the purchasing department's authorization to order the merchandise requisitioned.

Illustration 12–1
Purchase requisition

Adams Office Supplies	**PURCHASE REQUISITION**	
415 Concord Lane		Requisition No. B-114
Atlanta, Georgia 30312		

Required for ___Department A___   Date issued ___June 12, 1978___

Advise ___Mr. Adams___ on delivery   Date required ___June 30, 1978___

Quantity	Description
100 dz.	Item 1374 – No. 2 Lead pencils
100 dz.	Item 4856 – Black, fine point, ball-point pens
45 rms.	Item 7420 – 8½ x 11 Erasable bond typing paper

Approved by ___B.R. Jacobs___   Requisition placed by ___T.C. Abrams___

Purchasing Agent's Memorandum

Purchase Order No. ___179___   Issued to: General Supply Corp.
                                                        115 Berkley Dr.
Date ___June 12, 1978___   Nashville, Tenn. 37214

PURCHASE ORDER

A **purchase order** is a written order by a buyer for merchandise or other items recorded on the buyer's purchase requisition. Purchase orders are generally prepared on specially designed forms but may be prepared on a printed stock form or on forms provided by a vendor. Purchase orders are prepared in multiple copies and are numbered consecutively. Generally, but not always, the original copy goes to the vendor, the supplier from whom the goods are ordered. It is also common practice to send both the original and the duplicate copy to the supplier. In such a case, the duplicate is an "acknowledgement copy" on which the supplier will sign to indicate an acceptance of the order, creating a formal contract. This signed copy is then returned to the ordering firm. Who gets the remaining copies of the purchase order is a matter of policy within each firm. The department originating the requisition may get a copy, the receiving department may get a copy, or the accounting department may get a copy. The practice followed with respect to requisitioning, purchasing, receiving, recording, and paying for merchandise by each individual firm will govern the distribution of copies.

Illustration 12–2
Purchase order

PURCHASE ORDER

Adams Office Supplies
415 Concord Lane   Order No.   179
Atlanta, Georgia 30312

                                                          Date   June 12, 1978
                                                          Delivery by   June 30, 1978
   General Supply Corp.   Ship via   Speedy Trucking Co.
TO   115 Berkley Dr.
   Nashville, Tenn. 37214
                                                          FOB   Nashville
                                                          Terms   2/10, n/30

Quantity	Description	Unit Price
100 dz.	Item 1374 – No. 2 Lead pencils	0.60
100 dz.	Item 4856 – Black, fine point, ball-point pens	0.85
45 rms.	Item 7420 – 8½ x 11 Erasable bond typing paper	11.59

B. R. Jacobs

Illustration 12–2 is an example of a purchase order. This document contains the same information as the purchase requisition in Illustration 12–1. In addition, it shows unit prices which have been quoted by the supplier and at which the merchandise is expected to be billed.

INVOICE

An invoice, sometimes referred to as a **purchase invoice,** is a document prepared by a seller which states the items shipped, the cost of the merchandise, and the method of shipment. While this document is considered to be a purchase invoice by the buyer, it is a sales invoice from the seller's viewpoint.

Purchase invoices are normally received by the buyer before the shipment arrives but may be received after the shipment arrives. Upon receipt, the invoice is numbered (consecutively) and compared with a copy of the purchase order to insure that quantities, prices, description, and terms are correct and that the delivery date and method of shipment meet the specifications. A separate form may be used to verify this information, or a rubber stamp may be used to provide an approval section on the invoice. If a separate form is used, it must be attached to the invoice.

The invoice in Illustration 12–3 illustrates the use of a rubber stamp

Illustration 12–3
Invoice

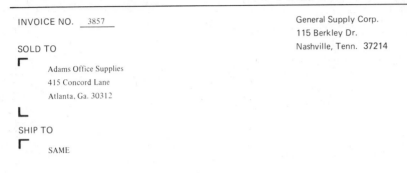

INVOICE NO. ___3857___

General Supply Corp.
115 Berkley Dr.
Nashville, Tenn. 37214

SOLD TO

┌
    Adams Office Supplies
    415 Concord Lane
    Atlanta, Ga. 30312
└

SHIP TO

┌
    SAME

└

INVOICE DATE	YOUR ORDER NO. & DATE		REQUISITION NO.	OUR ORDER NO.	DATE SHIPPED
June 20, 1978	179	June 12, 1978		4317	June 21, 1978

TERMS	FOB	CAR INITIALS & NO.	HOW SHIPPED	SHIPPED FROM	
2/10, n/30	Nashville		Speedy Trucking Co.	Nashville	

QUANTITY SHIPPED	DESCRIPTION	UNIT PRICE	EXTENSION
100 dz.	Item 1374 — No. 2 Lead pencils	.60	60.00
100 dz.	Item 4856 — Black, fine point, ball-point pens	.85	85.00
45 rms.	Item 7420 — 8½ x 11 Erasable bond typing paper	11.59	521.55
			666.55
		Freight	13.50
			680.05

Date received — *June 23*
Received by — *T. M.*
Items OK — *T. M.*
Prices OK — *T. M.*
Ext. and tot. OK — *R. J.*
Invoice no. — *347*
FOB —
Fr. bill no. —
Fr. charges — *13.50*
Approval for payment — *BRJ.*

for approval form. When merchandise is received, the receiving personnel may prepare a **receiving report** indicating the merchandise received, or the contents of the shipment may be compared with a copy of the purchase order. If a receiving report is prepared, it must be compared with the purchase order by personnel in either the accounting or purchasing department. When prices and extensions have been verified, the purchase can be entered in an invoice register (explained later in this chapter) and then posted to the creditor's account in the accounts payable ledger. The invoice is then filed in an unpaid invoice file until it is paid.

Back orders

Often the supplier is unable to fill the complete order at the time requested and must **back order** the items not shipped. In such a case the supplier may ship a partial order and send the invoice for the complete order, indicating what has been back ordered and when it will be shipped.

Trade discounts

Manufacturers and wholesalers of certain types of merchandise often quote list prices in their catalogs which are subject to substantial reductions known as **trade discounts.** This provides a means of revising prices without going through the costly process of revising the catalogs. Also, it provides a means of making price differentials among various classes of customers.

If an order is subject to a trade discount, the discount is generally shown on the face of the invoice as a deduction from the invoice total. If the invoice in Illustration 12–3 had been subject to a trade discount of 15 percent, the discount would be stated in the body of the invoice as shown in Illustration 12–4.

When the invoice is recorded in the invoice register and the accounts payable ledger, it is entered at the net amount after deducting the trade discount. Since trade discounts are merely price reductions, they are not to be entered in either the buyer's or the seller's books.

It is not uncommon to find more than one trade discount allowed on the same invoice. For example an invoice may be subject to a chain discount of 20, 15, and 5 percent. In computing the net invoice amount, the discounts are computed individually on the successive net invoice amounts.

Illustration 12–4

Quantity Shipped	Description	Unit Price	Extension
100 dz.	Item 1374 – No. 2 Lead pencils	0.60	$ 60.00
100 dz.	Item 4856 – Black, fine point, ball-point pens	0.85	85.00
45 rms.	Item 7420 – 8½ × 11 Erasable bond typing paper	11.59	521.55
			$666.55
		Less 15% Discount	99.98
			$566.57

To illustrate, assume that an invoice subject to trade discounts of 20, 15, and 5 percent has a gross amount of $500. The net invoice amount is computed as follows:

Gross invoice amount	$500
Less 20% (20% × $500)	100
Balance	$400
Less 15% (15% × $400)	60
Balance	$340
Less 5% (5% × $340)	17
Net Invoice Amount	$323

Again, when the invoice is recorded, only the net amount, $323, is to be entered. The same amounts can be calculated by multiplying the gross invoice amount by the complements of the discounts allowed. Complements are 100 percent minus the trade discount percentage. For example, the first trade discount is 20 percent, the complement is 100 percent − 20 percent, or 80 percent. In this illustration with trade discounts of 20, 15, and 5 percent, the respective complements are 80, 85, and 95 percent. Therefore, the net invoice amount is calculated by multiplying the gross invoice amount, $500, by $0.8 \times 0.85 \times 0.95$. This equals a net invoice amount of $323.

Cash discounts

While trade discounts are used to make price differentials among different classes of customers and as a means of avoiding catalog revisions, **cash discounts** are used primarily to induce prompt payment by customers. The payment terms should be clearly stated on the face of the invoice. Note that on the invoice in Illustration 12–3 the terms are clearly stated as "2/10, n/30." This means that if the invoice is paid within ten days from the invoice date (June 20 in this example), a discount of 2 percent will be allowed. Hence, should the invoice be paid on or before June 30, a discount of $13.33 (0.02 × $666.55) may be deducted from the invoice amount prior to payment. *Notice that the discount is NOT allowed on the freight charges.* The freight charges have been prepaid by the seller for the convenience of the buyer and must be refunded in full to the seller by the buyer. Thus in this example, assuming that the invoice is paid during the discount period, the amount paid to the vendor is $666.72 ($666.55 − $13.33 + $13.50). If the invoice is not paid within the discount period, the total invoice price plus freight ($680.05) must be paid to the vendor not later than July 20 which is 30 days after the invoice date.

When recording purchases, cash discounts are usually ignored and the invoice is entered at the total price. At the time of payment, the amount of the discount is deducted and a check issued for the net amount. When the check is recorded, the discount will be credited to a **Purchases Discounts account.** At the end of the accounting period the total credit balance of the Purchases Discounts account is shown as a deduction from purchases.

Occasionally an invoice is subject to both cash discounts and trade discounts. In the event of such an occurrence, the trade discounts are deducted from the gross amount of the invoice before the cash discount is applied. For example, assume that an invoice with a gross amount of $1,375 had trade discounts of 25, 10, and 5 percent and the terms were 2/10, n/30. The net amount payable within ten days of the invoice is computed as follows:

Gross invoice amount	$1,375.00
Less 25% (25% × $1,375)	343.75
Balance	$1,031.25
Less 10% (10% × $1,031.25)	103.12
Balance	$ 928.13
Less 5% (5% × $928.13)	46.41
Amount subject to cash discount	$ 881.72
Less 2% cash discount (2% × $881.72)	17.63
Net Amount Payable	$ 864.09

While vendors generally require that an entire invoice be paid within the specified time period in order to obtain the cash discount offered, some vendors allow the discount on partial payment. If such is the case, and a payment of $980 is made within the discount period on an invoice totaling $1,500 with terms of 2/10, n/30, the amount of the discount is computed as follows:

100 Percent = Amount for Which Customer Should Receive Credit
100 Percent − 2 Percent = 98 Percent
98 Percent = $980
$980 ÷ 98 Percent = $1,000
$1,000 − $980 = $20 Discount

To record this transaction the buyer would debit Accounts Payable for $1,000, credit Purchases Discounts for $20, and credit Cash for $980.

Accounts Payable	1,000	
Purchases Discount		20
Cash		980

To record payment on merchandise within the discount period.

COMMON TERMS

Explanations for some terms commonly used in connection with invoices are as follows:

2/10, n/30   This is read as "two ten, net thirty" and means that a 2 percent discount (2 percent of the gross invoice price of the merchandise) is allowed if payment is made within 10 days following the invoice date, and the gross invoice price is due 30 days from the invoice date.

2/EOM, n/60   This is read as "two EOM, net sixty" and means a 2 percent discount may be deducted if the invoice is paid by the end of the month. The discount may not be taken after the end of the month, and payment is due 60 days from the invoice date.

2/10/EOM, n/60   This is read as "two ten EOM, net sixty" and means that a 2 percent discount may be deducted if the invoice is paid by the tenth of the following month. No discount is allowed after that date, and the gross invoice amount is due 60 days from the invoice date.

F.O.B. destination   Free on board at destination. The seller has agreed to be ultimately responsible for all transportation costs and to assume all responsibility for the merchandise until it reaches the buyer's destination.

F.O.B. shipping point   Free on board at shipping point. The buyer has agreed to be ultimately responsible for the freight charges and to assume all risks at the time the merchandise is accepted for shipment by the carrier.

Freight collect   The buyer is to pay the freight when the merchandise arrives. If terms are f.o.b. destination, the buyer will be able to deduct the cost of the freight when paying the invoice.

Freight prepaid   The seller has paid the freight on the goods at the time of shipment. If the terms are f.o.b. shipping point, the seller will be able to collect the cost of the freight from the buyer.

MISCELLANEOUS FORMS ILLUSTRATED

The purchase of merchandise and other property involves the use of a number of forms not previously discussed. These forms, like other documents, must be properly processed. To use them properly, their function must be understood.

Bill of lading

A **bill of lading** is a receipt given to a shipper when merchandise is shipped by airfreight, highway freight, or railroad. The bill of lading is prepared in triplicate (original, shipping order, and memorandum). All three copies are signed by the freight agent who returns the original and memorandum copies to the shipper and retains the shipping copy for his or her records.

While a purchase invoice specified a given quantity of merchandise,

Illustration 12-5

STRAIGHT BILL OF LADING		SHIPPER NO. 4380
ORIGINAL — NOT NEGOTIABLE		CARRIER NO. 7145
CAROLINA FREIGHT CARRIERS CORP.		DATE 7/6/78

(NAME OF CARRIER)

TO:		FROM:	
CONSIGNEE Smith Bros.		SHIPPER Jones, Inc.	
STREET 105 Georgetown Drive		STREET 4481 Elm Street	
DESTINATION Albany, Georgia ZIP CODE 31700		ORIGIN Atlanta, Georgia ZIP CODE 30303	
ROUTE:		VEHICLE NUMBER	

NO. SHIPPING UNITS	KIND OF PACKAGING, DESCRIPTION OF ARTICLES, SPECIAL MARKS AND EXCEPTIONS	WEIGHT	SUBJECT TO CORR.	RATE	CHARGES (FOR CARRIER USE ONLY)
1	1 Carton Redwood Stain	45 lbs.			

REMIT C.O.D. TO	**COD** AMT: $	C.O.D. FEE PREPAID ☐ COLLECT ☐ $
ADDRESS		TOTAL CHARGES $

NOTE—Where the rate is dependent on value, shippers are required to state specifically in writing the agreed or declared value of the property. The agreed or declared value of the property is hereby specifically stated by the shipper to be not exceeding.

$ _____ per _____

Subject to Section 7 of the conditions, if this shipment is to be delivered to the consignee without recourse on the consignor, the consignor shall sign the following statement:
The carrier shall not make delivery of this shipment without payment of freight and all other lawful charges.

(Signature of Consignor)

FREIGHT CHARGES:
FREIGHT PREPAID   Check box except when box at right is checked   Check box if charges are to be collect ☐

RECEIVED, subject to the classifications and tariffs in effect on the date of the issue of this Bill of Lading, the property described above in apparent good order, except as noted (contents and condition of contents of packages unknown), marked, consigned, and destined as indicated above which said carrier (the word carrier being understood throughout this contract as meaning any person or corporation in possession of the property under the contract) agrees to carry to its usual place of delivery at said destination, if on its route, otherwise to deliver to another carrier on the route to said destination. It is mutually agreed as to each carrier of all or any of said property over all or any portion of said route to destination and as to each party at any time interested in all or any of said property, that every service to be performed hereunder shall be subject to all the bill of lading terms and conditions in the governing classification on the date of shipment.
Shipper hereby certifies that he is familiar with all the bill of lading terms and conditions in the governing classification and the said terms and conditions are hereby agreed to by the shipper and accepted for himself and his assigns.

SHIPPER	CARRIER CAROLINA FREIGHT CARRIERS CORP. Agent
PER	PER David C. Bailey
	DATE 7/6/78

the corresponding bill of lading may differ from the invoice as to quantity and description. The reason for this is that merchandise is shipped in crates, cartons, or other packages rather than the individual containers. The total number of packages and total weight are indicated on the bill of lading. Freight charges are based upon the total weight of the merchandise, the type of merchandise, and the distance it is being shipped. A bill of lading is shown in Illustration 12-5.

COD

Merchandise is often purchased under terms requiring payment upon delivery. This is known as collect on delivery or Cash on Delivery (**COD**). At the time of delivery, the cost of merchandise, transportation, and COD charges must be paid by the recipient. When COD shipments are made by freight, the bill of lading specifies the amount to be collected by the transportation company. The transportation company will then collect this amount plus a COD charge and will send the transportation charges to the shipper.

Freight and drayage

When merchandise is received for shipment by a transportation company, the agent of the transportation company prepares a waybill. This document describes the merchandise being shipped, shows the point of origin and destination, and indicates special handling requirements, if any. The original is forwarded to the transportation company's agent at the destination of the shipment. The agent prepares a **freight bill,** a bill for the transportation charges. The freight bill is similar to the bill of lading; however, in addition to the description of the shipment, freight charges are shown.

If it is necessary for the buyer to obtain services from a trucking company or delivery service to move the merchandise from the freight office to the buyer's location, additional costs known as **drayage** will be incurred. In this case the trucking company will prepare and submit a drayage bill to the recipient for services rendered.

Debit and credit memoranda

Merchandise is not always received in satisfactory condition or according to the terms agreed upon by the buyer. The shipment may be damaged, may be the wrong merchandise, or may be delivered too late.

Illustration 12–6
Debit memorandum

Adams Office Supplies	Debit Memorandum No. 24
415 Concord Lane	Date 8/6/78
Atlanta, Georgia 30312	

TO: General Supply Corp.
115 Berkley Dr.
Nashville, Tenn. 37214

Your account has been debited as follows:

In reference to your Invoice No. 4752 dated 8/3/78, six chairs arrived slightly damaged and must be sold as seconds. We believe we can sell the chairs at a satisfactory profit margin and will accept them if an allowance of $120 is granted. We believe this difference should be credited to our account.

Illustration 12–7
Credit memorandum

General Supply Corp.   Credit Memorandum No. 75
115 Berkley Dr.
Nashville, Tenn. 37214

TO: Adams Office Supplies
           415 Concord Lane
           Atlanta, Georgia 30312

Your account has been credited for $120 pertaining to an Invoice No. 4752.

We regret the inconvenience that the receipt of damaged merchandise may have caused you.
Your effort to sell the merchandise rather than returning it to us is greatly appreciated.

Illustration 12–8
Credit memorandum

CREDIT MEMORANDUM

General Supply Corp.   Date   July 8, 1978
115 Berkley Dr.
Nashville, Tenn. 37214

TO   Adams Office Supplies
       415 Concord Lane
       Atlanta, Georgia 30312

WE CREDIT YOUR ACCOUNT AS FOLLOWS

Description	Quantity	Unit Price	Extension	Total
Item 1374 – No. 2 Lead pencils	100 dz.	0.60	60.00	60.00

In such cases the buyer may return the shipment to the vendor, or may agree to keep the shipment if granted an allowance.

Assume first that the buyer has purchased 12 office chairs for resale and 6 are slightly damaged. Rather than return the chairs the buyer might request that an allowance be granted. Thus, a **debit memorandum** would be prepared as shown in Illustration 12-6.

After deciding that the amount of the adjustment is reasonable, General Supply Corporation would send a **credit memorandum** similar to the one in Illustration 12-7.

Occasionally, merchandise is received in such condition that it cannot be sold and must be returned. Upon notification and receipt of the merchandise, the vendor will issue a credit memorandum which might appear as shown in Illustration 12-8. This document shows that General Supply Corporation has given Adams Office Supplies credit for the return of 100 dozen pencils.

The accounting procedures followed in accounting for purchases are determined by the type and nature of the business, the volume of purchases, and the type and quantity of information desired. The following is a discussion and illustration of procedures that can be applied to numerous businesses in accounting for purchases.

INVOICE REGISTER

An **invoice register** is a book of original entry in which all invoices dealing with purchases on account, whether the purchases involve merchandise, supplies or other items, are recorded. The invoice register may be set up on a departmental basis to provide more information and perhaps better control.

Generally, property purchased consists of one of three things: (1) merchandise for resale; (2) supplies for use in the course of the business; or (3) equipment (long-lived assets) for use in operating the business. Therefore, an invoice register is set up to handle these types of transactions.

When an invoice register is used to record all incoming purchase invoices, adequate provision should be made for proper classification of debits and credits. Often, the Purchases accounts are kept on a departmental basis; therefore, a separate column is needed for recording the purchases of each department. The use of a separate column for each department permits summary posting. In addition, General Ledger debit and credit columns must also be provided in order to record items which must be posted individually to the general ledger accounts. Also, a column is needed for accounts payable since the purchases are made on account.

The use of the invoice register for recording incoming invoices for purchases on account will be illustrated below. A group of selected transactions will be recorded in the invoice register, the invoices will be posted to the accounts payable subsidiary ledger, and posting will be made from the invoice register to the general ledger account. There will not be a breakdown of purchases by departments.

This illustration involves Jones and Hicks, a retail plumbing supply business in Greenville, South Carolina. The accounts and corresponding account numbers involved in the purchase of merchandise and on account are as follows:

501	Purchases	143	Office Supplies
502	Purchases Discounts	151	Office Equipment
503	Purchase Returns and Allowances	161	Delivery Equipment
530	Transportation-In	251	Notes Payable
		260	Accounts Payable

Jones and Hicks use the form of invoice register shown in Illustration 12–9. A narrative of the transactions which have been entered in the register is given below. Each transaction should be examined and how it was entered in the register should be noted.

JONES AND HICKS
Narrative of Transactions

Date   Description
1978
July 1 Received Purchase Invoice No. 178 from Plumbing Fixtures, Inc., Atlanta, Ga.: bathtubs, $1,875; terms, June 29 – 2/10, n/30; freight prepaid and added to invoice, $54.75.
      2 Received Purchase Invoice No. 179 from Smith Office Supply Company, Greenville: office supplies, $118.50; terms, July 2 – net 30.
      2 Received Purchase Invoice No. 180 from Lincoln Lavatories, Winston Salem: lavatories, $956; terms, June 30 – 2/10, n/30; freight prepaid and added to invoice, $27.60.
      5 Received Purchase Invoice No. 181 from Business Machines, Raleigh: typewriter, $450; terms, July 2 – net 30; freight prepaid and added to invoice, $25.
      6 Received Purchase Invoice No. 182 from Thompson Metals, Asheville: metal piping, $2,540; terms, July 3 – 2/10, n/30; freight prepaid and added to invoice, $114.85.
      8 Received Purchase Invoice No. 183 from Smithwick Motors, Greenville: delivery truck, $4,250; terms, July 6 – 180-day note with interest at 9 percent.
      9 Received Purchase Invoice No. 184 from Plumbing Parts, Atlanta, Ga.: chrome faucets, $348.50; terms, July 8 – 2/10, n/30; freight collect.
     12 Received a corrected invoice from Thompson Metals, $2,600 excluding freight. See Invoice No. 182.
     12 Received a corrected invoice from Plumbing Fixtures, Inc., $1,850 excluding freight. See Invoice No. 178.
Transactions for the remainder of the months have been omitted.

Corrected purchase invoices

Often, an incorrect invoice will be received, and at a later date another purchase invoice will be received to correct the initial invoice. If the cor-

Illustration 12–9

INVOICE REGISTER

Month of July 1978 — Page 7

Debit — General Ledger								Credit		General Ledger		
Purchases	Acct. No.	Amount	✓	Day	Date of Invoice	Invoice No.	Name	Accounts Payable ✓	Acct. No.	Amount	✓
1,875.00	530	54.75	✓	1	6/29	178	Plumbing Fixtures, Inc.	1,929.75			
	143	118.50	✓	2	7/2	179	Smith Office Supply Company	118.50			
956.00	530	27.60	✓	2	6/30	180	Lincoln Lavatories	983.60			
	151	475.00	✓	5	7/2	181	Business Machines	475.00			
2,540.00	530	114.85	✓	6	7/3	182	Thompson Metals	2,654.85			
	161	4,250.00	✓	8	7/6	183	Smithwick Motors		251	4,250.00	✓
348.50				9	7/8	184	Plumbing Parts	348.50			
60.00	260	25.00	✓	12	7/3	182	Thompson Metals (corrected invoice)	60.00			
				12	6/30	178	Plumbing Fixtures, Inc. (corrected invoice)		501	25.00	✓
16,456.75	260	5,843.50	31					17,450.25		4,850.00	
(501)		(✓)						(260)		(✓)	

rected purchase invoice is received before the initial invoice has been entered in the invoice register, the initial invoice may be discarded and the corrected invoice may be entered in the invoice register. If the initial invoice has already been entered in the invoice register when the corrected invoice is received, only the difference between the two invoices is recorded. If the corrected invoice is for a greater amount than the initial invoice, the difference is debited to the proper account and credited to accounts payable. (See Invoice No. 182.) This amount is also posted to the proper creditor's account in the accounts payable subsidiary ledger.

If the amount of the corrected invoice is less than the amount of the initial invoice, the difference (a decrease) is debited to Accounts Payable and credited to the proper account. The amount is also posted to the proper creditor's account in the accounts payable subsidiary ledger. (See Invoice No. 178.) Also, the corrected invoice should be attached to the initial invoice.

Proof of the invoice register

At any point in time, the invoice register may be footed (totaled) and the total debits compared with the total credits to prove the invoice register. The total debits must equal the total credits. Jones and Hicks's invoice register was proved as of July 31 in the following manner:

Account Column	Debit	Credit
Purchases	$16,456.75	
General ledger	5,843.50	
Accounts payable		$17,450.25
General ledger		4,850.00
Totals	$22,300.25	$22,300.25

Posting procedure

Transactions are posted to both the general ledger and the accounts payable subsidiary ledger. This includes both summary posting and individual transaction posting. The ledgers used in the Jones and Hicks example include the general ledger (balance column accounts) in Illustration 12-10 and the accounts payable subsidiary ledger in Illustration 12-11. Upon entering each purchase invoice in the invoice register, the invoice was used to post to the proper creditor's account in the accounts payable subsidiary ledger. The invoice number is placed in the P.R. (Posting Reference) column in the accounts payable subsidiary ledger.

Posting to creditors' accounts directly from the invoice provides certain advantages over posting from the invoice register (which is also permissible). The invoice provides all the necessary information for

Illustration 12–10

GENERAL LEDGER (Partial)

Office Supplies   Account No. 143

Date		Explanation	P.R.	Debit	Credit	Balance
1978 July	1	Balance				67.50
	2		IR7	118.50		186.00

Office Equipment   Account No. 151

Date		Explanation	P.R.	Debit	Credit	Balance
1978 July	1	Balance				6,550.00
	5		IR7	475.00		7,025.00

Delivery Equipment   Account No. 161

Date		Explanation	P.R.	Debit	Credit	Balance
1978 July	1	Balance				8,475.00
	8		IR7	4,250.00		12,725.00

Notes Payable   Account No. 251

Date		Explanation	P.R.	Debit	Credit	Balance
1978 July	1	Balance				500.00
	8		IR7	4,250.00		4,750.00

Accounts Payable   Account No. 260

Date		Explanation	P.R.	Debit	Credit	Balance
1978 July	1	Balance				2,357.50
	12		IR7	25.00		2,332.50
	31		IR7		17,450.25	19,782.75

Purchases   Account No. 501

Date		Explanation	P.R.	Debit	Credit	Balance
1978 July	1	Balance				98,143.18
	12		IR7		25.00	98,118.18
	31		IR7	16,456.75		114,574.93

Illustration 12–10 (*continued*)

		Transportation-In			Account No. 530	
Date		Explanation	P.R.	Debit	Credit	Balance
1978 July	1	Balance				1,856.17
	1		IR7	54.75		1,910.92
	2		IR7	27.60		1,938.52
	6		IR7	114.85		2,053.37

Illustration 12–11

ACCOUNTS PAYABLE SUBSIDIARY LEDGER (Partial)

Business Machines

Date		Explanation	P.R.	Debit	Credit	Balance
1978 July	5	7/2 – net 30	181		450.00	450.00
	5	Freight prepaid	181		25.00	475.00

Lincoln Lavatories

Date		Explanation	P.R.	Debit	Credit	Balance
1978 July	1	Balance	✔			1,275.00
	2	6/30 – 2/10, n/30	180		956.00	2,231.00
	2	Freight prepaid	180		27.60	2,258.60

Plumbing Fixtures, Inc.

Date		Explanation	P.R.	Debit	Credit	Balance
1978 July	1	6/29 – 2/10, n/30	178		1,875.00	1,875.00
	1	Freight prepaid	178		54.75	1,929.75
	12	Corrected invoice	178	25.00		1,904.75

Plumbing Parts

Date		Explanation	P.R.	Debit	Credit	Balance
1978 July	1	Balance	✔			407.25
	9	7/8 – 2/10, n/30	184		348.50	755.75

Illustration 12–11 (*continued*)

Smith Office Supply Company

Date		Explanation	P.R.	Debit	Credit	Balance
1978 July	1	Balance	✓			248.65
	2	7/2 – net 30	179		118.50	367.15

Thompson Metals

Date		Explanation	P.R.	Debit	Credit	Balance
1978 July	1	Balance	✓			1,146.50
	6	7/3 – 2/10, n/30	182		2,540.00	3,686.50
	6	Freight prepaid	182		114.85	3,801.35
	12	Corrected invoice	182		60.00	3,861.35

proper posting, whereas additional information would have to be entered in the invoice register before it could be used for posting. For example, the invoice register does not contain the terms of a purchase invoice. In addition, certain errors can be eliminated. If an error is made in entering an invoice in the invoice register and posting to the accounts payable subsidiary ledger is done from the invoices, the same error is not likely to be made in the accounts payable subsidiary ledger. However, if the invoice register is used for posting to the accounts payable subsidiary ledger, an error in the invoice register will carry through to the accounts payable subsidiary ledger.

Posting directly to creditors' accounts from the invoices provides efficiency and a method of internal control. One person may enter the invoices in the invoice register and post from the invoice register to the general ledger while another person may post from the invoices to creditors' accounts in the accounts payable subsidiary ledger. This creates a separation of duties, and a check on accuracy can be obtained at any time by comparing the total of the accounts payable subsidiary ledger with the balance of the Accounts Payable control account maintained in the general ledger.

Summary posting

Summary posting is performed at the end of the month from the invoice register as illustrated in the Jones and Hicks example. The total of the column headed Purchases was debited to Purchases, Account No. 501, in the general ledger. The total of the column headed Accounts Payable was credited to Accounts Payable, Account No. 260, in the general ledger. As the total of each of these columns was posted, the account number was written in parentheses below the total in the invoice register to indicate that posting was complete. The page number of the invoice register was entered in the P.R. column of the general ledger as a cross-reference. A check mark (✔) was placed below the totals of the other columns of the invoice register to indicate that these totals were not posted.

Individual posting

Every invoice entered in the Accounts Payable column of the invoice register must be posted to the proper creditor's account in the accounts payable subsidiary ledger. If transportation charges are prepaid and stated separately, they must be posted separately from the merchandise or other property purchased. This procedure is necessary since discounts are not allowed on transportation charges.

In addition, it is necessary to individually post each item entered in the General Ledger debit and credit columns of the invoice register. This posting is generally performed daily, and a check mark (✔) is placed in the check (✔) column beside the amount posted. The invoice number is entered in the P.R. column of the subsidiary ledger account to which the amount is posted. (See the ledgers for Jones and Hicks, Illustrations 12–10 and 12–11.)

Cash and COD purchases

Cash and COD purchases are generally not entered in the invoice register. Purchases of these types are recorded in the cash disbursements journal. (Cash purchases may be recorded in the same manner as purchases on account, however.) If cash purchases are recorded in the cash disbursements journal, no entry is made in the individual creditors' accounts. The cost of property purchased under COD terms is the total amount paid (including COD charges and any transportation costs). Payment must be made prior to receipt of the property; hence, the COD purchase is essentially treated as a cash purchase. The cash disbursements journal is used for the initial recording, and the proper account is debited for the total cost, including transportation and COD charges, and cash is credited for the same amount.

Transportation costs

Shipping charges may be prepaid by the seller or paid by the buyer at the time of delivery. The merchandise may be delivered to the buyer or may be delivered to a freight office where the buyer obtains the merchandise or incurs the additional cost of having it delivered.

Prepaid freight.   If the shipper pays the transportation charges **(freight prepaid)**, the amount may or may not be added to the invoice, depending upon the terms of the sale. If the terms are FOB shipping point, it is understood that the buyer will pay the shipping costs in addition to the invoice price. If the terms are FOB destination, it is understood that the invoice price includes the shipping costs and the buyer is obligated to pay only the invoice price.

Freight collect.   If merchandise is shipped **FOB shipping point, freight collect,** the buyer must pay the shipping charges before obtaining possession of the merchandise. The method of recording these shipping charges is the same as for recording shipping charges prepaid by the seller and added to the invoice.

If merchandise is shipped **FOB destination,** freight collect, the buyer must pay the shipping charges before obtaining possession of the merchandise; however, the buyer deducts the transportation charges from the invoice amount when paying the creditor.

Recording transportation charges.   Transportation charges may be recorded as a debit to purchases; however, a more common practice is to record the transportation charges on incoming merchandise in a separate account titled **Transportation-In.** This account is treated as an extension of the Purchases account and is included in cost of goods sold.

In the Jones and Hicks illustration, the shipping charges are recorded as a separate item in a Transportation-In account. The only transportation charges reflected in the invoice register are those which have been prepaid by the seller and added to the invoice. All other transportation costs on merchandise purchased will be recorded in the cash disbursements journal.

Transportation costs on long-lived assets, such as office and delivery equipment, should be treated as part of the cost of the asset. (See Invoice No. 181 in the Jones and Hicks illustration.) It does not matter if the freight is prepaid or collect. The amount of freight is still recorded as a part of the asset cost in the asset account.

Insurance on merchandise.   Generally, merchandise shipped by parcel post mail is insured against loss or damage in transit. These insurance charges are rarely recorded as a separate item. Usually, they are either charged directly to the Purchases account or included with transportation costs in the Transportation-In account.

If the purchaser does not want merchandise insured, he or she assumes the risk of loss or damage in transit, since title to merchandise shipped by parcel post mail ordinarily passes to the purchaser when it is placed in the hands of the post office for delivery.

Purchase returns and allowances

A purchaser may receive a credit memorandum from the seller as a result of returning merchandise or being granted an allowance by the seller. In either instance, the transaction should be recorded by debiting Accounts Payable and crediting **Purchase Returns and Allowances.** Also, the creditor's account in the accounts payable subsidiary ledger should be debited for the amount of the credit memorandum.

AUTOMATED ACCOUNTING SYSTEMS

The purchasing process involves a number of steps including:

1. Requisitioning.
2. Issuing purchase orders.
3. Receiving and inspection.
4. Storing.
5. Checking accuracy of vendors' invoices with respect to prices, extensions, and footings.
6. Processing returns and allowances.
7. Maintaining adequate accounts payable records.
8. Making payments to vendors.

If a firm has a large volume of purchases, it might be feasible to use some automated purchasing system. Data may be keypunched on cards or paper tapes or recorded on magnetic tapes, and computers can be used to process the data and produce the desired records. Also, since purchases are directly related to inventories and cash disbursements, the automated accounting system might be designed to include cash disbursements and account for transactions including merchandise inventory.

GLOSSARY

Back orders orders or parts of orders that cannot be filled at the time requested but which will be shipped at a later date.

Bill of lading a receipt given to a shipper when merchandise is shipped by air freight, highway freight, or rail. It indicates the total number of packages, the total weight, and a description of the packages.

Cash discounts a means of inducing prompt payment by customers by allowing a deduction from the gross invoice amount if the invoice is paid within a specified time period. It is a sales discount to the seller and a purchases discount to the buyer.

COD   collect on delivery or cash on delivery meaning that payment is required at the time the merchandise is delivered.

Credit memorandum   a document that a seller uses to inform a buyer that the buyer's Accounts Receivable account on the seller's books has been credited due to errors, returns, or allowances.

Debit memorandum   a document that a buyer uses to inform a seller that the seller's Accounts Payable account on the buyer's books is being debited due to an error or an allowance for damaged merchandise.

Drayage   additional costs incurred when a buyer must obtain services from a trucking company or delivery service to move the merchandise from the freight office to the buyer's location.

F.O.B. destination   free on board at destination. Freight terms which indicate that the seller has agreed to be ultimately responsible for all transportation costs and to assume all responsibility for the merchandise until it reaches the buyer.

F.O.B. shipping point   free on board at shipping point. Freight terms which indicate that the buyer has agreed to be ultimately responsible for the freight charges and to assume all risks at the time the merchandise is accepted for shipment by the carrier.

Freight bill   a bill for the transportation charges. It is similar to a bill of lading, but it shows the freight charges in addition to a description of the shipment.

Freight collect   terms indicating that the buyer is to pay the freight when the merchandise arrives. If terms are f.o.b. destination, the buyer will be able to deduct the amount of the freight when paying the invoice.

Freight prepaid   terms indicating that the seller has paid the freight on the goods at the time of shipment. If the terms are f.o.b. shipping point, the seller will be able to collect the amount of the freight from the buyer.

Invoice register   a book of original entry in which all invoices dealing with purchases on account, whether the purchases involve merchandise, supplies, or other items, are recorded.

Purchase invoice   a document prepared by the seller which states the items shipped, the cost of the merchandise, and the method of shipment. It is a sales invoice to the seller and a purchase invoice to the buyer.

Purchase order   a form prepared by a buyer and sent to a seller requesting items indicated on the buyer's purchase requisition.

Purchase requisition   a form submitted by any department within an enterprise requesting the purchasing department to purchase merchandise or other items.

Purchase returns and allowances account   an account in which the cost of merchandise returned is recorded and in which deductions granted by the seller due to unsatisfactory merchandise are recorded. Its balance is shown as a deduction from purchases.

Purchases discounts account   an account in which the amount of cash discounts taken is recorded. At the end of the accounting period, its balance is shown as a deduction from purchases.

Receiving report a report prepared by the receiving personnel indicating the merchandise received. It should be compared with the purchase order.

Trade discounts reductions in the list prices of merchandise. They are a means of making price differentials among various classes of customers. They are also a means of revising prices without going through the costly process of revising the catalogs.

Transportation-In account an account in which transportation charges on incoming merchandise are recorded. It is an extension of the purchases account and, thus, is included in cost of goods sold.

Waybill a document prepared by an agent of the transportation company when merchandise is received for shipment. It describes the merchandise being shipped, shows points of origin and destination, and indicates any special handling requirements.

QUESTIONS AND EXERCISES

1. Distinguish among a purchase requisition, a purchase order, and a purchase invoice.

2. Distinguish between trade discounts and cash discounts.

3. What is a bill of lading? Why might the quantity specified on the bill of lading differ from the quantity shown on the purchase invoice?

4. What is meant by the following terms?

   a. 2/10, n/30.
   b. 2/EOM, n/60.
   c. 2/10/EOM, n/60.

5. Define the following terms:

   a. Waybill.
   b. Drayage.

6. What eight steps are involved in the purchasing process?

7. What types of transactions are recorded in a Purchase Returns and Allowances account?

8. Define the following terms:

   a. f.o.b. destination.
   b. f.o.b. shipping point.
   c. Freight collect.
   d. Freight prepaid.

9. How are transportation charges on (*a*) merchandise purchases and (*b*) long-lived assets commonly recorded?

10. What factors should be considered when computing the freight charges on a shipment of merchandise?

PROBLEMS

12-1. PART A   The Wells Garden Equipment Company ordered the following merchandise from the Byron Manufacturing Corporation:

Item	Quantity	Unit price
Shovels	50	$10.00
Hoes	30	7.50
Wheel barrows	10	35.25
Rakes	25	5.75

The gross invoice amount is subject to a trade discount of 15 percent. Shipping terms are f.o.b. shipping point, and the freight charges of $40 were prepaid by the Byron Manufacturing Corporation. The Wells Garden Equipment Company does not maintain an invoice register.

Required:

Prepare a general journal entry to record the receipt of the merchandise.

PART B   Assume that the Wells Garden Equipment Company purchased the merchandise listed in Part A under the following conditions:

a.   The gross invoice amount was subject to a chain discount of 20, 15, and 5 percent.
b.   Shipping terms were f.o.b. destination.
c.   Wells Garden Equipment Company paid the freight charges ($40) when the merchandise arrived.

Required:

Prepare general journal entries to record the receipt of the merchandise and the payment of the freight charges.

12-2.   The Cowboy Shop ordered the following items from the Ranchers Company:

Item	Quantity	Unit price
Boots	25 pairs	$30.00
Spurs	40 pairs	9.50
Chaps	32 pairs	28.00
Western shirts	50	20.00
Jeans	70 pairs	12.00

The gross amount of the invoice is subject to trade discounts of 25, 10, and 5 percent, and the payment terms are 2/10, n/30. The invoice date is April 15.

Required:

1. Compute the following items:

    a. Gross invoice amount.
    b. Amount subject to cash discount.
    c. Net amount payable within ten days of invoice date.

2. Make the general journal entry to record the receipt of the purchase invoice.
3. Make the general journal entry to record payment for the merchandise if the payment is made on April 24.
4. Make the general journal entry to record payment for the merchandise if the payment is made on May 10.

12–3. The Coaster Store ordered merchandise from the Carson Wholesale Company at a gross invoice amount of $3,600. This amount ($3,600) is subject to trade discounts of 20, 10, and 5 percent, and the payment terms are 2/10, n/60. The Carson Wholesale Company allows a discount to be taken when partial payment is made during the discount period.

Required:

1. Make the journal entry to record the receipt of the purchase invoice.
2. Make the journal entry to record payment for the entire shipment of merchandise during the discount period.
3. Make a journal entry to record a partial payment of $1,800 during the discount period.
4. Make a journal entry to record payment for the merchandise 30 days after the invoice date.

12–4. The King and Cole Sporting Goods Store completed the following purchase transactions during the month of May 1978.

1978

May 3 Received Purchase Invoice No. 201 from Roberts Wholesale for baseball equipment, $900; terms, May 1 – 2/10, n/30; freight prepaid and added to invoice, $45.50.

    6 Received Purchase Invoice No. 202 from Novak, Incorporated, for tennis equipment, $425; terms, May 1 – 2/10, n/30; freight collect.

   10 Received Purchase Invoice No. 203 from Palmer Golf Company for golf equipment, $1,080; terms, May 5 – 2/10, n/60; freight collect.

   13 Received Purchase Invoice No. 204 from Bradley Milton Company for indoor and outdoor games, $575; terms, May 10 – 2/10, n/30; freight prepaid and added to invoice, $32.

   17 Received Purchase Invoice No. 205 from Hargrove Supply Company for office supplies, $280; terms, May 14 – 2/10, n/60; freight collect.

May 20   Received Purchase Invoice No. 206 from Flemmen & Sons for store equipment, $650; terms, May 15 – n/60; freight prepaid and added to invoice, $85.

24   Received a corrected purchase invoice from Palmer Golf Company for $1,028. (See Invoice No. 203.)

Required:

Record each of the invoices in an invoice register like the one shown in Illustration 12–9. The following account numbers may be used:

160   Office Supplies
180   Store Equipment
210   Accounts Payable
510   Purchases
515   Transportation-In

12–5. The Printer's Shop is a retail store which sells books, office supplies, and school supplies. During the month of August, the following selected transactions occurred:

1978
Aug. 2   Received Purchase Invoice No. 410 from Reading, Incorporated, for reference books, $800; terms, July 28 – 2/10, n/30; freight collect.

6   Received Purchase Invoice No. 411 from Kano Supply Company for school supplies, $500; terms, August 3 – n/30; freight collect.

9   Received Purchase Invoice No. 412 from Daze & Son for store equipment, $350; terms, August 4 – 2/10, n/60; freight prepaid and added to invoice, $43.

13   Received Purchase Invoice No. 413 from Joe's Autos for a delivery car, $5,000; terms, August 10 – 2/10, n/60; freight prepaid and added to invoice, $185.

16   Received a corrected purchase invoice from Kano Supply Company for $550. (See Invoice No. 411.)

20   Received Purchase Invoice No. 414 from Reading, Incorporated, for educational books, $600; terms, August 16 – 2/10, n/30; freight collect.

23   Received Purchase Invoice No. 415 from Haas Supply Company for office supplies for resale, $489; terms, August 21 – n/30; freight prepaid and added to invoice, $36.

27   Received Purchase Invoice No. 416 from Odell Printing Company for Bibles and other religious books, $750; terms, August 23 – 2/10, n/60; freight prepaid and added to invoice, $62.

30   Received a corrected purchase invoice from Haas Supply Company for $469 plus $36 freight charges. (See Invoice No. 415.)

Required:

1.   Record each of the invoices in an invoice register like the one shown in Illustration 19–9, and post the invoice amount directly to the creditor's account in a subsidiary accounts payable ledger. (See balances below.)

2. Make the necessary individual postings and summary postings to the following accounts in the general ledger:

Account No.	Account Title	Balance, 7/31/78
148	Store equipment............................	$ 400
149	Delivery car.................................	0
221	Accounts payable.........................	10,000
511	Purchases...................................	21,000
518	Transportation-in	580

Subsidiary Accounts Payable Balances (*Partial*)
August 1, 1978

Daze & Son...	$200
Haas Supply Company	150
Joe's Autos..	0
Kano Supply Company	120
Odell Printing Company............................	500
Reading, Incorporated	200

12-6. The Snow Hardware Company has just completed its first month in business. During this month, the following purchase transactions occurred:

1978

Jan. 3   Received Purchase Invoice No. 10 from Abby's Wholesale for radios, $450; terms, December 29 — 2/10, n/30; freight prepaid and added to invoice, $18.

8   Received Purchase Invoice No. 11 from Cook's Appliances for appliances, $1,200; terms, January 3 — 2/10, n/60; freight collect.

10   Received Purchase Invoice No. 12 from Hansel Company for watches and clocks, $380; terms, January 7 — 2/10/E.O.M, n/60; freight collect.

14   Received Purchase Invoice No. 13 from Cobra Wholesale for athletic equipment, $950; terms, January 10 — 2/10, n/30; freight prepaid and added to invoice, $84.

17   Received Purchase Invoice No. 14 from Abby's Wholesale for toys and games, $620; terms, January 15 — 2/10, n/30; freight prepaid and added to invoice, $25.

19   Received a corrected purchase invoice from Cook's Appliances for $1,120. (See Invoice No. 11.)

21   Received Purchase Invoice No. 15 from King Supply Company for office supplies, $200, and store supplies, $500; terms, January 17 — 2/10, n/30; freight collect.

23   Received Purchase Invoice No. 16 from Florida Equipment Company for office equipment, $600; terms, January 16 — 2/10/EOM, n/60; freight prepaid and added to invoice, $45.

24   Received a corrected purchase invoice from Abby's Wholesale for $602 plus freight (No. 14).

24   Received Purchase Invoice No. 17 from Cobra Wholesale for guns and knives, $800; terms, January 20 — 2/10, n/30; freight prepaid and added to invoice, $80.

Jan. 28   Received Purchase Invoice No. 18 from Brooks Manufacturing Company for hand tools and power tools, $960; terms, January 23 – 2/10, n/60; freight collect.

   30   Received Purchase Invoice No. 19 from Byron's Bikes for bicycles, tricycles, and unicycles, $1,000; terms, January 23 – 2/10, n/60; freight prepaid and added to invoice, $125.

Required:

1. Record each of the invoices in an invoice register like the one shown in Illustration 19–9, and post the invoice amount directly to the creditor's account in a subsidiary accounts payable ledger.
2. Make the necessary individual and summary postings to the following accounts in the general ledger:

Account No.	*Account Title*
130	Office Supplies
131	Store Supplies
140	Office Equipment
212	Accounts Payable
401	Purchases
404	Transportation-In

3. Prepare a schedule of accounts payable on January 31, 1978.

Accounting for sales
Learning objectives

Accounting for sales may be thought of as the opposite of accounting for purchases since each transaction is a purchase to one business and a sale to another. The following material on sales repeats some of the items covered in Chapter 12 on purchases, but from a seller's point of view:

1. A discussion of the manner in which sales are normally made: cash, credit, approval, COD, consignment, and installment.

2. Accounting treatment and processing of incoming purchase orders.

3. Calculation of sales discounts and handling of sales returns and allowances.

4. Detailed illustration of procedures used in recording credit sales in the sales register and the subsequent posting of the sales register amounts to the appropriate accounts.

5. Accounting treatment of cash sales.

13

Accounting for sales

The procedures used in accounting for sales depend on several factors. A great deal depends on the type of business, organization of the sales department, type of goods sold, volume of sales, method of selling, and the sales terms. There are a number of steps in the accounting cycle for sales transactions. When the orders are received they must be examined for acceptability, terms determined, credit approved, a sales invoice prepared, merchandise packed and shipped or delivered, and finally collection is made before the sales cycle is complete.

The second step in the sales cycle is the determination of the appropriate terms of sale. The terms selected will necessarily affect the procedures used in handling the sales transaction. Below is a list of the terms on which sales are normally made:

1. For cash.
2. On credit.
3. On approval.
4. COD.
5. On consignment.
6. On installment.

SALES FOR CASH

While some businesses sell for cash or on credit, others sell for cash only. Examples include snack shops, newsstands, food stores, and some gas stations. Various procedures are used to handle cash sales. When cash sales are numerous, one or more types of cash registers are likely to be used. Sales may be accumulated on the cash register in several ways. Some registers have the ability to accumulate various subtotals in addition to the total sales amount. Depending on the keys punched, subtotals may be accumulated by department, by type of merchandise, or by salesperson. If a sales tax is required, it is usually recorded separately. Sales tickets are normally prepared in duplicate form. One copy is given to the customer as a receipt, and the second copy is retained in the register and later removed by a person in the accounting department who will analyze and record the sale. The cash register is a means of internal control since the total cash sales for the day should be reconciled to the cash in the register drawer. If more than one person operates the register, it is best to have a separate register drawer for each cashier.

SALES ON CREDIT

Sales on credit are often referred to as sales on account or charge sales. In such a sales transaction, the seller exchanges merchandise for the buyer's promise to pay at a later date. A credit sale is recorded by debiting or charging Accounts Receivable and by crediting the Sales account. The balance owed by each individual customer will be recorded in an accounts receivable subsidiary ledger. Most wholesale sales and a significant portion of retail sales are now made on credit. Since the business that sells on account assumes an additional risk, it is best to investigate the financial condition of the buyers. Larger businesses often have a credit department which establishes credit policies and approves or disapproves individual credit sales. Experienced credit managers have learned to establish credit policies that will neither be so tight as to reduce sales not so loose as to create excessive bad debt losses.

Salesclerks should be careful not to sell on credit to anyone who is not an approved credit customer. The problem is significantly lessened by providing established credit customers with credit cards or charge cards. Not only do the cards provide evidence that the buyer has an account, but they can be used in a mechanical device to print the customer's name, address, and account number on the sales ticket. In a wholesale business, a large portion of the sales orders are received by phone or mail. Such credit sales are approved in a routine manner before the goods are released. It is not necessary that credit sales orders received by phone or mail be processed immediately as the buyer is not personally waiting for the order.

It should be remembered that the presentation of a charge card by a prospective buyer does not necessarily mean that the card belongs to the bearer. To make sure the card belongs to the holder, the salesclerk may request further identification or may compare the signature on the charge card with the one on the sales ticket.

SALES ON APPROVAL

A **sale made on approval** means that the customer has the right to return the goods within a specified time period. Because of this, the sale is not final until the customer's intentions are known. Mail-order businesses engaged in the sale of stamps, coins, or books are examples of businesses which sell on approval. Approval sales may be handled as charge sales and returns treated as ordinary sales returns. They may also be handled as cash sales. When treated as such, a record is kept until it is known that the customer will keep the goods. By a specified date, the customer must either pay for the goods or return them. The accountant may wait until payment is received, and then it may be recorded as a cash sale.

Approval sales should not be confused with lay away sales or "will call" sales. Such sales may be made for cash or on credit. In either case, the buyer has agreed to purchase the goods with the understanding that the goods will be picked up and paid for at a later date. When the goods are purchased, a deposit may or may not be made. Although accounting for deposits is not uniform, they are usually handled in the same manner as cash sales. When the deposit is treated as a cash sale, the balance due is handled as a charge sale by preparing a sales ticket. The transaction is recorded by debiting Accounts Receivable and crediting the proper sales account. As with credit sales, the uncollected balance will be recorded in the accounts receivable subsidiary ledger.

When financial statements are prepared at the end of the accounting period, the cost of the goods being held for future delivery will not be included in the ending inventory. Since the goods have been accounted for as a sale, they are the property of the customer and should not be included in the inventory.

COD SALES

Merchandise may be sold for **cash on delivery (COD)**. Such terms call for payment by the buyer when the goods are delivered. The delivery and collection agent may be an employee of the seller, the post office, an express company, a trucking company, a railroad company, a steamship company, or any other common carrier.

Cash on delivery sales made by a retail business are usually recorded as cash sales. At the end of each day, the COD sales tickets are separated and a COD list is prepared for control purposes. Upon approval, the merchandise is delivered and the sales price is collected. After the money is turned in by the delivery agent, the agent is credited for the collection on the COD list and the sale is recorded in the same manner as that used for a cash sale. If the customer refuses the merchandise, it is returned to the stock room and the sale is canceled. It should be remembered that title to the goods purchased does not pass to the buyer until payment has been received. Therefore, the inventory is considered to be the property of the seller until payment is made. Although delivery may be made through the post office or other common carrier, retail merchants who sell on COD terms usually make their own deliveries and collections.

In contrast with retail merchants, wholesalers usually record COD sales in the same manner as charge sales. Sales to out-of-town customers are usually delivered by a common carrier. When shipment is made by parcel post or express, the delivery agent will retain possession of the merchandise until collection is made. Payments collected will then be sent to the seller by money order or check. When the payment is received by the seller, it is handled in the same manner as any other payment received in full or part settlement of an account.

SALES ON CONSIGNMENT

Sometimes a business will market goods on a **consignment** basis. When sold on a consignment basis, the merchandise is shipped to an agent dealer with the agreement that the agent dealer is not required to pay for the goods unless they are sold. Under such a method of selling, title to the goods consigned is retained by the shipper until the goods are sold by the agent dealer. The owner of the goods shipped on consignment is referred to as the **consignor.** The agent dealer is called the **consignee.** When the goods are shipped, an invoice of shipment is prepared. The invoice of shipment should not be referred to as a sales invoice since the consignment shipment is not a sale. The shipment invoice is used to inform the consignee of the goods shipped.

The consignee may work on a commission basis, or may earn a profit by making additional markups on the merchandise. Periodically, the consignee will prepare a "statement of consignment sales." This statement will show consigned goods on hand, consignment sales made, expenses chargeable to the consignor such as transportation, insurance, and storage expenses, and the amount due to the consignor.

Many types of goods such as livestock, vegetables, radios and televisions, garden equipment, power tools, and other products are often marketed on a consignment basis. The goods may be shipped to the consignee to be sold at a price specified by the consignor. If the consignee is not paid on a commission basis, certain discounts may be allowed from the consignor's list prices based upon sales volume.

INSTALLMENT SALES

Property such as appliances, stereo equipment, furniture, clothes, automobiles, real estate, and many other types of merchandise are sold on an **installment** basis. Such a method refers to a plan whereby the seller agrees to give the buyer physical possession of the goods in exchange for a promise to make payments periodically over a specified time interval. The agreement between the buyer and seller is referred to in legal terms as a conditional sales contract. Quite often a down payment is required. The sales contract will contain wording to the effect that the seller will retain title to the property until payment is made in full. The contract may state that the full sales price will become due immediately should the buyer default in making payment. The different types of contract wording bear out the fact that a buyer should carefully read and understand the contract terms before signing the contract.

Since the buyer does not receive title to the property until full payment is made, a business can be more lenient in extending credit to customers who buy on installment. A higher price is usually charged for goods sold on installment to offset the added risk imposed on the seller for waiting to collect payments and the additional record-keeping expenses involved.

Installment sales and consignment sales will not be further described as they are specialized areas of accounting for sales. For additional discussion on these subjects, a reliable intermediate accounting textbook should be consulted.

HANDLING OF INCOMING PURCHASE ORDERS

A wholesale merchant will usually receive sales orders by telephone, mail, or telegram. Purchase orders may be written on the purchase order form, letter head, or other stationery of the buyer, or on an order blank of the seller when received by mail. Orders received over the telephone should be carefully recorded on prepared forms. Regardless of the procedures used in handling purchase orders, it is important that well-organized procedures be established and followed. Such procedures should increase efficiency and aid in the prevention of clerical mistakes. The following steps will help assure that purchase orders are properly handled.

Examination

As each purchase order is received, it should be examined. The customer's identity should be determined, and the description and quantities of goods ordered should be reviewed. Incoming orders may be from old or new customers. If the customer has not been contacted by a salesperson and has never placed an order, the order may be difficult to identify. Due to the carelessness of some customers, the descriptions of goods ordered may be difficult to interpret. Sometimes merchandise is ordered by name, inventory number, or special code word. The person examining the purchase orders should make sure the inventory number or code word agrees with the merchandise description. Abbreviated inventory names and titles along with code words are often used when ordering by telegram or cablegram.

Credit approval

Part of the examination described above should include the separation of orders involving credit from all other incoming orders. The credit orders should be sent to the credit department for approval before any billing or shipping takes place. If the order is a COD order, it should also be approved by the credit department. If a customer does not customarily accept COD orders, the seller will have to bear the additional shipping charges when an order is returned. On the other hand, if a customer abuses the COD privilege, he or she may be asked to make full or partial payment before the order is shipped. It is not uncommon for sellers to require a partial cash payment to accompany all COD orders.

Review accuracy of purchase order

When the purchase order extensions and additions are reviewed, particular attention should be given to unit prices. Inaccurate pricing will result in incorrect billing as well as unnecessary customer ill will.

Transportation

As each order is processed, it is necessary to determine how the order will be shipped and who will bear the transportation expenses. Orders may be shipped by parcel post, express, rail, or by one of the firm's own delivery trucks. Orders transportated by a common carrier are usually insured. Express orders will go by rail or air while freight shipments may be delivered by truck, rail, air, or water.

When shipments are sent by parcel post, the transportation charges must be prepaid. Express or freight transportation charges may be paid by the seller or by the purchaser upon receipt of the goods. If the transportation charges are prepaid, the inclusion or exclusion of shipping charges on the invoice will depend on whether the invoice price was quoted for f.o.b. destination or f.o.b. shipping point.

Freight shipments require that shipment routes be predetermined. It is not uncommon for a buyer to specify how the order is to be shipped. If no preference is indicated by the buyer, the seller must decide among rail, truck, air, or water. Once the method of transportation is decided, the seller may have to decide what transportation company is to be used.

Shipments involving more than one method of transportation together with several transportation companies may add further complications.

Billing

After the purchase order is examined for accuracy of pricing and is approved for credit and the method of shipping is determined, a bill or sales invoice may be prepared. Shown in Illustration 13–1 is a purchase

Illustration 13–1
Purchase order received

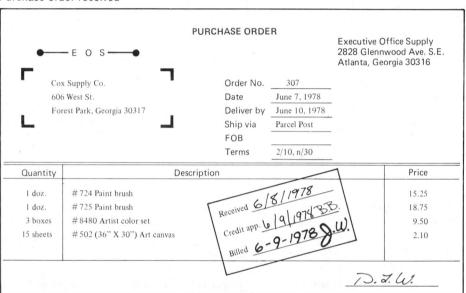

order received by Cox Supply Company from the Executive Office Supply Company. When the purchase order was received, it was rubber stamped, as shown, and the date of receipt was recorded in the space provided. Later, the date and initials of the persons responsible for credit approval and billing were recorded in the appropriate spaces. After the billing was completed, the purchase order was filed alphabetically by customer name, Executive Office Supply Company, for future reference.

Sales invoices are normally prepared in multicopy form. This may be done through the use of carbon paper, no carbon required invoice forms, or by some type of duplicating device. At least three copies are required. The original copy is sent to the customer, a copy is sent to the accounting department, and a copy is forwarded to the shipping department authorizing the shipment of the described merchandise. The sales invoice

Illustration 13–2
Customer copy of sales invoice

		COX SUPPLY CO. 606 West St. Forest Park, Ga. 30317		Invoice No. 3401 Terms: 2/10, n/30 Salesman: O. Scott.	

Sold to	Ship to		
Executive Office Supply		Invoice date	6/9/1978
2828 Glennwood Ave. S.E.	SAME	Customer order	309
Atlanta, Georgia 30316		Date order rec.	6/8/1978
		Date shipped	6/9/1978
		Shipped via	Parcel Post

Quantity	Description	Unit Price	Amount
1 doz.	# 724 Paint brush	15.25	15.25
1 doz.	# 725 Paint brush	18.75	18.75
3 boxes	# 8480 Artist color set	9.50	28.50
15 sheets	# 502 (36" X 30") Art canvas	2.10	31.50
			94.00
		Postage	4.25
			98.25

— CUSTOMER COPY —

shown in Illustration 13–2 was prepared for the purchase order received from the Executive Office Supply Company in Illustration 13–1. For control purposes, sales invoices should be prenumbered consecutively.

In addition to the sales invoice copies described above, other copies may be prepared. When the sale is made by a branch office, a copy may be forwarded to that office. Another copy may be sent to the salesperson making the sale. To make sure shipments are properly addressed, a copy may be sent to the shipping department. In such cases, the buyer's address may be separated from the sales invoice and used as a shipping label.

PURCHASES DISCOUNTS

Quite often suppliers will allow trade discounts to established customers. Such discounts are normally shown as a reduction in the total sales invoice amount. These discounts should not be reflected in the seller's accounts as they are simply reductions in the selling price of the merchandise.

As a means of encouraging prompt payment, cash discounts are frequently offered. Cash discounts are normally offered by wholesalers in contrast to retailers who seldom offer them. If a cash discount is to be offered, it should be noted in the terms of the sale. Since it is not known whether the discount will be taken at the time of the sale, the cash discount should be ignored when recording the sale. If the discount is taken and the payment determined to be correct, the discount may be treated as an expense, or as a reduction in sales. Although the discount can be treated as an expense, it is normally shown as a subtraction from gross sales on the earnings statement.

Although more than one sales account may exist (account for each department, territory, branch, etc.), the **sales discounts** taken are usually accumulated in a single account. This presents a problem when trying to determine the net sales for each sales unit. Even though a discount account could be maintained for each sales account, the increased accuracy is not worth the additional effort. The problem is usually solved by allocating the total sales discounts to the various sales accounts in proportion to the net sales of each department.

SALES RETURNS AND ALLOWANCES

If the merchandise shipped is damaged or unacceptable, the buyer may request a credit for merchandise returned or an allowance on the defective goods. Credit for the return or allowance is made by issuing a credit memorandum similar to the one shown in Illustration 12–7.

A separate **Sales Returns and Allowances account** is usually maintained for each Sales account. When the earnings statement is prepared, each sales returns and allowances account balance is subtracted from the related sales amount. An example of the sales section of the Cox Supply Company is shown in Illustration 13–3.

◀Illustration 13–3

COX SUPPLY COMPANY
Earnings Statement
For the Year Ended December 31, 1978

		Office Department		Art Department	Total
Sales		$108,784.76		$48,282.19	$157,066.95
Less: Sales returns and allowances		(3,530.45)		(1,230.01)	(4,760.46)
Sales discounts	(69%)	(1,853.33)	(31%)	(832.66)	(2,685.99)
Net Sales		$103,400.98		$46,219.52	$149,620.50

ACCOUNTING PROCEDURE

As indicated earlier in the chapter, Cox Supply Company is a wholesaler of office supplies. Two years ago the company added a line of art supplies. Sales in the office and art departments are recorded in separate accounts. Each of the charge sales is entered in a sales register. A separate column is used for the office supply and art supply departments. General Ledger debit and credit columns are included for items that will be posted individually. If a subsidiary accounts receivable ledger is kept, it is necessary to maintain an Accounts Receivable control account in the general ledger.

The accounting procedure for recording charge sales on a departmental or sales unit basis will be illustrated in the following pages. The documents and transactions of the Cox Supply Company will be used throughout the illustration. As mentioned earlier, Cox Supply Company is a wholesaler of office and art supplies. A description of the sales transactions is given in Illustration 13–4. The sales register used by Cox Supply Company is shown in Illustration 13–5. Illustrated postings to the general ledger and accounts receivable subsidiary accounts are presented in Illustrations 13–6 and 13–7, respectively.

Terms of 2/10, n/30 are given on all charge sales. Large orders involving considerable weight are usually sent by express or freight. When such shipments occur, the transportation charges are handled on a collect basis. Parcel post charges are simply added to the invoice price. Any prepaid postage is credited to Postage Stamps, Account No. 185 in the General Ledger column when the invoice is entered in the general ledger. Purchases by local retailers may be picked up or delivered by Cox Supply Company. A small charge is made for local deliveries greater than ten miles. Delivery charges are credited to Other Revenues, Account No. 909.

For recording purposes, the following accounts are used to account for the sales transactions of Cox Supply Company:

> 510 Sales – Office Department
> > 511   Sales Returns and Allowances – Office Department
>
> 520 Sales – Art Department
> > 521   Sales Returns and Allowances – Art Department

Recording sales

The charge sales made by Cox Supply Company during the period of August 1–6 have been recorded in the sales register in Illustration 13–5. Since all sales are made to retail dealers who intend to resell the merchandise, it is not necessary for Cox Supply Company to collect retail sales taxes. A description of the transactions recorded in the **sales**

register is shown in Illustration 13–4. A practical understanding of the procedures used in the sales register can be obtained by tracing each transaction in Illustration 13–4 to the sales register.

Sales invoice corrections. Since no system is error free, procedures should be provided for the correction of errors when they occur. If an error is discovered in an invoice before it is entered in the sales register,

Illustration 13–4

COX SUPPLY COMPANY
Description of Sales Transactions
August 1–6, 1978

August 1

Made the following charge sales:
    No. 807: The Paint Brush, art supplies, $66.75; postage of $6.43 added to invoice.
    No. 808: Baker Office Supply, Office Supplies, $693.18; express collect.
    No. 809: Standard Stationeries, Office Supplies, $125.44; insured parcel post, $12.68.
    No. 810: The Art Shop, art supplies, $54.92; to be delivered.

August 2

Made the following charge sale:
    No. 811: Alexander's, office supplies, $44.88; less credit of $5.08 for defective pencils which were returned. Accounts Receivable was debited for net amount. To be picked up.

August 3

    No. 812: Henson Office Supply, office supplies, $248.52; to be picked up.
    No. 813: The Gallery, art supplies, $164.25, to be delivered.

August 4

Sent Baker Office Supply a corrected invoice for the August 1 purchase of office supplies. The original invoice (No. 808) was for $693.18. The corrected invoice (No. 814) amounted to $698.43.

August 5

    No. 815: Clink Office Equipment Company, office supplies, $240.50; received a 45-day, 7 percent interest-bearing note (Notes Receivable, Account No. 125), to be delivered.

Sent the Paint Brush a corrected invoice for the August 1 purchase of art supplies. The original invoice (No. 807) was for $66.75. The corrected invoice (No. 816) amounted to $56.75. Postage charges remained the same.

August 6

Made the following charge sales:
    No. 817: The Paint Brush, art supplies, $75.15; to be delivered.
    No. 818: Standard Stationeries, office supplies, $108.91; delivery charge of $3.35 added to invoice.
    No. 819: Baker Office Supply, office supplies, $1,043.19; freight collect.
    No. 820: The Paint Brush, art supplies, $444.70; postage of $31.95 added to invoice.

Transactions for August 8 through August 31 are omitted.

Illustration 13–5

SALES REGISTER

	Debit							Credit				
	General Ledger							Sales		General Ledger		
Acct. No.	Amount	✓	Accounts Receivable	✓	Day	Name	Sale No.	Office Dept.	Art Dept.	Acct. No.	Amount	✓
			73.18	✓	1	The Paint Brush	807		66.75	185	6.43	✓
			693.18	✓	1	Baker Office Supply	808	693.18				
			138.12	✓	1	Standard Stationeries	809	125.44		185	12.68	✓
			54.92	✓	1	The Art Shop	810		54.92			
511	5.08	✓	39.80	✓	2	Alexander's	811	44.88				
			248.52	✓	3	Henson Office Supply	812	248.52				
			164.25	✓	3	The Gallery	813		164.25			
			5.25	✓	4	Baker Office Supply	814	5.25				
125	240.50	✓			5	Clink Office Equipment Co.	815	240.50				
520	10.00	✓			5	The Paint Brush	816			120	10.00	✓✓
			75.15	✓	6	The Paint Brush	817		75.15			
			112.26	✓	6	Standard Stationeries	818	108.91		909	3.35	✓
			1,043.19	✓	6	Baker Office Supply	819	1,043.19				
			476.65	✓	6	The Paint Brush	820		444.70	185	31.95	✓
455.82 (✓)			12,648.19 (120)		31			8,933.51 (510)	3,952.06 (520)		218.44 (✓)	

a corrected invoice should be prepared. The new invoice is entered in the sales register in the usual manner, and the original invoice is canceled. If the error is discovered after the original invoice has been entered and the postings completed, a corrected invoice should be prepared. When the corrected invoice is more than the original invoice, the increase is recorded in the sales register by debiting Accounts Receivable and by crediting the appropriate sales account (See Sale No. 814). The amount of increase should be posted as a debit to the customer's account in the accounts receivable subsidiary ledger.

The reverse procedure is used when the corrected invoice amount is less than the original invoice amount. The decrease is recorded by debiting the appropriate sales account and by crediting Accounts Receivable (see sale No. 816). The amount of decrease should be posted as a credit to the customer's account in the accounts receivable subsidiary ledger.

For future reference, a copy of the corrected invoice should be filed with the original invoice. A copy of the corrected invoice should be promptly forwarded to the customer.

Proving the sales register.   The sales register of Cox Supply Company is normally proved at the end of each month when the register is posted. However, when a page is completed, the register should be proved before proceeding to the next page. The register may be proved at any time by footing the columns and comparing the sum of the debit footings with the sum of the credit footings. The following schedule was prepared to prove the sales register of Cox Supply on August 31:

Account Column	Debit	Credit
General ledger	$ 455.82	
Accounts receivable	12,648.19	
Sales – office department		$ 8,933.51
Sales – art department		3,952.06
General ledger		218.44
Totals	$13,104.01	$13,104.01

Posting procedure

Both the general ledger and accounts receivable subsidiary ledger accounts used by Cox Supply Company are in the debit-credit-balance form. Those general ledger accounts used to record sales transactions are shown in Illustration 13–6. The accounts in the accounts receivable subsidiary ledger are presented in Illustration 13–7.

The presence of general ledger and subsidiary ledger accounts requires the use of both individual and summary postings. As each sales transaction is recorded in the sales register, it is also recorded in the appropri-

Illustration 13–6

GENERAL LEDGER (Partial)
Accounts Receivable   Account No. 120

Date		Explanation	P.R.	Debit	Credit	Balance
1978						
Aug.	1	Balance	✔			8,482.16
	5		SR33		10.00	8,472.16
	31		SR33	12,648.19		21,120.35

Notes Receivable   Account No. 125

Date		Explanation	P.R.	Debit	Credit	Balance
1978						
Aug.	1	Balance	✔			3,328.50
	5		SR33	240.50		3,569.00

Postage Stamps   Account No. 185

Date		Explanation	P.R.	Debit	Credit	Balance
1978						
Aug.	1	Balance	✔			67.92
	1		SR33		6.43	61.49
	1		SR33		12.68	48.81
	6		SR33		31.95	16.86

Sales—Office Department   Account No. 510

Date		Explanation	P.R.	Debit	Credit	Balance
1978						
Aug.	1	Balance	✔			68,492.25
	31		SR33		8,933.51	77,425.76

Sales—Art Department   Account No. 520

Date		Explanation	P.R.	Debit	Credit	Balance
1978						
Aug.	1	Balance	✔			28,301.20
	5		SR33	10.00		28,291.20
	31		SR33		3,952.06	32,243.26

Sales Returns and Allowances—Office Department   Account No. 511

Date		Explanation	P.R.	Debit	Credit	Balance
1978						
Aug.	1	Balance	✔			135.18
	2		SR33	5.08		140.26

Illustration 13–6 (*continued*)

Other Revenue					Account No. 909
Date	Explanation	P.R.	Debit	Credit	Balance
1978 Aug. 1	Balance	✔			784.15
6		SR33		3.35	787.50

ate customer account in the accounts receivable subsidiary ledger. Postings to individual customer accounts are made directly from the sales invoice. This is done to lessen the probability of duplicating any errors which may have been made in the sales register. Furthermore, posting from the sales register would require that additional information necessary for posting be recorded in the register. This would increase the size of the register making it more cumbersome and less efficient.

If performed properly, posting from the sales invoice will provide additional internal control. A sound system would require that one accountant enter the sales invoices in the sales register and perform the necessary postings to the general ledger. A second accountant would post directly from the sales invoices to the individual customer accounts. When the work is so divided, the employees' work can be proved by preparing a schedule of accounts receivable and comparing the subsidiary ledger total with the balance of the Accounts Receivable control account in the general ledger.

Postings to customer accounts in the subsidiary ledger may be performed manually or by some type of machine. The type of equipment used will normally depend on the volume of sales transactions. If only a few transactions are involved, the posting will probably be performed manually. A larger number of transactions may require that a manually operated posting machine be used. For businesses with a large volume of sales transactions, it may be advantageous to use an electronic computer. It is important to remember that the system should be large enough to handle expected sales growth but not so large to cause unnecessary expense because of excess capacity.

Posting individually. As each sales transaction is entered in the sales register, the recorded debit or credit must be posted to the customer's account in the subsidiary ledger. Debits may be the result of charge sales or invoice corrections while credits may result from invoice corrections or sales returns and allowances. If the sale involves prepaid shipping charges, the merchandise amount and shipping charges are recorded separately (see Sale No. 807 and related postings). Shipping charges are recorded separately since they are not subject to cash discounts for

Illustration 13–7

ACCOUNTS RECEIVABLE LEDGER (Partial)
The Paint Brush

Date		Explanation	P.R.	Debit	Credit	Balance
1978						
Aug.	1	Balance	✔			133.18
	1	Merchandise	807	66.75		199.93
	1	Postage	807	6.43		206.36
	5	Corrected invoice	816		10.00	196.36
	6	Merchandise	817	75.15		271.51
	6	Merchandise	820	444.70		716.21
	6	Postage	820	31.95		748.16

Baker Office Supply

Date		Explanation	P.R.	Debit	Credit	Balance
1978						
Aug.	1	Balance	✔			-0-
	1	Merchandise	808	693.18		693.18
	4	Corrected invoice	814	5.25		698.43
	6	Merchandise	819	1,043.19		1,741.62

Standard Stationeries

Date		Explanation	P.R.	Debit	Credit	Balance
1978						
Aug.	1	Balance	✔			25.32
	1	Merchandise	809	125.44		150.76
	1	Postage	809	12.68		163.44
	6	Merchandise	818	108.91		272.35
	6	Delivery charge	818	3.35		275.70

The Art Shop

Date		Explanation	P.R.	Debit	Credit	Balance
1978						
Aug.	1	Balance	✔			108.16
	1	Merchandise	810	54.92		163.08

Alexander's

Date		Explanation	P.R.	Debit	Credit	Balance
1978						
Aug.	1	Balance	✔			7.43
	2	Merchandise	811	39.80		47.23

Illustration 13–7 (*continued*)

Henson Office Supply

Date		Explanation	P.R.	Debit	Credit	Balance
1978 Aug.	1	Balance	✔			-0-
	3	Merchandise	812	248.52		248.52

The Gallery

Date		Explanation	P.R.	Debit	Credit	Balance
1978 Aug.	1	Balance	✔			206.75
	3	Merchandise	813	164.25		371.00

prompt payment. The selling terms of 2/10, n/30 only apply to the amount of merchandise purchased.

Individual postings are also required for items recorded in the General Ledger debit and credit columns of the sales register. Such postings are normally performed daily or as the items are recorded. As a means of indicating whether or not the amounts have been posted, a check mark (✔) is placed in the check column as the items are posted. To cross-reference the posting, the page number of the sales register is entered in the P.R. column of the affected general ledger or subsidiary ledger account.

Posting in summary. The following postings are made in summary at the end of each month:

1. The Accounts Receivable column total was posted as a debit to Accounts Receivable, Account No. 120, in the general ledger.
2. The Sales – Office Department column total was posted as a credit to Sales – Office Department, Account No. 510, in the general ledger.
3. The Sales – Art Department column total was posted as a credit to Sales – Art Department, Account No. 520, in the general ledger.

As each column total was posted, the account number of the account being posted to was recorded below the column total. To cross-reference the posting, the page number of the sales register was entered in the P.R. column of the general ledger account. To indicate that the General Ledger debit and credit columns are not to be posted, a check mark is placed below those column totals.

Cash sales

Since Cox Supply Company is a wholesale business, most of the sales are made on account. Although the practice will vary from firm to firm, Cox Supply Company only records credit sales in the sales register. When cash sales occur, they are recorded in the cash receipts record by debiting the bank or cash account and by crediting the appropriate sales account. Entries may be made in the cash receipts record as each cash sale is made or through the use of a summary entry at the end of each business day or other designated time period. Because no receivable arises from a cash sale, it is not necessary to post the sales transaction to individual customer accounts. The use of a cash receipts record is illustrated in Chapter 18.

COD sales

Cox Supply Company accounts for COD sales in the same manner as they do for charge sales. As with ordinary credit sales, several days may pass before a payment is received from an out-of-town customer who has ordered on COD terms. Under such a system, COD sales orders are entered in the sales register in the same manner as ordinary credit sales. As explained earlier in the chapter, the customer pays the carrying agent who in turn forwards the remittance to the seller. Upon receipt, the remittance is recorded in the cash receipts record along with other cash payments. Also, as individual payments are received, they should be posted to the accounts receivable subsidiary ledger.

Sales returns and allowances

Sales returns and allowances usually result from damaged or defective merchandise or from shipments that do not satisfy the customer's needs. Upon request, the seller will issue a credit memorandum to the buyer for the adjustment. The credit memo is recorded by debiting the appropriate sales returns and allowances account and by crediting Accounts Receivable. The adjustment should also be posted to the customer's account in the accounts receivable subsidiary ledger.

As an example, assume that The Paint Brush requested an allowance on an order of drawing paper that had received water damage during shipment. In response to the request, Cox Supply Company issued a credit memorandum for $41.52. The following general journal entry was used to record the allowance:

```
Sales Returns and Allowances—Art Department....................... 41.52
     Accounts Receivable—The Paint Brush.............................          41.52
Credit Memorandum No. 67 issued to The Paint Brush.
```

After the entry was recorded in the general journal, the allowance amount was posted to the customer's account (The Paint Brush) in the accounts receivable subsidiary ledger.

If credit memorandums are only issued occasionally, they can be recorded in the manner described above. When there is a significant number of credit memorandums issued, it may be advantageous to use a sales returns and allowances journal. Such a journal is similar to a sales register except that there are Returns and Allowances debit columns for each sales account and a credit column for accounts receivable. Since the sales register is used to record sales and the returns and allowances journal is used to cancel or partially cancel the sale, the columnar arrangement of the returns and allowances journal should be opposite from that of the sales register.

Shipping charges

When shipments are sent by parcel post, the postage charges and any related insurance charges must be prepaid. If the buyer is to bear these charges, they should be added to the face of the invoice. Unless the customer requests otherwise, Cox Supply Company sends all express and freight shipments on a transportation charges collect basis. When express and freight charges are prepaid, the charges are recorded by debiting **Transportation-Out,** Account No. 812, and by crediting the bank account. When the sale and related shipping charges are recorded in the sales register, the Transportation-Out account is credited for shipping charges. If all shipping charges were charged to the customers, the Transportation-Out account should have a zero balance at the end of the month. However, when shipments are made f.o.b. destination, the seller bears the shipping charges. In such a case, the Transportation-Out account will have a debit balance. The debit balance will represent the amount of selling expense incurred from the seller's bearing of shipping charges.

If a significant amount of shipping charges is prepaid, it may be helpful to provide a special credit column in the sales register to record the charges that are to be added to the customer's sales invoice. When postings are made, the column total will be posted in summary as a credit to Transportation-Out.

Automated processing of sales transactions

Businesses with a large volume of sales transactions may find it advisable to install a more advanced system to handle sales transactions. The degree of automation will vary depending on the system needed to satisfy the user's needs. Throughout the sales cycle, a number of transactions must be performed involving different forms. The more advanced systems will permit purchase order data to be punched on cards, recorded on magnetic tape, or entered in through a computer terminal. With proper programming, the system will analyze the purchase order for completeness, perform a credit check, prepare a sales invoice, issue shipping orders, adjust inventory levels, keep an accounts receivable subsidiary ledger, and make the necessary individual and summary postings to related accounts. Most systems with the capabilities described above will also be programmed to prepare the customer's monthly statements as well as to assist in the preparation of monthly reports.

GLOSSARY

COD sales   cash on delivery sales. Terms calling for payment by the buyer when the goods are delivered.

Consignee   an agent dealer who is not required to pay for goods unless they are sold.

Consignor   the owner of goods shipped on consignment. The consignor retains title to the goods consigned until they are sold by an agent dealer.

Installment sales   a method of selling whereby the seller agrees to give the buyer physical possession of the goods in exchange for a promise to make payments periodically over a specified time interval.

Sales Discounts account   an account in which cash discounts taken by customers are recorded. The balance in the account is subtracted from gross sales on the earnings statement.

Sales invoice   a document prepared by the seller which states the items shipped, the cost of the merchandise, and the method of shipment. It is a purchase invoice to the buyer.

Sales on approval   sales made on terms that allow the customer the right to return the goods within a specified time period. Sales on approval can be handled either as charge sales or as cash sales.

Sales on consignment   a method of selling that involves the shipment of merchandise from a consignor to an agent dealer or consignee with the agreement that the consignee is not required to pay for the goods unless they are sold.

Sales on credit   a sales transaction in which the seller exchanges merchandise for the buyer's promise to pay at a later date. Also referred to as sales on account or charge sales.

Sales register   a book of original entry in which credit sales and, sometimes, cash sales transactions are recorded.

Sales Returns and Allowances account   an account in which the selling price of returned merchandise and allowances (deductions from sales prices) granted to customers because of unsatisfactory merchandise are recorded. Its balance is shown as a deduction from sales on the earnings statement.

Transportation-Out account an account which is debited when the seller prepays express and freight charges and which is credited when the sale and related shipping charges are recorded in the sales register. A debit balance in the account represents the amount of selling expenses incurred from the seller's bearing of shipping charges.

QUESTIONS AND EXERCISES

1. What are some of the factors that must be considered when an accountant is trying to establish procedures to account for sales transactions?

2. List the steps that should be followed to account for sales transactions.

3. Identify (*a*) sales on credit and (*b*) sales on approval.

4. Explain how goods are sold on a consignment basis.

5. Identify the following terms:

   a. Consignor.
   b. Consignee.
   c. Invoice of shipment.
   d. Statement of consignment sales.

6. What is an installment sale? Name some goods that are sold on an installment basis.

7. The Caldwell Company has two sales departments. In 1978, Department A had sales of $208,000 and sales returns and allowances of $5,820, and Department B had sales of $109,600 and sales returns and allowances of $1,860. At December 31, 1978, the sales discounts account had a balance of $5,900. Prepare the sales section of the earnings statement for the Caldwell Company for the year ended December 31, 1978.

8. What procedures should be followed if an error is discovered in an invoice (*a*) before it is entered in the sales register and (*b*) after it is entered in the sales register and the postings are completed?

9. Why should postings to individual customer accounts be made directly from the sales invoice instead of from the sales register?

10. Why are shipping charges recorded separately from the amount of merchandise purchased?

PROBLEMS

13–1. R. E. Sigmon is a wholesale distributor of chemical supplies and pool supplies. Sigmon keeps merchandise accounts on a departmental basis. During the month of January 1978, Sigmon made the following charge sales:

Jan. 5 No. 100: Aldridge & Sons, chemical supplies, $250.
       8 No. 101: Holton and Pope, pool supplies, $560.
       9 No. 102: Frost Company, chemical supplies, $100, and pool sup-
          plies, $300.
      10 No. 103: Starnes and Staton, pool supplies, $150.
      15 No. 104: Hope Hunt Company, chemical supplies, $680.
      16 No. 105: Lindsey Brothers, chemical supplies, $490.
      17 No. 106: Sundry Supply Incorporated, pool supplies, $280.
      19 No. 107: Aldridge & Sons, chemical supplies, $305.
      22 No. 108: Bill Weiss, pool supplies, $195.
      23 No. 109: Oscar's Place, pool supplies, $308.
      24 No. 110: Frost Company, chemical supplies, $200.
      29 No. 111: Bill Weiss, pool supplies, $240.
      30 No. 112: Gray and White, chemical supplies, $306.
      31 No. 113: Wells and Wilson, pool supplies, $250 and chemical sup-
          plies, $485.

Required:

1. Record the above charge sales in a sales register like the one in Illustra-
    tion 13–5.
2. Foot and rule the sales register on January 31, 1978.

13–2. Richard Benton and Elane Kitchens own and operate a wholesale store
       which sells farm and garden supplies, tools, and equipment. The store is
       divided into two departments — the farm department and the garden depart-
       ment. Terms of 2/10, n/30 are given on all charge sales. During the month of
       May, the following charge sales were made:

1978
May 3 No. 303: Anderson & Sons, farm tools, $450; postage of $7 added
        to invoice.
     4 No. 304: Bailey Brothers, farm equipment, $950; express collect.
     6 No. 305: Canning Company, garden supplies, $308; postage of $6
        added to invoice.
     7 No. 306: Duckworth and Drane, garden equipment, $609; freight
        collect.
     8 No. 307: Estes Equipment Company, garden equipment, $498;
        farm equipment, $809; freight collect.
    10 No. 308: Franklin's Hardware Store, garden tools and supplies,
        $350; postage of $5 added to invoice.
    13 No. 309: Gilbert's Shop, garden tools, $205; to be picked up.
    15 Sent Franklin Hardware Store a corrected invoice for the May 10
        purchase of garden tools and supplies. The corrected invoice (No.
        310) amounted to $305. Postage charges remained the same.
    18 No. 311: Highland Company, garden equipment, $568; freight
        collect.
    20 No. 312: Anderson & Sons, garden supplies, $195; to be picked up.
    21 No. 313: Ingram House, farm equipment, $585; express collect.

May 22 No. 314: Jackson Brothers, garden tools, $150 and farm tools, $380; to be picked up.

25 No. 315: Kevin's Supply Store, farm supplies, $286; postage of $4 added to invoice.

27 Sent Ingram House a corrected invoice for the May 21 purchase of farm equipment. The corrected invoice (No. 316) amounted to $558.

29 No. 317: Lee and Lee, farm tools, $580; to be picked up.

31 No. 318: Morris & Sons, farm equipment, $650; freight collect.

Required:

1. Record the above transactions in a sales register like the one in Illustration 13–5. All prepaid postage should be credited to Postage Stamps, Account No. 145. Other accounts that might be needed are as follows:

505 Sales – Garden
506 Sales Returns and Allowances – Garden
510 Sales – Farm
511 Sales Returns and Allowances – Farm
112 Accounts Receivable

2. Foot and rule the sales register on May 31, 1978.

13–3. Ronald Akers and Daniel Ruffin operate a wholesale plumbing and electrical supplies store. Terms of 2/10, n/30 are given for all charge sales. The following charge sales were made during August, 1978:

1978
Aug. 2 No. 721: Ralph Baker, plumbing supplies, $106; to be picked up.

4 No. 722: Bruce Hill, electrical supplies, $96; to be picked up.

6 No. 723: Diana Moore, plumbing supplies, $290; postage of $6 added to invoice.

9 No. 724: Reed and Reagan, electrical supplies, $560; express collect.

11 No. 725: Barker and Britt, plumbing supplies, $300, and electrical supplies, $350; freight collect.

13 No. 726: Bradley Gable, electrical supplies, $255; postage of $3 added to invoice.

16 No. 727: Ralph Baker, plumbing supplies, $85; to be picked up.

18 No. 728: Taylor Company, plumbing supplies, $116; postage of $5 added to invoice.

20 Sent Bradley Gable a corrected invoice for the August 13 purchase of electrical supplies. The corrected invoice (No. 729) amounted to $245. Postage charges remained the same.

23 No. 730: Filbert and Ward, plumbing supplies, $78; to be picked up.

25 No. 731: Bruce Hill, electrical supplies, $110; to be picked up.

27 No. 732: Hilda Wesley, electrical supplies, $75, and plumbing supplies, $130. Postage of $6 added to invoice.

Aug. 30 No. 733: Carey Edenfield, plumbing supplies, $103; to be picked up.

31 No. 734: Lorenson Company, plumbing supplies, $450; freight collect.

Required

1. Record the above charge sales in a sales register like the one in Illustration 13–5. All prepaid postage should be credited to Postage Stamps, Account No. 166.

   Other relevant accounts are as follows:

   122   Accounts Receivable
   510   Sales — Plumbing
   511   Sales Returns and Allowances — Plumbing
   520   Sales — Electrical
   521   Sales Returns and Allowances — Electrical

2. Foot and rule the sales register on August 31, 1978.
3. Assuming that all postings, both individual and summary, have been completed, make the necessary check marks and other notations in the sales register.

13–4. L. White is a wholesaler of television and radio parts and supplies. White keeps merchandise accounts on a departmental basis and sells only to retailers. All charge sales carry the terms of 2/10, n/30. During November 1978, White made the following charge sales:

1978

Nov. 1 No. 946: Corporal Company, television parts, $542; express collect.

2 No. 947: Callaway Brothers, radio parts, $165; postage of $5 should be added to invoice.

3 No. 948: H. C. Allen & Sons, television parts, $250; to be picked up.

4 No. 949: Freeman and Oakley, radio supplies, $92; less credit of $8 for defective earphones which were returned. Accounts Receivable should be debited for the net amount. To be picked up.

5 No. 950: Homrich Brothers, television parts, $385; freight collect.

8 Sent Corporal Company a corrected invoice for the November 1 purchase of television parts. The corrected invoice (No. 951) amounted to $524.

9 No. 952: Callaway Brothers, radio parts, $105; postage of $3 should be added to invoice.

10 ˙ No. 953: Wall's, television parts, $400, and radio parts, $275; express collect.

11 No. 954: Todd Wells, radio parts, $138; postage of $4 should be added to invoice.

12 No. 955: Freeman and Oakley, radio supplies, $104; to be picked up.

Nov. 15 No. 956: Ramsey and Ray, television parts, $198; freight collect.
16 No. 957: Callaway Brothers, radio parts, $123; less credit of $45 for defective parts which were returned. Postage of $3 should be added to invoice. Accounts Receivable should be debited for net amount.
17 No. 958: H. C. Allen & Sons, television supplies, $111; to be picked up.
18 Sent Todd Wells a corrected invoice for the November 11 purchase of radio parts. The corrected invoice (No. 959) amounted to $133. Postage charges remained the same.
19 No. 960: Homrich Brothers, television supplies, $163; postage of $5 should be added to invoice.
22 No. 961: Triplex Company, radio parts, $675; express collect.
23 No. 962: Ramsey and Ray, television parts, $221; to be picked up.
24 No. 963: Wall's, television supplies, $175, and radio supplies, $75; postage of $10 should be added to invoice.
25 No. 964: Freeman and Oakley, radio supplies, $86; to be picked up.
26 Sent Homrich Brothers a corrected invoice for the November 19 purchase of television supplies. The corrected invoice (No. 965) amounted to $169. Postage charges remained the same.
29 No. 966: H. C. Allen & Sons, television parts, $395; express collect.
30 No. 967: Ramsey and Ray, television supplies, $113; to be picked up.

Required:

1. Open the following general ledger accounts and insert the November 1, 1978, balances:

Account
No.	*Account Title*	*Balance, 11/1/78*
113	Accounts receivable	$637
148	Postage stamps	75
505	Sales—television	28,000
506	Sales returns and allowances—television	420
510	Sales—radio	15,600
511	Sales returns and allowances—radio	240

2. Open the following subsidiary accounts receivable ledger accounts and insert the November 1, 1978 balances:

H. C. Allen & Sons	$ 62
Callaway Brothers	106
Corporal Company	55
Freeman and Oakley	22
Homrich Brothers	103
Ramsey and Ray	66

Wall's 102
Todd Wells 45
Triplex Company 76

3. Record the charge sales listed above in a sales register like the one shown in Illustration 13–5. Prepaid postage should be credited to Account No. 148. Post the charge sales directly to the customers' accounts in the subsidiary ledger.
4. Foot and rule the sales register on November 30, 1978.
5. Make the individual and summary postings to the general ledger accounts.
6. Prepare a schedule of accounts receivable on November 30, 1978.

13–5. The Hitchcock Wholesale Company is divided into two departments — Department A and Department B. All charge sales are made to retailers on terms of 2/10, n/30. The following charge sales were made during June 1978:

1978

June 1 No. 646: Medley Company, Department A, $350; postage of $8.50 should be added to invoice.

2 No. 647: Pathak and Patwardhan, Department A, $480, and Department B, $295; freight collect.

3 No. 648: Walbro, Department B, $260; to be picked up.

4 No. 649: Webb-Wax Company, Department A, $175, and Department B, $320; freight collect.

8 No. 650: Yang Company, Department B, $406; express collect.

9 Sent Medley Company a corrected invoice for the June 1 purchase of Department A merchandise. The corrected invoice (No. 651) amounted to $305. Postage charges remained the same.

10 No. 652: Walbro, Department A, $296; to be picked up.

11 No. 653: Kelley's Store, Department B, $323; postage of $10 should be added to invoice.

15 No. 654: Medley Company, Department B, $206; postage of $6.50 should be added to invoice.

16 No. 655: Webb-Wax Company, Department A, $126; postage of $5 should be added to invoice.

17 No. 656: Yang Company, Department B, $358; less credit of $85 for unacceptable merchandise which was returned. Accounts Receivable should be debited for the net amount; freight collect.

18 Sent Kelley's Store a corrected invoice for the June 11 purchase of Department B merchandise. The corrected invoice (No. 657) amounted to $332; postage charges remained the same.

22 No. 658: Pathak and Patwardhan, Department B, $198; to be picked up.

23 No. 659: Kelley's Store, Department A, $265; postage of $7 should be added to invoice.

24 Sent Webb-Wax Company a corrected invoice for the June 16 purchase of Department A merchandise. The corrected invoice (No. 660) amounted to $116. Postage charges remained the same.

25 No. 661: Walbro, Department B, $195; to be picked up.

June 29   No. 662: Yang Company, Department A, $260; postage of $5 should be added to invoice.

30   Sent Pathak and Patwardhan a corrected invoice for the June 22 purchase of Department B merchandise. The corrected invoice (No. 663) amounted to $189.

Required:

1. Open the following general ledger accounts, and insert the June 1, 1978, balances:

Account No.	Account Title	Balance, 6/1/78
115	Accounts receivable...............................	$ 968
155	Postage stamps	80
501	Sales – Department A	15,500
502	Sales returns and allowances – Dept. A.......	250
507	Sales – Department B.............................	18,900
508	Sales returns and allowances – Dept. B	475

2. Open a subsidiary ledger of accounts receivable and insert the June 1, 1978 balances:

Kelley's Store..............................	$225
Medley Company...........................	56
Pathak and Patwardhan..................	304
Walbro.......................................	74
Webb-Wax Company.....................	106
Yang Company.............................	203

3. Record the charge sales for June in a sales register like the one in Illustration 13–5. Post directly to the customers' account in the subsidiary ledger.

4. Foot and rule the sales register on June 30, 1978.

5. Make the individual and summary postings to the general ledger accounts.

6. Prepare a schedule of accounts receivable on June 30, 1978.

13–6. Jabro's Wholesale Clothing Store is divided into two departments – Men's and Women's. All charge sales are made to retailers on terms of 2/10, n/30. The following charge sales were made during February 1978:

1978

Feb. 2   No. 344: Marshall Brothers, Men's, $485; to be picked up.

3   No. 345: Delilah's Fashion Boutique, Women's, $696; freight collect.

4   No. 346: Hooper-Hayes, Men's, $590; Women's, $665; express collect.

5   No. 347: Weldon's Men's Shop, Men's, $378; to be picked up.

6   No. 348: Potter–Lind Company, Men's, $360; Women's, $480; express collect.

Feb. 7   No. 349: A. B. Smith & Sons, Women's, $403; to be picked up.
    9   Sent Marshall Brothers a corrected invoice for the February 2 purchase of Men's merchandise. The corrected invoice (No. 350) amounted to $458.
   10   No. 351: Gals' Place, Women's, $460; received a 60-day, 9 percent interest-bearing note; to be picked up.
   11   No. 352: Wallace and Valenti, Men's, $665; Women's, $420; express collect.
   12   No. 353: Oscar George Company, Women's, $596; less credit of $116 for unacceptable defective garments which were returned. Accounts Receivable should be debited for the net amount; express collect.
   13   No. 354: Weldon's Mens Shop, Men's, $422; to be picked up.
   14   No. 355: Rigsby–Teaford Company, Men's, $360; Women's, $489; freight collect.
   16   No. 356: Potter–Lind Company, Men's, $486; less credit of $120 for defective merchandise which was returned. Accounts Receivable should be debited for the net amount; to be picked up.
   17   No. 357: Delilah's Fashion Boutique, Women's, $367; freight collect.
   18   No. 358: A. B. Smith & Sons, Women's, $412; express collect.
   19   Sent Delilah's Fashion Boutique a corrected invoice for the February 17 purchase of Women's merchandise. The corrected invoice (No. 359) amounted to $376.
   20   No. 360: Linda's Fashions, Women's, $650; received a 60-day, 9 percent interest-bearing note; express collect.
   21   No. 361: Marshall Brothers, Men's, $508; freight collect.
   23   Sent A. B. Smith & Sons a corrected invoice for the February 18 purchase of Women's merchandise. The corrected invoice (No. 362) amounted to $402.
   24   No. 363: Wallace and Valenti, Men's, $489; express collect.
   25   No. 364: Rigsby–Teaford Company, Women's, $562; less credit of $82 for defective garments which were returned. Accounts Receivable should be debited for the net amount; freight collect.
   26   No. 365: Oscar George Company, Women's, $667; express collect.
   27   No. 366: Hooper-Hayes, Men's, $498; Women's, $575; freight collect.
   28   Sent a corrected invoice to Wallace and Valenti for the February 24 purchase of Men's merchandise. The corrected invoice (No. 367) amounted to $498.

Required:

1. Open the following general ledger accounts, and insert the February 1, 1978, balances:

Account
No.	*Account Title*	*Balance, 2/1/78*
120	Notes receivable...................................	$ 600
125	Accounts receivable	1,984
510	Sales—men's..	6,800
511	Sales returns and allowances—men's..........	250
520	Sales—women's.....................................	7,900
521	Sales returns and allowances—women's......	485

2. Open a subsidiary ledger of accounts receivable and insert the February 1, 1978 balances:

Delilah's Fashion Boutique	$408
Hooper-Hayes	230
Marshall Brothers..............................	360
Oscar George Company	105
Potter–Lind Company	120
Rigsby–Teaford Company....................	206
A. B. Smith & Sons	309
Wallace and Valenti	144
Weldon's Men's Shop.........................	102

3. Record the charge sales for February in a sales register like the one in Illustration 13–5. Post directly to the customers' accounts in the subsidiary ledger.
4. Foot and rule the sales register on February 28, 1978.
5. Make the individual and summary postings to the general ledger accounts.
6. Prepare a schedule of accounts receivable on February 28, 1978.

Merchandise inventory and prepaid expenses
Learning objectives

Merchandise inventories and prepaid expenses frequently comprise a significant portion of a merchant's current assets. A thorough study of the following material will provide an understanding of the accounting procedures used for these current assets.

1. Definition of what is included in merchandise inventory.
2. Purpose of and procedures used in taking a physical inventory.
3. Comparison of methods used in making inventory valuations.
4. Difference between asset and expense methods of accounting for prepaid expenses.
5. Use of insurance register in accounting for expired and unexpired insurance.

14

Merchandise inventory and prepaid expenses

Inventories and prepaid expenses derive their value from the expectation that they will benefit the owner in the future. In fact, anticipation of future use and earning power are the factors from which all assets receive their value. Since merchandise inventories and prepaid expenses are normally expected to benefit the owner in the coming accounting period or business operating cycle, they are reported in the current asset section of the statement of financial position. More often than not, the dollar value of merchandise inventories represents a material amount of the business's assets. Also, it will be noted that unless inventories and prepaid expenses are properly reported, periodic net earnings will be improperly stated. For these reasons, it is important that proper records be maintained. Inventories and prepaid expenses have been included in this chapter because both represent current expenses of the business for which payment has already been made.

MERCHANDISE INVENTORY

Not all inventories of a business are included in the statement of financial position under **"merchandise inventory."** As the title suggests, only those items held for resale are properly included. Inventories of office supplies, custodial supplies, and other inventories not held for resale are not included in merchandise inventory. They will be considered later since they are properly included as prepaid expenses. Merchandise inventory encompasses only items which the firm normally holds for resale in the ordinary course of business.

Purpose of taking inventory

There are a number of reasons for keeping an accurate record of merchandise inventories. The most important reason is that unless satisfactory accounting records are maintained, periodic net earnings of the firm will be misstated. If the records report that inventories on hand are less than they actually are, then the cost of goods sold will be overstated and net earnings will be understated. If inventory is overstated, then the reverse will be true, resulting in an overstatement of net earnings. Earnings in the next year will also be incorrect because the ending inventory of the first year is the beginning inventory of the second year. The above discussion is illustrated by the example in Illustration 14–1.

Often, the managers of a business are not the owners. If this is the case, one of management's functions is to make sure that assets are safeguarded. This involves taking the necessary steps to prevent theft, unnecessary spoilage, and excessive waste. Since inventories represent a relatively large asset, taking inventory and maintaining adequate records are means of fulfilling this duty. Another reason for maintaining accurate inventory records is that purchases should be made in accordance with business needs. Without proper records, inventories may be overstocked resulting in an unnecessary investment of business resources. Or, because of loose accounting, inventories may run out, resulting in a loss of sales and creating unhappy customers.

Taking inventory

Although it is not a normal duty of an accountant to take inventory, he or she may be called upon to do so. For this reason it is necessary to be familiar with the procedures used in taking inventory. In performing

Illustration 14–1

	Ending inventory				
	Correctly stated		Understated		Overstated
Sales.................................		$100,000		$100,000		$100,000
Beginning inventory............	$ 5,000		$ 5,000		$ 5,000	
Purchases..........................	50,000		50,000		50,000	
Goods available..................	$55,000		$55,000		$55,000	
Ending inventory	7,000		4,000		10,000	
Cost of goods sold..............		48,000		51,000		45,000
Gross profit........................		$ 52,000		$ 49,000		$ 55,000
Operating expenses............		30,000		30,000		30,000
Net earnings......................		$ 22,000		$ 19,000		$ 25,000

any accounting duty, the accountant should constantly be aware of the reason for performing a particular duty. Taking inventory is no exception. Periodic net earnings can only be as accurate as figures arrived at in taking inventory.

The key to a successful inventory count is preplanning. Determining the proper date to take inventory is most important. Often, inventory taking will be a sizable job. For this reason, a date should be selected when inventories are at their lowest amount. This is usually at a time during the year when business operations are at a low point. This low point is referred to as the end of the natural business year for a particular business. Often the business will select this natural business year as its fiscal year for reporting purposes.

In order to insure a proper count, inventory is often taken after business hours or while the business is closed for a few days. Without advance planning taking inventory during working hours can cause problems. It may be necessary to hire additional help in order to take inventory in as short a time as possible. Also, if taken during working hours, steps must be taken to assure that inventory items are not double counted or omitted. An inventory count should include only company property. Care must be exercised so that goods waiting shipment on which title has passed to the buyer are not included. If the count is made during working hours, control should be maintained over inventory, and a record should be kept of any movement of goods such as "rush" or "special" orders. Professional inventory firms are sometimes employed to take inventory.

On the day(s) inventory is taken, records are usually made on forms known as inventory sheets. During the inventory count, inventory takers work in pairs. One person counts the inventory and "calls out" the count to a partner who records the amount on the inventory sheet. On the pre-numbered sheets are spaces for date, description, quantity, and initials of persons calling, recording, pricing, extending, and examining sheets. Illustration 14–2 is a typical example of an inventory sheet for a hardware store.

After the inventory takers have recorded the counts, the inventory unit costs are recorded by a different person. Then, a fourth person performs the necessary extensions, that is, multiplying the units by the appropriate unit cost. As a final check, a fifth individual examines the inventory sheets for accuracy and completeness.

Valuation of inventory

The assignment of a cost to inventories is not as simple as might be expected. Often, the cost of a particular item is not known. This is particularly true if inventory consists of many like items. Items in inventory will most likely have been purchased at different times and at different prices. This creates a problem in determining the appropriate cost. It should be noted that not only will the quantity of inventory affect inventory cost and periodic net earnings but the cost assigned to inventory items will also affect net earnings. To help solve this problem of inventory costing, various methods of valuation have been developed. Three

Illustration 14–2
Inventory sheet

INVENTORY SHEET

Called by _BRW_   Store   Hill Hardware Co.

Recorded by _D.J.W._   June 30   19 78   Page   1

Costed by _HLR_   Sheet No.   1

Extended by _OKI_   Department   B

Checked by _D.A.W._   Location   Warehouse

Description	Quantity	Unit	Unit Cost	Extension
Power drills	11	each	$15.75	$173.25
Hammers	36	each	3.90	140.40
Tape measures	24	each	2.25	54.00
Tool boxes	10	each	9.50	95.00
Miter boxes	7	each	4.75	33.25
Total				$495.90

of the most popular are (1) first-in, first-out (Fifo); (2) last-in, first-out (Lifo); and (3) weighted average.

First-in; first-out.   Of the three methods, **first-in, first-out,** commonly known as the "Fifo" method, is the most widely used. Fifo assumes that the first items purchased are the first ones sold. In many situations this is the case with the result that the goods on hand represent the most recent purchases. This method is most realistic where inventories consist of items which have a short life and are apt to spoil. In this situation, the latest purchases are placed at the back of existing stock so that the oldest inventory will be sold first (milk and dairy products in a store). To illustrate the various methods of inventory valuation, the following data will be used:

Inventory at start of period, 200 units at $5 each	$1,000
Purchases during period:	
First,................... 300 units at $6 each	1,800
Second, ... 250 units at $7 each	1,750
Third,................... 200 units at $8 each	1,600
Fourth,................. 50 units at $9 each	450
Total Cost of Units Available for Sale	$6,600
Ending inventory of 275 units.	

Assuming that the first units purchased are the first ones sold, the ending inventory of 275 units would be priced as follows, starting with the most recent purchase.

Most recent purchase........................	50 units at $9 each................	$ 450
Next most recent purchase	200 units at $8 each	1,600
Next most recent purchase	25 units at $7 each	175
	275 units	
Cost Assigned to Ending Inventory...		$2,225

Fifo is widely used because of three basic reasons: (1) Fifo is most representative of the physical movement of the items sold, (2) Fifo results in the most current costs being assigned to inventory as shown on the statement of financial position, and (3) Fifo has long been used, and business executives are reluctant to change. Changes made in valuation methods cause records to be less comparable. When changes are made, consistency is destroyed. Business executives rely on consistent comparable records in making economic decisions.

Last-in, first-out. **Last-in, first-out,** referred to as "Lifo," is the opposite of Fifo. When using Lifo, it is assumed that sales during the period consist of the most recent purchases. Using the data given under Fifo and an ending inventory of 275 units, the following cost will be assigned using Lifo:

Earliest purchase—on hand at		
beginning of period........................	200 units at $5 each.............	$1,000
Next earliest purchase........................	75 units at $6 each.............	450
	275 units	
Cost Assigned to Ending Inventory...		$1,450

Lifo has been defended on the rather weak argument that Lifo represents the movement of goods in a business. This is seldom the case, and this argument has been abandoned in favor of stronger arguments. Probably the most convincing argument is that Lifo results in the most recent costs being matched with a period's revenues. This produces net earnings which are neither inflated nor deflated by price changes. Furthermore, when prices are rising, Lifo results in a lower net earnings figure because of the higher cost assigned to cost of goods sold. This lower net earnings figure results in lower income taxes.

Even though arguments for Lifo are notable, the Lifo valuation method is weak in at least two respects. Lifo does not normally represent the flow of goods; and most important, Lifo does not result in a meaningful inventory figure on the statement of financial position. In certain businesses where prices have steadily increased and inventories are material in amount, the use of Lifo will result in a significant understatement of current assets.

Weighted average. The third method used to value inventory is the **weighted average method.** It is a weighted average because the valuation involves the quantities as well as the costs of inventory items. In determining the weighted average, all of the units available for sale in a period are multiplied by their respective costs. The amounts are then summed and divided by the total units. This figure represents the weighted cost per unit during the period. Note: It should be observed that weighted average cost is an average of units multiplied by costs and is *not* a simple average of various unit costs during the period. Referring to data given in the Fifo discussion, the ending inventory is assigned a value of $1,815. This value is calculated by multiplying units by respective costs and dividing the sum by total units ($6,600 ÷ 1,000 = $6.60).

$$\frac{\text{Cost of Goods Available for Sale}}{\text{Number of Units Available}} = \text{Weighted Average Unit Cost}$$

The weighted average unit cost of $6.60 is then multiplied by the ending inventory of 275 units to arrive at a valuation of $1,815.

The three methods described above are normally referred to as methods of inventory valuation. It should be noted that the described methods are actually methods of cost assignment. This is true because cost of goods available for sale during the period will be assigned either to cost of goods sold or to ending inventory. These three methods of valuation make possible this assignment of costs. It is important that all costs be assigned in order that the earnings statement and the statement of financial position will be correctly stated.

Lower of cost or market. The **lower-of-cost-or-market method** is a combination method of inventory valuation. As the title suggests, the method involves the assignment of cost or market value, whichever is lower, to the inventory units. The method is an outgrowth of two financial concepts. The **realization concept** maintains that, except for unusual cases, unrealized profits should not be recorded. From this, it would seem that unrealized losses should not be recorded. This is where the concept of **conservatism** takes over. It has long been held that financial information should provide for all possible losses but should anticipate no gains. Current accounting trends indicate that the concept of conservatism is weakening as accountants are increasingly considering the recording of unrealized profits in justifiable situations. It is argued that conservatism introduces an element of bias in financial reporting, which often results in incorrect financial representations.

In the lower-of-cost-or-market method, the "cost" part stands for cost calculated on the Fifo or weighted average basis, whichever is lower. The Lifo cost method is not acceptable because of tax reasons. Since the tax law does not permit the use of lower of Lifo cost or market, it is not used. The "market" part of lower of cost or market represents the cost to replace the inventory unit.

Comparison of valuation methods. To compare the results of using the three methods, assume the same data as given above in discussing each method. Keep in mind that the example given in Illustration 14–3 is based on a period in which prices are rising. If prices had been falling, the cost of goods sold under Lifo would be lower than under Fifo, resulting in a higher net earnings figure for Lifo when compared to net earnings under the Fifo method of valuation.

It is observed that when compared with Fifo and weighted average, the lower-of-cost-or-market method does result in a conservative valuation of inventory. The arguments for using lower of cost or market are

Illustration 14–3

	Fifo		Weighted average		Lifo	
Sales		$10,000		$10,000		$10,000
Goods available for sale	$6,600		$6,600		$6,600	
Valuation of ending inventory	2,225		1,815		1,450	
Cost of goods sold		4,375		4,785		5,150
Gross profit		$ 5,625		$ 5,215		$ 4,850
Operating expenses		2,000		2,000		2,000
Net earnings		$ 3,625		$ 3,215		$ 2,850

	Fifo	Weighted average	Market	Lower of cost or market	Units		Amount
Fourth purchase	$9	$6.60	$6	$6	× 50	=	$ 300
Third purchase	8	6.60	6	6	× 200	=	1,200
Second purchase	7	6.60	6	6	× 25	=	150
					275		
Amount assigned to inventory of 275 units.							$1,650

based on the fact that recording inventories at the lower valuation will result in a no-less-than reasonable return on sales in the next accounting period. To be properly followed, the method should generally be applied to each inventory unit and not to the total inventory.

The cost of a unit of inventory is not always the invoice price. If purchases discounts are taken, they should be deducted from the invoice price. Each item of inventory need not be adjusted for purchases discounts. If the purchases for the period are $10,000 and discounts amount to $125, then the discounts represent $1\frac{1}{4}$ percent of purchases. Assuming an ending inventory of $2,000, the adjustment for discounts would equal $25 ($1\frac{1}{4}$ percent of $2,000). Thus, the ending inventory would be valued at $1,975 ($2,000 less $1\frac{1}{4}$ percent of $2,000). The above example is based on a Fifo method of valuation. If the lower-of-cost-or-market method were being used, the $1,975 inventory figure would be used unless the replacement (market) cost was lower.

As a final point to consider in valuing inventory, the shipping charges of inventory units must be mentioned. Since goods are only useful to the buyer when received, the shipping charges are properly included as an inventory cost. In fact, reasonable and necessary expenditures incurred to place any asset in condition and position for use constitute a part of an asset's cost. Often the shipping charges are an important part of the inventory cost, especially if long distance and/or special handling is required.

Maintaining record of inventory

It is important to have a reasonable idea of the cost of inventory on hand. Just taking a physical inventory once a year to help determine periodic net earnings is not enough. If the quantity of inventory on hand is not known at all times, inventories may run short, thus hindering production. On the other hand, inadequate records may cause excessive purchases to be made, resulting in costly storage and a tie-up of liquid assets (cash). To help keep abreast of inventory quantities and values, three methods are often used. They are (1) the gross profit method, (2) the retail method, and (3) the perpetual method. The first two methods aid in determining inventory cost, whereas the perpetual method is used to calculate both cost and quantity of items. All three methods are useful in preparing interim reports even though it is thought necessary to have the accuracy of physical inventory counts associated with year-end reports.

Gross profit method. The **gross profit method** involves the reduction of the sales figure by the normal gross profit percentage. This figure then represents the cost of goods sold which is subtracted from the cost of goods available for sale resulting in an estimation of the ending inventory.

As an illustration, assume a gross profit percentage of 40 percent. Beginning inventory is $20,000, and purchases to date amount to $80,000. Sales to date have been recorded at $125,000. Cost of goods sold for the period is assumed to be 60 percent of sales (100 percent − 40 percent gross profit). Therefore the cost of goods sold amounts to $75,000 ($125,000 × 60 percent). Since cost of goods available for sale is $100,000 (beginning inventory, $20,000 + purchases, $80,000), the ending inventory is equal to $100,000 − $75,000, or $25,000.

The gross profit method has other uses which make it a valuable tool. When inventory is being physically taken, the gross profit method can be used to test the reasonableness of inventory amounts. Another application of the gross profit method can be made when inventories have been destroyed by fire. Should such an occasion arise, the calculation will prove helpful in trying to negotiate an insurance settlement.

Although the gross profit method has proven to be a useful accounting tool, it is not without its weaknesses. The most obvious weakness is that unless the gross profit percentage has been fairly constant in the past and is expected to remain so in the future, the calculations will be inaccurate. It should be remembered that, at best, calculations made using this method are no more than reasonable estimates and should not be relied upon as being exact figures.

Retail method. In calculating the cost of goods sold and ending inventory, a variation of the gross profit method is often used. The **retail method** involves the maintenance of records showing both costs and retail prices of purchases on a current up-to-date basis. With this information, it is possible to calculate the ratio between the cost and retail selling price. The retail method is used by subtracting the period's sales from the retail value of goods available for sale. This results in an estimate of the retail value of the ending inventory. By multiplying the value of inventory at retail prices by the ratio of cost to retail, an estimate of the cost of ending inventory is obtained. An example using the retail method is shown in Illustration 14–4.

Illustration 14–4

	Cost	Retail
Inventory, beginning of period	$27,000	$35,000
Purchases during period (net)	33,000	45,000
	$60,000	$80,000
Deduct sales of period		50,000
Ending inventory at retail		$30,000
Ratio of cost to retail ($60,000 ÷ $80,000)		75%
Estimated Ending Inventory at Cost ($30,000 × 0.75)	$22,500	

The above example does not recognize the necessary adjustments because of markup and markdown in retail price during the period. Unless these adjustments are made, the cost-retail ratio will be inaccurate and the resulting valuation of inventory will be less than a good approximation.

An advantage of using the retail method is that the cost per unit of each inventory item need not be recorded. Only the aggregate cost of beginning inventory and purchases need be recorded for future reference. This facilitates the taking of inventory of goods once they have been priced at retail. By properly using the cost-retail ratio, a reasonable estimation of inventory cost can be obtained. The retail method can be used to estimate theft losses.

Perpetual method.   Depending on the type of inventory, some firms find it easier to keep records of inventories on a perpetual basis. The **perpetual inventory method** involves the maintenance of a running total of inventory quantities and aggregate value. The system works in a manner similar to an individual's checkbook or savings account. Each time purchases are made, the amount is added to the existing balance. As sales are made, the proper amounts are subtracted from the previous balance.

It is interesting to note that the perpetual method will result in the same inventory value as calculated using the Fifo method of valuation. (The results will be different if the Lifo or weighted average method is used.) Keeping inventory on the perpetual method does not eliminate the need for a periodic physical inventory count. There is always the possibility of human error or loss from theft in an inventory system. Taking a **periodic inventory** will help assure that the amounts determined on the perpetual basis are reasonable. In addition, a physical inventory count will allow differences between actual and recorded amounts to be corrected.

Not every business will find it desirable to keep inventory records on a perpetual basis. Stores with low-cost goods (such as grocery stores) will not find it desirable to keep a perpetual inventory. On the other hand, a firm with high-cost items (such as a furniture store or car dealer) will find it both convenient and economical to keep a perpetual inventory. Instead of using the perpetual system as a central method of maintaining inventory records, many firms use the perpetual method as a supplementary system for determining when to make purchases.

Although the perpetual method of maintaining inventory records has not been widely used in certain situations as described above, there is increasing evidence that this will not be the case in the near future. Technology is rapidly advancing, and retail stores are already installing electronic sensing devices at the point of sale. These sensors record the retail price as well as the stock number. Such information is then fed into a central system which maintains inventory records, sales, cost of sales, and signals for reorder of inventory. Such devices can be expected to change the procedures used to maintain inventory records in the future.

PREPAID EXPENSES

As with inventory, it is necessary to adjust the various prepaid expense accounts for amounts that were consumed during the period in order to determine periodic net earnings. In a typical business, the statement of financial position will report certain current assets which represent prepaid expenses. These assets represent business expenses which were not wholly consumed during the current period. Rent and interest may be paid in advance. Office and store supplies may exist at the period's end. Insurance may have been paid in advance. Expenditures for advertising may have been incurred to benefit present as well as future periods. The above are examples of **prepaid expenses.** They represent advance payments for benefits which are expected to be received in the future. Because they represent benefits to be received in the near future, they are reported as current assets. Prepaid expenses can be thought of as a method for recording as assets those expenses that were not consumed during the current period.

Accounting for prepayments

Prepayments can be recorded by using either the asset or the expense method. The asset method involves the recording of prepayments as assets. At the end of the period, calculations are made to determine the portion of the asset that was consumed during the period. This amount is then reported as an expense on the earnings statement.

The expense method involves the recording of prepayments as expenses. At the end of the period, the part of expense that was not consumed will be transferred to an asset account. This method will require an additional adjustment at the beginning of the following period which will be discussed later.

Asset method. The **asset method** is normally used when it is expected that the asset will not be completely consumed during the period. Of course, if it is reasonably assured that the asset will be completely consumed during the period, then it would be advisable to use the expense method.

Advertising. Advertising supplies and services is an example of a prepaid expense. Often the firm will design catalogs and purchase advertising supplies which are expected to benefit more than one period. In this case, the purchase results in a debit to Advertising Supplies and a credit to either Accounts Payable or Cash depending on whether the purchase was made on account or for cash.

When the period ends, an inventory of supplies is taken. The amount of supplies on hand is then subtracted from the amount recorded in the Advertising Supplies account to determine the advertising expense of the period. Assume that on December 31, the Advertising Supplies account has a debit balance of $450 and the inventory reveals that $175 of advertising supplies are on hand. Subtracting the $175 inventory from the $450 balance gives an expense for the period of $275. To account for the expense, the following adjustment is made:

```
Advertising Supplies Expense...................................................... 275
    Advertising Supplies...............................................................        275
        Amount of advertising supplies consumed during period.
```

After the Advertising Supplies account has been adjusted, the account will reflect a $175 balance which will be reported on the statement of financial position as a current asset. The expense of $275 will be shown as an operating expense on the earnings statement.

Rents. At year's end, it is not unusual to find prepaid rents in the current asset section of the statement of financial position. Rents are normally paid in advance, and those rents which have not been consumed in the current period are deferred to the succeeding period through the use of the Prepaid Rent account. Rents are consumed over time, requiring the calculation of consumed rents at the period's end.

Assume that on November 1, prepayment for rent is made for the next six months. At that time, Prepaid Rent is debited for $1,200 (6 months × $200 per month). On December 31, two months' rent has been used up. In order for earnings of the current period to be properly stated, it is necessary to record an expense for rents consumed of $400 (2 months × $200 per month). The rent expense will be recorded in the following manner:

```
Rent Expense........................................................................... 400
    Prepaid Rent.......................................................................        400
        To record rent expense for November and December.
```

After the above entry has been made, the Prepaid Rent Account will have a balance of $800 (4 months × $200 per month). The $800 debit balance represents prepaid rents for January, February, March, and April of the next year.

Office supplies. During the year, various office supplies such as paper, typewriter ribbons, ink, pencils, rubber bands, paper clips, carbon paper, envelopes, and other miscellaneous supplies are purchased and consumed. It is unrealistic to expect that all office supplies will be completely consumed at the year's end. For this reason, it is necessary to determine the amount of supplies used during the year. This is done by taking an inventory of the supplies on hand at December 31. This amount is then subtracted from the amount of supplies purchased during the year. Under the asset method of recording prepaid expenses, the amount purchased is represented by the debit balance in the Office Supplies account.

Assume that $500 worth of supplies were purchased during the year and debited to Office Supplies at the time of purchase. On December 31 it is determined by inventory count that $175 worth of supplies are on hand. By subtracting the inventory from the purchases made, it is determined that $325 worth of supplies were used during the year. The expense is recorded by the following entry:

Office Supplies Expense	325	
Office Supplies		325
To record office supplies consumed during the year.		

After making the above entry, the Office Supplies account will have a balance of $175 representing the supplies on hand at year's end. The $325 expense will be reported on the earnings statement as an operating expense.

Store supplies. Store supplies are accounted for in the same manner as office supplies. Normally included in store supplies are such items as paper bags, wrapping paper, tape, string, cleaning supplies, and other miscellaneous items. When supplies are purchased, they are debited to Store Supplies and a credit is made to either Accounts Payable or to Cash. The procedure used in calculating store supplies expense would be the same as that used in determining office supplies expense.

Interest. As with prepaid rent, prepayments of interest expire over time. When interest paid in advance does not expire in the current period, it is necessary to make an adjusting entry. Since the prepaid interest remaining at the end of the current period is expected to benefit the succeeding period, it is classified as a current asset on the statement of financial position.

As an example, assume that on December 1, a 90-day, 6 percent note for $2,000 was issued to a bank. The interest which amounts to $30 was paid in advance. On December 31, it is observed that one third of the interest expense has expired. To account for the expiration of interest, the following entry is made:

Interest Expense	10	
Prepaid Interest		10
Recording of expired amount of prepaid interest.		

After making the above entry, the Prepaid Interest account will have a debit balance of $20 representing the unexpired portion of prepaid interest. In the following period, an entry will be made debiting Interest Expense for $20 and crediting Prepaid Interest. Through the use of the adjusting entry above and the entry in the following period, the expired interest will be recorded in the period receiving such benefit. Had the entries referred to not been made, the reported earnings of both periods would be incorrect.

Illustration 14–5

INSURANCE REGISTER 1978

Date of Policy	Policy No.	Insurer	Property Insured	Amount	Term	Expiration Date	Unexpired Premium 1/1/78
8/1/77	70423	Midstate Insurance Co.	Office equipment	10,000	1	8/1/78	59.50
10/2/75	22204	Southern Fire & Casualty	Building	40,000	5	10/2/80	495.00
3/1/78	60206	Freedom Insurance Co.	Merchandise	30,000	1	3/1/79	126.00
4/4/75	11104	Atlantic Fire & Casualty	Public liability	200,000	3	4/4/78	33.75
8/1/78	89765	Midstate Insurance Co.	Office equipment	12,000	1	8/1/79	108.00
4/1/78	77706	Nationwide Insurance Co.	Public liability	200,000	3	4/1/81	432.00
							1,254.25

Insurance. In addition to the business risks of operating a business, consideration must also be given to the risk of loss due to fire, water, theft, wind, and other physical damages. In order to help insure against such losses, most businesses take out a contract with an insurance company. The contract is known as an insurance policy. The insurance company is known as the insurer and the person or business signing the contract is the insured. In exchange for protection in the event of loss, the insured agrees to make payments, commonly known as premiums, to the insurer. Premium payments are charged at a specified rate per $1,000 of insurance and are payable in advance. Since the insurance policy often covers more than one period, the premiums are debited to the Unexpired Insurance account. This account is reported in the current asset section of the statement of financial position.

As with interest and rents, prepaid insurance expires over time. In effect, a portion of the premiums expire daily. Since making daily adjusting entries for expired insurance would be unnecessary and time-consuming, the adjusting entries are usually made on a monthly or yearly basis. For the large business which may have several hundred policies, making adjustments on a monthly basis may still result in a time-consuming task. To simplify the making of the monthly adjustment, such firms normally use an **insurance register.** The register not only provides an organized record of policies but it also shows at a glance which policies will terminate and require renewal during the period.

The register has columns for the date the policy was issued, policy number, the insurer, property insured, amount of insurance, length of

Ilustration 14–5 (continued)

Expiring Premium													Unexpired Premium 12/31/78
Jan.	Feb.	Mar.	Apr.	May	June	July	Aug.	Sept.	Oct.	Nov.	Dec.	Total	
8.50	8.50	8.50	8.50	8.50	8.50	8.50						59.50	
15.00	15.00	15.00	15.00	15.00	15.00	15.00	15.00	15.00	15.00	15.00	15.00	180.00	315.00
		10.50	10.50	10.50	10.50	10.50	10.50	10.50	10.50	10.50	10.50	105.00	21.00
11.25	11.25	11.25										33.75	
							9.00	9.00	9.00	9.00	9.00	45.00	63.00
			12.00	12.00	12.00	12.00	12.00	12.00	12.00	12.00	12.00	108.00	324.00
34.75	34.75	45.25	46.00	46.00	46.00	46.00	46.50	46.50	46.50	46.50	46.50	531.25	723.00

policy, expiration date, and amount of unexpired premium at the beginning of the period. In addition, columns are provided for the amount of premiums expiring each month during the year, and, finally, a column shows the amount of unexpired premiums at the period's end. An example of an insurance register is shown in Illustration 14–5.

The amount of expiring premium is calculated by dividing the total premium payments by the term or length of coverage. Thus, if the premiums are $60 and the length of the policy is one year, then $5 will be the monthly insurance expense. In reference to Policy No. 60206 issued on March 1, 1978, the premium payment is $126 and the length of the policy is one year. Therefore, $10.50 will be recorded as expense each month. When the policy was issued, the insured debited Unexpired Insurance for $126 and credited Cash. If No. 60206 was the only policy, then the Unexpired Insurance account would have a debit balance of $21 on December 31.

When several policies are in force as indicated by the insurance register, the monthly or yearly expense is determined by adding up the premiums expiring each month. Assuming that adjustments are made on a monthly basis, the following entry would be made in July.

Insurance Expense – Office Equipment	8.50	
Insurance Expense – Building	15.00	
Insurance Expense – Merchandise	10.50	
Insurance Expense – Public Liability	12.00	
Unexpired Insurance		46.00
To record expiration of insurance during July.		

If the only adjusting entry was made at year-end, the amounts shown in the total column would be used. As the policies are issued, they are all debited to the Unexpired Insurance account. However, when the entries are made for monthly or yearly expense, separate expense accounts are used for each insured item. This is done so that expenses may be charged to the various segments of a business for planning and control purposes.

At the end of each year, a new register is made containing only the policies that are in force on December 31. Management has the duty to safeguard and protect the firm's assets. Obtaining insurance against possible loss is a justifiable means of fulfilling this duty. Maintaining an insurance register helps management assure themselves that they are effectively protecting the firm's assets.

Expense method. Instead of recording the initial prepayment as an asset, the **expense method** involves the recording of advance payments as expenses. The expense method is most useful when it is expected that the items or services purchased will be wholly consumed during the period. If prepaid expenses have been completely consumed during the period, no adjusting entry is required under the expense method. To illustrate, assume that during the period, $25 was spent for postage stamps and at the end of the period no stamps were left. Using the expense method, the following entry would be made at the time of purchase:

```
Postage Expense ......................................................................... 25
    Cash ..................................................................................        25
    To record purchase of postage stamps.
```

If postage stamps amounting to $4 had existed on December 31, the unused stamps would have to be transferred to an asset account. The transfer defers $4 worth of stamps to the next period in which they will be expensed (assuming stamps are used in the next period). The adjusting entry assures that postage expense will be recorded in the period in which stamps are used. To record the transfer, the following entry is required:

```
Postage Stamps ............................................................................ 4
    Postage Expense ....................................................................        4
    Postage stamps on hand.
```

The above entry sets up a temporary asset account. If the expense method is to be maintained, the adjusting entry will have to be reversed in the coming period (January 1). If the reversal were not made, the asset method would be in use in the following period, and an adjusting entry in the following period would be necessary to record the expense when the stamps were finally used. Reversing entries enable the accountant to record payments (expenses) and receipts (revenues) in a consistent manner from period to period. Adjusting entries requiring reversal are normally reversed on the first day of the next accounting period. The adjusting entry on December 31 and reversal on January 1 can be thought of as a means of deferring the expenses to a subsequent period.

Comparison of asset and expense methods. If the prepayments will expire during the period, the expense method will result in the least number of entries. This is true because prepayment will be recorded initially as an expense. Even though methods may differ as to entries involved in certain situations, it is important to remember that both methods achieve the same result. Since it is hard to predict conditions as they will exist at the period's end, unnecessary time should not be spent trying to figure out which method will result in fewer entries. Neither method varies significantly in amount of work involved. It is important that the firm select the method which is the most convenient to use under existing circumstances. Once a method is adopted, it should be used consistently, thereby lessening any chance of error from switching from one method to the other.

The following example illustrates the similar results achieved under both methods. Assume that advertising supplies amounting to $400 are purchased on August 12 on account. On December 31 the inventory reveals that $125 of supplies are on hand.

Asset Method

Aug. 12	Advertising Supplies	400	
	Accounts Payable		400
	Purchased advertising supplies		

Dec. 31	Advertising Expense	275	
	Advertising Supplies		275
	Advertising supplies consumed during period.		

Expense Method

Aug. 12	Advertising Expense	400	
	Accounts Payable		400
	Purchased supplies.		

Dec. 31	Advertising Supplies	125	
	Advertising Expense		125
	Advertising supplies on hand.		

After the above entries have been posted, both methods result in the Advertising Supplies and Advertising Expense accounts having balances of $125 and $275, respectively. The final results are the same. The December 31 adjusting entry under the expense method will have to be reversed on January 1 of the next year if the expense method is to be continued. The reversing entry would be made by debiting Advertising Expense for $125 and crediting Advertising Supplies for $125. Then all purchases of advertising supplies during the next year would be debited to the Advertising Expense account.

GLOSSARY

Asset method (of accounting for prepayments)   recording prepayments as assets and making calculations at the end of the period to determine the portion of the asset that was consumed during the period.

Conservatism   a concept which maintains that financial information should provide for all possible losses but should anticipate no gains.

Expense Method (of accounting for prepayments)   recording advance payments as expenses and at the end of the period, transferring the portion of expense that was not consumed to an asset account.

First-in, first-out (Fifo)   the most widely used inventory valuation method. It assumes that the first items purchased are the first ones sold. Thus, it assigns the most recent costs to merchandise inventory as shown on the statement of financial position.

Gross profit method   a method used to estimate the value of inventory. It involves the reduction of the sales figure by the normal gross profit percentage. This figure then represents the cost of goods sold which is subtracted from the cost of goods available for sale resulting in an estimation of ending inventory.

Insurance register   an organized record of insurance policies indicating the date the policy was issued, policy number, the insurer, property insured, amount of insurance, length of policy, expiration date, amount of unexpired premium at the beginning of the period, amount of premiums expiring each month, and the amount of unexpired premiums at the period's end.

Last-in, first-out (Lifo)   an inventory valuation method which assumes that sales during the period consist of the most recent purchases. Thus, the earliest costs are assigned to merchandise inventory as shown on the statement of financial position.

Lower-of-cost-or-market method   an inventory valuation method which involves the assignment of cost, calculated on the Fifo or weighted average basis, or market value, whichever is lower, to the inventory units.

Merchandise inventory   the amount of items on hand and available for resale.

Periodic inventory method   a procedure by which the cost of merchandise sold and the cost of merchandise on hand at the end of the period is determined by taking a physical count of the inventory units in stock.

Perpetual inventory method   the keeping of a running total of inventory quantities and aggregate values.

Prepaid expenses   a method for recording as assets those expenses that were not consumed during the current period. Examples are prepaid rent and office supplies on hand.

Realization concept   a financial concept which maintains that, except for unusual cases, unrealized profits should not be recorded.

Retail method   a method for estimating the value of inventory which involves the maintenance of records showing both costs and retail prices of purchases. A ratio is calculated between the cost and retail selling price. The period's sales are subtracted from the retail value of the goods available for sale which results in an estimate of the retail value of ending inventory. An estimate of the ending inventory cost is obtained by multiplying the retail value of inventory by the ratio of cost to retail.

Weighted average method   an inventory valuation method. All the units available for sale in a period are multiplied by their respective costs. The amounts are summed and divided by the total number of units. This figure is the weighted cost per unit. It is multiplied by the number of units in ending inventory to obtain a valuation for ending inventory.

QUESTIONS AND EXERCISES

1. What are the three methods of inventory valuation? What assumptions are made when using each method?

2. Give three reasons for the widespread use of Fifo.

3. How can one justify the use of Lifo? What are the weaknesses in this method?

4. What is the lower-of-cost-or-market method?

5. Explain the realization concept and the concept of conservatism.

6. How can a reasonable inventory cost figure be derived without taking a physical inventory?

7. Name some common prepaid expenses.

8. In accounting for prepayments, when should the asset method be used and when should the expense method be used?

9. The Stocking Company has just completed its first year of business. Its stock records reveal the following purchases:

    First............................... 5,000 units @ $5
    Second............................ 1,000 units @   4
    Third.............................. 2,000 units @   6

    At the end of the year, 1,000 units are on hand. Calculate three possible different costs for the ending inventory.

10. The Office Supplies account was debited for all purchases of office supplies made during the year. At the end of the year, its balance was $8,000. A physical inventory revealed that $500 worth of supplies were on hand at December 31, 1978. What adjusting entry should be made? If the $8,000 had originally been debited to Office Supplies Expense, what adjusting entry would be necessary?

PROBLEMS

14-1. Huff and Puff Corporation is in the wholesale electrical fixtures business. Stock records are kept on all merchandise handled. With respect to Item 43, data was assembled from the stock records and appeared as follows:

Quantity on hand at beginning of period .... 500 units
First purchase during period .... 750 units @ $15
Second purchase during period .... 550 units @ 13
Third purchase during period .... 650 units @ 18
Final purchase during period .... 600 units @ 16
Quantity on hand at end of period .... 625 units

Required:

Compute (1) the total cost of units on hand at the end of the period and (2) the total cost of the units sold during the period under (a) the Fifo method and (b) the Lifo method. Assume that the units on hand at the beginning of the period were assigned a cost of $14 under the Fifo method and $14.50 under the Lifo method.

14-2. Harper Brothers, Inc., is a wholesale appliance company with stock records kept on all merchandise handled. Data assembled from the stock records with regard to Item X appeared as follows:

Inventory at beginning of period .... 800 units @ $26.00
First purchase during period .... 200 units @ 28.00
Second purchase during period .... 760 units @ 25.00
Third purchase during period .... 890 units @ 27.50
Fourth purchase during period .... 950 units @ 29.00
Final purchase during period .... 650 units @ 28.75
Inventory at end of period .... 1,050 units

Required:

Compute (1) the total cost of the ending inventory and (2) the total cost of units sold during the period under (a) the weighted average method and (b) the Lifo method of cost assignment.

14-3. The Hunter Company values its inventory at retail. Given the following information from the Hunter Company's records, compute the cost of the ending inventory.

	Cost	Retail
Inventory, beginning of period	$ 54,000	$ 72,000
Purchases during period (net)	356,000	543,000
Sales during period		405,000

14-4. The J and J Company is a retailing concern providing both over-the-counter and mail-order services. Metered postage is used on all items except general postage on which stamps are used. All postage is initially charged to Prepaid Postage, Account No. 173, and the account is adjusted periodically to charge the postage used to the following expense accounts:

708 General Postage Expense
741 Parcel Post
763 Advertising Postage expense

On July 31, before adjusting entries were made, the Prepaid Postage account had a debit balance of $2,560. During the month of July, postage used on parcel post amounted to $1,250 and on advertising, $675. The unused metered postage on July 31 was $325, and unused stamps on hand amounted to $87.

Required:

1. Open the necessary "T-accounts" and enter the prepaid postage balance before adjustment.
2. Make the necessary journal entry to record all postage expense for the month and post to the accounts.
3. Balance and rule the Prepaid Postage account and bring down the balance as of August 1.

14-5. The Blue Sea Company sells three special types of aquariums – A, B, and C. The stock records reveal the following information on December 31, 1978:

Type of aquarium	*Amount on hand*	*Cost* Fifo	*Cost* Weighted average	*Cost to replace*	*Selling price*
A	500	$7.00	$6.50	$8.00	$15.00
B..........	600	6.00	6.75	6.50	11.00
C	1,000	5.00	4.25	3.50	8.00

Required:

Compute the total value of the inventory using (1) Fifo, (2) weighted average, (3) market, (4) lower of cost or market as applied to each individual category, and (5) lower of cost or market as applied to total inventory.

14-6. The Hardman Ton Company uses the asset method to account for prepayments. The relevant asset accounts had the following balances at the end of the year:

Prepaid rent...	$12,000
Unexpired insurance	1,500
Office supplies	4,000
Advertising supplies..	2,500
Store supplies	5,000

During the year, $6,000 of rent and $500 of insurance had expired. At the end of the year, physical inventories revealed that the following amounts of supplies were on hand:

Office supplies..	$1,500
Advertising supplies	300
Store supplies...	3,500

Required:

Make the journal entries to adjust the accounts at the end of the year.

14–7. For the past six years, the Cobbler Company has maintained a gross profit percentage of 35 percent sales. The following information is available for 1978:

Merchandise inventory, January 1	$ 26,000
Purchases	280,000
Sales	380,000

Required:

Use the gross profit method to estimate (1) cost of goods sold and (2) ending merchandise inventory for 1978.

14–8. The Bridge Box Company uses the expense method to record advance payments. On December 31, 1978, the relevant expense accounts had the following balances:

Rent expense	$14,000
Insurance expense	4,000
Office supplies expense	7,500
Advertising supplies expense	3,800
Postage expense	2,600

On December 31, 1978, $6,800 of rent and $1,000 of insurance had not expired. The following amounts of supplies were on hand at December 31, 1978:

Office supplies	$2,500
Advertising supplies	600
Postage stamps	150

Required:

Prepare journal entries to adjust the accounts at the end of the year.

14–9. Part A The Harper Berry Company values its inventory at retail. Given the following information from the Harper Berry Company's records, compute the cost of the ending inventory.

	Cost	Retail
Inventory, beginning of period	$ 25,000	$ 50,000
Purchases during period (net)	312,500	700,000
Sales during period		710,000

Part B For the past several years, the Callaway Company has maintained a gross profit percentage of 45 percent of sales. The following information is available for 1978:

Merchandise inventory, January 1	$ 42,000
Purchases	368,000
Sales	590,000

Required:

Use the gross profit method to estimate (1) cost of goods sold and (2) ending merchandise inventory for 1978.

14–10. The Billingsley Company uses the asset method to account for prepayments. The relevant asset accounts had the following balances at the end of the year:

Prepaid rent	$9,000
Unexpired insurance	2,000
Office supplies	6,800
Advertising supplies	900
Store supplies	4,200
Postage stamps	3,900

During the year, $7,200 of rent and $1,800 of insurance had expired. At the end of the year, physical inventories revealed that the following amounts of supplies were on hand:

Office supplies	$1,100
Advertising supplies	150
Store supplies	600
Postage stamps	950

Required:

Prepare journal entries to adjust the accounts at the end of the year.

Long-lived assets—tangible
Learning objectives

Many businesses invest significant amounts of equity in tangible long-lived assets. Regardless of the particular amounts, such investments have lasting effects on the earnings of the business. The material in this chapter is designed to provide an understanding of the accounting procedures surrounding tangible long-lived assets. The following material is introduced:

1. Discussion of the ways in which tangible assets may be classified on the statement of financial position.
2. Accounting methods used in determining depreciation expense.
3. Recording the purchase and disposal of long-lived assets.
4. Illustration of information included in an asset record.
5. Presentation of wasting assets and the calculation of related depletion charges.

15

Long-lived assets
— tangible

As a means of establishing and maintaining continuity, most businesses acquire assets with the expectation that they will benefit the current as well as future periods. Assets whose lives extend over several periods are referred to as **long-lived assets.** From a descriptive point of view, tangible long-lived assets best describe those assets with useful economic lives extending over several periods. Assets of this type are often referred to as plant assets, fixed assets, or capital assets. Long-lived assets can be classified on the basis of (1) legal characteristics, (2) physical characteristics, and (3) accounting treatment characteristics.

Legally, long-lived assets are classed as either real property or personal property. **Real property** refers to land and anything that is attached to the land. **Personal property** is defined as all assets owned other than real property. In most cases, real property is classified as long-lived assets. An exception would be made for temporary investments in real property such as real estate. Personal property may also be classed as long-lived assets in cases where the asset's life extends over several periods. Equipment, trucks, patents, copyrights, and office furniture are examples of long-lived personal assets owned by a business.

A second way of classifying assets is by physical properties. Assets which are physically present are referred to as **tangible assets,** while those not present are classed as **intangibles.** Some items of both real and personal property are tangible assets. Although not physically tangible, intangible assets exist in a legal or economic sense; that is, they usually represent contractual economic rights. Examples of intangibles are patents, leases, copyrights, trademarks, and business goodwill. Often, businesses will invest in stocks or bonds of another company. Based on classi-

377

fication by physical intangibility, it would seem that these investments should be classed as intangibles. However, because of the unusual nature of such assets, they are normally reported in either the current or long-term asset group in the statement of financial position depending on the length of the expected holding period.

The third method of asset classification is the method which will be discussed in this chapter. Classification by accounting treatment is a common way of reporting long-lived assets. Since accounting records are normally based on historical cost, the assets are recorded on the books by debiting the particular asset account for the cost and crediting Cash or a payable account. Because the accounting process attempts to match period benefits (revenues) with period sacrifices (expenses), the portion of a long-lived asset's cost that is used up in the period should be recorded as a period expense. Tangible long-lived assets are therefore said to **depreciate** during the asset's life. Not all long-lived real and personal property is depreciated. At present, land is the only tangible asset that is not depreciated. Since land does not normally deteriorate, a portion of its cost is not expensed each period. Examples of depreciable long-lived tangible assets are building, machinery, equipment, and furniture. Expensing of intangible assets is referred to as **amortization.** Although the word amortization is broad enough to cover both expensing of tangible and intangible assets, amortization is used as a method of distinguishing between the two.

In contrast to tangible long-lived assets which are depreciated over time, some assets are actually consumed or used up over time. Examples of such assets are oil wells, mines, and timber. These assets are called **wasting assets.** Instead of amortizing or depreciating wasting assets, period consumption or exhaustion is referred to as **depletion.**

By using the terms depreciation, amortization, and depletion, it is easier to understand what type of asset is being expensed. Although this discussion is primarily concerned with accounting for the more common tangible long-lived assets such as land, buildings, and machinery, accounting for wasting assets will be discussed at the end of the chapter.

DEPRECIATION

As mentioned earlier, accounting attempts to match revenues to the period in which they are earned and expenses to the period benefiting from expenditures. Since long-lived assets benefit more than one period, the cost of such assets must be allocated to periods receiving benefit in order to properly determine periodic net earnings. Depreciation or the loss in usefulness of an asset may be a result of physical and/or **functional depreciation.**

Physical depreciation of an asset involves the decline in usefulness due to physical wear and tear. Various factors determine how fast an asset deteriorates. Much of an asset's physical deterioration depends on how regularly the asset is used. Even though use is an important factor to consider, the maintenance or lack of maintenance of an asset will greatly affect the length of an asset's life. Another factor of physical depreciation is the environment in which the asset is used. A forklift truck that is used outdoors will deteriorate faster than one which is used indoors.

Functional depreciation refers to the loss in usefulness because of inadequacy or obsolescence. In certain situations, functional depreciation may be as important or more important than physical depreciation in determining the useful life of an asset. For example, in the computer industry technology is advancing electronic data processing systems faster than they can physically wear out. The asset in question may have several years of useful physical life left but be almost worthless due to obsolescence. Changes in demand often result when new methods or processes are developed which increase efficiency thereby lowering costs and/or raising quality.

Determining depreciation expense

Apportioning the cost of an asset over the periods expected to benefit from the asset's use involves at least two basic problems. First, only the net cost of an asset is expensed over its useful life. The net cost is the asset's cost less any salvage or scrap value it may have after it has served its purpose. Determining the salvage value of an asset is not easily accomplished. In situations where an asset has a relatively short life and has been replaced a number of times in the past, the salvage value can be estimated from experience. But, if the asset is expected to last 15 or 20 years, it may be very difficult to determine future salvage value.

A second problem is that of determining the useful life of an asset. As mentioned above, an asset may become obsolete due to changes in demand or technology. Since predicting the future is difficult if not impossible, it is not easy to project the number of years in an asset's useful life. If it was known for certain that an asset would last ten years, 10 percent of the net cost would be expensed each year. Once reasonable estimates of the asset's salvage value and useful life are determined, the calculation of the period's depreciation expense is reduced to a procedural problem.

In making the necessary projections and estimates to determine depreciation expense, an accountant may rely on past experience and on assets previously owned by the business. Another source of guidance is the results experienced by others. Often statistical information can be obtained from industry trade associations and government agencies. For unusual or highly specialized equipment, opinions of engineers and appraisers may be helpful. Even though past experience may be helpful, it is not always the best guide. Estimates of the past may prove to be reliable, but future projections should always be viewed with a certain amount of doubt.

Methods of calculating depreciation expense are limited only by the imagination. However, the method selected must be both appropriate and reasonable under the circumstances. The four methods to be described are:

1. Straight-line method.
2. Declining-balance method.
3. Sum-of-the-years'-digits method.
4. Units of production method.

Since depreciation at best is only an estimate, it should be kept in mind that there is no correct method. However, for a particular situation there is most likely a method which is best under the given circumstances. Although many businesses use the same depreciation method for both business and tax purposes as a matter of convenience, they are not required to do so. The tax laws will usually allow any method which is reasonable and justifiable for a particular situation.

Straight-line method. Of the four methods referred to above, the straight-line method is the easiest to use when calculating depreciation expense. As the term suggests, the straight-line method allocates an equal amount of an asset's net cost to each period during its useful life. Assume that an asset has a cost of $20,000 and is expected to last 40 years. It is estimated that the scrap or salvage value will be $2,000. Yearly depreciation expense of $450 would be computed as follows:

$$\frac{\$20,000 - \$2,000}{40} = \$450$$

The annual depreciation rate would be 2.25 percent ($450 ÷ $20,000). The formula for the annual depreciation rate is: Straight-Line Rate = 100 percent/N, where N = years of life. It should be remembered that each of the years of an asset's life will be charged with an equal amount of depreciation under the straight-line method. When shown on a graph (see Illustration 15–1 below), the method results in a straight line, which is how the method acquired its name. At any time during the asset's life, the asset's book value is equal to the asset's cost less the accumulated depreciation to date. The book value merely represents the asset's undepreciated cost and is not intended to equal an asset's market value.

Although an asset depreciates daily, entries for depreciation expense are normally made on a monthly basis. Accounting for depreciation on a monthly basis presents a problem when assets are purchased during a month, thus resulting in an accounting period which is less than a month.

Since it would be foolish to require management to purchase all assets on the 1st of the month, accountants use the rule that assets purchased before the 15th of the month are considered to be owned a full month. Those purchased after the 15th are treated as being acquired on the 1st of the next month.

Because many assets depreciate on a generally even basis, the straight-line method is favored because it most closely resembles the facts. Another advantage of using the method is its simplicity. It is argued that since all depreciation calculations are based on estimates, more elaborate and time-consuming computations are unwarranted.

Declining-balance method. The straight-line method assumes that repairs will be made evenly throughout the life of an asset and that the asset will steadily decline in value over its life. The declining-balance method takes into consideration the fact that repairs will probably be more frequent in later years. It is also argued that an asset is most useful during its early years and therefore should be depreciated at a faster rate in its initial years. For these reasons, it would seem desirable to calculate the depreciation expense in a manner that would allow for larger expense in the earlier years. These larger write-offs are accomplished through the use of the declining-balance method.

The method is called the declining-balance method because it results in a lower depreciation charge with each succeeding year. The declining charges are accomplished by applying a fixed percentage rate to the asset's book value each year. The salvage value is ignored under this method since any rate less than 100 percent would never reduce the cost to zero. Normally, a percentage rate of twice the straight-line rate is used. If the asset is expected to last five years, the depreciation rate using the straight-line method would be 20 percent (100 percent ÷ 5 years). The declining-balance method would double the straight-line rate, resulting in a declining-balance rate of 40 percent. Assuming the asset cost $800 and using the declining-balance rate of 40 percent, the following expenses and book values would be shown at the end of each year.

Year	Depreciation expense	Accumulated depreciation	Book value
0			$800.00
1	$320.00	$320.00	480.00
2	192.00	512.00	288.00
3	115.20	627.20	172.80
4	69.12	696.32	103.68
5	41.47	737.79	62.21

If it were discovered during year 3 that the salvage value would be significantly more or less than $62.21, the depreciation charges for the remaining years would be adjusted accordingly. There exists a formula for calculating the rate to be used to achieve a given salvage value. However, since tax laws allow a rate of twice the straight-line rate and since the calculations are complex when using the formula, the rate used is generally twice the straight-line rate. The formula for calculating depreciation under the double declining-balance method is:

$$\text{Depreciation Expense per Year} = (2) \left(\frac{100 \text{ percent}}{N}\right) \binom{\text{Book Value of the Asset at}}{\text{the Beginning of the Year}}$$

where N = number of years in the asset's expected useful life.

Sum-of-the-years'-digits method. Instead of using the declining-balance method, the sum-of-the-years'-digits method is often used to obtain smaller amounts of depreciation each year. However, the sum-of-the-years'-digits method allows depreciation expenses to be calculated so that the asset's book value is reduced to a predetermined salvage value at the end of the asset's useful life. Since depreciation calculations take salvage value into consideration, the write-offs each year are based on the asset's net cost. The yearly expense is determined by multiplying the asset's net cost by a fraction whose denominator consists of the sum of the years of the asset's expected life and whose numerator consists of the digit representing the number of expected years of service left in the asset at the beginning of the accounting period.

For example, assume that an asset costing $2,000 is purchased. Salvage value is estimated to be $200 at the end of a useful life of five years. The fraction's numerator would be determined by computing the sum-of-the-years' digits which are $5 + 4 + 3 + 2 + 1 = 15$. For the first year, $\frac{5}{15}$ of the net cost would be recorded as depreciation expense. The second year's depreciation expense would be $\frac{4}{15}$ of the asset's net cost; the third, $\frac{3}{15}$; the fourth, $\frac{2}{15}$; and the fifth, $\frac{1}{15}$. The following table illustrates the year-end results of the above calculations for each of the five years:

Year	Depreciation expense	Accumulated depreciation	Book value
0			$2,000
1	$600	$ 600	1,400
2	480	1,080	920
3	360	1,440	560
4	240	1,680	320
5	120	1,800	200

When using the sum-of-the-years'-digits method, finding the sum of the years to use in the fraction's denominator may be time-consuming. For example, an asset with a life of 25 years would require the addition of the digits 1 through 25. In order to save time, the following formula is often used.

$$\text{Denominator} = N\left(\frac{N+1}{2}\right)$$

where N = number of years in asset's expected useful life.

$$\text{Denominator} = 25\left(\frac{25+1}{2}\right) = 325$$

Depreciation expense is then calculated with the following formula:

$$\text{Depreciation Expense per Year} = \left(\frac{\text{Remaining Years of Life}}{\text{Sum-of-the-Years' Digits}}\right)\left(\begin{array}{c}\text{Depreciable}\\ \text{Cost}\end{array}\right)$$

Units of production method. Unlike the three methods described above, the depreciation expense cannot be determined ahead of time when using the units of production method. As the name suggests, the depreciation expense for each period is determined by the number of units produced. In some situations it is possible to estimate the number of units of production an asset is expected to produce during its useful life. Where this can be done, the net cost of the asset can be allocated to each of the units by dividing the asset's net cost by the total expected units of production.

This method results in depreciation being recorded only when the asset is being used. It is evident that this method of calculating depreciation is not applicable to all assets. The units of production method can only be used if the asset being depreciated produces goods or services which are measurable in units. Some think this method is better since it results in depreciation being recorded only in the period receiving benefit and only to the degree that benefits were realized.

As an example, assume that a machine is purchased which is expected to produce 400,000 units during its lifetime. The asset's cost is $35,000, and it is expected that after 400,000 units of production the asset will have a trade-in value of $3,000. The estimated depreciation per unit is 8 cents ($32,000 ÷ 400,000 units). If the machine produced 45,000 units during the first year, the depreciation expense to be recorded would be $3,600 (45,000 units × $0.08).

Comparison of methods. For comparative purposes, only the first three methods will be considered since the units of production method is based on a variable (production) and is not calculated in advance by using a formula. The table and graph in Illustration 15–1 show the results achieved under each of the methods. Calculations are based on an asset costing $1,000 with an expected salvage value of $100 at the end of five years.

Illustration 15–1

Year	Straight-line method		Declining-balance method		Sum-of-the-years'-digits method	
	Depreciation expense	Book value	Depreciation expense	Book value	Depreciation expense	Book value
0...............		$1,000.00		$1,000.00		$1,000.00
1...............	$180.00	820.00	$400.00	600.00	$300.00	700.00
2...............	180.00	640.00	240.00	360.00	240.00	460.00
3...............	180.00	460.00	144.00	216.00	180.00	280.00
4...............	180.00	280.00	86.40	129.60	120.00	160.00
5...............	180.00	100.00	51.84	77.76	60.00	100.00

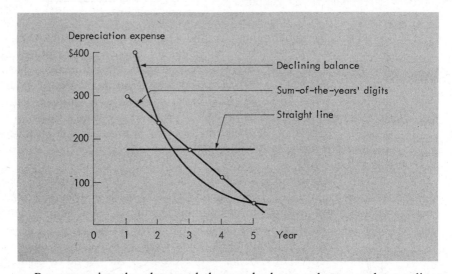

By comparing the chart and the graph above, a better understanding of the results achieved under the three methods can be obtained. The straight-line method results in a straight horizontal line. This is because of equal amounts of depreciation expense being recorded each year.

The declining-balance method results in a curved line. The line is curved because the depreciation charge each year is determined by multiplying the book value by 40 percent (twice the straight-line rate of 20 percent). In Illustration 15–1, the salvage value at the end of five years when using the declining-balance method is $77.76. To make the salvage value come out to $100, the depreciation charges for the later years would be adjusted downward. It should be noted that since the declining-balance method multiplies the asset's book value each year by a fixed percentage, the book value will never equal zero and will seldom equal the salvage value. For this reason, depreciation charges will usually need adjusting in the asset's later years.

The sum-of-the-years'-digits method results in a straight line that decreases each year by a fixed amount. In the above example, the depreciation expense declined each year by $60. It is observed that this is $\frac{1}{15}$ of the asset's net cost ($\frac{1}{15} \times \$900$). Since the fraction used each year decreases by $\frac{1}{15}$, the depreciation charges result in a straight downward sloping line.

Group depreciation. In certain situations it is possible to depreciate a group of assets rather than depreciate each asset separately. When depreciation is accounted for in this manner, it is important that the group consists of the same relative proportions of assets from period to period. Requiring that the groups of assets remain proportionately the same from period to period is necessary because group depreciation is based on an average depreciation rate.

The depreciation rate is determined by (1) calculating the annual depreciation charge for each asset, (2) totaling the annual depreciation charges for each asset, and (3) dividing the total charges by the total cost of the assets. For example, assume that a business has the following assets:

Asset No.	Cost	Salvage value	Estimated life	Annual depreciation
201	$ 25,000	$4,000	14 years	$1,500
202	30,000	2,000	20 years	1,400
203	24,000	3,000	21 years	1,000
204	44,000	4,000	16 years	2,500
Total	$123,000			$6,400

Group depreciation rate: $6,400 ÷ $123,000 = 5.203 Percent

The depreciation rate would probably be rounded to 5.2 percent. As long as the relative "mix" of the group remained unchanged, the annual depreciation charge for this particular group would be 5.2 percent of the group's total cost. The group method assumes that additions and retirements are made on a uniform basis which does not upset the group "mix." Because the group rate is based on averages, it should be remembered that unless the group is composed of the same relative proportions of assets from period to period, the use of a group rate will result in unreasonable depreciation charges.

ACCOUNTING FOR LONG-LIVED ASSETS

The extent of the accounting system used to record the acquisition, depreciation, and disposal of tangible long-lived assets will depend on the size of the business. If there are only a few assets of this type, a separate account for each will be maintained in the general ledger along with the asset's depreciation account (excluding land, which is not depreciated). Since each asset is accounted for separately, the periodic depreciation charge for each asset will be individually calculated.

Where there is a large number of long-lived assets, separate records for each asset will not be maintained in the general ledger. Instead, summary accounts will be used for each class of assets in the general ledger, and individual accounts will be recorded in a subsidiary ledger for each particular asset. The subsidiary records are often kept on cards or sheets with spaces provided for recording the asset's acquisition, depreciation, and ultimate disposition. The asset record cards enable the accountant to obtain, at a glance, the past and present accounting status of the asset. An asset record card will be further described and illustrated following a description of the basic journal entries used in accounting for tangible long-lived assets.

PURCHASE OF ASSETS

Accounting for the purchase of an asset is a relatively simple procedure. Since accountants generally record assets at their cost, the purchase is recorded by debiting the asset for its cost and crediting either cash or a payable or both. A situation in which both cash and a payable would be credited would be when an asset is purchased by making a partial cash payment and recording the balance as a payable. Also, it is possible that payment may be made by exchanging an existing asset (other than cash). In this situation, the asset traded will be credited instead of cash or a payable.

For example, assume that a piece of machinery is purchased for $5,000 cash. To record the purchase, the following general journal entry would be required:

```
Machinery ..........................................................................  5,000
    Cash ............................................................................            5,000
      Purchase of machinery for $5,000 cash.
```

If payment for the machinery had been other than cash, the appropriate account would have been credited.

DEPRECIATION OF ASSETS

Once depreciation schedules have been prepared, the monthly or yearly depreciation charges are easily made. Assume that depreciation charges are made on a yearly basis for a machine which costs $5,000. It is expected to have a salvage value of $500 at the end of ten years, and it is to be depreciated on a straight-line basis. The following general journal entry would be made at the end of each of the ten years:

```
Depreciation Expense—Machine............................................   450
   Accumulated Depreciation—Machine ...............................           450
   To record depreciation on machine No. 60423.
```

The above entry would be recorded in the books of a firm which makes individual entries for each asset. Such a situation would most likely exist when the firm has relatively few assets. In a larger firm, depreciation charges would be summarized in the subsidiary records, and an entry would be made in the general journal for each class of assets. The number of entries made will depend on the detail desired in the general journal and periodic statements.

As noted earlier, the asset's cost less the accumulated depreciation to date represents the asset's **book value.** Whenever an asset is disposed of, the depreciation must be brought up to date (to the nearest full month). Unless the depreciation is adjusted before the asset's disposal, the calculated gain or loss on disposal will be incorrect.

DISPOSAL OF ASSETS

An asset is normally disposed of in one of three ways:

1. Disposal through sale.
2. Disposal through exchange.
3. Disposal by retiring or discarding.

A fourth possibility for disposal exists when assets are destroyed as a result of a natural disaster. Although the basic principles to be discussed apply to involuntary disposal, the discussion to follow will be concerned with disposal during the ordinary course of business operations. Also, the following discussion relates to assets which are depreciated on an individual basis. If assets are depreciated on a group basis, a gain or loss is not recorded upon disposal. The asset group is simply credited for the asset's cost to remove the asset, and the asset's cost less any amount received upon disposal is charged to the group's accumulated depreciation account.

Disposal through sale

As mentioned above, it is necessary to know the book value of an asset to determine the proper gain or loss on the sale of the asset. The difference between the asset's cost and depreciation recorded to date is the asset's book value. Assume that an office machine costs $200 and is depreciated at a rate of 10 percent per year. After three and one-half years, the machine is sold. Before the entry is made to dispose of the asset, the depreciation must be recorded to date of sale. Assuming that depreciation is charged on a yearly basis, depreciation charged for the first three years would amount to $60. To record the depreciation charge for the last half year, the following general journal entry is required:

```
Depreciation Expense—Office Machine ..................................    10
    Accumulated Depreciation—Office Machine......................          10
    To record depreciation of last half year ($200  × 0.10  × ½ year).
```

No matter how the asset is disposed of, the depreciation charges must first be brought up to date. The following discussion of ways to dispose of assets will assume that depreciation has been recorded to the date of sale.

After the depreciation charge for the last one-half year has been recorded, the office machine has a book value of $130 ($200 − $70). If the asset is sold for $130, there is no gain or loss since the book value equals the sales price. Assuming the office machine is sold for cash, the following general journal entry is necessary:

```
Cash.................................................................................   130
    Accumulated Depreciation—Office Machine........................    70
    Office Machine...............................................................         200
    To record sale of office machine.
```

If the office machine were sold for $145, it would be necessary to record a gain of $15. The gain represents the excess of sales price over the asset's book value. Sale of the office machine for $145 would require the following general journal entry:

```
Cash................................................................................   145
Accumulated Depreciation—Office Machine............................    70
    Gain on Sale of Office Machine .........................................          15
    Office Machine...............................................................         200
    To record sale of office machine.
```

If the office machine were sold for $100, the following general journal entry would be necessary:

```
Cash................................................................................   100
Accumulated Depreciation—Office Machine............................    70
Loss on Sale of Office Machine ............................................    30
    Office Machine...............................................................         200
    To record sale of office machine.
```

In all of the above entries, it is important to note that (1) the asset is removed by crediting the particular asset account; (2) the accumulated depreciation account is debited, thus eliminating depreciation charges to date for the disposed asset; (3) an account is debited for the sales price of the asset (cash); and (4) the difference between the above debits and credits represents the gain or loss on disposal and is shown to be either a debit (loss) or a credit (gain). If the entry is properly made, it will have the effect of completely removing the asset and the related depreciation account from the books. This is a desirable effect since it represents the asset being removed from the business.

Disposal through exchange

When new equipment is purchased, the old asset being replaced is frequently traded as part of the payment for the new asset. The difference between the sales price and the trade-in allowance of the old asset is referred to as **"boot"** (the balance owed). If the trade-in allowance is less than the old asset's book value, there is a loss; if it is greater than the book value, there is a gain. However, according to *APB Opinion No. 29,* gains on the exchange of similar assets are not recognized on the books of the firm.

The asset being traded is often similar or of like kind to the asset being acquired. The income tax laws state that where assets are traded for similar assets, there will be no gain or loss. In such situations, the cost of the new asset is adjusted for any gain or loss resulting from the exchange.

For example, assume that a truck costing $6,000 has been owned for two years. Depreciation of $800 has been taken each year resulting in accumulated depreciation to date of $1,600. Therefore, the book value of the truck is $4,400 ($6,000 − $1,600). The owner is to be allowed a trade-in allowance of $4,000 in exchange for a new truck costing $7,200. The "boot" or cash to be paid is therefore $3,200 ($7,200 − $4,000). Assuming that the exchange is to be made without recording any gain or loss, the basis or cost of the new asset would be $7,600 ($4,400 + $3,200 cash). The general journal entry to record the exchange is as follows:

Truck (new)	7,600	
Accumulated Depreciation — Truck	1,600	
Truck (old)		6,000
Cash		3,200
Purchase of new truck.		

For exchanges which do not involve assets of like kind, gains and losses are recorded. For example, assume that a car is traded for a tractor. The car originally cost $4,000; and after recording depreciation to date, it has a book value of $1,500 ($4,000 cost − $2,500 accumulated depreciation). The new tractor costs $8,000 and a trade-in allowance of $1,000 is to be allowed for the car resulting in a cash payment of $7,000 ($8,000 − $1,000). The loss to be recorded is $500, representing the difference between the book value of the car ($1,500) and the trade-in allowance ($1,000). The transaction is recorded with the following general journal entry:

Tractor	8,000	
Accumulated Depreciation — Car	2,500	
Loss on Exchange of Car	500	
Car		4,000
Cash		7,000
Exchange of car for tractor.		

If the trade-in allowance had been greater than the book value of the car ($1,500), the entry above would have shown a gain as a result of the exchange. It should be noted that when assets are exchanged, it is as if the old asset were sold and the new asset were purchased in separate transactions. If two entries had been made, the net effect would be the entry as shown above.

Disposal by retiring or discarding

Sometimes assets are discarded or thrown away. The recording of a loss in such an event will depend on whether or not the asset has been fully depreciated. If the asset discarded has a book value (has not been fully depreciated), then the loss will equal the book value. For assets with no book value, there will be no loss upon disposal. The asset will be eliminated from the accounts by debiting the accumulated depreciation account and crediting the asset account for the cost of the asset.

Assume that an office desk costing $250 is discarded when it has a book value of $35. The following general journal entry reflects the disposal and loss of $35:

```
Accumulated Depreciation — Office Desk ...............................   215
Loss on Disposal of Desk ......................................................    35
     Office Desk ..................................................................               250
   Disposal of office desk.
```

It should be observed that each time a tangible long-lived asset is retired, the depreciation is first brought up to date; and secondly, the asset and related depreciation accounts are removed from the books.

STATEMENT PRESENTATION OF ASSETS

The manner in which assets are shown on the financial statements will depend on the amount of detail desired. Depreciation is usually considered an operating expense and is so classified on the earnings statement. Depreciation of assets used in selling may be deducted along with selling expenses while depreciation of assets used for administrative purposes (desks, chairs, and office equipment) may be recorded along with general and administrative expenses.

Because the accumulated depreciation accounts have a close relationship to the related asset accounts, the accumulated depreciation is often shown as a deduction from the cost of the asset. The net figure represents the asset's book value.

Although the net amount (cost-accumulated depreciation) is referred to as the asset's book value, it should not be regarded as the asset's market value. The net amount is not expected to equal the market value of the asset. What the asset is sold for or might be sold for has no effect on the asset's book value. The book value should only be viewed as the cost of the asset that has not been charged to operations.

ASSET RECORDS

To help keep records for each asset, information is usually recorded on asset record cards or sheets. The record cards describe the assets and give necessary information so that depreciation charges can be calculated. The following notes are descriptions of the information recorded on the asset record card shown in Illustration 15-2.

1975
July   1   Purchased a riding lawn mower from the Lazy Garden Shop for $1,000. with an estimated life of 4 years and estimated salvage value of $200.
Dec. 31   Annual depreciation of $100 (25 percent rate).
1976
Dec. 31   Annual depreciation of $200 (25 percent rate).
1977
Dec. 31   Annual depreciation of $200 (25 percent rate).
1978
June 30   Annual depreciation of $100 (25 percent rate).
      30   Sold mower for $450 cash.

Illustration 15-2
Asset record card

ASSET RECORD

Description	Riding lawn mower	Account	Yard equipment
Estimated life	4 years	Annual depreciation rate	25%
Estimated salvage value	$200	Annual depreciation	$200

Cost				Depreciation			
Date Purchased		Description	Amount	Year	Rate	Amount	Total to Date
July 1975	1	Riding lawn mower (Lazy Garden Shop)	1,000 00	1975	25%	100 00	100 00
				1976	25%	200 00	300 00
				1977	25%	200 00	500 00
Date Sold				1978	25%	100 00	600 00
June 1978	30	Sold mower for $450 Cash gain of $50					

After the depreciation for the first six months of 1978 has been recorded, the following general journal entry would be made to record the sale:

```
Cash ................................................................................   450
Accumulated Depreciation – Yard Equipment .........................   600
      Yard Equipment ........................................................              1,000
      Gain on Sale of Mower ................................................                 50
   To record sale of mower.
```

The use of asset record cards is most helpful when there are a large number of assets. Once the card is established, it provides the accountant with a simple method of keeping track of an asset's history and current status. In addition, it aids in recording periodic depreciation charges.

WASTING ASSETS

Wasting assets refers to real property which is consumed during production. Examples of wasting assets are natural resources such as timber, oil and gas wells, and mines. The term "wasting" is used because it is expected that valuable resources will eventually be completely exhausted. In some cases, such as oil and gas wells, only the resources below the surface are owned and not the actual land surface.

As discussed earlier, the expensing of wasting assets is called depletion since it best describes the manner in which the assets are consumed. Charges for depletion of wasting assets are similar to depreciation as calculated under the units of production method. The net cost of the property is determined by subtracting the expected salvage value from the property's cost. The net cost is then divided by the estimated number of units the property contains. The division results in the depletion expense per unit. Multiplying the unit expense by the number of units removed results in the depletion expense for the period.

Assume that the rights to drill for oil are acquired by the Maxwell Drilling Company for $1,000,000. It is estimated that there are 4,000,000 barrels of oil available for pumping. The first year resulted in the production of 900,000 barrels of oil. Depletion expense is computed as follows:

```
Cost of oil pumping rights ...........................   $1,000,000
                                                           ÷
Expected number of barrels of oil ................    4,000,000
Depletion expense per barrel .......................         25¢
                                                           ×
Production of first year ..............................     900,000
      First Year Depletion Expense ..............   $  225,000
```

The following general journal entry would reflect the first year's depletion expense:

```
Depletion Expense.......................................................... 225,000
    Accumulated Depletion — Oil Well ...............................        225,000
    Depletion of 900,000 barrels at 25 cents per barrel.
```

The difference between the cost of the oil well rights and the accumulated depletion is the book value of the asset:

```
Cost of oil well rights.................................... $1,000,000
    Less: Accumulated depletion .....................     225,000
        Book Value of Oil Well Rights .............. $  775,000
```

The depletion expense would be reported as an operating expense on the earnings statement, and the asset and related accumulated depletion accounts would be reported on the statement of financial position.

Because the number of units of production is an estimate and changes from time to time, it is necessary to revise the per unit depletion expense. Adjustment of previous depletion charges is not necessary. Instead, a new per unit depletion expense is calculated based on the asset's book value and the remaining estimated units of production. Assume that the oil well mentioned above yields 1,100,000 barrels of oil the second year. At the end of the year, it is estimated that there are 1,400,000 barrels of oil remaining. The revised depletion expense would be calculated as follows:

```
Book value of oil rights at beginning of year...............    $775,000
                                                                   ÷
Production this year (barrels) ...................................  1,100,000
Expected remaining production................................  1,400,000    2,500,000
Depletion expense per barrel....................................                   31¢
```

Depletion charges on the current year's production would be $341,000 (1,100,000 barrels × 31 cents per barrel).

GLOSSARY

Amortization   the expensing of intangible assets.

Book value (of long-lived asset)   cost of the asset less accumulated depreciation or accumulated depletion.

Boot   the amount of cash paid when an old asset is exchanged for a new asset. It is equal to the difference between the sales price of the new asset and the trade-in allowance of the old asset.

Depletion   expensing of wasting assets such as natural resources which are consumed or exhausted during production. Depletion expense is calculated by dividing the net cost (cost less salvage value) of the property by the estimated number of units the property contains. This results in the depletion expense per unit which is multiplied by the number of units removed to obtain the depletion expense for the period.

Depreciation   an estimate of the amount of a long-lived asset's cost that expires during a period. The periodic expense can be calculated using several different methods. The straight-line method allocates an equal amount of an asset's net cost to each period during its useful life. The declining-balance method involves the application of a fixed percentage rate to the asset's book value each year which results in a lower depreciation charge for each succeeding year. Using the sum-of-the-years'-digits method, depreciation expense is determined by multiplying the asset's net cost by a fraction whose denominator consists of the sum of the years of the asset's expected life and whose numerator consists of the digit representing the expected number of years of service left in the asset at the beginning of the accounting period.

Functional depreciation   the loss in usefulness of an asset because of inadequacy or obsolescence.

Intangible assets   assets which cannot be seen or touched but which do exist in a legal or economic sense. Patents, leases, copyrights, trademarks, and business goodwill are examples of intangible assets.

Long-lived assets   assets whose useful lives extend over several periods. The cost of such assets must be allocated to periods receiving benefits to determine properly periodic net earnings. Also referred to as plant assets, fixed assets, or capital assets.

Personal property   all assets owned other than real property. It includes equipment, trucks, patents, copyrights, office furniture, machinery, and tools.

Physical depreciation   an asset's decline in usefulness because of physical wear and tear.

Real property   land and anything that is attached to the land. It includes buildings, parking lots, loading docks, fences, and sidewalks.

Tangible assets   assets which can be seen and touched. Buildings, land, and equipment are examples of long-lived tangible assets.

Wasting assets   real property which is consumed or used over time. Examples are natural resources such as timber, oil wells, gas wells, and mines.

QUESTIONS AND EXERCISES

1. Distinguish between real and personal property, and give three examples of each.

2. Distinguish between physical and functional depreciation, and name the factors influencing each.

3. What are two estimates that are used in calculating depreciation expense?

4. The Burr Company paid $7,000 cash for a car that has a five-year useful life and a $600 salvage value. What general journal entries should be made to record the purchase and the first year's depreciation expense (straight-line method)?

5. What justification exists for using the declining-balance method of depreciation?

6. Name three ways to voluntarily dispose of an asset.

7. A tractor that originally cost $5,200 was sold for $600. The related accumulated depreciation account had a balance of $5,000 on the date of sale. What general journal entry should be made to record the sale?

8. What are wasting assets? Give some examples.

9. The Eddis Corporation paid $100,000 for rights to drill for oil. The well is expected to produce 400,000 barrels of oil. What is the depletion expense per barrel?

10. What is the book value of a coal mine that originally cost $2,000,000 and now has an accumulated depletion account balance of $500,000?

PROBLEMS

15–1. On January 1, 1978, the Goso Company purchased a truck for $36,100. The truck is expected to have a useful life of six years. At the end of six years, the company plans to sell the truck for $100. Calculate the annual depreciation expense using the straight-line method.

15–2. The Cone Corporation purchased a machine on March 1, 1976, for $45,000. Engineers have estimated that the machine will produce 200,000 units over its entire useful life and that it will have no salvage value. Using the units of production method and the following information, calculate the depreciation expense for 1976, 1977, and 1978.

Year	Number of units produced
1976	35,000
1977	50,000
1978	46,000

15–3. The Bobco Manufacturing Company installed a computer on January 3, 1976. Given the following information about the computer, calculate the depreciation expense and book value for each of the five years and give the general journal entry to record the expense in 1978.

> Cost: $500,000
> Salvage Value: 0
> Depreciation method: Double declining balance

15–4. The Jones Manufacturing Company purchased factory equipment costing $440,000. The equipment has a six-year useful life and a $20,000 salvage value. Using the sum-of-the-years'-digits method, calculate the depreciation expense for each of the six years.

15-5. Give the general journal entries to record the following transactions of the Betagam Company.

1978

Jan. 3 Purchased land costing $40,000 and a building costing $125,000. Paid $50,000 cash and charged the rest to its account. The building has a 40-year useful life and no salvage value.

Feb. 1 Purchased typewriter on account for $550. The typewriter has an estimated useful life of five years with an expected salvage value of $50.

Mar. 2 Purchased office desk for cash. The cost of the desk was $900, and it has an estimated useful life of eight years with an expected salvage value of $100.

Apr. 10 Purchased electronic desk calculator on account. The calculator cost $450 and has a $50 salvage value and an estimated useful life of five years.

May 12 Purchased on account a delivery truck costing $12,000. The truck has an expected useful life of eight years and a $2,000 salvage value.

Dec. 31 Record the depreciation expense for the year using the straight-line method for each item. (Make one compound general journal entry.) Compute depreciation to the nearest month.

15-6.

Asset	Cost	Date of purchase	Estimated useful life	Salvage value	Depreciation method
Truck	$12,500	June 30, 1972	8 years	$ 500	Straight line
Machine...	75,000	January 29, 1973	20 years	1,300	Units of production
Car	6,000	January 6, 1976	4 years	300	Sum-of-the-years' digits

The machine produced the following number of units each year. It was expected to produce a total of 368,500 units during its entire useful life.

Year	Number of units produced
1972.............................	25,000
1973.............................	15,000
1974.............................	27,000
1975.............................	35,000
1976.............................	40,000
1977.............................	18,000

Required:

1. Complete the following schedule showing the depreciation expense for each asset for each of the years 1972–1978.

Depreciation Expense Schedule
1972–1978

Years	Truck	Machine	Car	Annual Depreciation Expense
1972		–	–	
1973			–	
1974			–	
1975			–	
1976				
1977				
1978				
Accumulated depreciation as of December 31, 1978				

2. Total the rows to find the annual depreciation expense for each year and sum the columns to compute the accumulated depreciation account balances as of December 31, 1978.

3. Make the general journal entries to dispose of the assets on January 2, 1979, under the given circumstances.

   a. The truck was sold for $600.

   b. The machine became obsolete and was retired from service.

   c. The old car was exchanged for a new car that had an invoice price of $7,500. A $500 trade-in allowance was received on the exchange. (No gain or loss was to be recognized on the exchange.)

15-7. On February 27, 1977, the Minor Company acquired a coal mine at a cost of $1,200,000. It has been estimated that the mine contains 2,400,000 tons of coal. In 1977, 50,000 tons were mined, and 65,000 tons were mined in 1978.

Required:

1. Calculate the depletion expense per ton.

2. Make the general journal entries to record the depletion expense for 1977 and 1978.

3. Calculate the book value of the coal mine as of December 31, 1978.

Owner's equity: Proprietorship, partnerships
Learning objectives

To gain an understanding of the operational differences between accounting for a partnership and accounting for a proprietorship, this chapter considers the following topics:

1. The organization and accounting procedures of a sole proprietorship in contrast with the organization and accounting procedures of a partnership.
2. The treatment of owner's equity accounts for the sole proprietorship and partnership.
3. Presentation of owner's equity in the statement of financial position.
4. Admission and withdrawal of a partner.
5. Accounting procedures for liquidating a partnership.

16

Owner's equity: Proprietorship, partnerships

Whether operating as a proprietorship, partnership, or corporation, the assets of a business are normally subject to the claims of several parties. Creditors have a claim to the assets as represented by the liabilities on the statement of financial position. The difference between the assets and liabilities of a business is the amount of owner's equity.

THE PROPRIETORSHIP

By definition, the term proprietorship refers to a person who has the exclusive right of ownership of properties or assets in question. Even though creditors have a claim to a proprietorship's assets, the owner actually has exclusive title to business assets since the owner and not the business itself is personally liable for creditors' claims. The amount of owner's equity (assets − liabilities) on the statement of financial position is sometimes referred to as the net worth, net assets, or capital of the proprietorship. To identify the net amount invested, the term "capital" normally follows the name of the owner in the owner's equity section of the statement of financial position.

The proprietorship form of business is most common in small merchandising and personal service enterprises. Examples of businesses which are usually operated as proprietorships are those in the medical and dental professions, although there is a noticeable trend towards "professional corporations." An obvious reason for operating in the proprietorship form is the simplicity of operating as a sole owner. Since the proprietor is both manager and owner, he or she need not enter into legal or contractual agreements with others as to ownership and business

399

conduct. Compliance with state and local laws is all that is necessary to operate a sole proprietorship.

Proprietorship organization

Since the sole proprietor is the only investor, he or she alone decides the nature and amount of assets that will be invested in the business. The initial investment may consist only of cash or of cash along with other assets such as office and store equipment, buildings, land, and merchandise. In order to keep adequate business records, the property invested is usually segregated from other properties owned by the proprietor. An individual may invest in several enterprises, operating each as a separate proprietorship. Whenever such a situation exists, the proprietor may find that it is easier to manage each proprietorship if separate books are kept for each.

The sole proprietorship has several distinct advantages when compared to other forms of business organizations, such as:

1. Organizational simplicity.
2. Independence in making business decisions.
3. Reduced reporting and government control.

Although the sole proprietorship enjoys the above advantages, it is not without the following disadvantages:

1. Limited capital.
2. Proprietor's sole responsibility for business debts.
3. Limited business knowledge and experience.
4. Limited life.

Accounting procedure

The accounting procedure for ordinary business transactions does not vary with the organizational structure of the business. Differences in the legal structure of proprietorships, partnerships, and corporations have little effect on the routine transactions of a business. The differences become apparent when comparing the owner's equity section of the statement of financial position for each type of organization.

Equity accounts. The owner's equity section of a sole proprietorship contains two types of accounts. First, there are those accounts which remain from period to period; and secondly, there are those accounts which are temporary and are closed out at the end of each accounting period.

In the sole proprietorship, the only permanent account (or account which remains unclosed from period to period) is the capital account. As indicated above, the owner's equity in the business is identified by the owner's name followed by the term "capital," such as Smith, Capital.

The temporary owner's equity accounts are those which summarize the transactions of the period which affect owner's equity. Since the capital account is regarded as a permanent type of account, it is not adjusted for revenues, expenses, and cash withdrawals on a daily basis. Instead, a **summary account** is maintained for revenues and expenses, and a drawing account is used to record cash withdrawals of the owner. At the end of the accounting period, these temporary accounts are normally closed out to the capital account. The number of summary accounts will depend on the type of business operation. An account entitled Expense and Revenue Summary may be the only summary account for a service type proprietorship. If the proprietorship is a merchandising or manufacturing type business, an account titled Cost of Goods Sold may also be used.

At the end of the accounting period, the Cost of Goods Sold account is debited for the beginning inventory and for purchases during the period and is credited for purchase returns and allowances, purchase discounts allowed, and the merchandise inventory existing at the end of the period. The cost of goods sold during the period is represented by the resulting debit balance in the Cost of Goods Sold account. This balance is then transferred as a debit to the Expense and Revenue Summary account. In addition, all other expenses and revenues are transferred to the summary account. As a result, the balance in the summary account will represent a net loss (debit) or net earnings (credit) for the period. The summary accounts are only used to close the books at the end of the period.

Initial entries of a proprietorship. The accounts debited and credited to open the books of a proprietorship will depend on the type of assets transferred to the business. The owner may invest cash as well as other types of properties. If the assets transferred include real or personal property which has not been paid for, the related liabilities may also be transferred. For the individual who makes an initial investment consisting of cash only, the opening entry is simply a debit to Cash and a credit to Capital.

If other properties along with cash are transferred to the new business, the entry will involve debits to the cash and asset accounts for the amounts transferred and a credit to the capital account for the total amount invested. If there are liabilities attached to the various properties transferred, they will be recorded as credits in the opening entry. The liability accounts credited may involve items such as accounts payable, mortgages payable, notes payable, or any other liability attached to properties transferred. Where liabilities are recorded in the opening entry, the capital account is only credited for the excess of assets invested over the amount of liabilities recorded.

To illustrate the opening entry of a proprietorship, assume that A. B. Campbell transfers the following assets and liabilities: cash amounting to $2,000, delivery equipment worth $5,000, and office equipment costing $3,500. Campbell owes $500 on the office equipment and has a $1,000 note payable on the delivery equipment. Since all cash of the business is assumed to be immediately deposited in the bank, Cash in Bank will be debited for the cash transferred. To open the books of A. B. Campbell, the following general journal entry is used:

Cash in Bank	2,000	
Office Equipment	3,500	
Delivery Equipment	5,000	
Accounts Payable		500
Notes Payable		1,000
A. B. Campbell, Capital		9,000
To record investment in business.		

It is not uncommon to find small businesses which operate with little or no record keeping. The only records kept on a daily basis may be those recorded on check stubs. Accounts receivable and accounts payable are kept in an unorderly manner with no formal records as are usually found in a double-entry system along with the necessary journals. When the records are kept in a loose manner as described above, it is necessary to make rough calculations and estimates at the period's end in order to prepare an earnings statement. Statements prepared in such a haphazard manner are often incorrect as errors in calculations, and omission of information are likely to occur. For business records to be accurate, it is desirable that records be made soon after the transaction has taken place. In addition, the use of double-entry accounting provides a method of checking the mathematical accuracy of records as they are made.

It is not unusual to find a small business that has been in operation for a short time and after growing discovers that its record-keeping system is inadequate. Because this is often the case, it is best to begin with a record-keeping system that will allow for expansion and recall of past transactions. When it is decided that a double-entry system is needed, it is necessary to prepare a statement of financial position which will be used in formulating the opening entry.

Assume that J. J. Jones is the sole proprietor of a small janitorial business. Because of the lack of adequate records, Jones is finding it difficult to keep track of receivables and payables. Because of this inadequacy, Jones has had difficulty in determining business earnings. To establish a double-entry system, Jones, together with an accountant, prepares the statement of financial position shown in Illustration 16–1.

After all assets, liabilities and owner's equity amounts have been

Illustration 16–1

```
                          J. J. JONES
                   Statement of Financial Position
                        December 31, 1978

                             Assets
Cash in bank ...................................................................    $ 1,750
Accounts receivable ......................................................  $4,850
   Less: Allowance for doubtful accounts ...........................     700     4,150
Cleaning supplies............................................................            1,200
Service equipment..........................................................  $6,000
   Less: Accumulated depreciation ................................    1,250     4,750
      Total Assets..........................................................            $11,850

                           Liabilities
Accounts payable...........................................................  $1,100
Notes payable ...............................................................     500
      Total Liabilities .....................................................            $ 1,600

                        Owner's Equity
J. J. Jones, Capital                                                             $10,250
      Total Liabilities and Owner's Equity ..........................            $11,850
```

determined as shown in the above statement of financial position, the following general journal entry is used to open the general ledger:

```
Cash in Bank ...................................................................  1,750
Accounts Receivable ......................................................  4,850
Cleaning Supplies............................................................  1,200
Service Equipment..........................................................  6,000
   Accounts Payable......................................................            1,100
   Notes Payable............................................................             500
   Allowance for Doubtful Accounts ....................................            700
   Accumulated Depreciation .............................................          1,250
   J. J. Jones, Capital........................................................         10,250
      To open general ledger.
```

After the general journal has been opened by the above entry, the debits and credits of the opening entry are posted to the proper accounts. Each asset account is debited for the proper amount. Each liability and **contra asset account** (Allowance for Doubtful Accounts and Accumulated Depreciation) is credited for its respective amount. The capital account of J. J. Jones is credited for Jones's equity. Balances for the Accounts Receivable and Accounts Payable ledger accounts can be taken from the schedules of accounts receivable and accounts payable respectively.

It should be noted that the Accounts Receivable and Accounts Payable accounts are **controlling accounts.** A record is made in a subsidiary ledger for each customer and creditor. At any time, the balance of the Accounts Receivable general ledger account should equal the sum of the individual customers' balances in the accounts receivable subsidiary ledger. The same would be true for the accounts payable ledger.

Owner's equity transactions during the period. Transactions affecting the owner's drawing account or capital account are referred to as **owner's equity transactions.** Appearing below is a list of normal owner's equity transactions:

a. Additional investment in the business increasing owner's equity.
b. Reduction of assets with the intention of reducing owner's equity.
c. Payment of nonbusiness debts with business cash.
d. Cash withdrawals for personal use (earnings of business).

Because the owner is solely responsible for the debts of the business, he or she is free to increase or decrease personal investment in the business. When the owner makes withdrawals that are intended to be permanent decreases in owner's equity, they should be charged (debited) to the owner's capital account. If contributions of cash are intended to permanently increase equity, the owner's capital account should be credited.

Periodically, the owner will withdraw cash for personal use or to pay nonbusiness debts. In such cases, the owner's drawing account and not a business expense account should be charged for the withdrawal. Although cash withdrawals may represent salary or compensation to the owner, they should not be treated as a business expense since business earnings are considered personal earnings for tax purposes for a sole proprietor. Frequently, payment for the personal debts of the owner is made out of the same bank checking account as that used for business debts. Where such a situation exists, care should be taken to make sure that payments for business debts are charged to business expense accounts and that payments for personal debts are charged to the owner's drawing account.

Closing the Expense and Revenue Summary account. As mentioned earlier, the Expense and Revenue Summary account is a temporary account that is closed out at the end of each accounting period. The result of business operations is represented by a debit (loss) or a credit (earnings) balance in the account. To summarize the business earnings (loss), the balance in the Expense and Revenue Summary account is closed to the Capital account. The resulting balance in the Drawing account is then closed to the Capital account and represents the net increase or decrease in owner's equity for the period.

As an example, assume that before closing, the Expense and Revenue Summary account has a credit balance of $6,250. The owner's drawing account has a debit balance of $5,800, and the owner's capital account has a credit balance of $15,000. The following entries in general journal form are used to close the summary and drawing accounts of the K. T. Thomas proprietorship:

```
Expense and Revenue Summary ......................................... 6,250
    K. T. Thomas, Capital...................................................         6,250
    To close the expense and revenue
    summary account.

K. T. Thomas, Capital.......................................................... 5,800
    K. T. Thomas, Drawing .................................................         5,800
    To close the drawing account.
```

As a result of the above entries, the summary and drawing accounts have a zero balance and the capital account shows a balance of $15,450 ($15,000 + $6,250 − $5,800).

Presentation of owner's equity in the statement of financial position. Account titles used in financial statements will vary from business to business. But, the resulting statement of financial position should report (1) business assets, (2) business liabilities, and (3) owner's equity. As a method of disclosure, the owner's equity section should report the owner's capital balance at the beginning of the year, business net earnings (loss), withdrawals and the owner's capital balance at the end of the accounting period. The following presentation of owner's equity is based on the operations of K. T. Thomas as discussed above, assuming there were no investments or withdrawals of equity during the period.

Owner's Equity		
K. T. Thomas, capital: January 1, 1978..............................		$15,000
Net earnings...	$6,250	
Less: Withdrawals...	5,800	450
K. T. Thomas, capital, December 31, 1978..........................		$15,450

THE PARTNERSHIP

A partnership is a business enterprise in which two or more individuals have invested assets for a common business purpose. Partnerships are found in all types of business enterprises. Even though the partnership form exists in all types of businesses, it is typically found in service enterprises. Examples are often found in the medical, legal and accounting professions.

Partnership organization

In order to help regulate the formation and operation of partnerships, many states have adopted the **Uniform Partnership Act.** In part, the act states that "a partnership is an association of two or more persons who carry on, as co-owners, a business for profit." Although many partnerships operate under an implied or oral agreement, it is preferable that a written contract be signed by the would-be partners. This agreement is usually referred to as the articles of copartnership.

Even though some states seek to control the formation and operation of partnerships, there is no standard form of **partnership agreement.** However, since the articles of copartnership describe how a partnership will be operated, it should include:

1. Date of agreement and expected duration of partnership.
2. Names and signatures of partners.
3. Nature, scope, and location of business.
4. Initial investments of each partner.
5. Method of dividing profits and losses.
6. Rights, duties, and responsibilities of each partner.
7. Method of liquidation.
8. Salary, drawing, and interest on owner's equity to be allowed.
9. Any other special agreements between partners.

Except where agreed upon, each partner is personally liable for all business debts as is a sole proprietor. Partnerships in which all partners have unlimited liability are called general partnerships. Some states allow one or more partners to possess limited liability provided at least one partner remains a general partner with unlimited liability. Such a partnership is known as a limited partnership.

Advantages and disadvantages of a partnership

When compared with the sole proprietorship, the partnership has both advantages and disadvantages. Among the advantages is the fact that the business may gain from the combined resources, experience, and talents of the individual partners. Furthermore, because of the unlimited liability of each general partner, the partnership may be extended greater amounts of credit.

Although the partnership enjoys the advantages mentioned above, it has several disadvantages. One obvious disadvantage is that all general partners have unlimited liability. Each general partner is personally liable for all business debts. Also, a partner cannot transfer partnership interest without the consent of the other partners. In addition, should a partner go bankrupt, die, or commit an illegal act, the partnership is automatically dissolved.

From the above discussion, it is evident that an individual should consider both the advantages and disadvantages of a partnership before entering into an agreement. Should it be decided that an agreement will be entered into, the entering partner should make sure that the agreement is drafted in a suitable manner.

Accounting for a partnership

Except for the division of profits and losses among partners, accounting for a partnership is basically the same as accounting for a sole proprietorship. Separate owner's capital accounts are maintained for each partner's interest, and drawing accounts are usually provided for each partner. The basic problems in partnership accounting involve (1) the protection of each partner's interests when partners are admitted or withdrawn and (2) the allocation of partnership profits and losses.

Initial partnership entry. As with the sole proprietorship, the would-be partners may invest cash or cash and other property. If there are liabilities attached to contributed assets, the partnership may agree to assume them. For each partner, the opening entry will involve a debit to the assets transferred and credits to liabilities assumed and to the partner's capital account for his interest.

Assume that J. D. Holly and E. O. Green agree to form a partnership. Each is to contribute $10,000 as stated in the agreed-upon articles of copartnership. The opening entries in general journal form are as follows:

```
Cash in Bank...................................................................   10,000
     J. D. Holly, Capital.....................................................              10,000
   Investment in partnership.

Cash in Bank...................................................................   10,000
     E. O. Green, Capital ....................................................              10,000
   Investment in partnership.
```

The partnership entered into above by Holly and Green is the simplest type. Each partner simply contributes agreed-upon amounts of cash. It is not unusual for partners to contribute just cash or cash and other assets or just other assets. Assume that in the above example, Holly had contributed cash of $1,000, office equipment amounting to $10,000, and a truck valued at $4,000. In addition, the partnership is to assume the mortgage on the truck of $2,000 and the notes payable of $3,000 on the office equipment. To record the investment of Holly, the following general journal entry is used:

```
Cash in Bank...................................................................    1,000
Office Equipment.............................................................   10,000
Truck.............................................................................    4,000
     Notes Payable............................................................               3,000
     Mortgage Payable .......................................................               2,000
     J. D. Holly, Capital.....................................................              10,000
   Investment in partnership.
```

Combination of existing businesses. In order to benefit from the advantages of a partnership, two or more individuals with existing businesses may decide to form a partnership. In order to protect each individual's interest, it is necessary for the partners to agree upon the valuation

Illustration 16–2

O. C. BLACK
Statement of Financial Position
January 1, 1978

Assets

Cash in bank		$ 5,000
Accounts receivable	$4,000	
Less: Allowance for doubtful accounts	200	3,800
Supplies		1,500
Delivery equipment	$5,000	
Less: Accumulated depreciation	1,000	4,000
Total Assets		$14,300

Liabilities

Accounts payable	$1,200	
Notes payable	600	
Total Liabilities		$ 1,800

Owner's Equity

O. C. Black, capital		12,500
Total Liabilities and Owner's Equity		$14,300

J. L. TAYLOR
Statement of Financial Position
January 1, 1978

Assets

Cash in bank		$ 2,000
Accounts receivable	$3,500	
Less: Allowance for doubtful accounts	100	3,400
Merchandise		4,300
Office equipment	$6,300	
Less: Accumulated depreciation	1,200	5,100
Total Assets		$14,800

Liabilities

Accounts payable	$2,000	
Notes payable	2,200	
Total Liabilities		$ 4,200

Owner's Equity

J. L. Taylor, capital		10,600
Total Liabilities and Owner's Equity		$14,800

of assets and the amount of liabilities to be assumed by the partnership. Assume that on January 1, O. C. Black and J. L. Taylor agree to enter into a partnership agreement. Both agree that assets will be contributed and liabilities assumed as reported on each partner's statement of financial position. Profits and losses are to be shared equally, and dissolution will result in distribution of assets in relation to each partner's capital at that time. Each partner is to receive credit for his or her interest equal to the amount of net assets contributed. Shown in Illustration 16–2 is the agreed-upon statements of financial position for Black and Taylor to be used in recording the opening entries and in establishing each partner's capital.

Instead of reporting the long-lived assets at their cost and showing the accumulated depreciation to date on the partnership books, the assets transferred are recorded at their book values. The delivery equipment contributed by Black would be recorded at $4,000 (cost of $5,000 less accumulated depreciation of $1,000). The office equipment contributed by Taylor would be valued in the same manner.

If it were possible to determine which accounts receivable were in fact uncollectible, the accounts receivable balance would be adjusted before the partnership's opening entries were made. If there is a question as to the collectibility of the accounts, the accounts receivable balance is recorded as a debit along with the appropriate credit to allowance for doubtful accounts. Based on the above information, the entries in general journal form to open the books of the Black and Taylor partnership are as shown in Illustration 16–3.

In the above example, the amounts were taken directly from the statements of financial position for the separate proprietorships of Black and Taylor. However, this is not always the case. Assume that after examining the merchandise inventory belonging to Taylor, it is agreed upon that $4,000 is the current market valuation. Had such a case existed, the

Illustration 16–3

Cash in Bank	5,000	
Accounts Receivable	4,000	
Supplies	1,500	
Delivery Equipment	4,000	
Accounts Payable		1,200
Notes Payable		600
Allowance for Doubtful Accounts		200
O. C. Black, Capital		12,500
Investment of Black in partnership.		
Cash in Bank	2,000	
Accounts Receivable	3,500	
Merchandise	4,300	
Office Equipment	5,100	
Accounts Payable		2,000
Notes Payable		2,200
Allowance for Doubtful Accounts		100
J. L. Taylor, Capital		10,600
Investment of Taylor in partnership.		

merchandise would have been reduced to $4,000 and Taylor's capital would be $10,300 ($10,600 − $300). Regardless of the valuations used before the partnership was formed, the partners must examine each account and determine the amount at which it is to be recorded on the partnership books.

Black and Taylor have agreed to share profits and losses equally. It is noted that this ratio is not in relation to their owner's capital balances ($12,500 to $10,600). This fact should not be alarming since the manner in which profits and losses are distributed is not necessarily governed by the capital ratios. It is not uncommon to find one partner who invests most of the assets and spends little time working, while the second partner invests a small amount of assets and devotes full time to the business. In accounting for partnerships, it should be remembered that what may seem unreasonable to the accountant may not actually be so. The partners are free to distribute profits and losses in any agreed-upon manner, and it is the duty of the accountant to follow the partners' intentions as set forth in the articles of copartnership.

Partners' compensation.   As mentioned earlier in the chapter, the partners may receive varying amounts of compensation according to the partnership agreement. Other than dividing profits and losses in a predetermined manner, individual partners may receive additional compensation in the form of salaries, interest on capital, interest on loans, **royalties,** and bonuses. Salaries to partners may or may not be considered as a business expense in determining partnership earnings (loss). Tax laws state that unless salaries are guaranteed, they cannot be claimed as a deduction. Regardless of whether or not salaries are considered a deduction, they along with all other earnings of the partners resulting from the partnership are reported on the individual partners' tax returns as taxable earnings.

If salaries are treated as a partnership expense, a separate salary account is kept for each partner. In addition to a salary account, a drawing account may be used for each partner. Withdrawals that are not considered salary would be debited to the drawing account. If salaries are not deducted as partnership expenses, all salaries and withdrawals are debited to the drawing account when payment is made to the partner. Since the salary account means that salaries are being treated as a partnership expense, each salary account is closed to the Expense and Revenue Summary account at the end of the accounting period. After the profits and losses have been allocated to each partner's capital account, the balance in the drawing account is closed to the respective partner's capital account.

Partnership profits and losses.   At the end of each accounting period, it is necessary to divide or allocate all partnership profits and losses among the partners. Profits and losses are allocated among the partners as agreed upon in the partnership agreement. If **earnings and loss ratios** have not been established, profits and losses are shared equally among the partners regardless of the amount of each partner's equity. In situations where distribution of profits but not losses has been agreed upon, losses will be distributed in the same manner as profits.

After all expense and revenue accounts, including salary accounts (if used), have been closed to the Expense and Revenue Summary account, the summary account will either have a debit (loss), credit (earnings), or possibly a zero balance (break even). Whatever the balance is, it is allocated to the partners' capital accounts in the agreed-upon manner. After closing the summary account to the partners' capital accounts, the drawing accounts will be closed to the capital accounts.

The balance in the drawing account will either increase (credit balance) or decrease (debit balance) the partner's capital account. Debits in the drawing accounts result from any payment made to the partner except salaries when they are considered a partnership expense. Credits in the drawing account result from salaries (when salary account is not used) and other types of compensation. Assuming that capital accounts are not adjusted for withdrawals during the accounting period, the balance transferred from the drawing account to the capital account will reflect the net result of partner's withdrawals.

Partnership statement of financial position: Owner's equity. The owner's equity section of the statement of financial position is the same as that of the sole proprietor except that separate capital accounts are shown for each partner. Shown in Illustration 16–4 is an owner's equity section of a partnership statement of financial position. Note the effect that both earnings and withdrawals have on the capital balances of Clark and Kay.

Admission of a new partner. Whenever a new partner is admitted or an existing partner withdraws, the partnership agreement is voided, and a new agreement must be drafted and agreed upon by the remaining part-

Illustration 16–4

	Owners' Equity		
J. L. Clark, capital, January 1, 1978		$25,000	
Earnings (⅔ of $15,000)	$10,000		
Less: Withdrawals	11,250	(1,250)	
J. L. Clark, capital, December 31, 1978			$23,750
R. D. Kay, capital, January 1, 1978		$17,000	
Earnings (⅓ of $15,000)	$ 5,000		
Less: Withdrawals	1,500	3,500	
R. D. Kay, capital, December 31, 1978			20,500
Total Owners' Equity			$44,250

ners. An incoming partner may be admitted only upon consent of all remaining partners. However, under the Uniform Partnership Act, a partner can transfer his or her interest and right to earnings without the consent of the other partners. But, in order for the person acquiring interest to have a voice in the business, the person must be admitted by the consent of all partners.

An individual may acquire equity in the partnership either by purchasing a share of the existing partners' capital or by contributing assets to the partnership. If a purchase is made from existing partners' capital, the incoming partner simply makes payment to the partners' themselves. The only entry on the partnership books is an entry transferring capital from the existing partners to the new partner.

Assume that T. L. Knight and O. J. Carson each have capital balances of $60,000. To keep capital balances in proportion, they each agree to sell D. E. Land (new partner) one third of their capital. The entry in general journal form to record the purchase is as follows:

T. L. Knight, Capital	20,000	
O. J. Carson, Capital	20,000	
D. E. Land, Capital		40,000
Transfer of capital to Land.		

It should be noted that the above entry would be made under the given assumptions regardless of the amounts paid to Knight and Carson. Payments made to Knight and Carson do not affect the partnership; only the capital transferred is recorded.

Instead of purchasing capital from existing partners, the new partner may contribute cash or cash and other assets in exchange for capital in the partnership. When the new partner receives capital equal to the assets contributed, the admission is recorded by debiting the appropriate asset accounts and crediting the partner's capital account for the assets contributed.

In many instances, the existing partners agree to give the new partner an amount of capital greater than the amount of assets contributed. This is often because of expected benefits to be received (increased earnings) as a result of the new partner's admission. When this is done, it is necessary to debit an account in order to make the entry balance. Since the expectation of future earnings is an intangible asset, an intangible asset account entitled **"Goodwill"** is frequently debited. Assume that T. C. White contributes $10,000 cash in exchange for capital of $12,000. Using the intangible asset account "Goodwill," the following general journal entry is made to record White's admission:

Cash in Bank	10,000	
Goodwill	2,000	
T. C. White, Capital		12,000
To record admission of White.		

Although the goodwill method is used, accountants are reluctant to record goodwill since it involves assumptions and projections about the future. As an alternative, the existing partners may transfer part of their capital to the new partner. This method is referred to as the bonus method. It is so named because, the existing partners actually give a bonus (equity) to the new partner. The bonus given to the new partner is allocated between the old partners in accordance with the profit and loss ratio existing before the new partner is admitted. Using the information given above, assume that White is being admitted to the partnership of O. B. Owens and S. M. Jacobs who share profits and losses equally. The entry in general journal form to record the admission of White would be:

```
Cash in Bank....................................................................  10,000
O. B. Owens, Capital .......................................................   1,000
S. M. Jacobs, Capital.......................................................   1,000
    T. C. White, Capital ....................................................            12,000
    To record admission of White.
```

It is possible that the new partner may be willing to receive an amount of capital which is less than the assets he or she is to contribute. This may be done by the new partner with the expectation that the new partner will benefit financially from being associated with the partnership. In this case, goodwill can only be recorded if there is sufficient goodwill already on the books of the partnership to absorb the credit to Goodwill resulting from an excess in assets contributed over capital received.

Since it is hoped that the admission of a new partner will not result in negative (credit) goodwill, it is preferable that the bonus method be used when assets contributed by the incoming partner are more than capital received. Assume as in the example above that White is to be admitted to the partnership of Owens and Jacobs who share profits and losses equally. But, to receive capital of $12,000, White will have to contribute cash of $15,000. In this case, White is agreeing to pay a bonus to the existing partners to be admitted. The entry in general journal form to record the admission of White is as follows:

```
Cash in bank....................................................................  15,000
    O. B. Owens, Capital ..................................................             1,500
    S. M. Jacobs, Capital.................................................             1,500
    T. C. White, Capital ...................................................            12,000
    To record admission of White.
```

The goodwill method of adjusting for differences between assets contributed and capital received should be used only as a last resort. Where intangible assets exist and are identifiable, adjustment should be made to that particular account. If the difference results from assets that are over- or undervalued, the asset in question should be adjusted. Because the goodwill method involves assumptions which are difficult to verify, the bonus method and/or adjustment of specific accounts is preferable.

Withdrawal of a partner. Accounting for the withdrawal of a partner involves procedures which are the opposite of those used when a partner is admitted. Dissolution may result from a partner's death or from bankruptcy of the partnership. As with the admission of a new partner, the asset and capital accounts are reviewed by the partners to assure that each partner's capital account is properly stated before the entry is made to record the withdrawal. The withdrawal of a partner is similar to a partner's admission in that the partner may receive assets which are greater or less than his or her capital. Again, both the goodwill and the bonus methods can be used to account for the difference. For reasons discussed in the section above concerning the admission of a partner, the adjustment of specific assets and/or the use of the bonus method is preferable over the goodwill method in accounting for the difference between partner's capital and actual settlement made upon withdrawal.

Assume that the owners of a partnership have the following capital balances: A. M. Thompson, $11,000; B. L. Smith, $9,000; and C. B. Clark, $13,000. Also assume that Smith is withdrawing and is to be paid in cash for the full amount of his capital. To record the withdrawal, the following general journal entry is needed:

B. L. Smith, Capital	9,000	
Cash in Bank		9,000
To record withdrawal of Smith.		

If Smith were paid only $8,000 for his capital, he would be giving a bonus to Thompson and Clark. Assuming that the partners share profits and losses equally, the following general journal entry is required:

B. L. Smith, Capital	9,000	
A. M. Thompson, Capital		500
C. B. Clark, Capital		500
Cash in Bank		8,000
To record withdrawal of Smith.		

It is possible that in the above case the payment to Smith for less than his capital may have resulted from an overvaluation of partnership assets. If so, then the particular assets would be decreased instead of giving the remaining partners a bonus. In situations where payment to the withdrawing partner is in excess of his or her capital balance, the bonus method will generally be used since accountants are reluctant to write-up assets.

Liquidation of partnership. The mechanics of a liquidation will vary depending upon the agreement between partners. However, regardless of the manner in which the assets are to be distributed, there are several procedures which are common to all partnership liquidations. First, all creditors are paid by setting aside certain assets. After the creditors are paid, the remaining assets are either sold or valued for distribution to

Illustration 16–5

BAKER AND DUNCAN PARTNERSHIP
Statement of Liquidation — Complete
March 1–March 31, 1978

Earnings and Loss Ratio 50:50	Assets		Accounts Payable	Capital	
	Cash	Other than Cash		Baker	Duncan
March 1 — balance	$ 15,000	$ 12,000	$ 3,500	$ 11,500	$ 12,000
March 5 — payment of accounts payable	(3,500)		(3,500)		
Balance	$ 11,500	$ 12,000		$ 11,500	$ 12,000
March 25 — sale of assets for $9,000 and allocation of loss between partners	9,000	(12,000)		(1,500)	(1,500)
Balance	$ 20,500			$ 10,000	$ 10,500
March 31 — distribution of cash	(20,500)			(10,000)	(10,500)
Balance	-0-	-0-	-0-	-0-	-0-

partners. Before the assets are distributed, the gains and losses resulting from the sale and valuation of assets are allocated to the partners according to their profit and loss ratios. After all creditors have been satisfied and gains and losses have been allocated to partners, the remaining assets are distributed to partners in amounts as indicated by their capital balances. Illustration 16–5 is a simple example of the liquidation of the Baker and Duncan partnership.

The following journal entries reflect the partnership liquidation during March:

```
Mar.  5  Accounts Payable .............................................. 3,500
             Cash........................................................          3,500
         Paid creditors.

      25  Cash......................................................... 9,000
          Baker, Capital................................................... 1,500
          Duncan, Capital................................................ 1,500
             Assets (other than Cash)...............................          12,000
          Sale of assets for $9,000 and allocation of loss
          between partners.

      31  Baker, Capital................................................. 10,000
          Duncan, Capital............................................... 10,500
             Cash......................................................          20,500
          Distribution of cash.
```

GLOSSARY

Contra accounts   accounts which are used to record subtractions from related accounts which have positive balances. Examples of contra accounts include Allowance for Doubtful Accounts, Purchase Returns and Allowances, Accumulated Depreciation, and so on.

Controlling accounts   general ledger accounts that are supported by detailed information in subsidiary ledgers.

Earnings and loss ratio   the ratio by which earnings not distributed as salaries are divided among the various partners of a partnership.

Goodwill   an intangible asset which results primarily from the expectation that the entity has the ability to produce an above-average rate of earnings compared to similar entities in the same industry.

Owner's equity transactions   transactions which affect the owner's drawing account or capital account.

Partnership   a business undertaking in which two or more individuals have invested assets for a common business purpose.

Partnership agreement   an agreement among the partners of a partnership which states the bases and conditions upon which the partnership is formed and operated.

Proprietorship   a business organization owned by one person.

Royalties   compensation paid to the owner of a patent or copyright (or some real or personal property) for the use of it or the right to act under it.

Summary account   a temporary account maintained for revenues and expenses of a single proprietorship. It is normally closed to the Capital account at the end of the accounting period.

Uniform Partnership Act   a law which is used to resolve contested matters among the partners of a partnership which are not made clear in the partnership agreement.

QUESTIONS AND EXERCISES

1. List three advantages and three disadvantages of the proprietorship form of organization.

2. Dr. B. T. Wilson's professional practice contains business assets of $25,000 and business liabilities of $5,000. What is the amount of Dr. Wilson's owner's equity?

3. List three types of owner's equity transactions.

4. J. E. Brown opened a dry cleaning service in 1978. Brown's initial investment in the business consisted of $5,000 cash and a new delivery truck that cost $6,000. What journal entry should be made to record the formation of Brown's Dry Cleaning Service?

5. What is a partnership? Give some typical examples.

6. What is the articles of copartnership? What type of information does it contain?

7. List three advantages and three disadvantages of the partnership form of organization.

8. Bill Atlas and Bob World have agreed to form the Atlas-World Partnership. Bill will contribute $5,000 cash and a truck worth $3,000. The partnership will assume a $1,000 mortgage on the truck. Bob will contribute $6,000 cash and office furniture worth $1,000. What general journal entries should be made to record each partner's initial investment?

9. In addition to a share of the profits, what other types of compensation might a partner receive?

10. Ed Write has decided to sell his $20,000 partnership interest to Tom Read. Read has agreed to pay Write $22,000 for his interest. What general journal entry should be made on the partnership's books to record the transaction between Read and Write?

PROBLEMS

16-1. On February 13, 1978, T. L. Whim opened a grocery store in Woodland. Whim initially invested $10,000 cash, a delivery truck valued at $5,000, and a building valued at $30,000. There was a $5,000 mortgage on the building. On December 31, 1978, after the expense and revenue accounts were closed, the Expense and Revenue Summary account had a $20,000 credit balance; the drawing account had a $6,000 debit balance.

Required:
1. Make the general journal entry to record Whim's initial investment.
2. Close the Expense and Revenue Summary account and the drawing account.
3. Prepare a statement of owner's equity for the year ended December 31, 1978.

16–2.

ROBERT ALLEN
Adjusted Trial Balance
December 31, 1978

Account Title	Debit	Credit
Cash	$ 8,000	
Accounts receivable	5,000	
Office equipment	10,000	
Accumulated depreciation – office equipment		$ 3,000
Office furniture	30,000	
Accumulated depreciation – office furniture		6,000
Prepaid rent	1,200	
Unexpired insurance	1,000	
Accounts payable		10,000
Robert Allen, capital (January 1)		14,900
Robert Allen, drawing	15,000	
Professional fees		60,000
Rent expense	7,200	
Insurance expense	2,400	
Advertising expense	1,500	
Depreciation expense	3,000	
Salaries expense	9,600	
	$93,900	$93,900

Required:
1. Journalize the closing entries.
2. Prepare an earnings statement.
3. Prepare a statement of financial position.

16–3. Two dentists, Dr. Gum and Dr. Teeth, have decided to combine their practices into a partnership. Each dentist is to receive an interest in the partnership equal to the amount of net assets contributed. Using the statements of financial position shown on page 419, make the necessary journal entries to record the formation of the partnership.

DR. GUM
Statement of Financial Position
September 14, 1978

Assets

Cash		$10,000
Accounts receivable	$ 6,000	
Less: Allowance for doubtful accounts	500	5,500
Dental supplies		800
Dental equipment	$30,000	
Less: Accumulated depreciation	10,000	20,000
Total Assets		$36,300

Liabilities

Accounts payable	$ 2,000	
Notes payable	1,000	
Total Liabilities		$ 3,000

Owner's Equity

Dr. Gum, capital		33,300
Total Liabilities and Owner's Equity		$36,300

DR. TEETH
Statement of Financial Position
September 14, 1978

Assets

Cash		$ 6,000
Accounts receivable	$ 3,000	
Less: Allowance for doubtful accounts	100	2,900
Dental supplies		500
Dental equipment	$10,000	
Less: Accumulated depreciation	2,000	8,000
Total Assets		$17,400

Liabilities

Accounts payable	$ 500	
Notes payable	2,000	
Total Liabilities		$ 2,500

Owner's Equity

Dr. Teeth, capital		14,900
Total Liabilities and Owner's Equity		$17,400

16–4. Baker, Carter, and Masche are all general partners in the BCM Company. Given the following independent assumptions (*a*) and (*b*), complete the chart below showing the distribution of earnings and losses for 1976, 1977, and 1978.

    a. The partnership agreement does not specify how earnings and losses are to be distributed.

    b. The partnership agreement states that the earnings and loss sharing ratio for Baker, Carter, and Masche is 50:40:10.

			Distribution of Partnership Earnings and Losses		
Assumption	Year	Net Earnings (Loss)	Baker	Carter	Masche
a.	1976	$36,000			
	1977	(9,900)			
	1978	4,500			
b.	1976	36,000			
	1977	(9,900)			
	1978	4,500			

16–5. P. T. Bone and M. E. Debs each have a $50,000 interest in the Epitome Company. They have recently decided to admit a third partner, A. S. Samson. What journal entry should be made to record the admission of Samson under each of the following unrelated assumptions?

    a. Samson pays each partner $12,000 for one fifth of his interest.

    b. Samson contributes $10,000 cash to the partnership and receives capital equal to the value of the asset contributed.

    c. Samson contributes $10,000 cash in exchange for capital of $9,000.

    d. Samson contributes $10,000 cash in exchange for capital of $15,000:

        (1) Goodwill Method

        (2) Bonus Method

16–6.

THE JORCON HARDWARE STORE
Adjusted Trial Balance
December 31, 1978

Account Title	Debit	Credit
Cash	$ 7,000	
Accounts receivable	20,000	
Allowance for doubtful accounts		$ 1,500
Inventory	50,000	
Unexpired insurance	1,000	
Office supplies	500	
Building	40,000	
Accumulated depreciation – building		10,000
Office equipment	5,000	
Accumulated depreciation – office equipment		1,500
Delivery equipment	10,000	
Accumulated depreciation – delivery equipment		2,000
Service equipment	15,000	
Accumulated depreciation – service equipment		5,000
Accounts payable		8,000
Interest payable		100
Notes payable		10,000
Mortgage payable		20,000
L. J. Jordan, capital		40,200
K. B. Conner, capital		44,000
L. J. Jordan, drawing	10,000	
K. B. Conner, drawing	9,000	
Sales		150,000
Cost of goods sold	100,000	
Depreciation expense	7,500	
Wages expense	14,000	
Insurance expense	1,200	
Office supplies expense	700	
Bad debts expense	300	
Other expense	1,100	
	$292,300	$292,300

Required:

1. Prepare the necessary closing entries. (Jordan and Conner share earnings and losses equally.)
2. Prepare an earnings statement for the year ended December 31, 1978.
3. Prepare a statement of financial position as of December 31, 1978.

Owners' equity: Corporation
Learning objectives

To gain an understanding of the corporate form of business ownership, this chapter introduces the following material:

1. The legal rights and responsibilities and the resulting advantages and disadvantages of the corporate form of business.
2. The legal requirements for obtaining a corporate charter.
3. Management and ownership of the business when licensed as a corporation.
4. Accounting procedures used in recording the issuance of corporate stock and distribution of earnings.
5. An understanding of the following terms: common stock subscribed, subscriptions receivable, par value, retained earnings, dividends, premium on stock, stock dividends, and date of record.

17

Owners' equity: Corporation

The **corporation,** unlike the proprietorship or partnership, is created by law and is separate from its owners. Even though the owners, referred to as **shareholders** or stockholders, own the corporation, they themselves are not the corporation. Chief Justice Marshall in the Dartmouth College Case stated: "A corporation is an artificial being, invisible, intangible, and existing only in contemplation of the law." Although there are a larger number of proprietorships than corporations, the dollar amount of business transacted by corporations is much more than that of proprietorships and partnerships. When compared to the forms of business discussed in the preceding chapter, the corporate form of business has a number of advantages as well as some distinct disadvantages.

CORPORATE ADVANTAGES

As noted above, one advantage of the corporation is that it is legally separate from its owners. Since the corporation is a legal entity, it has the power to hold property in its own name. It has the right to sue and be sued. Also, through its agents, it has the right to enter into legal contracts. In short, the corporation enjoys all of the legal rights and responsibilities of an individual except, of course, the right to vote or to marry. Because the corporation is legally separate from its owners, it has continuity of life. Continued life arises from the fact that the owners' equity in a corporation is represented by shares of stock which may be transferred at will. Therefore, the corporation's life is not related to the owners' lives as is the case with proprietorships and partnerships.

The corporation offers several advantages from the shareholders'

423

point of view. Because the corporation is an entity separate from its owners, the shareholder is not responsible for the debts and obligations of the corporation. Unlike the sole proprietor or general partners, the owners' (shareholders') only risk is that of losing amounts invested in the corporation. Even though the shareholder runs this risk, the risk is limited to the invested amounts. The shareholder does not assume unlimited liability for corporate or shareholders' obligations.

An individual shareholder has no power to bind the corporation or other shareholders to contracts and legal obligations. And, because the shareholder is not bound by the acts of the corporation or fellow shareholders, investment in a corporation can be made with less consideration than would be necessary when investing in a partnership. Since each general partner has unlimited liability, greater care must be taken when selecting partners than is necessary when electing corporate officers.

CORPORATE DISADVANTAGES

One of the disadvantages of a corporation when compared to a partnership or sole proprietorship is that corporations are created by state law. Incorporation under state laws will bring about a certain amount of supervision and control that is not experienced by the partnership or sole proprietorship. And, since corporate laws vary from state to state, careful study must be made of the corporate laws of the state in which incorporation is to take place.

A further disadvantage of the corporate form concerns the taxation of the corporation. Because the corporation is a separate legal entity, it is taxed separately. It should be noted that the earnings of the partnership and sole proprietorship are taxed through the individual proprietor or partner. However, the earnings of a corporation are taxed as the corporate level before distribution and are taxed again at the individual level after the earnings are distributed. The tax rate on the first $25,000 of earnings is 20 percent. All earnings between $25,000 and $50,000 are taxed at a rate of 22 percent and all earnings in excess of $50,000 are taxed at 48 percent. (These rates are subject to congressional change.)

Even though limiting shareholders' liability is an advantage, it is also a disadvantage. It was noted in the chapter on partnerships that the partnership normally has a greater ability to borrow than does the sole proprietorship because each general partner is personally liable for the partnership debts. For the small corporation, the limited liability of shareholders proves to be a disadvantage because only the assets of the corporation can be used to satisfy creditors should bankruptcy occur. Because of this, it is possible for a partnership to borrow greater amounts of money than a corporation of equal size. This disadvantage is often circumvented by a shareholder personally signing for corporate notes and obligations. Of course, any shareholder who cosigns corporate obligations must be personally able to satisfy the obligations should the corporation be unable to do so.

CORPORATE ORGANIZATION

As mentioned earlier, the corporation laws of the state in which incorporation is to take place must be carefully studied. The corporation is legally formed when a **charter** from the state is issued. The persons applying for incorporation are known as the **incorporators.** The incorporators must draft a proposed charter showing:

1. The name of the proposed corporation.
2. Address of corporation.
3. Purpose of corporate organization.
4. The limitations, qualifications, restrictions, and rights of each class stock, if more then one class is issued.
5. Amounts of authorized stock.
6. Names, addresses, occupations, number of shares held, and amounts paid for shares for each of the incorporators.
7. The names, addresses, and length of appointment for the original directors and trustees.

After the charter is drafted, all of the incorporators must sign the charter. Each incorporator must possess the competence to contract and must subscribe to one or more shares of stock, and some or all of the incorporators must be citizens of the state in which the charter is to be filed. After the charter has been filed and incorporation fees have been paid, the charter is examined by the proper state officials. If all requirements have been fulfilled, a charter or certificate of incorporation is issued.

Once the charter has been issued, the corporation becomes a legal body. Even though the charter contains basic information about corporate organization, a set of **bylaws** governing the actions of corporate directors and officers is adopted at the first shareholders' meeting. The bylaws designate:

1. The number of directors, duties, qualifications, and length of office.
2. The duties, authority, and length of office for corporate officers other than directors.
3. Rules and regulations governing corporate officers and rules governing the election of directors and the appointment of officers.

Because the corporate charter is the basic legal document, it is important that the bylaws of the corporation be constructed in a manner that will not contradict or violate the charter. At all times the directors and officers must conduct their duties in accordance with procedures set forth in the charter and the accompanying bylaws.

CORPORATE MANAGEMENT

Since the shareholders are the owners of the corporation, they are the individuals who have ultimate control over the corporation. However, in most large corporations, the shareholders are spread over a large portion of the country. Furthermore, many of the shareholders do not have the knowledge or do not possess the capability of running a large corporation. To manage the corporation, the shareholders elect a board of directors. The shareholders have voting rights in proportion to the number of shares held. The directors are elected in accordance with the bylaws.

The **board of directors** is given the responsibility of managing the corporation. They are responsible to the shareholders. The directors and not the shareholders are the legal agents of the corporation. The board of directors consists of three or more shareholders. If a large number of directors is elected, an executive committee is appointed and given authority to manage the corporation.

After the shareholders elect a board of directors, the board in turn elects the corporate officers. The corporate officers normally include a president, vice president, secretary, and treasurer. In a large corporation, an individual will be elected for each of the executive offices. In a small corporation, it is not uncommon to find the same person holding two positions, such as secretary and treasurer. The officers are directly responsible to the board of directors and receive their instructions from the board. Aside from the authority given to the officers by the board to carry out specified duties, the officers have no other authority, They are required to perform their duties as outlined in the bylaws and are liable for fraud or for actions which exceed the duties and authority delegated to them in the bylaws. The difference between the board of directors and corporate officers is that the directors make company plans and policies whereas the officers carry out the plans in accordance with company policies.

Illustration 17–1 shows a typical corporation organizational chart. Note the relationships between shareholders, directors, officers, and company employees.

CORPORATE OWNERSHIP

To make it possible for many people to have equity in a corporation, the ownership of a corporation is divided into shares. When a corporation is formed, the incorporators and other interested people wishing to be-

Illustration 17–1

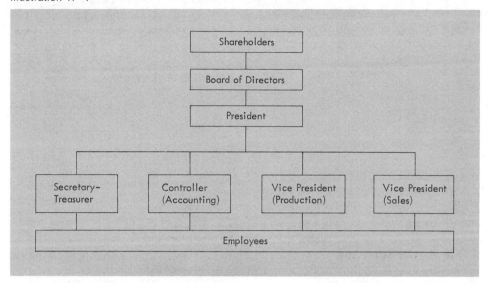

come owners subscribe for a certain number of shares. Each agrees to pay a specified amount for each share. Payment may be made by transferring cash or other assets to the corporation. Stock may be subscribed to before or after incorporation. If the **subscription** takes place before incorporation, the subscription is actually an agreement to subscribe for stock. Since the corporation does not exist until after incorporation, the subscription is an agreement entered into between the incorporator and the **subscriber** and not between the corporation and the subscriber.

The amount of stock that can be legally issued is specified in the corporate charter. Any amount of stock issued above the **capital stock authorized** by the state in which incorporation takes place is an illegal stock transaction. The stock is issued in the form of **stock certificates.** The certificate identifies the issuing company, the subscriber, date issued, and number of shares issued. The company officers sign the certificate, and it may also be impressed with the company seal.

The **par value** of stock will vary from state to state and from corporation to corporation. Depending on the state's corporate laws, it may not be necessary for stock to have a par value. Although the par value of stock does not have much practical significance, par value is the smallest amount a corporation may accept without the subscriber incurring a liability to the corporation or to the corporation's creditors upon liquidation. In those states where par value is not required, the stock may have a stated value which is similar to par value. Stock is normally issued at or above par value at incorporation.

If a corporation issues only one kind of stock, the shareholders are owners "in common" and the stock is called common stock. The common stock shareholders have two basic rights. They have the right to vote for corporate directors and other issues put to a shareholder vote, and they have the right to share in company distributions of assets resulting from corporation liquidation. No matter what type of stock is owned, the rights of the owner are always in direct proportion to the number of shares held. It is noted that this is quite different from the partnership where distributions are made in accordance with the agreement set forth in the articles of copartnership and not in accordance with the amount of each partner's owner's equity or capital.

It is not uncommon for corporation to have more than one class of stock. The differences in stock classes arise from the fact that owners of different classes of stock have different rights. Besides common stock, a corporation may issue one or more classes of preferred stock. **Preferred stock** is so named because it entitles the owner to have certain rights and preferences over the holders of common stock. The owners of preferred stock often have the right to receive a fixed amount of earnings before the holders of common stock receive any distributions. Sometimes the right to earnings will be cumulative, thus requiring that all current as well as previous unpaid distributions on preferred stock be made before the holders of common stock receive any distributions. Preferred stock will normally have a stated **liquidation value.** This assures holders of preferred stock that they will have claim to any remaining company assets upon liquidation before the holders of common stock participate in any distributions.

From the above discussion, it is clear that the holder of preferred stock assumes a lesser risk than does the holder of common stock. Because of this, the distributions of preferred stockholders may be smaller than what they could receive on other investments of a similar amount. Also, it is not unusual for preferred stock to be issued without voting rights. The differences between preferred and common stock illustrate the fact that returns on investments are usually related to the risks assumed. Although the holders of preferred stock enjoy the prior claims to earnings and assets in liquidation, they do not stand to gain as much as holders of common stock. Should company earnings increase, distributions on common would probably increase whereas distributions on preferred would remain fixed. Even though the holder of high-risk investments stands to gain the most, it should be pointed out that investments with a high risk also stand to lose the most.

The **book value** per share of common stock for a company which has only one class of stock is equal to total equity divided by the number of shares outstanding. As with the sole proprietorship and partnership, the equity of a business is determined by subtracting total liabilities from total assets. If a company has a class of preferred stock outstanding, the amount allocated to the preferred stock (liquidation value) is subtracted from total owners' equity, and the resulting figure is divided by the number of outstanding shares of common stock in determining book value per share.

As is the case with the book value of depreciable assets, the book value per share of stock is not expected to equal the market value per share. If the company's stock is actively traded on a stock exchange, the quoted price will be a fair representation of the stock market value. The market value per share is influenced by several factors. Probably the most important factor is the expected success of the company in the future. If higher earnings are anticipated, the market price will probably rise; and if earnings are declining, prices will also decline. The par value, book value, and market value will, in most cases, be three different amounts.

CORPORATE ACCOUNTING PROCEDURE

The normal accounting procedures for revenues and expenses of a corporation are nearly the same as those used for the sole proprietorship and partnership. The basic differences are found in the owners' equity section of a corporation's statement of financial position. As accounting for owners' equity is described in the following pages, it will also be observed that a receivable and a payable account may also arise as a result of transactions affecting owners' equity.

In examining the owners' equity section of a corporation's statement of financial position, it is noted that the earnings of a corporation are kept separate from the amounts invested by the shareholders. Thus, the owners' equity is composed of two amounts—the equity invested by shareholders and the equity resulting from profitable operations (retained earnings). It is possible for the Retained Earnings account to have a debit balance (unprofitable operations), in which case the owners' equity is equal to invested equity less the amount of operating **deficit.** Keeping invested equity separate from retained earnings is quite different from the sole proprietorship or partnership in which investments and earnings are combined into one owner's capital account.

The basic entry in the owners' equity section is that of recording the sale of stock. When stock is sold at par or stated value, the proper account is debited for cash and/or other assets received, and the stock account is credited. If more than one class of stock exists, a separate account is used for each class. If more than the par or stated value is paid for stock, the difference is credited to Paid in Equity in Excess of Stated Value. As an example, assume that 100 shares of common stock with a par value of $25 are sold for $30 per share. The entry in general journal form is:

```
Cash in Bank.................................................................  3,000
    Common Stock.........................................................          2,500
    Paid in Equity in Excess of Stated Value .......................            500
To record sale of stock.
```

As discussed earlier, a corporation may obtain subscriptions for its stock. In a stock subscription, the subscriber agrees to buy a certain number of shares at a stated price. The subscriber also agrees to pay for the shares either all at one time or in installments over a predetermined length of time. When shares are subscribed to, the transaction is recorded by debiting Subscriptions Receivable and crediting *Common Stock Subscribed* (assuming the subscription is for par value). To illustrate, assume that a subscription is received for 50 shares of common stock for $10 (par value). The general journal entry to record the subscription is as follows:

```
Subscriptions Receivable.................................................   500
    Common Stock Subscribed...........................................          500
To record stock subscriptions of 50 shares.
```

Payments on the subscription should be debited to Cash in Bank (or other asset received) and credited to Subscriptions Receivable. It is important to note that the stock is not issued until payment has been made in full for the subscription. If payment is made in installments, the Subscriptions Receivable account is reduced by the amount of each payment, and the stock is issued when subscriptions have been paid in full. Based on the information given in the previous entry, assume that a cash payment is made for the full **subscription price.** The entries to record the receipt of cash and issuance of stock in general journal form are as follows:

```
Cash in Bank .................................................................   500
    Subscriptions Receivable .............................................          500
To record the payment on subscriptions receivable.
Common Stock Subscribed................................................   500
    Common Stock........................................................          500
To record issuance of stock.
```

If a statement of financial position was constructed on a date when subscriptions had not been paid in full, the Subscriptions Receivable account would represent an asset and would be reported in the current asset section. The Common Stock Subscribed account would be shown in the owners' equity section of the statement of financial position and would represent the amount of equity that will eventually be added to common stock.

After the shares of stock have been issued, the sale and exchange of shares between shareholders has no effect upon the assets, liabilities, or owners' equity of a corporation. This, again, is different from the partnership in which a capital account is maintained for each owner. All outstanding shares of a particular class of stock are represented by the credit to that particular stock account. The record of the number of shares held by each shareholder is recorded in the stock records kept by the company. Transfer of stock between shareholders is recognized by appropriate notation in the stock records.

At the close of each accounting period, each expense and revenue account is closed to the Expense and Revenue Summary account. The balance in the Expense and Revenue Summary account is transferred to the Retained Earnings account. If the company has operated at a loss during the accounting period, the Summary account will have a debit balance before being closed to Retained Earnings. The Summary account is closed in this case by debiting Retained Earnings and crediting the Summary account. If operations have been profitable, the Summary account will have a credit balance and will be closed by debiting the Summary account and crediting Retained Earnings. If the Retained Earnings account has a debit balance after closing the Expense and Revenue Summary account, the debit balance is referred to as an operating deficit and is shown as a deduction in the owners' equity section of the statement of financial position.

A distribution by a corporation to its stockholders is called a **dividend.** The decision to pay a dividend must be approved by the board of directors and is commonly known as a declaration of dividends. The distribution may be in the form of cash, assets, or the corporation's own stock. Cash dividends are the most common and are usually stated as so many dollars per share. As an example, assume that a corporation declared a cash dividend of $1.25 per share of common stock. If a shareholder owns 100 shares, he or she will receive $125 ($1.25 × 100). Distributions of assets or of a corporation's own stock are also distributed on a per share basis.

Three dates surround the distribution of a dividend. The board of directors will normally declare a dividend on a date to be paid on a later date to shareholders of record on a third date (date between declaration and payment dates). For example, the board may declare a dividend on December 22, to be paid on January 9 to shareholders of record on January 7. It is important to note that regardless of who holds the shares on the date of record (January 7), unless the shares are registered in the corporation's stock records under the holder's name, the holder will not receive the dividend payment. The time lag between the **date of declaration** and **date of record** gives the shareholder time to register his or her stock on the corporation's stock records, if the shareholder has not already done so.

Although the shareholders own the company, they have no legal right to dividends until they are declared by the board of directors. Between the date of declaration and the **date of payment,** the declared dividends represent a current liability of the corporation. As an example, assume that the board of directors of the Scott Manufacturing Company declare a cash dividend of $1 per share on May 9, payable on May 25 to shareholders of record on May 20. No entry is necessary on the date of record, May 20. Assuming the Scott Manufacturing Company has 10,000 shares of common stock outstanding, the entries in general journal form to record the declaration and subsequent payment are as follows:

May	9	Retained Earnings..	10,000	
		Dividends Payable..		10,000
		To record declared dividend.		
	20	No entry—date of record.		
	25	Dividends Payable..	10,000	
		Cash in Bank..		10,000
		To record dividend payment.		

Distributions may also be made in the form of stock dividends. Stock dividends may be distributed when the company is short of cash or when the board of directors think it to be in the shareholders' best interest if a cash distribution is not made. When a stock dividend is declared, a charge equal to the market value of the shares to be distributed is made to the Retained Earnings account. An amount equal to the par or stated value of the shares is credited to Stock Dividend Distributable. The excess of market value over par is credited to Premium on Common Stock. It is noted that the Stock Dividend Distributable account is not a liability as no money will be distributed. When the stock is distributed, the Stock Dividend Distributable account is debited and the Common Stock account is credited. The dates of declaration, record, and distribution (payment) are used for a stock dividend in the same manner as for a cash dividend. If a statement of financial position were constructed between the dates of declaration and distribution, the Stock Dividend Distributable account would be shown as part of owners' equity.

For example, assume that the board of directors of the Shallow Mine Company declares a 20 percent common stock dividend on August 12 to be distributed on September 1 to shareholders of record on August 25. The 20 percent dividend means that one share will be distributed for every five shares outstanding. Assuming that the common stock of Shallow Mine Company has a par value of $10 and a market value of $15 and that 20,000 shares are outstanding, the following general journal entries are needed to record the declaration and distribution of the stock dividend:

```
Aug. 12  Retained Earnings.............................................. 60,000
              Premium on Common Stock .........................          20,000
              Common Stock Dividend Distributable .............          40,000
           To record stock dividend of 4,000 shares
           (0.20 × 20,000 = 4,000).

     25  No entry—date of record

Sept. 1  Common Stock Dividend Distributable ................... 40,000
              Common Stock...........................................          40,000
           To record distribution of stock.
```

It should be noted that a stock dividend does not affect the assets or liabilities of a corporation. It only transfers part of the retained earnings to the stock accounts. The stock dividend does not increase the owners' equity. It only changes the structure of the owners' equity section on the statement of financial position. Since the increased number of shares held by shareholders represents the same amount of equity, stock dividends are not regarded as income and are not included in the shareholder's taxable income.

Incorporating a sole proprietorship

Incorporating a sole proprietorship involves the same steps as those used in organizing a new corporation. Since the sole proprietor is the owner of the proprietorship, he or she will normally be the principal shareholder when the business is incorporated. The corporation may assume the assets and liabilities of the proprietorship in exchange for common stock. The corporation may use the existing proprietorship books, or a new set of books may be used.

To illustrate the incorporation of a sole proprietorship, assume that the sole proprietorship of A. R. King is to be incorporated as the King Company, Inc. Shown in Illustration 17–2 is the statement of financial position of the King proprietorship. King intends to subscribe for 180 shares of common stock at $100 per share. A $2,500 contribution will be made by King to the corporation, which when added to the equity of King's proprietorship will equal the proposed owner's equity of the corporation ($18,000).

Regardless of whether King uses the existing books of the proprietorship or begins with a new set of books, the following general journal entry will be made in the books to record the common stock subscription:

```
Subscriptions Receivable.................................................. 18,000
     Common Stock Subscribed .........................................          18,000
   To record King's subscription for 180 shares.
```

Illustration 17–2

```
                          A. R. KING
                 Statement of Financial Position
                        April 15, 1978


                            Assets
Cash in bank ...................................................        $ 3,000
Accounts receivable ......................................  $4,300
    Less: Allowance for doubtful accounts ...........      400         3,900

Supplies.........................................................                4,600
Office equipment.............................................  $3,000
    Less: Accumulated Depreciation...................   1,500          1,500
Service equipment..........................................  $7,000
    Less: Accumulated depreciation ..................   2,600          4,400
        Total Assets.........................................                 $17,400



                          Liabilities
Accounts payable...........................................  $1,500
Notes payable ...............................................     400
        Total Liabilities ....................................                 $ 1,900



                        Owner's Equity
A. R. King, capital..........................................                  15,500
        Total Liabilities and Owner's Equity .........                 $17,400
```

If King decides to use the proprietorship books, the following general journal entry is needed to transfer the assets and liabilities to the corporation:

```
A. R. King, Capital.............................................. 15,500
    Subscriptions Receivable .............................               15,500
    To record transfer of equity of King to corporation
    at book value.
```

If a new set of books is to be used, an entry is made to record each of the assets and liabilities to be transferred to the corporation's books. The long-lived depreciable assets will ordinarily be recorded on the corporation's books at their net value. Any other adjustment in assets and liabilities should be made when they are transferred. Assuming that a new set of books is used, the following general journal entry is made to record the transfer:

```
Cash in Bank.......................................................................  3,000
Accounts Receivable.......................................................  4,300
Supplies............................................................................  4,600
Office Equipment.............................................................  1,500
Service Equipment...........................................................  4,400
    Accounts Payable ......................................................              1,500
    Notes Payable..............................................................               400
    Allowance for Doubtful Accounts................................               400
    Subscriptions Receivable............................................            15,500
    To record transfer of equity of King to corporation
    at book value.
```

After King makes the $2,500 cash payment, the entries to record the receipt of cash and issuance of stock in general journal form are as follows:

```
Cash in Bank......................................................................  2,500
    Subscriptions Receivable..............................................             2,500
    To record receipt of balance owed by King on
    common stock subscription.

Common Stock Subscribed................................................ 18,000
    Common Stock...........................................................            18,000
    To record issuance of 180 shares of
    common stock to A. R. King.
```

It should be noted that the Common Stock account has now replaced the owner's capital account of the sole proprietorship. Future earnings of the corporation will be credited to the Retained Earnings account and not to the Owner's Capital account (owner's equity) as was done in the proprietorship form of business.

Incorporating a partnership

In the previous chapter, it was stated that a partnership could be terminated for several reasons, such as death, bankruptcy, or committing an illegal act. Incorporation of a partnership is an additional reason for termination of a partnership. As with the sole proprietorship, the existing partnership books or a new set of books may be used. For example, assume that the Royal Company, Inc., is incorporated with an authorized equity of $45,000. The Royal Company will take over the business conducted by the partnership of Royal and Blair. The partners subscribe for common stock as follows:

```
J. D. Royal, 500 shares @ $45 per share........................................ $22,500
E. O. Blair, 400 shares @ $45 per share .........................................  18,000
```

Royal and Blair are to receive credit towards their subscriptions for their respective partnership equities. Illustration 17–3 is a statement of financial position prepared just prior to July 1, the date of incorporation:

Illustration 17–3

```
                           ROYAL AND BLAIR
                     Statement of Financial Position
                             June 30, 1978
                                Assets
Cash in bank ..................................................................        $ 8,500
Notes receivable..............................................................          1,200
Accounts receivable ..........................................          $4,000
   Less: Allowance for doubtful accounts............................             300     3,700

Merchandise inventory.......................................................         14,500
Store equipment .............................................          $5,500
   Less: Accumulated depreciation ..................................           2,000     3,500
Office equipment.............................................          $3,500
   Less: Accumulated depreciation ...................................          1,400     2,100
        Total Assets.........................................................        $33,500


                              Liabilities
Accounts payable.......................................................          $4,000
Notes payable................................................................            900


        Total Liabilities .....................................................        $ 4,900
                            Owners' Equity
J. D. Royal, capital..........................................................         15,000
E. O. Blair, capital ..........................................................         13,600
        Total Liabilities and Owners' Equity .......................        $33,500
```

The subscriptions of Royal and Blair are recorded by the following general journal entry:

```
Subscriptions Receivable...................................................  40,500
   Common Stock subscribed ...........................................           40,500
   To record common stock subscriptions:
   J. D. Royal, 500 shares.
   E. O. Blair, 400 shares.
```

If Royal and Blair decide to use the existing partnership books, the partners' equities (capital) may be transferred to the corporation by the following general journal entry:

```
J. D. Royal, Capital ..........................................................  15,000
E. O. Blair, Capital.............................................................  13,600
   Subscriptions Receivable ..............................................           28,600
   To record transfer of equities of Royal and Blair to
   corporation at book value.
```

Should Royal and Blair decide to use a new set of books, the following general journal entry would be made on the books of the corporation to record the transfer of assets and liabilities to the corporation.

Cash in Bank	8,500	
Notes Receivable	1,200	
Accounts Receivable	4,000	
Merchandise Inventory	14,500	
Store Equipment	3,500	
Office Equipment	2,100	
Accounts Payable		4,000
Notes Payable		900
Allowance for Doubtful Accounts		300
Subscriptions Receivable		28,600

To record transfer of equity of Royal and Blair
to corporation at book value.

It should be noted that the long-lived depreciable assets are transferred at their book values. If they and any other asset or liability had been transferred at amounts other than book value, appropriate adjustments would have been made prior to transfer.

The following general journal entries are used to record the amounts owed by Royal and Blair on their stock subscriptions and to record the issuance of stock certificates:

Cash in Bank	11,900	
Subscriptions Receivable		11,900

To record final payment on stock subscriptions:
J. D. Royal, $7,500 ($22,500 − $15,000).
E. O. Blair, $4,400 ($18,000 − $13,600).

Common Stock Subscribed	40,500	
Common Stock		40,500

To record issuance of stock certificates.

Owners' equity section

The owners' equity section of the corporation's statement of financial position represents the difference between the total assets and total liabilities of the corporation. The owners' equity section is composed of equities from two sources. Equity arises from investments by shareholders and from the retention of earnings. Assuming that the Royal Company retained $8,000 of its earnings in the first year and that there were no stock transactions subsequent to incorporation, the owners' equity section of the company's statement of financial position would appear as follows:

Owners' Equity

Common stock, $45 par value	
(1,000 shares authorized; 900 shares issued)	$40,500
Retained earnings	8,000
Total Owners' Equity	$48,500

It should be noted that the owners' equity section will vary for different corporations depending on the number of classes of stock and the amounts paid for each. Also, there may be a deficit resulting from unprofitable operations. Should such a deficit exist, it would be shown as a deduction in the owners' equity section.

GLOSSARY

Articles of incorporation   a document submitted to the state by those persons wishing to form a corporation. It contains significant information about the proposed corporation.

Board of directors   a group of persons elected by the stockholders of a corporation. It is given the responsibility of directing the affairs of the corporation.

Book value   the proceeds which each shareholder of a corporation would receive if all the corporation's assets were liquidated at amounts stated on the books and all its debts and obligations were paid.

Bylaws   a set of rules and regulations adopted by the shareholders of a corporation to govern the conduct of the affairs of the corporation within the general laws of the state and the policies and purposes found in the corporate charter.

Capital stock authorized   the type and amount of capital stock which a corporation may issue as specified in the corporate charter.

Corporate charter   a document granted by the state which acknowledges a corporation's legal existence.

Corporation   a business organization created by law. It is viewed as an entity separate from its owners and creditors. Ownership in the corporation is usually shown by shares of capital stock.

Date of declaration   the date on which the board of directors of a corporation states formally that the corporation will pay a dividend.

Date of payment   the date on which dividends that have been declared will be paid.

Date of record   the date on which the corporation will determine to whom dividends are to be paid.

Deficit   a debit balance in the Retained Earnings account.

Dividend   a distribution by a corporation to its stockholders. It may be in the form of cash, assets, or the corporation's own stock.

Incorporators   those persons applying for the incorporation of an organization.

Liquidation value   the amount per share (of preferred stock) which will be paid to preferred stockholders upon liquidation of the corporation.

Par value   an arbitrary amount assigned to each share of capital stock of a given class. It normally has no correlation with the market value or selling price of the stock.

Preferred stock a class of corporate capital stock which carries certain privileges and rights not given to all outstanding shares of stock. Holders of preferred stock are usually entitled to a specified dividend before any dividend payment may be made on common stock. Preferred stocks usually have no voting rights.

Shareholders basically, the owners of a corporation.

Stock certificate a document which shows proof of ownership in a corporation.

Subscribed stock stock which individuals have agreed to purchase but for which stock certificates have not yet been issued.

Subscriber a person who agrees to purchase shares of stock of a corporation.

Subscription an agreement to purchase shares of stock of a corporation.

Subscription price the price a subscriber agrees to pay for shares of stock in a subscription contract.

QUESTIONS AND EXERCISES

1. Discuss the advantages and disadvantages of the corporate form of organization.

2. What items are contained in a corporation's charter? In its bylaws?

3. Describe the organizational chart of a corporation. What is the difference between directors and officers?

4. How does the owners' equity section of the statement of financial position for a corporation differ from the owner's equity section for a proprietorship or partnership?

5. Distinguish among par value, book value, and market value of common stock.

6. Distinguish between common stock and preferred stock.

7. What three dates surround the distribution of a dividend?

8. Why might a company decide to distribute stock dividends?

9. John Miller subscribed to 60 shares of Slimey Corporation stock on May 1. The stock has a par value of $10, but John agreed to pay $15 per share. He paid for the stock on June 1, and Slimey Corporation issued the stock upon the receipt of the cash. What general journal entries should be made to record the subscription, the receipt of cash, and the issuance of the stock?

10. On December 8, the SSR Company declared a cash dividend of 50 cents per common share on 10,000 shares outstanding. The dividend is payable on January 30 to the stockholders of record on January 15. What journal entry should be made on each of the three mentioned dates?

PROBLEMS

17-1. The Collicat Corporation received a charter from the state of Georgia that authorized it to issue 10,000 shares of $25 par value common stock. What journal entries should be made to record the following owners' equity transactions?

1978

Jan.　5　Sold and issued 1,000 shares at par.

Apr. 14　Received subscriptions to 2,000 shares at $35 per share. The subscriptions were accompanied by a $10 per share down payment.

May 18　Received the balance due on the April 14 subscriptions and issued the stock.

Dec. 31　Closed the Expense and Revenue Summary account which had a credit balance of $60,000.

1979

Jan.　8　Declared a dividend of $2 per share payable on February 8 to stockholders of record on January 21.

Feb.　8　Paid the dividend.

17-2. R. B. Roast has decided to incorporate her sole proprietorship as the Roast Corporation. She plans to subscribe to 200 shares of common stock at $100 per share. In addition to her proprietorship equity, she will contribute $5,000 cash to the corporation. Based on the information given above and on Ms. Roast's statement of financial position shown below, make the journal entries to incorporate the proprietorship under each of the following assumptions:

a. The Roast Corporation uses the existing books of the proprietorship.

b. The Roast Corporation begins with a new set of books.

R. B. ROAST

Statement of Financial Position

September 17, 1978

Assets

Cash		$ 3,000
Accounts receivable	$ 5,000	
Less: Allowance for doubtful accounts	500	4,500
Inventory		10,000
Building	$30,000	
Less: Accumulated depreciation	5 000	25,000
Total Assets		$42,500

Liabilities

Accounts payable.. $ 7,500
Mortgage payable.. 20,000
     Total Liabilities $27,500

Owner's Equity

R. B. Roast, capital 15,000
     Total Liabilities and Owner's Equity $42,500

17-3. The Bullgeese Corporation has been granted a charter and has been authorized to issue 10,000 shares of $10 par value preferred stock and 50,000 shares of $20 par value common stock. Record the following owners' equity transactions in general journal form.

1978

Jan.   5   Sold and issued 5,000 shares of preferred at par.
        11   Received subscriptions to 3,000 shares of common at $25 per share.
Feb. 11   Received a $15 per share payment on all January 11 subscriptions.
Mar. 11   Received balance due on January 11 subscriptions and issued the stock.
June 18   Received subscriptions to 1,000 shares of preferred at $20 per share.
July   3   Sold and issued 4,000 shares of common at par.
      19   Received payment for June 18 subscriptions and issued the stock.
Dec. 31   Closed the Expense and Revenue Summary account which had a $40,000 credit balance.

1979

Mar. 31   Declared dividends of $3 per common share and $1 per preferred share. The dividends are payable on May 15 to the stockholders of record on April 15.
May 15   Paid the dividends.
Aug. 14   Sold and issued 2,000 shares of common at $50 per share.
Dec. 31   Closed the Expense and Revenue Summary account which had a $20,000 debit balance.

1980

Mar. 31   Declared a 20 percent common stock dividend distributable on May 5 to common stockholders of record on April 15. The market value of the stock is $40 per share.
May   5   Distributed the stock dividend.
      31   Declared a $1 per share dividend on preferred stock. The dividend is payable on July 20 to the preferred stockholders of record on June 20.
July 20   Paid the preferred cash dividend.
Dec. 31   Closed the Expense and Revenue Summary account which had a $95,000 credit balance.

17–4. The Landrow Corporation has been authorized to issue 5,000 shares of $10 par value common stock. The corporation will take over the business of the Land and Harrow partnership. The partners have subscribed for common stock as follows:

> S. M. Harrow, 2,000 shares @ $10 per share $20,000
> D. W. Land, 2,000 shares @ $10 per share $20,000

The partners will receive credit towards their subscriptions for their respective partnership equities. Each partner will contribute cash to pay the balance owed on his subscription.

Based on the information in the preceding paragraph and on the Land and Harrow statement of financial position shown below, make the journal entries that are necessary to incorporate the partnership under each of the following conditions:

a. The Landrow Corporation uses the existing books of the partnership.

b. The Landrow Corporation opens a new set of books.

LAND AND HARROW
Statement of Financial Position
October 17, 1978

Assets

Cash..		$ 6,000
Accounts receivable		6,000
Inventory		10,000
Prepaid rent...		6,000
Delivery truck...	$8,000	
Less: Accumulated depreciation.....................	4,000	4,000
Total Assets		$32,000

Liabilities

Accounts payable	$ 5,000

Owners' Equity

D. W. Land, capital.......................................	14,000
S. M. Harrow, capital....................................	13,000
Total Liabilities and Owners' Equity..........	$32,000

17–5. When the Moore Corporation was organized, it was authorized to issue 40,000 shares of $10 par value common stock and 10,000 shares of $20 par value preferred stock. The preferred stock has a liquidation value of $25 per share. The following owners' equity section appeared on the Moore Corporation's statement of financial position on December 31, 1978.

Owners' Equity

Preferred stock, $20 par, 8,000 shares issued.................. $160,000
Common stock, $10 par, 30,000 shares issued................. 300,000
Retained earnings... 500,000

Total Owners' Equity....................................... $960,000

Required:

Compute the book value per share for each class of stock.

17–6.

THE MEHRABONNER CORPORATION
Adjusted Trial Balance
December 31, 1978

Account Title	Debit	Credit
Cash..	$ 10,000	
Accounts receivable	20,000	
Allowance for doubtful accounts		$ 3,000
Inventory	80,000	
Unexpired insurance	2,000	
Prepaid rent...	9,600	
Office supplies..	1,000	
Store equipment	25,000	
Accumulated depreciation — store equipment ...		5,000
Office furniture...	20,000	
Accumulated depreciation — office furniture		2,500
Accounts payable		10,500
Interest payable...		250
Wages payable		2,000
Notes payable		5,000
Common stock ($10 par).............................		80,000
Premium on common stock		8,000
Retained earnings		41,500
Sales..		497,000
Cost of goods sold	420,000	
Insurance expense	1,000	
Rent expense	9,600	
Wages expense..	48,000	
Bad debts expense	2,500	
Depreciation expense	3,500	
Office supplies expense..............................	2,000	
Other expense...	550	
	$654,750	$654,750

Required:

1. Make the necessary closing entries.
2. Prepare an earnings statement.
3. Prepare a statement of financial position.

Accrual accounting—wholesale business
Learning objectives

To obtain a working knowledge of the accounting practices and procedures applicable to the wholesale business, this chapter contains the following material:

1. A description of the factors affecting the accounting records used by a wholesale business.
2. The organization and content of the records and the chart of accounts kept by a wholesaler.
3. The manner in which supplementary records are used to assist the wholesaler in maintaining the general business records.
4. A detailed illustration of the day-by-day accounting procedure needed to record the transactions of a wholesale business.

18

Accrual accounting – wholesale business

Often referred to as the "middle man," a **wholesale merchandising enterprise** purchases products directly from manufacturers and importers which are then sold to retailers who in turn sell to the individual consumer. The typical wholesaler has storage facilities which enable the wholesaler to make purchases in large quantities at a lower cost per unit. The bulk or lot purchases are then marked up and sold to the retailer in smaller quantities. The markup in wholesale cost will often seem small in comparison to the markup at the retail level. This is due to the fact that wholesalers depend on volume rather than large cost markups to produce revenues. Although wholesalers may purchase and sell for cash or on account, credit transactions are used extensively in the wholesale business.

ITEMS AFFECTING ACCOUNTING RECORDS USED

The books of original entry as well as the auxiliary records to be used in a wholesale business involve several considerations. Items of particular concern are discussed below. These points may be used in determining the record requirements for most enterprises:

1. Type of business

A wholesale business may be operated as a sole proprietorship, a partnership, or as a corporation. When operated as a sole proprietorship or partnership, no distinguishing records are necessary. However, when operated as a corporation, a **book of minutes,** a record of shares owned, and a **shareholders' ledger** are usually maintained. The owner's equity structure of the business will have a direct impact on the accounts used. If operated as a sole proprietorship, only two equity accounts are necessary — one for the proprietor's capital and another for the proprietor's personal withdrawals. A partnership requires that separate equity accounts be maintained for each partner. When a wholesale business is operated as a corporation, separate accounts must be kept for retained earnings, dividends payable, and the various classes of stock.

2. Business volume

In addition to the type of business organization, the volume or potential volume of a business should be carefully considered when determining the type and number of accounts to be used. It is evident that an enterprise with annual sales of $10 million a year will be noticeably different from one with sales of $25,000 a year. As the volume of business increases, there is an increased need for adequate control. Such controls are often achieved through the use of statistical and analytical data which further expands the number of records and volume of paperwork.

The number of persons engaged in keeping a firm's accounting records will depend on the size of the business and on the extent to which accounting machines are used. If the records are kept on a manual basis, the number of people engaged in record keeping will be closely related to the size of the business. When a manual system is used, the accounting functions and related procedures will be divided in some logical manner. Separate records and books of original entry will be maintained along with the appropriate ledgers for the various business transactions. Special journals may be kept for sales, purchases, cash receipts, and checks drawn, and a general journal may be kept to record transactions not properly included in a special journal. Subsidiary ledgers are often maintained for many of the general ledger accounts in order to provide sufficient detail.

By functionally dividing the accounting activities among the accounting employees, the following advantages are realized:

a.   Provides an equitable distribution of work among employees.
b.   Provides internal checks and controls.
c.   Allows transactions to be classified in the books of original entry in a detailed manner.
d.   Permits transaction details to be summarized and posted to the general ledger on a periodic basis.

3. Desired information

An accounting system is of little value unless it provides management with the desired information with which to operate the business. Management is interested in the financial position of the business as well as the results of operations from period to period. As mentioned earlier, statistical and analytical data may be desired in addition to traditional accounting information. Management may want information concerning inventory quantities in addition to dollar amounts. An important responsibility is that of providing information needed for federal, state, and local tax authorities. Also, if the company's stock is publicly traded, it will be necessary to provide information required by the various regulatory agencies.

4. Office machines

Since office equipment machines replace manual procedures, the accounting system will be affected. Office equipment technology makes it possible for the small business executive to afford and operate various accounting machines. Even though computers and posting machines have replaced manual operations, the need for separation of accounting procedures has not been eliminated. Where computers are used, accounting controls are maintained at the points of input and output in addition to the controls built into the computer itself.

The extent to which office machines are used does not reduce the need for adherence to fundamental principles involved in keeping accounting records. Accounting theory must be applied regardless of the extent to which office machines are used.

RECORDS AND CHART OF ACCOUNTS

Bailey and Brown are partners engaged in the wholesale plumbing and electrical supply business. Plumbing supplies are handled in the plumbing department; electrical supplies are handled in the electrical department. All supplies and equipment are purchased on account from various manufacturers. Discounts on purchases range from 1 to 3 percent for cash in from 10 to 30 days. Sales by Bailey and Brown are to local dealers and distributors for cash or on account. Sales on account are given a 2 percent discount if paid within 10 days, net amount due if paid within 30 days. Hereafter, the discount will be referred to as 2/10, n/30.

Bailey and Brown maintain the following records:

1. Books of original entry.

    a. Sales register.
    b. Record of cash receipts.
    c. Invoice register.
    d. Record of checks drawn.
    e. General journal.

2. Books of final entry.

    a. General ledger.
    b. Subsidiary ledgers.
        (1) Accounts receivable ledger.
        (2) Accounts payable ledger.
        (3) Operating expense ledger.

3. Supplementary records.

    a. Daily bank statement.
    b. Petty cash record.
    c. Insurance register.
    d. Notes receivable records.
    e. Inventory records.
    f. Long-lived asset record.

Sales register

Bailey and Brown use the sales register as shown in Illustration 18–1. The register provides columns for accounts receivable, customer, and sales by department. Columns are also provided for date, for sale number, and for miscellaneous debits and credits to the general ledger.

Record of cash receipts

The cash receipts record used by Bailey and Brown has been reproduced in Illustration 18–2. Debit columns are provided for bank, sales discount, and general ledger. Credit columns are used for accounts receivable, general ledger, and cash sales by department. All cash received is debited to the bank account. This procedure means that all receipts are deposited in the bank and that all disbursements, except petty cash, are made by check.

The cash receipts record may be proved daily or periodically by footing the debit and credit columns and comparing the totals. Should a page be filled before the record is normally proved, it should be footed and proved before starting another page. These totals are then forwarded to the top of the next page. It should be noted that a new page is normally

Illustration 18–1

Month of December 1978 SALES REGISTER Page 10

Acct. No.	Amount	✓	Accounts Receivable	✓	Day	Name	Sale No.	Plumbing	Electrical	Acct. No.	Amount	✓
								Debit → General Ledger / Accounts Receivable; **Credit** → Sales / General Ledger				
			665.74	✓	1	Sharp Contractors	220	482.60	183.14			
			67.42	✓	1	B. L. Thompson	221		67.42			
			132.14	✓	4	Anderson Builders	222		132.14			
			243.00	✓	4	Normal Hardware	223	243.00				
			325.00	✓	5	McDonald Construction Co.	224		325.00			
			23.00 1,456.30	✓	5	O. B. Smith	225	23.00 748.60	707.70			
			389.05	✓	8	Farmers Hardware	226	389.05				
			350.44	✓	8	Peoples Hardware	227		345.60	153	4.84	✓
			143.18	✓	8	Fred Smith	228		143.18			
			514.83	✓	10	Sharp Contractors	229	208.88	305.95			
			408.15	✓	10	Quick Contractors	230		408.15			
			88.09	✓	13	B. L. Thompson	231		88.09			
			143.25	✓	13	Anderson Builders	232		143.25			
			56.70	✓	13	Green Plumbing Co.	233	56.70				
			3,549.99					1,403.23	2,141.92		4.84	
			215.00	✓	31	McDonald Construction Co.	250		215.00			
			88.52	✓	31	Sturdy Builders	251	88.52				
			6,853.51		31			2,591.75	4,181.92		79.84	
			(130)					(410)	(420)		(✓)	

Illustration 18-2

Month of December 1978 · CASH RECEIPTS RECORD · Page 20

Debit — General Ledger Acct. No.	Amount	✓	Sales Discounts	Bank Net Amt.	Day	Received From	Accounts Receivable	✓	Credit — Cash Sales Plumbing	Electrical	General Ledger Acct. No.	Amount	✓
			16.49	807.76	1	T. C. Scott	824.25	✓					
				776.60	6	Cash sales			387.00	389.60			
			16.49	1,584.36	8	George Glass	824.25	✓	387.00	389.60			
			9.84	482.33			492.17						
			13.31	652.43	9	Sharp Contractors	665.74	✓					
			1.35	66.07	9	B. L. Thompson	67.42	✓					
				401.38	9	Cash sales			112.00	289.38			
				493.32	10	Cash sales			398.24	95.08			
			2.64	129.50	11	Anderson Builders	132.14	✓					
				182.14	11	Slow Contractors	182.14	✓					
				491.05	11	Cash sales			88.42	402.63			
			4.86	238.14	12	Normal Hardware	243.00	✓					
				117.53	13	Cash sales			53.09	64.44			
			48.49	4,838.25	15	Discounted note	2,606.86		1,038.75	1,241.13	131	400.00	✓
				401.53							710	1.53	✓
				25.00	15	Interest revenue — govt. bonds					710	25.00	✓
				668.67	31	Cash sales			668.67				
				408.15	31	Quick Contractors	408.15	✓					
			2.72	133.50	31	Fred Smith	136.22	✓					
	(✓)		64.32	9,474.99			4,351.23		2,407.42	2,241.13		539.53	
			(422)	(110)			(130)		(410)	(420)		(✓)	

started at the beginning of each month for the record of cash receipts and for each of the registers, records, and journals described in the following pages.

Posting the cash receipts record. Items involving the General Ledger debit and credit columns are posted individually. These individual items are posted on a daily basis. As each item is posted, a check mark is entered in the check (✓) column beside the amount being posted. As a method of cross-reference, the initials "cr" along with the page number of the cash receipts record are entered in the P.R. column of the general ledger account to which the amount is being posted.

Summary totals of the remaining columns are posted on a monthly basis. The posting involves the following procedure:

1. The Sales Discounts column is totaled and posted as a debit to Sales Discounts, Account No. 422, in the general ledger.
2. The Bank column is totaled and posted as a debit to National Bank, Account No. 110, in the general ledger.
3. The Accounts Receivable column total is posted as a credit to Accounts Receivable, Account No. 130, in the general ledger. (Note, postings to individual customer accounts are made when cash is received.)
4. The columns for sales of the plumbing and electrical departments are totaled and credited to Sales — Plumbing Department, Account No. 410, and to Sales — Electrical Department, Account No. 420, respectively, in the general ledger.

As each total is posted, the account number should be recorded below the total in the cash receipts record. As a means of cross-reference, the initials "cr" and the cash receipts record page number are entered in the P.R. column of the general ledger account being posted. A check mark or other symbol should be recorded below the total of the General Ledger debit and credit columns to indicate that these totals are not to be posted since the items included in the total were posted individually.

Invoice register

The invoice register used by Bailey and Brown has been reproduced in Illustration 18–3. The register contains columns for purchases charged to the plumbing and electrical departments or to the general ledger accounts for nondepartmental purchases. Other columns are provided for the days of the month, invoice date, invoice number, creditor, and credits to accounts payable and general ledger accounts. (For an additional description of invoice register procedures, refer to Chapter 12.)

Illustration 18–3

Month of December 1978   **INVOICE REGISTER**   Page 10

Day	Date of Invoice	Invoice No.	Name	Debit: Purchases Plumbing	Purchases Electrical	Gen. Ledger Acct. No.	Gen. Ledger Amount	✓	Credit: Accounts Payable	✓	Gen. Ledger Acct. No.	Gen. Ledger Amount	✓
3	12/2	649	National Electrical Co.		345.00				345.00	✓			
3	12/3	650	Southern Supply Co.	232.48					232.48	✓			
3	12/3	651	Bendix Office Supplies Co.			151	42.19	✓	42.19	✓			
4	12/3	652	Eastern Supply Co.		245.18				245.18	✓			
				232.48	590.18		42.19	✓	864.85				
10	12/9	653	Republic Electrical Co.		308.14				308.14	✓			
10	12/8	654	Atlantic Manufacturing Co.	440.15					440.15	✓			
10	12/10	655	Peters Supply Co.			152	52.80	✓	52.80	✓			
10	12/10	656	Butler & Sons Inc.			150	18.00	✓	18.00	✓			
12	12/12	657	National Electrical Co.		108.00				108.00	✓			
12	12/11	658	Southern Supply Co.	304.19					304.19	✓			
12	12/10	659	Great Manufacturing Co.	208.01					208.01	✓			
				1,184.83	1,006.32		112.99		2,304.14				
15	12/14	660	Owens Equipment Co.			170	300.00	✓	275.00	✓	170	125.00	✓
						171	100.00	✓					
31	12/30	681	National Electrical Co.		112.14				112.14	✓			
31	12/29	682	Chattanooga Marble Co.	348.49					348.49	✓			
31				3,033.32	2,118.46		592.99		5,539.77			205.00	
				(510)	(520)		(✓)		(250)			(✓)	

Record of checks drawn

The record of checks drawn used by Baily and Brown is shown in Illustration 18–4. Debit columns are provided for the general ledger, operating expenses, and accounts payable. A column is provided for the payee, and credit columns for general ledger, purchases discounts, and bank are included. The record of checks drawn may be footed and proved on a daily or periodic basis. The record is proved by comparing the debit footings with the credit footings. When a page is full or at the beginning of a month, the columns are footed and a new page is started by entering the totals on the top of the next page.

Posting the record of checks drawn. As with the record of cash receipts, the posting of checks drawn involves both individual and summary posting. Individual posting is required for the General Ledger debit and credit columns and for the Operating Expenses columns. The individual posting is normally done on a daily basis. As each item is posted, a check mark is recorded in the check (✔) column beside the amount being posted. To cross-reference the posting, the initials "cd" and the page number of the record of checks drawn are recorded in the P.R. column of the ledger account being posted.

At the end of each month, the summary posting, which involves the following procedure, is performed:

1. The Operating Expenses column is footed and posted as a debit to Operating Expenses, Account No. 610, in the general ledger.
2. The Accounts Payable column total is posted as a debit to Accounts Payable, Account No. 250, in the general ledger. (Note: Postings to individual creditors' accounts are performed when payment is made.)
3. The Purchases Discounts column total is posted as a credit to Purchases Discounts, Account No. 522, in the general ledger.
4. The Bank column total is posted as a credit to National Bank, Account No. 110, in the general ledger.

When the column total is posted, the account number should be written below the total indicating that the total has been posted. The page number and initials "cd" should be recorded in the P.R. column of the ledger account being posted to as a means of cross-reference. A check mark or other appropriate symbol should be placed below the General Ledger debit and credit column totals indicating that they are not to be posted.

General journal

The general journal used by Bailey and Brown is shown in Illustration 18–5. In addition to the General Ledger debit and credit columns, debit

Illustration 18–4

RECORD OF CHECKS DRAWN

Month of December 1978

Debit — General Ledger Acct. No.	Amount	✓	Operating Expenses Acct. No.	Amount	✓	Accounts Payable	✓	Day	Drawn to the Order Of	Credit — General Ledger Acct. No.	Amount	✓	Purchases Discounts	Ck. No.	Bank Net Amt.
			6125	250.00	✓			1	Small Realtors					643	250.00
						556.88	✓	2	Republic Electrical Co.				16.70	644	540.18
154	150.00	✓						2	H. H. Insurance Co.					645	150.00
						356.10	✓	4	National Electrical Co.				7.12	646	348.98
						185.85	✓	6	E-Z Drain Manufacturing Co.				3.71	647	182.14
	150.00			250.00		1,098.83							27.53		1,471.30
						322.21	✓	8	Atlantic Manufacturing Co.				6.44	648	315.77
						423.56	✓	9	Copper Pipe Company				8.47	649	415.09
						321.25	✓	10	National Electrical Co.				6.43	650	314.82
						232.48	✓	11	Southern Supply Co.				4.65	651	227.83
			6106	95.00	✓			11	Randall Company					652	95.00
153	10.00	✓						11	Postage					653	10.00
	160.00			345.00		2,398.33							53.52		2,849.81
			6101	450.00	✓			15	Payroll	210	33.31	✓		654	1,549.00
			6102	215.00	✓					230	57.69	✓			
			6103	250.00	✓										
			6121	450.00	✓										
			6122	275.00	✓										
210	133.24	✓						15	National Bank					655	248.62
230	115.38	✓													
						187.75	✓	31	Southern Supply Co.				3.75	667	184.00
						120.59	✓	31	West Manufacturing Co.				2.41	668	118.18
	541.62			2,355.00		3,214.67		31	Carried forward		99.00		62.68		5,949.61

Illustration 18–4 (continued)

RECORD OF CHECKS DRAWN

Month of December 1978   Page 22

	Debit										Credit				
General Ledger			Operating Expenses			Accounts Payable	✓	Day	Drawn to the Order Of	General Ledger			Purchases Discounts	Ck. No.	Bank Net Amt.
Acct. No.	Amount	✓	Acct. No.	Amount	✓					Acct. No.	Amount	✓			
	541.62			2,355.00		3,214.67		31	Amounts Brought forward		99.00		62.68		5,949.61
180	42.00	✓						31	Industrial Supply Co.					669	42.00
			6101	450.00				31	Payroll	210	33.31	✓		670	1,549.00
										230	57.69	✓			
			6102	215.00	✓										
			6103	250.00	✓										
			6121	450.00	✓										
			6122	275.00	✓										
			6105	8.42	✓			31	Petty Cash					671	92.53
			6107	14.15	✓										
			6109	5.00	✓										
			6114	2.65	✓										
			6117	15.32	✓										
			6123	6.00	✓										
			6124	18.00	✓										
			6129	1.25	✓										
			6133	21.74	✓										
	583.62			4,087.53		3,214.67		31			190.00		62.68		7,633.14
	(✓)			(610)		(250)					(✓)		(522)		(110)

Illustration 18–5

GENERAL JOURNAL

Month of December 1978   Page ____

Operating Expenses Acct. No.	Operating Expenses Amount	✓	Accounts Payable	✓	General Ledger (Debit) Acct. No.	General Ledger (Debit) Amount	✓	Day	Description	General Ledger (Credit) Acct. No.	General Ledger (Credit) Amount	✓	Accounts Receivable	✓
					411	9.83	✓	9	Normal Hardware, C.M. 128				9.83	✓
			23.75	✓				10	National Electrical Co. CB10	521	23.75	✓		
			23.75			9.83					23.75	✓	9.83	
6131	58.47	✓						15	Payroll taxes	210	33.31	✓		
										220	2.96	✓		
	58.47		23.75			9.83				240	22.20	✓	9.83	
											82.22			
					161	65.00	✓	15	Discarding desk	160	65.00	✓		
					131	20.00	✓	15	J. J. Clark				20.00	✓
					421	10.39	✓	15	B. L. Thompson, C.M. 129				10.39	✓
≈≈≈	≈≈≈	≈	≈≈≈	≈	≈≈≈	≈≈≈	≈	≈	≈≈≈	≈≈≈	≈≈≈	≈	≈≈≈	≈
6131	58.47	✓						31	Payroll taxes	210	33.31	✓		
										220	2.96	✓		
								31		240	22.20	✓		
	179.72		44.25			185.22					268.97		140.22	
	(610)		(250)			(✓)					(✓)		(130)	

columns are provided for operating expenses and accounts payable. A Credit column for accounts receivable are also provided. Adjusting, closing, and reversing entries along with entries representing transactions not recorded in the special journals are entered in the general journal.

The general journal can be footed and proved daily or periodically by comparing the debit and credit totals. Column totals are forwarded to a new page when the page is full or at the start of a month.

Posting the general journal. Both individual and summary posting is involved when posting from the general journal. The general ledger debits and credits require individual posting to the appropriate accounts. Postings are usually made on a daily basis and are so indicated by placing a check mark in the check ($\checkmark$) column beside the general journal amount. The initial "G" along with the general journal page number is entered in the P.R. column of the general ledger account being posted. The operating expenses debits are also posted in a similar manner.

Summary postings at the end of the month involve the following procedures:

1. The Operating Expenses column total should be posted as a debit to Operating Expenses, Account No. 610, in the general ledger.
2. The total of the Accounts Payable debit column is posted as a debit to Accounts Payable, Account No. 250, in the general ledger.
3. The total of the Accounts Payable credit column is posted as a credit to Accounts Payable, Account No. 250, in the general ledger.
4. The Accounts Receivable column total is posted as a credit to Accounts Receivable, Account No. 130, in the general ledger.

The operating expenses, the accounts payable debits and credits, and the accounts receivable credits are also posted to the subsidiary ledgers as the transactions occur. The appropriate account number should be written below each column total that is posted. Those totals not posted should be noted with a check mark or other symbol. The letter "G" and the page number of the general journal should be placed beside the amount in the P.R. column of the general ledger account being posted.

General ledger

The general ledger accounts used by Bailey and Brown are shown in Illustration 18-6. The chart of accounts lists each of the general ledger accounts in numerical order. Several accounts listed in the chart of accounts need further explanation. These accounts are mentioned below.

Government Bonds, Account No. 120. At present, Bailey and Brown are holding temporary investments in the form of U.S. government bonds. Whenever the partners have excess cash, they make temporary invest-

Illustration 18–6

BAILEY AND BROWN
General Ledger Chart of Accounts

Assets:

Cash
  110 National Bank
  111 Petty Cash
Short-Term Investments
  120 Government Bonds
Receivables
  130 Accounts Receivable
    131 Allowance for Doubtful Accounts
  132 Notes Receivable
  133 Accrued Interest Receivable
Merchandise Inventory
  140 Merchandise Inventory—
    Plumbing Department
  145 Merchandise Inventory—
    Electrical Department
Supplies and Prepayments
  150 Store Supplies
  151 Office Supplies
  152 Advertising Supplies
  153 Postage Stamps
  154 Unexpired Insurance
Long-Lived Assets
  160 Store Equipment
    161 Accumulated Depreciation—
      Store Equipment
  170 Office Equipment
    171 Accumulated Depreciation—
      Office Equipment
  180 Delivery Equipment
    181 Accumulated Depreciation—
      Delivery Equipment

Liabilities:

210 F.I.C.A. Taxes Payable
220 F.U.T.A. Taxes Payable
230 Income Taxes Payable—Federal
    employee
240 State Unemployment Taxes Payable
250 Accounts Payable
260 Notes Payable
270 Accrued Interest Payable

Owners' Equity:

310 M. O. Brown, Capital
311 M. O. Brown, Drawing
320 W. E. Bailey, Capital
321 W. E. Bailey, Drawing
330 Expense and Revenue Summary

Revenues:

410 Sales—Plumbing Department
  411 Sales Returns and Allowances—
    Plumbing Department
420 Sales—Electrical Department
  421 Sales Returns and Allowances—
    Electrical Department
  422 Sales Discounts

Cost of Goods Sold:

510 Purchases—Plumbing Department
  511 Purchase Returns and Allowances—
    Plumbing Department
520 Purchases—Electrical Department
  521 Purchase Returns and Allowances—
    Electrical Department
  522 Purchases Discounts
540 Transportation-In—Plumbing Dept.
550 Transportation-In—Electrical Dept.
560 Cost of Goods Sold—Plumbing Dept.
570 Cost of Goods Sold—Electrical Dept.

Operating Expenses:

610 Operating Expenses

Other Revenue:

710 Interest Revenue

Other Expenses:

810 Interest Expense
820 Collection Expense

ments to add to earnings from normal operations. **Temporary investments** of this type are of low risk and can be readily liquidated. Since they are held on a short-term basis, they are classified as current assets on the statement of financial position.

Sales Discounts, Account No. 422. As an incentive for prompt payment of purchases, most wholesale businesses offer their customers a cash discount if payment is made within a certain period. The discount allowed by Bailey and Brown is 2 percent if the amount owed is paid within ten days of the sale. Since Bailey and Brown have no way of knowing whether or not the customer will pay within the discount period, the sales are billed at the gross amount If the customer pays within ten days, the remittance is recorded by debiting National Bank for the amount received and Sales Discounts for the allowed discount and crediting Accounts Receivable for the gross amount. Even though sales discounts could be treated as an expense, the normal procedure is to subtract the discounts given along with sales returns and allowances to determine the amount of net sales.

Cost of Goods Sold — Plumbing Department, Account No. 560, and Cost of Goods Sold — Electrical Department, Account No. 570. These two accounts are used to close out the appropriate accounts needed to calculate cost of goods sold for each department. The debit balances of the beginning inventory of merchandise, transportation-in (discussed below), and purchases, and the credit balances of purchase returns and allowances and purchases discounts are closed to the respective department's cost of goods sold account. After the ending inventory is taken and credited to the Cost of Goods Sold account, the remaining balance represents the cost of goods sold for the department in question. The cost of goods sold balances are then closed to the Expense and Revenue Summary account.

Transportation-In — Plumbing Department, Account No. 540, and Transportation-In — Electrical Department, Account No. 550. The freight charges on purchases of Bailey and Brown are charged to these two accounts. As indicated above, the year-end balances of these accounts are transferred as debits to the cost of goods sold accounts.

Accounts receivable ledger

Bailey and Brown use the debit-credit-balance form of ledger for accounts receivable. The Accounts Receivable control account (Account No. 130) is kept in the general ledger. The ledger accounts are maintained in alphabetical order, and at the end of each month a **schedule of accounts receivable** is prepared. The schedule total should equal the Accounts Receivable control account balance.

Posting to the individual customer accounts may be done from the books of original entry, from the customer billing slip, or from other transaction documents. To lessen the probability of transcription errors, Bailey and Brown follow the procedure of posting from the transaction documents.

Accounts payable ledger

As with the accounts receivable ledger, Bailey and Brown use the debit-credit-balance ledger form for accounts payable. The accounts are kept in alphabetical order and are represented in the general ledger by the Accounts Payable control account (Account No. 250). A **schedule of accounts payable** is prepared at the end of each month and compared with the balance of the Accounts Payable control account.

Posting to the accounts payable ledger may be done from the books of original entry or from the transaction documents. Bailey and Brown use the latter procedure.

Operating expense ledger

The operating expense ledger of Bailey and Brown is maintained in the debit-credit-balance form. The accounts are kept in numerical order as indicated in the operating expense chart of accounts of Illustration 18–7. The control account (Account No. 610) for operating expenses is kept in the general ledger. At the end of each month, the subsidiary ledger balance is compared with the control account balance.

The books of original entry are used in posting to the Operating Expenses accounts. The page number and initials of the journal from which the posting is made are recorded in the P.R. column beside each posted amount.

Supplementary records

Bailey and Brown maintain the following supplementary records: a daily bank statement, a petty cash record, an insurance register, notes

Illustration 18–7

BAILEY AND BROWN
Operating Expense Ledger Chart of Accounts

Selling Expenses:		Administrative Expenses:	
6101	M. O. Brown, Salary Expense	6121	W. E. Bailey, Salary Expense
6102	Truck Drivers' Wages Expense	6122	Office Salaries Expense
6103	Store Clerks' Salary Expense	6123	Power and Water Expense
6104	M. O. Brown, Travel Expense	6124	Telephone Expense
6105	Advertising Expense	6125	Rent Expense
6106	Garage Rent Expense	6126	Property Tax Expense
6107	Truck Repairs Expense	6127	Office Supplies Expense
6108	Truck Operating Expense	6128	Bad Debts Expense
6109	Shipping Expense	6129	Postage Expense (Administration)
6110	Merchandise Insurance Expense	6130	Office Equipment Insurance Expense
6111	Delivery Equipment Insurance Expense	6131	Payroll Taxes Expense
6112	Store Equipment Insurance Expense	6132	Depreciation of Office Equipment
6113	Postage Expense (Selling)	6133	Miscellaneous General Expense
6114	Store Supplies Expense		
6115	Depreciation of Store Equipment		
6116	Depreciation of Delivery Equipment		
6117	Miscellaneous Selling Expense		

receivable records, inventory records, and a long-lived asset record. The daily bank statement and petty cash record used by Bailey and Brown are shown in Illustrations 18–9 and 18–10. The insurance register and notes receivable record are similar to those shown in Illustrations 18–1 and 18–2, respectively.

Daily bank statement. As a method of keeping track of the bank balance on a daily basis, Bailey and Brown use a **daily bank statement.** The statement is similar to the records kept on an individual's check stubs in that it is used to record the checks written and deposits made each day. The December statement is shown in Illustration 18–9. Since the statement is used to keep track of the daily bank balance, a running balance on the check stubs is not needed. Bailey and Brown use the check stubs to record information necessary to maintain the record of checks drawn and to post to the appropriate creditor accounts in the accounts payable ledger.

Inventory record. The **inventory record** shown in Illustration 18–8 is used by Bailey and Brown. The record provides inventory control and is used as an aid to good business management. The inventory record is particularly valuable when determining when to reorder. Even though an inventory record is kept, a physical inventory count should be taken at least once each year to eliminate any discrepancies between the records and the actual amounts on hand. Unless some form of inventory record or estimate is used, a physical count will be required when preparing interim statements (monthly or quarterly) and year-end reports. An inventory record allows the physical count to be taken in stages or in parts during the year. This proves to be an advantage when preparing statements.

Information from the purchase invoices, sales invoices, sales returns, and purchase returns is used in maintaining the inventory record. It is noted that only quantities are recorded. When minimum quantities are

Illustration 18–8

INVENTORY RECORD				
Date	Invoice No.	Received	Issued	Balance
Mar. 2				488
3	1042	204		692
4	667		30	662
9	675		50	612
10	683		120	492
13	1050	300		792
20	700		60	732

Article	Description	Minimum	Department
Light switches	White w/night light	500	Electrical

reached, a purchase order is prepared. Some inventory records provide columns for items on order but not yet received. The sum of quantities on order and quantities on hand is then used to determine when to reorder.

Long-lived asset record. Bailey and Brown use the group method of depreciation (described on page 385). Because of this, an individual record for each depreciable asset is not maintained. If each asset was depreciated individually, asset record cards similar to the example shown in Illustration 15–2 would be used.

ACCOUNTING PROCEDURE ILLUSTRATED

The records of Bailey and Brown are kept on a calendar year basis. The sales register, cash receipts record, invoice register, record of checks drawn, and general journal (the books of original entry) are shown in Illustrations 18–1, 18–2, 18–3, 18–4, and 18–5. The supplementary records of the daily bank statement and petty cash disbursements have been reproduced in Illustrations 18–9 and 18–10, respectively. The remaining supplementary records and the general and subsidiary ledgers are not shown. A narrative of the transactions of Bailey and Brown during the month of December is given on the following pages.

BAILEY AND BROWN
Plumbing and Electrical Supply Wholesalers
Narrative of Transactions

December 1

Sales on account:

No. 220: Sharp Contractors, City; plumbing, $482.60; electrical, $183.14; terms, 2/10, n/30.
No. 221: B. L. Thompson, City; electrical, $67.42; terms, 2/10, n/30.

After the sale is made, the accountant obtains the necessary information from a carbon copy of the sales invoice prepared by the store clerk. As the amounts are entered in the sales register, a check mark is placed in the check (✔) column to indicate that the amounts will be posted to the individual creditors' accounts. The invoices are then posted to the accounts receivable ledger. An additional copy of the sales invoice is used to make the appropriate entries in the inventory records (see inventory record shown in Illustration 18–8).

Issued Check No. 643 for $250 to Small Realtors for the December rent.

Received a check for $807.76 from T. C. Scott for our invoice of November 25, $824.25, less the 2 percent discount.

As a means of determining if the discount and check amount were properly stated, the accountant examined the Accounts Receivable

Illustration 18–9

Daily Bank Statement
For Month of December 1978

Outstanding Checks			Daily Bank Balance			
Check Number	Amount	Memorandum	Day	Deposits	Checks	Balance
		Balance—previous month				8425 16
			1	807 76	250 00	8982 92
			2		690 18	8292 74
			3			8292 74
			4		348 98	7943 76
			5			7943 76
			6	776 60	182 14	8538 22
			7			8538 22
			8	482 33	315 77	8704 78
			9	1119 88	415 09	9409 57
			10	493 32	314 82	9588 07
			11	802 69	332 83	10057 93
			12	238 14		10296 07
			13	117 53		10413 60
			14			10413 60
			15	426 53	1797 62	9042 51
			31	1210 32	1985 71	10267 01
				9474 99	7633 14	

ledger account of T. C. Scott. The ledger indicated that on November 25, Scott had made purchases amounting to $824.25. Since the payment was made within ten days, the discount was properly taken. The amount was verified as follows:

Invoice amount	$824.25
Less: 2% discount	16.49
Amount Due	$807.76

After the check amount was verified, it was posted to the acount of T. C. Scott in the accounts receivable ledger. The amount of the check, $807.76, was entered on one line, and the $16.49 discount was entered on the next line. The check was then entered in the cash receipts record

Illustration 18–10

Petty Cash Disbursements Record
December 1978

Day	Description	Voucher Number	Total Amount		6105	6107	6109
	Balance $100.00						
9	Adding machine repairs	84	8 50				
9	Truck repair	85	14 15			14 15	
10	Newspaper advertisement	86	8 42		8 42		
10	Masking tape	87	7 14				5 00
11	Shipping labels	88	6 42				
11	Telephone bill	89	18 00				
11	Water bill	90	6 00				
15	Adding machine tape	91	68 63 / 2 65		8 42	14 15	5 00
31	Postage due	95	1 25				
			92 53		8 42	14 15	5 00
	Balance $ 7.47						
	Received 92.53						
	$ 100.00						

by debiting Sales Discounts for $16.49 and Bank for the amount of the check, $807.76, and by crediting Accounts Receivable for $824.25, the total invoice amount. A check mark was placed in the check column to indicate that the appropriate postings had been made to the T. C. Scott account.

At the close of each day, the total amount of checks issued and the total amount of deposits made are recorded in the daily bank statement. Since December 1 was the first working day of the month, the ending bank balance for November, $8,425.16, was forwarded to the top of the next page. The deposit of $807.76 and the check issued for $250 were entered in the daily bank statement, and the new balance was extended.

December 2

Issued checks as follows:

No. 644: Republic Electrical Company, $540.18, in payment of its November 24 invoice for $556.88 less 3 percent discount.

Page 12

Distribution Charges				Account	Amount	
6117	6123	6124	6133			
			8 50			
			2 14			
642						
		18 00				
642	6 00 / 6 00	18 00	10 64	6114	2 65	
				6129	1 25	
15 32	6 00	18 00	21 74		3 90	

No. 645: H. H. Insurance Company, $150, in payment for one-year policy on merchandise.

As the checks were drawn, check marks were placed in the check columns beside the Accounts Payable and General Ledger debit columns to indicate that the checks will be posted to the proper subsidiary ledgers.

The total of the checks issued on December 2 was recorded on the daily bank statement, and the balance was extended.

December 3

Received the following invoices:

National Electrical Company, City; light fixtures, $345; terms, December 2 — 2/10, n/30.

Southern Supply Company, City; pipe fittings, $232.48; terms, December 3 — 2/10, n/30.

Bendix Office Supplies Company, City; office supplies, $42.19; terms, December 3 — n/30.

As the invoices were received, they were numbered consecutively, beginning with No. 649, and were recorded in the invoice register. Check marks were placed in the check column following the amounts shown in the Accounts Payable credit column to indicate that the invoices had been posted to the appropriate creditor accounts in the accounts payable ledger. Invoices were also used to record relevant information on the inventory record cards.

December 4

Issued Check No. 646 for $348.98 to National Electrical Company in payment of its November 27 invoice for $356.10 less 2 percent discount.

Received invoice from Eastern Supply Company, City; electric wire, $245.18; terms, December 3 − 2/10, n/30; shipped directly to McDonald Construction Company, Monroe, freight collect.

Because of the warehouse limitations of Bailey and Brown, they do not stock the complete line of products carried by their suppliers. The above shipment of wire was of a special type which is not often requested. In such cases, Bailey and Brown instruct the supplier to bill them and ship the merchandise to the indicated address. Upon receipt of the invoice, the accountant for Bailey and Brown will post the invoice to the accounts payable ledger and then bill the customer (McDonald Construction Company) for the purchase.

Made the following sales on account:

No. 222: Anderson Builders, City; electrical supplies, $132.14; terms, 2/10, n/30.
No. 223: Normal Hardware, City; plumbing fittings, $243; terms, 2/10, n/30.

December 5

Made the following sales on account:

No. 224: McDonald Construction Company, Monroe; electric wire, $325; terms, 2/10, n/30; shipped directly from factory (see invoice of December 3 from Eastern Supply Company).
No. 225: O. B. Smith, City; pipe, $23; terms, 2/10, n/30.

December 6

Made the following cash sales:

No. 343: T. C. Owens; pipe fittings, $242.
No. 344: Moore Hardware; electrical supplies, $389.60.
No. 345: Benjimen Builders, plumbing supplies, $145.

At the close of each business day, the carbon copies of the cash sales tickets are analyzed to determine the total sales by department. An entry is then made in the cash receipts record debiting Bank and crediting the departments for the appropriate amounts.

Issued Check No. 647 for $182.14 to E-Z Drain Manufacturing Company in payment for invoice of November 28 for $185.85 less 2 percent discount.

End-of-the-Week Accounting Procedures

1. Totaled the amount columns in the invoice register, sales register, cash receipts record, general journal, and record of checks drawn, and proved the footings.

2. Finished individual postings from books of original entry to the general and operating expense ledger accounts.

3. Proved the bank balance as follows:

Balance, December 1	$ 8,425.16
Add: Total receipts December 1–6 (cash receipts record)	1,584.36
Total	$10,009.52
Less: Checks issued December 1–6 (record of checks drawn)	1,471.30
Balance, December 6	$ 8,538.22

(Note balance of daily bank statement—December 6.)

December 8

Received a check for $482.33 from George Glass (plumber) for merchandise sold on November 29 amounting to $492.17, less 2 percent discount.

Made the following sales on account:

No. 226: Farmers Hardware, Winterville; plumbing supplies, $389.05; terms, 2/10, n/30.

No. 227: Peoples Hardware, City; electrical supplies, $345.60; postage, $4.84; terms, 2/10, n/30.

No. 228: Fred Smith (electrician), City; wire, fuse box, $143.18; terms, 2/10, n/30.

In recording Sales Invoice No. 227, the postage was charged to the Peoples Hardware account and credited to Postage Stamps, Account No. 153. In posting to the accounts receivable ledger, the amount of merchandise sold, $345.60, was entered on one line and the prepaid postage of $4.84 was entered on the next line.

Issued Check No. 648 for $315.77 to the Atlantic Manufacturing Company in payment of November 29 invoice for $322.21 less 2 percent discount.

December 9

Issued Check No. 649 for $415.09 to the Copper Pipe Company in payment of invoice of November 29 for $423.56 less 2 percent discount.

Received the following checks: Sharp Contractors, $652.43, in payment of merchandise sold on December 1 amounting to $665.74 less 2 percent discount; and B. L. Thompson, $66.07, in payment of merchandise sold on December 1 amounting to $67.42 less 2 percent discount.

Issued Credit Memorandum No. 128 to Normal Hardware, $9.83, for pipe returned. Made the following cash sales.

No. 346: J. R. Rynold; plumbing, $112; electrical, $94,88.
No. 347: W. M. Stone; electrical, $194.50.

Made the following petty cash disbursements (petty cash has $100 balance):

Adding machine repairs, $8.50; Voucher No. 84.
Repair on truck, $14.15; Voucher No. 85.

December 10

Issued charge-back Invoice No. 10 to National Electrical Company, $23.75, for electric wire returned; purchased on December 2.

Made the following cash sales:

No. 348: C. B. Clark; plumbing, $188.10.
No. 349: A. C. Maxwell; electrical, $95.08.
No. 350: N. L. Wilson; plumbing, $210.14.

Made the following petty cash disbursements:

Newspaper advertisement, $8.42, Voucher No. 86.
Masking tape, $7.14; Shipping expense, $5.00; and miscellaneous general expense, $2.14. Voucher No. 87.

Made the following sales on account:

No. 229: Sharp Contractors, City; plumbing, $208.88; electrical, $305.95; terms, 2/10, n/30.
No. 230: Quick Contractors, City; electrical, $408.15; terms, 2/10, n/30.

Issued Check No. 650 for $314.82 to the National Electrical Company in payment of balance due on invoice of December 2, $321.25 less 2 percent discount.

In order to determine the amount due the National Electrical Company, it is necessary to refer to the accounts payable ledger. The amount payable was determined by making the following calculations:

Invoice of December 2	$345.00
Less: Merchandise returned on December 10	23.75
Amount subject to discount	$321.25
Less: 2% discount	6.43
Amount Due	$314.82

Received the following invoices:

Republic Electrical Company, Atlanta; electrical supplies, $308.14; terms, December 9 — 2/10, n/30.

Atlantic Manufacturing Company, Boston; pipe fittings, $440.15; terms, December 8 — 2/10, n/30.

Peters Supply Company, City; advertising supplies, $52.80; terms, December 10 — 2/10, n/30.

Butler & Sons Inc., City; store supplies, $18; terms, December 10 — 2/10 n/30.

December 11

Issued the following checks:

No. 651: Southern Supply Company; $227.83 in payment of December 3 invoice for $232.48 less 2 percent discount.

No. 652: Randall Company; $95 in payment of December garage rent (due by 15th).

No. 653: $10 payable to Postage; cashed check at bank and purchased stamps.

Made the following petty cash disbursements:

Shipping labels, $6.42; Voucher No. 88.
Telephone bill, $18; Voucher No. 89.
Water bill, $6; Voucher No. 90.

Received the following checks:

Anderson Builders, $129.50, in payment of merchandise sold December 4 amounting to $132.14 less 2 percent discount.

Slow Contractors, $182.14, in payment of merchandise sold on November 15 amounting to $182.14 (no discount).

Made the following cash sales:

No. 351: H. H. Banks; electrical, $170.45.
No. 352: Blank Hardware; electrical, $232.18.
No. 353: T. C. Owens; plumbing, $88.42.

December 12

Received the following invoices:

National Electrical Company, City; light switches, ground wire, $108; terms, December 12 — 2/10, n/30.
Southern Supply Company, City; bathroom fixtures, $304.19; terms, December 11 — 2/10, n/30.
Great Manufacturing Company, New York; plastic pipe and fittings, $208.01; terms, December 10 — 2/10, n/30.

Received a check from Normal Hardware for $238.14 in payment of merchandise sold on December 4 amounting to $243 less 2 percent discount.

December 13

Made the following sales on account:

No. 231: B. L. Thompson, City; electrical, $88.09; terms, 2/10, n/30.
No. 232: Anderson Builders, City; wire, $143.25; terms, 2/10, n/30.
No. 233: Green Plumbing Company, City; plumbing supplies, $56.70; terms, 2/10, n/30.

Made the following cash sales:

No. 354: O. R. Blair; plumbing, $53.09.
No. 355: H. B. Simpson; electrical, $64.44.

End-of-the-Week Accounting Procedures

1. Totaled the amount columns in the invoice register, sales register, cash receipts record, petty cash disbursements record, general journal, and record of checks drawn, and proved the footings.
2. Finished individual postings from books of original entry to the general and operating expense ledger accounts.
3. Proved the bank balance as follows:

Balance, December 8 .... $ 8,538.22
Add: Total receipts December 8–13 (cash receipts record) 3,253.89
Total... $11,792.11
Less: Checks issued December 8–13 (record of checks drawn) ... 1,378.51
Balance, December 13... $10,413.60

(Note balance of daily bank statement — December 13.)

December 15

Made a petty cash disbursement of $2.65 for adding machine tape — store, Voucher No. 91.

Received invoice from Owens Equipment Company for cost of new typewriter, $300, less trade-in allowance for exchange of old typewriter, $25; terms, December 14 — n/30.

The cost of the old typewriter was $125. Because the group method of depreciation is used, the accumulated depreciation account must be charged with the cost of the old typewriter less the $25 trade-in allowance. The transaction was recorded by debiting Office Equipment, Account No. 170, for $300, the cost of the new typewriter; by debiting Accumulated Depreciation — Office Equipment, Account No. 171, for $100, the difference between the cost and the trade-in allowance on the old typewriter; by crediting Office Equipment, Account No. 170, for $125, the cost of the old typewriter; and by crediting Accounts Payable, Account No. 250, for $275 (balance due on new typewriter).

Discounted note from Able Contractors for $400 at the National Bank at 7 percent and deposited the proceeds which amounted to $401.53. The note had been held since November 25 (20 days).

Clipped interest coupons amounting to $25 from the government bonds and deposited them in the National Bank.

Issued Check No. 654 payable to Payroll for $1,549.

Bailey and Brown pay their employees on the 15th and the last day of each month. Employee wages and salaries are subject to the following taxes and contribution requirements:

1. Federal Insurance Contribution Act — old-age benefits and hospital insurance.
2. Federal Unemployment Tax Act — unemployment insurance.
3. State unemployment compensation fund.
4. Federal income tax.

In addition to the above deductions, Bailey and Brown have agreed that they are to receive a monthly salary of $900, payable semimonthly. Although the partners' salaries are treated as a business expense, they do not represent "wages" as stated in the social security and income tax laws. Therefore, they are not subject to the above deductions. Partnership earnings will be reported on each partner's individual tax return and taxed accordingly.

At the end of each pay period, the payroll statement is prepared:

Payroll Statement December 1–December 15				
	Deductions			
Classification	Gross Earnings	F.I.C.A. Taxes	Federal Income Taxes	Net Amount Payable
Office salaries	$ 275.00	$12.38	$24.19	$ 238.43
Store clerk—salaries	250.00	11.25	19.42	219.33
Truck driver—wages	215.00	9.68	14.08	191.24
Partners' salaries:				
M. O. Brown	450.00	None	None	450.00
W. E. Bailey	450.00	None	None	450.00
	$1,640.00	$33.31	$57.69	$1,549.00

Employer's payroll taxes:
F.I.C.A. taxes $33.31
Unemployment compensation taxes:
    State unemployment taxes...................... $22.20
    F.U.T.A. taxes.. 2.96   25.16
        Total.. $58.47

A check payable to Payroll was prepared and cashed at the National Bank. Currency in the proper denominations to meet individual payroll requirements was obtained. The accountant deposited the salaries of Bailey and Brown in their respective bank accounts as instructed and provided them with duplicate deposit slips.

The payroll check was entered in the record of checks drawn by debiting the proper payroll accounts and crediting the proper liability accounts for deductions and by crediting the bank account for the net payroll amount. The payroll taxes on the employer are recorded in the general journal by debiting Payroll Taxes Expense, Account No. 6131, and by crediting the appropriate liability accounts.

Issued Check No. 655 for $248.62 to the National Bank in payment of the following taxes (the National Bank is a U.S. depository).

Employees' federal income taxes
    (withheld during November).. $115.38
On employee (withheld during November) $66.62
On employer... 66.62   133.24
    Total.. $248.62

Discarded desk in storage room. Desk was included in assets being depreciated on a group basis. Original cost was $65. The transaction was recorded by debiting Accumulated Depreciation—Store Equipment, Account No. 161, and by crediting Store Equipment, Account No. 160, for $65.

After deciding that the $20 owed by J. J. Clark was uncollectible, Bailey and Brown decided to write off the account. The entry was recorded by debiting Allowance for Doubtful Accounts, Account No. 131, and by crediting Accounts Receivable, Account No. 130.

Issued Credit Memorandum No. 129 to B. L. Thompson for electrical supplies returned. Credit amounted to $10.39.

(Transactions between December 15 and December 31 have been omitted.)

December 31

Received the following invoices:

National Electrical Company, City; electrical supplies, $112.14; terms, December 30—2/10, n/30.

Chattanooga Marble Company, Chattanooga; marble sink tops, $348.49; terms, December 29—2/10, n/30.

Made the following sales on account:

No. 250: McDonald Construction Company, Monroe; electrical, $215; terms, 2/10, n/30.

No. 251: Sturdy Builders, City; drain pipe, $88.52; terms, 2/10, n/30.

Made the following cash sales:

No. 376: A. A. Adams; plumbing, $214.99.
No. 357: O. J. Rich; plumbing, $175.50.
No. 378: J & J Hardware; plumbing, $278.18.

Made a petty cash disbursement of $1.25 for package received with postage due. Voucher No. 95 (charge to Account No. 6129).

Issued the following checks:

No. 667: Southern Supply Company; $184 in payment of December 23 invoice for $187.75 less 2 percent discount.

No. 668: West Manufacturing Company, $118.18 in payment of December 22 invoice for $120.59 less 2 percent discount.

No. 669: Industrial Supply Company, $42. Cash purchase of two dollies for use in store and on delivery truck.

No. 670: Payroll, $1,549. Payroll is the same as for the first half of the month.

No. 671: $92.53 payable to Petty Cash to reimburse the petty cash fund. December petty cash disbursements are as follows:

December Petty Cash Disbursements

Account No.	Account Title	Amount
6105	Advertising expense	$ 8.42
6107	Truck repairs expense	14.15
6109	Shipping expense	5.00
6114	Store supplies expense	2.65
6117	Miscellaneous selling expense	15.32
6123	Power and water expense	6.00
6124	Telephone expense	18.00
6129	Postage expense (administrative)	1.25
6133	Miscellaneous general expense	21.74
	Total disbursements	$92.53

Received the following checks:

Quick Contractors, $408.15, in payment of merchandise sold on December 10 amounting to $408.15.

Fred Smith, $133.50, in payment of merchandise sold on December 22 amounting to $136.22 less 2 percent discount.

End-of-the-Month Accounting Procedures

1. Proved the books of original entry and petty cash disbursements record by footing the amount columns and comparing totals.

2. Proved the bank balance as shown below:

Balance, December 1	$ 8,425.16
Add: Total receipts December 1–31 (cash receipts record)	9,474.99
Total	$17,900.15
Less: Checks issued December 1–31 (record of checks drawn)	7,633.14
Balance, December 31	$10,267.01

(Note balance of daily bank statement—December 31.)

3. Finished postings from books of original entry to the general and operating expense ledger accounts.

4. Ruled all amount columns in books of original entry.

5. Posted totals of the appropriate columns of the books of original entry to the general ledger accounts.

6. Prepared trial balance of general ledger accounts.

7. Prepared schedules of accounts receivable, accounts payable, and operating expenses.

Steps 6 and 7 would ordinarily be carried out at the end of each month. Since this is the end of the year for Bailey and Brown, additional procedures will be performed. The trial balance and schedule of operating expenses will be used to prepare worksheets to aid in preparation of financial statements for the year ending December 31.

The additional procedures necessary to prepare financial statements will be taken up in the following chapter.

GLOSSARY

Book of minutes   a record book in which actions taken at shareholders' and the board of directors' meetings are recorded.

Daily bank statement   a supplementary record which keeps track of an enterprise's bank balance on a daily basis.

Inventory record   a supplementary record used in inventory control. It is particularly useful in determining physical inventory on hand when preparing interim financial statements.

Schedule of accounts payable   a list of all creditors' accounts found in the subsidiary accounts payable ledger. Its total should equal the Accounts Payable control account balance.

Schedule of accounts receivable   a list of all customer accounts found in the accounts receivable subsidiary ledger. Its total should equal the Accounts Receivable control account balance.

Shareholders' ledger   a subsidiary ledger controlled by the capital stock account which shows the number of shares of stock held by each stockholder at any time.

Temporary investments   investments which will be converted into cash during the normal operating cycle of the business. Since they are held on a short-term basis, they are classified as current assets on the statement of financial position.

Wholesale merchandising enterprise   an enterprise which purchases products directly from manufacturers and importers and then sells them to retailers who in turn sell them to individual customers.

QUESTIONS AND EXERCISES

1. Describe the operation of a wholesale merchandising enterprise in the chain of product distribution.

2. What factors affect the accounting records to be used in a wholesale merchandising enterprise?

3. What impact does the owner's equity structure of a business have on the accounts used?

4. What advantages can be realized by functionally dividing the accounting activities among the accounting employees?

5. List several books of original entry, books of final entry, and supplementary records that might be kept by a wholesale merchandising business.

6. When and why might a wholesale business buy U.S. treasury bills? How would the treasury bills be classified as far as financial statements are concerned?

7. What are sales discounts? How are they treated on financial statements?

8. What are some advantages of maintaining an inventory record?

9. On March 1, Ailene Barker purchased merchandise from Wistuff's Wholesale Company. The gross amount of the invoice was $950, and payment terms were 2/10, n/30. On March 9, Wistuff's Wholesale received a check from Ms. Barker. What should be the amount of the check is Ms. Barker wishes to take advantage of the cash discount?

10. The Geiger Wholesale Company uses the group method for depreciating long-lived assets. During the month of March, it discarded a typewriter. What general journal entry should be made to record the disposal of the asset if its original cost was $175.

PROBLEMS

18-1. Yogi and Endora Barechi operate a wholesale furniture and appliance store. During the month of January 1978, the Barechis completed the following selected transactions (sales on account):

1978
Jan. 5 No. 300: Broadman Furniture Company, City; bookcases, $250; square commodes, $500; hexagonal commodes, $250; cocktail tables, $350; terms, 2/20, n/60.

6 No. 301: Rose's Appliances, Volney; toasters, $50; irons, $125; electric fry pans, $150; terms, 2/10, n/30.

7 No. 302: Agarwall Company, Hastings; vacuum cleaners, $640; sewing machines, $740; terms, 2/20, n/60.

8 No. 303: Wheless, Incorporated, Lincoln; percolators, $130; electric heaters, $100; table lamps, $315; terms, 2/10, n/30.

12 No. 304: Doug Hogan Enterprises, Adel; carpet shampooers, $160; dishwashers, $1,120; ice makers, $1,800; terms, 2/20, n/90.

13 No. 305: Trinity & Sons, Thomson; microwave ovens, $2,000; terms, 2/20, n/60.

15 No. 306: Pitts Furniture Store, Conway; sofas, $750; chairs, $720; end tables, $480; coffee table, $260; terms, 2/20, n/60.

16 No. 307: Roger's Store, Canton; dinette sets, $1,250; pedestal tables, $250; terms, 2/20, n/60.

17 No. 308: Lassie's, Cayuga; canopy beds, $186, trundle beds, $564; terms, 2/20, n/60.

20 No. 309: Rhonda's Showcase, Harris; dresses, $330; five-drawer chests, $315; bunk beds, $360; terms, 2/20, n/60.

21 No. 310: Phyliss & Sons, Brevard; oval mirrors, $102; rectangular mirrors, $160; terms, 2/10, n/30.

Jan. 23 No. 311: Broadman Furniture Company, City; bookcases, $150; end tables, $201; terms, 2/10, n/30.

26 No. 312: Brannon Brothers, City; panel beds, $245; powder tables, $145; dressers, $312; terms, 2/20, n/60.

28 No. 313: Day Sisters, City; waffle irons, $80; electric can openers, $90; meat grinders, $120; terms, 2/10, n/30.

29 No. 314: Estes Company, Pelham; portable ovens, $280; blenders, $100; electric mixers, $144; terms, 2/10, n/30.

31 No. 315: Debbie's Place, Americus; nightstands, $48; roll-top desks, $550; desk chairs, $45; Boston rockers, $105; terms, 2/20, n/60.

Required:

1. Record the transactions in a sales register like the one shown in Illustration 18–1. (have columns for (1) furniture and (2) appliances).
2. Foot and rule the sales register.

18–2. Doug Head and Chris Legg have just begun operating a wholesale store that sells power tools and lawn and garden equipment. During the first month of operation, Head and Legg completed the following selected transactions:

1978

Mar. 1 Doug Head invested $10,000 cash in the business. Chris Legg invested $20,000 cash and office equipment amounting to $500 in the business. Issued Check No. 101 to Andrews Realty Company in payment of the March rent, $300.

2 Issued Check No. 102 for $75 to Jordan's Newspaper for advertisements. Issued Check No. 103 to Handy Equipment Company for store equipment, $900.

3 Issued Check No. 104 to Garden Manufacturing Company for garden and lawn equipment, $2,000. Issued Check No. 105 to Boss Manufacturing Company for power tools, $1,500.

4 Issued Check No. 106 to Smith Supply Company for office supplies, $300, and store supplies, $400.
Made the following cash sales:
No. 1: Hayley Kent; chain saw, $75.
No. 2: Kenneth Corley; lawn mower, $150.

5 Made the following cash sales:
No. 3: Gordy Chatfield, drill press, $60.
No. 4: Donald Wilson; tools, $60.

8 Made the following cash sales:
No. 5: Helen Johns; garden equipment, $500.
No. 6: Furber Company; power tools, $350.
Issued Check No. 107 to U.S. Post Office for stamps, $10.

9 Issued the following checks:
No. 108: Rawlins Equipment Company for office equipment, $600.
No. 109: Garden Manufacturing Company for garden and lawn equipment, $600.

Mar. 10   Made the following cash sales:
      No. 7: Bob Edenfield; chain saws; $120.
      No. 8: John Stevens; garden equipment, $405.
      No. 9: Sarah Butler; garden equipment, $225.

    11   Received the following check: Della's, Incorporated, $441 for merchandise sold on March 5 amounting to $450 less 2 percent discount.
        Issued the following check: No. 110 for $627.20 to Niemi's Power Tools for its invoice of March 2 amounting to $640 less 2 percent discount.

    12   Received the following checks: Jan Akins, $242.50, for merchandise sold on March 5 amounting to $250 less 3 percent discount; and Lewis Alexander, $349.20, for merchandise sold on March 5 amounting to $360 less 3 percent discount.

    15   Issued the following checks:
      No. 111: $150 to WKTV for television advertisements.
      No. 112: $690.90 to Hutto Manufacturers for its May 5 invoice amounting to $705 less 2 percent discount.

    16   Made the following cash sales:
      No. 10: Rhett Gable; power tools, $220.
      No. 11: Clark Butler; garden equipment, $400.
        Received a check for $300 from Kay Cassell for merchandise sold on March 5 amounting to $300.

    17   Issued the following checks:
      No. 113: $1,018.50 to Meeker's Manufacturing Company for its March 8 invoice amounting to $1,050 less 3 percent discount.
      No. 114: $150 to WZKT radio station for advertisements

    18   Made the following cash sales:
      No. 12: Diane Bone; sabre saws, $66.
      No. 13: Buck Birdsong; circular saws, $150.
        Received the following check: Tina Bridges, $465.60 for merchandise sold on March 8 amounting to $480 less 3 percent discount.

    19   Issued the following checks:
      No. 115: $2,425 to Sheryl's Haven for its March 9 invoice amounting to $2,500 less 3 percent discount.
      No. 116: $75 to the United Fund.

    22   Received a check for $500 from Marilyn West for merchandise sold on March 8 amounting to $500. Issued a check (No. 117) to Luke & Sons for $1,400 for its March 8 invoice amounting to $1,400.

    23   Made the following cash sales:
      No. 14: Sunit Pathak; chain saws, $85.
      No. 15: Satish Mehra; power tools, $660.

    24   Made the following cash sale:
      No. 16: Samir Akruk; garden equipment, $474.

    25   Received a check for $275 from Elaine Halsey for merchandise sold on March 10 amounting to $275. Issued Check No. 118 for $65 to the March of Dimes.

Mar. 26 Received the following checks: Carolyn Wood, $171.50 for merchandise sold on March 16 amounting to $175 less 2 percent discount; and Bryan Scoggins, $220.50, for merchandise sold on March 16 amounting to $225 less 2 percent discount.

29 Issued the following check:

No. 119: Garden Manufacturing Company for lawn and garden equipment, $800.

Made the following cash sale:

No. 17: Wayne Stout; garden hoses, $15.

30 Received a check for $994.25 from Ellerbee Company for merchandise sold on March 22 amounting to $1,025 less 3 percent discount.

31 Made the following cash sales:

No. 18: Gayla Eubanks; lawn mowers, $400.

No. 19: Debra Boggs; garden equipment, $217.

No. 20: Ralph Edwards; power tools, $185.

Issued Check No. 120 to Boss Manufacturing Company for power tools, $900.

Required:

1. Record the transactions in the appropriate book of original entry (cash receipts record or record of checks drawn).
2. Prepare a daily bank statement.
3. Foot and rule the books of original entry on March 31, 1978.
4. Prove the bank balance on March 31, 1978.

HEAD AND LEGG

Chart of Accounts (Partial)

Account No.   *Account Title*

Account No.	Account Title
101	Bank
110	Accounts Receivable
150	Office Equipment
160	Store Equipment
210	Accounts Payable
300	Doug Head, Capital
310	Chris Legg, Capital
401	Sales — Tools
411	Sales — Lawn and Garden Equipment
415	Sales Discounts
501	Purchases — Tools
511	Purchases — Lawn and Garden Equipment
515	Purchases Discounts
601	Rent Expense
607	Advertising Expense
610	Office Supplies Expense
612	Store Supplies Expense
618	Postage Expense
690	Charitable Contributions Expense

18–3. James R. Buchanan runs a wholesale chemical supply store. On April 1, 1978, Mr. Buchanan created a $150 petty cash fund. During April the following disbursements were made from the petty cash fund:

1978
Apr. 3 Voucher No. 1: truck repairs, $20.
       6 Voucher No. 2: water bill, $12.
       8 Voucher No. 3: newspaper advertisement, $10.
     10 Voucher No. 4: telephone bill, $15.
     13 Voucher No. 5: postage stamps, $8.
     15 Voucher No. 6: truck repairs, $8.
     19 Voucher No. 7: electricity bill, $19.
     23 Voucher No. 8: newspaper advertisement, $10.
     26 Voucher No. 9: adding machine repairs, $7.
     29 Voucher No. 10: typewriter repairs, $11.
     30 Voucher No. 11: postage stamps, $5.

The fund was replenished on April 30, 1978.

Required:

1. Prepare the general journal entry to establish the petty cash fund on April 1, 1978.
2. Record the above transactions in a petty cash disbursements record. The charges should be distributed among the following accounts:

        6101 Truck Repairs Expense
        6106 Power and Water Expense
        6112 Advertising Expense
        6118 Telephone Expense
        6125 Miscellaneous Expense
        6130 Postage Expense

3. Total the amount columns and prove the footings.
4. Prepare a general journal entry to replenish the fund on April 30, 1978.

The following chart of accounts is to be used in Problems 4 and 5:

LEONARD'S WHOLESALE TV AND RADIO SUPPLIES
AND PARTS
General Ledger Chart of Accounts

Assets:

101	Bank of Upson
102	Petty Cash
111	Marketable Securities
121	Accounts Receivable
122	Allowing for Doubtful Accounts
123	Notes Receivable
124	Accrued Interest Receivable
131	Merchandise Inventory — TV Supplies and Parts
132	Merchandise Inventory — Radio Supplies and Parts
141	Store Supplies
142	Office Supplies
143	Unexpired Insurance
151	Store Equipment
152	Accumulated Department — Store Equipment
153	Office Equipment
154	Accumulated Department — Office Equipment
155	Delivery Truck
156	Accumulated Department — Delivery Truck

Liabilities:

201	F.I.C.A. Taxes Payable
202	F.U.T.A. Taxes Payable
203	Income Taxes Payable — Federal Employee
204	State Unemployment Taxes Payable
211	Accounts Payable
212	Notes Payable
213	Accrued Interest Payable

Owner's Equity:

301	G. R. Leonard, Capital
302	G. R. Leonard, Drawing
311	Expense and Revenue Summary

Revenues:

401	Sales — TV Supplies and Parts
402	Sales Returns and Allowances — TV Supplies and Parts
411	Sales — Radio Supplies and Parts
412	Sales Returns and Allowances — Radio Supplies and Parts
421	Sales Discounts

Cost of Goods Sold:

501	Purchases — TV Supplies and Parts
502	Purchase Returns and Allowances — TV Supplies and Parts
511	Purchases — Radio Supplies and Parts
512	Purchase Returns and Allowances — Radio Supplies and Parts
521	Purchases Discounts
531	Transportation-In — TV Supplies and Parts
541	Transportation-In — Radio Supplies and Parts
551	Cost of Goods Sold — TV Supplies and Parts
561	Cost of Goods Sold — Radio Supplies and Parts
601	Operating Expenses
701	Interest Revenue
801	Interest Expense
811	Collection Expense

18-4. G. R. Leonard operates a wholesale store which sells TV and radio supplies and parts to retail stores. During the month of June 1978, Leonard completed the following purchases and sales transactions:

1978
June 1 Sales on account:
    No. 106: Conyers Repair Shop, City; TV parts, $206; terms, 2/10, n/30.
    No. 107: Lance Denall, City; radio parts, $122; terms, 2/10, n/30.

  2 Sales on account:
    No. 108: Clay Dennis, Comer; TV supplies and parts, $400; terms, 2/10, n/30.
    Received the following invoices:
    No. 75: Helen Manufacturing Company, City; radio parts, $345; terms, June 2 − 2/10, n/30.
    No. 76: Folk Manufacturing Company, Macon; TV parts, $690; terms, May 29 − 2/10, n/60.
    No. 77: Reeves Supply Company, City; office supplies, $85; terms, June 2 − 2/10, n/30.

  3 Received the following invoice:
    No. 78: Haywood TV Company, Columbus; TV supplies and parts, $850; terms, May 28 − 2/10, n/60.

  4 Sales on account:
    No. 109: Love's Repair Service, City; radio parts and supplies, $110; terms, 2/10, n/30.

  8 Sales on account:
    No. 110: Lynn Eden, City; radio parts, $80; terms, 2/10, n/30.
    No. 111: Henry Lovett, Monroe; TV parts and supplies, $175; terms, 2/10, n/30.

  9 Sales on account:
    No. 112: Huckleberry's Repair Company, Winder; radio parts and supplies, $125, and TV parts and supplies, $200; terms, 2/10, n/30.

 10 Received the following invoice:
    No. 79: Shaw's Equipment Company, Albany; typewriter, $300; terms, June 7 − 2/10, n/30.

 11 Received the following invoices:
    No. 80: Lloyd's Company, City; store supplies, $60; terms, June 11 − n/30.
    No. 81: Frank Baker, City; calculator, $90; terms, June 11 − n/30.

 15 Sales on account:
    No. 113: Kathy Ryals, Bogart; radio supplies, $50; terms, n/30.
    No. 114: Rhonda Hilley, Byron; radio supplies, $80, and TV supplies, $125; terms, 2/10, n/30.

 16 Sales on account:
    No. 115: Mike's Repair Shop, Athens; TV parts and supplies, $290; terms, 2/10, n/30.

No. 116: Buford's Hardware Store, City; radio parts and supplies, $60; terms, n/30.

June 17 Sales on account:

No. 117: Yung's Supply Store, Augusta; radio supplies and parts, $160; terms, 2/10, n/30.

18 Received the following invoice:

No. 82: Calley's Equipment Company, City; store equipment, $200; terms, June 18 − 2/10, n/30.

22 Received the following invoices:

No. 83: Houston Supplies, Cordele; radio supplies and parts, $560; terms, June 18 − 2/10, n/60.

No. 84: Helen Manufacturing Company, City; radio supplies and parts, $300; terms, June 22 − 2/10, n/30.

No. 85: Roscoe's Radio Company, Forsyth; radio parts, $200; terms, June 19 − 2/10, n/30.

23 Sales on account:

No. 118: Buckley's Repair Shop, Shady Dale; TV supplies and parts, $150; terms, 2/10, n/30.

24 Sales on account:

No. 119: Michael Ware, City; TV parts, $50; terms, n/30.

No. 120: Phil Masten Company, Cairo; TV supplies and parts, $220; terms, 2/10, n/30.

Received the following invoices:

No. 86: Bobo Equipment Company, New York; multiple-purpose accounting machine, $1,800; terms, June 18 − 2/20, n/120.

No. 87: Lee Manufacturing Company, Dallas; radio supplies and parts, $400 and TV supplies and parts, $500; terms, June 20 − 2/10, n/90.

25 Sales on account:

No. 121: David Trice, Thomaston; radio supplies and parts, $80; terms, n/30.

29 Received the following invoices:

No. 88: Folk Manufacturing Company, Macon; TV parts, $400; terms, June 26 − 2/10, n/30.

No. 89: Bates TV Company, Manchester; TV supplies and parts, $500; terms, June 26 − 2/10, n/30.

No. 90: T & R Manufacturing Company, Atlanta; TV parts, $250, and radio parts, $300; terms, June 27 − 2/10, n/30.

30 Sales on account:

No. 122: George Wells, Bishop; radio supplies, $75; terms, n/30.

No. 123: Heidi Kiger, Valdosta; TV supplies and parts, $325; terms, 2/10, n/30.

Received the following invoices:

No. 91: Huxley's, Columbus; radio supplies and parts, $510; terms, June 26 − 2/10, n/60.

No. 92: Windal's, Moultrie; TV supplies, $250; terms, June 27 − 2/10, n/30.

Required:

1. Prepare a sales register like the one shown in Illustration 18–1 for the month of June.
2. Prepare an invoice register like the one shown in Illustration 18–3 for the month of June.
3. Foot and rule the registers prepared in 1 and 2 above.

18–5. G. R. Leonard (see Problem 4) completed the following selected transactions during the month of June 1978:

1978

June 1 Issued Check No. 708 for $300 to Ruffin Realty Company for the June rent (Account No. 6010). Issued Check No. 709 for $240.10 to Deen Manufacturers in payment of its May 22 invoice for $245 less 2 percent discount.

2 Made the following cash sales:

No. 350: Leroy Allen; radio parts, $105.

No. 351: James Kellum; TV parts, $210.

No. 352: Charles Ford; radio supplies, $96.

Issued Check No. 710 for $388 to Cordell Equipment Company in payment of its May 23 invoice for $400 less 3 percent discount.

3 Received a check for $318.50 from Carl Franko for merchandise sold on May 27 amounting to $325 less 2 percent discount.

Made the following cash sales:

No. 353: Andy Melton; TV parts, $400.

No. 354: Stephen T. Hayes; TV parts, $160.

4 Issued Check No. 711 for $666.40 to Mackey's Shack in payment of its May 26 invoice for $680 less 2 percent discount. Received a check for $176.40 from Troy Milsap for merchandise sold on May 27 amounting to $180 less 2 percent discount.

8 Made the following cash sales:

No. 355: Joe Garland; radio parts, $50 and television parts, $250.

No. 356: Terrell Wilson; TV supplies, $75.

9 Issued the following checks:

No. 712: $171.50 to Margot's Supply Company in payment of its May 31 invoice for $175 less 2 percent discount.

No. 713: $426.80 to Binet Manufacturing Company in payment of its May 31 invoice for $440 less 3 percent discount.

Made the following cash sale:

No. 357: Martin King; radio parts, $105.

10 Received the following checks: Conyers Repair Shop, $201.88, for merchandise sold on June 1 amounting to $206 less 2 percent discount; and Clay Dennis, $392, for merchandise sold on June 2 amounting to $400 less 2 percent discount.

Issued the following checks:

No. 714: $690 to Folk Manufacturing Company in payment of its May 29 invoice.

No. 715: $850 to Haywood TV Company in payment of its May 28 invoice.

June 11 Issued the following checks:

No. 716: $50 to Sumter Journal for local newspaper advertisements (Account No. 6015).

No. 717: $212 to Hobo's Motor Company for repairs to the delivery truck (Account No. 6019).

Received the following checks: Lance Denall, $119.56, for merchandise sold on June 1 amounting to $122 less 2 percent discount; and Kelly Potts, $218, for merchandise sold on May 15 amounting to $218.

15 Received the following check: Love's Repair Service, $110 for merchandise sold on June 4 amounting to $110.

Issued the following checks:

No. 718: $345 to Helen Manufacturing Company in payment of its June 2 invoice.

No. 719: $85 to Reeves Supply Company in payment of its June 2 invoice.

16 Issued the following check:

No. 720: $294 to Shaw's Equipment Company in payment of its June 7 invoice for $300 less 2 percent discount.

17 Made the following cash sales:

No. 358: Richard Jones: TV parts, $300.

No. 359: Barbra Ronstall; radio parts, $175.

Issued the following checks:

No. 721: $60 to Lloyd's Company in payment of its June 11 invoice.

No. 722: $90 to Frank Baker in payment of his June 11 invoice.

18 Received the following checks: Lynn Eden, $78.40, for merchandise sold on June 8 amounting to $80 less 2 percent discount; and Henry Lovett, $171.50, for merchandise sold on June 8 amounting to $175 less 2 percent discount.

18 Huckleberry's Repair Company, $312, for merchandise sold on June 9 amounting to $325 less 4 percent discount.

Issued the following check:

No. 723: $125 to Southern Independence Telephone Company for the telephone bill (Account No. 6020).

22 Made the following cash sales:

No. 360: Bill Brinkley; TV supplies, $85.

No. 361: Scott Alexander; radio parts, $75.

No. 362: Debbie Bell; radio parts, $50.

23 Received the following check: Kathy Ryals, $50 for merchandise sold on June 15.

Made the following cash sale:

No. 363: Tim Wheless; TV parts, $75.

24 Issued the following checks:

No. 724: $196 to Calley's Equipment Company in payment of its June 18 invoice for $200 less 2 percent discount.

No. 725: $300 to G. R. Leonard for personal expenses.

Received the following checks: Rhonda Hilley, $122.50, for merchandise sold on June 15 amounting to $125 less 2 percent discount; and Mike's Repair Shop, $284.20, for merchandise sold on June 16 amounting to $290 less 2 percent discount.

June 25   Received the following checks: Buford's Hardware Store, $60, for merchandise sold on June 16; and Yung's Supply Store, $156.80, for merchandise sold on June 17 amounting to $160 less 2 percent discount.

25   Issued the following check:

No. 726: $548.80 to Houston Supplies in payment of its June 18 invoice for $560 less 2 percent discount.

29   Issued the following check:

No. 727: $196 to Roscoe's Radio Company in payment of its June 19 invoice for $200 less 2 percent discount.

30   Issued the following check:

No. 728: $882 to Lee Manufacturing Company for its June 20 invoice of $900 less 2 percent discount.

Made the following cash sales:

No. 364: Byron Wells; TV supplies and parts, $206 and radio parts, $44.

No. 365: Satish Mehra; radio parts, $125.

Paid the payroll for the month of June with Check Nos. 729, 730, and 731. Payroll data is shown below:

Gross earnings		$2,400.00
Less: F.I.C.A. Tax	140.00	
Federal income tax.................	400.00	540.40
Net Earnings........................		$1,859.60

Check no.	Employee	Net earnings
729	Joseph French	$697.35
730	Faye Smothers....................	603.20
731	Adam Tucker	559.05

The employer's payroll tax expenses are also recorded in the record of checks drawn.

(Salaries Expense—Account No. 6030.)

(Payroll Tax Expense—Account No. 6040.)

F.I.C.A. tax—employer..................	$140.40
F.U.T.A. tax...............................	4.50
State unemployment tax	24.30

Required:

1. Record each of the above transactions in either the cash receipts record or the record of checks drawn, whichever is correct.

2. Prepare a daily bank statement. (Cash balance, May 31, 1978—$6,411.65.)

3. Foot and rule the records prepared in (1) above.
4. Prove the bank balance on June 30, 1978.

18–6. Thomas Cooper and Laura Dooley own and operate C and D Wholesale House. The store is divided into two departments — Department C which sells clothing and Department G which sells groceries. During the month of February 1978, the C and D Wholesale House was involved in the following transactions:

1978
Feb. 2 Issued Check No. 807 to Kendrick Realty Company for the February rent, $400.
Sales on account:
   No. 250: Tiller's Corner Grocery, City; groceries, $500; terms, 2/10, n/30.
   No. 251: Kemp's Variety Shop, City; groceries, $125; clothing, $300; terms, n/30.
   No. 252: Wayne's Market, City; groceries, $250; terms, n/30.
  3 Received a check for $275 from Tim Gowan for merchandise sold on January 6 amounting to $275.
Made the following cash sale:
   No. 519: Goolsby Store; clothing, $275.
  4 Received the following invoices:
   No. 400: Rice Manufacturing Company, Atlanta; clothing, $800; terms, February 2 — 2/10, n/30.
   No. 401: Ridley Brothers, City; groceries, $705; terms, February 4 — 2/10, n/30.
Issued Check No. 808 to Independent Telephone Company for the January phone bill, $150.
  5 Sales on account:
   No. 253: Hood's Clothes, City; clothing, $500; terms, 2/10, n/30.
   No. 254: Ford's Men's Store; clothing, $450; terms, n/30.
  6 Issued the following checks:
   No. 809: $75 to Aubrey's Supply Company for office supplies.
   No. 810: $425 to Fleming Manufacturing Company in payment of its invoice of January 7 amounting to $425.
Made the following cash sales:
   No. 520: Fred Fish; groceries, $300.
   No. 521: Rebecca Fields; clothing, $215.
Received a check for $627.20 from Sikes' Grocery Store for merchandise sold on January 30 amounting to $640 less 2 percent discount.
  9 Received the following invoices:
   No. 402: Griffin Manufacturing Company, Augusta; clothing, $650; terms, February 5 — 2/10, n/30.
   No. 403: Lindsay Equipment Company, Detroit; office equipment, $750; terms, January 31 — 2/20, n/60.

Sales on account:
    No. 255: Dorothy Cavan, City; groceries, $275; terms, n/30.
    No. 256: Julian Liles, City; groceries, $580; terms, 2/10, n/30.
Made the following cash sale:
    No. 522: Patrick Norton, Valdosta, clothing, $330.

Feb. 10   Issued the following checks:
    No. 811: $135 to Nunn Brothers for store supplies.
    No. 812: $427.28 to Seabro Company in payment of its January
    31 invoice of $436 less 2 percent discount.
Received a check for $478.24 from Howard Day for merchandise
sold on January 12 amounting to $478.24.

11   Received the following invoices:
    No. 404: Morrison Foods, Smithville; groceries, $585; terms,
    February 10 − 2/10, n/30.
    No. 405: Henrietta's Cottons, Dallas; clothing, $759; terms,
    February 5 − 2/10, n/30.

12   Issued Check No. 813 for $784 to Rice Manufacturing Company in
payment of its February 2 invoice for $800 less 2 percent discount.
Received a check for $490 from Tiller's Corner Grocery for mer-
chandise sold on February 2 amounting to $500 less 2 percent
discount.

13   Made the following cash sales:
    No. 523: Mark Christo, City; groceries, $239.
    No. 524: Dana Javo, City; clothing, $312.
Issued the following checks:
    No. 814 for $690.90 to Ridley Brothers in payment of its Feb-
    ruary 4 invoice for $705 less 2 percent discount.
    No. 815 for $637 to Griffin Manufacturing Company in pay-
    ment of its February 5 invoice for $650 less 2 percent discount.
    No. 816 for $743.82 to Henrietta's Cottons in payment of its
    February 5 invoice for $759 less 2 percent discount.
Received a check for $490 from Hood's Clothes for merchandise
sold on February 5 amounting to $500 less 2 percent discount.

16   Sales on account:
    No. 257: James Turner, Thomasville; clothing, $650; terms,
    2/10, n/30.
    No. 258: Gerald Pierce, City; clothing, $180; groceries, $410;
    terms, 2/10, n/30.

17   Made the following cash sales:
    No. 525: Willis Hill, Americus; groceries, $267.
    No. 526: Leslie Roper, City; clothing, $342.

18   Received the following invoices.
    No. 406: Corbett's Groceries, City; groceries, $395; terms,
    February 18 − n/30.
    No. 407: Clinton's Clothing Company, Columbus; Clothing,
    $562; terms, February 17 − 2/10, n/30.
Issued Check No. 817 for $735 to Lindsay Equipment Company
    for its January 31 invoice of $750 less 2 percent discount.

Feb. 19 Issued the following checks:

No. 818: $573.30 to Morrison Foods for its February 10 invoice amounting to $585 less 2 percent discount.

No. 819: $55 to Times—Free Press for local newspaper advertising.

Received a check for $568.40 from Julian Liles for merchandise sold on February 9 amounting to $580 less 2 percent discount.

20 Sales on account:

No. 259: Steve Sailors, City; clothing, $702; terms, 2/10, n/30.

No. 260: Jack Trapnell, Leesburg; Groceries, $610; terms, 2/10, n/30.

Received the following invoice:

No. 408: Rice Manufacturing Company, Atlanta; clothing, $700; terms, February 17—2/10, n/30.

23 Received the following checks: Kemp's Variety Shop, $425, for merchandise sold on February 2 amounting to $425; and Wayne's Market, $250, for merchandise sold on February 2 amounting to $250.

Received the following invoice:

No. 409: Ridley Brothers, City; groceries, $911; terms, February 23—2/10, n/30.

24 Made the following cash sales:

No. 527: Kermit & Son, City; groceries, $308.

No. 528: Barbra Reinholt, City; clothing, $509.

25 Received the following checks: Ford's Men's Store, $450, for merchandise sold on February 5 amounting to $450; and Dorothy Cavan, $275, for merchandise sold on February 9 amounting to $275.

26 Received the following checks: James Turner, $637, for merchandise sold on February 16 amounting to $650 less 2 percent discount; and Gerald Pierce, $578.20 for merchandise sold on February 16 amounting to $590 less 2 percent discount.

Issued the following checks:

No. 820: $550.76 to Clinton's Clothing Company for its February 17 invoice of $562 less 2 percent discount.

No. 821: $686 to Rice Manufacturing Company for its February 20 invoice of $700 less 2 percent discount.

27 Issued the following check:

No. 822: $395 to Corbett's Groceries for its February 18 invoice of $395.

Required:

1. Record the transactions in the appropriate book of original entry—invoice register, sales register, cash receipts record, or record of checks drawn.

2. Prepare a daily bank statement for February. The bank balance was $3,417.54 on February 1.

3. Foot and rule the books of original entry.
4. Prepare a proof of the bank balance on February 28, 1978.

C AND D WHOLESALE HOUSE
Chart of Accounts (Partial)

Account No.	*Account Title*
100	Bank
120	Accounts Receivable
140	Store Supplies
142	Office Supplies
150	Store· Equipment
160	Office Equipment
240	Accounts Payable
300	Thomas Cooper, Capital
301	Thomas Cooper, Drawing
310	Laura Dooley, Capital
311	Laura Dooley, Drawing
400	Sales – Department C
410	Sales – Department G
420	Sales Discounts
500	Purchases – Department C
510	Purchases – Department G
520	Purchases Discounts
610	Rent Expense
611	Telephone Expense
612	Advertising Expense

Year-end accounting procedure—
wholesale business
Learning objectives

To obtain a basic understanding of the year-end
accounting procedures necessary to prepare timely
financial statements, the following material is presented
in this chapter:

1. A discussion of the construction and completion
   of summary and supporting work sheets used in the
   preparation of financial statements.
2. A detailed illustration of the adjusting entries
   normally required in the presentation of timely
   financial reports.
3. Journalizing and posting the adjusting and closing
   entries.
4. The reasons for and procedures used in preparing
   a post-closing trial balance.
5. An illustration of the completed earnings statement
   and the statement of financial position.

19

Year-end accounting procedure – wholesale business

Periodic financial reports are prepared to help management and other interested parties to analyze the activities of a particular business. Since preparation of financial statements is the end product of the accounting system, the statements are a primary reason for maintaining accounting records. Statement users will require as a minimum that they be supplied with an earnings statement and a statement of financial position. In order to collect and summarize the information necessary to prepare the statements, a **worksheet** is usually prepared. The worksheet has columns for the year-end trial balance and **adjusting entries.** After the accounts are adjusted, the amounts are extended to the appropriate financial statement columns. When the worksheet is completed, the data required to construct the various financial statements can be taken directly from the worksheet statement columns.

SUMMARY AND SUPPORTING WORKSHEETS

In the previous chapter, the transactions and related accounting procedures for the partnership of Bailey and Brown were illustrated. This chapter will be concerned with construction of year-end worksheets necessary to prepare statements for Bailey and Brown. The discussion will center around the use of a ten-column summary worksheet and a supporting three-column **operating expense worksheet.** The general ledger and operating expense account titles and numbers are the same as those used in the previous chapter (Illustrations 18–6 and 18–7, respectively). The transactions of Bailey and Brown in the previous chapter were for the month of December 1978, and were recorded in the books of original

493

entry and other auxiliary records. The books of original entry were shown as they would appear after posting the transactions to the accounts. It may be assumed that a trial balance was taken upon completion of posting and that the general ledger accounts as well as the controlling and subsidiary ledger accounts were in balance.

Summary worksheet

The summary worksheet used by Bailey and Brown is shown in Illustration 19–1. After the trial balance is taken and the accounts are in balance, a worksheet is prepared. The worksheet provides spaces for each account title and number. All accounts are listed in order by account number except for Expense and Revenue Summary. Account No. 330 is not shown on the worksheet since it is used only in adjusting and closing the accounts. The cost of goods sold accounts (Nos. 560 and 570) are used to combine several account balances into a single amount. The **cost of goods sold** is determined by combining:

1. Beginning inventory.
2. Purchases.
3. Transportation-in.
4. Purchase returns and allowances.
5. Purchases discounts.
6. Ending inventory.

As a part of the adjusting process, these amounts are combined into a single amount which is then extended to the Earnings Statement columns as the cost of goods sold. Because the combination of the above accounts involves several debits and credits, several lines are used on the worksheet for cost of goods sold. After the account balances are entered on the worksheet and shown to be in balance (total debits equal total credits), the worksheet is ready for the necessary adjustments to be made.

Adjustments to determine cost of goods sold. The following entries were used to adjust the inventory and inventory-related accounts to determine the cost of goods sold.

Adjustment (a): The beginning inventory for the plumbing department, $124,314.99, was transferred to Cost of Goods Sold – Plumbing Department by debiting Account No. 560 and by crediting Merchandise Inventory – Plumbing Department, Account No. 140.

Adjustment (b): The beginning inventory for the electrical department, $78,705.10, was transferred to Cost of Goods Sold – Electrical Department by debiting Account No. 570 and by crediting Merchandise Inventory – Electrical Department, Account No. 145.

Adjustment (c): Purchases of the plumbing department amounting to $376,867.25 were transferred to Cost of Goods Sold – Plumbing Department by debiting Account No. 560 and by crediting Purchases— Plumbing Department, Account No. 510.

Adjustment (d): Purchases of the electrical department amounting to $235,334.71, were transferred to Cost of Goods Sold—Electrical Department by debiting Account No. 570 and by crediting Purchases— Electrical Department, Account No. 520.

Adjustment (e): Transportation-in for the plumbing department amounting to $2,563.07 was transferred to Cost of Goods Sold—Plumbing Department by debiting Account No. 560 and by crediting Transportation-In—Plumbing Department, Account No. 540.

Adjustment (f): Transportation-in for the electrical department amounting to $1,218.60 was transferred to Cost of Goods Sold—Electrical Department by debiting Account No. 570 and by crediting Transportation-in—Electrical Department, Account No. 550.

Adjustment (g): Purchase returns and allowances of $1,562.15 for the plumbing department were transferred to the related cost of goods sold account by debiting Purchase Returns and Allowances—Plumbing Department, Account No. 511, and by crediting Cost of Goods Sold— Plumbing Department, Account No. 560.

Adjustment (h): Purchase returns and allowances of $981.03 for the electrical department were transferred to the related cost of goods sold account by debiting Purchase Returns and Allowances—Electrical Department, Account No. 521, and by crediting Cost of Goods Sold— Electrical Department, Account No. 570.

Adjustment (i): During the year, purchases discounts amounting to $10,183.88 were taken. This amount was allocated between the cost of goods sold accounts in relation to the amount of purchases (less purchase returns and allowances) of the two departments. The following schedule was used in determining the allocation of purchases discounts:

Department	Purchases less returns	Percent	Purchases discount	Department allocation
Plumbing	$375,305.10	62	$10,183.88	$ 6,314.01
Electrical	234,353.68	38	10,183.88	3,869.87
	$609,658.78	100		$10,183.88

Based on the above calculations, the purchases discounts were allocated to the cost of goods sold accounts by debiting Purchases Discounts, Account No. 522, for $10,183.88, and by crediting Cost of Goods Sold—Plumbing Department, Account No. 560, for $6,314.01, and Cost of Goods Sold—Electrical Department, Account No. 570, for $3,869.87.

Illustration 19–1

Bailey and Brown
Worksheet
For the Year Ended December 31, 1978

Account	Account Number	Trial Balance Debit	Trial Balance Credit	Adjustments Debit	Adjustments Credit
National Bank	110	10267 01			
Petty cash	111	100 00			
Government bonds	120	5000 00			
Accounts receivable	130	26592 67			
Allowance for doubtful accounts	131		1161 88		(v) 777 39
Notes receivable	132	3042 15			
Accrued interest receivable	133			(L) 22 09	
Merchandise inv.-plumbing dept.	140	124314 99		(i) 125218 67	(a) 124314 99
Merchandise inv.-elec. dept.	145	78705 10		(k) 80015 11	(b) 78705 10
Store supplies	150	3016 75			(n) 2940 87
Office supplies	151	2224 18			(o) 2176 17
Advertising supplies	152	847 19			(p) 769 44
Postage stamps	153	615 00			(q) 599 60
Unexpired insurance	154	804 72			(R) 445 39
Store equipment	160	3255 70			
Accumulated depreciation - store equipment	161		832 34		(s) 325 57
Office equipment	170	3005 65			
Accumulated depreciation - office equipment	171		789 83		(t) 300 57
Delivery equipment	180	5790 12			
Accumulated depreciation - delivery equipment	181		349 50		(u) 574 51
FICA taxes payable	210		133 24		
FUTA taxes payable	220		53 28		
Employees' income taxes payable	230		115 38		
State unemployment taxes payable	240		97 72		
Accounts payable	250		8942 78		(w) 15 50
Notes payable	260		2400 00		
Accrued interest payable	270				(M) 15 65
M.O. Brown, capital	310		105333 18		
M.O. Brown, drawing	311	17945 88			
W.E. Bailey, capital	320		105523 00		
W.E. Bailey, drawing	321	17450 00			
Sales - plumbing dept.	410		468041 34		
Sales returns & allowances - plumb. dept.	411	5907 48			
Sales - electrical dept.	420		282041 09		
Sales returns & allowances - electrical dept.	421	2119 62			
Sales discounts	0430	8371 44			
Totals - forward		319375 65	974014 56	205255 87	211960 75

Adjusted Trial Balance		Earnings Statement		Statement of Financial Position	
Debit	Credit	Debit	Credit	Debit	Credit
1026701				1026701	
10000				10000	
500000				500000	
2659267				2659267	
	193927				193927
304215				304215	
2209				2209	
12521867				12521867	
8001511				8001511	
7588				7588	
4801				4801	
7775				7775	
1540				1540	
35933				35933	
325570				325570	
	115791				115791
300565				300565	
	109040				109040
579012				579012	
	92401				92401
	13324				13324
	5328				5328
	11538				11538
	9772				9772
	895828				895828
	240000				240000
	1565				1565
	10353318				10353318
1794588				1794588	
	10552300				10552300
1745000				1745000	
	46804134		46804134		
590748		590748			
	28204109		28204109		
211962		211962			
837144		837144			
31467996	97602375	1639854	75008243	29828142	22594132

Illustration 19–1 (*continued*)

Bailey and Brown
Worksheet
For the Year Ended December 31, 1978

Account	Account Number	Trial Balance Debit	Trial Balance Credit	Adjustments Debit	Adjustments Credit
Balances forward		31937565	97401456	20525587	21196075
Purchases – plumbing dept.	510	3768675			(c) 3768675
Purchase returns & allowances – plumb. dept.	511		156215	(q) 156215	
Purchases – electrical dept.	520	2353347			(d) 2353347
Purchase returns & allowances – electrical dept.	521		98103	(h) 98103	
Purchases discounts	522		1018388	(i) 1018388	
Transportation-in-plumbing dept	540	256307			(e) 256307
Transportation-in-electrical dept.	550	121860			(f) 121860
Cost of goods sold – plumbing dept.	560			(a) 1243149	(q) 156215
				(c) 3768675	(i) 631401
				(e) 256307	(j) 12521867
Cost of goods sold – electrical dept.	570			(b) 7870510	(h) 98103
				(d) 2353347	(i) 386987
				(f) 121860	(k) 8001511
Operating expenses	610	512284 5		(n-w) 892501	
Interest revenue	710		10241		(l) 2209
Interest expense	810	20405		(m) 1565	
Collection expense	820	5225			
		98684403	98684403	104592731	104592731
Net earnings					

Adjustment (j): On December 31, a physical inventory was taken and a cost of $125,218.67 was assigned to the merchandise inventory of the plumbing department. The inventory was recorded by debiting Merchandise Inventory—Plumbing Department, Account No. 140, and by crediting Cost of Goods Sold—Plumbing Department, Account No. 560. Bailey and Brown use the first-in, first-out method for inventory costing purposes. A more accurate cost assignment to inventory could be made by including transportation-in and deducting purchases discounts associated with the inventory on hand. Since these amounts are small in relation to total inventory, they are ignored in determining inventory cost. After the physical inventory is taken, the inventory records are adjusted for any discrepancies between the stock records and the actual inventory counts.

| Adjusted Trial Balance | | Earnings Statement | | Statement of Financial Position | |
Debit	Credit	Debit	Credit	Debit	Credit
314679 96	976023 75	16398 54	750082 43	298281 42	225941 32
370650 48		370650 48			
230392 40		230392 40			
60153 46		60153 46			
	124 50		124 50		
219 70		219 70			
52 25		52 25			
976148 25	976148 25	677866 83	750206 93	298281 42	225941 32
		72340 10			72340 10
		750206 93	750206 93	298281 42	298281 42

Adjustment (k): The December 31 physical inventory assigned a cost of $80,015.11 to the merchandise inventory in the electrical department. The inventory was recorded by debiting Merchandise Inventory—Electrical Department, Account No. 145, and by crediting Cost of Goods Sold—Electrical Department, Account No. 570.

Interest adjustments. The proper determination of both interest expense and interest revenue involves the use of accrual accounting since all collections and payments of interest are not made on December 31. The schedule in Illustration 19–2 was prepared in determining the amount of accrued interest on notes receivable.

Bailey and Brown also own five $1,000 U.S. treasury bonds. Two of these bonds earn interest at a rate of 2.5 percent which was collected on December 15. Accrued interest on these bonds for 16 days amounts to

Illustration 19–2

	Schedule of Accrued Interest on Notes Receivable For the Year Ended December 31, 1978 (assume a 365-day year)				
No.	Principal Amount	Rate of Interest	Date of Note	Days Accrued	Accrued Interest
123	$ 800.00	7%	Nov. 2	59	$ 9.05
124	375.00	—	Nov. 8	—	—
130	725.00	7	Nov. 15	46	6.39
134	292.15	7	Dec. 17	14	0.78
135	850.00	7	Dec. 28	3	0.48
	$3,042.15				$16.70

$2.19. On December 18, three additional bonds were purchased (3 percent interest rate). Accrued interest on the December 18 bonds amounts to $3.20. Therefore, total accrued interest receivable on December 31 was $22.09 ($16.70 + $2.19 + $3.20).

Adjustment (l): Accrued interest receivable on December 31 was recorded by debiting Account No. 132 for $22.09 and by crediting Interest Revenue, Account No. 710, for $22.09.

On December 31, Bailey and Brown had a single note outstanding amounting to $2,400. It was a 90-day, 7 percent note dated November 27. As of December 31, the note had been outstanding for 34 days, and interest amounting to $15.65 had accrued.

Adjustment (m): The accrued interest payable was recorded by debiting Interest Expense, Account No. 810, and by crediting Accrued Interest Payable, Account No. 270, for $15.65.

Supporting worksheet—operating expenses

To make the general ledger more manageable, Bailey and Brown keep a subsidiary ledger for the various operating expense accounts. The subsidiary ledger is represented in the general ledger by the controlling account, Operating Expenses (No. 610). To bring the operating expense accounts up to date, a number of accounts must be adjusted. The adjustments involve debits to the subsidiary accounts and credits to the related general ledger accounts. The total debits to the subsidiary accounts are shown as a debit adjustment to the controlling account, Operating Expenses, in the general ledger.

Illustration 19–3 is the operating expense worksheet used by Bailey and Brown to adjust the operating expense accounts. Not only does the

Illustration 19–3

Bailey and Brown
Operating Expense Worksheet
Year Ended December 31, 1978

	Account Number	Trial Balance Debit	Adjustments Debit	Adjusted Trial Balance Debit
M. O. Brown, salary expense	6101	10800 00		10800 00
Truck drivers' wages expense	6102	5160 00		5160 00
Store clerks' salary expense	6103	6000 00		6000 00
M. O. Brown, travel expense	6104	943 18		943 18
Advertising expense	6105	2105 54	(p) 769 44	2874 98
Garage rent expense	6106	450 00		450 00
Truck repairs expense	6107	343 25	(w) 15 50	358 75
Truck operating expense	6108	1688 19		1688 19
Shipping expense	6109	25 00		25 00
Merchandise ins. expense	6110		(r) 201 19	201 19
Delivery equip. ins. expense	6111		(r) 152 40	152 40
Store equip. ins. expense	6112		(r) 54 92	54 92
Postage expense (selling)	6113		(q) 322 18	322 18
Store supplies expense	6114		(n) 2940 87	2940 87
Depreciation of store equip.	6115		(s) 325 57	325 57
Depreciation of delivery equip.	6116		(u) 574 51	574 51
Miscellaneous selling expense	6117	302 47		302 47
W. E. Bailey, salary expense	6121	10800 00		10800 00
Office salaries expense	6122	6600 00		6600 00
Power and water expense	6123	122 59		122 59
Telephone expense	6124	204 81		204 81
Rent expense	6125	3000 00		3000 00
Property tax expense	6126	425 70		425 70
Office supplies expense	6127		(o) 2176 17	2176 17
Bad debts expense	6128		(v) 777 39	777 39
Postage expense (admin.)	6129		(q) 277 42	277 42
Office equip. ins. expense	6130		(r) 36 88	36 88
Payroll taxes expense	6131	1969 44		1969 44
Depreciation of office equip.	6132		(t) 300 57	300 57
Miscellaneous general expense	6133	288 28		288 28
		51228 45	8925 01	60153 46

worksheet aid in adjusting the operating expense accounts, it also provides detailed information to be used in preparing the earnings statement and supporting schedule of operating expenses. An appropriate heading identifies the worksheet along with the period covered, and columns are provided for (1) the trial balance amounts, (2) adjustments, and (3) the adjusted trial balance amounts. As with the summary (general ledger) worksheet, the operating expense worksheet was prepared by listing the expense accounts by number as shown on the chart of accounts in Illustration 18–7. The trial balance amount for each account was entered in the Trial Balance column. It is noted that the trial balance contained a number of accounts with a zero balance. After the trial balance amounts

Illustration 19–4

Schedule of Supplies Used For the Year Ended December 31, 1978				
Asset	Acct. No.	Balance Dec. 31, 1978	On Hand Dec. 31, 1978	Expense for Year
Store supplies	150	$3,016.75	$75.88	$2,940.87
Office supplies	151	2,224.18	48.01	2,176.17
Advertising supplies	152	847.19	77.75	769.44
Postage stamps	153	615.00	15.40	599.60

were entered, the column was totaled and compared with the controlling account balance. If the total had not agreed with the controlling account balance of $51,228.45 in the general ledger, the error would have been corrected before making the adjustments.

Each of the adjusting entries involves debits to one or more operating expense accounts on the operating expense worksheet and credits to one or more general ledger accounts on the summary worksheet.

Supplies expense adjustments. Bailey and Brown maintain supplies accounts in the general ledger for (1) store supplies, (2) office supplies, (3) advertising supplies, and (4) postage stamps. All supplies are recorded as assets when purchased. At the end of the accounting period, a physical inventory of unused supplies and stamps is taken. The difference between each account balance and the amount on hand represents the amount to be charged as an expense in the adjusting entry for each account. The schedule shown in Illustration 19–4 was used in determining the necessary adjustments.

After constructing the schedule, the following adjusting entries were made:

Adjustment (n): The store supplies expense for the year was recorded by debiting Account No. 6114 and by crediting Store Supplies, Account No. 150, for $2,940.87.

Adjustment (o): The office supplies expense for the year was recorded by debiting Account No. 6127 and by crediting Office Supplies, Account No. 151, for $2,176.17.

Adjustment (p): The advertising supplies expense for the year was recorded by debiting Account No. 6105 and by crediting Advertising Supplies, Account No. 152, for $769.44.

Adjustment (q): During the year, postage stamps were used by both the selling and the administrative areas of the business. Upon examining the records kept by the mail clerk, it was determined that $322.18 was a selling expense and that $277.42 was an administrative expense. The postage expense was recorded by debiting Postage Expense (Selling), Account No. 6113, for $322.18 and Postage Expense (Administrative), Account No. 6129, for $277.42 and by crediting Postage Stamps, Account No. 153, for $599.60.

Insurance expense adjustments. Bailey and Brown account for prepaid insurance premiums by recording the amount paid as an asset when payment is made. When payments are made, they are debited to Unexpired Insurance, Account No. 154, in the general ledger. On December 31, the insurance expense for the year is calculated by examining each insurance policy to determine the proportion of the total term coverage of the policy that has expired during the year. The proportion that has expired is multiplied by the original premium to determine the dollar amount of insurance expense. Each policy is classified according to the type of asset insured so that the proper expense account will be charged. Bailey and Brown maintain insurance expense accounts for merchandise, the delivery truck, store equipment, and office equipment in the operating expense ledger.

To simplify calculations necessary to determine insurance expenses each December 31, Bailey and Brown use an insurance register similar to the one shown in Illustration 14–5, on pages 366–67.

Illustration 19–5

Schedule of Insurance Expense
For the Year Ended December 31, 1978

Property Insured	Expense for Year
Office equipment	$ 36.88
Store equipment	54.92
Merchandise	201.19
Delivery equipment	152.40
Total	$445.39

The following adjustment was prepared from the information presented in the schedule:

Adjustment (*r*): Insurance expense for the year was recorded by debiting Office Equipment Insurance Expense, Account No. 6130, for $36.88; by debiting Store Equipment Insurance Expense, Account No. 6112, for $54.92; by debiting Merchandise Insurance Expense, Account No. 6110, for $201.19; by debiting Delivery Equipment Insurance Expense, Account No. 6111, for $152.40; and by crediting Unexpired Insurance, Account No. 154, for $445.39.

Depreciation expense adjustment. As mentioned earlier, Bailey and Brown use the group method to account for and to depreciate long-lived assets. The general ledger contains asset accounts for office equipment, store equipment, and delivery equipment along with the related accumulated depreciation accounts. The operating expense ledger contains depreciation expense accounts for each of the long-lived assets mentioned above. For depreciation purposes, Bailey and Brown consider assets purchased on or before the 15th of the month to be owned for the whole month. Assets that are purchased after the 15th of the month are considered to have been purchased on the first day of the following month. Assets disposed of on or by the 15th are considered to be removed on the first day of the month, and those disposed of after the 15th are deemed to have been removed on the first day of the following month.

In determining the amount of depreciation expense for the year, it is necessary to review the asset accounts for any changes which occurred during the last month (particularly the last 15 days). Unless a review is made, depreciation expense may be misstated because of the inclusion or omission of assets. Based on the rules for including or excluding an asset when determining depreciation expense as described above, the Delivery Equipment account should be decreased by $45. This reduction is because of the purchase of two dollies on December 31. The discarding of an old desk (store equipment) and exchange of typewriters (office equipment) do not require adjustments to the asset accounts since the transactions occurred on December 15 (considered to have been made on December 1).

After making the necessary adjustments to calculate depreciation expense, the schedule in Illustration 19–6 was prepared.

The following adjustments were prepared from the schedule. Each adjustment involves a debit on the operating expense worksheet and a credit on the summary (general ledger) worksheet.

Adjustment (*s*): Depreciation of store equipment was recorded by debiting Account No. 6115 and by crediting Accumulated Depreciation — Store Equipment, Account No. 161, for $325.57.

Adjustment (*t*): Depreciation of office equipment was recorded by debiting Account No. 6132 and by crediting Accumulated Depreciation — Office Equipment, Account No. 171, for $300.57.

Illustration 19–6

Schedule of Depreciation Expense – Straight Line For the Year Ended December 31, 1978			
Assets	Cost	Annual Rate of Depreciation	Depreciation Expense
Store equipment	$3,255.70	10%	$325.57
Office equipment	3,005.65	10	300.57
Delivery equipment	5,745.12*	10	574.51

* $5,790.12 − $45.00 = $5,745.12 (dollies purchased on December 31).

Adjustment (u): Depreciation of delivery equipment was recorded by debiting Account No. 6116 and by crediting Accumulated Depreciation – Delivery Equipment, Account No. 181, for $574.51.

Bad debts expense adjustments. Bailey and Brown have found from past experience that $4/10$ of 1 percent of credit sales are uncollectable. During the current year ended December 31, 1978, sales on account amount to $194,348.16 resulting in an estimated bad debts expense of $777.39 ($194,348.16 × 0.004). The following entry was made to record the **bad debts expense.**

Adjustment (v): Debit Bad Debts Expense, Account No. 6128, and credit Allowance for Doubtful Accounts, Account No. 131, for $777.39.

Miscellaneous adjustments. During the process of completing the operating expense worksheet, the accountant for Bailey and Brown discovered a bill for truck repairs of $15.50. The charge for repairs made on December 27 had not been recorded. Normally, this transaction would have been recorded before the trial balance was taken. The truck repairs expense was recorded by making the following adjustment.

Adjustment (w): Debit Truck Repairs Expense, Account No. 6107, and credit Accounts Payable, Account No. 250, for $15.50.

Completion of worksheets

Operating expense worksheet. To complete the operating expense worksheet, the amounts shown in the Trial Balance column were combined with amounts shown in the Adjustments column (if any) and entered in the Adjusted Trial Balance column. If there was no trial balance amount, the adjustment amount was simply extended to the Adjusted Trial Balance column.

After the Adjustments and Adjusted Trial Balance columns were totaled, the total of the first column $51,228.45 was added to the sum of the second column, $8,925.01 and compared with the total of the Adjusted Trial Balance column, $60,153.46. The fact that the sum of the first two columns equals the third column total does not necessarily indicate that the adjustments were properly made. Its equality only proves that the worksheet additions were correct.

Summary worksheet. It is noted that all of the adjustments (*n–w*) on the operating expense worksheet were debits. Since Operating Expenses, Account No. 610, is the controlling account for the subsidiary accounts shown on the operating expense worksheet, it was debited for the total amount of the operating expense adjustments, $8,925.01. The debit to the controlling account was identified as (*n–w*), representing the total of adjustments *n* through *w* on the operating expense worksheet. This debit was offset by the credits which were entered on the summary worksheet as a result of each of the adjustments.

The next step was to total the Adjustments columns on the summary worksheet to prove their equality. The Adjusted Trial Balance column was completed by combining the amounts in the Trial Balance columns with the amounts shown in the Adjustments column. After combining the column amounts, the Adjusted Trial Balance columns were totaled to prove the equality of the debits and credits. Each of the amounts in the Adjusted Trial Balance columns was extended to the appropriate Earnings Statement or Financial Position columns, depending on the nature of the account. The columns were then totaled. The excess of the credit column total over the debit column total amounted to $72,340.10 representing the net earnings for the year. This amount was labeled as net earnings and entered as a debit in the Earnings Statement columns and a credit in the Financial Position columns. The Earnings Statement and the Financial Position columns were then totaled to prove the equality of each statement's debit and credit columns. To complete the worksheet, each column was double ruled.

The earnings statement (Illustration 19–7) and the statement of financial position (Illustration 19–8) were prepared from the summary worksheet. The operating expense schedule (Illustration 19–9) was prepared from the operating expense worksheet.

ADJUSTING ENTRIES—JOURNALIZING

The adjusting entries were made so that each account would be properly stated as of December 31. Since the adjustments reflect actual changes in the accounts, the adjusting entries were recorded in the general journal. The form of general journal used by Bailey and Brown along with the adjusting entries (*a–w*) are shown in Illustration 19–10. To save space, the Accounts Receivable and Accounts Payable columns have been omitted (see Illustration 19–10 for complete journal). In forming the adjusting entries, only the debits and credits in the general ledger and debits in the operating expense ledger were involved. Therefore, only

Illustration 19–7

BAILEY AND BROWN
Earnings Statement
For the Year Ended December 31, 1978

	Plumbing Department	Electrical Department	Total
Sales	$468,041.34	$282,041.09	$750,082.43
Less: Sales returns and allow.	(5,907.48)	(2,119.62)	(8,027.10)
Sales discounts	(5,190.29)	(3,181.15)	(8,371.44)
Net sales	$456,943.57	$276,740.32	$733,683.89
Cost of goods sold:			
Merchandise inventory, January 1	$124,314.99	$78,705.10	$203,020.09
Purchases	$376,867.25	$235,334.71	$612,201.96
Less: Purchase returns and allow.	(1,562.15)	(981.03)	(2,543.18)
Purchases discounts	(6,314.01)	(3,869.87)	(10,183.88)
Net purchases	$368,991.09	$230,483.81	$599,474.90
Transportation—in	2,563.07	1,218.60	3,781.67
Merchandise available for sale	$495,869.15	$310,407.51	$806,276.66
Less: Merchandise inventory, December 31	125,218.67	80,015.11	205,233.78
Cost of goods sold	370,650.48	230,392.40	601,042.88
Gross profit	$ 86,293.09	$ 46,347.92	$132,641.01
Operating expenses			60,153.46
Net operating earnings			$ 72,487.55
Other revenue			124.50
Interest revenue			$ 72,612.05
Other expenses:			
Interest expense		$ 219.70	
Collection expense		52.25	
Total Other Expenses			271.95
Net Earnings			$ 72,340.10

Illustration 19–8

BAILEY AND BROWN
Statement of Financial Position
December 31, 1978

Assets

Current Assets:

Cash		$ 10,367.01	
Government bonds		5,000.00	
Accrued interest receivable	$ 22.09		
Notes receivable	3,042.15		
Accounts receivable	26,592.67		
	$ 29,656.91		
Less: Allowance for doubtful accounts	1,939.27	27,717.64	

Merchandise inventories:

Plumbing department	$125,218.67		
Electrical department	80,015.11	205,233.78	

Supplies and prepayments:

Store supplies	$ 75.88		
Office supplies	48.01		
Advertising supplies	77.75		
Postage stamps	15.40		
Unexpired insurance	359.33	576.37	
Total Current Assets			$248,894.80

Long-Lived Assets:

Store equipment	$ 3,255.70		
Less: Accumulated depreciation	1,157.91	$ 2,097.79	
Office equipment	$ 3,005.65		
Less: Accumulated depreciation	1,090.40	1,915.25	
Delivery equipment	$ 5,790.12		
Less: Accumulated depreciation	924.01	4,866.11	
Total Long-Lived Assets			8,879.15
Total Assets			$257,773.95

Liabilities

Current Liabilities:

F.I.C.A. taxes payable	$ 133.24	
F.U.T.A. taxes payable	53.28	
Income taxes payable—federal employee	115.38	
State unemployment taxes payable	97.72	
Accounts payable	8,958.28	
Notes payable	2,400.00	
Accrued interest payable	15.65	
Total Current Liabilities		$ 11,773.55

Illustration 19–8 (continued)

Owner's Equity

M. O. Brown Capital, January 1, 1978 .... $103,533.18		
Net earnings (½ of $72,340.10) $36,170.05		
Less Withdrawals 17,945.88 .... 18,224.17		
M. O. Brown Capital, December 31, 1978	121,757.35	
W. E. Bailey Capital, January 1, 1978 .... $105,523.00		
Net earnings (½ of $72,340.10) $36,170.05		
Less: Withdrawals 17,450.00 .... 18,720.05		
W. E. Bailey Capital, December 31, 1978	124,243.05	
Total Owner's Equity		246,000.40
Total Liabilities and Owner's Equity		$257,773.95

these three columns are used in the general journal when journalizing the adjusting entries.

In journalizing the adjusting entries, it is noted that account numbers and not account titles are used to identify the accounts. The account titles are only used in describing the entry in the Description column. The entries are journalized in alphabetical order (*a*) through (*w*) as shown on the related worksheets. Although journalizing in alphabetical order is not necessary, it helps to reduce the chance of omitting an entry. As a final step in recording the entries, the columns were totaled to prove the equality of the debits and credits, and the columns were ruled.

ADJUSTING ENTRIES—POSTING

After the adjusting entries were journalized, the journal entry amounts were posted to the appropriate accounts. The postings were made by account number, and a check mark (✔) was placed beside each amount in the general journal after it was posted. Those entries involving the operating expense accounts were posted to the related accounts in the operating expense ledger. The total of the general journal operating expense column, $8,925.01, was posted to the control account Operating Expenses, Account No. 610, in the general ledger. To identify the posting of the operating expense total, the number "610" was placed below the column total. The general ledger debit and credit columns were not posted in total and were so identified by placing a check mark (✔) below each column total. As each posting was made in the general ledger and the operating expense ledger, the posting was referenced to the general

Illustration 19–9

BAILEY AND BROWN
Schedule of Operating Expenses
For the Year Ended December 31, 1978

Selling expenses:

M. O. Brown, salary expense	$10,800.00
Truck drivers' wages expense	5,160.00
Store clerks' salary expense	6,000.00
M. O. Brown, travel expense	943.18
Advertising expense	2,874.98
Garage rent expense	450.00
Truck repairs expense	358.75
Truck operating expense	1,688.19
Shipping expense	25.00
Merchandise insurance expense	201.19
Delivery equipment insurance expense	152.40
Store equipment insurance expense	54.92
Postage expense (selling)	322.18
Store supplies expense	2,940.87
Depreciation of store equipment	325.57
Depreciation of delivery equipment	574.51
Miscellaneous selling expense	302.47
Total Selling Expenses	$33,174.21

Administrative expenses:

W. E. Bailey, salary expense	$10,800.00
Office salaries expense	6,600.00
Power and water expense	122.59
Telephone expense	204.81
Rent expense	3,000.00
Property tax expense	425.70
Office supplies expense	2,176.17
Bad debts expense	777.39
Postage expense (administrative)	277.42
Office equipment insurance expense	36.88
Payroll taxes expense	1,969.44
Depreciation of office equipment	300.57
Miscellaneous general expense	288.28
Total Administrative Expenses	$26,979.25
Total Operating Expenses	$60,153.46

journal by recording the general journal page number (G56) by each posting.

CLOSING ENTRIES—JOURNALIZING

The required **closing entries** are shown Illustration 19–10. Note that the account titles as well as their numbers were used to identify the accounts to be debited and credited. The titles of those accounts which

Illustration 19–10

Month of December 1978

GENERAL JOURNAL

Page 56

Operating Expenses Acct. No.	Amount	✔	Debit General Ledger Acct. No.	Amount	✔	Day	Description	Credit General Ledger Acct. No.	Amount	✔
						31	Adjusting Entries			
			560	124,314.99	✔		Transfer beginning inventories to	140	124,314.99	✔
			570	78,705.10	✔		cost of goods sold	145	78,705.10	✔
			560	376,867.25	✔		Transfer purchases to	510	376,867.25	✔
			570	235,334.71	✔		cost of goods sold	520	235,334.71	✔
			560	2,563.07	✔		Transfer transportation-in to	540	2,563.07	✔
			570	1,218.60	✔		cost of goods sold	550	1,218.60	✔
			511	1,562.15	✔		Transfer purchase returns and allowances to	560	1,562.15	✔
			521	981.03	✔		cost of goods sold	570	981.03	✔
			522	10,183.88	✔		Transfer purchases discounts to	560	6,314.01	✔
							cost of goods sold	570	3,869.87	✔
			140	125,218.67	✔		To record ending	560	125,218.67	✔
			145	80,015.11	✔		inventories	570	80,015.11	✔
			133	22.09	✔		Interest revenue	710	22.09	✔
			810	15.65	✔		Interest expense	270	15.65	✔
6114	2,940.87	✔					Store supplies expenses	150	2,940.87	✔
6127	2,176.17	✔					Office supplies expense	151	2,176.17	✔
6105	769.44	✔					Advertising expense	152	769.44	✔
6113	322.18	✔					Postage stamps used	153	599.60	✔
6129	277.42	✔								
6110	201.19	✔					Expired insurance	154	445.39	✔
6111	152.40	✔								
6112	54.92	✔								
6130	36.88	✔								
6115	325.57	✔					Depreciation of store equipment	161	325.57	✔
6132	300.57	✔					Depreciation of office equipment	171	300.57	✔
6116	574.51	✔					Depreciation of delivery equipment	181	574.51	✔
6128	777.39	✔					Bad debts expense	131	777.39	✔
6107	15.50	✔					Truck repairs expense	250	15.50	✔
	8,925.01			1,037,002.30	✔				1,045,927.31	
	(610)									

Illustration 19–10 (continued)

GENERAL JOURNAL

Month of December 1978 — Page 57

Debit Operating Expenses Acct. No.	Amount	✓	Debit General Ledger Acct. No.	Amount	✓	Day	Description	Credit General Ledger Acct. No.	Amount	✓
						31	Closing Entries			
			410	468,041.34	✓		Sales—plumbing department			
			420	282,041.09	✓		Sales—electrical			
			710	124.50	✓		Interest revenue			
							Expense and revenue summary	330	750,206.93	✓
			330	677,866.83	✓		Expense and revenue summary			
							Sales R and A—plumbing department	411	5,907.48	✓
							Sales R and A—electrical department	421	2,119.62	✓
							Sales discounts	422	8,371.44	✓
							Cost of goods sold—plumbing department	560	370,650.48	✓
							Cost of goods sold—electrical department	570	230,392.40	✓
							Operating expenses	610	60,153.46	✓
							Interest expense	810	219.70	✓
							Collection expense	820	52.25	✓
			330	72,340.10	✓		Expense and revenue summary			
							M. O. Brown, capital	310	36,170.05	✓
							W. E. Bailey, capital	320	36,170.05	✓
			310	17,945.88	✓		M. O. Brown, capital			
							M. O. Brown, drawing	311	17,945.88	✓
			320	17,450.00	✓		W. E. Bailey, capital			
							W. E. Bailey, drawing	321	17,450.00	✓
				1,535,809.74					1,535,809.74	

GENERAL JOURNAL

Month of January 1979 — Page 58

Debit General Ledger Acct. No.	Amount	✓	Day	Description	Credit General Ledger Acct. No.	Amount	✓
			1	Reversing Entries			
710	22.09	✓		To reverse adjusting entries for	133	22.09	✓
270	15.65	✓		accrued interest	810	15.65	✓

were credited were slightly indented. Even though the closing entries do not have to be journalized in any particular order, some logical sequence should be used to make sure that all accounts are closed. Quite often, the accounts are closed in the following order: (1) revenue accounts, (2) expense accounts, (3) expense and revenue summary, and (4) distribution of earnings. As a final step, the General Ledger columns were footed to prove the equality of the debits and credits and were double ruled.

Illustration 19–11

		Truck Repairs Expense			Account No. 6107	
Date	Description	P.R.	Debit	Credit	Balance
1978 Dec. 1	Balance	✓			329.10
9		PC12	14.15		343.25
27		GJ56	15.50		358.75
31		GJ57		358.75	-0-

In the part of the general journal shown in Illustration 19–10 which contains the closing entries, it should be noted that the expense accounts in the operating expense ledger are not credited in making the closing entries. Instead, the controlling account Operating Expenses, Account No. 610, is credited for $60,153.46, the total of the adjusted account debits in the subsidiary ledger. A basic reason for not crediting each subsidiary account in the general journal is that the general journal does not have a column in which credits can be made to the operating expense accounts. The infrequency of transactions involving credits to operating expense accounts does not warrant a column in the general journal for such transactions. When such a credit does arise, both the control account number (610) and the subsidiary account being credited are recorded in the Account No. column. The credit is then posted to both the control and subsidiary accounts.

Even though the credits involved in closing the operating expense accounts are too numerous to record in the general journal, it should be understood that all 30 of the subsidiary accounts must be closed. Whenever a controlling account is closed, an accountant should know that the subsidiary accounts to the controlling account should also be closed. Each of the subsidiary accounts were closed in a manner similar to Illustration 19–11 for Truck Repairs Expense, Account No. 6107.

Illustration 19–12

		Expense and Revenue Summary			Account No. 330	
Date		Description	P.R.	Debit	Credit	Balance
1978						
Dec.	31	Sales—plumbing department	GJ57		468,041.34	468,041.34
	31	Sales—electrical department	GJ57		282,041.09	750,082.43
	31	Interest revenue	GJ57		124.50	750,206.93
	31	Sales returns and allowances—plumbing	GJ57	5,907.48		744,299.45
	31	Sales returns and allowances—electrical	GJ57	2,119.62		742,179.83
	31	Sales discounts	GJ57	8,371.44		733,808.39
	31	Cost of goods sold—plumbing	GJ57	370,650.48		363,157.91
	31	Cost of goods sold—electrical	GJ57	230,392.40		132,765.51
	31	Operating expense	GJ57	60,153.46		72,612.05
	31	Interest expense	GJ57	219.70		72,392.35
	31	Collection expense	GJ57	52.25		72,340.10
	31	M. O. Brown, capital	GJ57	36,170.05		36,170.05
	31	W. E. Bailey, capital	GJ57	36,170.05		-0-

Illustration 19–13

		Cost of Goods Sold—Plumbing Department			Account No. 560	
Date		Description	P.R.	Debit	Credit	Balance
1978						
Dec.	31	Beginning inventory	GJ56	124,314.99		124,314.99
	31	Purchases	GJ56	376,867.25		501,182.24
	31	Transportation-in	GJ56	2,563.07		503,745.31
	31	Purchase returns and allowances	GJ56		1,562.15	502,183.16
	31	Purchases discounts	GJ56		6,314.01	495,869.15
	31	Ending inventory	GJ56		125,218.67	370,650.48
	31	Expense and revenue summary	GJ56		370,650.48	-0-

		Cost of Goods Sold—Electrical Department			Account No. 570	
Date		Description	P.R.	Debit	Credit	Balance
1978						
Dec.	31	Beginning inventory	GJ56	78,705.10		78,705.10
	31	Purchases	GJ56	235,334.71		314,039.81
	31	Transportation-in	GJ56	1,218.60		315,258.41
	31	Purchase returns and allowances	GJ56		981.03	314,277.38
	31	Purchases discounts	GJ56		3,869.87	310,407.51
	31	Ending inventory	GJ56		80,015.11	230,392.40
	31	Expense and revenue summary	GJ56		230,392.40	-0-

CLOSING ENTRIES—POSTING

Postings were made to each of the accounts involved in the closing entries. A check mark (✔) was placed in the (✔) column beside each amount that was posted. As a cross-reference, the general journal page (GJ57) was recorded in the P.R. column of each account posted. Refer to the Truck Repairs Expense account in Illustration 19–11 for an example of the cross-referencing used when posting the closing entries.

After posting the adjusting and closing entries, the Expense and Revenue Summary account (Illustration 19–12) and the two cost of goods sold accounts (Illustration 19–13) would appear as shown. These accounts are summary accounts and are used only at the end of the accounting period. When perpetual inventories are maintained, the cost of goods sold is known as each inventory unit is sold making it possible to use the cost of goods sold account throughout the year. Since Bailey and Brown keep a perpetual inventory of quantities only, the cost of goods sold account is used as a summary account at the end of the period. Note that the Expense and Revenue Summary account was posted in detail (items representing the debits and credits in the closing entries were posted individually instead of in total).

POST-CLOSING TRIAL BALANCE

After all adjusting and closing entries were posted, a **post-closing trial balance** of the remaining general ledger accounts with balances (open) was taken. This was done to prove the equality of the debit and credit balances of the general ledger accounts. The post-closing trial balance of Bailey and Brown is shown in Illustration 19–14.

Although a post-closing trial balance is not required, it is a desirable procedure. If a post-closing trial balance is taken, it can be used to help resolve any errors that might arise in the accounts at a later date.

REVERSING ENTRIES

In preparing the adjusting entries on December 31, two entries of the "accrual type" were made. **Reversing entries** enable the accountant to record payments (expenses) and receipts (revenues) in a consistent manner from period to period. Adjusting entries requiring reversal are normally reversed on the first day of the next accounting period. Bailey and Brown made two reversing entries—one for the accrued interest receivable of $22.09 and another for the accrued interest payable of $15.65. The reversing entries are shown in the general journal.

Illustration 19–14

BAILEY AND BROWN
Post-Closing Trial Balance
December 31, 1978

Account No.	Account Title	Debit	Credit
110	National Bank	$ 10,267.01	
111	Petty cash	100.00	
120	Government bonds	5,000.00	
130	Accounts receivable	26,592.67	
131	Allowance for doubtful accounts		$ 1,939.27
132	Notes receivable	3,042.15	
133	Accrued interest receivable	22.09	
140	Merchandise inventory—plumbing department	125,218.67	
145	Merchandise inventory—electrical department	80,015.11	
150	Store supplies	75.88	
151	Office supplies	48.01	
152	Advertising supplies	77.75	
153	Postage stamps	15.40	
154	Unexpired insurance	359.33	
160	Store equipment	3,255.70	
161	Accumulated depreciation—store equipment		1,157.91
170	Office equipment	3,005.65	
171	Accumulated depreciation—office equipment		1,090.40
180	Delivery equipment	5,790.12	
181	Accumulated depreciation—delivery equipment		924.01
210	F.I.C.A. taxes payable		133.24
220	F.U.T.A. taxes payable		53.28
230	Income taxes payable—federal employee		115.38
240	State unemployment taxes payable		97.72
250	Accounts payable		8,958.28
260	Notes payable		2,400.00
270	Accrued interest payable		15.65
310	M. O. Brown, capital		121,757.35
320	W. E. Bailey, capital		124,243.05
		$262,885.54	$262,885.54

GLOSSARY

Adjusting entries   journal entries made at the end of an accounting period so that the accounts will reflect the correct balances in the financial statements. These entries are necessary because some transactions have an effect upon more than one accounting period, and their effects must be apportioned over the accounting periods affected.

Bad debts expense   an expense incurred by a business when it grants credit to customers. It occurs because some customers fail to pay their accounts.

Closing entries   those entries made at the end of an accounting period which transfer the balances in the expense and revenue accounts to the Expense and Revenue Summary account.

Cost of goods sold an expense incurred consisting of the cost to the seller of goods sold to customers. It is computed as Beginning Inventory + (Purchases + Transportation-In – Purchase Returns and Allowances – Purchase Discounts) – Ending Inventory.

Operating expense worksheet a supporting worksheet used to adjust operating expense accounts.

Post-closing trial balance a trial balance taken after the expense and revenue accounts have been closed.

Reversing entries entries which enable the accountant to record payments and receipts in a consistent manner from period to period. Adjusting entries requiring reversal are normally reversed on the first day of the next accounting period.

Worksheet an informal accounting statement which summarizes the trial balance and other information needed to prepare the financial statements and closing entries.

QUESTIONS AND EXERCISES

1. Why is the Expense and Revenue Summary account left out of the summary worksheet?

2. What account balances must be combined in order to determine the cost of goods sold?

3. The Huff Wholesale Store has two departments—A and B. During 1978, purchases for Department A totaled $425,000 and purchases for Department B totaled $282,000. Purchase returns and allowances amounted to $12,750 for Department A and $11,280 for Department B. Purchases discounts for 1978 amounted to $12,600. This amount is to be allocated between the cost of goods sold accounts in relation to the amount of purchases (less purchase returns and allowances) of the two departments. What general journal entry should be made to allocate the purchases discounts amount between the two departments?

4. On December 31, 1978, the Harbuck Wholesale Company had two notes receivable—an $850, 8 percent, 90-day note dated December 1, and a $360, 7 percent, 60-day note dated December 16. What adjustment is necessary to record accrued interest on December 31, 1978? (Assume a 360-day year.)

5. Store Supplies, Account No. 125, has a balance of $3,725 on December 31, 1978. A physical inventory count reveals that $560 worth of store supplies are on hand at December 31, 1978. What adjustment is necessary to record store supplies expense for 1978?

6. The long-lived asset accounts of the J and S Wholesale Store have the following balances on December 31, 1978:

Store equipment...................... $4,600
Office equipment 2,725
Delivery equipment 6,890

The annual rates of depreciation are 10 percent for store and office equipment and 20 percent for delivery equipment. What adjustments are necessary to record depreciation expense for 1978?

7. What logical sequence is often used to journalize closing entries?

8. What three amount columns appear on an operating expense worksheet?

9. Pessa and Miller have found from past experience that $\frac{1}{2}$ of 1 percent of all credit sales become uncollectible. During the current year, credit sales amounted to $2,425,000. What adjustment is necessary to record the estimated bad debts expense?

10. Akins and Alexander have a single note payable outstanding on December 31. It is a $2,500, 90-day, 8 percent note dated November 16. What adjusting entry should be made on December 31, and what reversing entry should be made on January 1? (Assume a 360-day year.)

PROBLEMS

19–1. Nancy Finn and Gordon Fisher own and operate a wholesale clothing store. The trial balance for Finn and Fisher for the year ended December 31, 1978, is shown below:

FINN AND FISHER
Trial Balance
December 31, 1978

Account No.	Account Title	Debit	Credit
105	First National Bank	$ 12,000	
108	Petty cash	100	
110	Accrued interest receivable		
112	Notes receivable	600	
115	Accounts receivable.....................................	15,800	
116	Allowance for doubtful accounts		$ 1,200
120	Merchandise inventory	86,000	
125	Office supplies	800	
126	Store supplies	1,200	
127	Postage stamps	1,400	
128	Unexpired insurance	2,300	
130	Store equipment	4,600	
131	Accumulated depreciation—store equipment.....		1,380
140	Office equipment	3,800	
141	Accumulated depreciation—office equipment ...		1,140
150	Delivery equipment	10,400	

Account No.	Account Title	Debit	Credit
151	Accumulated depreciation—delivery equipment		4,800
205	F.I.C.A. taxes payable		600
206	Employees' income taxes payable..................		1,300
212	Accounts payable......................................		14,000
305	Nancy Finn, capital		68,200
306	Nancy Finn, drawing	13,665	
312	Gordon Fisher, capital		48,200
313	Gordon Fisher, drawing.............................	10,500	
405	Sales		988,000
406	Sales returns and allowances	10,320	
407	Sales discounts..	9,680	
505	Purchases..	822,100	
506	Purchase returns and allowances...................		8,000
507	Purchases discounts..................................		12,000
508	Transportation-in.....................................	6,800	
515	Cost of goods sold....................................		
605	Operating expenses...................................	136,800	
705	Interest revenue		45
		$1,148,865	$1,148,865

Finn and Fisher maintain subsidiary ledgers for accounts receivable, accounts payable, and operating expenses. A trial balance for the operating expense accounts is shown below:

Account No.	Account Title	Balance
6051	Salaries expense...	$ 80,000
6052	Wages expense	25,000
6053	Travel expense	2,800
6054	Advertising expense	11,200
6055	Rent expense...	4,800
6056	Insurance expense..	
6057	Truck repairs expense.....................................	800
6058	Truck operating expense	1,500
6059	Shipping expense	1,500
6061	Postage expense..	
6062	Store supplies expense	
6063	Office supplies expense	
6064	Depreciation expense......................................	
6065	Utilities expense	2,500
6066	Telephone expense...	500
6067	Bad Debts expense...	
6068	Payroll taxes expense	5,700
6069	Miscellaneous expense....................................	500
		$136,800

Required:

Prepare (1) a ten-column summary worksheet for the year ended December 31, 1978, and (2) a supporting worksheet for operating expenses for the year ended December 31, 1978. (Note: Leave three lines for cost of goods sold.)

Data for adjustments is as follows:

> Merchandise inventory, December 31, 1978, $92,000.
> Office supplies on hand, December 31, 1978, $50.
> Store supplies on hand, December 31, 1978, $200.
> Postage stamps on hand, December 31, 1978, $450.
> Unexpired insurance, December 31, 1978, $1,100.

Bad debts expense is estimated to be $3/_{10}$ of 1 percent of net sales. No new equipment was purchased after June 30, 1978. Therefore, one year's depreciation is to be taken on the equipment. Depreciation rates are 10 percent for office and store equipment and 15 percent for delivery equipment.

Finn and Fisher own one note receivable. It is a $600, 10 percent, 90-day note dated December 1, 1978.

19–2. The worksheets completed in Problem 19–1 for Finn and Fisher will be needed to work this problem.

Required:

1. Using a general journal like the one shown in Illustration 19–10, prepare the adjusting entries for the year ended December 31, 1978. After the entries have been made, rule the amount columns.
2. Prepare the closing entries on December 31, 1978. Distribute the Expense and Revenue Summary account balance (Account No. 320) equally among the partners. Once again, foot the amount columns.
3. Prepare the reversing entry on January 1, 1979.
4. Assuming that all posting, both individual and summary, has been completed, make the necessary check marks and other notations in the general journal.

Required:

19–3. Using the worksheets prepared in Problem 1 for Finn and Fisher, prepare the following items:

1. Earnings statement.
2. Schedule of operating expenses.
3. Statement of financial position.
4. Post-closing trial balance.

19–4. The Sasser Wholesale Corporation is divided into two departments—A and B. The corporation has just completed business for the year ended December 31, 1978. Susan Baker, an accountant for the corporation, has prepared the following trial balance:

THE SASSER WHOLESALE CORPORATION
Trial Balance
December 31, 1978

Account No.	Account Title	Debit	Credit
101	Second National Bank	$ 11,800	
102	Petty cash	100	
105	Marketable securities	1,200	
110	Accounts receivable	15,800	
111	Allowance for doubtful accounts		$ 400
114	Notes receivable	1,200	
115	Accrued interest receivable		
120	Merchandise inventory — Department A	40,000	
125	Merchandise inventory — Department B	32,000	
130	Store supplies	2,300	
132	Office supplies	1,800	
133	Unexpired insurance	3,600	
140	Store equipment	7,200	
141	Accumulated depreciation — store equipment		1,300
150	Office equipment	5,600	
151	Accumulated depreciation — office equipment		800
160	Delivery equipment	45,000	
161	Accumulated depreciation — delivery equipment		6,800
170	Building	82,000	
171	Accumulated depreciation — building		11,000
180	Land	10,000	
201	F.I.C.A. taxes payable		1,100
202	F.U.T.A. taxes payable		150
203	Employees' income taxes payable		1,000
204	State unemployment taxes payable		250
210	Accounts payable		13,000
211	Notes payable		800
212	Accrued interest payable		
301	Common stock		80,000
302	Premium on common stock		48,000
305	Retained earnings		50,910
401	Sales — Department A		650,000
402	Sales returns and allowances — Department A	19,000	
410	Sales — Department B		480,000
411	Sales returns and allowances — Department B	8,000	
412	Sales discounts	20,000	
501	Purchases — Department A	529,000	
502	Purchase returns and allowances — Department A		20,000
510	Purchases — Department B	410,000	
511	Purchase returns and allowances — Department B		5,000
512	Purchases discounts		18,000
520	Transportation-in — Department A	3,100	

Problem 4 (*continued*)

Account No.	Account Title	Debit	Credit
521	Transportation-in – Department B	1,600	
530	Cost of goods sold – Department A		
535	Cost of goods sold – Department B...............		
540	Operating expenses....................................	138,200	
601	Interest revenue		30
701	Interest expense..	40	
		$1,388,540	$1,388,540

Ms. Baker also prepared the following trial balance of operating expenses:

Operating Expenses Trial Balance

Account No.	Account Title	Balance
5400	Salaries expense (selling)................................	$ 40,000
5401	Wages expense	35,000
5402	Travel expense	3,000
5403	Advertising expense	4,500
5404	Truck repairs expense...................................	1,400
5405	Truck operating expense	3,000
5406	Merchandise insurance expense.......................	
5407	Delivery equipment insurance expense	
5408	Store equipment insurance expense..................	
5409	Building insurance expense............................	
5410	Postage expense (selling)..............................	300
5411	Store supplies expense.................................	
5412	Depreciation of store equipment......................	
5413	Depreciation of delivery equipment..................	
5414	Depreciation of building................................	
5415	Miscellaneous selling expense	100
5416	Office salaries expense.................................	36,000
5417	Power and water expense	3,000
5418	Telephone expense.......................................	800
5419	Property tax expense....................................	1,200
5420	Office supplies expense	
5421	Bad debts expense.......................................	
5422	Postage expense (administrative)......................	400
5423	Office equipment insurance expense	
5424	Payroll taxes expense	9,100
5425	Depreciation of office equipment......................	
5426	Miscellaneous general expense	400
		$138,200

Required:

Prepare (1) a ten-column summary worksheet for the year ended December 31, 1978, and (2) a supporting worksheet for operating expenses for the year ended December 31, 1978. (Note: Leave three lines for each cost of goods sold account.)

Data for adjustments is as follows:

Purchases discounts are to be allocated between the cost of goods sold accounts in relation to the amount of purchases (less purchase returns and allowances) of the two departments. Merchandise inventories, December 31, 1978.

Department A, $38,000.
Department B, $29,000.

Sixty days' interest at 10 percent has accrued on the notes receivable. Ninety days' interest at 10 percent has accrued on the notes payable.

Supplies on hand, December 31, 1978:

Store supplies, $500.
Office supplies, $600.

The following amounts of insurance expired during 1978:

Merchandise insurance	$200
Delivery equipment insurance	350
Store equipment insurance	200
Building insurance	500
Office equipment insurance	150

No long-lived assets were purchased or disposed of during 1978. Depreciation rates are 10 percent for office and store equipment, 15 percent for delivery equipment, and 5 percent for building.

Bad debts expense is estimated to be $2/10$ of 1 percent of total net sales for 1978.

19–5. The worksheets completed in Problem 19–4 for the Sasser Wholesale Corporation will be needed to work this problem.

Required:

1. Using a general journal like the one shown in Illustration 19–10, prepare the adjusting entries for the year ended December 31, 1978. After the entries have been made, rule the amount columns.
2. Prepare the closing entries on December 31, 1978. (Expense and Revenue Summary is Account No. 310.)
   Foot the amount columns after the closing entries have been made.
3. Prepare the reversing entries on January 1, 1979.
4. Assuming that all posting, both individual and summary, has been completed, make the necessary check marks and other notations in the general journal.

Required:

19-6. Using the worksheets prepared in Problem 19–4 for the Sasser Wholesale Corporation, prepare the following items:

1. Earnings statement.
2. Schedule of operating expenses.
3. Statement of financial position.
4. Post-closing trial balance.

Voucher system
Learning objectives

Control over cash disbursements is an important function of any business. This chapter contains the following material on the contents and use of a voucher system:

1. A description of the registers and accounts in a voucher system.
2. The mechanics of preparing, recording, paying, and filing disbursement vouchers.
3. An illustration of the voucher check often used in a voucher system.
4. Treatment of purchase returns and allowances and invoice corrections when using a voucher system. system.

20 Voucher system

As a method of handling cash and controlling expenditures, many companies use what is known as a **voucher system.** Control over each cash disbursement is achieved by requiring that written approval be obtained for each cash payment. In a system of this type, specific corporate officers may be authorized to approve specific expenditures, and a cashier will be authorized to issue checks for approved payments. A voucher system will usually include the following items:

1. Vouchers.
2. Voucher register.
3. Vouchers Payable account (general ledger).
4. Voucher checks.
5. Check register.

A number of accounting procedures are applicable to the voucher system. Voucher systems may be used for materials, payrolls, supplies, taxes, interest, payables, and other expenditures. Even though voucher systems are quite flexible and can be used in most situations involving cash expenditures, they are not appropriate under all circumstances. They are best used when one or more of the following conditions exist:

1. When invoices are paid in full at maturity rather than making partial or installment payments.
2. When the volume of transactions is large enough to make expenditure controls necessary.
3. When it is desirable to record invoices when received rather than when payment is made.

PURCHASE INVOICE

Purchase invoices received by a business may come from purchases of materials, supplies, services, inventories, and long-lived assets. When a shipment is received, the receiving clerk prepares a **receiving report** describing the type, quantity, and condition of goods received. The purchasing agent will verify prices, grades, sizes, and terms of payment with the original purchase order. The accounting department will then verify the accuracy of the extensions and additions and compare the purchase invoice with the receiving report. When the invoice amounts are deemed to be properly substantiated, the accountant will indicate the account or accounts to be charged. Invoices representing services received are normally verified by the department receiving the service.

Shown in Illustration 20–1 is an invoice received by the Star Manufacturing Company from Southern Supply, Inc., for materials purchased on account. The receiving clerk prepared the receiving report for the materials received. The prices and quantities were verified by the purchasing agent. The accounting department checked the extensions and compared the purchase invoice with the receiving report. The accountant

Illustration 20–1
Purchase invoice

No. 3482

Southern Supply, Inc.
6103 Broad Street S.E.
Atlanta, Georgia 30303

Sold to	Star Manufacturing Co.	Date	March 1, 1978
	228 Cherry St.	Terms	2/10, n/30
	Macon, Georgia 31204	Shipped via	Motor express

Quantity	Description	Price	Total
25 gal.	Glue-it glue	$3.00	$75.00
20 gross	Brass screws	4.50	90.00
10 doz.	hinges	8.75	87.50
15 boxes	staples	3.00	45.00
			$297.50

Account # 202

noted that Materials Inventory, Account No. 202, should be charged for the amount of the invoice.

VOUCHER PREPARATION

As described in this chapter, a **voucher** is a document used to record information about the purchase of goods or services. The document usually contains spaces for accounts to be charged, dollar amounts, approval of voucher, and authorization of payment along with other details.

Vouchers are prepared for each invoice received except for invoices which represent minor expenses. Such expenses are usually paid out of a petty cash fund. The form of vouchers will vary from business to business as there is no standard form. The form used depends on the type of business, the accounts involved, and the voucher's routing through the business system. After the purchase invoice has been verified, the voucher clerk or other authorized person will prepare a voucher for the related invoice. After the voucher is prepared, the purchase invoice is attached to it and forwarded to the accounting department. The accounting department compares the voucher with the verified invoice and related receiving report for completeness and agreement before making payment. Note that the back of each voucher contains a payment summary. The date of payment, amount, and check number are recorded in the spaces provided.

Illustration 20–2
Voucher—Face

VOUCHER

The STAR Manufacturing Co.

Date	March 3, 1978		Voucher No.	401

Payee   Southern Supply, Inc.
6103 Broad Street S.E.
Atlanta, Georgia 30303

Date	Details	Amount
March 1	Materials	$297.50

Attach supporting documents

Illustration 20–2 (*continued*)
Voucher—back

		DISTRIBUTION					
	Manufacturing Expense		Operating Expenses		Sundry Accounts		
Materials	Acct. No.	Amount	Acct. No.	Amount	Acct. No.	Amount	
297 50							

Voucher Summary		Payment Summary	
Amount	297.50	Date	
Adjustment		Amount	
Discount	5.95	Check No.	
Net	291.55	Approved	Treasurer
Approved 𝒟.𝒵.𝒲.	Controller	Recorded	
Recorded			

The front and back of a voucher used by the Star Manufacturing Company are shown in Illustration 20–2. The voucher information was taken from the invoice shown in Illustration 20–1.

Illustration 20–3

Month of March 1978   **VOUCHER REGISTER**   Page 12

Material Purchases, Dr.	Manufacturing Exp., Dr.			Operating Expense, Dr.			Sundry Accounts, Dr.		
	Acct. No.	Amount	✓	Acct. No.	Amount	✓	Acct. No.	Amount	✓
297.50							208	18.08	✓
							303	5,842.88	✓
1,052.25									
	6402	45.05	✓				210	165.00	✓
	7410	408.19	✓						
	6019	683.75	✓	7403	543.18	✓	601	888.18	✓
				7404	1,328.02	✓			
				7405	748.50	✓			

VOUCHER RECORDING

When it has been determined that the voucher, invoice, and receiving report are complete and in agreement, the voucher is recorded in the voucher register. Since the **voucher register** is used to record the purchase of assets and services, it can be thought of as an enlarged purchases journal. It is also similar to an invoice register. The number and type of columns in the register will depend on the nature of the business and classification of accounts. It would be incorrect to assume that a manufacturing firm would make the same type of purchases as a service business.

The Star Manufacturing Company uses the form of voucher register shown in Illustration 20–3. Voucher No. 401 (Illustration 20–2) is the first entry in the register. The voucher was recorded by debiting Materials Inventory, Account No. 202, and by crediting **Vouchers Payable** for $297.50.

Shown below is a summary listing of selected vouchers recorded in the voucher register through March 15:

1978
Mar. 3 No. 401: Southern Supply, Inc., 6103 Broad Street, S.E., Atlanta; Materials, Account No. 202; terms, March 1 – 2/10, n/30, $297.50.
3 No. 402: Butler Supply, 2020 Hawkins Ave; Office Supplies, Account No. 208; terms, March 2 – n/30, $18.08.
4 No. 403: Riverside Truck Company, 5340 Riverside Dr.; Delivery Truck, Account No. 303; terms, March 3 – n/30, $5,842.88. Charge to Delivery Equipment.
5 No. 404: Mid-South Lumber Company, 304 First Street, Dalton; Materials, Account No. 202; terms, March 3 – 2/10, n/30, $1,052.25.

| Day | Voucher No. | Payee | Sundry Accounts, Cr. | | | Vouchers Payable Cr. | Paid | |
			Acct. No.	Amount	✔		Date	Ck. No.
3	401	Southern Supply, Inc.				297.50	3/7	304
3	402	Butler Supply				18.08	3/16	309
4	403	Riverside Truck Co.				5,842.88		
5	404	Mid-South Lumber Co.				1,052.25	3/11	305
6	405	Sharp Suppliers				45.05	3/14	306
7	406	National Fire and Casualty Co.				165.00		
8	407	Tri-State Power Co.				408.19	3/15	307
15	432	Payroll (March 1–15)	404	188.59	✔	3,451.23	3/15	308
			407	551.81	✔			

6 No. 405: Sharp Suppliers, 1010 Oak Rd; Factory Supplies, Account No. 6402; terms, March 6−2/10, n/30, $45.05.

7 No. 406: National Fire and Casualty Company, 101 Courtland Ave; factory insurance premium, Account No. 210; terms, March 5−n/60, $165.

8 No. 407: Tri-State Power Company, 1084 Jackson Street; factory power bill, Account No. 7410; terms, March 6−n/10, $408.19.

15 No. 432: Payroll, March 1−15. Distributed as follows: Office Salaries Expense, Account No. 7403, $543.18; Officers' Salaries Expense. Account No. 7404, $1,328.02; Sales Salaries Expense, Account No. 7405, $748.50; Direct Labor, Account No. 601, $888.18; Indirect Labor, Account No. 6019, $683.75; Taxes Withheld; F.I.C.A. Taxes Payable, Account No. 404, $188.59; Employees' Income Taxes Payable, Account No. 407, $551.81.

Voucher No. 432 was based on a payroll schedule prepared by the payroll clerk. The amount payable was determined by deducting the taxes withheld. Wages and salaries earned during the March 1−15 period amounted to $4,191.63. The total was based on the following payroll distribution.

Distribution	*Amount*
Office salaries	$ 543.18
Officers' salaries	1,328.02
Sales salaries	748.50
Direct labor	888.18
Indirect labor	683.75
Total	$4,191.63

In order to record Voucher No. 432, it was necessary to use three lines in the voucher register. This was because three separate labor accounts in the operating expense ledger were involved. To meet legal requirements related to the payroll, it was necessary to record the payroll taxes imposed on the employer. The general journal entry used to record these taxes is shown below:

Operating Expenses	116.81	
Manufacturing Expenses	200.24	
F.I.C.A. Taxes Payable		188.59
F.U.T.A. Taxes Payable		16.30
State Unemployment Taxes Payable		112.16

Note that the tax liabilities recorded in the above entry were debited to general ledger control accounts. Because the amounts were debited to control accounts, it was also necessary to record the amounts in detail in the subsidiary ledgers. The debit of $116.81 to Operating Expenses was recorded in the subsidiary operating expense ledger by debiting Payroll Taxes − Administrative, Account No. 7418, for $83.44, and by debiting Payroll Taxes − Sales, Account No. 7427, for $33.37. The debit of

$200.24 to Manufacturing Expenses was recorded in the subsidiary manufacturing expenses ledger by debiting Payroll Taxes — Factory, Account No. 6023, for $200.24.

The Star Manufacturing Company uses the following procedure to record the payroll expenses and related tax liabilities:

1. Employee timecards are checked for completeness and reasonableness. After recorded hours are shown to be correct, the gross earnings are determined for each employee. A payroll clerk then prepares a payroll summary report showing:

    a. Classification of wages earned (classification will usually determine accounts to be charged).
    b. Total earnings to be charged to each account.
    c. Total deductions (taxes, insurance).
    d. Net amount of wages payable.

2. A voucher is prepared to record the payroll and is entered in the voucher register. The voucher will include debits to the proper labor accounts and credits to the related tax liability accounts and a credit to Vouchers Payable for the net amount of wages payable.

3. After the payroll voucher is prepared and approved, the treasurer or other authorized officer will issue a check in payment of the payroll voucher. The check will be made payable to Payroll. The check can then be used to meet the payroll in one or more of the following three ways:

    a. Check is cashed at bank and funds are obtained in proper denominations to pay employees in cash.
    b. Check may be cashed and funds deposited directly in employees' bank accounts.
    c. Individual payroll checks can be drawn after the check has been deposited in a special payroll checking account. The check issued for the net amount of the payroll is recorded by debiting Vouchers Payable and by crediting the proper bank account.

4. A general journal entry is made to record the employer's liability for payroll taxes. Payroll taxes imposed on the employer may be recorded each payday or at the end of each month.

Regardless of whether the payroll taxes are recorded each payday or at the end of each month, a voucher should be prepared when such taxes become due. After the voucher has been authorized, it is recorded in the voucher register by debiting the appropriate liability accounts and by crediting Vouchers Payable. When the taxes are paid, the check(s) will be recorded by debiting Vouchers Payable and by crediting the proper bank account.

The number of accounts that are debited in recording the payroll taxes will depend on the type of business and the detail desired in the accounting records. A manufacturing business may wish to separate expenses related to the factory wages, administrative salaries, and sales salaries. In this case, separate expense accounts for taxes will be maintained for each type of wages. Note from earlier discussion that the Star Manufacturing Company used separate expense accounts for payroll taxes of the factory, administrative, and sales departments.

The voucher register is proved by footing each column in the register and comparing the sum of the debits with the sum of the credits for equality. The register should be proved before carrying footings forward to the next page and before making summary postings.

FILING UNPAID VOUCHERS

There is no set procedure for filing unpaid vouchers. Once the vouchers are recorded in the voucher register, they may be filed alphabetically, or they may be filed numerically by date due. When the vouchers are filed numerically by date due, it is only necessary to examine the vouchers at the front of the file to determine which ones are due. Regardless of the method of filing, the invoices represented by the vouchers should be paid according to their terms. Late payments not only result in lost discounts but may also damage a company's credit standing.

VOUCHER REGISTER POSTING

Amounts in the voucher register are posted both individually and in summary. Items in the Manufacturing Expenses debit column are posted individually to the proper accounts in the manufacturing expense subsidiary ledger. Other individual postings include amounts in the Operating Expense debit column to the operating expense subsidiary ledger and items in the Sundry Accounts debit and credit columns to the designated accounts in the general ledger. As each item is posted, a check mark is made in the check (ν) column beside the amount being posted in the voucher register. Also, the page number of the voucher register should be entered in the P.R. column of the ledger account being posted.

At the end of each month or specified period, the following summary postings are made from the voucher register:

1. The Materials Purchases debit column total is posted as a debit to the Materials Purchases account in the general ledger.

2. Manufacturing Expense debit column total is posted as a debit to the Manufacturing Expense account in the general ledger.
3. The Operating Expense debit column total is posted as a debit to the Operating Expense account in the general ledger.
4. The Vouchers Payable credit column total is posted as a credit to the Vouchers Payable account in the general ledger.

Note that each of the above postings are made to control accounts in the general ledger. As each column total is posted, the number of the account posted to is recorded below the column total. The page number of the voucher register is recorded in the P.R. column of the ledger account posted to. To avoid posting the totals of the Sundry Accounts debit and credit columns, it is a common practice to place a check mark (✔) below these column totals. This serves as an indication that these column totals should not be posted in summary.

VOUCHER PAYMENTS

As mentioned earlier in the chapter, a voucher is used to control expenditures. When payment is due or shortly before it is due, the treasurer or other authorized person must approve the expenditure before the pay-

Illustration 20–4

Last National Bank					66-101 2304		
			Date March 7, 1978		No. 304		
Pay to the order of Southern Supply, Inc.				$ 291.55			
two hundred ninety-one and 55/100				Dollars			
				The STAR Manufacturing Co.			
				Dwight Matthews Treasurer			

Detach statement before depositing check

THE STAR MANUFACTURING CO.

Attached check is for full settlement of the following   Date   March 7, 1978

Invoice		Details	Invoice Amount		Deductions		Net Amount	
Date	Number							
March 1	3482	Materials	297	50	5	95 (discount)	291	55

ment can actually be made. Once the voucher expenditure is approved, it is delivered to the proper disbursing officer for payment. Payment may be made by ordinary check, or by a special form of check called a **voucher check** may be used. A voucher check has space for recording information from the invoice for which payment is being made. The form of voucher check used by the Star Manufacturing Company is shown in Illustration 20–4. The check was issued to Southern Supply, Inc., in payment of its March 1 invoice. The statement attached to the check describes the items purchased, date of invoice, invoice number, invoice amount, any deductions, and the net amount. Voucher checks are used to identify items for which payment is being made which is a benefit for the payee.

FILING PAID VOUCHERS

Paid vouchers may be filed in any convenient manner. The method used should be one which will permit easy access to the voucher for later reference. This is often accomplished by filing either numerically or alphabetically by creditor. Quite often the canceled check or a copy of the canceled check is filed with the voucher.

RECORDING VOUCHER CHECKS

All checks issued by the Star Manufacturing Company are recorded in the check register shown in Illustration 20–5. It is not necessary to identify the accounts to be charged in the **check register** as this has already been done in the voucher register. However, quite often a column will be included in the check register to record deductions made at the time of payment. Note that the check register in Illustration 20–5 contains a column for purchases discount deductions. As checks are written

Illustration 20–5

Month of March 1978			CHECK REGISTER			Page 3
Vouchers Payable, Dr.		Day	Payee	Purchases Discount, Cr.	Bank, Cr.	
No.	Amount				Ck. No.	Amount
401	297.50	7	Southern Supply, Inc.	5.95	304	291.55
404	1,052.25	11	Mid-South Lumber Co.	21.04	305	1,031.21
405	45.05	14	Sharp Suppliers	0.90	306	44.15
407	408.19	15	Tri-State Power Co.		307	408.19
432	3,451.23	15	Payroll		308	3,451.23
402	18.08	16	Butler Supply		309	18.08

and recorded in the check register, appropriate notation should also be made in the voucher register. When a check is issued, the date and number of the check is recorded in the voucher register to indicate that the voucher has been paid.

Shown below is a description of the checks recorded in the check register in Illustration 20–5.

1978
Mar. 7   No. 304: Southern Supply, Inc., $291.55, in payment of Voucher No. 401 for $297.50 less 2 percent discount.
    11   No. 305: Mid-South Lumber Company, $1,031.21, in payment of Voucher No. 404 for $1,052.25 less 2 percent discount.
    14   No. 306: Sharp Suppliers, $44.15, in payment of Voucher No. 405 for $45.05 less 2 percent discount.
    15   No. 307: Tri-State Power Company, $408.19, in payment of Voucher No. 407.
    15   No. 308: Payroll, $3,451.23, in payment of Voucher No. 432.
    16   No. 309: Butler Supply, $18.08, in payment of Voucher No. 402.

The check register is proved by footing the columns and determining that the Vouchers Payable debit column total is equal to the sum of the Purchases Discount credit and Bank credit column totals. The check register should be proved before making the summary postings and before column totals are carried forward to the next page.

CHECK REGISTER POSTING

Since the check register only involves three general ledger accounts, no individual postings are necessary. At the end of each month or period, the check register is proved, and the column footings are posted.

The following posting procedures are used when making the summary postings from the check register:

1.   The Vouchers Payable debit column total is posted as a debit to the Vouchers Payable account in the general ledger.
2.   The Purchases Discount credit column total is posted as a credit to the Purchases Discount account in the general ledger.
3.   The Bank credit column total is posted as a credit to the bank account in the general ledger.

As the column totals are posted, the number of the account being posted to is recorded below the column total. The P.R. column of the account posted to is used to record the page number of the check register.

VERIFYING VOUCHERS PAYABLE

Before a trial balance is taken, the Vouchers Payable account balance should be verified. This can be done by preparing a list of all unpaid vouchers. The total of unpaid vouchers should equal the balance of the general ledger Vouchers Payable account.

FRACTIONAL PAYMENTS

One of the reasons for using a voucher system is that full rather than partial payments are made when a voucher system is used. A voucher system is generally not suitable when it is the custom of a business to make partial payments. However, such situations do arise when a voucher system is used. Special handling of these payments is required, and when it is known that partial payments will be made, separate vouchers should be prepared for each intended payment.

If partial payments are to be made on a voucher that is already prepared, it is best that the original voucher be canceled and that two or more new ones be prepared. The sum of the new vouchers should equal the amount of the old voucher. When recording the new vouchers in the voucher register, the debit may be to Vouchers Payable. This will offset the credit made to Vouchers Payable in recording the original invoice. Those accounts debited in recording the original voucher will remain from the old voucher.

The following general journal entries illustrate the procedures that may be used when new vouchers are prepared to replace an old one:

Materials	2,000	
Vouchers Payable		2,000
Original voucher prepared for purchase of materials amounting to $2,000.		

Vouchers Payable	2,000	
Vouchers Payable		1,000
Vouchers Payable		750
Vouchers Payable		250
Entry used to cancel original voucher and to record new vouchers representing the fractional payments to be made in the amounts of $1,000, $750, and $250.		

Appropriate notation should be made in the voucher register indicating that the original voucher has been canceled and showing the numbers of the new vouchers issued. Later payments for the new vouchers will be recorded in the customary manner.

TEMPORARY VOUCHER SETTLEMENT

It is not uncommon for a business to give a note in temporary settlement of a voucher that is due. Such a settlement may be recorded by debiting Vouchers Payable and crediting Notes Payable. Notation should be made on the original voucher and in the voucher register indicating that the voucher was temporarily settled with a note. A new voucher is authorized when the note becomes due and is recorded in the voucher register. The voucher register entry is a debit to Notes Payable for the amount of the note, a debit to Interest Expense for the interest on the note, and a credit to Vouchers Payable for the amount of the voucher check.

If a new note is issued in settlement of an old note and accrued interest, the entry may be a debit to Notes Payable for the amount of the old note, a debit to Interest Expense for the accrued interest on the old note, and a credit to Notes Payable for the amount of the new note. A voucher will be prepared in the usual manner when the new note becomes due.

Sometimes a check will be issued in payment of interest and for a partial payment of an outstanding note. In this situation, a new note is issued for the balance, and a voucher is prepared for the amount to be paid in cash. The voucher is recorded in the voucher register by debiting Notes Payable for the principal paid, by debiting Interest Expense for the accrued interest, and by crediting Vouchers Payable for the total amount. The voucher is then paid in the usual manner. The new note is issued for the remaining portion of the original note and is recorded in the general journal by debiting Notes Payable and by crediting Notes Payable for the face amount of the new note. This entry effectively cancels the old note and records the new one. When the new note is due, a voucher will be prepared, recorded, and paid in the usual manner.

PURCHASE RETURNS AND ALLOWANCES

The use of a voucher system will not prevent purchase returns and allowances. The effect of such transactions must be reflected in the voucher register and related accounts. If a credit memo is received for returned merchandise, the Vouchers Payable balance should be reduced.

Returns and allowances may be recorded in several ways. If the return or allowance is related to a voucher that has been recorded in the current month, a correction can be made in the voucher register. If the purchase return involves an item in the Operating Expense debit column, the correction can be made by recording the adjustment above the amount in question and also by recording the adjustment above the related amount in the Vouchers Payable credit column. To draw attention, the adjustment is usually made in a different color of ink or is circled if made in the color of the original ink. The correction should also be noted on the voucher itself. If the corrections are separately totaled for the Materials debit and Vouchers Payable credit columns, the materials total can be posted as a credit to the material Purchase Returns and Allowances account, and the total of the vouchers payable adjustments can be posted as a debit to Vouchers Payable. Keep in mind that the above adjustment procedure can only be used in the same month that the voucher was recorded and before any summary postings involving the adjusted purchases have been made. Adjustments involving manufacturing expense, operating expense, or sundry account purchases must be posted individually.

If the return or allowance involves a voucher recorded in the previous month, the old voucher should be canceled and the adjustment recorded in the general journal. A new voucher is then prepared for the adjusted amount. Appropriate notation concerning the canceled voucher should be made in the register. Some accountants do not approve of the correction procedure described in the preceding paragraph and recommend that all returns and allowances be handled by canceling the old voucher and preparing a new one.

A procedure often used to record returns and allowances involves (1) noting adjustment on voucher and attaching credit memo to voucher; (2) recording correction in voucher register beside voucher being reduced; and (3) recording a general journal entry to reflect the transaction. The general journal entry would involve a debit to Vouchers Payable and a credit to the account charged for the purchase (Purchase Returns and Allowances if for materials).

INVOICE CORRECTIONS

As a result of mistakes in billing, a correct invoice may be received after the original invoice has been recorded in the voucher register. The correction may either increase or decrease the amount of the original voucher. A general journal entry should be made to reflect the change in the original voucher. Proper notation should be made on the original voucher, and the corrected invoice should be attached to the original invoice and voucher. As with purchase returns and allowances, some accountants prefer to cancel the original voucher and prepare a new one.

VOUCHERS PAYABLE SUBSIDIARY LEDGER

The voucher system makes it unnecessary to keep a subsidiary accounts payable ledger. The Vouchers Payable account balance is supported by the unpaid voucher file. The voucher register also provides support in that each blank line in the Paid column indicates an unpaid voucher.

If a subsidiary accounts payable ledger is not kept and unpaid vouchers are filed by date due, there is no way of rapidly determining the amount owed to a particular creditor. Such detailed information may not be considered important since business executives tend to think in terms of the total amount payable rather than the amounts owed to individual creditors. If specific creditor information is desired, a subsidiary creditors' ledger may be kept by filing copies of vouchers by creditor.

VOUCHER SYSTEM AND THE PETTY CASH FUND

A petty cash fund eliminates the need for writing checks for small cash payments. A petty cash fund may be kept by either an imprest or journal method. The imprest method was discussed in Chapter 4. The imprest method requires that cash on hand plus disbursements equal the balance of the petty cash fund in the general ledger.

The journal method differs from the imprest method in that disbursements are recorded in a journal under the journal method. Under this method, each payment is recorded by debiting the proper account and crediting Petty Cash. Postings to the accounts involved are made directly from the journal. Under the imprest method, a journal entry is prepared from the information summarized in the petty cash disbursements record, and posting is done from this entry.

The voucher system does not affect the manner in which the petty cash fund is operated. The only difference is that a voucher must be prepared when the fund is replenished. These vouchers are recorded in the voucher register in the usual manner. When the imprest method is used, a voucher is prepared to create the fund, debiting Petty Cash and crediting Vouchers Payable. Subsequent replenishment of the fund is accomplished by preparing vouchers, debiting the proper accounts, and crediting Vouchers Payable. Under the journal method, vouchers issued for the petty cash fund are recorded by debiting Petty Cash and by crediting Vouchers Payable.

Checks issued to petty cash under both methods are recorded by debiting Vouchers Payable and by crediting the bank account.

GLOSSARY

Check register   a special register in which all checks written are recorded in numerical sequence.

Paid voucher file   a permanent file where vouchers which have been paid may be filed in any convenient manner, either alphabetically or numerically.

Purchase invoice   a document prepared by the seller which states the items shipped, the cost of the merchandise, and the method of shipment.

Receiving report   a report which describes the types, quantity, and condition of goods received.

Unpaid vouchers file   a file in which unpaid vouchers may be filed either alphabetically or numerically by date due.

Voucher a form on which is recorded information about the liability being incurred. It also has spaces for approval signatures, the date of the check used for payment, and the check number.

Voucher checks checks which are issued in payment of vouchers. The canceled check or a copy of the canceled check is filed with the voucher in the paid voucher file.

Voucher register a journal in which prenumbered vouchers are recorded in numerical sequence.

Vouchers Payable account similar to an Accounts Payable account, it is used when a voucher system is maintained.

Voucher system a system which provides tight internal control over all cash disbursements.

QUESTIONS AND EXERCISES

1. What items are usually included in a voucher system?

2. Name some conditions under which it would be appropriate to use a voucher system.

3. What is a voucher?

4. Why should vouchers be paid according to their terms?

5. How can the Vouchers Payable account balance be verified?

6. On May 1, a voucher was prepared for the purchase of a truck costing $8,000. On May 16, the company decided to make partial payments of $4,000, $2,500, and $1,500. What general journal entries are required to record (1) the purchase of the truck and (2) the decision to make partial payments?

7. What journal entry should be made when a note is issued in temporary settlement of a voucher that is due? What voucher register entry should be made when the note becomes due?

8. What correction should be made in the voucher register if a return of office supplies is related to a voucher that has been recorded in the current month?

9. What correction procedure is necessary if a purchase return or allowance involves a voucher recorded in the previous month?

10. What effect does a voucher system have on the petty cash fund?

PROBLEMS

20–1. The Woodson Manufacturing Company uses a voucher register like the one shown in Illustration 20–3. Vouchers are recorded in the voucher register at their gross amounts. During the first two weeks of April 1978, the following purchase invoices were received:

1978

Apr. 1   No. 308: Larson Supply Company, 618 Kingston Ave; Office Supplies, Account No. 538; terms, April 1 – 2/10, n/30, $80.

2   No. 309: Howard's Distributors, 407 Peach Road, Birmingham; Materials, Account No. 128; terms, March 30 – 2/10, n/30, $350.

3   No. 310: Wilson & Daughters, 109 Fairy Street; Factory Supplies, Account No. 6318; terms, April 13 – n/30, $90.

5   No. 311: Times-Banner Herald, 450 Center Street; Advertising, Account No. 568; terms, April 3 – net 10, $65.

6   No. 312: Colby and Davis, 910 Alpha Circle; Materials, Account No. 128; terms, April 5 – 2/10, n/30, $500.

7   No. 313: WW and W Company, 515 Edwards Lane, Lansing; Factory Equipment, Account No. 165; terms, April 2 – 2/10, n/30, $2,500.

8   No. 314: DB and D Company, 619 Edwards Lane, Lansing; Office Equipment, Account No. 160; terms, April 3 – 2/10, n/30, $700.

9   No. 315: Brent's Repair Shop, 491 Eastwood Road; Delivery Truck Repairs, Account No. 544; terms, April 9 – 2/10, n/30, $450.

10   No. 316: Randall Hughes, 503 Nebula Road; Repairs to Factory Equipment, Account No. 6332; terms, April 10 – 2/10, n/30, $600.

12   No. 317: State Power Company, 210 Barnes Road; Factory Power Bill, Account No. 6226; terms, April 10 – n/10, $390.

13   No. 318: Bell's Insurance Agency, 806 Dellview Avenue; Factory Insurance Premium, Account No. 130; terms, April 12 – n/30, $185.

14   No. 319: Barron Motor Company, 2918 Hilton Drive; Delivery Truck, Account No. 175; terms, April 14 – 2/10, n/60, $5,680.

Required:

1. Record the invoices in a voucher register. Assume the voucher number is the same as the invoice number.

2. Foot the amount columns of the voucher register.

20-2. The Guy Store maintains a check register like the one in Illustration 20–5 and a voucher register like the one in Illustration 20–3. During the first two weeks of June, the following checks were issued in payment of vouchers:

1978

June 1   No. 720: Cradle Company, $543.90, in payment of Voucher No. 556 for $555 less 2 percent discount.

2   No. 721: Brown's Supply Store, $125, in payment of Voucher No. 557 for $125.

3   No. 722: State Power Company, $275, in payment of Voucher No. 572.

4   No. 723: Hayes Manufacturers, $643.86, in payment of Voucher No. 560 for $657 less 2 percent discount.

June 5   No. 724: Tankersley Equipment Company, $824.50, in payment of Voucher No. 559 for $850 less 3 percent discount.

7   No. 725: Gurley Company, $86, in payment of Voucher No. 546.

8   No. 726: Independence Telephone Company, $55, in payment of Voucher No. 570.

9   No. 727: Evans Supply Company, $218.54, in payment of Voucher No. 562 for $223 less 2 percent discount.

10   No. 728: Ervin and Eubanks, $374.36, in payment of Voucher No. 563 for $382 less 2 percent discount.

11   No. 729: Blizzard & Sons, $125, in payment of Voucher No. 550.

12   No. 730: Fulghum Motors, $6,105.40, in payment of Voucher No. 565 for $6,230 less 2 percent discount.

14   No. 731: Hawk and Fryer, $343, in payment of Voucher No. 564 for $350 less 2 percent discount.

Required:

1.   Record the checks in a check register.
2.   Foot the amount columns of the check register.

20–3.   Tiffin and Till is a wholesale store that sells a variety of merchandise to retailers. A voucher register is one of the accounting records used by Tiffin and Till. The voucher register contains debit columns for purchases, operating expenses, and sundry accounts and credit columns for vouchers payable and sundry accounts. During July 1978 the following transactions relating to vouchers occurred:

1978
July   1   Received an invoice for $400 from Coolidge Realtors, 617 Jordan Avenue, for rent, Account No. 536.

2   Received a telephone bill for $75 from Franklin Telephone Company, 2110 Lancelot Place (Account No. 544).

3   Received an invoice for $500 from Stonehead Manufacturing Company, 692 Cherokee Avenue, Charlotte, for merchandise purchases; terms, July 1 − 2/10, n/30.

5   Received an invoice for $150 from Cal's Supply Company, 1020 Kingston Road, for office supplies, Account No. 540; terms, net 20.

6   Received an invoice for $650 from Stewart's Distributors, 540 Pope Street, Kansas City, for merchandise purchases; terms, July 2 − 2/10, n/30.

7   Received an invoice for $350 from Galahad Equipment Company, 418 Buckhead Road, Montgomerey, for office equipment, Account No. 145; terms, July 5 − 2/10, n/30.

8   Received an invoice for $125 from Farmington Advertising Company, 598 Christmas Lane, for advertising, Account No. 542.

9   Received an invoice for $860 from Stomper-Tack Manufacturers, 302 South Green Street, Augusta, for merchandise purchases; terms, July 7 − 2/10, n/30.

July 12 Received an invoice for $250 from Kersey Suppliers, 198 Wood-
lake Plaza, for store supplies, Account No. 538; terms, July 12 –
net 20.

13 Received an invoice for $45 from Lane's Repair Shop, 211 Scott
Road, for repairs to office equipment, Account No. 552; terms,
July 13 – net 5.

15 Prepared a voucher for the payroll. Payroll was distributed as
follows: Office Salaries Expense, Account No. 524, $525; Officers'
Salaries Expense, Account No. 525, $890; Sales Salaries Expense,
Account No. 526, $1,250; F.I.C.A. Taxes Payable, Account No.
205, $160; Employees' Income Taxes Payable, Account No. 206,
$465.

19 Received an invoice for $50 from the Concord Times, 111 North
Avenue, for advertising, Account No. 542.

20 Received an invoice for $680 from Twin Equipment Company,
984 Parkview Square, for store equipment, Account No. 155;
terms, July 20 – n/30.

21 Received an invoice for $55 from Cal's Supply Company, 1020
Kingston Road, for office supplies, Account No. 540; terms, net 20.

22 Received an invoice for $750 from Johnson and Myers Company,
2666 Briarcliff Avenue, Albany, for merchandise purchases; terms,
July 19 – 2/10, n/30.

23 Received an invoice for $380 from Williams Brothers, 505 Kings
Road, for merchandise purchases; terms, July 23 – 2/10, n/20.

26 Prepared a voucher for $75 to establish a petty cash fund, Account
No. 105.

27 Prepared a voucher for $30 to purchase postage stamps, Account
No. 546.

28 Received an invoice for $75 from Fox Insurance Agency, 888 Free-
port Drive, for insurance, Account No. 534.

29 Received an invoice for $250 from Bond-Patton Equipment Com-
pany, 4849 Peach Avenue, Birmingham, for office equipment,
Account No. 145; terms, July 27 – 2/10, n/30.

30 Received an invoice for $485 from Stewart's Distributors, 540
Pope Street, Kansas City, for merchandise purchases; terms,
July 27 – 2/10, n/30.

31 Prepared a voucher for the payroll. Payroll was distributed as
follows: Office Salaries Expense, Account No. 524, $650; Officers'
Salaries Expense, Account No. 525, $780; Sales Salaries Expense,
Account No. 526, $1,400; F.I.C.A. Taxes Payable, Account No.
205, $165; Employees' Income Taxes Payable, Account No. 206,
$485.

Required:

Record the transactions in a voucher register; foot and rule the voucher
register. Number the vouchers consecutively, beginning with No. 82.

20-4. The Spring Store's treasurer issued the following checks during the month of May 1978:

1978

May 1 Check No. 546 to Kent Lane Realty Company in payment of Voucher No. 483, $250.

3 Check No. 547 to Corporal Telephone Company in payment of Voucher No. 486, $45.

4 Check No. 548 to Leitch Supply Company in payment of Voucher No. 475, $150.

5 Check No. 549 for $352.80 to Carrel Distributors in payment of Voucher No. 476, $360 less 2 percent discount.

6 Check No. 550 for $573.30 to Morris Manufacturers in payment of Voucher No. 478, $585 less 2 percent discount.

7 Check No. 551 for $637 to Simmons Manufacturing Company in payment of Voucher No. 480, $650 less 2 percent discount.

8 Check No. 552 to Alamo Newspaper in payment of Voucher No. 492, $65.

10 Check No. 553 to Seabrook Power Company in payment of Voucher No. 493, $105.

11 Check No. 554 for $182.28 to King Brothers in payment of Voucher No. 482, $186 less 2 percent discount.

12 Check No. 555 to Bluff Suppliers in payment of Voucher No. 484, $135.

13 Check No. 556 to Allen's Equipment Company in payment of Voucher No. 469, $502.

14 Check No. 557 for $456.68 to Davenport Company in payment of Voucher No. 488, $466 less 2 percent discount.

15 Check No. 558 to Payroll in payment of Voucher No. 498, $6,500.

17 Check No. 559 to Cliburn Brothers in payment of Voucher No. 490, $59.

18 Check No. 560 to Buffington Cleaners in payment of Voucher No. 497, $42.

19 Check No. 561 to Mason and Dixon in payment of Voucher No. 491, $163.

20 Check No. 562 for $377.30 to Warren Hart Manufacturing Company in payment of Voucher No. 489, $385 less 2 percent discount.

21 Check No. 563 for $523.80 to Hodges Manufacturers in payment of Voucher No. 494, $540 less 3 percent discount.

22 Check No. 564 for $86 to Carter's Repair Shop in payment of Voucher No. 496.

24 Check No. 565 for $94 to WKZK Radio Station in payment of Voucher No. 499.

25 Check No. 566 for $592.90 to Elmo Manufacturing Company in payment of Voucher No. 495, $605 less 2 percent discount.

26 Check No. 567 for $100 to Petty Cash in payment of Voucher No. 506.

May 27   Check No. 568 for $317.52 to Carrel Distributors in payment of Voucher No. 550, $324 less 2 percent discount.

28   Check No. 569 to Bates Supply Company in payment of Voucher No. 487, $175.

29   Check No. 570 for $761.46 to Hamby Manufacturers in payment of Voucher No. 501, $777 less 2 percent discount.

31   Check No. 571 to Payroll in payment of Voucher No. 512, $6,650.

Required:

1.   Record the issuance of the checks in a check register like the one shown in Illustration 20–5.
2.   Foot and rule the check register on May 31, 1978.

20–5.   The Arbor Dell Manufacturing Corporation was granted its charter in January 1978. It began operating on February 2. The following selected transactions occurred during the first month of operations:

1978
Feb. 2   Received an invoice for $600 from Cobbler Company 4593 Bender Road, for materials; terms, January 30 – 2/10, n/30.

3   Received an invoice for $800 from Ellis Realtors, 502 Parkway Drive, for rent, Account No. 5162. Issued Check No. 101 in payment of the rent.

4   Received an invoice for $250 from Brownlee Suppliers, Account No. 5166; terms, February 4 – n/30.

5   Received an invoice for $5,000 from Norton Equipment Company, 1050 Eagle Drive, Griffin, for factory equipment, Account No. 140; terms, February 3, n/60.

6   Received an invoice for $1,500 from Porter Equipment Company, 5194 Cherokee Road, Miami, for office equipment, Account No. 150; terms, February 3 – n/30.

7   A voucher was prepared to establish a petty cash fund of $150. Check No. 102 was cashed for that amount. (Petty Cash is Account No. 105.)

7   Received an invoice for $550 from Beck Supply Company, 811 Wildwood Place, for factory supplies, Account No. 6142; terms, February 7 – n/30.

9   Issued Check No. 103 to Cobbler Company in payment of Voucher No. 1 less 2 percent discount.

10   Received an invoice for $1,380 from Harding Steel Company, 301 Pinecrest Drive, Atlanta, for materials; terms, February 9 – 2/10, n/30.

11   Received an invoice for $820 from Hancock, Incorporated, 4133 Cascade Road, Dublin, for materials; terms, February 9 – 2/10, n/30.

12   Issued Check No. 104 to Brownlee Suppliers in payment of Voucher No. 3.

Feb. 13 Received an invoice for $75 from WFDT Radio Station, 611 Church Street, for advertising, Account No. 5172; terms, February 12 − n/5.

14 Issued Check No. 105 to WFDT Radio Station in payment of Voucher No. 10.

14 Decided to pay Norton Equipment Company with fractional payments of $1,500, $1,500, and $2,000 instead of $5,000 as noted on Voucher No. 4. Canceled Voucher No. 4 and issued three new vouchers for $1,500, $1,500, and $2,000.

16 Issued Check No. 106 to Norton Equipment Company in payment of Voucher No. 11.

17 Received an invoice for $650 from Robert Newman, Attorney, 6109 Fairfax Parkway, Atlanta, for legal fees, Account No. 5175.

18 Issued Check No. 107 to Harding Steel Company in payment of Voucher No. 8 less 2 percent discount.

18 Issued Check No. 108 to Hancock, Incorporated, in payment of Voucher No. 9 less 2 percent discount.

19 Received an invoice for $150 from Smith Supply Store, 420 Fifth Avenue, for office supplies, Account No. 5166; terms, February 19 − net 10.

20 Issued Check No. 109 to Robert Newman, attorney, in payment of Voucher No. 14.

21 Received an invoice for $580 from Cobbler Company, 4593 Bender Road, for materials; terms, February 19 − 2/10, n/30.

23 Issued Check No. 110 to Porter Equipment Company in payment of Voucher No. 5.

24 Received an invoice for $50 from T-Town Press, 4119 Goshen Road, for newspaper advertising, Account No. 5172; terms, February 23 − net 5.

25 Issued Check No. 111 to Beck Supply Company in payment of Voucher No. 7.

26 Issued Check No. 112 to T-Town Press in payment of Voucher No. 17.

27 Issued Check No. 113 to Cobbler Company in payment of Voucher No. 16 less 2 percent discount.

28 Issued Check No. 114 to Smith Supply Store in payment of Voucher No. 15.

Required:

1. Record the transactions in the voucher register or check register, whichever is appropriate. Number the vouchers consecutively beginning with No. 1.

2. Foot and rule the registers on February 28, 1978. (Note: Vouchers Payable is Account No. 250.)

20–6. Jefferson Footwears, Incorporated, is a new wholesale shoe store which has just opened in Griffin, Georgia. During the first month of business, the following selected transactions occurred:

1978

Jan. 5 Received an invoice for $750 from Silva Manufacturers, 217 Forest Avenue, Columbus, for shoes; terms, January 2 — 2/10, n/30.

6 Received a bill for $300 from Hunt Realty Company, 185 East Road, for rent, Account No. 532; terms, January 6 — net 5.

8 Received an invoice for $570 from Morgan's Shoes, 901 Woodland Drive, Atlanta, for shoes; terms, January 7 — 2/10, n/30.

9 Issued Check No. 101 to Hunt Realty Company in payment of Voucher No. 2.

10 Received an invoice for $960 from Bluster Shoe Company, 105 Chalfont Avenue, Albany, for shoes; terms, January 8 — 2/10, n/30.

10 Received an invoice for $200 from Kevin's Supply Store, 359 Hilton Street, for office supplies, Account No. 536; terms, January 10 — n/10.

10 Issued Check No. 102 to Silva Manufacturers in payment of Voucher No. 1 less 2 percent discount.

12 Received an invoice for $6,000 from Kody Motor Company, 191 Carter Drive, for a delivery truck, Account No. 160; terms, January 9 — n/60. Fractional payments of $2,000 each are to be made three times.

13 Received a bill for $75 from WKRX-TV, 408 Lakewood Plaza, for advertising, Account No. 542; terms, January 12 — n/5.

15 Received an invoice for $500 from Kenton Equipment Company, 104 Whitehall Road, for office equipment, Account No. 150; terms, January 14 — n/30.

16 Issued Check No. 103 to WKRX-TV in payment of Voucher No. 9.

16 Issued Check No. 104 to Morgan's Shoes in payment of Voucher No. 3 less 2 percent discount.

17 Issued Check No. 105 to Bluster Shoe Company in payment of Voucher No. 4 less 2 percent discount.

19 Received an invoice for $450 from Silva Manufacturers, 217 Forest Avenue, Columbus, for shoes; terms, January 16 — 2/10, n/30.

20 Issued Check No. 106 to Kevin's Supply Store in payment of Voucher No. 5.

22 Received an invoice for $1,200 from Kinsaul Shoe Manufacturers, 650 Greenwood Road, Chicago, for shoes; terms, January 17 — 2/10, n/30.

23 Received an invoice for $550 from Hasty Shoe Company, 122 Spring Road, Athens, for shoes; terms, January 22 — 2/10, n/30.

24 Issued Check No. 107 to Silva Manufacturers in payment of Voucher No. 11 less 2 percent discount.

26 Issued Check No. 108 to Kinsaul Shoe Manufacturers in payment of Voucher No. 12 less 2 percent discount.

27 Received an invoice for $250 from Dorsey Suppliers, 206 Avalon Way, for store supplies, Account No. 538; terms, January 27 — net 10.

Jan. 29 Issued Check No. 109 to Kody Motor Company in payment of Voucher No. 6 ($2,000).

   30 Issued Check No. 110 to Hasty Shoe Company in payment of Voucher No. 13 less 2 percent discount.

   30 Received an invoice for $80 from Griffin Free Press, 120 Granger Drive, for advertising, Account No. 542; terms, net 5.

   31 Received an invoice for $680 from Morgan's Shoes, 901 Woodland Drive, Atlanta, for shoes; terms, January 30 − 2/10, n/30.

Required:

1. Record the transactions in a voucher register or check register, whichever is appropriate. The check register should look like the one in Illustration 20–5, and the voucher register will be similar to the one in Illustration 20–3 except there will be no need for a Manufacturing Expense column. The first column should be labeled "purchases." Vouchers should be numbered consecutively beginning with number 1.
2. Foot and rule the voucher register and the check register.
3. Post the footings of the Vouchers Payable columns in each register to the Vouchers Payable account (Account No. 230).
4. Prepare a schedule of unpaid vouchers as of January 31, 1978, and compare the total to the Vouchers Payable account balance.

Index

A

Accomodation endorsement, 284
Account, 12
    defined, 17
Accountant, 3
Accounting, 2
    defined, 17
    distinguished from bookkeeping, 2
    double-entry, 11
    elements of, 3
        assets, 3
        expenses, 7
        liabilities, 3
        owner's equity, 3
        revenues, 7
    financial, 2
    functions of, 2
    governmental, 2
    management, 2
    purpose of, 1
Accounting cycle, 189
    defined, 194
Accounting equation, 4, 12, 17
    illustrated, 6
Accounts payable, 30, 217
    defined, 40
    invoice method, 216
    ledger account system, 218
    schedule of, 228
Accounts Payable account, 229
Accounts payable ledger, 459
Accounts receivable, 9, 211
    defined, 18
    individual ledger accounts, 212

Accounts receivable—Cont.
    sales invoice method, 212
    schedule of, 228
Accounts Receivable account, 229
Accounts receivable ledger, 459
Accrual basis of accounting, 203
    defined, 229
Accrued liability, defined, 257
Accumulated Depreciation account, 180
    defined, 194
Adjusting, 177, 183
Adjusting entries, 177, 194, 493
    asset expiration, 190
    asset growth, 191
    defined, 516
    journalizing, 251, 506
    liability expiration, 190
    liability growth, 191
    posting, 509
Allowance for Doubtful Accounts account, 193
    defined, 194
Allowance method of accounting for bad debts, 192
    defined, 194
Amortization, 378
    defined, 393
Articles of incorporation, defined, 438
Asset method (of accounting for prepayments) defined, 370
Asset record card, 391
Assets, 3
    decreases in, 13
    defined, 18
    depreciation of, 386

Assets—*Cont.*
  exchange of, 389
  increases in, 13
  purchase of, 386
  retiring or discarding of, 390
  sale, 387
Automated Accounting Systems, 313
  purchasing process, 313

B

Back order, 297
  defined, 313
Bad debts, 191
Bad debts expense, 192
  allowance method, 192
  defined, 195, 516
  direct write-off method, 192
Bad debt recoveries, 193
  allowance method, 194
  direct write-off method, 193
Balance column account, illustrated, 16
Balance sheet, 4
Bank balance, 101
Bank credit card transactions, 84, 208–9
  bank statement, 104
  merchant draft, 86
  purchases, 85
  sales slips, 86
Bank reconciliation, 101
  bank balance, 102
  book balance, 102
  defined, 105
  deposits in transit, 102
  illustrated, 102
  journalizing of, 103
  outstanding checks, 101
  service charges, 101
Bank statement, 100
  beginning balance, 101
  canceled checks, 101
  checks and deductions, 101
  defined, 105
  deposits, 101
  ending balance, 101
  form of, 101
Bill of lading, 300
  defined, 313
  distribution of copies, 300
  illustrated, 301
Blank endorsement, defined, 284
Board of directors, defined, 438
Book balance, 102
Book of minutes, 446
  defined, 475
Book of original entry, 26, 70, 147
Book value, 390, 428
  defined, 393, 438

Boot, 389
  defined, 393
Business papers, 25
  defined, 40
Bylaws, defined, 438

C

Capital, 4
  defined, 18
Capital stock authorized, 427
  defined, 438
Carrying value, asset, 250
  defined, 257
Cash, 69
  bank drafts, 69
  defined, 87
  money orders, 69
Cash basis of accounting, 143
  assets acquisition, 144
  defined, 164
  expenses, 144
  revenues, 143
Cash disbursements, 70
  checks, 70
  currency, 70
  receipts for, 70
Cash disbursements journal, 77
  defined, 87
  footing, 79
  form of, 77
  general account columns, 81
  illustrated, 78
  posting of, 79
  special columns, 78
Cash discounts, 298
  defined, 313
Cash journal, 70, 147
  cash columns, 70
  defined, 87
  description column, 70
  end-of-month procedures, 155
  end-of-week procedures, 148
  footing, 71
  general account columns, 70
  illustrated, 71
  posting, 72
  proving, 71
Cash on Delivery (COD), 301
Cash receipts, 70
  verifying, 70
Cash receipts journal, 74
  accounts receivable, 77
  defined, 87
  footing, 77
  form of, 74
  general accounts, 77
  illustrated, 75

Cash receipts journal — *Cont.*
  posting of, 76
  sales discounts, 76
Cash receipts record, illustrated, 451
Cash short and over, 73
  closing, 73
  defined, 87
Certified check, 98
  defined, 105
Certified Public Accountant (CPA), 2
  defined, 18
Chain discounts, 297
Chart of accounts, 27, 145
  account classifications, 27
  defined, 40
  illustrated, 28, 146
Check, 69, 93, 96
  amount in figures, 97
  amount in words, 97
  authorized signature, 97
  cashiers, 69
  certified, 98
  defined, 105
  dishonored, 95
  IOUs, 69
  payee, 97
  personal, 69
  postdated, 69
  traveler's, 69
Check register, 536
  defined, 541
  posting, 547
Checkbook, 99
  form of, 99
  illustrated, 99
Checking account, 93
  elements of, 93
  purpose of, 93
  special, 103
    dividend, 103
    payroll, 103
Checkwriter, 97
  defined, 105
Classified financial statements, 247
  defined, 257
Clock card, illustrated, 113
Closing, 57, 183
  defined, 61
  purpose of, 57
Closing entries, 57, 188
  defined, 61, 195, 516
  journalizing, 251, 510
  posting, 515
COD, defined, 314
Common stock, 428
  book value, 428
  par value, 427
Common stock subscribed, 430
Compound journal entry, 27

Conservatism, 359
  defined, 370
Consignee, 326
  defined, 342
Consignor, 326
  defined, 342
Contingent liability, 271
  defined, 285
  reporting of, 275
Contra account, 195
  defined, 416
Contra assets account, 180, 403
Control account, 212
  defined, 229
Controlling accounts, 403
  defined, 416
Corporate charter, defined, 438
Corporation, 423
  advantages, 423
  board of directors, 426
  bylaws, 425
  charter, 425
  defined, 438
  disadvantages, 424
  incorporators, 425
  management, 426
  organization, 425
  stockholders, 423
Cosigner (of a note), 279
  defined, 284
Cost of goods sold, 219, 494
  defined, 229, 517
  determination of, 494
Credit (Cr.), 12
  defined, 18
  illustrated, 13
Credit memorandum (memo), 98, 304
  defined, 314
  illustrated, 303
Creditors, decisions, 1
Cross-reference, 35
Cross-reference system, 149
  defined, 164
Cross-referencing, defined, 40
Current liabilities, 256
  defined, 257
Current assets, 249
  defined, 257

D

Daily bank statement, 461
  defined, 475
Date of declaration (for dividends), 431
  defined, 438
Date of payment (for dividends), 432
  defined, 438
Date of record (for dividends), 431
  defined, 438

Debit (Dr.), 12
    defined, 18
    illustrated, 13
Debit memorandum (memo), 97, 304
    defined, 314
    illustrated, 98, 302
Declining-balance method, depreciation,
    381
Deficit, 429
    defined, 438
Dependents, 115
    defined, 134
Depletion, 378
    defined, 393
Deposit slip, 70
    defined, 87
    verifying, 70
Deposit ticket, 94
    defined, 105
    illustrated, 94
Deposits, 96
    mail, 96
    night, 96
Depreciate, 378
Depreciation, 144
    defined, 164, 394
    functional, 378
    group, 385
    physical, 378
Depreciation expense, 144, 379
    defined, 164
    determination of, 379
        asset life, 379
        salvage value, 379
Depreciation methods, 380
    comparison of methods, 383
    straight-line, 380
    sum-of-the-years'-digits, 382
    units of production, 383
Direct write-off method of accounting for
    bad debts, 192
    defined, 195
Discount, 268
Discount (on a noninterest-bearing note)
    defined, 284
Discount (on purchases), 297
    cash, 298
    chain, 297
    terms of, 300
    trade, 297
Discounting notes receivable, 284
Dishonored check, defined, 106
Dishonored note, defined, 284
Dividend, 431
    date of declaration, 431
    date of payment, 432
    date of record, 438

Drawing account, 32
    closing of, 60
    defined, 40
Drayage, 302
    defined, 314

E

Earnings and loss ratio, 412
    defined, 416
Earnings record, 120, 126
    defined, 134
    illustrated, 127
Earnings statement, 9, 54, 247
    defined, 18, 134
    flow concept, 55
    format of, 55
    illustrated, 10, 55, 507
    merchandising firm, 247
    payroll, 124
Employees, decisions, 1
Employee's Withholding Allowance Cer-
    tificate (Form W-4), 115
Endorsement, 95
    blank, 95
    defined, 106
    full, 95
    restrictive, 95
Endorsing a payment, defined, 285
Entity, defined, 18
Entity concept, 4
Exemptions, 119
    defined, 134
Expense, 7
    defined, 18
Expense accounts, closing, 58
Expense method (of accounting for prepay-
    ments), 370
Expense and Revenue Summary account,
    58
    closing of, 59
    defined, 61

F

Federal Fair Labor Standards Act, 114
    defined, 134
Fees earned, 58
F.I.C.A. taxes, 115
    defined, 134
Financial accounting, 2
Financial information, 1
    users of, 1
Financial statements, 9
    earnings statement, 9
    statement of financial position, 10
    statement of owner's equity, 11
First-in; first-out (FiFo), 356
    compared with LiFo, 359

First-in; first-out (FiFo)—*Cont.*
  defined, 370
  lower of cost or market, 359
Fiscal year, 239
  defined, 258
F.O.B. destination, 300
  defined, 314
F.O.B. shipping point, 300
  defined, 314
Foot, 16
  defined, 18
Freight bill, 302
  defined, 314
Freight collect, 300
  defined, 314
Freight prepaid, 300
  defined, 314
Functional depreciation, defined, 394
F.U.T.A. taxes, 130
  defined, 134

G

General journal, 453
  illustrated, 456
General ledger, 34, 147, 457
Goodwill, 412
  defined, 416
Governmental accounting, 2
Governmental units, decisions, 1
Gross earnings, 114
  deductions from, 114
Gross margin, 219
  defined, 229
Gross profit, 219
Gross profit method, 360
  defined, 370
Group depreciation, 385

I

Imprest fund, 81
Income taxes withheld, 115
Incorporators, defined, 438
Independent contractor, 112
  defined, 134
Installment sales, 342
Insurance register, 367
  defined, 370
Intangible assets, 250
  defined, 258, 394
Intangibles, 377
Interest, 269
  computation of, 269
    interest rate, 269
    principal, 269
    time period, 269
  defined, 285
Interest payable, accrual of, 284

Interest receivable, accrual of, 283
Inventory, 354
  counting (taking) of, 354
    procedure, 355
    purpose, 354
  valuation of, 355
    comparison of methods, 359
    first-in; first-out, 356
    last-in; first-out, 357
    lower of cost or market, 359
    weighted average method, 358
Inventory methods, 360
  gross profit, 360
  perpetual, 362
  retail, 361
Inventory record, 461
  defined, 475
Inventory sheets, 355
Invoice corrections, 540
Invoice method, 216
  defined, 229
Invoice register, 304, 451
  cash purchases, 311
  defined, 314
  illustrated, 306, 452
  posting, 307
  proof of, 307
  summary posting, 310
  transportation costs, 311
    freight collect, 312
    insurance on merchandise, 312
    prepaid freight, 312
    recording of, 312

J

Journal, 26
  defined, 40
  illustrated, 26
  proving, 34
Journal entry, 26
  components, 26
  compound, 27
  defined, 40
  posting, 35
Journal procedure, 27
Journalizing, 26
  defined, 28
  illustrated, 28, 41
  process, 29

L

Last-in; first-out (LiFo), 357
  compared with FiFo, 359
  defined, 370
Ledger, 34
  defined, 41
Ledger account system, 218

Ledger accounts, illustrated, 183–88
Liabilities, 3
  decreases in, 14
  defined, 18
  increases in, 13
Liquidation value, 428
  defined, 438
Liquidity, 69
  defined, 87
Long-lived assets, 377
  classification of, 377
    accounting treatment characteristics,
      378
    legal characteristics, 377
    physical characteristics, 377
  defined, 394
  depreciation, 386
  disposal, 387
    exchange, 389
    retiring or discarding, 390
    sale, 387
  purchase, 386
  statement presentation, 390
Long-term investments, 249
  defined, 258
Long-term liability, 250
  defined, 258
Lower-of-cost-or-market method, 358
  defined, 370

M

Maker, 268
  defined, 285
Management, decisions, 1
Management accounting, 2
Matching concept, 191
  defined, 195
Maturity value, 271
  defined, 285
Merchandise inventory, 212, 353
  defined, 229, 370
Merchandising firm, 203
  accounting procedures, illustrated, 220,
    228
  defined, 229
Merchant draft, 86
Merit rating, defined, 135
Merit-rating system, 131

N

"Negative" account valances, 226
  defined, 229
Net book value, 250
  defined, 258
Net earnings, 11
  defined, 18
Net loss, 11
  defined, 18

Net purchases, 219
  defined, 229
Net sales, 219
  defined, 229
Notes payable, 268, 279, 282
  for cash loan, 279
  endorsing the payment, 279
  in exchange for goods and services, 280
  for extension of payment time on a pre-
    vious obligation, 280
  payment of, 281
  renewal of, 281
Notes payable register, defined, 285
Notes receivable, 268, 273, 278
  accomodation endorsement, 279
  blank endorsement, 278
  for cash loan, 273
  collection, 275
  discounted, 274
  dishonored, 276
  endorsement of, 276
  in exchange for goods and services, 280
  for extension of payment time on a pre-
    vious obligation, 273
  renewal of, 276
  special endorsement, 276
Notes receivable register, 276
  defined, 285
  illustrated, 277

O

Operating expense ledger, 460
Operating expense worksheet, 493
  defined, 517
Owners, decisions, 1
Owner's equity, 3
  decreases in, 14
  defined, 18
  determination of, 11
  increases in, 13
  withdrawals, 32
Owner's equity transactions, 404
  defined, 416

P

Paid voucher file, defined, 541
Partnership, 405
  accounting for, 407
  admission of new partner, 411
  advantantages, 406
  combination of existing businesses, 407
    goodwill, 412
  defined, 416
  disadvantages, 406
  incorporating of, 435
  initial partnership entry, 407
  liquidation, 414
  partners' compensation, 410

Partnership—*Cont.*
  profits and losses, 410
  statement of financial position, 411
  withdrawal of partner, 414
Partnership agreement, 406
  defined, 416
Par value, 427
  defined, 438
Payee, 268
  defined, 285
Payroll accounting, 111
  computation of gross earnings, 112
  deductions from gross earnings, 114
    F.I.C.A. taxes, 115
    income taxes withheld, 115
    miscellaneous, 119
  defined, 135
Payroll check, 120, 122
  defined, 135
  illustrated, 124–25
Payroll deductions, 128
Payroll records, components of, 119
Payroll register (journal), 120
  defined, 135
  illustrated, 121
Payroll taxes, 130
  F.I.C.A. taxes, 130
  filing tax returns, 132
    illustrated, 133
  F.U.T.A. taxes, 130
  state unemployment taxes, 130
Percentage rate method, 119
  defined, 135
Periodic inventory method, defined, 371
Periodic inventory system, 212
  defined, 229
Perpetual inventory method, 362
  defined, 370
Personal property, 377
  defined, 394
Petty cash, 81
Petty cash book, 84
Petty cash fund, 81
  custodian, 81
  decreases in, 82
  defined, 87
  illustrated, 82
  imprest, 81
  increases in, 82
  replenishment, 81
Petty cash voucher, 81
  defined, 87
Physical depreciation, defined, 394
Physical inventory, 360
Plant assets, 250
  defined, 258
Post-closing trial balance, 61, 188, 515
  accounts included, 61

Post-closing trial balance—*Cont.*
  defined, 61, 195, 517
  illustrated, 188
  preparation of, 61
  purpose of, 61
Posting, 34, 227
  defined, 41
Posting reference (P.R.), 72
P.R. column, 147
  defined, 165
Preferred stock, 428
  defined, 439
  liquidation value, 428
Prepaid expenses, 249, 363
  defined, 258, 370
Prepayments, accounting for, 363
  asset method, 363
  comparison of asset and expense methods, 369
  expense method, 368
Present value (of a note), 270
  defined, 285
Principal, 269
  defined, 285
Promissory note, 267
  defined, 285
  illustrated, 268
  legal attributes, 267
Proprietorship, 399
  advantages, 400
  defined, 416
  disadvantages, 400
  equity accounts, 401
  summary account, 401
Proving the journal, 34
Public accounting firms, 1
Purchase invoice, 214, 295, 528
  corrected, 305
  defined, 229, 314, 541
  illustrated, 296, 528
Purchase order, 294
  acknowledgement copy, 294
  defined, 314
  distribution of copies, 294
  illustrated, 295
  incoming, 327
    accuracy of, 328
    billing, 329
    credit approval, 328
    examination of, 327
    transportation, 328
Purchase requisition, 293
  defined, 314
  illustrated, 294
Purchases, 213, 293
Purchases account, defined, 230
Purchases journal, 215
  defined, 230

Purchases returns and allowances, 214, 313,
    539
  defined, 230, 314
Purchasing process, 313

R

Real property, 377
  defined, 394
Realization concept, 358
  defined, 371
Receiving report, 296, 528
  defined, 314, 541
Record of cash receipts, 448
Record of checks drawn, 453
  illustrated, 454, 455
  posting of, 453
Retail method, 361
  defined, 371
Retail sales tax, 205
  defined, 230
Revenue, 7
  defined, 18
  recording of, 205
Revenue accounts, closing, 58
Reversing entries, 515
  defined, 517
Royalties, 410
  defined, 416

S

Salary, 112
  defined, 135
Sales, 323
  cash, 323, 340
  COD, 325, 340
  consignment, 326
  credit, 324
  installment, 327
  on approval, 325
  recording of, 332
Sales on approval, 325
  defined, 342
Sales on consignment, defined, 342
Sales on credit, defined, 342
Sales account, 204
  defined, 230
Sales discounts, 331
Sales discounts account, defined, 342
Sales invoice (ticket), 207, 329
  corrections, 332
  defined, 230, 342
  distribution of copies, 329
  illustrated, 330
Sales invoice method, 212
Sales journal, 209
  defined, 230
Sales register, 448
  defined, 342

Sales register—*Cont.*
  illustrated, 334, 449
  posting, 335
  proving of, 335
Sales returns and allowances, 207, 331, 340
  defined, 230, 342
Sales Tax Payable account, 206
  defined, 230
Sales ticket, 207
Salvage value, 380
Savings accounts, 104
Schedule of accounts payable, 228, 460
  defined, 230, 475
Schedule of accounts receivable, 228
  defined, 230, 475
Service bureau, 127
  defined, 135
Service charge, 104
Service enterprise, 143
  defined, 165
Shareholders, 423
  defined, 439
Signature card, 93
  defined, 106
Special endorsement, defined, 285
Statement of financial position, 4, 10, 56, 248
  defined, 18
  format of, 56
  illustrated, 10
  merchandising firm, 248
Statement of owner's equity, 11
Stock certificates, 427
  defined, 439
Stockholders' ledger, 446
  defined, 475
Straight-line method, depreciation, 380
Subscribed stock, defined, 439
Subscriber, 427
  defined, 439
Subscription, 427
  defined, 439
Subscription price, defined, 439
Subsidiary account, 212
Subsidiary ledger, defined, 230
Summary account, defined, 416
Summary posting, 217
  defined, 230
Summary worksheet, 494
  illustrated, 496
Sum-of-the-years'-digits methods, depreciation, 382
Supporting worksheet, 500

T

T-account, 12
  illustrated, 14
Tangible assets, 377
  defined, 394

Temporary investments, defined, 475
Temporary owner's equity accounts, 57
  defined, 61
  purpose of, 57
Time clock, 112
  defined, 135
Trade discount, 297
  chain, 297
  defined, 314
Transaction worksheet, illustrated, 6, 8
Transactions, 5
  defined, 18
  illustrated, 14
Transportation costs, 312
  freight collect, 312
  freight prepaid, 312
  insurance, 312
Transportation-in account, defined, 314
Transportation-out, 341
  defined, 343
Trial balance, 17, 36, 163, 240
  defined, 18
  illustrated, 164
  preparation of, 39
  purpose of, 38

U

Uniform Partnership Act, 405
  defined, 416
Units of production method, depreciation, 383
Unpaid vouchers file, defined, 541

V

Voucher, 529
  defined, 542
  fractional payments, 538
  paid, filing of, 536
  payment of, 535
  temporary settlement, 538
Voucher checks, 536
  defined, 542
  illustrated, 535
  recording, 536

Voucher register, 531
  defined, 542
  posting, 534
Voucher system, 527
  defined, 542
  invoice corrections, 540
  petty cash fund, 541
  purchase returns and allowances, 529
Vouchers payable, 531
  defined, 542
  verifying, 537
Vouchers payable subsidiary ledger, 540

W

Wage-bracket method, 117, 119
  defined, 135
Wages, 112
  defined, 135
Wasting assets, 378, 392
  defined, 394
Waybill, 302
  defined, 314
Weighted average method (inventory), 358
  defined, 371
Wholesale merchandising enterprise, 445
  defined, 475
  records required, 445
    business volume, 446
    desired information, 447
    office machines, 447
    type of business, 445
Withholding allowances, 116
  defined, 135
Worksheet, 51, 177, 241, 493
  adjusted trial balance columns, 179
  defined, 62, 517
  earnings statement columns, 52
  form of, 51
  illustrated, 52, 178–79
  merchandising firm, 241
    illustrated, 242–43
  preparation of, 179, 182
  statement of financial position columns, 52
  trial balance columns, 52

This book has been set in 10 point and 9 point Times Roman, leaded two points. Chapter numbers are 60 point Weiss; chapter titles are 20 point Helvetica. The maximum type area is 30 by 45½ picas.